Weymouth New Testament in Modern Speech

1912

RICHARD FRANCIS WEYMOUTH

TABLE OF CONTENTS

BOOK 62 1 JOHN

001:001 That which was from the beginning, which we have listened to, which we have seen with our own eyes, and our own hands have handled concerning the Word of Life- 001:002 the Life was manifested, and we have seen and bear witness, and we declare unto you the Life of the Ages which was with the Father and was manifested to us- 001:003 that which we have seen and listened to we now announce to you also, in order that you also may have fellowship in it with us, and this fellowship with us is fellowship with the Father and with His Son Jesus Christ. 001:004 And we write these things in order that our joy may be made complete. 001:005 This is the Message which we have heard from the Lord Jesus and now deliver to you-God is Light, and in Him there is no darkness. 001:006 If, while we are living in darkness, we profess to have fellowship with Him, we speak falsely and are not adhering to the truth. 001:007 But if we live in the light as He is in the light, we have fellowship with one another, and the blood of Jesus, His Son, cleanses us from all sin. 001:008 If we claim to be already free from sin, we lead ourselves astray and the truth has no place in our hearts. 001:009 If we confess our sins, He is so faithful and just that He forgives us our sins and cleanses us from all unrighteousness. 001:010 If we deny that we have sinned, we make Him a liar, and His Message has no place in our hearts. 002:001 Dear children, I write thus to you in order that you may not sin. If any one sins, we have an Advocate with the Father-Jesus Christ the righteous; 002:002 and He is an atoning sacrifice for our sins, and not for ours only, but also for the sins of the whole world. 002:003 And by this we may know that we know Him-if we obey His commands. 002:004 He who professes to know Him, and yet does not obey His commands, is a liar, and the truth has no place in his heart. 002:005 But whoever obeys His

Message, in him love for God has in very deed reached perfection. By this we can know that we are in Him. 002:006 The man who professes to be continuing in Him is himself also bound to live as He lived. 002:007 My dearly-loved friends, it is no new command that I am now giving you, but an old command which you have had from the very beginning. By the old command I mean the teaching which you have already received. 002:008 And yet I *am* giving you a new command, for such it really is, so far as both He and you are concerned: because the darkness is now passing away and the light, the true light, is already beginning to shine. 002:009 Any one who professes to be in the light and yet hates his brother man is still in darkness. 002:010 He who loves his brother man continues in the light, and his life puts no stumbling-block in the way of others. 002:011 But he who hates his brother man is in darkness and is walking in darkness; and he does not know where he is going- because the darkness has blinded his eyes. 002:012 I am writing to you, dear children, because for His sake your sins are forgiven you. 002:013 I am writing to you, fathers, because you know Him who has existed from the very beginning. I am writing to you, young men, because you have overcome the Evil one. I have written to you, children, because you know the Father. 002:014 I have written to you, fathers, because you know Him who has existed from the very beginning. I have written to you, young men, because you are strong and God's Message still has a place in your hearts, and you have overcome the Evil one. 002:015 Do not love the world, nor the things in the world. If any one loves the world, there is no love in his heart for the Father. 002:016 For the things in the world-the cravings of the earthly nature, the cravings of the eyes, the show and pride of life- they all come, not from the Father, but from the world. 002:017 And the world, with its cravings, is passing away, but he who does God's will continues for ever. 002:018 Dear children, the last hour has come; and as you once heard that there was to be an anti-Christ, so even now many anti-Christs have appeared. By this we may know that the last hour has come. 002:019 They have gone forth from our midst, but they did not really belong to us; for had they belonged to us, they would have remained with us. But they left us that it might be manifest that professed believers do not all belong to us. 002:020 As for you, you have an anointing from the holy One and have perfect knowledge. 002:021 I have written to you, not because you are ignorant of the truth, but because you know it, and you know that nothing false comes from the truth. 002:022 Who is a liar compared with him who denies that Jesus is the Christ? He who disowns the Father and the Son is the anti-Christ. 002:023 No one who disowns the Son has the Father. He who acknowledges the Son has also the Father. 002:024 As for you, let the teaching which you have received from the very beginning continue in your hearts. If that teaching does continue in your hearts, you also will continue to be in union with the

Son and with the Father. 002:025 And this is the promise which He Himself has given us- the Life of the Ages. 002:026 I have thus written to you concerning those who are leading you astray. 002:027 And as for you, the anointing which you received from Him remains within you, and there is no need for any one to teach you. But since His anointing gives you instruction in all things- and is true and is no falsehood-you are continuing in union with Him even as it has taught you to do. 002:028 And now, dear children, continue in union with Him; so that, if He re-appears, we may have perfect confidence, and may not shrink away in shame from His presence at His Coming. 002:029 Since you know that He is righteous, be assured also that the man who habitually acts righteously is a child of His. 003:001 See what marvellous love the Father has bestowed upon us- that we should be called God's children: and that is what we are. For this reason the world does not recognize us-because it has not known Him. 003:002 Dear friends, we are now God's children, but what we are to be in the future has not yet been fully revealed. We know that if Christ reappears we shall be like Him, because we shall see Him as He is. 003:003 And every man who has this hope fixed on Him, purifies himself so as to be as pure as He is. 003:004 Every one who is guilty of sin is also guilty of violating Law; for sin is the violation of Law. 003:005 And you know that He appeared in order to take away sins; and in Him there is no sin. 003:006 No one who continues in union with Him lives in sin: no one who lives in sin has seen Him or knows Him. 003:007 Dear children, let no one lead you astray. The man who acts righteously is righteous, just as He is righteous. 003:008 He who is habitually guilty of sin is a child of the Devil, because the Devil has been a sinner from the very beginning. The Son of God appeared for the purpose of undoing the work of the Devil. 003:009 No one who is a child of God is habitually guilty of sin. A God-given germ of life remains in him, and he cannot habitually sin-because he is a child of God. 003:010 By this we can distinguish God's children and the Devil's children: no one who fails to act righteously is a child of God, nor he who does not love his brother man. 003:011 For this is the Message you have heard from the beginning- that we are to love one another. 003:012 We are not to resemble Cain, who was a child of the Evil one and killed his own brother. And why did he kill him? Because his own actions were wicked and his brother's actions righteous. 003:013 Do not be surprised, brethren, if the world hates you. 003:014 As for us, we know that we have already passed out of death into Life-because we love our brother men. He who is destitute of love continues dead. 003:015 Every one who hates his brother man is a murderer; and you know that no murderer has the Life of the Ages continuing in him. 003:016 We know what love is-through Christ's having laid down His life on our behalf; and in the same way we ought to lay down our lives for our brother men. 003:017 But if any one has this world's wealth and sees that his brother man is in need, and yet hardens his heart against him- how can such a one continue to love God? 003:018 Dear children, let us not love in words only nor with the lips, but in deed and in truth. 003:019 And in this way we shall come to know that we are loyal to the truth, and shall satisfy our consciences in His presence 003:020 in whatever matters our hearts condemn us-because God is greater than our hearts and knows everything. 003:021 Dear friends, if our hearts do not condemn us, we have perfect confidence towards God; 003:022 and whatever we ask for we obtain from Him, because we obey His commands and do the things which are pleasing in His sight. 003:023 And this is His command-that we are to believe in His Son Jesus Christ and love one another, just as He has commanded us to do. 003:024 The man who obeys His commands continues in union with God, and God continues in union with him; and through His Spirit whom He has given us we can know that He continues in union with us. 004:001 Dear friends, do not believe every spirit, but put the spirits to the test to see whether they are from God; for many false teachers have gone out into the world. 004:002 The test by which you may recognize the Spirit of God is that every spirit which acknowledges that Jesus Christ has come as man is from God, 004:003 and that no spirit is from God which does not acknowledge this about Jesus. Such is the spirit of the anti-Christ; of whose coming you have heard, and it is already in the world. 004:004 As for you, dear children, you are God's children, and have successfully resisted them; for greater is He who is in you than he who is in the world. 004:005 They are the world's children, and so their language is that of the world, and the world listens to them. We are God's children. 004:006 The man who is beginning to know God listens to us, but he who is not a child of God does not listen to us. By this test we can distinguish the Spirit of truth from the spirit of error. 004:007 Dear friends, let us love one another; for love has its origin in God, and every one who loves has become a child of God and is beginning to know God. 004:008 He who is destitute of love has never had any knowledge of God; because God is love. 004:009 God's love for us has been manifested in that He has sent His only Son into the world so that we may have Life through Him. 004:010 This is love indeed-we did not love God, but He loved us and sent His Son to be an atoning sacrifice for our sins. 004:011 Dear friends, if God has so loved us, we also ought to love one another. 004:012 No one has ever yet seen God. If we love one another, God continues in union with us, and His love in all its perfection is in our hearts. 004:013 We can know that we are continuing in union with Him and that He is continuing in union with us, by the fact that He has given us a portion of His Spirit. 004:014 And we have seen and bear witness that the Father has sent the Son to be the Saviour of the world. 004:015 Whoever acknowledges that Jesus is the Son of God-God continues in union with him, and he continues in union with God. 004:016 And, as for us, we know the love which God has for us, and we confide in it. God is love, and he who continues to love continues in union with God, and God continues in union with him. 004:017 Our love will be manifested in all its perfection by our having complete confidence on the day of the Judgement; because just what He is, we also are in the world. 004:018 Love has in it no element of fear; but perfect love drives away fear, because fear involves pain, and if a man gives way to fear, there is something imperfect in his love. 004:019 We love because God first loved us. 004:020 If any one says that he loves God, while he hates his brother man, he is a liar; for he who does not love his brother man whom he has seen, cannot love God whom he has not seen. 004:021 And the command which we have from Him is that he who loves God must love his brother man also. 005:001 Every one who believes that Jesus is the Christ is a child of God; and every one who loves the Father loves also Him who is the Father's Child. 005:002 The fact that we love God Himself, and obey His commands, is a proof that we love God's children. 005:003 Love for God means obedience to His commands; and His commands are not irksome. 005:004 For every child of God overcomes the world; and the victorious principle which has overcome the world is our faith. 005:005 Who but the man that believes that Jesus is the Son of God overcomes the world? 005:006 Jesus Christ is He who came with water and blood; not with the water only, but with the water and with the blood. And it is the Spirit who gives testimony-because the Spirit is the Truth. 005:007 For there are three that give testimony-the Spirit, the water, and the blood; 005:008 and there is complete agreement between these three. 005:009 If we accept the testimony of men, God's testimony is greater: for God's testimony consists of the things which He has testified about His Son. 005:010 He who believes in the Son of God has the testimony in his own heart: he who does not believe God has made Him a liar, in that he has refused to accept the testimony which God has given about His Son. 005:011 And that testimony is to the effect that God has given us the Life of the Ages, and that this Life is in His Son. 005:012 He who has the Son has the Life: he who has not the Son of God has not the Life. 005:013 I write all this to you in order that you who believe in the Son of God may know for certain that you already have the Life of the Ages. 005:014 And we have an assured confidence that whenever we ask anything in accordance with His will, He listens to us. 005:015 And since we know that He listens to us, then whatever we ask, we know that we have the things which we have asked from Him. 005:016 If any one sees a brother man committing a sin which is not unto death, he shall ask and God shall give him life- for those who do not sin unto death. There is such a thing as sin unto death; for that I do not bid him make request. 005:017 Any kind of wrongdoing is sin; but there is sin which is not unto death. 005:018 We know that no one who is a child of God lives in sin, but He who is God's Child keeps him, and the Evil one cannot touch him. 005:019 We know that we are children of God, and that the whole world lies in the power of the Evil one. 005:020 And we know that the Son of God has come, and has given us understanding so that we know the true One, and are in union with the true One-that is, we are in union with His Son Jesus Christ. He is the true God and the Life of the Ages. 005:021 Dear children, guard yourselves from idols.

BOOK 60 1 PETER

001:001 Peter, an Apostle of Jesus Christ: To God's own people scattered over the earth, who are living as foreigners in Pontus, Galatia, Cappadocia, Roman Asia, and Bithynia, 001:002 chosen in accordance with the foreknowledge of God the Father, through the sanctifying work of the Spirit, with a view to their obedience and to their being sprinkled with the blood of Jesus Christ. May more and more grace and peace be granted to you. 001:003 Blessed be the God and Father of our Lord Jesus Christ, who in His great mercy has begotten us anew to an ever-living hope through the resurrection of Jesus Christ from the dead, 001:004 to an inheritance imperishable, undefiled and unfading, which has been reserved in Heaven for you, 001:005 whom God in His power is guarding through faith for a salvation that even now stands ready for unveiling at the End of the Age. 001:006 Rejoice triumphantly in the prospect of this, even if now, for a short time, you are compelled to sorrow amid various trials. 001:007 The sorrow comes in order that the testing of your faith- being more precious than that of gold, which perishes and yet is proved by fire-may be found to result in praise and glory and honour at the re-appearing of Jesus Christ. 001:008 Him you love, though your eyes have never looked on Him. In Him, though at present you cannot see Him, you nevertheless trust, and triumph with a joy which is unspeakable and is crowned with glory, 001:009 while you are securing as the outcome of your faith the salvation of your souls. 001:010 There were Prophets who earnestly inquired about that salvation, and closely searched into it-even those who spoke beforehand of the grace which was to come to you. 001:011 They were eager to know the time which the Spirit of Christ within them kept indicating, or the characteristics of that time, when they solemnly made known beforehand the sufferings that were to come upon Christ and the glories which would follow. 001:012 To them it was revealed that they were serving not themselves but you, when they foretold the very things which have now been openly declared to you by those who, having been taught by the Holy Spirit which had been sent from Heaven, brought you the Good News. Angels long to stoop and look into these things. 001:013 Therefore gird up your minds and fix your hopes calmly and unfalteringly upon the boon that is soon to be yours, at the re-appearing of Jesus Christ. 001:014 And, since you delight in obedience, do not shape your lives by the cravings which used to dominate you in the time of your ignorance, 001:015 but-in imitation of the holy One who has called you- you also must be holy in all your habits of life. 001:016 Because it stands written, "You are to be holy, because I am holy." 001:017 And if you address as your Father Him who judges impartially in accordance with each man's actions, then spend in fear the time of your stay here on earth, 001:018 knowing, as you do, that it was not with a ransom of perishable wealth, such as silver or gold, that you were set free from your frivolous habits of life which had been handed down to you from your forefathers, 001:019 but with the precious blood of Christ-as of an unblemished and spotless lamb. 001:020 He was pre-destined indeed to this work, even before the creation of the world, but has been plainly manifested in these last days for the sake of you who, through Him, 001:021 are faithful to God, who raised Him from among the dead and gave Him glory, so that your faith and hope are resting upon God. 001:022 Now that, through your obedience to the truth, you have purified your souls for cherishing sincere brotherly love, you must love another heartily and fervently. 001:023 For you have been begotten again by God's ever-living and enduring word from a germ not of perishable, but of imperishable life. 001:024 "All mankind resemble the herbage, and all their beauty is like its flowers. The herbage dries up, and its flowers drop off; 001:025 But the word of the Lord remains for ever." And that means the Message which has been proclaimed among you in the Good News. 002:001 Rid yourselves therefore of all ill-will and all deceitfulness, of insincerity and envy, and of all evil speaking. 002:002 Thirst, like newly-born infants, for pure milk for the soul, that by it you may grow up to salvation; 002:003 if you have had any experience of the goodness of the Lord. 002:004 Come to Him, the ever-living Stone, rejected indeed by men as worthless, but in God's esteem chosen and held in honour. 002:005 And be yourselves also like living stones that are being built up into a spiritual house, to become a holy priesthood to offer spiritual sacrifices acceptable to God through Jesus Christ. 002:006 For it is contained in Scripture, "See, I am placing on Mount Zion a Cornerstone, chosen, and held in honour, and he whose faith rests on Him shall never have reason to feel ashamed." 002:007 To you believers, therefore, that honour belongs; but for unbelievers-"A Stone which the builders rejected has been made the Cornerstone," 002:008 and "a Stone for the foot to strike against, and a

Rock to stumble over." Their foot strikes against it because they are disobedient to God's Message, and to this they were appointed. 002:009 But you are a chosen race, a priesthood of kingly lineage, a holy nation, a people belonging specially to God, that you may make known the perfections of Him who called you out of darkness into His marvellous light. 002:010 Once you were not a people, but now you are the people of God. Once you had not found mercy, but now you have. 002:011 Dear friends, I entreat you as pilgrims and foreigners not to indulge the cravings of your lower natures: for all such cravings wage war upon the soul. 002:012 Live honourable lives among the Gentiles, in order that, although they now speak against you as evil-doers, they may yet witness your good conduct, and may glorify God on the day of reward and retribution. 002:013 Submit, for the Lord's sake, to every authority set up by man, whether it be to the Emperor as supreme ruler, 002:014 or to provincial Governors as sent by him for the punishment of evil-doers and the encouragement of those who do what is right. 002:015 For it is God's will that by doing what is right you should thus silence the ignorant talk of foolish persons. 002:016 Be free men, and yet do not make your freedom an excuse for base conduct, but be God's bondservants. 002:017 Honour every one. Love the brotherhood, fear God, honour the Emperor. 002:018 Household servants, be submissive to your masters, and show them the utmost respect-not only if they are kind and thoughtful, but also if they are unreasonable. 002:019 For it is an acceptable thing with God, if, from a sense of duty to Him, a man patiently submits to wrong, when treated unjustly. 002:020 If you do wrong and receive a blow for it, what credit is there in your bearing it patiently? But if when you do right and suffer for it you bear it patiently, this is an acceptable thing with God. 002:021 And it is to this you were called; because Christ also suffered on your behalf, leaving you an example so that you should follow in His steps. 002:022 He never sinned, and no deceitful language was ever heard from His mouth. 002:023 When He was reviled, He did not answer with reviling; when He suffered He uttered no threats, but left His wrongs in the hands of the righteous Judge. 002:024 The burden of our sins He Himself carried in His own body to the Cross and bore it there, so that we, having died so far as our sins are concerned, may live righteous lives. By His wounds yours have been healed. 002:025 For you were straying like lost sheep, but now you have come back to the Shepherd and Protector of your souls. 003:001 Married women, in the same way, be submissive to your husbands, so that even if some of them disbelieve the Message, they may, apart from the Message, be won over by the daily life of their wives, after watching your daily life- 003:002 so full of reverence, and so blameless! 003:003 Your adornment ought not to be a merely outward thing-one of plaiting the hair, putting on jewelry, or wearing beautiful dresses. 003:004 Instead of that, it should be a new nature within-the imperishable ornament of a gentle and peaceful spirit, which is indeed precious in the sight of God. 003:005 For in ancient times also this was the way the holy women who set their hopes upon God used to adorn themselves, being submissive to their husbands. 003:006 Thus, for instance, Sarah obeyed Abraham, acknowledging his authority over her. And you have become Sarah's children if you do what is right and permit nothing whatever to terrify you. 003:007 Married men, in the same way, live with your wives with a clear recognition of the fact that they are weaker than you. Yet, since you are heirs with them of God's free gift of Life, treat them with honour; so that your prayers may not be hindered. 003:008 In conclusion, all of you should be of one mind, quick to sympathize, kind to the brethren, tenderhearted, lowly-minded, 003:009 not requiting evil with evil nor abuse with abuse, but, on the contrary, giving a blessing in return, because a blessing is what you have been called by God to inherit. 003:010 For "He who wishes to be well-satisfied with life and see happy days-let him restrain his tongue from evil, and his lips from deceitful words; 003:011 Let him turn from evil, and do good; Let him inquire for peace and go in pursuit of it. 003:012 For the eyes of the Lord are upon the righteous, and His ears are open to their supplication; but the face of the Lord is set against evil-doers." 003:013 And who will be able to harm you, if you show yourselves zealous for that which is good? 003:014 But even if you suffer for righteousness' sake, you are to be envied. So do not be alarmed by their threats, nor troubled; 003:015 but in your hearts consecrate Christ as Lord, being always ready to make your defence to any one who asks from you a reason for the hope which you cherish. 003:016 Yet argue modestly and cautiously, keeping your consciences free from guilt, so that, when you are spoken against, those who slander your good Christian lives may be put to shame. 003:017 For it is better that you should suffer for doing right, if such be God's will, than for doing evil; 003:018 because Christ also once for all died for sins, the innocent One for the guilty many, in order to bring us to God. He was put to death in the flesh, but made alive in the spirit, 003:019 in which He also went and proclaimed His Message to the spirits that were in prison, 003:020 who in ancient times had been disobedient, while God's longsuffering was patiently waiting in the days of Noah during the building of the Ark, in which a few persons- eight in number-were brought safely through the water. 003:021 And, corresponding to that figure, the water of baptism now saves you- not the washing off of material defilement, but the craving of a good conscience after God-through the resurrection of Jesus Christ, 003:022 who is at God's right hand, having gone into Heaven, angels and authorities and powers having been made subject to Him. 004:001 Since, then, Christ has suffered in the flesh, you also must arm yourselves with a determination to do the same- because he who has suffered in the flesh has done with sin- 004:002 that in future you may spend the rest of your earthly lives, governed not by human passions, but by the will of God. 004:003 For you have given time enough in the past to the doing of the things which the Gentiles delight in-pursuing, as you did, a course of habitual licence, debauchery, hard drinking, noisy revelry, drunkenness and unholy image-worship. 004:004 At this they are astonished-that you do not run into the same excess of profligacy as they do; and they speak abusively of you. 004:005 But they will have to give account to Him who stands ready to pronounce judgement on the living and the dead. 004:006 For it is with this end in view that the Good News was proclaimed even to some who were dead, that they may be judged, as all mankind will be judged, in the body, but may be living a godly life in the spirit. 004:007 But the end of all things is now close at hand: therefore be sober-minded and temperate, so that you may give yourselves to prayer. 004:008 Above all continue to love one another fervently, for love throws a veil over a multitude of faults. 004:009 Extend ungrudging hospitality towards one another. 004:010 Whatever be the gifts which each has received, you must use them for one another's benefit, as good stewards of God's many-sided kindness. 004:011 If any one preaches, let it be as uttering God's truth; if any one renders a service to others, let it be in the strength which God supplies; so that in everything glory may be given to God in the name of Jesus Christ, to whom belong the glory and the might to the Ages of the Ages. Amen. 004:012 Dear friends, do not be surprised at finding that that scorching flame of persecution is raging among you to put you to the test- as though some surprising thing were accidentally happening to you. 004:013 On the contrary, in the degree that you share in the sufferings of the Christ, rejoice, so that at the unveiling of His glory you may also rejoice with triumphant gladness. 004:014 You are to be envied, if you are being reproached for bearing the name of Christ; for in that case the Spirit of glory- even the Spirit of God-is resting upon you. 004:015 But let not one of you suffer as a murderer or a thief or an evil-doer, or as a spy upon other people's business. 004:016 If, however, any one suffers because he is a Christian, let him not be ashamed, but let him glorify God for being permitted to bear that name. 004:017 For the time has come for judgement to begin, and to begin at the house of God; and if it begins with us, what will be the end of those who reject God's Good News? 004:018 And if it is difficult even for a righteous man to be saved, what will become of irreligious men and sinners? 004:019 Therefore also, let those who are suffering in accordance with the will of God entrust their souls in well-doing to a faithful Creator. 005:001 So I exhort the Elders among you-I who am their fellow Elder and have been an eye-witness of the sufferings of the Christ, and am also a sharer in the glory which is soon to be revealed. 005:002 Be shepherds of God's flock which is among you. Exercise the oversight not reluctantly but eagerly, in accordance with the will of God;

not for base gain but with cheerful minds; 005:003 not lording it over your Churches but proving yourselves patterns for the flock to imitate. 005:004 And then, when the chief Shepherd appears, you will receive the never-withering wreath of glory. 005:005 In the same way you younger men must submit to your elders; and all of you must gird yourselves with humility towards one another, for God sets Himself against the proud, but gives grace to the humble. 005:006 Humble yourselves therefore beneath the mighty hand of God, so that at the right time He may set you on high. 005:007 Throw the whole of your anxiety upon Him, because He Himself cares for you. 005:008 Curb every passion, and be on the alert. Your great accuser, the Devil, is going about like a roaring lion to see whom he can devour. 005:009 Withstand him, firm in your faith; knowing that your brethren in other parts of the world are passing through just the same experiences. 005:010 And God, the giver of all grace, who has called you to share His eternal glory, through Christ, after you have suffered for a short time, will Himself make you perfect, firm, and strong. 005:011 To Him be all power unto the Ages of the Ages! Amen. 005:012 I send this short letter by Silas, our faithful brother- for such I regard him-in order to encourage you, and to bear witness that what I have told you is the true grace of God. In it stand fast. 005:013 The Church in Babylon, chosen like yourselves by God, sends greetings, and so does Mark my son. 005:014 Greet one another with a kiss of love. Peace be with all of you who are in Christ.

BOOK 52 1 THESSALONIANS

001:001 Paul, Silas, and Timothy: To the Church of the Thessalonians which is in God the Father and the Lord Jesus Christ. May grace and peace be granted to you. 001:002 We continually give thanks to God because of you all, while we make mention of you in our prayers. 001:003 For we never fail to remember your works of faith and labours of love and your persistent and unwavering hope in our Lord Jesus Christ in the presence of our God and Father; 001:004 knowing as we do, brethren, that you are beloved by God and that He has chosen you. 001:005 The Good News that we brought you did not come to you in words only, but also with power and with the Holy Spirit and with much certainty, for you know the sort of men we became among you, as examples for your sakes. 001:006 And you followed the pattern set you by us and by the Master, after you had received the Message amid severe persecution, and yet with the joy which the Holy Spirit gives, 001:007 so that you became a pattern to all the believers throughout Macedonia and Greece. 001:008 For it was not only from you that the Master's Message sounded forth throughout Macedonia and Greece; but everywhere your faith in God has become known, so that it is unnecessary for us to say anything about it. 001:009 For when others speak of us they report the reception we had from you, and how you turned from your idols to God, to be bondservants of the true and ever-living God, 001:010 and to await the return from Heaven of His Son, whom He raised from among the dead-even Jesus, our Deliverer from God's coming anger. 002:001 For you yourselves, brethren, know that our visit to you did not fail of its purpose. 002:002 But, as you will remember, after we had already met with suffering and outrage at Philippi, we summoned up boldness, by the help of our God, to tell you God's Good News amid much opposition. 002:003 For our preaching was not grounded on a delusion, nor prompted by mingled motives, nor was there fraud in it. 002:004 But as God tested and approved us before entrusting us with His Good News, so in what we say we are seeking not to please men but to please God, who tests and approves our motives. 002:005 For, as you are well aware, we have never used the language of flattery nor have we found pretexts for enriching ourselves- God is our witness; 002:006 nor did we seek glory either from you or from any other mere men, although we might have stood on our dignity as Christ's Apostles. 002:007 On the contrary, in our relations to you we showed ourselves as gentle as a mother is when she tenderly nurses her own children. 002:008 Seeing that we were thus drawn affectionately towards you, it would have been a joy to us to have imparted to you not only God's Good News, but to have given our very lives also, because you had become very dear to us. 002:009 For you remember, brethren, our labour and toil: how, working night and day so as not to become a burden to any one of you, we came and proclaimed among you God's Good News. 002:010 You yourselves are witnesses-and God is witness-how holy and upright and blameless our dealings with you believers were. 002:011 For you know that we acted towards every one of you as a father does towards his own children, encouraging and cheering you, 002:012 and imploring you to live lives worthy of fellowship with God who is inviting you to share His own Kingship and glory. 002:013 And for this further reason we render unceasing thanks to God, that when you received God's Message from our lips, it was as no mere message from men that you embraced it, but as-what it really is-God's Message, which also does its work in the hearts of you who believe. 002:014 For you, brethren, followed the example of the Churches of God in Christ Jesus which are in Judaea; seeing that you endured the same ill-treatment at the hands of your countrymen, as they did at the hands of the Jews. 002:015 Those Jewish persecutors killed both the Lord Jesus and the Prophets, and drove us out of their midst. They are displeasing to God, and are the enemies of all mankind; 002:016 for they still try to prevent our preaching to the Gentiles so that they may find salvation. They thus continually fill up the measure of their own sins, and God's anger in its severest form has overtaken them. 002:017 But we, brethren, having been for a short time separated from you in bodily presence, though not in heart, endeavoured all the more earnestly, with intense longing, to see you face to face. 002:018 On this account we wanted to come to you-at least I Paul wanted again and again to do so-but Satan hindered us. 002:019 For what is our hope or joy, or the crown of which we boast? Is it not you yourselves in the presence of our Lord Jesus at His Coming? 002:020 Yes, you are our glory and our joy. 003:001 So when we could endure it no longer, we decided to remain behind in Athens alone; 003:002 and sent Timothy our brother and God's minister in the service of Christ's Good News, that he might help you spiritually and encourage you in your faith; 003:003 that none of you might be unnerved by your present trials: for you yourselves know that they are our appointed lot. 003:004 For even when we were with you, we forewarned you, saying, "We are soon to suffer affliction;" and this actually happened, as you well know. 003:005 For this reason I also, when I could no longer endure the uncertainty, sent to know the condition of your faith, lest perchance the Tempter might have tempted you and our labour have been lost. 003:006 But now that Timothy has recently come back to us from you, and has brought us the happy tidings of your faith and love, and has told us how you still cherish a constant and affectionate recollection of us, and are longing to see us as we also long to see you- 003:007 for this reason in our distress and trouble we have been comforted about you, brethren, by your faith. 003:008 For now life is for us life indeed, since you are standing fast in the Lord. 003:009 For what thanksgiving on your behalf can we possibly offer to God in return for all the joy which fills our souls before our God for you, 003:010 while night and day, with intense earnestness, we pray that we may see your faces, and may bring to perfection whatever may be still lacking in your faith? 003:011 But may our God and Father Himself-and our Lord Jesus- guide us on our way to you; 003:012 and as for you, may the Lord teach you to love one another and all men, with a growing and a glowing love, resembling our love for you. 003:013 Thus He will build up your characters, so that you will be faultlessly holy in the presence of our God and Father at the Coming of our Lord Jesus with all His holy ones. 004:001 Moreover, brethren, as you learnt from our lips the lives which you ought to live, and do live, so as to please God, we beg and exhort you in the name of the Lord Jesus to live them more and more truly. 004:002 For you know the commands which we laid upon you by the authority of the Lord Jesus. 004:003 For this is God's will-your purity of life, that you abstain from fornication; 004:004 that each man among you shall know how to procure a wife who shall be his own in purity and honour; 004:005 that you be not overmastered by lustful cravings, like the Gentiles who have no knowledge of God; 004:006 and that in this matter there be no encroaching on the rights of a brother Christian and no overreaching him. For the Lord is an avenger in all such cases, as we have already taught you and solemnly warned you. 004:007 God has not called us to an unclean life, but to one of purity. 004:008 Therefore a defiant spirit in such a case provokes not man but God, who puts His Holy Spirit into your hearts. 004:009 But on the subject of love for the brotherhood it is unnecessary for me to write to you, for you yourselves have been taught by God to love one another; 004:010 and indeed you do love all the brethren throughout Macedonia. And we exhort you to do so more and more, 004:011 and to vie with one another in eagerness for peace, every one minding his own business and working with his hands, as we ordered you to do: 004:012 so as to live worthy lives in relation to outsiders, and not be a burden to any one. 004:013 Now, concerning those who from time to time pass away, we would not have you to be ignorant, brethren, lest you should mourn as others do who have no hope. 004:014 For if we believe that Jesus has died and risen again, we also believe that, through Jesus, God will bring with Him those who shall have passed away. 004:015 For this we declare to you on the Lord's own authority- that we who are alive and continue on earth until the Coming of the Lord, shall certainly not forestall those who shall have previously passed away. 004:016 For the Lord Himself will come down from Heaven with a loud word of command, and with an archangel's voice and the trumpet of God, and the dead in Christ will rise first. 004:017 Afterwards we who are alive and are still on earth will be caught up in their company amid clouds to meet the Lord in the air. 004:018 And so we shall be with the Lord for ever. Therefore encourage one another with these words. 005:001 But as to times and dates it is unnecessary that anything be written to you. 005:002 For you yourselves know perfectly well that the day of the Lord comes like a thief in the night. 005:003 While they are saying "Peace and safety!" then in a moment destruction falls upon them, like birth-pains on a woman who is with child; and escape there is none. 005:004 But you, brethren, are not in darkness, that daylight should surprise you like a thief; 005:005 for all of you are sons of Light and sons of the day. We belong neither to the night nor to darkness. 005:006 So then let us not sleep, like the rest of the world, but let us keep awake and be sober. 005:007 For those who sleep, sleep at night, and those who drink freely, drink at night. 005:008 But let us, belonging-as we do-to the day, be sober, putting on the breastplate of faith and love, and for a helmet the hope of salvation. 005:009 For God has not pre-destined us to meet His anger, but to obtain salvation through our Lord Jesus Christ; 005:010 who died on our behalf, so that whether we are awake or are sleeping we may share His Life. 005:011 Therefore encourage one another, and let each one help to strengthen his friend, as in fact you do. 005:012 Now we beg you, brethren, to show respect for those who labour among you and are your leaders in Christian work, and are your advisers; 005:013 and to esteem them very highly in love for their work's sake. Be at peace among yourselves. 005:014 And we exhort you, brethren, admonish the unruly, comfort the timid, sustain the weak, and be patient towards all. 005:015 See to it that no one ever repays another with evil for evil; but always seek opportunities of doing good both to one another and to all the world. 005:016 Be always joyful. 005:017 Be unceasing in prayer. 005:018 In every circumstance of life be thankful; for this is God's will in Christ Jesus respecting you. 005:019 Do not quench the Spirit. 005:020 Do not think meanly of utterances of prophecy; 005:021 but test all such, and retain hold of the good. 005:022 Hold yourselves aloof from every form of evil. 005:023 And may God Himself who gives peace, make you entirely holy; and may your spirits, souls and bodies be preserved complete and be found blameless at the Coming of our Lord Jesus Christ. 005:024 Faithful is He who calls you, and He will also perfect His work. 005:025 Brethren, pray for us. 005:026 Greet all the brethren with a holy kiss. 005:027 I solemnly charge you in the Lord's name to have this Letter read to all the brethren. 005:028 May the grace of our Lord Jesus Christ be with you.

BOOK 54 1 TIMOTHY

001:001 Paul, an Apostle of Christ Jesus by the will of God our Saviour and Christ Jesus our hope: 001:002 To Timothy, my own true son in the faith. May grace, mercy and peace be granted to you from God the Father and Christ Jesus our Lord. 001:003 When I was on my journey to Macedonia I begged you to remain on in Ephesus that you might remonstrate with certain persons because of their erroneous teaching 001:004 and the attention they bestow on mere fables and endless pedigrees, such as lead to controversy rather than to a true stewardship for God, which only exists where there is faith. And I make the same request now. 001:005 But the end sought to be secured by exhortation is the love which springs from a pure heart, a clear conscience and a sincere faith. 001:006 From these some have drifted away, and have wandered into empty words. 001:007 They are ambitious to be teachers of the Law, although they do not understand either their own words or what the things are about which they make such confident assertions. 001:008 Now we know that the Law is good, if a man uses it in the way it should be used, 001:009 and remembers that a law is not enacted to control a righteous man, but for the lawless and rebellious, the irreligious and sinful, the godless and profane-for those who strike their fathers or their mothers, for murderers, 001:010 fornicators, sodomites, slave-dealers, liars and false witnesses; and for whatever else is opposed to wholesome teaching 001:011 and is not in accordance with the Good News of the blessed God with which I have been entrusted. 001:012 I am thankful to Him who made me strong-even Christ Jesus our Lord-because He has judged me to be faithful and has put me into His service, 001:013 though I was previously a blasphemer and a persecutor and had been insolent in outrage. Yet mercy was shown me, because I had acted ignorantly, not having as yet believed; 001:014 and the grace of our Lord came to me in overflowing fulness, conferring faith on me and the love which is in Christ Jesus. 001:015 Faithful is the saying, and deserving of universal acceptance, that Christ Jesus came into the world to save sinners; among whom I stand foremost. 001:016 But mercy was shown me in order that in me as the foremost of sinners Christ Jesus might display the fulness of His long-suffering patience as an example to encourage those who would afterwards be resting their faith on Him with a view to the Life of the Ages. 001:017 Now to the immortal and invisible King of the Ages, who alone is God, be honour and glory to the Ages of the Ages! Amen. 001:018 This is the charge which I entrust to you, my son Timothy, in accordance with the inspired instructions concerning you which were given me long ago, that being equipped with them as your armour you may be continually fighting the good fight, 001:019 holding fast to faith and a clear conscience, which some have cast aside and have made shipwreck of their faith. 001:020 Among these are Hymenaeus and Alexander, whom I have delivered to Satan so that they may be taught not to blaspheme. 002:001 I exhort then, first of all, that supplications, prayers, intercessions and thanksgivings be offered on behalf of all men; 002:002 including kings and all who are in high station, in order that we may live peaceful and tranquil lives with all godliness and gravity. 002:003 This is right, and is pleasing in the sight of God our Saviour, 002:004 who is willing for all mankind to be saved and come to a full knowledge of the truth. 002:005 For there is but one God and but one Mediator between God and men- Christ Jesus, Himself man; 002:006 who gave Himself as the redemption price for all-a fact testified to at its own appointed time, 002:007 and of which I have been appointed a herald and an Apostle (I am speaking the truth: it is not a fiction), a teacher of the Gentiles in faith and truth. 002:008 So then I would have the men everywhere pray, lifting to God holy hands which are unstained with anger or strife; 002:009 and I would have the women dress becomingly, with modesty and self-control, not with plaited hair or gold or pearls or costly clothes, 002:010 but-as befits women making a claim to godliness- with the ornament of good works. 002:011 A woman should quietly learn from others with entire submissiveness. 002:012 I do not permit a woman to teach, nor have authority over a man, but she must remain silent. 002:013 For Adam was formed first, and then Eve; 002:014 and Adam was not deceived, but his wife was thoroughly deceived, and so became involved in transgression. 002:015 Yet a woman will be brought safely through childbirth if she and her husband continue to live in faith and love and growing holiness, with habitual self-restraint. 003:001 Faithful is the saying, "If any one is eager to have the oversight of a Church, he desires a noble work." 003:002 A minister then must be a man of irreproachable character, true to his one wife, temperate, sober-minded, well-behaved, hospitable to strangers, and with a gift for teaching; 003:003 not a hard drinker nor given to blows; not selfish or quarrelsome or covetous; 003:004 but ruling his own household wisely and well, with children kept under control with true dignity. 003:005 (If a man does not know how to rule his own household, how shall he have the Church of God given into his care?) 003:006 He ought not to be a new convert, for fear he should be blinded with pride and come under the same condemnation as the Devil. 003:007 It is needful also that he bear a good character with people outside the Church, lest he fall into reproach or a snare of the Devil. 003:008 Deacons, in the same way, must be men of serious demeanour, not double-tongued, nor addicted to much wine, nor greedy of base gain, 003:009 but holding the secret truths of the faith with a clear conscience. 003:010 And they must also be well-tried men, and when found to be of unblemished character then let them serve as deacons. 003:011 Deaconesses, in the same way, must be sober-minded women, not slanderers, but in every way temperate and trustworthy. 003:012 A deacon must be true to his one wife, and rule his children and his own household wisely and well. 003:013 For those who have filled the deacon's office wisely and well, are already gaining for themselves an honourable standing, and are acquiring great freedom of speech in proclaiming the faith which rests on Christ Jesus. 003:014 All this I write to you, though I am hoping before long to come to see you. 003:015 But, for fear I may be hindered, I now write, so that you may have rules to guide you in dealing with God's household. For this is what the Church of the ever-living God is, and it is the pillar and foundation-stone of the truth. 003:016 And, beyond controversy, great is the mystery of our religion- that Christ appeared in human form, and His claims justified by the Spirit, was seen by angels and proclaimed among Gentile nations, was believed on in the world, and received up again into glory. 004:001 Now the Spirit expressly declares that in later times some will fall away from the faith, giving heed to deceiving spirits and the teachings of demons; 004:002 through the hypocrisy of men who teach falsely and have their own consciences seared as with a hot iron; 004:003 forbidding people to marry, and insisting on abstinence from foods which God has created to be partaken of, with thankfulness, by those who believe and have a clear knowledge of the truth. 004:004 For everything that God has created is good, and nothing is to be cast aside, if only it is received with thanksgiving. 004:005 For it is made holy by the word of God and by prayer. 004:006 If you warn the brethren of these dangers you will be a good and faithful servant of Christ Jesus, inwardly feeding on the lessons of the faith and of the sound teaching of which you have been, and are, so close a follower. 004:007 But worldly stories, fit only for credulous old women, have nothing to do with. 004:008 Train yourself in godliness. Exercise for the body is not useless, but godliness is useful in every respect, possessing, as it does, the promise of Life now and of the Life which is soon coming. 004:009 Faithful is this saying and deserving of universal acceptance: 004:010 and here is the motive of our toiling and wrestling, because we have our hopes fixed on the ever-living God, who is the Saviour of all mankind, and especially of believers. 004:011 Command this and teach this. 004:012 Let no one think slightingly of you because you are a young man; but in speech, conduct, love, faith and purity, be an example for your fellow Christians to imitate. 004:013 Till I come, bestow your attention on reading, exhortation and teaching. 004:014 Do not be careless about the gifts with which you are endowed, which were conferred on you through a divine revelation when the hands of the elders were placed upon you. 004:015 Habitually practise these duties, and be absorbed in them; so that your growing proficiency in them may be evident to all. 004:016 Be on your guard as to yourself and your teaching. Persevere in these things; for by doing this you will make certain your own salvation and that of your hearers. 005:001 Never administer a sharp reprimand to a man older than yourself; but entreat him as if he were your father, and the younger men as brothers; 005:002 the elder women too as mothers, and the younger women as sisters, with perfect modesty. 005:003 Honour widows who are really in need. 005:004 But if a widow has children or grandchildren, let these learn first to show piety towards their own homes and to prove their gratitude to their parents; for this is well pleasing in the sight of God. 005:005 A widow who is really in need, friendless and desolate, has her hopes fixed on God, and continues at her supplications and prayers, night and day; 005:006 but a pleasure-loving widow is dead even while still alive. 005:007 Press these facts upon them, so that they may live lives free from reproach. 005:008 But if a man makes no provision for those dependent on him, and especially for his own family, he has disowned the faith and is behaving worse than an unbeliever. 005:009 No widow is to be put on the roll who is under sixty years of age. 005:010 She must have been true to her one husband, and well reported of for good deeds, as having brought up children, received strangers hospitably, washed the feet of God's people, given relief to the distressed, and devoted herself to good works of every kind. 005:011 But the younger widows you must not enrol; for as soon as they begin to chafe against the yoke of Christ, they want to marry, 005:012 and they incur disapproval for having broken their original vow. 005:013 And at the same time they also learn to be idle as they go round from house to house; and they are not only idle, but are gossips also and busybodies, speaking of things that ought not to be spoken of. 005:014 I would therefore have the younger women marry, bear children, rule in domestic matters, and furnish the Adversary with no excuse for slander. 005:015 For already some of them have gone astray, following Satan. 005:016 If a believing woman has widows dependent on her, she should relieve their wants, and save the Church from being burdened- so that the Church may relieve the widows who are really in need. 005:017 Let the Elders who perform their duties wisely and well be held worthy of double honour, especially those who labour in preaching and teaching. 005:018 For the Scripture says, "You are not to muzzle the ox while it is treading out the grain;" and the workman deserves his pay. 005:019 Never entertain an accusation against an Elder except on the evidence of two of three witnesses. 005:020 Those who persist in sin reprove in the presence of all, so that it may also be a warning to the rest. 005:021 I solemnly call upon you, in the presence of God and of Christ Jesus and of the elect angels, to carry out these instructions of mine without prejudice, and to do nothing from partiality. 005:022 Do not ordain any one hastily; and do not be a partaker in the sins of others; keep *yourself* pure. 005:023 (No longer be a water-drinker; but take a little wine for the sake of your digestion and your frequent ailments.) 005:024 The sins of some men are evident to the world, leading the way to your estimate of their characters, but the sins of others lag behind. 005:025 So also the right actions of some are evident to the world, and those that are not cannot remain for ever out of sight. 006:001 Let all who are under the yoke of slavery hold their own masters to be deserving of honour, so that the name of God and the Christian teaching may not be spoken against. 006:002 And those who have believing masters should not be wanting in respect towards them because they are their brethren, but should serve them all the more willingly because those who profit by the faithful service rendered are believers and are friends. 006:003 So teach and exhort. If any one is a teacher of any other kind of doctrine, and refuses assent to wholesome instructions- those of our Lord Jesus Christ-and the teaching that harmonizes with true godliness, 006:004 he is puffed up with pride and has no true knowledge, but is crazy over discussions and controversies about words which give rise to envy, quarrelling, revilings, ill-natured suspicions, 006:005 and persistent wranglings on the part of people whose intellects are disordered and they themselves blinded to all knowledge of the truth; who imagine that godliness means gain. 006:006 And godliness *is* gain, when associated with contentment; 006:007 for we brought nothing into the world, nor can we carry anything out of it; 006:008 and if we have food and clothing, with these we will be satisfied. 006:009 But people who are determined to be rich fall into temptation and a snare, and into many unwise and pernicious ways which sink mankind in destruction and ruin. 006:010 For from love of money all sorts of evils arise; and some have so hankered after money as to be led astray from the faith and be pierced through with countless sorrows. 006:011 But you, O man of God, must flee from these things; and strive for uprightness, godliness, good faith, love, fortitude, and a forgiving temper. 006:012 Exert all your strength in the honourable struggle for the faith; lay hold of the Life of the Ages, to which you were called, when you made your noble profession of faith before many witnesses. 006:013 I charge you-as in the presence of God who gives life to all creatures, and of Christ Jesus who at the bar of Pontius Pilate made a noble profession of faith- 006:014 that you keep God's commandments stainlessly and without reproach till the Appearing of our Lord Jesus Christ. 006:015 For, as its appointed time, this will be brought about by the blessed and only Sovereign, the King of kings and Lord of lords, 006:016 who alone possesses immortality, dwelling in unapproachable light, and whom no man has seen or can see. To Him be eternal honour and power! Amen. 006:017 Impress on those who are rich in the present age that they must not be haughty nor set their hopes on riches- that unstable foundation-but on God who provides us richly with all things for our enjoyment. 006:018 They must be beneficent, rich in noble deeds, open-handed and liberal; 006:019 storing up for themselves that which shall be a solid foundation for the future, that they may lay hold of the Life which is life indeed. 006:020 O Timothy, guard the truths entrusted to you, shunning irreligious and frivolous talk, and controversy with what is falsely called `knowledge'; 006:021 of which some have spoken boastfully in connexion with the true faith, and have erred. Grace be with you all.

BOOK 47 2 CORINTHIANS

001:001 Paul, an Apostle of Christ Jesus by the will of God- and our brother Timothy: To the Church of God in Corinth, with all God's people throughout Greece. 001:002 May grace and peace be granted to you from God our Father and the Lord Jesus Christ. 001:003 Heartfelt thanks be to the God and Father of our Lord Jesus Christ- the Father who is full of compassion and the God who gives all comfort. 001:004 He comforts us in our every affliction so that we may be able to comfort those who are in any kind of affliction by means of the comfort with which we ourselves are comforted by God. 001:005 For just as we have more than our share of suffering for the Christ, so also through the Christ we have more than our share of comfort. 001:006 But if, on the one hand, we are enduring affliction, it is for your comfort and salvation; and if, on the other hand, we are receiving comfort, it is for your comfort which is produced within you through your patient fortitude under the same sufferings as those which we also are enduring. 001:007 And our hope for you is stedfast; for we know that as you are partners with us in the sufferings, so you are also partners in the comfort. 001:008 For as for our troubles which came upon us in the province of Asia, we would have you know, brethren, that we were exceedingly weighed down, and felt overwhelmed, so that we renounced all hope even of life. 001:009 Nay, we had, as we still have, the sentence of death within our own selves, in order that our confidence may repose, not on ourselves, but on God who raised the dead to life. 001:010 He it is who rescued us from so imminent a death, and will do so again; and we have a firm hope in Him that He will also rescue us in all the future, 001:011 while you on your part lend us your aid in entreaty for us, so that from many lips thanksgivings may rise on our behalf for the boon granted to us at the intercession of many. 001:012 For the reason for our boasting is this-the testimony of our own conscience that it was in holiness and with pure motives before God, and in reliance not on worldly wisdom but on the gracious help of God, that we have conducted ourselves in the world, and above all in our relations with you. 001:013 For we are writing to you nothing different from what we have written before, or from what indeed you already recognize as truth and will, I trust, recognize as such to the very end; 001:014 just as some few of you have recognized us as your reason for boasting, even as you will be ours, on the day of Jesus our Lord. 001:015 It was because I entertained this confidence that I intended to visit you before going elsewhere-so that you might receive a twofold proof of God's favour-001:016 and to pass by way of Corinth into Macedonia. Then my plan was to return from Macedonia to you, and be helped forward by you to Judaea. 001:017 Did I display any vacillation or caprice in this? Or the purposes which I form-do I form them on worldly principles, now crying "Yes, yes," and now "No, no"? 001:018 As certainly as God is faithful, our language to you is not now "Yes" and now "No." 001:019 For Jesus Christ the Son of God-He who was proclaimed among you by us, that is by Silas and Timothy and myself- did not show Himself a waverer between "Yes" and "No." But it was and always is "Yes" with Him. 001:020 For all the promises of God, whatever their number, have their confirmation in Him; and for this reason through Him also our "Amen" acknowledges their truth and promotes the glory of God through our faith. 001:021 But He who is making us as well as you stedfast through union with the Anointed One, and has anointed us, is God, 001:022 and He has also set His seal upon us, and has put His Spirit into our hearts as a pledge and foretaste of future blessing. 001:023 But as for me, as my soul shall answer for it, I appeal to God as my witness, that it was to spare you pain that I gave up my visit to Corinth. 001:024 Not that we want to lord it over you in respect of your faith- we do, however, desire to help your joy-for in the matter of your faith you are standing firm. 002:001 But, so far as I am concerned, I have resolved not to have a painful visit the next time I come to see you. 002:002 For if I of all men give you pain, who then is there to gladden my heart, but the very persons to whom I give pain? 002:003 And I write this to you in order that when I come I may not receive pain from those who ought to give me joy, confident as I am as to all of you that my joy is the joy of you all. 002:004 For with many tears I write to you, and in deep suffering and depression of spirit, not in order to grieve you, but in the hope of showing you how brimful my heart is with love for you. 002:005 Now if any one has caused sorrow, it has been caused not so much to me, as in some degree-for I have no wish to exaggerate- to all of you. 002:006 In the case of such a person the punishment which was inflicted by the majority of you is enough. 002:007 So that you may now take the opposite course, and forgive him rather and comfort him, for fear he should perhaps be driven to despair by his excess of grief. 002:008 I beg you therefore fully to reinstate him in your love. 002:009 For in writing to you I have also this object in view- to discover by experience whether you are prepared to be obedient in every respect. 002:010 When you forgive a man an offence I also forgive it; for in fact what I have forgiven, if I have forgiven anything, has always been for your sakes in the presence of Christ, 002:011 for fear Satan should gain an advantage over us. For we are not ignorant of his devices. 002:012 Now when I came into the Troad to spread there the Good News about the Christ, even though in the Lord's providence a door stood open before me, 002:013 yet, obtaining no relief for my spirit because I did not find our brother Titus, I bade them farewell and went on into Macedonia. 002:014 But to God be the thanks who in Christ ever heads our triumphal procession, and by our hands waves in every place that sweet incense, the knowledge of Him. 002:015 For we are a fragrance of Christ grateful to God in those whom He is saving and in those who are perishing; 002:016 to the last-named an odor of death predictive of death, and to the others an odor of life predictive of life. And for such service as this who is competent? 002:017 We are; for, unlike most teachers, we are not fraudulent hucksters of God's Message; but with transparent motives, as commissioned by God, in God's presence and in communion with Christ, so we speak. 003:001 Do you say that this is self-recommendation once more? Or do we need, as some do, letters of recommendation to you or from you? 003:002 Our letter of recommendation is yourselves-a letter written on our hearts and everywhere known and read. 003:003 For all can see that you are a letter of Christ entrusted to our care, and written not with ink, but with the Spirit of the ever-living God-and not on tablets of stone, but on human hearts as tablets. 003:004 Such is the confidence which we have through Christ in the presence of God; 003:005 not that of ourselves we are competent to decide anything by our own reasonings, but our competency comes from God. 003:006 It is He also who has made us competent to serve Him in connexion with a new Covenant, which is not a written code but a Spirit; for the written code inflicts death, but the Spirit gives Life. 003:007 If, however, the service that proclaims death-its code being engraved in writing upon stones-came with glory, so that the children of Israel could not look steadily on the face of Moses because of the brightness of his face- a vanishing brightness; 003:008 will not the service of the Spirit be far more glorious? 003:009 For if the service which pronounces doom had glory, far more glorious still is the service which tells of righteousness. 003:010 For, in fact, that which was once resplendent in glory has no glory at all in this respect, that it pales before the glory which surpasses it. 003:011 For if that which was to be abolished came with glory, much more is that which is permanent arrayed in glory. 003:012 Therefore, cherishing a hope like this, we speak without reserve, and we do not imitate Moses, 003:013 who used to throw a veil over his face to hide from the gaze of the children of Israel the passing away of what was but transitory. 003:014 Nay, their minds were made dull; for to this very day during the reading of the book of the ancient Covenant, the same veil remains unlifted, because it is only in Christ that it is to be abolished. 003:015 Yes, to this day, whenever Moses is read, a veil lies upon their hearts. 003:016 But whenever the heart of the nation shall have returned to the Lord, the veil will be withdrawn. 003:017 Now by "the Lord" is meant the Spirit; and where the Spirit of the Lord is, freedom is enjoyed. 003:018 And all of us, with unveiled faces, reflecting like bright mirrors the glory of the Lord, are being transformed into the same likeness, from one degree of radiant holiness to another, even as derived from the Lord the Spirit. 004:001 Therefore, being engaged in this service and being mindful of the mercy which has been shown us, we are not cowards. 004:002 Nay, we have renounced the secrecy which marks a feeling of shame. We practice no cunning tricks, nor do we adulterate God's Message. But by a full clear statement of the truth we strive to commend ourselves in the presence of God to every human conscience. 004:003 If, however, the meaning of our Good News has been veiled, the veil has been on the hearts of those who are on the way to perdition, 004:004 in whom the god of this present age has blinded their unbelieving minds so as to shut out the sunshine of the Good News of the glory of the Christ, who is the image of God. 004:005 (For we do not proclaim ourselves, but we proclaim Christ Jesus as Lord, and ourselves as your bondservants for the sake of Jesus.) 004:006 For God who said, "Out of darkness let light shine," is He who has shone in our hearts to give us the light of the knowledge of God's glory, which is radiant on the face of Christ. 004:007 But we have this treasure in a fragile vase of clay, in order that the surpassing greatness of the power may be seen to belong to God, and not to originate in us. 004:008 We are hard pressed, yet never in absolute distress; perplexed, yet never utterly baffled; 004:009 pursued, yet never left unsuccoured; struck to the ground, yet never slain; 004:010 always, wherever we go, carrying with us in our bodies the putting to death of Jesus, so that in our bodies it may also be clearly shown that Jesus lives. 004:011 For we, alive though we are, are continually surrendering ourselves to death for the sake of Jesus, so that in this mortal nature of ours it may also be clearly shown that Jesus lives. 004:012 Thus we are constantly dying, while you are in full enjoyment of Life. 004:013 But possessing the same Spirit of faith as he who wrote, "I believed, and therefore I have spoken," we also believe, and therefore we speak. 004:014 For we know that He who raised the Lord Jesus from the dead will raise us also to be with Jesus, and will cause both us and you to stand in His own presence. 004:015 For everything is for your sakes, in order that grace, being more richly bestowed because of the thanksgivings of the increased number, may more and more promote the glory of God. 004:016 Therefore we are not cowards. Nay, even though our outward man is wasting away, yet our inward man is being renewed day by day. 004:017 For this our light and transitory burden of suffering is achieving for us a preponderating, yes, a vastly preponderating, and eternal weight of glory; 004:018 while we look not at things seen, but things unseen; for things seen are temporary, but things unseen are eternal. 005:001 For we know that if this poor tent, our earthly house, is taken down, we have in Heaven a building which God has provided, a house not built by human hands, but eternal. 005:002 For in this one we sigh, because we long to put on over it our dwelling which comes from Heaven- 005:003 if indeed having really put on a robe we shall not be found to be unclothed. 005:004 Yes, we who are in this tent certainly do sigh under our burdens, for we do not wish to lay aside that with which we are now clothed, but to put on more, so that our mortality may be absorbed in Life. 005:005 And He who formed us with this very end in view is God, who has given us His Spirit as a pledge and foretaste of that bliss. 005:006 We have therefore a cheerful confidence. We know that while we are at home in the body we are banished from the Lord; 005:007 for we are living a life of faith, and not one of sight. 005:008 So we have a cheerful confidence, and we anticipate with greater delight being banished from the body and going home to the Lord. 005:009 And for this reason also we make it our ambition, whether at home or in exile, to please Him perfectly. 005:010 For we must all of us appear before Christ's judgement-seat in our true characters, in order that each may then receive an award for his actions in this life, in accordance with what he has done, whether it be good or whether it be worthless. 005:011 Therefore, because we realize how greatly the Lord is to be feared, we are endeavouring to win men over, and God recognizes what our motives are, and I hope that you, in your hearts, recognize them too. 005:012 We are not again commending ourselves to your favour, but are furnishing you with a ground of boasting on our behalf, so that you may have a reply ready for those with whom superficial appearances are everything and sincerity of heart counts for nothing. 005:013 For if we have been beside ourselves, it has been for God's glory; or if we are now in our right senses, it is in order to be of service to you. 005:014 For the love of Christ overmasters us, the conclusion at which we have arrived being this-that One having died for all, His death was their death, 005:015 and that He died for all in order that the living may no longer live to themselves, but to Him who died for them and rose again. 005:016 Therefore for the future we know no one simply as a man. Even if we have known Christ as a man, yet now we do so no longer. 005:017 So that if any one is in Christ, he is a new creature: the old state of things has passed away; a new state of things has come into existence. 005:018 And all this is from God, who has reconciled us to Himself through Christ, and has appointed us to serve in the ministry of reconciliation. 005:019 We are to tell how God was in Christ reconciling the world to Himself, not charging men's transgressions to their account, and that He has entrusted to us the Message of this reconciliation. 005:020 On Christ's behalf therefore we come as ambassadors, God, as it were, making entreaty through our lips: we, on Christ's behalf, beseech men to be reconciled to God. 005:021 He has made Him who knew nothing of sin to be sin for us, in order that in Him we may become the righteousness of God. 006:001 And you also we, as God's fellow workers, entreat not to be found to have received His grace to no purpose. 006:002 For He says, "At a time of welcome I have listened to you, and on a day of salvation I have succoured you." Now is the time of loving welcome! Now is the day of salvation! 006:003 We endeavour to give people no cause for stumbling in anything, lest the work we are doing should fall into discredit. 006:004 On the contrary, as God's servants, we seek their full approval- by unwearied endurance, by afflictions, by distress, by helplessness; 006:005 by floggings, by imprisonments; by facing riots, by toil, by sleepless watching, by hunger and thirst; 006:006 by purity of life, by knowledge, by patience, by kindness, by the Holy Spirit, by sincere love; 006:007 by the proclamation of the truth, by the power of God; by the weapons of righteousness, wielded in both hands; 006:008 through honour and ignominy, through calumny and praise. We are looked upon as impostors and yet are true men; 006:009 as obscure persons, and yet are well known; as on the point of death, and yet, strange to tell, we live; as under God's discipline, and yet we are not deprived of life; 006:010 as sad, but we are always joyful; as poor, but we bestow wealth on many; as having nothing, and yet we securely possess all things. 006:011 O Corinthians, our lips are unsealed to you: our heart is expanded. 006:012 There is no narrowness in our love to you: the narrowness is in your own feelings. 006:013 And in just requital-I speak as to my children-let your hearts expand also. 006:014 Do not come into close association with unbelievers, like oxen yoked with asses. For what is there in common between righteousness and lawlessness? Or what partnership has light with darkness? 006:015 Where can harmony between Christ and Belial be found? Or what participation has a believer with an unbeliever? 006:016 And what compact has the Temple of God with idols? For *we* are the Temple of the ever-living God; as God has said, "I will dwell among them, and walk about among them; and will be their God, and it is they who shall be My people." 006:017 Therefore, "`Come out from among them and separate yourselves,' says the Lord, `and touch nothing impure; and I will receive you, and will be a Father to you, 006:018 and you shall be My sons and daughters,' says the Lord the Ruler of all." 007:001 Having therefore these promises, beloved friends, let us purify ourselves from all defilement of body and of spirit, and secure perfect holiness through the fear of God. 007:002 Make room for us in your hearts. There is not one of you whom we have wronged, not one to whom we have done harm, not one over whom we have gained any selfish advantage. 007:003 I do not say this to imply blame, for, as I have already said, you have such a place in our hearts that we would die with you or live with you. 007:004 I have great confidence in you: very loudly do I boast of you. I am filled with comfort: my heart overflows with joy amid all our affliction. 007:005 For even after our arrival in Macedonia we could get no relief such as human nature craves. We were greatly harassed; there were conflicts without and fears within. 007:006 But He who comforts the depressed-even God-comforted us by the coming of Titus, and not by his coming only, 007:007 but also by the fact that he had felt comforted on your account, and by the report which he brought of your eager affection, of your grief, and of your jealousy on my behalf, so that I rejoiced more than ever. 007:008 For if I gave you pain by that letter, I do not regret it, though I did regret it then. I see that that letter, even though for a time it gave you pain, had a salutary effect. 007:009 Now I rejoice, not in your grief, but because the grief led to repentance; for you sorrowed with a godly sorrow, which prevented you from receiving injury from us in any respect. 007:010 For godly sorrow produces repentance leading to salvation, a repentance not to be regretted; but the sorrow of the world finally produces death. 007:011 For mark the effects of this very thing-your having sorrowed with a godly sorrow-what earnestness it has called forth in you, what eagerness to clear yourselves, what indignation, what alarm, what longing affection, what jealousy, what meting out of justice! You have completely wiped away reproach from yourselves in the matter. 007:012 Therefore, though I wrote to you, it was not to punish the offender, nor to secure justice for him who had suffered the wrong, but it was chiefly in order that your earnest feeling on our behalf might become manifest to yourselves in the sight of God. 007:013 For this reason we feel comforted; and-in addition to this our comfort-we have been filled with all the deeper joy at Titus's joy, because his spirit has been set at rest by you all. 007:014 For however I may have boasted to him about you, I have no reason to feel ashamed; but as we have in all respects spoken the truth to you, so also our boasting to Titus about you has turned out to be the truth. 007:015 And his strong and tender affection is all the more drawn out towards you when he recalls to mind the obedience which all of you manifested by the timidity and nervous anxiety with which you welcomed him. 007:016 I rejoice that I have absolute confidence in you. 008:001 But we desire to let you know, brethren, of the grace of God which has been bestowed on the Churches of Macedonia; 008:002 how, while passing through great trouble, their boundless joy even amid their deep poverty has overflowed to increase their generous liberality. 008:003 For I can testify that to the utmost of their power, and even beyond their power, they have of their own free will given help. 008:004 With earnest entreaty they begged from us the favour of being allowed to share in the service now being rendered to God's people. 008:005 They not only did this, as we had expected, but first of all in obedience to God's will they gave their own selves to the Lord and to us. 008:006 This led us to urge Titus that, as he had previously been the one who commenced the work, so he should now go and complete among you this act of beneficence also. 008:007 Yes, just as you are already very rich in faith, readiness of speech, knowledge, unwearied zeal, and in the love that is in you, implanted by us, see to it that this grace of liberal giving also flourishes in you. 008:008 I am not saying this by way of command, but to test by the standard of other men's earnestness the genuineness of your love also. 008:009 For you know the condescending goodness of our Lord Jesus Christ- how for your sakes He became poor, though He was rich, in order that you through His poverty might grow rich. 008:010 But in this matter I give you an opinion; for my doing this helps forward your own intentions, seeing that not only have you begun operations, but a year ago you already had the desire to do so. 008:011 And now complete the doing also, in order that, just as there was then the eagerness in desiring, there may now be the accomplishment in proportion to your means. 008:012 For, assuming the earnest willingness, the gift is acceptable according to whatever a man has, and not according to what he has not. 008:013 I do not urge you to give in order that others may have relief while you are unduly pressed, 008:014 but that, by equalization of burdens, your superfluity having in the present emergency supplied their deficiency, their superfluity may in turn be a supply for your deficiency later on, so that there may be equalization of burdens. 008:015 Even as it is written, "He who gathered much had not too much, and he who gathered little had not too little." 008:016 But thanks be to God that He inspires the heart of Titus with the same deep interest in you; 008:017 for Titus welcomed our request, and, being thoroughly in earnest, comes to you of his own free will. 008:018 And we send with him the brother whose praises for his earnestness in proclaiming the Good News are heard throughout all the Churches. 008:019 And more than that, he is the one who was chosen by the vote of the Churches to travel with us, sharing our commission in the administration of this generous gift to promote the Lord's glory and gratify our own strong desire. 008:020 For against one thing we are on our guard-I mean against blame being thrown upon us in respect to these large and liberal contributions which are under our charge. 008:021 For we seek not only God's approval of our integrity, but man's also. 008:022 And we send with them our brother, of whose zeal we have had frequent proof in many matters, and who is now more zealous than ever through the strong confidence which he has in you. 008:023 As for Titus, remember that he is a partner with me, and is my comrade in my labours for you. And as for our brethren, remember that they are delegates from the Churches, and are men in whom Christ is glorified. 008:024 Exhibit therefore to the Churches a proof of your love, and a justification of our boasting to these brethren about you. 009:001 As to the services which are being rendered to God's people, it is really unnecessary for me to write to you. 009:002 For I know your earnest willingness, on account of which I habitually boast of you to the Macedonians, pointing out to them that for a whole year you in Greece have been ready; and the greater number of them have been spurred on by your ardour. 009:003 Still I send the brethren in order that in this matter our boast about you may not turn out to have been an idle one; so that, as I have said, you may be ready; 009:004 for fear that, if any Macedonians come with me and find you unprepared, we-not to say you yourselves-should be put to the blush in respect to this confidence. 009:005 I have thought it absolutely necessary therefore to request these brethren to visit you before I myself come, and to make sure beforehand that the gift of love which you have already promised may be ready as a gift of love, and may not seem to have been something which I have extorted from you. 009:006 But do not forget that he who sows with a niggardly hand will also reap a niggardly crop, and that he who sows bountifully will also reap bountifully. 009:007 Let each contribute what he has decided upon in his own mind, and not do it reluctantly or under compulsion. "It is a cheerful giver that God loves." 009:008 And God is able to bestow every blessing on you in abundance, so that richly enjoying all sufficiency at all times, you may have ample means for all good works. 009:009 As it is written, "He has scattered abroad, he has given to the poor, his almsgiving remains for ever." 009:010 And God who continually supplies seed for the sower and bread for eating, will supply you with seed and multiply it, and will cause your almsgiving to yield a plentiful harvest. 009:011 May you be abundantly enriched so as to show all liberality, such as through our instrumentality brings thanksgiving to God. 009:012 For the service rendered in this sacred gift not only helps to relieve the wants of God's people, but it is also rich in its results and awakens a chorus of thanksgiving to God. 009:013 For, by the practical proof of it which you exhibit in this service, you cause God to be extolled for your fidelity to your professed adherence to the Good News of the Christ, and for the liberality of your contributions for them and for all who are in need, 009:014 while they themselves also in supplications on your behalf pour out their longing love towards you because of God's surpassing grace which is resting upon you. 009:015 Thanks be to God for His unspeakably precious gift! 010:001 But as for me Paul, I entreat you by the gentleness and self-forgetfulness of Christ-I who when among you have not an imposing personal presence, but when absent am fearlessly outspoken in dealing with you. 010:002 I beseech you not to compel me when present to make a bold display of the confidence with which I reckon I shall show my `courage' against some who reckon that we are guided by worldly principles.

010:003 For, though we are still living in the world, it is no worldly warfare that we are waging. 010:004 The weapons with which we fight are not human weapons, but are mighty for God in overthrowing strong fortresses. 010:005 For we overthrow arrogant `reckonings,' and every stronghold that towers high in defiance of the knowledge of God, and we carry off every thought as if into slavery- into subjection to Christ; 010:006 while we hold ourselves in readiness to punish every act of disobedience, as soon as ever you as a Church have fully shown your obedience. 010:007 Is it outward appearances you look to? If any man is confident as regards himself that he specially belongs to Christ, let him consider again and reflect that just as he belongs to Christ, so also do we. 010:008 If, however, I were to boast more loudly of our Apostolic authority, which the Lord has given us that we may build you up, not pull you down, I should have no reason to feel ashamed. 010:009 Let it not seem as if I wanted to frighten you by my letters. 010:010 For they say "His letters are authoritative and forcible, but his personal presence is unimpressive, and as for eloquence, he has none." 010:011 Let such people take this into their reckoning, that whatever we are in word by our letters when absent, the same are we also in act when present. 010:012 For we have not the `courage' to rank ourselves among, or compare ourselves with, certain persons distinguished by their self-commendation. Yet they are not wise, measuring themselves, as they do, by one another and comparing themselves with one another. 010:013 We, however, will not exceed due limits in our boasting, but will keep within the limits of the sphere which God has assigned to us as a limit, which reaches even to you. 010:014 For there is no undue stretch of authority on our part, as though it did not extend to you. We pressed on even to Corinth, and were the first to proclaim to you the Good News of the Christ. 010:015 We do not exceed our due limits, and take credit for other men's labours; but we entertain the hope that, as your faith grows, we shall gain promotion among you- still keeping within our own sphere-promotion to a larger field of labour, 010:016 and shall tell the Good News in the districts beyond you, not boasting in another man's sphere about work already done by him. 010:017 But "whoever boasts, let his boast be in the Lord." 010:018 For it is not the man that commends himself who is really approved, but he whom the Lord commends. 011:001 I wish you could have borne with a little foolish boasting on my part. Nay, do bear with me. 011:002 I am jealous over you with God's own jealousy. For I have betrothed you to Christ to present you to Him like a faithful bride to her one husband. 011:003 But I am afraid that, as the serpent in his craftiness deceived Eve, so your minds may be led astray from their single-heartedness and their fidelity to Christ. 011:004 If indeed some visitor is proclaiming among you another Jesus whom we did not proclaim, or if you are receiving a Spirit different from the One you have already received or a Good News different from that which you have

already welcomed, your toleration is admirable! 011:005 Why, I reckon
myself in no respect inferior to those superlatively great Apostles. 011:006
And if in the matter of speech I am no orator, yet in knowledge I am not
deficient. Nay, we have in every way made that fully evident to you. 011:007
Is it a sin that I abased myself in order for you to be exalted, in that I
proclaimed God's Good News to you without fee or reward? 011:008
Other Churches I robbed, receiving pay from them in order to do you
service. 011:009 And when I was with you and my resources failed, there
was no one to whom I became a burden-for the brethren when they came
from Macedonia fully supplied my wants- and I kept myself from being in
the least a burden to you, and will do so still. 011:010 Christ knows that it is
true when I say that I will not be stopped from boasting of this anywhere in
Greece. 011:011 And why? Because I do not love you? God knows that I
do. 011:012 But I will persist in the same line of conduct in order to cut the
ground from under the feet of those who desire an opportunity of getting
themselves recognized as being on a level with us in the matters about
which they boast. 011:013 For men of this stamp are sham apostles,
dishonest workmen, assuming the garb of Apostles of Christ. 011:014 And
no wonder. Satan, their master, can disguise himself as an angel of light.
011:015 It is therefore no great thing for his servants also to disguise
themselves as servants of righteousness. Their end will be in accordance
with their actions. 011:016 To return to what I was saying. Let no one
suppose that I am foolish. Or if you must, at any rate make allowance for
me as being foolish, in order that I, as well as they, may boast a little.
011:017 What I am now saying, I do not say by the Lord's command, but as
a fool in his folly might, in this reckless boasting. 011:018 Since many boast
for merely human reasons, I too will boast. 011:019 Wise as you yourselves
are, you find pleasure in tolerating fools. 011:020 For you tolerate it, if any
one enslaves you, lives at your expense, makes off with your property, gives
himself airs, or strikes you on the face. 011:021 I use the language of self-
disparagement, as though I were admitting our own feebleness. Yet for
whatever reason any one is `courageous'-I speak in mere folly- I also am
courageous. 011:022 Are they Hebrews? So am I. Are they Israelites? So am
I. Are they descendants of Abraham? So am I. 011:023 Are they servants of
Christ? (I speak as if I were out of my mind.) Much more am I His servant;
serving Him more thoroughly than they by my labours, and more
thoroughly also by my imprisonments, by excessively cruel floggings, and
with risk of life many a time. 011:024 From the Jews I five times have
received forty lashes all but one. 011:025 Three times I have been beaten
with Roman rods, once I have been stoned, three times I have been
shipwrecked, once for full four and twenty hours I was floating on the open
sea. 011:026 I have served Him by frequent travelling, amid dangers in
crossing rivers, dangers from robbers; dangers from my own countrymen,

dangers from the Gentiles; dangers in the city, dangers in the Desert, dangers by sea, dangers from spies in our midst; 011:027 with labour and toil, with many a sleepless night, in hunger and thirst, in frequent fastings, in cold, and with insufficient clothing. 011:028 And besides other things, which I pass over, there is that which presses on me daily-my anxiety for all the Churches. 011:029 Who is weak, and I am not weak? Who is led astray into sin, and I am not aflame with indignation? 011:030 If boast I must, it shall be of things which display my weakness. 011:031 The God and Father of our Lord Jesus Christ-He who is blessed throughout the Ages-knows that I am speaking the truth. 011:032 In Damascus the governor under King Aretas kept guards at the gates of the city in order to apprehend me, 011:033 but through an opening in the wall I was let down in a basket, and so escaped his hands. 012:001 I am compelled to boast. It is not a profitable employment, but I will proceed to visions and revelations granted me by the Lord. 012:002 I know a Christian man who fourteen years ago-whether in the body I do not know, or out of the body I do not know; God knows-was caught up (this man of whom I am speaking) even to the highest Heaven. 012:003 And I know that this man-whether in the body or apart from the body I do not know; 012:004 God knows-was caught up into Paradise and heard unspeakable things which no human being is permitted to repeat. 012:005 Of such a one I will boast; but of myself I will not boast, except in my weaknesses. 012:006 If however I should choose to boast, I should not be a fool for so doing, for I should be speaking the truth. But I forbear, lest any one should be led to estimate me more highly than what his own eyes attest, or more highly than what he hears from my lips. 012:007 And judging by the stupendous grandeur of the revelations-therefore lest I should be over-elated there has been sent to me, like the agony of impalement, Satan's angel dealing blow after blow, lest I should be over-elated. 012:008 As for this, three times have I besought the Lord to rid me of him; 012:009 but His reply has been, "My grace suffices for you, for power matures in weakness." Most gladly therefore will I boast of my infirmities rather than complain of them- in order that Christ's power may overshadow me. 012:010 In fact I take pleasure in infirmities, in the bearing of insults, in distress, in persecutions, in grievous difficulties- for Christ's sake; for when I am weak, then I am strong. 012:011 It is foolish of me to write all this, but you have compelled me to do so. Why, you ought to have been my vindicators; for in no respect have I been inferior to these superlatively great Apostles, even though in myself I am nothing. 012:012 The signs that characterize the true Apostle have been done among you, accompanied by unwearied fortitude, and by tokens and marvels and displays of power. 012:013 In what respect, therefore, have you been worse dealt with than other Churches, except that I myself never hung as a dead weight upon you? Forgive the injustice I thus did you! 012:014 See, I am now for the third time prepared to visit you, but I will not be a dead weight to you. I desire not your money, but yourselves; for children ought not to put by for their parents, but parents for their children. 012:015 And as for me, most gladly will I spend all I have and be utterly spent for your salvation. 012:016 If I love you so intensely, am I the less to be loved? Be that as it may: I was not a burden to you. But being by no means scrupulous, I entrapped you, they say! 012:017 Have I gained any selfish advantage over you through any one of the messengers I have sent to you? 012:018 I begged Titus to visit you, and sent our other brother with him. Did Titus gain any selfish advantage over you? Were not he and I guided by one and the same Spirit, and did we not walk in the same steps? 012:019 You are imagining, all this time, that we are making our defense at your bar. In reality it is as in God's presence and in communion with Christ that we speak; but, dear friends, it is all with a view to your progress in goodness. 012:020 For I am afraid that perhaps when I come I may not find you to be what I desire, and that you may find me to be what you do not desire; that perhaps there may be contention, jealousy, bitter feeling, party spirit, ill-natured talk, backbiting, undue eulogy, unrest; 012:021 and that upon re-visiting you I may be humbled by my God in your presence, and may have to mourn over many whose hearts still cling to their old sins, and who have not repented of the impurity, fornication, and gross sensuality, of which they have been guilty. 013:001 This intended visit of mine is my third visit to you. "On the evidence of two or three witnesses every charge shall be sustained." 013:002 Those who cling to their old sins, and indeed all of you, I have forewarned and still forewarn (as I did on my second visit when present, so I do now, though absent) that, when I come again, I shall not spare you; 013:003 since you want a practical proof of the fact that Christ speaks by my lips-He who is not feeble towards you, but powerful among you. 013:004 For though it is true that He was crucified through weakness, yet He now lives through the power of God. We also are weak, sharing His weakness, but with Him we shall be full of life to deal with you through the power of God. 013:005 Test yourselves to discover whether you are true believers: put your own selves under examination. Or do you not know that Jesus Christ is within you, unless you are insincere? 013:006 But I trust that you will recognize that we are not insincere. 013:007 And our prayer to God is that you may do nothing wrong; not in order that our sincerity may be demonstrated, but that you may do what is right, even though our sincerity may seem to be doubtful. 013:008 For we have no power against the truth, but only for the furtherance of the truth; 013:009 and it is a joy to us when we are powerless, but you are strong. This we also pray for-the perfecting of your characters. 013:010 For this reason I write thus while absent, that when present I may not have to act severely in the exercise of the authority which the Lord has given me for building up, and not for pulling down. 013:011 Finally, brethren, be joyful, secure perfection of character, take courage, be of one mind, live in peace. And then God who gives love and peace will be with you. 013:012 Salute one another with a holy kiss. 013:013 All God's people here send greetings to you. 013:014 May the grace of the Lord Jesus Christ, the love of God, and the fellowship of the Holy Spirit, be with you all.

BOOK 63 2 JOHN

001:001 The Elder to the elect lady and her children. Truly I love you all, and not I alone, but also all who know the truth, 001:002 for the sake of the truth which is continually in our hearts and will be with us for ever. 001:003 Grace, mercy and peace will be with us from God the Father, and from Jesus Christ the Son of the Father, in truth and love. 001:004 It is an intense joy to me to have found some of your children living true Christian lives, in obedience to the command which we have received from the Father. 001:005 And now, dear lady, I pray you-writing to you, as I do, not a new command, but the one which we have had from the very beginning-let us love one another. 001:006 The love of which I am speaking consists in our living in obedience to God's commands. God's command is that you should live in obedience to what you all heard from the very beginning. 001:007 For many deceivers have gone out into the world-men who do not acknowledge Jesus as Christ who has come in human nature. Such a one is `the deceiver' and `the anti-Christ.' 001:008 Keep guard over yourselves, so that you may not lose the results of your good deeds, but may receive back a full reward. 001:009 No one has God, who instead of remaining true to the teaching of Christ, presses on in advance: but he who remains true to that teaching has both the Father and the Son. 001:010 If any one who comes to you does not bring this teaching, do not receive him under your roof nor bid him Farewell. 001:011 He who bids him Farewell is a sharer in his evil deeds. 001:012 I have a great deal to say to you all, but will not write it with paper and ink. Yet I hope to come to see you and speak face to face, so that your happiness may be complete. 001:013 The children of your elect sister send greetings to you.

BOOK 61 2 PETER

001:001 Simon Peter, a bondservant and Apostle of Jesus Christ: To those to whom there has been allotted the same precious faith as that which is ours through the righteousness of our God and of our Saviour Jesus Christ. 001:002 May more and more grace and peace be granted to you in a full knowledge of God and of Jesus our Lord, 001:003 seeing that His divine power has given us all things that are needful for life and godliness, through our knowledge of Him who has appealed to us by His own glorious perfections. 001:004 It is by means of these that He has granted us His precious and wondrous promises, in order that through them you may, one and all, become sharers in the very nature of God, having completely escaped the corruption which exists in the world through earthly cravings. 001:005 But for this very reason-adding, on your part, all earnestness- along with your faith, manifest also a noble character: along with a noble character, knowledge; 001:006 along with knowledge, self-control; along with self-control, power of endurance; 001:007 along with power of endurance, godliness; along with godliness, brotherly affection; and along with brotherly affection, love. 001:008 If these things exist in you, and continually increase, they prevent your being either idle or unfruitful in advancing towards a full knowledge of our Lord Jesus Christ. 001:009 For the man in whom they are lacking is blind and cannot see distant objects, in that he has forgotten that he has been cleansed from his old sins. 001:010 For this reason, brethren, be all the more in earnest to make sure that God has called you and chosen you; for it is certain that so long as you practise these things, you will never stumble. 001:011 And so a triumphant admission into the eternal Kingdom of our Lord and Saviour Jesus Christ will be freely granted to you. 001:012 For this reason I shall always persist in reminding you of these things, although you know them and are stedfast believers in truth which you already possess. 001:013 But I think it right, so long as I remain in the body, my present dwelling-place, to arouse you by such reminders. 001:014 For I know that the time for me to lay aside my body is now rapidly drawing near, even as our Lord Jesus Christ has revealed to me. 001:015 So on every possible occasion I will also do my best to enable you to recall these things after my departure. 001:016 For when we made known to you the power and Coming of our Lord Jesus Christ, we were not eagerly following cleverly devised legends, but we had been eye-witnesses of His majesty. 001:017 He received honour and glory from God the Father, and out of the wondrous glory words such as these were spoken to Him, "This is My dearly-loved Son, in whom I take delight." 001:018 And we ourselves heard these words come from Heaven, when we were with Him on the holy mountain. 001:019 And in the written word of prophecy we have something more permanent; to which you do well to pay attention- as to a lamp shining in a dimly-lighted place-until day dawns and the morning star rises in your hearts. 001:020 But, above all, remember that no prophecy in Scripture will be found to have come from the prophet's own prompting; 001:021 for never did any prophecy come by human will, but men sent by God spoke as they were impelled by the Holy Spirit. 002:001 But there were also false prophets among the people, as there will be teachers of falsehood among you also, who will cunningly introduce fatal divisions, disowning even the Sovereign Lord who has redeemed them, and bringing on themselves swift destruction. 002:002 And in their immoral ways they will have many eager disciples, through whom religion will be brought into disrepute. 002:003 Thirsting for riches, they will trade on you with their canting talk. From of old their judgement has been working itself out, and their destruction has not been slumbering. 002:004 For God did not spare angels when they had sinned, but hurling them down to Tartarus consigned them to caves of darkness, keeping them in readiness for judgement. 002:005 And He did not spare the ancient world, although He preserved Noah, a herald of righteousness, with seven others, when He brought a deluge on the world of the ungodly. 002:006 He reduced to ashes the cities of Sodom and Gomorrah, and condemned them to overthrow, making them an example to people who might in future be living godless lives. 002:007 But when righteous Lot was sore distressed by the gross misconduct of immoral men He rescued him. 002:008 (For their lawless deeds were torture, day after day, to the pure soul of that righteous man-all that he saw and heard whilst living in their midst.) 002:009 Since all this is so, the Lord knows how to rescue godly men from temptation, and on the other hand how to keep the unrighteous under punishment in readiness for the Day of Judgement, 002:010 and especially those who are abandoned to sensuality- craving, as they do, for polluted things, and scorning control. Fool-hardy and self-willed, they do not tremble when speaking evil of glorious beings; 002:011 while angels, though greater than they in might and power, do not bring any insulting accusation against such in the presence of the Lord. 002:012 But these men, like brute beasts, created (with their natural instincts) only to be captured or destroyed, are abusive in matters of which they are ignorant, and in their corruption will perish, 002:013 being doomed to receive a requital for their guilt. They reckon it pleasure to feast daintily in broad daylight. They are spots and blemishes, while feeding luxuriously at their love-feasts, and banqueting with you. 002:014 Their very eyes are full of adultery-being eyes which never cease from sin. These men set traps to catch unstedfast souls, their own hearts being well trained in greed. They are fore-doomed to God's curse! 002:015 Forsaking the straight road, they have gone astray, having eagerly followed in the steps of Balaam, the son of Beor, who was bent on securing the wages of unrighteousness. 002:016 But he was rebuked for his transgression: a dumb ass spoke with a human voice and checked the madness of the Prophet. 002:017 These people are wells without water, mists driven along by a storm, men for whom the dense darkness has been reserved. 002:018 For, while they pour out their frivolous and arrogant talk, they use earthly cravings-every kind of immorality- as a bait to entrap men who are just escaping from the influence of those who live in error. 002:019 And they promise them freedom, although they are themselves the slaves of what is corrupt. For a man is the slave of any one by whom he has been worsted in fight. 002:020 For if, after escaping from the pollutions of the world through a full knowledge of our Lord and Saviour Jesus Christ, people are once more entangled in these pollutions and are overcome, their last state has become worse than their first. 002:021 For it would have been better for them not to have fully known the way of righteousness, than, after knowing it, to turn back from the holy commandments in which they were instructed. 002:022 Their case is that described in the true proverb, "A dog returns to what he has vomited," and also in the other proverb, "The sow has washed itself and now goes back to roll in its filth." 003:001 This letter which I am now writing to you, dear friends, is my second letter. In both my letters I seek to revive in your honest minds the memory of certain things, 003:002 so that you may recall the words spoken long ago by the holy Prophets, and the commandments of our Lord and Saviour given you through your Apostles. 003:003 But, above all, remember that, in the last days, men will come who make a mock at everything-men governed only by their own passions, 003:004 and, asking, "What has become of His promised Return? For from the time our forefathers fell asleep all things continue as they have been ever since the creation of the world." 003:005 For they are wilfully blind to the fact that there were heavens which existed of old, and an earth, the latter arising out of water and extending continuously through water, by the command of God; 003:006 and that, by means of these, the then existing race of men was overwhelmed with water and perished. 003:007 But the present heavens and the present earth are, by the command of the same God, kept stored up, reserved for fire in preparation for a day of judgement and of destruction for the ungodly. 003:008 But there is one thing, dear friends, which you must not forget. With the Lord one day resembles a thousand years and a thousand years resemble one day. 003:009 The Lord is not slow in fulfilling His promise, in the sense in which some men speak of slowness. But He bears patiently with you, His desire being that no one should perish but that all should come to repentance. 003:010 The day of the Lord will come like a thief-it will be a day on which the heavens will pass away with a rushing noise, the elements be destroyed in the fierce heat, and the earth and all the works of man be utterly burnt up. 003:011 Since all these things are thus pre-destined to dissolution, what sort of men ought you to be found to be in all holy living and godly conduct, 003:012 eagerly looking forward to the coming of the day of God, by reason of which the heavens, all ablaze, will be destroyed, and the elements will melt in the fierce heat? 003:013 But in accordance with His promise we are expecting new heavens and a new earth, in which righteousness will dwell. 003:014 Therefore, dear friends, since you have these expectations, earnestly seek to be found in His presence, free from blemish or reproach, in peace. 003:015 And always regard the patient forbearance of our Lord as salvation, as our dear brother Paul also has written to you in virtue of the wisdom granted to him. 003:016 That is what he says in all his letters, when speaking in them of these things. In those letters there are some statements hard to understand, which ill-taught and unprincipled people pervert, just as they do the rest of the Scriptures, to their own ruin. 003:017 You, therefore, dear friends, having been warned beforehand, must continually be on your guard so as not to be led astray by the false teaching of immoral men nor fall from your own stedfastness. 003:018 But be always growing in the grace and knowledge of our Lord and Saviour Jesus Christ. To Him be all glory, both now and to the day of Eternity!

BOOK 53 2 THESSALONIANS

001:001 Paul, Silas, and Timothy: To the Church of the Thessalonians which is in God our Father and the Lord Jesus Christ. 001:002 May grace and peace be granted to you from God our Father and the Lord Jesus Christ. 001:003 Unceasing thanks are due from us to God on your behalf, brethren. They are appropriate because your faith is growing greatly, and the love of every one of you for all the others goes on increasing. 001:004 It so increases that we ourselves make honourable mention of you among the Churches of God because of your patience and faith amid all your persecutions and amid the afflictions which you are enduring. 001:005 For these are a plain token of God's righteous judgement, which has in view your being deemed worthy of admission to God's Kingdom, for the sake of which, indeed, you are sufferers. 001:006 A plain token of God's righteous judgement, I say, since it is a righteous thing for Him to requite with affliction those who are now afflicting you; 001:007 and to requite with rest you who are suffering affliction now- rest with us at the re-appearing of the Lord Jesus from Heaven, attended by His mighty angels. 001:008 He will come in flames of fire to take vengeance on those who have no knowledge of God, and do not obey the Good News as to Jesus, our Lord. 001:009 They will pay the penalty of eternal destruction, being banished from the presence of the Lord and from His glorious majesty, 001:010 when He comes on that day to be glorified in His people and to be wondered at among all who have believed, including you- because you believed the testimony which we brought for your acceptance. 001:011 It is with this view also that we continually pray to our God for you, asking that He will count you worthy of His call, and by His mighty power fully gratify your every desire for what is truly good and make your work of faith complete; 001:012 in order that the name of our Lord Jesus may be glorified in you, and that you may be glorified in Him-so wonderful is the grace of our God and of the Lord Jesus Christ! 002:001 But with respect to the Coming of our Lord Jesus Christ and our being gathered to meet Him, we entreat you, brethren, 002:002 not readily to become unsettled in mind or troubled-either by any pretended spiritual revelation or by any message or letter claiming to have been sent by us-through fancying that the day of the Lord is now here. 002:003 Let no one in any way deceive you, for that day cannot come without the coming of the apostasy first, and the appearing of the man of sin, the son of perdition, who sets himself against, 002:004 and exalts himself above, every so-called `god' or object of worship, and goes the length of taking his seat in the very temple of God, giving it out that he himself is God. 002:005 Do you not remember that while I was still with you I used to tell you all this? 002:006 And now you know what restrains him, in order that his true character may be revealed at his appointed time. 002:007 For lawlessness is already at work in secret; but only until the man who is now exercising a restraining influence is removed, 002:008 and then the Lawless one will be revealed, whom the Lord Jesus will sweep away with the tempest of His anger, and utterly overwhelm by the awful splendour of His Coming. 002:009 The appearing of the Lawless one will be attended by various miracles and tokens and delusive marvels-for so Satan works- 002:010 and by every kind of wicked deception for those who are on the way to perdition because they did not welcome into their hearts the love of the truth, so that they might be saved. 002:011 And for this reason God sends them a misleading influence that they may believe the lie; 002:012 in order that all may come under judgement who have refused to believe the truth and have taken pleasure in unrighteousness. 002:013 And from us thanks are always due to God on your behalf- brethren whom the Lord loves-because God from the beginning has chosen you for salvation through the Spirit's sanctifying influence and your belief in the truth. 002:014 To this blessing God has called you by our Good News, so that you may have a share in the glory of our Lord Jesus Christ. 002:015 So then, brethren, stand your ground, and hold fast to the teachings which you have received from us, whether by word of mouth or by letter. 002:016 And may our Lord Jesus Christ Himself-and God our Father who has loved us and has given us in His grace eternal consolation and a bright hope-002:017 comfort your hearts and make you stedfast in every good work and word. 003:001 Finally, brethren, pray for us, asking that the Lord's Message may be spread rapidly and its glory be displayed, as it was displayed among you; 003:002 and that we may be delivered from wrong-headed and wicked men; for it is not everybody who has faith. 003:003 But the Lord is faithful, and He will make you stedfast and will guard you from the Evil one. 003:004 And we have confidence in the Lord in regard to you that you are doing, and will do, what we command. 003:005 And may the Lord guide your hearts into the love of God and into the patience of Christ. 003:006

But, by the authority of the Lord, we command you, brethren, to stand aloof from every brother whose life is disorderly and not in accordance with the teaching which all received from us. 003:007 For you yourselves know that it is your duty to follow our example. There was no disorder in our lives among you, 003:008 nor did we eat any one's bread without paying for it, but we laboured and toiled, working hard night and day in order not to be a burden to any of you. 003:009 This was not because we had not a claim upon you, but it arose from a desire to set you an example-for you to imitate us. 003:010 For even when we were with you, we laid down this rule for you: "If a man does not choose to work, neither shall he eat." 003:011 For we hear that there are some of you who live disorderly lives and are mere idle busybodies. 003:012 To persons of that sort our injunction-and our command by the authority of the Lord Jesus Christ-is that they are to work quietly and eat their own honestly-earned bread. 003:013 But you, brethren, must not grow weary in the path of duty; 003:014 and if any one refuses to obey these our written instructions, mark that man and hold no communication with him- so that he may be made to feel ashamed. 003:015 And yet do not regard him as an enemy, but caution him as a brother. 003:016 And may the Lord of peace Himself continually grant you peace in every sense. The Lord be with you all. 003:017 I Paul add the greeting with my own hand, which is the credential in every letter of mine. 003:018 This is my handwriting. May the grace of our Lord Jesus Christ be with you all.

BOOK 55 2 TIMOTHY

001:001 Paul, an Apostle of Christ Jesus, by the will of God, for proclaiming the promise of the Life which is in Christ Jesus: 001:002 To Timothy my dearly-loved child. May grace, mercy and peace be granted to you from God the Father and Christ Jesus our Lord. 001:003 I thank God, whom I serve with a pure conscience-as my forefathers did-that night and day I unceasingly remember you in my prayers, 001:004 being always mindful of your tears, and longing to see you that I may be filled with joy. 001:005 For I recall the sincere faith which is in your heart- a faith which dwelt first in your grandmother Lois and then in your mother Eunice, and, I am fully convinced, now dwells in you also. 001:006 For this reason let me remind you to rekindle God's gift which is yours through the laying on of my hands. 001:007 For the Spirit which God has given us is not a spirit of cowardice, but one of power and of love and of sound judgement. 001:008 Do not be ashamed then to bear witness for our Lord and for me His prisoner; but rather share suffering with me in the service of the Good News, strengthened by the power of God. 001:009 For He saved us and called us with a holy call, not in accordance with our desserts, but in accordance with His own purpose and the free grace which He bestowed on us in Christ Jesus before the commencement of the Ages, 001:010 but which has now been plainly revealed through the Appearing of our Saviour, Christ Jesus. He has put an end to death and has brought Life and Immortality to light through the Good News, 001:011 of which I have been appointed a preacher, Apostle and teacher, to the Gentiles. 001:012 That indeed is the reason why I suffer as I do. But I am not ashamed, for I know in whom my trust reposes, and I am confident that He has it in His power to keep what I have entrusted to Him safe until that day. 001:013 Provide yourself with an outline of the sound teaching which you have heard from my lips, and be true to the faith and love which are in Christ Jesus. 001:014

That precious treasure which is in your charge, guard through the Holy Spirit who has His home in our hearts. 001:015 Of this you are aware, that all the Christians in Roman Asia have deserted me: and among them Phygelus and Hermogenes. 001:016 May the Lord show mercy to the household of Onesiphorus; for many a time he cheered me and he was not ashamed of my chain. 001:017 Nay, when he was here in Rome, he took great pains to inquire where I was living, and at last he found me. 001:018 (The Lord grant that he may obtain mercy at His hands on that day!) And you yourself well know all the services which he rendered me in Ephesus. 002:001 You then, my child, must be strong in the grace that is in Christ Jesus. 002:002 All that you have been taught by me in the hearing of many witnesses, you must hand on to trusty men who shall themselves, in turn, be competent to instruct others also. 002:003 As a good soldier of Christ Jesus accept your share of suffering. 002:004 Every one who serves as a soldier keeps himself from becoming entangled in the world's business-so that he may satisfy the officer who enlisted him. 002:005 And if any one takes part in an athletic contest, he gets no prize unless he obeys the rules. 002:006 The harvestman who labours in the field must be the first to get a share of the crop. 002:007 Mark well what I am saying: the Lord will give you discernment in everything. 002:008 Never forget that Jesus Christ has risen from among the dead and is a descendant of David, as is declared in the Good News which I preach. 002:009 For preaching the Good News I suffer, and am even put in chains, as if I were a criminal: yet the word of God is not imprisoned. 002:010 For this reason I endure all things for the sake of God's own people; so that they also may obtain salvation-even the salvation which is in Christ Jesus-and with it eternal glory. 002:011 Faithful is the saying: "If we died with Him, we shall also live with Him; 002:012 "If we patiently endure pain, we shall also share His Kingship; "If we disown Him, He will also disown us; 002:013 "And even if *our* faith fails, He remains true-He cannot prove false to Himself." 002:014 Bring all this to men's remembrances, solemnly charging them in the presence of God not to waste time in wrangling about mere words, a course which is altogether unprofitable and tends only to the ruin of the hearers. 002:015 Earnestly seek to commend yourself to God as a servant who, because of his straightforward dealing with the word of truth, has no reason to feel any shame. 002:016 But from irreligious and frivolous talk hold aloof, for those who indulge in it will proceed from bad to worse in impiety, 002:017 and their teaching will spread like a running sore. Hymenaeus and Philetus are men of that stamp. 002:018 In the matter of the truth they have gone astray, saying that the Resurrection is already past, and so they are overthrowing the faith of some. 002:019 Yet God's solid foundation stands unmoved, bearing this inscription, "The Lord knows those who really belong to Him." And this also, "Let every one who names the Name of the Lord renounce all wickedness." 002:020 Now in a great house there are not only articles of gold and silver, but also others of wood and of earthenware; and some are for specially honourable, and others for common use. 002:021 If therefore a man keeps himself clear of these latter, he himself will be for specially honourable use, consecrated, fit for the Master's service, and fully equipped for every good work. 002:022 Keep a strong curb, however, on your youthful cravings; and strive for integrity, good faith, love, peace, in company with all who pray to the Lord with pure hearts. 002:023 But avoid foolish discussions with ignorant men, knowing-as you do- that these lead to quarrels; 002:024 and a bondservant of the Lord must not quarrel, but must be inoffensive towards all men, a skilful teacher, and patient under wrongs. 002:025 He must speak in a gentle tone when correcting the errors of opponents, in the hope that God will at last give them repentance, for them to come to a full knowledge of the truth 002:026 and recover sober-mindedness and freedom from the Devil's snare, though they are now entrapped by him to do his will. 003:001 But of this be assured: in the last days grievous times will set in. 003:002 For men will be lovers of self, lovers of money, boastful, haughty, profane. They will be disobedient to parents, thankless, irreligious, 003:003 destitute of natural affection, unforgiving, slanderers. They will have no self-control, but will be brutal, opposed to goodness, 003:004 treacherous, headstrong, self-important. They will love pleasure instead of loving God, 003:005 and will keep up a make-believe of piety and yet live in defiance of its power. Turn away from people of this sort. 003:006 Among them are included the men who make their way into private houses and carry off weak women as their prisoners- women who, weighed down by the burden of their sins, are led by ever-changing caprice, 003:007 and are always learning something new, and yet are never able to arrive at real knowledge of the truth. 003:008 And just as Jannes and Jambres withstood Moses, so also these false teachers withstand the truth-being, as they are, men of debased intellects, and of no real worth so far as faith is concerned. 003:009 But they will have no further success; for their folly will be as clearly manifest to all men, as that of the opponents of Moses came to be. 003:010 But you have intimately known my teaching, life, aims, faith, patience, love, resignation, 003:011 and the persecutions and sufferings which I have endured; the things which happened to me in Antioch, Iconium and Lystra. You know the persecutions I endured, and how the Lord delivered me out of them all. 003:012 And indeed every one who is determined to live a godly life as a follower of Christ Jesus will be persecuted. 003:013 But bad men and impostors will go on from bad to worse, misleading and being misled. 003:014 But you must cling to the things which you have learnt and have been taught to believe, knowing who your teachers were, 003:015 and that from infancy you have known the sacred writings which are able to make you wise to obtain salvation through faith in Christ Jesus. 003:016 Every Scripture is inspired by God and is useful for teaching, for convincing, for correction of error, and for instruction in right doing; 003:017 so that the man of God may himself be complete and may be perfectly equipped for every good work. 004:001 I solemnly implore you, in the presence of God and of Christ Jesus who is about to judge the living and the dead, and by His Appearing and His Kingship: 004:002 proclaim God's message, be zealous in season and out of season; convince, rebuke, encourage, with the utmost patience as a teacher. 004:003 For a time is coming when they will not tolerate wholesome instruction, but, wanting to have their ears tickled, they will find a multitude of teachers to satisfy their own fancies; 004:004 and will turn away from listening to the truth and will turn aside to fables. 004:005 But as for you, you must exercise habitual self-control, and not live a self-indulgent life, but do the duty of an evangelist and fully discharge the obligations of your office. 004:006 I for my part am like a drink-offering which is already being poured out; and the time for my departure is now close at hand. 004:007 I have gone through the glorious contest; I have run the race; I have guarded the faith. 004:008 From this time onward there is reserved for me the crown of righteousness which the Lord, the righteous Judge, will award to me on that day, and not only to me, but also to all who love the thought of His Appearing. 004:009 Make an effort to come to me speedily. 004:010 For Demas has deserted me-loving, as he does, the present age- and has gone to Thessalonica; Crescens has gone to Galatia, and Titus to Dalmatia. 004:011 Luke is the only friend I now have with me. Call for Mark on your way and bring him with you, for he is a great help to me in my ministry. 004:012 Tychicus I have sent to Ephesus. 004:013 When you come, bring with you the cloak which I left behind at Troas at the house of Carpus, and the books, but especially the parchments. 004:014 Alexander the metal-worker showed bitter hostility towards me: the Lord will requite him according to his doings. 004:015 You also should beware of him; for he has violently opposed our preaching. 004:016 At my first defence I had no one at my side, but all deserted me. May it not be laid to their charge. 004:017 The Lord, however, stood by me and filled me with inward strength, that through me the Message might be fully proclaimed and that all the Gentiles might hear it; and I was rescued from the lion's jaws. 004:018 The Lord will deliver me from every cruel attack and will keep me safe in preparation for His heavenly Kingdom. To Him be the glory until the Ages of the Ages! Amen. 004:019 Greet Prisca and Aquila, and the household of Onesiphorus. 004:020 Erastus stayed in Corinth; Trophimus I left behind me at Miletus, ill. 004:021 Make an effort to come before winter. Eubulus greets you, and so do Pudens, Linus, Claudia, and all the brethren. 004:022 The Lord be with your spirit. Grace be with you all.

BOOK 64 3 JOHN

001:001 The Elder to his dear friend Gaius. Truly I love you. 001:002 My dear friend, I pray that you may in all respects prosper and enjoy good health, just as your soul already prospers. 001:003 For it is an intense joy to me when brethren come and bear witness to your fidelity to the truth-that you live in obedience to the truth. 001:004 I have no greater joy than to hear that my children are living in obedience to the truth. 001:005 My dear friend, you are acting faithfully in all your behaviour towards the brethren, even when they are strangers to you. 001:006 They have testified, in the presence of the Church, to your love; and you will do well to help them on their journey in a manner worthy of your fellowship with God. 001:007 For it is for Christ that they have gone forth, accepting nothing from the Gentiles. 001:008 It is therefore our duty to show hospitality to such men, so that we may be fellow workers in promoting the truth. 001:009 I wrote to the Church, but Diotrephes, who loves to have the first place among them, refuses to listen to us. 001:010 For this reason, if I come, I shall not forget his conduct, nor his idle and mischievous talk against us. And he does not stop there: he not only will not receive the brethren, but those who desire to do this he hinders, and excludes them from the Church. 001:011 My dear friend, do not follow wrong examples, but right ones. He who habitually does what is right is a child of God: he who habitually does what is wrong has not seen God. 001:012 The character of Demetrius has the approval of all men, and of the truth itself. We also express our approval of it, and you know that we only give our approval to that which is true. 001:013 I have a great deal to say to you, but I do not wish to go on writing it with ink and pen. 001:014 But I hope to see you very soon, and then we will speak face to face. Peace be with you. Our friends send greetings to you. Greet our friends individually.

BOOK 44 ACTS

001:001 My former narrative, Theophilus, dealt with all that Jesus did and taught as a beginning, down to the day on which, 001:002 after giving instruction through the Holy Spirit to the Apostles whom He had chosen, He was taken up to Heaven. 001:003 He had also, after He suffered, shown Himself alive to them with many sure proofs, appearing to them at intervals during forty days, and speaking of the Kingdom of God. 001:004 And while in their company He charged them not to leave Jerusalem, but to wait for the Father's promised gift. "This you have heard of," He said, "from me. 001:005 For John indeed baptized with water, but before many days have passed you shall be baptized with the Holy Spirit." 001:006 Once when they were with Him, they asked Him, "Master, is this the time at which you are about to restore the kingdom of Israel?" 001:007 "It is not for you," He replied, "to know times or epochs which the Father has reserved within His own authority; 001:008 and yet you will receive power when the Holy Spirit has come upon you, and you will be my witnesses in Jerusalem and in all Judaea and Samaria and to the remotest parts of the earth." 001:009 When He had said this, and while they were looking at Him, He was carried up, and a cloud closing beneath Him hid Him from their sight. 001:010 But, while they stood intently gazing into the sky as He went, suddenly there were two men in white garments standing by them, 001:011 who said, "Galilaeans, why stand looking into the sky? This same Jesus who has been taken up from you into Heaven will come in just the same way as you have seen Him going into Heaven." 001:012 Then they returned to Jerusalem from the mountain called the Oliveyard, which is near Jerusalem, about a mile off. 001:013 They entered the city, and they went up to the upper room which was now their fixed place for meeting. Their names were Peter and John, James and Andrew, Philip and Thomas, Bartholomew and Matthew, James the son of Alphaeus, Simon the Zealot, and Judas the brother of James. 001:014 All of these with one mind continued earnest in prayer, together with some women, and Mary the mother of Jesus, and His brothers. 001:015 It was on one of these days that Peter stood up in the midst of the brethren-the entire number of persons present being about 120-and said, 001:016 "Brethren, it was necessary that the Scripture should be fulfilled- the prediction, I mean, which the Holy Spirit uttered by the lips of David, about Judas, who acted as guide to those who arrested Jesus. 001:017 For Judas was reckoned as one of our number, and a share in this ministry was allotted to him." 001:018 (Now having bought a piece of ground with the money paid for his wickedness he fell there with his face downwards, and, his body bursting open, he became disembowelled. 001:019 This fact became widely known to the people of Jerusalem, so that the place received the name, in their language, of Achel-damach, which means `The Field of Blood.') 001:020 "For it is written in the Book of Psalms, "`Let his encampment be desolate: let there be no one to dwell there'; and "`His work let another take up.' 001:021 "It is necessary, therefore, that of the men who have been with us all the time that the Lord Jesus went in and out among us- 001:022 beginning from His baptism by John down to the day on which He was taken up again from us into Heaven-one should be appointed to become a witness with us as to His resurrection." 001:023 So two names were proposed, Joseph called Bar-sabbas- and surnamed Justus-and Matthias. 001:024 And the brethren prayed, saying, "Thou, Lord, who knowest the hearts of all, show clearly which of these two Thou hast chosen 001:025 to occupy the place in this ministry and Apostleship from which Judas through transgression fell, in order to go to his own place." 001:026 Then they drew lots between them. The lot fell on Matthias, and a place among the eleven Apostles was voted to him. 002:001 At length, on the day of the Harvest Festival, they had all met in one place; 002:002 when suddenly there came from the sky a sound as of a strong rushing blast of wind. This filled the whole house where they were sitting; 002:003 and they saw tongues of what looked like fire distributing themselves over the assembly, and on the head of each person a tongue alighted. 002:004 They were all filled with the Holy Spirit, and began to speak in foreign languages according as the Spirit gave them words to utter. 002:005 Now there were Jews residing in Jerusalem, devout men from every part of the world. 002:006 So when this noise was heard, they came crowding together, and were amazed because everyone heard his own language spoken. 002:007 They were beside themselves with wonder, and exclaimed, "Are not all these speakers Galilaeans? 002:008 How then does each of us hear his own native language spoken by them? 002:009 Some of us are Parthians, Medes, Elamites. Some are inhabitants of Mesopotamia, of Judaea or Cappadocia, of Pontus or the Asian Province, of Phrygia or Pamphylia, 002:010 of Egypt or of the parts of Africa towards Cyrene.

Others are visitors from Rome-being either Jews or converts from heathenism-and others are Cretans or Arabians. 002:011 Yet we all alike hear these Galilaeans speaking in our own language about the wonderful things which God has done." 002:012 They were all astounded and bewildered, and asked one another, "What can this mean?" 002:013 But others, scornfully jeering, said, "They are brim-full of sweet wine." 002:014 Peter however, together with the Eleven, stood up and addressed them in a loud voice. "Men of Judaea, and all you inhabitants of Jerusalem," he said, "be in no uncertainty about this matter but pay attention to what I say. 002:015 For this is not intoxication, as you suppose, it being only the third hour of the day. 002:016 But that which was predicted through the Prophet Joel has happened: 002:017 "And it shall come to pass in the last days, God says, that I will pour out My Spirit upon all mankind; and your sons and your daughters shall prophesy, and your young men shall see visions, and your old men shall have dreams; 002:018 and even upon My bondservants, both men and women, at that time, I will pour out My Spirit, and they shall prophesy. 002:019 I will display marvels in the sky above, and signs on the earth below, blood and fire, and pillars of smoke. 002:020 The sun shall be turned into darkness and the moon into blood, to usher in the day of the Lord-that great and illustrious day; 002:021 and every one who calls on the name of the Lord shall be saved.' 002:022 "Listen, Israelites, to what I say. Jesus, the Nazarene, a man accredited to you from God by miracles and marvels and signs which God did among you through Him, as you yourselves know, Him- 002:023 delivered up through God's settled purpose and foreknowledge- you by the hands of Gentiles have nailed to a cross and have put to death. 002:024 But God has raised Him to life, having terminated the throes of death, for in fact it was not possible for Him to be held fast by death. 002:025 For David says in reference to Him, "`I constantly fixed my eyes upon the Lord, because He is at my right hand in order that I may continue unshaken. 002:026 For this reason my heart is glad and my tongue exults. My body also shall rest in hope. 002:027 For Thou wilt not leave me in the Unseen World forsaken, nor give up Thy holy One to undergo decay. 002:028 Thou hast made known to me the ways of Life: Thou wilt fill me with gladness in Thy presence.' 002:029 "As to the patriarch David, I need hardly remind you, brethren, that he died and was buried, and that we still have his tomb among us. 002:030 Being a Prophet, however, and knowing that God had solemnly sworn to him to seat a descendant of his upon his throne, 002:031 with prophetic foresight he spoke of the resurrection of the Christ, to the effect that He was not left forsaken in the Unseen World, nor did His body undergo decay. 002:032 This Jesus, God has raised to life-a fact to which all of us testify. 002:033 "Being therefore lifted high by the mighty hand of God, He has received from the Father the promised Holy Spirit and has poured out this which you see and hear. 002:034 For David did not ascend into Heaven, but he says himself, "`The Lord said to my Lord, Sit at My right hand 002:035 until I make thy foes a footstool under thy feet.' 002:036 "Therefore let the whole House of Israel know beyond all doubt that God has made Him both LORD and CHRIST- this Jesus whom you crucified." 002:037 Stung to the heart by these words, they said to Peter and the rest of the Apostles, "Brethren, what are we to do?" 002:038 "Repent," replied Peter, "and be baptized, every one of you, in the name of Jesus Christ, with a view to the remission of your sins, and you shall receive the gift of the Holy Spirit. 002:039 For to you belongs the promise, and to your children, and to all who are far off, whoever the Lord our God may call." 002:040 And with many more appeals he solemnly warned and entreated them, saying, "Escape from this crooked generation." 002:041 Those, therefore, who joyfully welcomed his Message were baptized; and on that one day about three thousand persons were added to them; 002:042 and they were constant in listening to the teaching of the Apostles and in their attendance at the Communion, that is, the Breaking of the Bread, and at prayer. 002:043 Fear came upon every one, and many marvels and signs were done by the Apostles. 002:044 And all the believers kept together, and had everything in common. 002:045 They sold their lands and other property, and distributed the proceeds among all, according to every one's necessities. 002:046 And, day by day, attending constantly in the Temple with one accord, and breaking bread in private houses, they took their meals with great happiness and single-heartedness, 002:047 praising God and being regarded with favour by all the people. Also, day by day, the Lord added to their number those whom He was saving. 003:001 One day Peter and John were going up to the Temple for the hour of prayer-the ninth hour-and, just then, 003:002 some men were carrying there one who had been lame from birth, whom they were wont to place every day close to the Beautiful Gate (as it was called) of the Temple, for him to beg from the people as they went in. 003:003 Seeing Peter and John about to go into the Temple, he asked them for alms. 003:004 Peter fixing his eyes on him, as John did also, said, "Look at us." 003:005 So he looked and waited, expecting to receive something from them. 003:006 "I have no silver or gold," Peter said, "but what I have, I give you. In the name of Jesus Christ, the Nazarene-walk!" 003:007 Then taking his hand Peter lifted him up, and immediately his feet and ankles were strengthened. 003:008 Leaping up, he stood upright and began to walk, and went into the Temple with them, walking, leaping, and praising God. 003:009 All the people saw him walking and praising God; 003:010 and recognizing him as the man who used to sit at the Beautiful Gate of the Temple asking for alms, they were filled with awe and amazement at what had happened to him. 003:011 While he still clung to Peter and John, the people, awe-struck, ran up crowding round them in what was known as Solomon's Portico. 003:012 Peter, seeing this, spoke to the people. "Israelites," he said, "why do you wonder at this man? Or why gaze at us, as though by any power or piety of our own we had enabled him to walk? 003:013 The God of Abraham, Isaac, and Jacob, the God of our forefathers, has conferred this honour on His Servant Jesus, whom you delivered up and disowned in the presence of Pilate, when he had decided to let Him go. 003:014 Yes, you disowned the holy and righteous One, and asked as a favour the release of a murderer. 003:015 The Prince of Life you put to death; but God has raised Him from the dead, and we are witnesses as to that. 003:016 It is His name-faith in that name being the condition-which has strengthened this man whom you behold and know; and the faith which He has given has made this man sound and strong again, as you can all see. 003:017 "And now, brethren, I know that it was in ignorance that you did it, as was the case with your rulers also. 003:018 But in this way God has fulfilled the declarations He made through all the Prophets, that His Christ would suffer. 003:019 Repent, therefore, and reform your lives, so that the record of your sins may be cancelled, and that there may come seasons of revival from the Lord, 003:020 and that He may send the Christ appointed beforehand for you-even Jesus. 003:021 Heaven must receive Him until those times of which God has spoken from the earliest ages through the lips of His holy Prophets- the times of the reconstitution of all things. 003:022 Moses declared, "`The Lord your God will raise up a Prophet for you from among your brethren as He has raised me. In all that He says to you, you must listen to Him. 003:023 And every one, without exception, who refuses to listen to that Prophet shall be utterly destroyed from among the People.' 003:024 Yes, and all the Prophets, from Samuel onwards-all who have spoken- have also announced the coming of this present time. 003:025 "You are the heirs of the Prophets, and of the Covenant which God made with your forefathers when He said to Abraham, `And through your posterity all the families of the world shall be blessed.' 003:026 It is to you first that God, after raising His Servant from the grave, has sent Him to bless you, by causing every one of you to turn from your wickedness." 004:001 While they were saying this to the people, the Priests, the Commander of the Temple Guard, and the Sadducees came upon them, 004:002 highly incensed at their teaching the people and proclaiming in the case of Jesus the Resurrection from among the dead. 004:003 They arrested the two Apostles and lodged them in custody till the next day; for it was already evening. 004:004 But many of those who had listened to their preaching believed; and the number of the adult men had now grown to be about 5,000. 004:005 The next day a meeting was held in Jerusalem of their Rulers, Elders, and Scribes, 004:006 with Annas the High Priest, Caiaphas, John, Alexander, and the other members of the high-priestly family. 004:007 So they made the Apostles stand in the centre, and demanded of them, "By what power or in what name have you done this?" 004:008 Then Peter was filled with the Holy Spirit, and he replied, "Rulers and Elders of the people, 004:009 if we to-day are under examination concerning the benefit conferred on a man helplessly lame, as to how this man has been cured; 004:010 be it known to you all, and to all the people of Israel, that through the name of Jesus the Anointed, the Nazarene, whom *you* crucified, but whom *God* has raised from among the dead-through that name this man stands here before you in perfect health. 004:011 This Jesus is the Stone treated with contempt by you the builders, but it has been made the Cornerstone. 004:012 And in no other is the great salvation to be found; for, in fact, there is no second name under Heaven that has been given among men through which we are to be saved." 004:013 As they looked on Peter and John so fearlessly outspoken- and also discovered that they were illiterate persons, untrained in the schools-they were surprised; and now they recognized them as having been with Jesus. 004:014 And seeing the man standing with them-the man who had been cured- they had no reply to make. 004:015 So they ordered them to withdraw from the Sanhedrin while they conferred among themselves. 004:016 "What are we to do with these men?" they asked one another; for the fact that a remarkable miracle has been performed by them is well known to every one in Jerusalem, and we cannot deny it. 004:017 But to prevent the matter spreading any further among the people, let us stop them by threats from speaking in the future in this name to any one whatever." 004:018 So they recalled the Apostles, and ordered them altogether to give up speaking or teaching in the name of Jesus. 004:019 But Peter and John replied, "Judge whether it is right in God's sight to listen to you instead of listening to God. 004:020 As for us, what we have seen and heard we cannot help speaking about." 004:021 The Court added further threats and then let them go, being quite unable to find any way of punishing them on account of the people, because all gave God the glory for the thing that had happened. 004:022 For the man was over forty years of age on whom this miracle of restoration to health had been performed. 004:023 After their release the two Apostles went to their friends, and told them all that the High Priests and Elders had said. 004:024 And they, upon hearing the story, all lifted up their voices to God and said, "O Sovereign Lord, it is Thou who didst make Heaven and earth and sea, and all that is in them, 004:025 and didst say through the Holy Spirit by the lips of our forefather David Thy servant, "`Why have the nations stamped and raged, and the peoples formed futile plans? 004:026 The kings of the earth came near, and the rulers assembled together against the Lord and against His Anointed.'" 004:027 "They did indeed assemble in this city in hostility to Thy holy Servant Jesus whom Thou hadst anointed-Herod and Pontius Pilate with the Gentiles and also the tribes of Israel- 004:028 to do all that Thy power and Thy will had predetermined should be done. 004:029 And now, Lord, listen to their threats, and enable Thy servants to proclaim Thy Message with fearless courage, 004:030 whilst Thou stretchest out Thine arm to cure men, and to give signs and marvels through the name of Thy holy Servant Jesus." 004:031 When they had prayed, the place in which they were assembled shook, and they were, one and all, filled with the Holy Spirit, and proceeded to tell God's Message with boldness. 004:032 Among all those who had embraced the faith there was but one heart and soul, so that none of them claimed any of his possessions as his own, but everything they had was common property; 004:033 while the Apostles with great force of conviction delivered their testimony as to the resurrection of the Lord Jesus; and great grace was upon them all. 004:034 And, in fact, there was not a needy man among them, for all who were possessors of lands or houses sold them, and brought the money which they realised, 004:035 and gave it to the Apostles, and distribution was made to every one according to his wants. 004:036 In this way Joseph, whom the Apostles gave the name of Bar-nabas- signifying `Son of Encouragement'-a Levite, a native of Cyprus, 004:037 sold a farm which he had, and brought the money and gave it to the Apostles. 005:001 There was a man of the name of Ananias who, with his wife Sapphira, sold some property but, 005:002 with her full knowledge and consent, dishonestly kept back part of the price which he received for it, though he brought the rest and gave it to the Apostles. 005:003 "Ananias," said Peter, "why has Satan taken possession of your heart, that you should try to deceive the Holy Spirit and dishonestly keep back part of the price paid you for this land? 005:004 While it remained unsold, was not the land your own? And when sold, was it not at your own disposal? How is it that you have cherished this design in your heart? It is not to men you have told this lie, but to God." 005:005 Upon hearing these words Ananias fell down dead, and all who heard the words were awe-struck. 005:006 The younger men, however, rose, and wrapping the body up, carried it out and buried it. 005:007 About three hours had passed, when his wife came in, knowing nothing of what had happened. 005:008 Peter at once questioned her. "Tell me," he said, "whether you sold the land for so much." "Yes," she replied, "for so much." 005:009 "How was it," replied Peter, "that you two agreed to try an experiment upon the Spirit of the Lord? The men who have buried your husband are already at the door, and they will carry you out." 005:010 Instantly she fell down dead at his feet, and the young men came in and found her dead. So they carried her out and buried her by her husband's side. 005:011 This incident struck terror into the whole Church, and into the hearts of all who heard of it. 005:012 Many signs and marvels continued to be done among the people by the Apostles; and by common consent they all met in Solomon's Portico. 005:013 But none of the others dared to attach themselves to them. Yet the people held them in high honour- 005:014 and more and more believers in the Lord joined them, including great numbers both of men and women- 005:015 so that they would even bring out their sick friends into the streets and lay them on light couches or mats, in order that when Peter came by, at least his shadow might fall on one or other of them. 005:016 The inhabitants, too, of the towns in the neighbourhood of Jerusalem came in crowds, bringing sick persons and some who were harassed by foul spirits, and they were cured, one and all. 005:017 This roused the High Priest. He and all his party-the sect of the Sadducees-were filled with angry jealousy 005:018 and laid hands upon the Apostles, and put them into the public jail. 005:019 But during the night an angel of the Lord opened the prison doors and brought them out, and said, 005:020 "Go and stand in the Temple, and go on proclaiming to the people all this Message of Life." 005:021 Having received that command they went into the Temple, just before daybreak, and began to teach: So when the High Priest and his party came, and had called together the Sanhedrin as well as all the Elders of the descendants of Israel, they sent to the jail to fetch the Apostles. 005:022 But the officers went and could not find them in the prison. So they came back and brought word, 005:023 saying, "The jail we found quite safely locked, and the warders were on guard at the doors, but upon going in we found no one there." 005:024 When the Commander of the Temple Guards and the High Priests heard this statement, they were utterly at a loss with regard to it, wondering what would happen next. 005:025 And some one came and brought them word, saying, "The men you put in prison are actually in the Temple, standing there, teaching the people." 005:026 Upon this the Commander went with the officers, and brought the Apostles; but without using violence; for they were afraid of being stoned by the people. 005:027 So they brought them and made them stand in front of the Sanhedrin. And then the High Priest questioned them. 005:028 "We strictly forbad you to teach in that name-did we not?" he said. "And see, you have filled Jerusalem with your teaching, and are trying to make us responsible for that man's death!" 005:029 Peter and the other Apostles replied, "We must obey God rather than man. 005:030 The God of our forefathers has raised Jesus to life, whom you crucified and put to death. 005:031 God has exalted Him to His right hand as Chief Leader and as Saviour, to give Israel repentance and forgiveness of sins. 005:032 And we-and the Holy Spirit whom God has given to those who obey Him- are witnesses as to these things." 005:033 Infuriated at getting this answer, they were disposed to kill the Apostles. 005:034 But a Pharisee of the name of Gamaliel, a teacher of the Law, held in honour by all the people, rose from his seat and requested that they should be sent outside the court for a few minutes. 005:035 "Israelites," he said, "be careful what you are about to do in dealing with these men. 005:036 Years ago Theudas appeared, professing to be a person of importance, and a body of men, some four hundred in number, joined him. He was killed, and all his followers were dispersed and annihilated. 005:037 After him, at the time of the Census, came Judas, the Galilaean, and was the leader in a revolt. He too perished, and all his followers were scattered. 005:038 And now I tell you to hold aloof from these men and leave them alone-for if this scheme or work is of human origin, it will come to nothing. 005:039 But if it is really from God, you will be powerless to put them down-lest perhaps you find yourselves to be actually fighting against God." 005:040 His advice carried conviction. So they called the Apostles in, and- after flogging them- ordered them not to speak in the name of Jesus, and then let them go. 005:041 They, therefore, left the Sanhedrin and went their way, rejoicing that they had been deemed worthy to suffer disgrace on behalf of the NAME. 005:042 But they did not desist from teaching every day, in the Temple or in private houses, and telling the Good News about Jesus, the Christ. 006:001 About this time, as the number of disciples was increasing, complaints were made by the Greek-speaking Jews against the Hebrews because their widows were habitually overlooked in the daily ministration. 006:002 So the Twelve called together the general body of the disciples and said, "It does not seem fitting that we Apostles should neglect the delivery of God's Message and minister at tables. 006:003 Therefore, brethren, pick out from among yourselves seven men of good repute, full of the Spirit and of wisdom, and we will appoint them to undertake this duty. 006:004 But, as for us, we will devote ourselves to prayer and to the delivery of the Message." 006:005 The suggestion met with general approval, and they selected Stephen, a man full of faith and of the Holy Spirit, Philip, Prochorus, Nicanor, Timon, Parmenas, and Nicolas, a proselyte of Antioch. 006:006 These men they brought to the Apostles, and, after prayer, they laid their hands upon them. 006:007 Meanwhile God's Message continued to spread, and the number of the disciples in Jerusalem very greatly increased, and very many priests obeyed the faith. 006:008 And Stephen, full of grace and power, performed great marvels and signs among the people. 006:009 But some members of the so-called `Synagogue of the Freed-men,' together with some Cyrenaeans, Alexandrians, Cilicians and men from Roman Asia, were roused to encounter Stephen in debate. 006:010 They were quite unable, however, to resist the wisdom and the Spirit with which he spoke. 006:011 Then they privately put forward men who declared, "We have heard him speak blasphemous things against Moses and against God." 006:012 In this way they excited the people, the Elders, and the Scribes. At length they came upon him, seized him with violence, and took him before the Sanhedrin. 006:013 Here they brought forward false witnesses who declared, "This fellow is incessantly speaking against the Holy Place and the Law. 006:014 For we have heard him say that Jesus, the Nazarene, will pull this place down to the ground and will change the customs which Moses handed down to us." 006:015 At once the eyes of all who were sitting in the Sanhedrin were fastened on him, and they saw his face looking just like the face of an angel. 007:001 Then the High Priest asked him, "Are these statements true?" 007:002 The reply of Stephen was, "Sirs-brethren and fathers-listen to me. God Most Glorious appeared to our forefather Abraham when he was living in Mesopotamia, before he settled in Haran, 007:003 and said to him, "`Leave your country and your relatives, and go into whatever land I point out to you.' 007:004 "Thereupon he left Chaldaea and settled in Haran till after the death of his father, when God caused him to remove into this country where you now live. 007:005 But he gave him no inheritance in it, no, not a single square yard of ground. And yet He promised to bestow the land as a permanent possession on him and his posterity after him- and promised this at a time when Abraham was childless. 007:006 And God declared that Abraham's posterity should for four hundred years make their home in a country not their own, and be reduced to slavery and be oppressed. 007:007 "`And the nation, whichever it is, that enslaves them, I will judge,' said God; `and afterwards they shall come out, and they shall worship Me in this place.' 007:008 "Then He gave him the Covenant of circumcision, and under this Covenant he became the father of Isaac-whom he circumcised on the eighth day. Isaac became the father of Jacob, and Jacob became the father of the twelve Patriarchs. 007:009 "The Patriarchs were jealous of Joseph and sold him into slavery in Egypt. But God was with him 007:010 and delivered him from all his afflictions, and gave him favour and wisdom when he stood before Pharaoh, king of Egypt, who appointed him governor over Egypt and all the royal household. 007:011 But there came a famine throughout the whole of Egypt and Canaan- and great distress-so that our forefathers could find no food. 007:012 When, however, Jacob heard that there was wheat to be had, he sent our forefathers into Egypt; that was the first time. 007:013 On their second visit Joseph made himself known to his brothers, and Pharaoh was informed of Joseph's parentage. 007:014 Then Joseph sent and invited his father Jacob and all his family, numbering seventy-five persons, to come to him, 007:015 and Jacob went down into Egypt. There he died, and so did our forefathers, 007:016 and they were taken to Shechem and were laid in the tomb which Abraham had bought from the sons of Hamor at Shechem for a sum of money paid in silver. 007:017 "But as the time drew near for the fulfilment of the promise which God had made to Abraham, the people became many times more numerous in Egypt, 007:018 until there arose a foreign king over Egypt who knew nothing of Joseph. 007:019 He adopted a crafty policy towards our race, and oppressed our forefathers, making them cast out their infants so that they might not be permitted to live. 007:020 At this time Moses was born-a wonderfully beautiful child; and for three months he was cared for in his father's house. 007:021 At length he was cast out, but Pharaoh's daughter adopted him, and brought him up as her own son. 007:022 So Moses was educated in all the learning of the Egyptians, and possessed great influence through his eloquence and his achievements. 007:023 "And when he was just forty years old, it occurred to him to visit his brethren the descendants of Israel. 007:024 Seeing one of them wrongfully treated he took his part, and secured justice for the ill-treated man by striking down the Egyptian. 007:025 He supposed his brethren to be aware that by him God was sending them deliverance; this, however, they did not understand. 007:026 The next day, also, he came and found two of them fighting, and he endeavoured to make peace between them. "`Sirs,' he said, `you are brothers. Why are you wronging one another?' 007:027 "But the man who was doing the wrong resented his interference, and asked, "`Who appointed you magistrate and judge over us? 007:028 Do you mean to kill me as you killed the Egyptian yesterday?' 007:029 "Alarmed at this question, Moses fled from the country and went to live in the land of Midian. There he became the father of two sons. 007:030 "But at the end of forty years there appeared to him in the Desert of Mount Sinai an angel in the middle of a flame of fire in a bush. 007:031 When Moses saw this he wondered at the sight; but on his going up to look further, the voice of the Lord was heard, saying, 007:032 "`I am the God of your forefathers, the God of Abraham, of Isaac, and of Jacob.' "Quaking with fear Moses did not dare gaze. 007:033 "`Take off your shoes,' said the Lord, `for the spot on which you are standing is holy ground. 007:034 I have seen, yes, I have seen the oppression of My people who are in Egypt and have heard their groans, and I have come down to deliver them. And now I will send you to Egypt.' 007:035 "The Moses whom they rejected, asking him, `Who appointed you magistrate and judge?'-that same Moses we find God sending as a magistrate and a deliverer by the help of the angel who appeared to him in the bush. 007:036 This was he who brought them out, after performing marvels and signs in Egypt and at the Red Sea, and in the Desert for forty years. 007:037 This is the Moses who said to the descendants of Israel, "`God will raise up a Prophet for you, from among your brethren, just as He raised me up.' 007:038 `This is he who was among the Congregation in the Desert, together with the angel who spoke to him on Mount Sinai and with our forefathers, who received ever-living utterances to hand on to us. 007:039 "Our forefathers, however, would not submit to him, but spurned his authority and in their hearts turned back to Egypt. 007:040 They said to Aaron, "`Make gods for us, to march in front of us; for as for this Moses who brought us out of the land of Egypt, we do not know what has become of him.' 007:041 "Moreover they made a calf at that time, and offered a sacrifice to the idol and kept rejoicing in the gods which their own hands had made. 007:042 So God turned from them and gave them up to the worship of the Host of Heaven, as it is written in the Book of the Prophets, "'Were they victims and sacrifices which you offered Me, forty years in the Desert, O House of Israel? 007:043 Yes, you lifted up Moloch's tent and the Star of the God Rephan- the images which you made in order to worship them; and I will remove you beyond Babylon.' 007:044 "Our forefathers had the Tent of the Testimony in the Desert, built as He who spoke to Moses had instructed him to make it in imitation of the model which he had seen. 007:045 That Tent was bequeathed to the next generation of our forefathers. Under Joshua they brought it with them when they were taking possession of the land of the Gentile nations, whom God drove out before them. So it continued till David's time. 007:046 David obtained favour with God, and asked leave to provide a dwelling-place for the God of Jacob. 007:047 But it was Solomon who built a house for Him. 007:048 Yet the Most High does not dwell in buildings erected by men's hands. But, as the Prophet declares, 007:049 "`The sky is My throne, and earth is the footstool for My feet. What kind of house will you build for Me, says the Lord, or what resting place shall I have? 007:050 Did not My hand form this universe.' 007:051 "O stiff-necked men, uncircumcised in heart and ears, you also are continually at strife with the Holy Spirit- just as your forefathers were. 007:052 Which of the Prophets did not your forefathers persecute? Yes, they killed those who announced beforehand the advent of the righteous One, whose betrayers and murderers you have now become- 007:053 you who received the Law given through angels, and yet have not obeyed it." 007:054 As they listened to these words, they became infuriated and gnashed their teeth at him. 007:055 But, full of the Holy Spirit and looking up to Heaven, Stephen saw the glory of God, and Jesus standing at God's right hand. 007:056 "I can see Heaven wide open," he said, "and the Son of Man standing at God's right hand." 007:057 Upon this, with a loud outcry they stopped their ears, rushed upon Stephen in a body, 007:058 dragged him out of the city, and stoned him, the witnesses throwing off their outer garments and giving them into the care of a young man called Saul. 007:059 So they stoned Stephen, while he prayed, "Lord Jesus, receive my spirit." 007:060 Then, rising on his knees, he cried aloud, "Lord, do not reckon this sin against them." And with these words he fell asleep. 008:001 And Saul fully approved of his murder. At this time a great persecution broke out against the Church in Jerusalem, and all except the Apostles were scattered throughout Judaea and Samaria. 008:002 A party of devout men, however, buried Stephen, and made loud lamentation over him. 008:003 But Saul cruelly harassed the Church. He went into house after house, and, dragging off both men and women, threw them into prison. 008:004 Those, however, who were scattered abroad went from place to place spreading the Good News of God's Message; 008:005 while Philip went down to the city of Samaria and proclaimed Christ there.

008:006 Crowds of people, with one accord, gave attention to what they heard from him, listening, and witnessing the signs which he did. 008:007 For, with a loud cry, foul spirits came out of many possessed by them, and many paralytics and lame persons were restored to health. 008:008 And there was great joy in that city. 008:009 Now for some time past there had been a man named Simon living there, who had been practising magic and astonishing the Samaritans, pretending that he was more than human. 008:010 To him people of all classes paid attention, declaring, "This man is the Power of God, known as the great Power." 008:011 His influence over them arose from their having been, for a long time, bewildered by his sorceries. 008:012 But when Philip began to tell the Good News about the Kingdom of God and about the Name of Jesus Christ, and they embraced the faith, they were baptized, men and women alike. 008:013 Simon himself also believed, and after being baptized remained in close attendance on Philip, and was full of amazement at seeing such signs and such great miracles performed. 008:014 When the Apostles in Jerusalem heard that the Samaritans had accepted God's Message, they sent Peter and John to visit them. 008:015 They, when they came down, prayed for them that they might receive the Holy Spirit: 008:016 for He had not as yet fallen upon any of them. They had only been baptized into the name of the Lord Jesus. 008:017 Then the Apostles placed their hands upon them, and they received the Holy Spirit. 008:018 When, however, Simon saw that it was through the laying on of the Apostles' hands that the Spirit was bestowed, he offered them money. 008:019 "Give me too," he said, "that power, so that every one on whom I place my hands will receive the Holy Spirit." 008:020 "Perish your money and yourself," replied Peter, "because you have imagined that you can obtain God's free gift with money! 008:021 No part or lot have you in this matter, for your heart is not right in God's sight. 008:022 Repent, therefore, of this wickedness of yours, and pray to the Lord, in the hope that the purpose which is in your heart may perhaps be forgiven you. 008:023 For I perceive that you have fallen into the bitterest bondage of unrighteousness." 008:024 "Pray, both of you, to the Lord for me," answered Simon, "that nothing of what you have said may come upon me." 008:025 So the Apostles, after giving a solemn charge and delivering the Lord's Message, travelled back to Jerusalem, making known the Good News also in many of the Samaritan villages. 008:026 And an angel of the Lord said to Philip, "Rise and proceed south to the road that runs down from Jerusalem to Gaza, crossing the Desert." 008:027 Upon this he rose and went. Now, as it happened, an Ethiopian eunuch who was in a position of high authority with Candace, queen of the Ethiopians, as her treasurer, had visited Jerusalem to worship there, 008:028 and was now on his way home; and as he sat in his chariot he was reading the Prophet Isaiah. 008:029 Then the Spirit said to Philip, "Go and enter that chariot." 008:030

So Philip ran up and heard the eunuch reading the Prophet Isaiah. "Do you understand what you are reading?" he asked. 008:031 "Why, how can I," replied the eunuch, "unless some one explains it to me?" And he earnestly invited Philip to come up and sit with him. 008:032 The passage of Scripture which he was reading was this: "Like a sheep He was led to slaughter, and just as a lamb before its shearer is dumb so He opened not His mouth. 008:033 In His humiliation justice was denied Him. Who will make known His posterity? For He is destroyed from among men." 008:034 "Pray, of whom is the Prophet speaking?" inquired the eunuch; "of himself or of some one else?" 008:035 Then Philip began to speak, and, commencing with that same portion of Scripture, told him the Good News about Jesus. 008:036 So they proceeded on their way till they came to some water; and the eunuch exclaimed, "See, here is water; what is there to prevent my being baptized?" 008:037 [] 008:038 So he stopped the chariot; and both of them-Philip and the eunuch- went down into the water, and Philip baptized him. 008:039 But no sooner had they come up out of the water than the Spirit of the Lord caught Philip away, and the eunuch did not see him again. With a glad heart he resumed his journey; 008:040 but Philip found himself at Ashdod. Then visiting town after town he everywhere made known the Good News until he reached Caesarea. 009:001 Now Saul, whose every breath was a threat of destruction for the disciples of the Lord, 009:002 went to the High Priest and begged from him letters addressed to the synagogues in Damascus, in order that if he found any believers there, either men or women, he might bring them in chains to Jerusalem. 009:003 But on the journey, as he was getting near Damascus, suddenly there flashed round him a light from Heaven; 009:004 and falling to the ground he heard a voice which said to him, "Saul, Saul, why are you persecuting Me?" 009:005 "Who art thou, Lord?" he asked. "I am Jesus, whom you are persecuting," was the reply. 009:006 "But rise and go to the city, and you will be told what you are to do. 009:007 Meanwhile the men who travelled with Saul were standing dumb with amazement, hearing a sound, but seeing no one. 009:008 Then he rose from the ground, but when he had opened his eyes, he could not see, and they led him by the arm and brought him to Damascus. 009:009 And for two days he remained without sight, and did not eat or drink anything. 009:010 Now in Damascus there was a disciple of the name of Ananias. The Lord spoke to him in a vision, saying, "Ananias!" "I am here, Lord," he answered. 009:011 "Rise," said the Lord, "and go to Straight Street, and inquire at the house of Judas for a man called Saul, from Tarsus, for he is actually praying. 009:012 He has seen a man called Ananias come and lay his hands upon him so that he may recover his sight." 009:013 "Lord," answered Ananias, "I have heard about that man from many, and I have heard of the great mischief he has done to Thy people in Jerusalem; 009:014 and here he is authorized by the High

Priests to arrest all who call upon Thy name." 009:015 "Go," replied the Lord; "he is a chosen instrument of Mine to carry My name to the Gentiles and to kings and to the descendants of Israel. 009:016 For I will let him know the great sufferings which he must pass through for My sake." 009:017 So Ananias went and entered the house; and, laying his two hands upon Saul, said, "Saul, brother, the Lord-even Jesus who appeared to you on your journey-has sent me, that you may recover your sight and be filled with the Holy Spirit." 009:018 Instantly there dropped from his eyes what seemed to be scales, and he could see once more. Upon this he rose and received baptism; 009:019 after which he took food and regained his strength. Then he remained some little time with the disciples in Damascus. 009:020 And in the synagogues he began at once to proclaim Jesus as the Son of God; 009:021 and his hearers were all amazed, and began to ask one another, "Is not this the man who in Jerusalem tried to exterminate those who called upon that Name, and came here on purpose to carry them off in chains to the High Priests?" 009:022 Saul, however, gained more and more influence, and as for the Jews living in Damascus, he bewildered them with his proofs that Jesus is the Christ. 009:023 At length the Jews plotted to kill Saul; 009:024 but information of their intention was given to him. They even watched the gates, day and night, in order to murder him; 009:025 but his disciples took him by night and let him down through the wall, lowering him in a hamper. 009:026 So he came to Jerusalem and made several attempts to associate with the disciples, but they were all afraid of him, being in doubt as to whether he himself was a disciple. 009:027 Barnabas, however, came to his assistance. He brought Saul to the Apostles, and related to them how, on his journey, he had seen the Lord, and that the Lord had spoken to him, and how in Damascus he had fearlessly taught in the name of Jesus. 009:028 Henceforth Saul was one of them, going in and out of the city, 009:029 and speaking fearlessly in the name of the Lord. And he often talked with the Hellenists and had discussions with them. 009:030 But they kept trying to take his life. On learning this, the brethren brought him down to Caesarea, and then sent him by sea to Tarsus. 009:031 The Church, however, throughout the whole of Judaea, Galilee and Samaria, had peace and was spiritually built up; and grew in numbers, living in the fear of the Lord and receiving encouragement from the Holy Spirit. 009:032 Now Peter, as he went to town after town, came down also to God's people at Lud. 009:033 There he found a man of the name of Aeneas, who for eight years had kept his bed, through being paralysed. 009:034 Peter said to him, "Aeneas, Jesus Christ cures you. Rise and make your own bed." He at once rose to his feet. 009:035 And all the people of Lud and Sharon saw him; and they turned to the Lord. 009:036 Among the disciples at Jaffa was a woman called Tabitha, or, as the name may be translated, `Dorcas.' Her life was wholly devoted to the good and charitable actions which she was constantly doing. 009:037 But, as it happened, just at that time she was taken ill and died. After washing her body they laid it out in a room upstairs. 009:038 Lud, however, being near Jaffa, the disciples, who had heard that Peter was at Lud, sent two men to him with an urgent request that he would come across to them without delay. 009:039 So Peter rose and went with them. On his arrival they took him upstairs, and the widow women all came and stood by his side, weeping and showing him the underclothing and cloaks and garments of all kinds which Dorcas used to make while she was still with them. 009:040 Peter, however, putting every one out of the room, knelt down and prayed, and then turning to the body, he said, "Tabitha, rise." Dorcas at once opened her eyes, and seeing Peter, sat up. 009:041 Then, giving her his hand, he raised her to her feet and, calling to him God's people and the widows, he / 7 gave her back to them alive. 009:042 This incident became known throughout Jaffa, and many believed in the Lord; 009:043 and Peter remained for a considerable time at Jaffa, staying at the house of a man called Simon, a tanner. 010:001 Now a Captain of the Italian Regiment, named Cornelius, was quartered at Caesarea. 010:002 He was religious and God-fearing-and so was every member of his household. He was also liberal in his charities to the people, and continually offered prayer to God. 010:003 About three o'clock one afternoon he had a vision, and distinctly saw an angel of God enter his house, who called him by name, saying, "Cornelius!" 010:004 Looking steadily at him, and being much alarmed, he said, "What do you want, Sir?" "Your prayers and charities," he replied, "have gone up and have been recorded before God. 010:005 And now send to Jaffa and fetch Simon, surnamed Peter. 010:006 He is staying as a guest with Simon, a tanner, who has a house close to the sea." 010:007 So when the angel who had been speaking to him was gone, Cornelius called two of his servants and a God-fearing soldier who was in constant attendance on him, 010:008 and, after telling them everything, he sent them to Jaffa. 010:009 The next day, while they were still on their journey and were getting near the town, about noon Peter went up on the house-top to pray. 010:010 He had become unusually hungry and wished for food; but, while they were preparing it, he fell into a trance. 010:011 The sky had opened to his view, and what seemed to be an enormous sail was descending, being let down to the earth by ropes at the four corners. 010:012 In it were all kinds of quadrupeds, reptiles and birds, 010:013 and a voice came to him which said, "Rise, Peter, kill and eat." 010:014 "On no account, Lord," he replied; "for I have never yet eaten anything unholy and impure." 010:015 Again a second time a voice was heard which said, "What God has purified, you must not regard as unholy." 010:016 This was said three times, and immediately the sail was drawn up out of sight. 010:017 While Peter was greatly perplexed as to the meaning of the vision which he had seen, just then the men sent by Cornelius, having by inquiry found out Simon's house, 010:018 had come to the door and had called the servant, and were asking, "Is Simon, surnamed Peter, staying here?" 010:019 And Peter was still earnestly thinking over the vision, when the Spirit said to him, "Three men are now inquiring for you. 010:020 Rise, go down, and go with them without any misgivings; for it is I who have sent them to you." 010:021 So Peter went down and said to the men, "I am the Simon you are inquiring for. What is the reason of your coming?" 010:022 Their reply was, "Cornelius, a Captain, an upright and God-fearing man, of whom the whole Jewish nation speaks well, has been divinely instructed by a holy angel to send for you to come to his house and listen to what you have to say." 010:023 Upon hearing this, Peter invited them in, and gave them a lodging. The next day he set out with them, some of the brethren from Jaffa going with him, 010:024 and the day after that they reached Caesarea. There Cornelius was awaiting their arrival, and had invited all his relatives and intimate friends to be present. 010:025 When Peter entered the house, Cornelius met him, and threw himself at his feet to do him homage. 010:026 But Peter lifted him up. "Stand up," he said; "I myself also am but a man." 010:027 So Peter went in and conversed with him, and found a large company assembled. 010:028 He said to them, "You know better than most that a Jew is strictly forbidden to associate with a Gentile or visit him; but God has taught me to call no one unholy or unclean. 010:029 So for this reason, when sent for, I came without raising any objection. I therefore ask why you sent for me." 010:030 "Just at this hour, three days ago," replied Cornelius, "I was offering afternoon prayer in my house, when suddenly a man in shining raiment stood in front of me, 010:031 who said, "`Cornelius, your prayer has been heard, and your charities have been put on record before God. 010:032 Send therefore to Jaffa, and invite Simon, surnamed Peter, to come here. He is staying as a guest in the house of Simon, a tanner, close to the sea.' 010:033 "Immediately, therefore, I sent to you, and I thank you heartily for having come. That is why all of us are now assembled here in God's presence, to listen to what the Lord has commanded you to say." 010:034 Then Peter began to speak. "I clearly see," he said, "that God makes no distinctions between one man and another; 010:035 but that in every nation those who fear Him and live good lives are acceptable to Him. 010:036 The Message which He sent to the descendants of Israel, when He announced the Good News of peace through Jesus Christ-He is Lord of all-that Message you cannot but know; 010:037 the story, I mean, which has spread through the length and breadth of Judaea, beginning in Galilee after the baptism which John proclaimed. 010:038 It tells how God anointed Jesus of Nazareth with the Holy Spirit and with power, so that He went about everywhere doing acts of kindness, and curing all who were being continually oppressed by the Devil-for God was with Jesus. 010:039 "And we are witnesses as to all

He did both in the country of the Jews and in Jerusalem. But they even put Him to death, by crucifixion. 010:040 That same Jesus God raised to life on the third day, and permitted Him to appear unmistakably, 010:041 not to all the people, but to witnesses-men previously chosen by God-namely, to us, who ate and drank with Him after He rose from the dead. 010:042 And He has commanded us to preach to the people and solemnly declare that this is He who has been appointed by God to be the Judge of the living and the dead. 010:043 To Him all the Prophets bear witness, and testify that through His name all who believe in Him receive the forgiveness of their sins." 010:044 While Peter was speaking these words, the Holy Spirit fell on all who were listening to the Message. 010:045 And all the Jewish believers who had come with Peter were astonished that on the Gentiles also the gift of the Holy Spirit was poured out. 010:046 For they heard them speaking in tongues and extolling the majesty of God. Then Peter said, 010:047 "Can any one forbid the use of water, and object to these persons being baptized-men who have received the Holy Spirit just as we did?" 010:048 And he directed that they should be baptized in the name of Jesus Christ. Then they begged him to remain with them for a time. 011:001 Now the Apostles, and the brethren in various parts of Judaea, heard that the Gentiles also had received God's Message; 011:002 and, when Peter returned to Jerusalem, the champions of circumcision found fault with him. 011:003 "You went into the houses of men who are not Jews," they said, "and you ate with them." 011:004 Peter, however, explained the whole matter to them from the beginning. 011:005 "While I was in the town of Jaffa, offering prayer," he said, "in a trance I saw a vision. There descended what seemed to be an enormous sail, being let down from the sky by ropes at the four corners, and it came close to me. 011:006 Fixing my eyes on it, I examined it closely, and saw various kinds of quadrupeds, wild beasts, reptiles and birds. 011:007 I also heard a voice saying to me, "`Rise, Peter, kill and eat.' 011:008 "`On no account, Lord,' I replied, `for nothing unholy or impure has ever gone into my mouth.' 011:009 "But a voice answered, speaking a second time from the sky, "`What God has purified, you must not regard as unholy.' 011:010 "This was said three times, and then everything was drawn up again out of sight. 011:011 "Now at that very moment three men came to the house where we were, having been sent from Caesarea to find me. 011:012 And the Spirit told me to accompany them without any misgivings. There also went with me these six brethren who are now present, and we reached the Centurion's house. 011:013 Then he described to us how he had seen the angel come and enter his house and say, "`Send to Jaffa and fetch Simon, surnamed Peter. 011:014 He will teach you truths by which you and all your family will be saved.'" 011:015 "And," said Peter, "no sooner had I begun to speak than the Holy Spirit fell upon them, just as He fell upon us at the first.

011:016 Then I remembered the Lord's words, how He used to say, "`John baptized with water, but you shall be baptized in the Holy Spirit.' 011:017 "If therefore God gave them the same gift as He gave us when we first believed on the Lord Jesus Christ, why, who was I to be able to thwart God?" 011:018 This statement of Peter's silenced his opponents. They extolled the goodness of God, and said, "So, then, to the Gentiles also God has given the repentance which leads to Life." 011:019 Those, however, who had been driven in various directions by the persecution which broke out on account of Stephen made their way to Phoenicia, Cyprus and Antioch, delivering the Message to none but Jews. 011:020 But some of them were Cyprians and Cyrenaeans, who, on coming to Antioch, spoke to the Greeks also and told them the Good News concerning the Lord Jesus. 011:021 The power of the Lord was with them, and there were a vast number who believed and turned to the Lord. 011:022 When tidings of this reached the ears of the Church in Jerusalem, they sent Barnabas as far as Antioch. 011:023 On getting there he was delighted to see the grace which God had bestowed; and he encouraged them all to remain, with fixed resolve, faithful to the Lord. 011:024 For he was a good man, and was full of the Holy Spirit and of faith; and the number of believers in the Lord greatly increased. 011:025 Then Barnabas paid a visit to Tarsus to try to find Saul. 011:026 He succeeded, and brought him to Antioch; and for a whole year they attended the meetings of the Church, and taught a large number of people. And it was in Antioch that the disciples first received the name of `Christians.' 011:027 At that time certain Prophets came down from Jerusalem to Antioch, 011:028 one of whom, named Agabus, being instructed by the Spirit, publicly predicted the speedy coming of a great famine throughout the world. (It came in the reign of Claudius.) 011:029 So the disciples decided to send relief, every one in proportion to his means, to the brethren living in Judaea. 011:030 This they did, forwarding their contributions to the Elders by Barnabas and Saul. 012:001 Now, about that time, King Herod arrested certain members of the Church, in order to ill-treat them; 012:002 and James, John's brother, he beheaded. 012:003 Finding that this gratified the Jews, he proceeded to seize Peter also; these being the days of Unleavened Bread. 012:004 He had him arrested and lodged in jail, handing him over to the care of sixteen soldiers; and intended after the Passover to bring him out again to the people. 012:005 So Peter was kept in prison; but long and fervent prayer was offered to God by the Church on his behalf. 012:006 Now when Herod was on the point of taking him out of prison, that very night Peter was asleep between two soldiers, bound with two chains, and guards were on duty outside the door. 012:007 Suddenly an angel of the Lord stood by him, and a light shone in the cell; and, striking Peter on the side, he woke him and said, "Rise quickly." Instantly the chains dropped off his wrists. 012:008 "Fasten your girdle," said the angel, "and tie on your sandals." He did so. Then the angel said, "Throw your cloak round you, and follow me." 012:009 So Peter went out, following him, yet could not believe that what the angel was doing was real, but supposed that he saw a vision. 012:010 And passing through the first ward and the second, they came to the iron gate leading into the city. This opened to them of itself; and, going out, they passed on through one of the streets, and then suddenly the angel left him. 012:011 Peter coming to himself said, "Now I know for certain that the Lord has sent His angel and has rescued me from the power of Herod and from all that the Jewish people were anticipating." 012:012 So, after thinking things over, he went to the house of Mary, the mother of John surnamed Mark, where a large number of people were assembled, praying. 012:013 When he knocked at the wicket in the door, a maidservant named Rhoda came to answer the knock; 012:014 and recognizing Peter's voice, for very joy she did not open the door, but ran in and told them that Peter was standing there. 012:015 "You are mad," they said. But she strenuously maintained that it was true. "It is his guardian angel," they said. 012:016 Meanwhile Peter went on knocking, until at last they opened the door and saw that it was really he, and were filled with amazement. 012:017 But he motioned with his hand for silence, and then described to them how the Lord had brought him out of the prison. "Tell all this to James and the brethren," he added. Then he left them, and went to another place. 012:018 When morning came, there was no little commotion among the soldiers, as to what could possibly have become of Peter. 012:019 And when Herod had had him searched for and could not find him, after sharply questioning the guards he ordered them away to execution. He then went down from Judaea to Caesarea and remained there. 012:020 Now the people of Tyre and Sidon had incurred Herod's violent displeasure. So they sent a large deputation to wait on him; and having secured the good will of Blastus, his treasurer, they begged the king to be friendly with them again, because their country was dependent on his for its food supply. 012:021 So, on an appointed day, Herod, having arrayed himself in royal robes, took his seat on the tribunal, and was haranguing them; 012:022 and the assembled people kept shouting, "It is the voice of a god, and not of a man!" 012:023 Instantly an angel of the Lord struck him, because he had not given the glory to God, and being eaten up by worms, he died. 012:024 But God's Message prospered, and converts were multiplied. 012:025 And Barnabas and Saul returned from Jerusalem, having discharged their mission, and they brought with them John, surnamed Mark. 013:001 Now there were in Antioch, in the Church there-as Prophets and teachers-barnabas, Symeon surnamed `the black,' Lucius the Cyrenaean, Manaen (who was Herod the Tetrarch's foster-brother), and Saul. 013:002 While they were worshipping the Lord and fasting, the Holy Spirit said, "Set apart for Me, now at once, Barnabas and

Saul, for the work to which I have called them." 013:003 So, after fasting and prayer and the laying on of hands, they let them go. 013:004 They therefore, being thus sent out by the Holy Spirit, went down to Seleuceia, and from there sailed to Cyprus. 013:005 Having reached Salamis, they began to announce God's Message in the synagogues of the Jews. And they had John as their assistant. 013:006 When they had gone through the whole length of the island as far as Paphos, they there met with a Jewish magician and false prophet, Bar-Jesus by name, 013:007 who was a friend of the Proconsul Sergius Paulus. The Proconsul was a man of keen intelligence. He sent for Barnabas and Saul, and asked to be told God's Message. 013:008 But Elymas (or `the Magician,' for such is the meaning of the name) opposed them, and tried to prevent the Proconsul from accepting the faith. 013:009 Then Saul, who is also called Paul, was filled with the Holy Spirit, and, fixing his eyes on Elymas, 013:010 said, "You who are full of every kind of craftiness and unscrupulous cunning-you son of the Devil and foe to all that is right-will you never cease to misrepresent the straight paths of the Lord? 013:011 The Lord's hand is now upon you, and you will be blind for a time and unable to see the light of day." Instantly there fell upon him a mist and a darkness, and, as he walked about, he begged people to lead him by the hand. 013:012 Then the Proconsul, seeing what had happened, believed, being struck with amazement at the teaching of the Lord. 013:013 From Paphos, Paul and his party put out to sea and sailed to Perga in Pamphylia. John, however, left them and returned to Jerusalem. 013:014 But they themselves, passing through from Perga, came to Antioch in Pisidia. Here, on the Sabbath day, they went into the synagogue and sat down. 013:015 After the reading of the Law and the Prophets, the Wardens of the synagogue sent word to them. "Brethren," they said, "if you have anything encouraging to say to the people, speak." 013:016 So Paul rose, and motioning with his hand for silence, said, "Israelites, and you others who fear God, pay attention to me. 013:017 The God of this people of Israel chose our forefathers, and made the people great during their stay in Egypt, until with wondrous power He brought them out from that land. 013:018 For a period of about forty years, He fed them, like a nurse, in the Desert. 013:019 Then, after overthrowing seven nations in the land of Canaan, He divided that country among them as their inheritance for about four hundred and fifty years; 013:020 and afterwards He gave them judges down to the time of the Prophet Samuel. 013:021 Next they asked for a king, and God gave them Saul the son of Kish, a Benjamite, who reigned forty years. 013:022 After removing him, He raised up David to be their king, to whom He also bore witness when He said, "`I have found David the son of Jesse, a man I love, who will obey all My commands.' 013:023 "It is from among David's descendants that God, in fulfilment of His promise, has raised up a Saviour for Israel, even Jesus. 013:024 Before the coming of

Jesus, John had proclaimed to all the people of Israel a baptism of repentance. 013:025 But John, towards the end of his career, repeatedly asked the people, "`What do you suppose me to be? I am not the Christ. But there is One coming after me whose sandal I am not worthy to unfasten.' 013:026 "Brethren, descendants of the family of Abraham, and all among you who fear God, to us has this Message of salvation been sent. 013:027 For the people of Jerusalem and their rulers, by the judgement they pronounced on Jesus, have actually fulfilled the predictions of the Prophets which are read Sabbath after Sabbath, through ignorance of those predictions and of Him. 013:028 Without having found Him guilty of any capital offence they urged Pilate to have Him put to death; 013:029 and when they had carried out everything which had been written about Him, they took Him down from the cross and laid Him in a tomb. 013:030 "But God raised Him from the dead. 013:031 And, after a few days, He appeared to the people who had gone up with Him from Galilee to Jerusalem and are now witnesses concerning Him to the Jews. 013:032 And we bring you the Good News about the promise made to our forefathers, 013:033 that God has amply fulfilled it to our children in raising up Jesus; as it is also written in the second Psalm, `Thou art My Son: to-day I have become Thy Father.' 013:034 And as to His having raised Him from among the dead, never again to be in the position of one soon to return to decay, He speaks thus: `I will give you the holy and trustworthy promises made to David.' 013:035 Because in another Psalm also He says, `Thou wilt not give up Thy Holy One to undergo decay.' 013:036 For David, after having been useful to his own generation in accordance with God's purpose, did fall asleep, was gathered to his forefathers, and did undergo decay. 013:037 But He whom God raised to life underwent no decay. 013:038 "Understand therefore, brethren, that through this Jesus forgiveness of sins is announced to you; 013:039 and in Him every believer is absolved from all offences, from which you could not be absolved under the Law of Moses. 013:040 Beware, then, lest what is spoken in the Prophets should come true of you: 013:041 `Behold, you despisers, be astonished and perish, because I am carrying on a work in your time-a work which you will utterly refuse to believe, though it be fully declared to you.'" 013:042 As Paul and Barnabas were leaving the synagogue, the people earnestly begged to have all this repeated to them on the following Sabbath. 013:043 And, when the congregation had broken up, many of the Jews and of the devout converts from heathenism continued with Paul and Barnabas, who talked to them and urged them to hold fast to the grace of God. 013:044 On the next Sabbath almost the whole population of the city came together to hear the Lord's Message. 013:045 Seeing the crowds, the Jews, filled with angry jealousy, opposed Paul's statements and abused him. 013:046 Then, throwing off all reserve, Paul and Barnabas said, "We were bound to proclaim God's Message to you first. But since you spurn it and judge yourselves to be unworthy of the Life of the Ages-well, we turn to the Gentiles. 013:047 For such is the Lord's command to us. "`I have placed Thee,' He says of Christ, `as a light to the Gentiles, in order that Thou mayest be a Saviour as far as the remotest parts of the earth.'" 013:048 The Gentiles listened with delight and extolled the Lord's Message; and all who were pre-destined to the Life of the Ages believed. 013:049 So the Lord's Message spread through the whole district. 013:050 But the Jews influenced the gentlewomen of rank who worshipped with them, and also the leading men in the city, and stirred up persecution against Paul and Barnabas and drove them out of the district. 013:051 But they shook off the dust from their feet as a protest against them and came to Iconium; 013:052 and as for the disciples, they were more and more filled with joy and with the Holy Spirit. 014:001 At Iconium the Apostles went together to the Jewish synagogue and preached, with the result that a great number both of Jews and Greeks believed. 014:002 But the Jews who had refused obedience stirred up the Gentiles and embittered their minds against the brethren. 014:003 Yet Paul and Barnabas remained there for a considerable time, speaking freely and relying on the Lord, while He bore witness to the Message of His grace by permitting signs and marvels to be done by them. 014:004 At length the people of the city split into parties, some siding with the Jews and some with the Apostles. 014:005 And when a hostile movement was made by both Gentiles and Jews, with the sanction of their magistrates, to maltreat and stone them, 014:006 the Apostles, having become aware of it, made their escape into the Lycaonian towns of Lystra and Derbe, and the neighbouring country. 014:007 And there they continued to tell the Good News. 014:008 Now a man who had no power in his feet used to sit in the streets of Lystra. He had been lame from his birth and had never walked. 014:009 After this man had listened to one of Paul's sermons, the Apostle, looking steadily at him and perceiving that he had faith to be cured, 014:010 said in a loud voice, "Stand upright upon your feet!" 014:011 So he sprang up and began to walk about. Then the crowds, seeing what Paul had done, rent the air with their shouts in the Lycaonian language, saying, "The gods have assumed human form and have come down to us." 014:012 They called Barnabas `Zeus,' and Paul, as being the principal speaker, `Hermes.' 014:013 And the priest of Zeus-the temple of Zeus being at the entrance to the city-brought bullocks and garlands to the gates, and in company with the crowd was intending to offer sacrifices to them. 014:014 But the Apostles, Barnabas and Paul, heard of it; and tearing their clothes they rushed out into the middle of the crowd, exclaiming, "Sirs, why are you doing all this? 014:015 We also are but men, with natures kindred to your own; and we bring you the Good News that you are to turn from these unreal things, to worship the ever-living God, the Creator of earth and sky and sea and of everything that is in them.

014:016 In times gone by He allowed all the nations to go their own ways; 014:017 and yet by His beneficence He has not left His existence unattested- His beneficence, I mean, in sending you rain from Heaven and fruitful seasons, satisfying your hearts with food and joyfulness." 014:018 Even with words like these they had difficulty in preventing the thronging crowd from offering sacrifices to them. 014:019 But now a party of Jews came from Antioch and Iconium, and, having won over the crowd, they stoned Paul and dragged him out of the town, believing him to be dead. 014:020 When, however, the disciples had collected round him, he rose and went back into the town. The next day he went with Barnabas to Derbe; 014:021 and, after proclaiming the Good News to the people there and gaining a large number of converts, they retraced their steps to Lystra, Iconium, and Antioch. 014:022 Everywhere they strengthened the disciples by encouraging them to hold fast to the faith, and warned them saying, "It is through many afflictions that we must make our way into the Kingdom of God." 014:023 And in every Church, after prayer and fasting, they selected Elders by show of hands, and commended them to the Lord on whom their faith rested. 014:024 Then passing through Pisidia they came into Pamphylia; 014:025 and after telling the Message at Perga they came down to Attaleia. 014:026 Thence they sailed to Antioch, where they had previously been commended to the grace of God in connexion with the work which they had now completed. 014:027 Upon their arrival they called the Church together and proceeded to report in detail all that God, working with them, had done, and how He had opened for the Gentiles the door of faith. 014:028 And they remained a considerable time in Antioch with the disciples. 015:001 But certain persons who had come down from Judaea tried to convince the brethren, saying, "Unless you are circumcised in accordance with the Mosaic custom, you cannot be saved." 015:002 Between these new comers and Paul and Barnabas there was no little disagreement and controversy, until at last it was decided that Paul and Barnabas and some other brethren should go up to consult the Apostles and Elders in Jerusalem on this matter. 015:003 So they set out, being accompanied for a short distance by some other members of the Church; and as they passed through Phoenicia and Samaria, they told the whole story of the conversion of the Gentiles and inspired all the brethren with great joy. 015:004 Upon their arrival in Jerusalem they were cordially received by the Church, the Apostles, and the Elders; and they reported in detail all that God, working with them, had done. 015:005 But certain men who had belonged to the sect of the Pharisees but were now believers, stood up in the assembly, and said, "Yes, Gentile believers ought to be circumcised and be ordered to keep the Law of Moses." 015:006 Then the Apostles and Elders met to consider the matter; 015:007 and after there had been a long discussion Peter rose to his feet. "It is within your own knowledge," he said, "that God originally made choice among you that from my lips the Gentiles were to hear the Message of the Good News, and believe. 015:008 And God, who knows all hearts, gave His testimony in their favour by bestowing the Holy Spirit on them just as He did on us; 015:009 and He made no difference between us and them, in that He cleansed their hearts by their faith. 015:010 Now, therefore, why try an experiment upon God, by laying on the necks of these disciples a yoke which neither our forefathers nor we have been able to bear? 015:011 On the contrary, we believe that it is by the grace of the Lord Jesus that we, as well as they, shall be saved." 015:012 Then the whole assembly remained silent while they listened to the statement made by Paul and Barnabas as to all the signs and marvels that God had done among the Gentiles through their instrumentality. 015:013 When they had finished speaking, James said, "Brethren, listen to me. 015:014 Symeon has related how God first looked graciously on the Gentiles to take from among them a People to be called by His name. 015:015 And this is in harmony with the language of the Prophets, which says: 015:016 "`"Afterwards I will return, and will rebuild David's fallen tent. Its ruins I will rebuild, and I will set it up again; 015:017 In order that the rest of mankind may earnestly seek the Lord- even all the nations which are called by My name," 015:018 Says the Lord, who has been making these things known from ages long past.' 015:019 "My judgement, therefore, is against inflicting unexpected annoyance on those of the Gentiles who are turning to God. 015:020 Yet let us send them written instructions to abstain from things polluted by connexion with idolatry, from fornication, from meat killed by strangling, and from blood. 015:021 For Moses from the earliest times has had his preachers in every town, being read, as he is, Sabbath after Sabbath, in the various synagogues." 015:022 Thereupon it was decided by the Apostles and Elders, with the approval of the whole Church, to choose suitable persons from among themselves and send them to Antioch, with Paul and Barnabas. Judas, called Bar-sabbas, and Silas, leading men among the brethren, were selected, 015:023 and they took with them the following letter: "The Apostles and the elder brethren send greeting to the Gentile brethren throughout Antioch, Syria and Cilicia. 015:024 As we have been informed that certain persons who have gone out from among us have disturbed you by their teaching and have unsettled your minds, without having received any such instructions from us; 015:025 we have unanimously decided to select certain men and send them to you in company with our dear friends Barnabas and Paul, 015:026 who have endangered their very lives for the sake of our Lord Jesus Christ. 015:027 We have therefore sent Judas and Silas, who are themselves bringing you the same message by word of mouth. 015:028 For it has seemed good to the Holy Spirit and to us to lay upon you no burden heavier than these necessary requirements- 015:029 You must abstain from things sacrificed to idols, from blood, from things strangled, and from fornication. Keep yourselves clear of these things, and it will be well with you. Farewell." 015:030 They, therefore, having been solemnly sent, came down to Antioch, where they called together the whole assembly and delivered the letter. 015:031 The people read it, and were delighted with the comfort it brought them. 015:032 And Judas and Silas, being themselves also Prophets, gave them a long and encouraging talk, and strengthened them in the faith. 015:033 After spending some time there they received an affectionate farewell from the brethren to return to those who had sent them. 015:034 [] 015:035 But Paul and Barnabas remained in Antioch, teaching and, in company with many others, telling the Good News of the Lord's Message. 015:036 After a while Paul said to Barnabas, "Suppose we now revisit the brethren in the various towns in which we have made known the Lord's Message-to see whether they are prospering!" 015:037 Barnabas, however, was bent on taking with them John, whose other name was Mark, 015:038 while Paul deemed it undesirable to have as their companion one who had deserted them in Pamphylia and had not gone on with them to the work. 015:039 So there arose a serious disagreement between them, which resulted in their parting from one another, Barnabas taking Mark and setting sail for Cyprus. 015:040 But Paul chose Silas as his travelling companion; and set out, after being commended by the brethren to the grace of the Lord; 015:041 and he passed through Syria and Cilicia, strengthening the Churches. 016:001 He also came to Derbe and to Lystra. At Lystra he found a disciple, Timothy by name-the son of a Christian Jewess, though he had a Greek father. 016:002 Timothy was well spoken of by the brethren at Lystra and Iconium, 016:003 and Paul desiring that he should accompany him on his journey, took him and circumcised him on account of the Jews in those parts, for they all knew that his father was a Greek. 016:004 As they journeyed on from town to town, they handed to the brethren for their observance the decisions which had been arrived at by the Apostles and Elders in Jerusalem. 016:005 So the Churches went on gaining a stronger faith and growing in numbers from day to day. 016:006 Then Paul and his companions passed through Phrygia and Galatia, having been forbidden by the Holy Spirit to proclaim the Message in the province of Asia. 016:007 When they reached the frontier of Mysia, they were about to enter Bithynia, but the Spirit of Jesus would not permit this. 016:008 So, passing along Mysia, they came to Troas. 016:009 Here, one night, Paul saw a vision. There was a Macedonian who was standing, entreating him and saying, "Come over into Macedonia and help us." 016:010 So when he had seen the vision, we immediately looked out for an opportunity of passing on into Macedonia, confidently inferring that God had called us to proclaim the Good News to the people there. 016:011 Accordingly we put out to sea from Troas, and ran a straight course to Samothrace. The next day we came to Neapolis, 016:012 and thence to Philippi, which is a city in Macedonia, the first in its district, a Roman colony. And there we stayed some little time. 016:013 On the Sabbath we went beyond the city gate to the riverside, where we had reason to believe that there was a place for prayer; and sitting down we talked with the women who had come together. 016:014 Among our hearers was one named Lydia, a dealer in purple goods. She belonged to the city of Thyateira, and was a worshipper of the true God. The Lord opened her heart, so that she gave attention to what Paul was saying. 016:015 When she and her household had been baptized, she urged us, saying, "If in your judgement I am a believer in the Lord, come and stay at my house." And she made us go there. 016:016 One day, as we were on our way to the place of prayer, a slave girl met us who claimed to be inspired and was accustomed to bring her owners large profits by telling fortunes. 016:017 She kept following close behind Paul and the rest of us, crying aloud, "These men are the bondservants of the Most High God, and are proclaiming to you the way of salvation." 016:018 This she persisted in for a considerable time, until Paul, wearied out, turned round and said to the spirit, "I command you in the name of Jesus Christ to come out of her." And it came out immediately. 016:019 But when her owners saw that their hopes of gain were gone, they seized Paul and Silas and dragged them off to the magistrates in the public square. 016:020 Then they brought them before the praetors. "These men," they said, "are creating a great disturbance in our city. 016:021 They are Jews, and are teaching customs which we, as Romans, are not permitted to adopt or practise." 016:022 The crowd, too, joined in the outcry against them, till at length the praetors ordered them to be stripped and beaten with rods; 016:023 and, after severely flogging them, they threw them into jail and bade the jailer keep them safely. 016:024 He, having received an order like that, lodged them in the inner prison, and secured their feet in the stocks. 016:025 About midnight Paul and Silas were praying and singing hymns to God, and the prisoners were listening to them, 016:026 when suddenly there was such a violent shock of earthquake that the prison shook to its foundations. Instantly the doors all flew open, and the chains fell off from every prisoner. 016:027 Starting up from sleep and seeing the doors of the jail wide open, the jailer drew his sword and was on the point of killing himself, supposing that the prisoners had escaped. 016:028 But Paul shouted loudly to him, saying, "Do yourself no injury: we are all here. 016:029 Then, calling for lights, he sprang in and fell trembling at the feet of Paul and Silas; 016:030 and, bringing them out of the prison, he exclaimed, "O sirs, what must I do to be saved?" 016:031 "Believe on the Lord Jesus," they replied, "and both you and your household will be saved." 016:032 And they told the Lord's Message to him as well as to all who were in his house. 016:033 Then he took them, even at that time of night, washed their wounds, and he and all his household were immediately baptized; 016:034 and bringing the Apostles up into his house, he spread a meal for them, and was filled with gladness, with his whole household, his faith resting on God. 016:035 In the morning the praetors sent their lictors with the order, "Release those men." 016:036 So the jailer brought Paul word, saying, "The praetors have sent orders for you to be released. Now therefore you can go, and proceed on your way in peace." 016:037 But Paul said to them, "After cruelly beating us in public, without trial, Roman citizens though we are, they have thrown us into prison, and are they now going to send us away privately? No, indeed! Let them come in person and fetch us out." 016:038 This answer the lictors took back to the praetors, who were alarmed when they were told that Paul and Silas were Roman citizens. 016:039 Accordingly they came and apologized to them; and, bringing them out, asked them to leave the city. 016:040 Then Paul and Silas, having come out of the prison, went to Lydia's house; and, after seeing the brethren and encouraging them, they left Philippi. 017:001 Then, passing through Amphipolis and Apollonia, they went to Thessalonica. Here there was a synagogue of the Jews. 017:002 Paul-following his usual custom-betook himself to it, and for three successive Sabbaths reasoned with them from the Scriptures, 017:003 which he clearly explained, pointing out that it had been necessary for the Christ to suffer and rise again from the dead, and insisting, "The Jesus whom I am announcing to you is the Christ." 017:004 Some of the people were won over, and attached themselves to Paul and Silas, including many God-fearing Greeks and not a few gentlewomen of high rank. 017:005 But the jealousy of the Jews was aroused, and, calling to their aid some ill-conditioned and idle fellows, they got together a riotous mob and filled the city with uproar. They then attacked the house of Jason and searched for Paul and Silas, to bring them out before the assembly of people. 017:006 But, failing to find them, they dragged Jason and some of the other brethren before the magistrates of the city, loudly accusing them. "These men," they said, "who have raised a tumult throughout the Empire, have come here also. 017:007 Jason has received them into his house; and they all set Caesar's authority at defiance, declaring that there is another Emperor- one called Jesus." 017:008 Great was the excitement among the crowd, and among the magistrates of the city, when they heard these charges. 017:009 They required Jason and the rest to find substantial bail, and after that they let them go. 017:010 The brethren at once sent Paul and Silas away by night to Beroea, and they, on their arrival, went to the synagogue of the Jews. 017:011 The Jews at Beroea were of a nobler disposition than those in Thessalonica, for they very readily received the Message, and day after day searched the Scriptures to see whether it was as Paul stated. 017:012 As the result many of them became believers, and so did not a few of the Greeks-gentlewomen of good position, and men.

017:013 As soon, however, as the Jews of Thessalonica learnt that God's Message had been proclaimed by Paul at Beroea, they came there also, and incited the mob to a riot. 017:014 Then the brethren promptly sent Paul down to the sea-coast, but Silas and Timothy remained behind. 017:015 Those who were caring for Paul's safety went with him as far as Athens, and then left him, taking a message from him to Silas and Timothy, asking them to join him as speedily as possible. 017:016 While Paul was waiting for them in Athens, his spirit was stirred within him when he noticed that the city was full of idols. 017:017 So he had discussions in the synagogue with the Jews and the other worshippers, and in the market place, day after day, with those whom he happened to meet. 017:018 A few of the Epicurean and Stoic philosophers also encountered him. Some of them asked, "What has this beggarly babbler to say?" "His business," said others, "seems to be to cry up some foreign gods." This was because he had been telling the Good News of Jesus and the Resurrection. 017:019 Then they took him and brought him up to the Areopagus, asking him, "May we be told what this new teaching of yours is? 017:020 For the things you are saying sound strange to us. We should therefore like to be told exactly what they mean." 017:021 (For all the Athenians and their foreign visitors used to devote their whole leisure to telling or hearing about something new.) 017:022 So Paul, taking his stand in the centre of the Areopagus, spoke as follows: "Men of Athens, I perceive that you are in every respect remarkably religious. 017:023 For as I passed along and observed the things you worship, I found also an altar bearing the inscription, `TO AN UNKNOWN GOD.' "The Being, therefore, whom you, without knowing Him, revere, Him I now proclaim to you. 017:024 GOD who made the universe and everything in it-He, being Lord of Heaven and earth, does not dwell in sanctuaries built by men. 017:025 Nor is He ministered to by human hands, as though He needed anything- but He Himself gives to all men life and breath and all things. 017:026 He caused to spring from one forefather people of every race, for them to live on the whole surface of the earth, and marked out for them an appointed span of life and the boundaries of their homes; 017:027 that they might seek God, if perhaps they could grope for Him and find Him. Yes, though He is not far from any one of us. 017:028 For it is in closest union with Him that we live and move and have our being; as in fact some of the poets in repute among yourselves have said, `For we are also His offspring.' 017:029 Since then we are God's offspring, we ought not to imagine that His nature resembles gold or silver or marble, or anything sculptured by the art and inventive faculty of man. 017:030 Those times of ignorance God viewed with indulgence. But now He commands all men everywhere to repent, 017:031 seeing that He has appointed a day on which, before long, He will judge the world in righteousness, through the instrumentality of a man whom He has pre-destined to this work, and has made the fact certain to every one by raising Him from the dead." 017:032 When they heard Paul speak of a resurrection of dead men, some began to scoff. But others said, "We will hear you again on that subject." 017:033 So Paul went away from them. 017:034 A few, however, attached themselves to him and believed, among them being Dionysius a member of the Council, a gentlewoman named Damaris, and some others. 018:001 After this he left Athens and came to Corinth. 018:002 Here he found a Jew, a native of Pontus, of the name of Aquila. He and his wife Priscilla had recently come from Italy because of Claudius's edict expelling all the Jews from Rome. So Paul paid them a visit; 018:003 and because he was of the same trade-that of tent-maker- he lodged with them and worked with them. 018:004 But, Sabbath after Sabbath, he preached in the synagogue and tried to win over both Jews and Greeks. 018:005 Now at the time when Silas and Timothy came down from Macedonia, Paul was preaching fervently and was solemnly telling the Jews that Jesus is the Christ. 018:006 But upon their opposing him with abusive language, he shook his clothes by way of protest, and said to them, "Your ruin will be upon your own heads. I am not responsible: in future I will go among the Gentiles." 018:007 So he left the place and went to the house of a person called Titius Justus, a worshipper of the true God. His house was next door to the synagogue. 018:008 And Crispus, the Warden of the synagogue, believed in the Lord, and so did all his household; and from time to time many of the Corinthians who heard Paul believed and received baptism. 018:009 And, in a vision by night, the Lord said to Paul, "Dismiss your fears: go on speaking, and do not give up. 018:010 I am with you, and no one shall attack you to injure you; for I have very many people in this city." 018:011 So Paul remained in Corinth for a year and six months, teaching among them the Message of God. 018:012 But when Gallio became Proconsul of Greece, the Jews with one accord made a dead set at Paul, and brought him before the court. 018:013 "This man," they said, "is inducing people to offer unlawful worship to God." 018:014 But, when Paul was about to begin his defence, Gallio said to the Jews, "If it had been some wrongful act or piece of cunning knavery I might reasonably have listened to you Jews. 018:015 But since these are questions about words and names and your Law, you yourselves must see to them. I refuse to be a judge in such matters." 018:016 So he ordered them out of court. 018:017 Then the people all set upon Sosthenes, the Warden of the synagogue, and beat him severely in front of the court. Gallio did not concern himself in the least about this. 018:018 After remaining a considerable time longer in Corinth, Paul took leave of the brethren and set sail for Syria; and Priscilla and Aquila were with him. He had shaved his head at Cenchreae, because he was bound by a vow. 018:019 They put in at Ephesus, and there Paul left his companions behind. As for himself, he went to the synagogue and had a discussion with the Jews. 018:020 When they asked him to remain longer he did not consent, 018:021 but took leave of them with the promise, "I will return to you, God willing." So he set sail from Ephesus. 018:022 Landing at Caesarea, he went up to Jerusalem and inquired after the welfare of the Church, and then went down to Antioch. 018:023 After spending some time in Antioch, Paul set out on a tour, visiting the whole of Galatia and Phrygia in order, and strengthening all the disciples. 018:024 Meanwhile a Jew named Apollos came to Ephesus. He was a native of Alexandria, a man of great learning and well versed in the Scriptures. 018:025 He had been instructed by word of mouth in the way of the Lord, and, being full of burning zeal, he used to speak and teach accurately the facts about Jesus, though he knew of no baptism but John's. 018:026 He began to speak boldly in the synagogue, and Priscilla and Aquila, after hearing him, took him home and explained God's way to him more accurately. 018:027 Then, as he had made up his mind to cross over into Greece, the brethren wrote to the disciples in Corinth begging them to give him a kindly welcome. Upon his arrival he rendered valuable help to those who through grace had believed; 018:028 for he powerfully and in public overcame the Jews in argument, proving to them from the Scriptures that Jesus is the Christ. 019:001 During the stay of Apollos in Corinth, Paul, after passing through the inland districts, came to Ephesus, where he found a few disciples. 019:002 "Did you receive the Holy Spirit when you first believed?" he asked them. "No," they replied, "we did not even hear that there is a Holy Spirit." 019:003 "Into what then were you baptized?" he asked. "Into John's baptism," they replied. 019:004 "John," he said, "administered a baptism of repentance, bidding the people believe on One who was to come after him; namely, on Jesus." 019:005 On hearing this, they were baptized into the name of the Lord Jesus; 019:006 and when Paul laid his hands upon them, the Holy Spirit came on them, and they began to speak in tongues and to prophesy. 019:007 They numbered in all about twelve men. 019:008 Afterwards he went into the synagogue. There for three months he continued to preach fearlessly, explaining in words which carried conviction the truths which concern the Kingdom of God. 019:009 But some grew obstinate in unbelief and spoke evil of the new faith before all the congregation. So Paul left them, and, taking with him those who were disciples, held discussions daily in Tyrannus's lecture-hall. 019:010 This went on for two years, so that all the inhabitants of the province of Asia, Jews as well as Greeks, heard the Lord's Message. 019:011 God also brought about extraordinary miracles through Paul's instrumentality. 019:012 Towels or aprons, for instance, which Paul had handled used to be carried to the sick, and they recovered from their ailments, or the evil spirits left them. 019:013 But there were also some wandering Jewish exorcists who undertook to invoke the name of Jesus over those who had the evil spirits, saying, "I command you by that Jesus whom Paul preaches." 019:014 There were seven sons of one Sceva, a Jew of high-priestly family, who were doing this. 019:015 "Jesus I know," the evil spirit answered, "and Paul I have heard of, but who are you?" 019:016 And the man in whom the evil spirit was sprang on two of them, over-mastered them both, and treated them with such violence, that they fled from the house stripped of their clothes and wounded. 019:017 All the people of Ephesus, Jews as well as Greeks, came to know of this. There was widespread terror, and they began to hold the name of the Lord Jesus in high honour. 019:018 Many also of those who believed came confessing without reserve what their conduct had been, 019:019 and not a few of those who had practised magical arts brought their books together and burnt them in the presence of all. The total value was reckoned and found to be 50,000 silver coins. 019:020 Thus mightily did the Lord's Message spread and triumph! 019:021 When matters had reached this point, Paul decided in his own mind to travel through Macedonia and Greece, and go to Jerusalem. "After that," he said, "I must also see Rome." 019:022 But he sent two of his assistants, Timothy and Erastus, to Macedonia, while he himself remained for a while in Roman Asia. 019:023 Now just at that time there arose no small commotion about the new faith. 019:024 There was a certain Demetrius, a silversmith, who made miniature silver sanctuaries of Diana, a business which brought great gain to the mechanics in his employ. 019:025 He called his workmen together, and others who were engaged in similar trades, and said to them, "You men well know that our prosperity depends on this business of ours; 019:026 and you see and hear that, not in Ephesus only but throughout almost the whole province of Asia, this fellow Paul has led away a vast number of people by inducing them to believe that they are not gods at all that are made by men's hands. 019:027 There is danger, therefore, not only that this our trade will become of no account, but also that the temple of the great goddess Diana will fall into utter disrepute, and that before long she will be actually deposed from her majestic rank- she who is now worshipped by the whole province of Asia; nay, by the whole world." 019:028 After listening to this harangue, they became furiously angry and kept calling out, "Great is the Ephesian Diana!" 019:029 The riot and uproar spread through the whole city, till at last with one accord they rushed into the Theatre, dragging with them Gaius and Aristarchus, two Macedonians who were fellow travellers with Paul. 019:030 Then Paul would have liked to go in and address the people, but the disciples would not let him do so. 019:031 A few of the public officials, too, who were friendly to him, sent repeated messages entreating him not to venture into the Theatre. 019:032 The people, meanwhile, kept shouting, some one thing and some another; for the assembly was all uproar and confusion, and the greater part had no idea why they had come together. 019:033 Then some of the people crowded round Alexander, whom the Jews had pushed forward; and Alexander, motioning with his hand to get silence, was prepared to make a defence to the people. 019:034 No sooner, however, did they see that he was a Jew, than there arose from them all one roar of shouting, lasting about two hours. "Great is the Ephesian Diana," they said. 019:035 At length the Recorder quieted them down. "Men of Ephesus," he said, "who is there of all mankind that needs to be told that the city of Ephesus is the guardian of the temple of the great Diana and of the image which fell down from Zeus? 019:036 These facts, then, being unquestioned, it becomes you to maintain your self-control and not act recklessly. 019:037 For you have brought these men here, who are neither robbers of temples nor blasphemers of our goddess. 019:038 If, however, Demetrius and the mechanics who support his contention have a grievance against any one, there are Assize-days and there are Proconsuls: let the persons interested accuse one another. 019:039 But if you desire anything further, it will have to be settled in the regular assembly. 019:040 For in connexion with to-day's proceedings there is danger of our being charged with attempted insurrection, there having been no real reason for this riot; nor shall we be able to justify the behaviour of this disorderly mob." 019:041 With these words he dismissed the assembly. 020:001 When the uproar had ceased, Paul sent for the disciples; and, after speaking words of encouragement to them, he took his leave, and started for Macedonia. 020:002 Passing through those districts he encouraged the disciples in frequent addresses, and then came into Greece, and spent three months there. 020:003 The Jews having planned to waylay him whenever he might be on the point of taking ship for Syria, he decided to travel back by way of Macedonia. 020:004 He was accompanied as far as the province of Asia by Sopater the Beroean, the son of Pyrrhus; by the Thessalonians, Aristarchus and Secundus; by Gaius of Derbe, and Timothy; and by the Asians, Tychicus and Trophimus. 020:005 These brethren had gone on and were waiting for us in the Troad. 020:006 But we ourselves sailed from Philippi after the days of Unleavened Bread, and five days later joined them in the Troad, where we remained for a week. 020:007 On the first day of the week, when we had met to break bread, Paul, who was going away the next morning, was preaching to them, and prolonged his discourse till midnight. 020:008 Now there were a good many lamps in the room upstairs where we all were, 020:009 and a youth of the name of Eutychus was sitting at the window. This lad, gradually sinking into deep sleep while Paul preached at unusual length, overcome at last by sleep, fell from the second floor and was taken up dead. 020:010 Paul, however, went down, threw himself upon him, and folding him in his arms said, "Do not be alarmed; his life is still in him." 020:011 Then he went upstairs again, broke bread, and took some food; and after a long conversation which was continued till daybreak, at last he

parted from them. 020:012 They had taken the lad home alive, and were
greatly comforted. 020:013 The rest of us had already gone on board a ship,
and now we set sail for Assos, intending to take Paul on board there; for so
he had arranged, he himself intending to go by land. 020:014 Accordingly,
when he met us at Assos, we took him on board and came to Mitylene.
020:015 Sailing from there, we arrived the next day off Chios. On the next
we touched at Samos; and on the day following reached Miletus. 020:016
For Paul's plan was to sail past Ephesus, so as not to spend much time in
the province of Asia; since he was very desirous of being in Jerusalem, if
possible, on the day of the Harvest Festival. 020:017 From Miletus he sent
to Ephesus for the Elders of the Church to come to him. 020:018 Upon
their arrival he said to them, "You Elders well know, from the first day of
my setting foot in the province of Asia, the kind of life I lived among you
the whole time, 020:019 serving the Lord in all humility, and with tears, and
amid trials which came upon me through the plotting of the Jews- 020:020
and that I never shrank from declaring to you anything that was profitable,
or from teaching you in public and in your homes, 020:021 and urging upon
both Jews and Greeks the necessity of turning to God and of believing in
Jesus our Lord. 020:022 "And now, impelled by a sense of duty, I am on my
way to Jerusalem, not knowing what will happen to me there, 020:023
except that the Holy Spirit, at town after town, testifies to me that
imprisonment and suffering are awaiting me. 020:024 But even the sacrifice
of my life I count as nothing, if only I may perfect my earthly course, and
be faithful to the duty which the Lord Jesus has entrusted to me of
proclaiming, as of supreme importance, the Good News of God's grace.
020:025 "And now, I know that none of you among whom I have gone in
and out proclaiming the coming of the Kingdom will any longer see my
face. 020:026 Therefore I protest to you to-day that I am not responsible
for the ruin of any one of you. 020:027 For I have not shrunk from
declaring to you God's whole truth. 020:028 "Take heed to yourselves and
to all the flock among which the Holy Spirit has placed you to take the
oversight for Him and act as shepherds to the Church of God, which He
has bought with His own blood. 020:029 I know that, when I am gone,
cruel wolves will come among you and will not spare the flock; 020:030 and
that from among your own selves men will rise up who will seek with their
perverse talk to draw away the disciples after them. 020:031 Therefore be
on the alert; and remember that, night and day, for three years, I never
ceased admonishing every one, even with tears. 020:032 "And now I
commend you to God and to the word of His grace. He is able to build you
up and to give you your inheritance among His people. 020:033 No one's
silver or gold or clothing have I coveted. 020:034 You yourselves know that
these hands of mine have provided for my own necessities and for the
people with me. 020:035 In all things I have set you an example, showing

you that, by working as I do, you ought to help the weak, and to bear in mind the words of the Lord Jesus, how He Himself said, "`It is more blessed to give than to receive.'" 020:036 Having spoken thus, Paul knelt down and prayed with them all; 020:037 and with loud lamentation they all threw their arms round his neck, and kissed him lovingly, 020:038 grieved above all things at his having told them that after that day they were no longer to see his face. And they went with him to the ship. 021:001 When, at last, we had torn ourselves away and had set sail, we ran in a straight course to Cos; the next day to Rhodes, and from there to Patara. 021:002 Finding a ship bound for Phoenicia, we went on board and put to sea. 021:003 After sighting Cyprus and leaving that island on our left, we continued our voyage to Syria and put in at Tyre; for there the ship was to unload her cargo. 021:004 Having searched for the disciples and found them, we stayed at Tyre for seven days; and, taught by the Spirit, they repeatedly urged Paul not to proceed to Jerusalem. 021:005 When, however, our time was up, we left and went on our way, all the disciples and their wives and children coming to see us off. Then, after kneeling down on the beach and praying, 021:006 we took leave of one another; and we went on board, while they returned home. 021:007 As for us, our voyage was over when having sailed from Tyre we reached Ptolemais. here we inquired after the welfare of the brethren, and remained a day with them. 021:008 On the morrow we left Ptolemais and went on to Caesarea, where we came to the house of Philip the Evangelist, who was one of the seven, and stayed with him. 021:009 Now Philip had four unmarried daughters who were prophetesses; 021:010 and during our somewhat lengthy stay a Prophet of the name of Agabus came down from Judaea. 021:011 When he arrived he took Paul's loincloth, and bound his own feet and arms with it, and said, "Thus says the Holy Spirit, `So will the Jews in Jerusalem bind the owner of this loincloth, and will hand him over to the Gentiles.'" 021:012 As soon as we heard these words, both we and the brethren at Caesarea entreated Paul not to go up to Jerusalem. 021:013 His reply was, "What can you mean by thus breaking my heart with your grief? Why, as for me, I am ready not only to go to Jerusalem and be put in chains, but even to die there for the sake of the Lord Jesus." 021:014 So when he was not to be dissuaded, we ceased remonstrating with him and said, "The Lord's will be done!" 021:015 A few days afterwards we loaded our baggage-cattle and continued our journey to Jerusalem. 021:016 Some of the disciples from Caesarea also joined our party, and brought with them Mnason, a Cyprian, one of the early disciples, at whose house we were to lodge. 021:017 At length we reached Jerusalem, and there the brethren gave us a hearty welcome. 021:018 On the following day we went with Paul to call on James, and all the Elders of the Church came also. 021:019 After exchanging friendly greetings, Paul told in detail all that God had done among the Gentiles through his instrumentality. 021:020

And they, when they had heard his statement, gave the glory to God. Then they said, "You see, brother, how many tens of thousands of Jews there are among those who have accepted the faith, and they are all zealous upholders of the Law. 021:021 Now what they have been repeatedly told about you is that you teach all the Jews among the Gentiles to abandon Moses, and that you forbid them to circumcise their children or observe old-established customs. 021:022 What then ought you to do? They are sure to hear that you have come to Jerusalem; 021:023 so do this which we now tell you. We have four men here who have a vow resting on them. 021:024 Associate with these men and purify yourself with them, and pay their expenses so that they can shave their heads. Then everybody will know that there is no truth in these stories about you, but that in your own actions you yourself scrupulously obey the Law. 021:025 But as for the Gentiles who have accepted the faith, we have communicated to them our decision that they are carefully to abstain from anything sacrificed to an idol, from blood, from what is strangled, and from fornication." 021:026 So Paul associated with the men; and the next day, having purified himself with them, he went into the Temple, giving every one to understand that the days of their purification were finished, and there he remained until the sacrifice for each of them was offered. 021:027 But, when the seven days were nearly over, the Jews from the province of Asia, having seen Paul in the Temple, set about rousing the fury of all the people against him. 021:028 They laid hands on him, crying out, "Men of Israel, help! help! This is the man who goes everywhere preaching to everybody against the Jewish people and the Law and this place. And besides, he has even brought Gentiles into the Temple and has desecrated this holy place." 021:029 (For they had previously seen Trophimus the Ephesian with him in the city, and imagined that Paul had brought him into the Temple.) 021:030 The excitement spread through the whole city, and the people rushed in crowds to the Temple, and there laid hold of Paul and began to drag him out; and the Temple gates were immediately closed. 021:031 But while they were trying to kill Paul, word was taken up to the Tribune in command of the battalion, that all Jerusalem was in a ferment. 021:032 He instantly sent for a few soldiers and their officers, and came down among the people with all speed. At the sight of the Tribune and the troops they ceased beating Paul. 021:033 Then the Tribune, making his way to him, arrested him, and, having ordered him to be secured with two chains, proceeded to ask who he was and what he had been doing. 021:034 Some of the crowd shouted one accusation against Paul and some another, until, as the uproar made it impossible for the truth to be ascertained with certainty, the Tribune ordered him to be brought into the barracks. 021:035 When Paul was going up the steps, he had to be carried by the soldiers because of the violence of the mob; 021:036 for the whole mass of the people pressed on in the rear, shouting, "Away with him!" 021:037 When he was about to be taken into the barracks, Paul said to the Tribune, "May I speak to you?" "Do you know Greek?" the Tribune asked. 021:038 "Are you not the Egyptian who some years ago excited the riot of the 4,000 cut-throats, and led them out into the Desert?" 021:039 "I am a Jew," replied Paul, "belonging to Tarsus in Cilicia, and am a citizen of no unimportant city. Give me leave, I pray you, to speak to the people." 021:040 So with his permission Paul stood on the steps and motioned with his hand to the people to be quiet; and when there was perfect silence he addressed them in Hebrew. 022:001 "Brethren and fathers," he said, "listen to my defence which I now make before you." 022:002 And on hearing him address them in Hebrew, they kept all the more quiet; and he said, 022:003 "I am a Jew, born at Tarsus in Cilicia, but brought up in this city. I was carefully trained at the feet of Gamaliel in the Law of our forefathers, and, like all of you to-day, was zealous for God. 022:004 I persecuted to death this new faith, continually binding both men and women and throwing them into prison; 022:005 as the High Priest also and all the Elders can bear me witness. It was, too, from them that I received letters to the brethren in Damascus, and I was already on my way to Damascus, intending to bring those also who had fled there, in chains to Jerusalem, to be punished. 022:006 "But on my way, when I was now not far from Damascus, about noon a sudden blaze of light from Heaven shone round me. 022:007 I fell to the ground and heard a voice say to me, "`Saul, Saul, why are you persecuting Me?' 022:008 "`Who art thou, Lord?' I asked. "`I am Jesus, the Nazarene,' He replied, `whom you are persecuting.' 022:009 "Now the men who were with me, though they saw the light, did not hear the words of Him who spoke to me. 022:010 And I asked, "`What am I to do, Lord?' "And the Lord said to me, "`Rise, and go into Damascus. There you shall be told of all that has been appointed for you to do.' 022:011 "And as I could not see because the light had been so dazzling, those who were with me had to lead me by the arm, and so I came to Damascus. 022:012 "And a certain Ananias, a pious man who obeyed the Law and bore a good character with all the Jews of the city, 022:013 came to me and standing at my side said, "`Brother Saul, recover your sight.' "I instantly regained my sight and looked up at him. 022:014 Then he said, `The God of our forefathers has appointed you to know His will, and to see the righteous One and hear Him speak. 022:015 For you shall be a witness for Him, to all men, of what you have seen and heard. 022:016 And now why delay? Rise, get yourself baptized, and wash off your sins, calling upon His name.' 022:017 "After my return to Jerusalem, and while praying in the Temple, I fell into a trance. 022:018 I saw Jesus, and He said to me, "`Make haste and leave Jerusalem quickly, because they will not accept your testimony about Me.' 022:019 "`Lord,' I replied, `they themselves well know how active I was in imprisoning, and in flogging in synagogue after synagogue those who believe in Thee; 022:020 and when they were shedding the blood of Stephen, Thy witness, I was standing by, fully approving of it, and I held the clothes of those who were killing him.' 022:021 "`Go,' He replied; `I will send you as an Apostle to nations far away.'" 022:022 Until they heard this last statement the people listened to Paul, but now with a roar of disapproval they cried out, "Away with such a fellow from the earth! He ought not to be allowed to live." 022:023 And when they continued their furious shouts, throwing their clothes into the air and flinging dust about, 022:024 the Tribune ordered him to be brought into the barracks, and be examined by flogging, in order to ascertain the reason why they thus cried out against him. 022:025 But, when they had tied him up with the straps, Paul said to the Captain who stood by, "Does the Law permit you to flog a Roman citizen-and one too who is uncondemned?" 022:026 On hearing this question, the Captain went to report the matter to the Tribune. "What are you intending to do?" he said. "This man is a Roman citizen." 022:027 So the Tribune came to Paul and asked him, "Tell me, are you a Roman citizen?" "Yes," he said. 022:028 "I paid a large sum for my citizenship," said the Tribune. "But I was born free," said Paul. 022:029 So the men who had been on the point of putting him under torture immediately left him. And the Tribune, too, was frightened when he learnt that Paul was a Roman citizen, for he had had him bound. 022:030 The next day, wishing to know exactly what charge was being brought against him by the Jews, the Tribune ordered his chains to be removed; and, having sent word to the High Priests and all the Sanhedrin to assemble, he brought Paul down and made him stand before them. 023:001 Then Paul, fixing a steady gaze on the Sanhedrin, said, "Brethren, it is with a perfectly clear conscience that I have discharged my duties before God up to this day." 023:002 On hearing this the High Priest Ananias ordered those who were standing near Paul to strike him on the mouth. 023:003 "Before long," exclaimed Paul, "God will strike you, you white-washed wall! Are you sitting there to judge me in accordance with the Law, and do you yourself actually break the Law by ordering me to be struck?" 023:004 "Do you rail at God's High Priest?" cried the men who stood by him. 023:005 "I did not know, brethren," replied Paul, "that he was the High Priest; for it is written, `Thou shalt not speak evil of a ruler of Thy people.'" 023:006 Noticing, however, that the Sanhedrin consisted partly of Sadducees and partly of Pharisees, he called out loudly among them, "Brethren, I am a Pharisee, the son of Pharisees. It is because of my hope of a resurrection of the dead that I am on my trial." 023:007 These words of his caused an angry dispute between the Pharisees and the Sadducees, and the assembly took different sides. 023:008 For the Sadducees maintain that there is no resurrection, and neither angel nor spirit; but the Pharisees acknowledge the existence of both. 023:009 So there arose a great uproar; and some of the Scribes belonging to the sect of the Pharisees sprang to their feet and fiercely contended, saying, "We find no harm in the man. What if a spirit has spoken to him, or an angel!" 023:010 But when the struggle was becoming violent, the Tribune, fearing that Paul would be torn to pieces by the people, ordered the troops to go down and take him from among them by force and bring him into the barracks. 023:011 The following night the Lord came and stood at Paul's side, and said, "Be of good courage, for as you have borne faithful witness about me in Jerusalem, so you must also bear witness in Rome." 023:012 Now, when daylight came, the Jews formed a conspiracy and solemnly swore not to eat or drink till they had killed Paul. 023:013 There were more than forty of them who bound themselves by this oath. 023:014 They went to the High Priests and Elders and said to them, "We have bound ourselves under a heavy curse to take no food till we have killed Paul. 023:015 Now therefore you and the Sanhedrin should make representations to the Tribune for him to bring him down to you, under the impression that you intend to inquire more minutely about him; and we are prepared to assassinate him before he comes near the place." 023:016 But Paul's sister's son heard of the intended attack upon him. So he came and went into the barracks and told Paul about it; 023:017 and Paul called one of the Captains and said, "Take this young man to the Tribune, for he has information to give him." 023:018 So he took him and brought him to the Tribune, and said, "Paul, the prisoner, called me to him and begged me to bring this youth to you, because he has something to say to you." 023:019 Then the Tribune, taking him by the arm, withdrew out of the hearing of others and asked him, "What have you to tell me?" 023:020 "The Jews," he replied, "have agreed to request you to bring Paul down to the Sanhedrin to-morrow for the purpose of making yourself more accurately acquainted with the case. 023:021 I beg you not to comply; for more than forty men among them are lying in wait for him, who have solemnly vowed that they will neither eat nor drink till they have assassinated him; and even now they are ready, in anticipation of receiving that promise of you." 023:022 So the Tribune sent the youth home, cautioning him. "Do not let any one know that you have given me this information," he said. 023:023 Then, calling to him two of the Captains, he gave his orders. "Get ready two hundred men," he said, "to march to Caesarea, with seventy cavalry and two hundred light infantry, starting at nine o'clock to-night." 023:024 He further told them to provide horses to mount Paul on, so as to bring him safely to Felix the Governor. 023:025 He also wrote a letter of which these were the contents: 023:026 "Claudius Lysias to his Excellency, Felix the Governor: all good wishes. 023:027 This man Paul had been seized by the Jews, and they were on the point of killing him, when I came upon them with the troops and rescued him, for I had been informed that he was a Roman citizen. 023:028 And, wishing to know with certainty the offense of which they were accusing him, I brought him down into their Sanhedrin, 023:029 and I discovered that the charge had to do with questions of their Law, but that he was accused of nothing for which he deserves death or imprisonment. 023:030 But now that I have received information of an intended attack upon him, I immediately send him to you, directing his accusers also to state before you the case they have against him." 023:031 So, in obedience to their orders, the soldiers took Paul and brought him by night as far as Antipatris. 023:032 The next day the infantry returned to the barracks, leaving the cavalry to proceed with him; 023:033 and, the cavalry having reached Caesarea and delivered the letter to the Governor, they brought Paul also to him. 023:034 Felix, after reading the letter, inquired from what province he was; and being told "from Cilicia," 023:035 he said, "I will hear all you have to say, when your accusers also have come." And he ordered him to be detained in custody in Herod's Palace. 024:001 Five days after this, Ananias the High Priest came down to Caesarea with a number of Elders and a pleader called Tertullus. They stated to the Governor the case against Paul. 024:002 So Paul was sent for, and Tertullus began to impeach him as follows: "Indebted as we are," he said, "to you, most noble Felix, for the perfect peace which we enjoy, and for reforms which your wisdom has introduced to this nation, 024:003 in every instance and in every place we accept them with profound gratitude. 024:004 But-not to detain you too long-I beg you in your forbearance to listen to a brief statement from us. 024:005 For we have found this man Paul a source of mischief and a disturber of the peace among all the Jews throughout the Empire, and a ringleader in the heresy of the Nazarenes. 024:006 He even attempted to profane the Temple, but we arrested him. 024:007 [] 024:008 You, however, by examining him, will yourself be able to learn the truth as to all this which we allege against him." 024:009 The Jews also joined in the charge, maintaining that these were facts. 024:010 Then, at a sign from the Governor, Paul answered, "Knowing, Sir, that for many years you have administered justice to this nation, I cheerfully make my defence. 024:011 For you have it in your power to ascertain that it is not more than twelve days ago that I went up to worship in Jerusalem; 024:012 and that neither in the Temple nor in the synagogues, nor anywhere in the city, did they find me disputing with any opponent or collecting a crowd about me. 024:013 Nor can they prove the charges which they are now bringing against me. 024:014 But this I confess to you-that in the way which they style a heresy, I worship the God of our forefathers, believing everything that is taught in the Law or is written in the Prophets, 024:015 and having a hope directed towards God, which my accusers themselves also entertain, that before long there will be a resurrection both of the righteous and the unrighteous. 024:016 This too is my own earnest endeavour-always to have a clear conscience in relation to God and man. 024:017 "Now after an interval of

several years I came to bring alms to my nation, and to offer sacrifices.
024:018 While I was busy about these, they found me in the Temple
purified, with no crowd around me and no uproar; but there were certain
Jews from the province of Asia. 024:019 They ought to have been here
before you, and to have been my prosecutors, if they have any charge to
bring against me. 024:020 Or let these men themselves say what
misdemeanour they found me guilty of when I stood before the Sanhedrin,
024:021 unless it was in that one expression which I made use of when I
shouted out as I stood among them, "`The resurrection of the dead is the
thing about which I am on my trial before you to-day.'" 024:022 At this
point Felix, who was fairly well informed about the new faith, adjourned
the trial, saying to the Jews, "When the Tribune Lysias comes down, I will
enter carefully into the matter." 024:023 And he gave orders to the Captain
that Paul was to be kept in custody, but be treated with indulgence, and that
his personal friends were not to be prevented from showing him kindness.
024:024 Not long after this, Felix came with Drusilla his wife, a Jewess, and
sending for Paul, listened to him as he spoke about faith in Christ Jesus.
024:025 But when he dealt with the subjects of justice, self-control, and the
judgement which was soon to come, Felix became alarmed and said, "For
the present leave me, and when I can find a convenient opportunity I will
send for you." 024:026 At the same time he hoped that Paul would give him
money; and for this reason he sent for him the oftener to converse with
him. 024:027 But after the lapse of fully two years Felix was succeeded by
Porcius Festus; and being desirous of gratifying the Jews, Felix left Paul still
in prison. 025:001 Festus, having entered on his duties as governor of the
province, two days later went up from Caesarea to Jerusalem. 025:002 The
High Priests and the leading men among the Jews immediately made
representations to him against Paul, and begged him- 025:003 asking it as a
favour, to Paul's prejudice-to have him brought to Jerusalem. They were
planning an ambush to kill him on the way. 025:004 Festus, however,
replied that Paul was in custody in Caesarea, and that he was himself going
there very soon. 025:005 "Therefore let those of you," he said, "who can
come, go down with me, and impeach the man, if there is anything amiss in
him." 025:006 After a stay of eight or ten days in Jerusalem-not more- he
went down to Caesarea; and the next day, taking his seat on the tribunal, he
ordered Paul to be brought in. 025:007 Upon Paul's arrival, the Jews who
had come down from Jerusalem stood round him, and brought many grave
charges against him which they were unable to substantiate. 025:008 But, in
reply, Paul said, "Neither against the Jewish Law, nor against the Temple,
nor against Caesar, have I committed any offence whatever." 025:009 Then
Festus, being anxious to gratify the Jews, asked Paul, "Are you willing to go
up to Jerusalem, and there stand your trial before me on these charges?"
025:010 "I am standing before Caesar's tribunal," replied Paul, "where alone

I ought to be tried. The Jews have no real ground of complaint against me, as in fact you yourself are beginning to see more clearly. 025:011 If, however, I have done wrong and have committed any offence for which I deserve to die, I do not ask to be excused that penalty. But if there is no truth in what these men allege against me, no one has the right to give me up to them as a favour. I appeal to Caesar." 025:012 Then, after conferring with the Council, Festus replied, "To Caesar you have appealed: to Caesar you shall go." 025:013 A short time after this, Agrippa the king and Bernice came to Caesarea to pay a complimentary visit to Festus; 025:014 and, during their rather long stay, Festus laid Paul's case before the king. "There is a man here," he said, "whom Felix left a prisoner, 025:015 about whom, when I went to Jerusalem, the High Priests and the Elders of the Jews made representations to me, begging that sentence might be pronounced against him. 025:016 My reply was that it is not the custom among the Romans to give up any one for punishment before the accused has had his accusers face to face, and has had an opportunity of defending himself against the charge which has been brought against him. 025:017 "When, therefore, a number of them came here, the next day I took my seat on the tribunal, without any loss of time, and ordered the man to be brought in. 025:018 But, when his accusers stood up, they did not charge him with the misdemeanours of which I had been suspecting him. 025:019 But they quarrelled with him about certain matters connected with their own religion, and about one Jesus who had died, but- so Paul persistently maintained-is now alive. 025:020 I was at a loss how to investigate such questions, and asked Paul whether he would care to go to Jerusalem and there stand his trial on these matters. 025:021 But when Paul appealed to have his case kept for the Emperor's decision, I ordered him to be kept in prison until I could send him up to Caesar." 025:022 "I should like to hear the man myself," said Agrippa. "to-morrow," replied Festus, "you shall." Accordingly, the next day, Agrippa and Bernice came in state 025:023 and took their seats in the Judgement Hall, attended by the Tribunes and the men of high rank in the city; and, at the command of Festus, Paul was brought in. 025:024 Then Festus said, "King Agrippa and all who are present with us, you see here the man about whom the whole nation of the Jews made suit to me, both in Jerusalem and here, crying out that he ought not to live any longer. 025:025 I could not discover that he had done anything for which he deserved to die; but as he has himself appealed to the Emperor, I have decided to send him to Rome. 025:026 I have nothing very definite, however, to tell our Sovereign about him. So I have brought the man before you all- and especially before you, King Agrippa-that after he has been examined I may find something which I can put into writing. 025:027 For, when sending a prisoner to Rome, it seems to me to be absurd not to state the charges against him." 026:001 Then Agrippa said to Paul,

"You have permission to speak about yourself." So Paul, with outstretched arm, proceeded to make his defence. 026:002 "As regards all the accusations brought against me by the Jews," he said, "I think myself fortunate, King Agrippa, in being about to defend myself to-day before you, 026:003 who are so familiar with all the customs and speculations that prevail among the Jews; and for this reason, I pray you, give me a patient hearing. 026:004 "The kind of life I have lived from my youth upwards, as exemplified in my early days among my nation and in Jerusalem, is known to all the Jews. 026:005 For they all know me of old-if they would but testify to the fact- how, being an adherent of the strictest sect of our religion, my life was that of a Pharisee. 026:006 And now I stand here impeached because of my hope in the fulfilment of the promise made by God to our forefathers- 026:007 the promise which our twelve tribes, worshipping day and night with intense devotedness, hope to have made good to them. It is on the subject of this hope, Sir, that I am accused by the Jews. 026:008 Why is it deemed with all of you a thing past belief if God raises the dead to life? 026:009 "I myself, however, thought it a duty to do many things in hostility to the name of Jesus, the Nazarene. 026:010 And that was how I acted in Jerusalem. Armed with authority received from the High Priests I shut up many of God's people in various prisons, and when they were about to be put to death I gave my vote against them. 026:011 In all the synagogues also I punished them many a time, and tried to make them blaspheme; and in my wild fury I chased them even to foreign towns. 026:012 "While thus engaged, I was travelling one day to Damascus armed with authority and a commission from the High Priests, 026:013 and on the journey, at noon, Sir, I saw a light from Heaven- brighter than the brightness of the sun-shining around me and around those who were travelling with me. 026:014 We all fell to the ground; and I heard a voice which said to me in Hebrew, "`Saul, Saul, why are you persecuting Me? You are finding it painful to kick against the ox-goad.' 026:015 "`Who art Thou, Lord?' I asked. "`I am Jesus whom you are persecuting,' the Lord replied. 026:016 `But rise, and stand on your feet; for I have appeared to you for the very purpose of appointing you My servant and My witness both as to the things you have already seen and as to those in which I will appear to you. 026:017 I will save you from the Jewish people and from the Gentiles, to whom I send you to open their eyes, 026:018 that they may turn from darkness to light and from the obedience to Satan to God, in order to receive forgiveness of sins and an inheritance among those who are sanctified through faith in Me.' 026:019 "Therefore, King Agrippa, I was not disobedient to the heavenly vision; 026:020 but I proceeded to preach first to the people in Damascus, and then to those in Jerusalem and in all Judaea, and to the Gentiles, that they must repent and turn to God, and live lives consistent with such repentance. 026:021 "It was on this account that the Jews seized me in the Temple and tried to kill me. 026:022 Having, however, obtained the help which is from God, I have stood firm until now, and have solemnly exhorted rich and poor alike, saying nothing except what the Prophets and Moses predicted as soon to happen, 026:023 since the Christ was to be a suffering Christ, and by coming back from the dead was then to be the first to proclaim a message of light both to the Jewish people and to the Gentiles." 026:024 As Paul thus made his defence, Festus exclaimed in a loud voice, "You are raving mad, Paul; and great learning is driving you mad." 026:025 "I am not mad, most noble Festus," replied Paul; "I am speaking words of sober truth. 026:026 For the King, to whom I speak freely, knows about these matters. I am not to be persuaded that any detail of them has escaped his notice; for these things have not been done in a corner. 026:027 King Agrippa, do you believe the Prophets? I know that you believe them." 026:028 Agrippa answered, "In brief, you are doing your best to persuade me to become a Christian." 026:029 "My prayer to God, whether briefly or at length," replied Paul, "would be that not only you but all who are my hearers to-day, might become such as I am-except these chains." 026:030 So the King rose, and the Governor, and Bernice, and those who were sitting with them; 026:031 and, having withdrawn, they talked to one another and said, "This man is doing nothing for which he deserves death or imprisonment." 026:032 And Agrippa said to Festus, "He might have been set at liberty, if he had not appealed to Caesar." 027:001 Now when it was decided that we should sail for Italy, they handed over Paul and a few other prisoners into the custody of Julius, a Captain of the Augustan battalion; 027:002 and going on board a ship of Adramyttium which was about to sail to the ports of the province of Asia, we put to sea; Aristarchus, the Macedonian, from Thessalonica, forming one of our party. 027:003 The next day we put in at Sidon. There Julius treated Paul with thoughtful kindness and allowed him to visit his friends and profit by their generous care. 027:004 Putting to sea again, we sailed under the lee of Cyprus, because the winds were against us; 027:005 and, sailing the whole length of the sea that lies off Cilicia and Pamphylia, we reached Myra in Lycia. 027:006 There Julius found an Alexandrian ship bound for Italy, and put us on board of her. 027:007 It took several days of slow sailing for us to come with difficulty off Cnidus; from which point, as the wind did not allow us to get on in the direct course, we ran under the lee of Crete by Salmone. 027:008 Then, coasting along with difficulty, we reached a place called `Fair Havens,' near the town of Lasea. 027:009 Our voyage thus far had occupied a considerable time, and the navigation being now unsafe and the Fast also already over, Paul warned them. 027:010 "Sirs," he said, "I perceive that before long the voyage will be attended with danger and heavy loss, not only to the cargo and the ship but to our own lives also." 027:011 But Julius let himself be persuaded by the pilot and by the owner rather than by Paul's arguments; 027:012 and as the harbour was inconvenient for wintering in, the majority were in favour of putting out to sea, to try whether they could get to Phoenix-a harbour on the coast of Crete facing north-east and south-east-to winter there. 027:013 And a light breeze from the south sprang up, so that they supposed they were now sure of their purpose. So weighing anchor they ran along the coast of Crete, hugging the shore. 027:014 But it was not long before a furious north-east wind, coming down from the mountains, burst upon us and carried the ship out of her course. 027:015 She was unable to make headway against the gale; so we gave up and let her drive. 027:016 Then we ran under the lee of a little island called Cauda, where we managed with great difficulty to secure the boat; 027:017 and, after hoisting it on board, they used frapping-cables to undergird the ship, and, as they were afraid of being driven on the Syrtis quicksands, they lowered the gear and lay to. 027:018 But, as the storm was still violent, the next day they began to lighten the ship; 027:019 and, on the third day, with their own hands they threw the ship's spare gear overboard. 027:020 Then, when for several days neither sun nor stars were seen and the terrific gale still harassed us, the last ray of hope was now vanishing. 027:021 When for a long time they had taken but little food, Paul, standing up among them, said, "Sirs, you ought to have listened to me and not have sailed from Crete. You would then have escaped this suffering and loss. 027:022 But now take courage, for there will be no destruction of life among you, but of the ship only. 027:023 For there stood by my side, last night, an angel of the God to whom I belong, and whom also I worship, 027:024 and he said, "`Dismiss all fear, Paul, for you must stand before Caesar; and God has granted you the lives of all who are sailing with you.' 027:025 "Therefore, Sirs, take courage; for I believe God, and am convinced that things will happen exactly as I have been told. 027:026 But we are to be stranded on a certain island." 027:027 It was now the fourteenth night, and we were drifting through the Sea of Adria, when, about midnight, the sailors suspected that land was close at hand. 027:028 So they hove the lead and found twenty fathoms of water; and after a short time they hove again and found fifteen fathoms. 027:029 Then for fear of possibly running on rocks, they threw out four anchors from the stern and waited impatiently for daylight. 027:030 The sailors, however, wanted to make their escape from the ship, and had lowered the boat into the sea, pretending that they were going to lay out anchors from the bow. 027:031 But Paul, addressing Julius and the soldiers, said, "Your lives will be sacrificed, unless these men remain on board." 027:032 Then the soldiers cut the ropes of the ship's boat and let her fall off. 027:033 And continually, up till daybreak, Paul kept urging all on board to take some food. "This is the fourteenth day," he said, "that you have been anxiously waiting for the storm to cease, and have fasted, eating little or nothing. 027:034 I therefore strongly advise you to take some food. This is essential for your safety. For not a hair will perish from the head of any one of you." 027:035 Having said this he took some bread, and, after giving thanks to God for it before them all, he broke it in pieces and began to eat it. 027:036 This raised the spirits of all, and they too took food. 027:037 There were 276 of us, crew and passengers, all told. 027:038 After eating a hearty meal they lightened the ship by throwing the wheat overboard. 027:039 When daylight came, they tried in vain to recognise the coast. But an inlet with a sandy beach attracted their attention, and now their object was, if possible, to run the ship aground in this inlet. 027:040 So they cut away the anchors and left them in the sea, unloosing at the same time the bands which secured the paddle-rudders. Then, hoisting the foresail to the wind, they made for the beach. 027:041 But coming to a place where two seas met, they stranded the ship, and her bow sticking fast remained immovable, while the stern began to go to pieces under the heavy hammering of the sea. 027:042 Now the soldiers recommended that the prisoners should be killed, for fear some one of them might swim ashore and effect his escape. 027:043 But their Captain, bent on securing Paul's safety, kept them from their purpose and gave orders that those who could swim should first jump overboard and get to land; 027:044 and that the rest should follow, some on planks, and others on various things from the ship. In this way they all got safely to land. 028:001 Our lives having been thus preserved, we discovered that the island was called Malta. 028:002 The strange-speaking natives showed us remarkable kindness, for they lighted a fire and made us all welcome because of the pelting rain and the cold. 028:003 Now, when Paul had gathered a bundle of sticks and had thrown them on the fire, a viper, driven by the heat, came out and fastened itself on his hand. 028:004 When the natives saw the creature hanging to his hand, they said to one another, "Beyond doubt this man is a murderer, for, though saved from the sea, unerring Justice does not permit him to live." 028:005 He, however, shook the reptile off into the fire and was unhurt. 028:006 They expected him soon to swell with inflammation or suddenly fall down dead; but, after waiting a long time and seeing no harm come to him, they changed their minds and said that he was a god. 028:007 Now in the same part of the island there were estates belonging to the Governor, whose name was Publius. He welcomed us to his house, and for three days generously made us his guests. 028:008 It happened, however, that his father was lying ill of dysentery aggravated by attacks of fever; so Paul went to see him, and, after praying, laid his hands on him and cured him. 028:009 After this, all the other sick people in the island came and were cured. 028:010 They also loaded us with honours, and when at last we sailed they put supplies on board for us. 028:011 Three months passed before we set sail in an Alexandrian vessel, called the `Twin Brothers,' which had wintered at the island. 028:012 At Syracuse we put in and stayed for two days. 028:013 From there we came round and reached Rhegium; and a day later, a south wind sprang up which brought us by the evening of the next day to Puteoli. 028:014 Here we found brethren, who invited us to remain with them for a week; and so we reached Rome. 028:015 Meanwhile the brethren there, hearing of our movements, came as far as the Market of Appius and the Three Huts to meet us; and when Paul saw them he thanked God and felt encouraged. 028:016 Upon our arrival in Rome, Paul received permission to live by himself, guarded by a soldier. 028:017 After one complete day he invited the leading men among the Jews to meet him; and, when they were come together, he said to them, "As for me, brethren, although I had done nothing prejudicial to our people or contrary to the customs of our forefathers, I was handed over as a prisoner from Jerusalem into the power of the Romans. 028:018 They, after they had sharply questioned me, were willing to set me at liberty, because they found no offence in me for which I deserve to die. 028:019 But, at last, the opposition of the Jews compelled me to appeal to Caesar; not however that I had any charge to bring against my nation. 028:020 For these reasons, then, I have invited you here, that I might see you and speak to you; for it is for the sake of Him who is the hope of Israel that this chain hangs upon me." 028:021 "For our part," they replied, "we have not received any letters from Judaea about you, nor have any of our countrymen come here and reported or stated anything to your disadvantage. 028:022 But we should be glad to hear from you what it is that you believe; for as for this sect all we know is that it is everywhere spoken against." 028:023 So they arranged a day with him and came to him in considerable numbers at the house of the friends who were entertaining him. And then, with solemn earnestness, he explained to them the subject of the Kingdom of God, endeavouring from morning till evening to convince them about Jesus, both from the Law of Moses and from the Prophets. 028:024 Some were convinced; others refused to believe. 028:025 Unable to agree among themselves, they at last left him, but not before Paul had spoken a parting word to them, saying, "Right well did the Holy Spirit say to your forefathers through the Prophet Isaiah: 028:026 "`Go to this people and tell them, you will hear and hear, and by no means understand; and will look and look, and by no means see. 028:027 For this people's mind has grown callous, their hearing has become dull, and their eyes they have closed; to prevent their ever seeing with their eyes, or hearing with their ears, or understanding with their minds, and turning back, so that I might cure them.' 028:028 "Be fully assured, therefore, that this salvation- God's salvation- has now been sent to the Gentiles, and that they, at any rate, will give heed." 028:029 [] 028:030 After this Paul lived for fully two years in a hired house of his own, receiving all who came to see him. 028:031 He announced the coming of the Kingdom of God, and taught concerning the Lord Jesus Christ without let or hindrance.

BOOK 51 COLOSSIANS

001:001 Paul, an Apostle of Christ Jesus by the will of God- and Timothy our brother: 001:002 To the people of God and the believing brethren at Colossae who are in Christ. May grace and peace be granted to you from God our Father. 001:003 We give thanks to God, the Father of our Lord Jesus Christ, constantly praying for you as we do, 001:004 because we have heard of your faith in Christ Jesus and of the love which you cherish towards all God's people, 001:005 on account of the hope treasured up for you in Heaven. Of this hope you have already heard in the Message of the truth of the Good News. 001:006 For it has reached you, and remains with you, just as it has also spread through the whole world, yielding fruit there and increasing, as it has done among you from the day when first you heard it and came really to know the grace of God, 001:007 as you learned it from Epaphras our dearly-loved fellow servant. He is to you a faithful minister of Christ in our stead, 001:008 and moreover he has informed us of your love, which is inspired by the Spirit. 001:009 For this reason we also, from the day we first received these tidings, have never ceased to pray for you and to entreat that you may be filled with a clear knowledge of His will accompanied by thorough wisdom and discernment in spiritual things; 001:010 so that your lives may be worthy of the Lord and perfectly pleasing to Him, while you exhibit the results of right action of every sort and grow into a fuller knowledge of God. 001:011 Since His power is so glorious, may you be strengthened with strength of every kind, and be prepared for cheerfully enduring all things with patience and long-suffering; 001:012 and give thanks to the Father who has made us fit to receive our share of the inheritance of God's people in Light. 001:013 It is God who has delivered us out of the dominion of darkness, and has transferred us into the Kingdom of His dearly-loved Son, 001:014 in whom we have our redemption-the forgiveness of our sins. 001:015 Christ is the visible representation of the invisible God, the Firstborn and Lord of all creation. 001:016 For in Him was created the universe of things in heaven and on earth, things seen and things unseen, thrones, dominions, princedoms, powers-all were created, and exist through and for Him. 001:017 And HE IS before all things and in and through Him the universe is a harmonious whole. 001:018 Moreover He is the Head of His Body, the Church. He is the Beginning, the Firstborn from among the dead, in order that He Himself may in all things occupy the foremost place. 001:019 For it was the Father's gracious will that the whole of the divine perfections should dwell in Him. 001:020 And God purposed through Him to reconcile the universe to Himself, making peace through His blood, which was shed upon the Cross- to reconcile to Himself through Him, I say, things on earth and things in Heaven. 001:021 And you, estranged as you once were and even hostile in your minds, amidst your evil deeds, 001:022 He has now, in His human body, reconciled to God by His death, to bring you, holy and faultless and irreproachable, into His presence; 001:023 if, indeed, you are still firmly holding to faith as your foundation, without ever shifting from your hope that rests on the Good News that you have heard, which has been proclaimed in the whole creation under Heaven, and in which I Paul have been appointed to serve. 001:024 Now I can find joy amid my sufferings for you, and I fill up in my own person whatever is lacking in Christ's afflictions on behalf of His Body, the Church. 001:025 I have been appointed to serve the Church in the position of responsibility entrusted to me by God for your benefit, so that I may fully deliver God's Message- 001:026 the truth which has been kept secret from all ages and generations, but has now been revealed to His people, 001:027 to whom it was His will to make known how vast a wealth of glory for the Gentile world is implied in this truth- the truth that `Christ is in you, the hope of glory.' 001:028 Him we preach, admonishing every one and instructing every one, with all possible wisdom, so that we may bring every one into God's presence, made perfect through Christ. 001:029 To this end, like an earnest wrestler, I exert all my strength in reliance upon the power of Him who is mightily at work within me. 002:001 For I would have you know in how severe a struggle I am engaged on behalf of you and the brethren in Laodicea and of all who have not known me personally, 002:002 in order that their hearts may be cheered, they themselves being welded together in love and enjoying all the advantages of a reasonable certainty, till at last they attain the full knowledge of God's truth, which is Christ Himself. 002:003 In Him all the treasures of wisdom and knowledge are stored up, hidden from view. 002:004 I say this to prevent your being misled by any one's plausible sophistry. 002:005 For although, as you say, I am absent from you in body, yet in spirit I am present with you and am delighted to witness your good discipline and the solid front presented by your faith in Christ. 002:006 As therefore you have received the Christ, even Jesus our Lord, live and act in vital union with Him; 002:007 having the roots of your being firmly planted in Him, and continually building yourselves up in Him, and always being increasingly confirmed in the faith as you were taught it, and abounding in it with thanksgiving. 002:008 Take care lest there be some one who leads you away as prisoners by means of his philosophy and idle fancies, following human traditions and the world's crude notions instead of following Christ. 002:009 For it is in Christ that the fulness of God's nature dwells embodied, and in Him you are made complete, 002:010 and He is the Lord of all princes and rulers. 002:011 In Him also you were circumcised with a circumcision not performed by hand, when you threw off your sinful nature in true Christian circumcision; 002:012 having been buried with Him in your baptism, in which you were also raised with Him through faith produced within you by God who raised Him from among the dead. 002:013 And to you-dead as you once were in your transgressions and in the uncircumcision of your natural state-He has nevertheless given Life with Himself, having forgiven us all our transgressions. 002:014 The bond, with its requirements, which was in force against us and was hostile to us, He cancelled, and cleared it out of the way, nailing it to His Cross. 002:015 And the hostile princes and rulers He shook off from Himself, and boldly displayed them as His conquests, when by the Cross He triumphed over them. 002:016 Therefore suffer no one to sit in judgement on you as to eating or drinking or with regard to a festival, a new moon or a sabbath. 002:017 These were a shadow of things that were soon to come, but the substance belongs to Christ. 002:018 Let no one defraud you of your prize, priding himself on his humility and on his worship of the angels, and taking his stand on the visions he has seen, and idly puffed up with his unspiritual thoughts. 002:019 Such a one does not keep his hold upon Christ, the Head, from whom the Body, in all its parts nourished and strengthened by its points of contact and its connections, grows with a divine growth. 002:020 If you have died with Christ and have escaped from the world's rudimentary notions, why, as though your life still belonged to the world, do you submit to such precepts as 002:021 "Do not handle this;" "Do not taste that;" "Do not touch that other thing"- 002:022 referring to things which are all intended to be used up and perish- in obedience to mere human injunctions and teachings? 002:023 These rules have indeed an appearance of wisdom where self-imposed worship exists, and an affectation of humility and an ascetic severity. But not one of them is of any value in combating the indulgence of our lower natures. 003:001 If however you have risen with Christ, seek the things that are above, where Christ is, enthroned at God's right hand. 003:002 Give your minds to the things that are above, not to the things that are on the earth. 003:003 For you have died, and your life is hidden with Christ in God. 003:004 When Christ appears-He is our true Life-then you also will appear with Him in glory. 003:005 Therefore put to death your earthward inclinations- fornication, impurity, sensual passion, unholy desire, and all greed, for that is a form of idolatry. 003:006 It is on account of these very sins that God's anger is coming, 003:007 and you also were once addicted to them, while you were living under their power. 003:008 But now you must rid yourselves of every kind of sin- angry and passionate outbreaks, ill-will, evil speaking, foul-mouthed abuse-so that these may never soil your lips. 003:009 Do not speak falsehoods to one another, for you have stripped off the old self with its doings, 003:010 and have clothed yourselves with the new self which is being remoulded into full knowledge so as to become like Him who created it. 003:011 In that new creation there is neither Greek nor Jew, circumcision nor uncircumcision, barbarian, Scythian, slave nor free man, but Christ is everything and is in all of us. 003:012 Clothe yourselves therefore, as God's own people holy and dearly loved, with tender-heartedness, kindness, lowliness of mind, meekness, long-suffering; 003:013 bearing with one another and readily forgiving each other, if any one has a grievance against another. Just as the Lord has forgiven you, you also must forgive. 003:014 And over all these put on love, which is the perfect bond of union; 003:015 and let the peace which Christ gives settle all questionings in your hearts, to which peace indeed you were called as belonging to His one Body; and be thankful. 003:016 Let the teaching concerning Christ remain as a rich treasure in your hearts. In all wisdom teach and admonish one another with psalms, hymns, and spiritual songs, and sing with grace in your hearts to God. 003:017 And whatever you do, in word or in deed, do everything in the name of the Lord Jesus, and let it be through Him that you give thanks to God the Father. 003:018 Married women, be submissive to your husbands, as is fitting in the Lord. 003:019 Married men, be affectionate to your wives, and do not treat them harshly. 003:020 Children be obedient to your parents in everything; for that is right for Christians. 003:021 Fathers, do not fret and harass your children, or you may make them sullen and morose. 003:022 Slaves, be obedient in everything to your earthly masters; not in acts of eye service, as aiming only to please men, but with simplicity of purpose, because you fear the Lord. 003:023 Whatever you are doing, let your hearts be in your work, as a thing done for the Lord and not for men. 003:024 For you know that it is from the Lord you will receive the inheritance as your reward. Christ is the Master whose bondservants you are. 003:025 The man who perpetrates a wrong will find the wrong repaid to him; and with God there are no merely earthly distinctions. 004:001 Masters, deal justly and equitably with your slaves, knowing that you too have a Master in Heaven. 004:002 Be earnest and unwearied in prayer, being on the alert in it and in your giving of thanks. 004:003 And pray at the same time for us also, that God may open for us a door for preaching, for us to tell the truth concerning Christ for the sake of which I am even a prisoner. 004:004 Then I shall proclaim it fully, as it is my duty to do. 004:005 Behave wisely in relation to the outside world, buying up your opportunities. 004:006 Let your language be always seasoned with the salt of grace, so that you may know how to give every man a fitting answer. 004:007 Tychicus, our much-loved brother, a trusty assistant and fellow servant with us in the Lord's work, will give you every information about me. 004:008 And for this very purpose I send him to you that you may know how we are faring; and that he may cheer your hearts. 004:009 And with him I send our dear and trusty brother Onesimus, who is one of yourselves. They will inform you of everything here. 004:010 Aristarchus my fellow prisoner sends greeting to you, and so does Barnabas's cousin Mark. You have received instructions as to him; if he comes to you, give him a welcome. 004:011 Jesus, called Justus, also sends greeting. These three are Hebrew converts. They alone among such have worked loyally with me for the Kingdom of God-they are men who have been a comfort to me. 004:012 Epaphras, who is one of yourselves, a bondservant of Jesus Christ, sends greetings to you, always wrestling on your behalf in his prayers, that you may stand firm-Christians of ripe character and of clear conviction as to everything which is God's will. 004:013 For I can bear witness to the deep interest he takes in you and in the brethren at Laodicea and in those at Hierapolis. 004:014 Luke, the dearly-loved physician, salutes you, and so does Demas. 004:015 Christian greetings to the brethren at Laodicea, especially to Nymphas, and to the Church that meets at their house. 004:016 And when this Letter has been read among you, let it be read also in the Church of the Laodiceans, and you in turn must read the one I am sending to Laodicea. 004:017 And tell Archippus to discharge carefully the duties devolving upon him as a servant of the Lord. 004:018 I Paul add with my own hand this final greeting. Be mindful of me in my imprisonment. Grace be with you.

BOOK 49 EPHESIANS

001:001 Paul, an Apostle of Christ Jesus by the will of God: To God's people who are in Ephesus-believers in Christ Jesus. 001:002 May grace and peace be granted to you from God our Father and the Lord Jesus Christ. 001:003 Blessed be the God and Father of our Lord Jesus Christ, who has crowned us with every spiritual blessing in the heavenly realms in Christ; 001:004 even as, in His love, He chose us as His own in Christ before the creation of the world, that we might be holy and without blemish in His presence. 001:005 For He pre-destined us to be adopted by Himself as sons through Jesus Christ-such being His gracious will and pleasure- 001:006 to the praise of the splendour of His grace with which He has enriched us in the beloved One. 001:007 It is in Him, and through the shedding of His blood, that we have our deliverance-the forgiveness of our offences- so abundant was God's grace, 001:008 the grace which He, the possessor of all wisdom and understanding, lavished upon us, 001:009 when He made known to us the secret of His will. And this is in harmony with God's merciful purpose 001:010 for the government of the world when the times are ripe for it- the purpose which He has cherished in His own mind of restoring the whole creation to find its one Head in Christ; yes, things in Heaven and things on earth, to find their one Head in Him. 001:011 In Him we Jews have been made heirs, having been chosen beforehand in accordance with the intention of Him whose might carries out in everything the design of His own will, 001:012 so that we should be devoted to the extolling of His glorious attributes-we who were the first to fix our hopes on Christ. 001:013 And in Him you Gentiles also, after listening to the Message of the truth, the Good News of your salvation-having believed in Him-were sealed with the promised Holy Spirit; 001:014 that Spirit being a pledge and foretaste of our inheritance, in anticipation of its full redemption-the inheritance which He has purchased to be specially His for the extolling of His glory. 001:015 For this reason I too, having heard of the faith in the Lord Jesus which prevails among you, and of your love for all God's people, 001:016 offer never ceasing thanks on your behalf while I make mention of you in my prayers. 001:017 For I always beseech the God of our Lord Jesus Christ- the Father most glorious-to give you a spirit of wisdom and penetration through an intimate knowledge of Him, 001:018 the eyes of your understanding being enlightened so that you may know what is the hope which His call to you inspires, what the wealth of the glory of His inheritance in God's people, 001:019 and what the transcendent greatness of His power in us believers as seen in the working of His infinite might 001:020 when He displayed it in Christ by raising Him from the dead and seating Him at His own right hand in the heavenly realms, 001:021 high above all other government and authority and power and dominion, and every title of sovereignty used either in this Age or in the Age to come. 001:022 God has put all things under His feet, and has appointed Him universal and supreme Head of the Church, which is His Body, 001:023 the completeness of Him who everywhere fills the universe with Himself. 002:001 To you Gentiles also, who were dead through your offences and sins, 002:002 which were once habitual to you while you walked in the ways of this world and obeyed the Prince of the powers of the air, the spirits that are now at work in the hearts of the sons of disobedience-to you God has given Life. 002:003 Among them all of us also formerly passed our lives, governed by the inclinations of our lower natures, indulging the cravings of those natures and of our own thoughts, and were in our original state deserving of anger like all others. 002:004 But God, being rich in mercy, because of the intense love which He bestowed on us, 002:005 caused us, dead though we were through our offences, to live with Christ-it is by grace that you have been saved- 002:006 raised us with Him from the dead, and enthroned us with Him in the heavenly realms as being in Christ Jesus, 002:007 in order that, by His goodness to us in Christ Jesus, He might display in the Ages to come the transcendent riches of His grace. 002:008 For it is by grace that you have been saved through faith; and that not of yourselves. It is God's gift, and is not on the ground of merit- 002:009 so that it may be impossible for any one to boast. 002:010 For we are God's own handiwork, created in Christ Jesus for good works which He has predestined us to practise. 002:011 Therefore, do not forget that formerly you were Gentiles as to your bodily condition. You were called the Uncircumcision by those who style themselves the Circumcised-their circumcision being one which the knife has effected. 002:012 At that time you were living apart from Christ, estranged from the Commonwealth of Israel, with no share by birth in the Covenants which are based on the Promises, and you had no hope and no God, in all the world. 002:013 But now in Christ Jesus you who once were so far away have been brought near through the death of Christ. 002:014 For He is our peace-He who has made Jews and Gentiles one, and in His own human nature has broken down the hostile dividing wall, 002:015 by setting aside the Law with its commandments, expressed, as they were, in definite decrees. His design was to unite the two sections of humanity in Himself so as to form one new man, 002:016 thus effecting peace, and to reconcile Jews and Gentiles in one body to God, by means of His cross-slaying by it their mutual enmity. 002:017 So He came and proclaimed good news of peace to you who were so far away, and peace to those who were near; 002:018 because it is through Him that Jews and Gentiles alike have access through one Spirit to the Father. 002:019 You are therefore no longer mere foreigners or persons excluded from civil rights. On the contrary you share citizenship with God's people and are members of His family. 002:020 You are a building which has been reared on the foundation of the Apostles and Prophets, the cornerstone being Christ Jesus Himself, 002:021 in union with whom the whole fabric, fitted and closely joined together, is growing so as to form a holy sanctuary in the Lord; 002:022 in whom you also are being built up together to become a fixed abode for God through the Spirit. 003:001 For this reason I Paul, the prisoner of Christ Jesus on behalf of you Gentiles- 003:002 if, that is, you have heard of the work which God has graciously entrusted to me for your benefit, 003:003 and that by a revelation the truth hitherto kept secret was made known to me as I have already briefly explained it to you. 003:004 By means of that explanation, as you read it, you can judge of my insight into the truth of Christ 003:005 which in earlier ages was not made known to the human race, as it has now been revealed to His holy Apostles and Prophets through the Spirit- 003:006 I mean the truth that the Gentiles are joint heirs with us Jews, and that they form one body with us, and have the same interest as we have in the promise which has been made good in Christ Jesus through the Good News, 003:007 in which I have been appointed to serve, in virtue of the work which God, in the exercise of His power within me, has graciously entrusted to me. 003:008 To me who am less than the least of all God's people has this work been graciously entrusted-to proclaim to the Gentiles the Good News of the exhaustless wealth of Christ, 003:009 and to show all men in a clear light what my stewardship is. It is the stewardship of the truth which from all the Ages lay concealed in the mind of God, the Creator of all things- 003:010 concealed in order that the Church might now be used to display to the powers and authorities in the heavenly realms the innumerable aspects of God's wisdom. 003:011 Such was the eternal purpose which He had formed in Christ Jesus our Lord, 003:012 in whom we have this bold and confident access through our faith in Him. 003:013 Therefore I entreat you not to lose heart in the midst of my sufferings on your behalf, for they bring you honour. 003:014 For this reason, on bended knee I beseech the

Father, 003:015 from whom the whole family in Heaven and on earth derives its name, 003:016 to grant you-in accordance with the wealth of His glorious perfections-to be strengthened by His Spirit with power penetrating to your inmost being. 003:017 I pray that Christ may make His home in your hearts through your faith; so that having your roots deep and your foundations strong, in love, you may become mighty to grasp the idea, 003:018 as it is grasped by all God's people, of the breadth and length, the height and depth- 003:019 yes, to attain to a knowledge of the knowledge-surpassing love of Christ, so that you may be made complete in accordance with God's own standard of completeness. 003:020 Now to Him who, in exercise of His power that is at work within us, is able to do infinitely beyond all our highest prayers or thoughts- 003:021 to Him be the glory in the Church and in Christ Jesus to all generations, world without end! Amen. 004:001 I, then, the prisoner for the Master's sake, entreat you to live and act as becomes those who have received the call that you have received- 004:002 with all lowliness of mind and unselfishness, and with patience, bearing with one another lovingly, and earnestly striving to maintain, 004:003 in the uniting bond of peace, the unity given by the Spirit. 004:004 There is but one body and but one Spirit, as also when you were called you had one and the same hope held out to you. 004:005 There is but one Lord, one faith, one baptism, 004:006 and one God and Father of all, who rules over all, acts through all, and dwells in all. 004:007 Yet to each of us individually grace was given, measured out with the munificence of Christ. 004:008 For this reason Scripture says: "He re-ascended on high, He led captive a host of captives, and gave gifts to men." 004:009 (Now this "re-ascended"-what does it mean but that He had first descended into the lower regions of the earth? 004:010 He who descended is the same as He who ascended again far above all the Heavens in order to fill the universe.) 004:011 And He Himself appointed some to be Apostles, some to be Prophets, some to be evangelists, some to be pastors and teachers, 004:012 in order fully to equip His people for the work of serving- for the building up of Christ's body- 004:013 till we all of us arrive at oneness in faith and in the knowledge of the Son of God, and at mature manhood and the stature of full-grown men in Christ. 004:014 So we shall no longer be babes nor shall we resemble mariners tossed on the waves and carried about with every changing wind of doctrine according to men's cleverness and unscrupulous cunning, making use of every shifting device to mislead. 004:015 But we shall lovingly hold to the truth, and shall in all respects grow up into union with Him who is our Head, even Christ. 004:016 Dependent on Him, the whole body-its various parts closely fitting and firmly adhering to one another-grows by the aid of every contributory link, with power proportioned to the need of each individual part, so as to build itself up in a spirit of love. 004:017 Therefore I warn you, and I implore you in the name of the Master, no longer to live as the Gentiles in their perverseness live, 004:018 with darkened understandings, having by reason of the ignorance which is deep-seated in them and the insensibility of their moral nature, no share in the Life which God gives. 004:019 Such men being past feeling have abandoned themselves to impurity, greedily indulging in every kind of profligacy. 004:020 But these are not the lessons which you have learned from Christ; 004:021 if at least you have heard His voice and in Him have been taught- and this is true Christian teaching- 004:022 to put away, in regard to your former mode of life, your original evil nature which is doomed to perish as befits its misleading impulses, 004:023 and to get yourselves renewed in the temper of your minds and clothe yourselves 004:024 with that new and better self which has been created to resemble God in the righteousness and holiness which come from the truth. 004:025 For this reason, laying aside falsehood, every one of you should speak the truth to his fellow man; for we are, as it were, parts of one another. 004:026 If angry, beware of sinning. Let not your irritation last until the sun goes down; 004:027 and do not leave room for the Devil. 004:028 He who has been a thief must steal no more, but, instead of that, should work with his own hands in honest industry, so that he may have something of which he can give the needy a share. 004:029 Let no unwholesome words ever pass your lips, but let all your words be good for benefiting others according to the need of the moment, so that they may be a means of blessing to the hearers. 004:030 And beware of grieving the Holy Spirit of God, in whom you have been sealed in preparation for the day of Redemption. 004:031 Let all bitterness and all passionate feeling, all anger and loud insulting language, be unknown among you- and also every kind of malice. 004:032 On the contrary learn to be kind to one another, tender-hearted, forgiving one another, just as God in Christ has also forgiven you. 005:001 Therefore be imitators of God, as His dear children. 005:002 And live and act lovingly, as Christ also loved you and gave Himself up to death on our behalf as an offering and sacrifice to God, yielding a fragrant odor. 005:003 But fornication and every kind of impurity, or covetousness, let them not even be mentioned among you, for they ought not to be named among God's people. 005:004 Avoid shameful and foolish talk and low jesting-they are all alike discreditable-and in place of these give thanks. 005:005 For be well assured that no fornicator or immoral person and no money-grubber-or in other words idol-worshipper-has any share awaiting him in the Kingdom of Christ and of God. 005:006 Let no one deceive you with empty words, for it is on account of these very sins that God's anger is coming upon the disobedient. 005:007 Therefore do not become sharers with them. 005:008 There was a time when you were nothing but darkness. Now, as Christians, you are Light itself. 005:009 Live and act as sons of Light-for the effect of the Light is seen in every kind of goodness, uprightness and truth- 005:010 and learn in your own experiences what is fully pleasing to the Lord. 005:011 Have nothing to do with the barren unprofitable deeds of darkness, but, instead of that, set your faces against them; 005:012 for the things which are done by these people in secret it is disgraceful even to speak of. 005:013 But everything can be tested by the light and thus be shown in its true colors; for whatever shines of itself is light. 005:014 For this reason it is said, "Rise, sleeper; rise from among the dead, and Christ will shed light upon you." 005:015 Therefore be very careful how you live and act. Let it not be as unwise men, but as wise. 005:016 Buy up your opportunities, for these are evil times. 005:017 On this account do not prove yourselves wanting in sense, but try to understand what the Lord's will is. 005:018 Do not over-indulge in wine-a thing in which excess is so easy- 005:019 but drink deeply of God's Spirit. Speak to one another with psalms and hymns and spiritual songs. Sing and offer praise in your hearts to the Lord. 005:020 Always and for everything let your thanks to God the Father be presented in the name of our Lord Jesus Christ; 005:021 and submit to one another out of reverence for Christ. 005:022 Married women, submit to your own husbands as if to the Lord; 005:023 because a husband is the Head of his wife as Christ also is the Head of the Church, being indeed the Saviour of this His Body. 005:024 And just as the Church submits to Christ, so also married women should be entirely submissive to their husbands. 005:025 Married men, love your wives, as Christ also loved the Church and gave Himself up to death for her; 005:026 in order to make her holy, cleansing her with the baptismal water by the word, 005:027 that He might present the Church to Himself a glorious bride, without spot or wrinkle or any other defect, but to be holy and unblemished. 005:028 So too married men ought to love their wives as much as they love themselves. He who loves his wife loves himself. 005:029 For never yet has a man hated his own body. On the contrary he feeds and cherishes it, just as Christ feeds and cherishes the Church; 005:030 because we are, as it were, parts of His Body. 005:031 "For this reason a man is to leave his father and his mother and be united to his wife, and the two shall be as one." 005:032 That is a great truth hitherto kept secret: I mean the truth concerning Christ and the Church. 005:033 Yet I insist that among you also, each man is to love his own wife as much as he loves himself, and let a married woman see to it that she treats her husband with respect. 006:001 Children, be obedient to your parents as a Christian duty, for it is a duty. 006:002 "Honour your father and your mother"-this is the first Commandment which has a promise added to it- 006:003 "so that it may be well with you, and that you may live long on the earth." 006:004 And you, fathers, do not irritate your children, but bring them up tenderly with true Christian training and advice. 006:005 Slaves, be obedient to your earthly masters, with respect and eager anxiety to please and with simplicity of motive as if you were obeying Christ. 006:006 Let it not be in acts of eye-service as if you had but to please men, but as Christ's bondservants who are doing God's will from the heart. 006:007 With right good will, be faithful to your duty as service rendered to the Lord and not to man. 006:008 You well know that whatever right thing any one does, he will receive a requital for it from the Lord, whether he is a slave or a free man. 006:009 And you masters, act towards your slaves on the same principles, and refrain from threats. For you know that in Heaven there is One who is your Master as well as theirs, and that merely earthly distinctions there are none with Him. 006:010 In conclusion, strengthen yourselves in the Lord and in the power which His supreme might imparts. 006:011 Put on the complete armour of God, so as to be able to stand firm against all the stratagems of the Devil. 006:012 For ours is not a conflict with mere flesh and blood, but with the despotisms, the empires, the forces that control and govern this dark world-the spiritual hosts of evil arrayed against us in the heavenly warfare. 006:013 Therefore put on the complete armour of God, so that you may be able to stand your ground on the day of battle, and, having fought to the end, to remain victors on the field. 006:014 Stand therefore, first fastening round you the girdle of truth and putting on the breastplate of uprightness 006:015 as well as the shoes of the Good News of peace-a firm foundation for your feet. 006:016 And besides all these take the great shield of faith, on which you will be able to quench all the flaming darts of the Wicked one; 006:017 and take the helmet of salvation, and the sword of the Spirit which is the word of God. 006:018 Pray with unceasing prayer and entreaty on every fitting occasion in the Spirit, and be always on the alert to seize opportunities for doing so, with unwearied persistence and entreaty on behalf of all God's people, 006:019 and ask on my behalf that words may be given to me so that, outspoken and fearless, I may make known the truths (hitherto kept secret) of the Good News- 006:020 to spread which I Book 48 Galatians

001:001 Paul, an Apostle sent not from men nor by any man, but by Jesus Christ and by God the Father, who raised Jesus from among the dead- 001:002 and all the brethren who are with me: To the Churches of Galatia. 001:003 May grace and peace be granted to you from God the Father, and from our Lord Jesus Christ, 001:004 who gave Himself to suffer for our sins in order to rescue us from the present wicked age in accordance with the will of our God and Father. 001:005 To Him be the glory to the Ages of the Ages! Amen. 001:006 I marvel that you are so readily leaving Him who called you by the grace of Christ, and are adhering to a different Good News. 001:007 For other "Good News" there is none; but there are some persons who are troubling you, and are seeking to distort the Good News concerning Christ. 001:008 But if even we or an angel from Heaven should bring you a Good News different from that which we have already brought you, let him be accursed. 001:009 What I have just said I repeat-if any one is preaching to you a Good News other than that which you originally received, let him be accursed. 001:010 For is it man's favour or God's that I aspire to? Or am I seeking to please men? If I were still a man-pleaser, I should not be Christ's bondservant. 001:011 For I must tell you, brethren, that the Good News which was proclaimed by me is not such as man approves of. 001:012 For, in fact, it was not from man that I received or learnt it, but by a revelation from Jesus Christ. 001:013 For you have heard of my early career in Judaism-how I furiously persecuted the Church of God, and made havoc of it; 001:014 and how in devotion to Judaism I outstripped many men of my own age among my people, being far more zealous than they on behalf of the traditions of my forefathers. 001:015 But when He who set me apart even from my birth, and called me by His grace, 001:016 saw fit to reveal His Son within me in order that I might tell among the Gentiles the Good News concerning Him, at once I did not confer with any human being, 001:017 nor did I go up to Jerusalem to those who were my seniors in the Apostleship, but I went away into Arabia, and afterwards came back to Damascus. 001:018 Then, three years later, I went up to Jerusalem to inquire for Peter, and I spent a fortnight with him. 001:019 I saw none of the other Apostles, except James, the Lord's brother. 001:020 In making these assertions I am speaking the truth, as in the sight of God. 001:021 Afterwards I visited Syria and Cilicia. 001:022 But to the Christian Churches in Judaea I was personally unknown. 001:023 They only heard it said, "He who was once our persecutor is now telling the Good News of the faith of which he formerly made havoc." 001:024 And they gave glory to God on my account. 002:001 Later still, after an interval of fourteen years, I again went up to Jerusalem in company with Barnabas, taking Titus also with me. 002:002 I went up in obedience to a revelation of God's will; and I explained to them the Good News which I proclaim among the Gentiles. To the leaders of the Church this explanation was made in private, lest by any means I should be running, or should already have run, in vain. 002:003 But although my companion Titus was a Greek they did not insist upon even his being circumcised. 002:004 Yet there was danger of this through the false brethren secretly introduced into the Church, who had stolen in to spy out the freedom which is ours in Christ Jesus, in order to rob us of it. 002:005 But not for an hour did we give way and submit to them; in order that the Good News might continue with you in its integrity. 002:006 From those leaders I gained nothing new. Whether they were men of importance or not, matters nothing to me- God recognizes no external distinctions. To me, at any rate, the leaders imparted nothing new. 002:007 Indeed, when they saw that I was entrusted with the preaching of the Good News to the Gentiles as Peter had been with that to the Jews- 002:008 for He who had been at work within Peter with a view to his Apostleship to the Jews had also been at work within me with a view to my Apostleship to the Gentiles- 002:009 and when they perceived the mission which was graciously entrusted to me, they (that is to say, James, Peter, and John, who were considered to be the pillars of the Church) welcomed Barnabas and me to their fellowship on the understanding that we were to go to the Gentiles and they to the Jews. 002:010 Only they urged that we should remember their poor-a thing which was uppermost in my own mind. 002:011 Now when Peter visited Antioch, I remonstrated with him to his face, because he had incurred just censure. 002:012 For until certain persons came from James he had been accustomed to eat with Gentiles; but as soon as these persons came, he withdrew and separated himself for fear of the Circumcision party. 002:013 And along with him the other Jews also concealed their real opinions, so that even Barnabas was carried away by their lack of straightforwardness. 002:014 As soon as I saw that they were not walking uprightly in the spirit of the Good News, I said to Peter, before them all, "If you, though you are a Jew, live as a Gentile does, and not as a Jew, how can you make the Gentiles follow Jewish customs? 002:015 You and I, though we are Jews by birth and not Gentile sinners, 002:016 know that it is not through obedience to Law that a man can be declared free from guilt, but only through faith in Jesus Christ. We have therefore believed in Christ Jesus, for the purpose of being declared free from guilt, through faith in Christ and not through obedience to Law. For through obedience to Law no human being shall be declared free from guilt. 002:017 But if while we are seeking in Christ acquittal from guilt we ourselves are convicted of sin, Christ then encourages us to sin! No, indeed. 002:018 Why, if I am now rebuilding that structure of sin which I had demolished, I am thereby constituting myself a transgressor; 002:019 for it is by the Law that I have died to the Law, in order that I may live to God. 002:020 I have been crucified with Christ, and it is no longer I that live, but Christ that lives in me; and the life which I now live in the body I live through faith in the Son of God who loved me and gave Himself up to death on my behalf. 002:021 I do not nullify the grace of God; for if acquittal from guilt is obtainable through the Law, then Christ has died in vain." 003:001 You foolish Galatians! Whose sophistry has bewitched you- you to whom Jesus Christ has been vividly portrayed as on the Cross? 003:002 Answer me this one question, "Is it on the ground of your obedience to the Law that you received the Spirit, or is it because, when you heard, you believed?" 003:003 Are you so foolish? Having begun by the Spirit, are you now going to reach perfection through what is external? 003:004 Have you endured such sufferings to no purpose-if indeed it has been to no purpose? 003:005 He who gives you His Spirit and works miracles among you- does He do so on the ground of your obedience to the Law, or is it the result of your having heard and believed: 003:006 even as Abraham believed God, and his faith was placed to his account as righteousness? 003:007 Notice therefore that those who possess faith are true sons of Abraham. 003:008 And the Scripture, foreseeing that in consequence of faith God would declare the nations to be free from guilt, sent beforehand the Good News to Abraham, saying, "In you all the nations shall be blessed." 003:009 So we see that it is those who possess faith that are blessed with believing Abraham. 003:010 All who are depending upon their own obedience to the Law are under a curse, for it is written, "Cursed is every one who does not remain faithful to all the precepts of the Law, and practise them." 003:011 It is evident, too, that no one can find acceptance with God simply by obeying the Law, because "the righteous shall live by faith," 003:012 and the Law has nothing to do with faith. It teaches that "he who does these things shall live by doing them." 003:013 Christ has purchased our freedom from the curse of the Law by becoming accursed for us-because "Cursed is every one who is hanged upon a tree." 003:014 Our freedom has been thus purchased in order that in Christ Jesus the blessing belonging to Abraham may come upon the nations, so that through faith we may receive the promised Spirit. 003:015 Brethren, even a covenant made by a man-to borrow an illustration from daily life-when once formally sanctioned is not liable to be set aside or added to. 003:016 (Now the promises were given to Abraham and to his seed. God did not say "and to seeds," as if speaking of many, but "and to your seed," since He spoke of only one- and this is Christ.) 003:017 I mean that the Covenant which God had already formally made is not abrogated by the Law which was given four hundred and thirty years later-so as to annul the promise. 003:018 For if the inheritance comes through obedience to Law, it no longer comes because of a promise. But, as a matter of fact, God has granted it to Abraham in fulfilment of a promise. 003:019 Why then was the Law given? It was imposed later on for the sake of defining sin, until the seed should come to whom God had made the promise; and its details were laid down by a mediator with the help of angels. 003:020 But there cannot be a mediator where only one individual is concerned. 003:021 God, however, is only one. Is the Law then opposed to the promises of God? No, indeed; for if a Law had been given which could have conferred Life, righteousness would certainly have come by the Law. 003:022 But Scripture has shown that all mankind are the prisoners of sin, in order that the promised blessing, which depends on faith in Jesus Christ, may be given to those who believe. 003:023 Before this faith came, we Jews were perpetual prisoners under the Law, living under restraints and limitations in preparation for the faith which was soon to be revealed. 003:024 So that the Law has acted the part of a tutor-slave to lead us to Christ, in order that through faith we may be declared to be free from guilt. 003:025 But now that this faith has come, we are no longer under a tutor-slave. 003:026 You are all sons of God through faith in Christ Jesus; 003:027 for all of you who have been baptized into Christ, have clothed yourselves with Christ. 003:028 In Him the distinctions between Jew and Gentile, slave and free man, male and female, disappear; you are all one in Christ Jesus. 003:029 And if you belong to Christ, then you are indeed true descendants of Abraham, and are heirs in fulfilment of the promise. 004:001 Now I say that so long as an heir is a child, he in no respect differs from a slave, although he is the owner of everything, 004:002 but he is under the control of guardians and trustees until the time his father has appointed. 004:003 So we also, when spiritually we were children, were subject to the world's rudimentary notions, and were enslaved. 004:004 But, when the time was fully come, God sent forth His Son, born of a woman, born subject to Law, 004:005 in order to purchase the freedom of all who were subject to Law, so that we might receive recognition as sons. 004:006 And because you are sons, God has sent out the Spirit of His Son to enter your hearts and cry "Abba! our Father!" 004:007 Therefore you are no longer a slave, but a son; and if a son, then an heir also through God's own act. 004:008 But at one time, you Gentiles, having no knowledge of God, were slaves to gods which in reality do not exist. 004:009 Now, however, having come to know God- or rather to be known by Him- how is it you are again turning back to weak and worthless rudimentary notions to which you are once more willing to be enslaved? 004:010 You scrupulously observe days and months, special seasons, and years. 004:011 I am alarmed about you, and am afraid that I have perhaps bestowed labour upon you to no purpose. 004:012 Brethren, become as I am, I beseech you; for I have also become like you. In no respect did you behave badly to me. 004:013 And you know that in those early days it was on account of bodily infirmity that I proclaimed the Good News to you, 004:014 and yet the bodily infirmity which was such a trial to you, you did not regard with contempt or loathing, but you received me as if I had been an angel of God or Christ Jesus Himself! 004:015 I ask you, then, what has become of your self-congratulations? For I bear you witness that had it been possible you would have torn out your own eyes and have given them to me. 004:016 Can it be that I have become your enemy through speaking the truth to you? 004:017 These men pay court to you, but not with honourable motives. They want to exclude you, so that you may pay court to them. 004:018 It is always an honourable thing to be courted in an honourable cause; always, and not only when I am with you, my children- 004:019 you for whom I am again, as it were, undergoing the pains of childbirth, until Christ is fully formed within you. 004:020 Would that I were with you and could change my tone, for I am perplexed about you. 004:021 Tell me-you who want to continue to be subject to Law- will you not listen to the Law? 004:022 For it is written that Abraham had two sons, one by the slave-girl and one by the free woman. 004:023 But we see that the child of the slave-girl was born in the common course of nature; but the child of the free woman in fulfilment of the promise. 004:024 All this is allegorical; for the women represent two Covenants. One has its origin on Mount Sinai, and bears children destined for slavery. 004:025 This is Hagar; for the name Hagar stands for Mount Sinai in Arabia, and corresponds to the present Jerusalem, which is in bondage together with her children. 004:026 But the Jerusalem which is above is free, and *she* is *our* mother. 004:027 For it is written, "Rejoice, thou barren woman that bearest not, break forth into a joyful cry, thou that dost not travail with child. For the desolate woman has many children- more indeed than she who has the husband." 004:028 But you, brethren, like Isaac, are children born in fulfilment of a promise. 004:029 Yet just as, at that time, the child born in the common course of nature persecuted the one whose birth was due to the power of the Spirit, so it is now. 004:030 But what says the Scripture? "Send away the slave-girl and her son, for never shall the slave-girl's son share the inheritance with the son of the free woman." 004:031 Therefore, brethren, since we are not the children of a slave-girl, but of the free woman- 005:001 Christ having made us gloriously free-stand fast and do not again be hampered with the yoke of slavery. 005:002 Remember that it is I Paul who tell you that if you receive circumcision Christ will avail you nothing. 005:003 I once more protest to every man who receives circumcision that he is under obligation to obey the whole Law of Moses. 005:004 Christ has become nothing to any of you who are seeking acceptance with God through the Law: you have fallen away from grace. 005:005 *We* have not, for through the Spirit we wait with longing hope for an acceptance with God which is to come through faith. 005:006 For in Christ Jesus neither circumcision nor uncircumcision is of any importance; but only faith working through love. 005:007 You were running the race nobly! Who has interfered and caused you to swerve from the truth? 005:008 No such teaching ever proceeded from Him who is calling you. 005:009 A little yeast corrupts the whole of the dough. 005:010 For my part I have strong confidence in you in the Lord that you will adopt my view of the matter. But the man- be he who he may-who is troubling you, will have to bear the full weight of the judgement to be pronounced on him. 005:011 As for me, brethren, if I am still a preacher of circumcision, how is it that I am still suffering persecution? In that case the Cross has ceased to be a stumbling-block! 005:012 Would to God that those who are unsettling your faith would even mutilate themselves. 005:013 You however, brethren, were called to freedom. Only do not turn your freedom into an excuse for giving way to your lower natures; but become bondservants to one another in a spirit of love. 005:014 For the entire Law has been obeyed when you have kept the single precept, which says, "You are to love your fellow man equally with yourself." 005:015 But if you are perpetually snarling and snapping at one another, beware lest you are destroyed by one another. 005:016 This then is what I mean. Let your lives be guided by the Spirit, and then you will certainly not indulge the cravings of your lower natures. 005:017 For the cravings of the lower nature are opposed to those of the Spirit, and the cravings of the Spirit are opposed to those of the lower nature; because these are antagonistic to each other, so that you cannot do everything to which you are inclined. 005:018 But if the Spirit is leading you, you are not subject to Law. 005:019 Now you know full well the doings of our lower natures. Fornication, impurity, indecency, idol-worship, sorcery; 005:020 enmity, strife, jealousy, outbursts of passion, intrigues, dissensions, factions, envyings; 005:021 hard drinking, riotous feasting, and the like. And as to these I forewarn you, as I have already forewarned you, that those who are guilty of such things will have no share in the Kingdom of God. 005:022 The Spirit, on the other hand, brings a harvest of love, joy, peace; patience towards others, kindness, benevolence; 005:023 good faith, meekness, self-restraint. 005:024 Against such things as these there is no law. Now those who belong to Christ Jesus have crucified their lower nature with its passions and appetites. 005:025 If we are living by the Spirit's power, let our conduct also be governed by the Spirit's power. 005:026 Let us not become vain-glorious, challenging one another, envying one another. 006:001 Brethren, if anybody be detected in any misconduct, you who are spiritual should restore such a one in a spirit of meekness. And let each of you keep watch over himself, lest he also fall into temptation. 006:002 Always carry one another's burdens, and so obey the whole of Christ's Law. 006:003 For if there is any one who thinks himself to be somebody when he is nobody, he is deluding himself. 006:004 But let every man scrutinize his own conduct, and then he will find out, not with reference to another but with reference to himself, what he has to boast of. 006:005 For every man will have to carry his own load. 006:006 But let those who receive instruction in Christian truth share with their instructors all temporal blessings. 006:007 Do not deceive yourselves. God is not to be scoffed at. For whatever a man sows, that he will also reap. 006:008 He who sows in the field of his lower nature, will from that nature reap destruction; but he who sows to serve the Spirit will from the Spirit reap the Life of the Ages. 006:009 Let us not abate our courage in doing what is right; for in due time we shall reap a reward, if we do not faint. 006:010 So then, as we have opportunity, let us labour for the good of all, and especially of those who belong to the household of the faith. 006:011 See in what large letters I am writing to you with my own hand. 006:012 All who desire to display their zeal for external observances try to compel you to receive circumcision, but their real object is simply to escape being persecuted for the Cross of

Christ. 006:013 For these very men do not really keep the Law of Moses, but they would have you receive circumcision in order that they may glory in *your* bodies. 006:014 But as for me, God forbid that I should glory in anything except the Cross of our Lord Jesus Christ, upon which the world is crucified to me, and I am crucified to the world. 006:015 For neither circumcision nor uncircumcision is of any importance; but only a renewed nature. 006:016 And all who shall regulate their lives by this principle- may peace and mercy be given to them-and to the true Israel of God. 006:017 From this time onward let no one trouble me; for, as for me, I bear, branded on my body, the scars of Jesus as my Master. 006:018 May the grace of our Lord Jesus Christ be with your spirits, brethren. Amen.

But in order that you also may know how I am doing, Tychicus our dearly-loved brother and faithful helper in the Lord's service will tell you everything. 006:022 I have sent him to you for the very purpose-that you may know about us and that he may encourage you. 006:023 Peace be to the brethren, and love combined with faith, from God the Father and the Lord Jesus Christ. 006:024 May grace be with all who love our Lord Jesus Christ with perfect sincerity.

BOOK 58 HEBREWS

001:001 God, who in ancient days spoke to our forefathers in many distinct messages and by various methods through the Prophets, 001:002 has at the end of these days spoken to us through a Son, who is the pre-destined Lord of the universe, and through whom He made the Ages. 001:003 He brightly reflects God's glory and is the exact representation of His being, and upholds the universe by His all-powerful word. After securing man's purification from sin He took His seat at the right hand of the Majesty on high, 001:004 having become as far superior to the angels as the Name He possesses by inheritance is more excellent than theirs. 001:005 For to which of the angels did God ever say, "My Son art Thou: I have this day become Thy Father;" and again, "I will be a Father to Him, and He shall be My Son"? 001:006 But speaking of the time when He once more brings His Firstborn into the world, He says, "And let all God's angels worship Him." 001:007 Moreover of the angels He says, "He changes His angels into winds, and His ministering servants into a flame of fire." 001:008 But of His Son, He says, "Thy throne, O God, is for ever and for ever, and the sceptre of Thy Kingdom is a sceptre of absolute justice. 001:009 Thou hast loved righteousness and hated lawlessness; therefore God, Thy God, has anointed Thee with the oil of gladness beyond Thy companions." 001:010 It is also of His Son that God says, "Thou, O Lord, in the beginning didst lay the foundations of the earth, and the heavens are the work of Thy hands. 001:011 The heavens will perish, but Thou remainest; and they will all grow old like a garment, 001:012 and, as though they were a mantle Thou wilt roll them up; yes, like a garment, and they will undergo change. But Thou art the same, and Thy years will never come to an end." 001:013 To which of the angels has He ever said, "Sit at My right hand till I make Thy foes a footstool for Thy feet"? 001:014 Are not all angels spirits that serve Him-whom He sends out to render service for the benefit of those who, before long, will inherit salvation? 002:001 For this reason we ought to pay the more earnest heed to the things which we have heard, for fear we should drift away from them. 002:002 For if the message delivered through angels proved to be true, and every transgression and act of disobedience met with just retribution, 002:003 how shall *we* escape if we are indifferent to a salvation as great as that now offered to us? This, after having first of all been announced by the Lord Himself, had its truth made sure to us by those who heard Him, 002:004 while God corroborated their testimony by signs and marvels and various miracles, and by gifts of the Holy Spirit distributed in accordance with His own will. 002:005 It is not to angels that God has assigned the sovereignty of that coming world, of which we speak. 002:006 But, as we know, a writer has solemnly said, "How poor a creature is man, and yet Thou dost remember him, and a son of man, and yet Thou dost come to him! 002:007 Thou hast made him only a little inferior to the angels; with glory and honour Thou hast crowned him, and hast set him to govern the works of Thy hands. 002:008 Thou hast put everything in subjection under his feet." For this subjecting of the universe to man implies the leaving nothing not subject to him. But we do not as yet see the universe subject to him. 002:009 But Jesus-who was made a little inferior to the angels in order that through God's grace He might taste death for every human being-we already see wearing a crown of glory and honour because of His having suffered death. 002:010 For it was fitting that He for whom, and through whom, all things exist, after He had brought many sons to glory, should perfect by suffering the Prince Leader who had saved them. 002:011 For both He who sanctifies and those whom He is sanctifying have all one Father; and for this reason He is not ashamed to speak of them as His brothers; 002:012 as when He says: "I will proclaim Thy name to My brothers: in the midst of the congregation I will hymn Thy praises;" 002:013 and again, "As for Me, I will be one whose trust reposes in God;" and again, "Here am I, and here are the children God has given Me." 002:014 Since then the children referred to are all alike sharers in perishable human nature, He Himself also, in the same way, took on Him a share of it, in order that through death He might render powerless him who had authority over death, that is, the Devil, 002:015 and might set at liberty all those who through fear of death had been subject to lifelong slavery. 002:016 For assuredly it is not to angels that He is continually reaching a helping hand, but it is to the descendants of Abraham. 002:017 And for this purpose it was necessary that in all respects He should be made to resemble His brothers, so that He might become a compassionate and faithful High Priest in things relating to God, in order to atone for the sins of the people. 002:018 For inasmuch as He has Himself felt the pain of temptation and trial, He is also able instantly to help those who are tempted and tried. 003:001 Therefore, holy brethren, sharers with others in a heavenly invitation, fix your thoughts on Jesus, the Apostle and High Priest whose followers we profess to be. 003:002 How faithful He was to Him who appointed Him, just as Moses also was faithful in all God's house! 003:003 For Jesus has been counted worthy of greater glory than Moses, in so far as he who has built a house has higher honour than the house itself. 003:004 For every house has had a builder, and the builder of all things is God. 003:005 Moreover, Moses was faithful in all God's house as a servant in delivering the message given him to speak; 003:006 but Christ was faithful as a Son having authority over God's house, and we are that house, if we hold firm to the End the boldness and the hope which we boast of as ours. 003:007 For this reason-as the Holy Spirit warns us, "To-day, if you hear His voice, 003:008 do not harden your hearts as your forefathers did in the time of the provocation on the day of the temptation in the Desert, 003:009 where your forefathers so sorely tried My patience and saw all that I did during forty years. 003:010 Therefore I was greatly grieved with that generation, and I said, `They are ever going astray in heart, and have not learnt to know My paths.' 003:011 As I swore in My anger, they shall not be admitted to My rest"- 003:012 see to it, brethren, that there is never in any one of you- as perhaps there may be-a sinful and unbelieving heart, manifesting itself in revolt from the ever-living God. 003:013 On the contrary encourage one another, day after day, so long as To-day lasts, so that not one of you may be hardened through the deceitful character of sin. 003:014 For we have, all alike, become sharers with Christ, if we really hold our first confidence firm to the End; 003:015 seeing that the warning still comes to us, "To-day, if you hear His voice, do not harden your hearts as your forefathers did in the time of the provocation." 003:016 For who were they that heard, and yet provoked God? Was it not the whole of the people who had come out of Egypt under the leadership of Moses? 003:017 And with whom was God so greatly grieved for forty years? Was it not with those who had sinned, and whose dead bodies fell in the Desert? 003:018 And to whom did He swear that they should not be admitted to His rest, if it was not to those who were disobedient? 003:019 And so we see that it was owing to lack of faith that they could not be admitted. 004:001 Therefore let us be on our guard lest perhaps, while He still leaves us a promise of being admitted to His rest, some one of you should be found to have fallen short of it. 004:002 For Good News has been brought to us as truly as to them; but the message they heard failed to benefit them, because they were not one in faith with those who gave heed to it. 004:003 We who have believed are soon to be admitted to the true rest; as He has said, "As I swore in My anger, they shall not be admitted to My rest," although God's works had been going on ever since the creation of the world. 004:004 For, as we know, when speaking of the seventh day He has used the words, "And God rested on the seventh day from all His works;" 004:005 and He has also declared, "They shall not be admitted to My rest." 004:006 Since, then, it is still true that some will be admitted to that rest, and that because of disobedience those who formerly had Good News proclaimed to them were not admitted, 004:007 He again definitely mentions a certain day, "To-day," saying long afterwards, by David's lips, in the words already quoted, "To-day, if you hear His voice, do not harden your hearts." 004:008 For if Joshua had given them the true rest, we should not afterwards hear God speaking of another still future day. 004:009 It follows that there still remains a sabbath rest for the people of God. 004:010 For He who has been admitted to His rest, has rested from His works as God did from His. 004:011 Let it then be our earnest endeavour to be admitted to that rest, so that no one may perish through following the same example of unbelief. 004:012 For God's Message is full of life and power, and is keener than the sharpest two-edged sword. It pierces even to the severance of soul from spirit, and penetrates between the joints and the marrow, and it can discern the secret thoughts and purposes of the heart. 004:013 And no created thing is able to escape its scrutiny; but everything lies bare and completely exposed before the eyes of Him with whom we have to do. 004:014 Inasmuch, then, as we have in Jesus, the Son of God, a great High Priest who has passed into Heaven itself, let us hold firmly to our profession of faith. 004:015 For we have not a High Priest who is unable to feel for us in our weaknesses, but one who was tempted in every respect just as we are tempted, and yet did not sin. 004:016 Therefore let us come boldly to the throne of grace, that we may receive mercy and find grace to help us in our times of need. 005:001 For every High Priest is chosen from among men, and is appointed to act on behalf of men in matters relating to God, in order to offer both gifts and sin-offerings, 005:002 and must be one who is able to bear patiently with the ignorant and erring, because he himself also is beset with infirmity. 005:003 And for this reason he is required to offer sin-offerings not only for the people but also for himself. 005:004 And no one takes this honourable office upon himself, but only accepts it when called to it by God, as Aaron was. 005:005 So Christ also did not claim for Himself the honour of being made High Priest, but was appointed to it by Him who said to Him, "My Son art Thou: I have to-day become Thy Father;" 005:006 as also in another passage He says, "Thou art a priest for ever, belonging to the order of Melchizedek." 005:007 For Jesus during his earthly life offered up prayers and entreaties, crying aloud and weeping as He pleaded with Him who was able to bring Him in safety out of death, and He was delivered from the terror from which He shrank. 005:008 Although He was God's Son, yet He learned obedience from the sufferings which He endured; 005:009 and so, having been made perfect, He became to all who obey Him the source and giver of eternal salvation. 005:010 For God Himself addresses Him as a High Priest for ever, belonging to the order of Melchizedek. 005:011 Concerning Him we have much to say, and much that it would be difficult to make clear to you, since you have become so dull of apprehension. 005:012 For although, considering the long time you have been believers, you ought now to be teachers of others, you really need some one to teach you over again the very rudiments of the truths of God, and you have come to require milk instead of solid food. 005:013 By people who live on milk I mean those who are imperfectly acquainted with the teaching concerning righteousness. 005:014 Such persons are mere babes. But solid food is for adults- that is, for those who through constant practice have their spiritual faculties carefully trained to distinguish good from evil. 006:001 Therefore leaving elementary instruction about the Christ, let us advance to mature manhood and not be continually re-laying a foundation of repentance from lifeless works and of faith in God, 006:002 or of teaching about ceremonial washings, the laying on of hands, the resurrection of the dead, and the last judgement. 006:003 And advance we will, if God permits us to do so. 006:004 For it is impossible, in the case of those who have once for all been enlightened, and have tasted the sweetness of the heavenly gift, and have been made partakers of the Holy Spirit, 006:005 and have realized how good the word of God is and how mighty are the powers of the coming Age, and then fell away- 006:006 it is impossible, I say, to keep bringing them back to a new repentance, for, to their own undoing, they are repeatedly crucifying the Son of God afresh and exposing Him to open shame. 006:007 For land which has drunk in the rain that often falls upon it, and brings forth vegetation useful to those for whose sakes, indeed, it is tilled, has a share in God's blessing. 006:008 But if it only yields a mass of thorns and briers, it is considered worthless, and is in danger of being cursed, and in the end will be destroyed by fire. 006:009 But we, even while we speak in this tone, have a happier conviction concerning you, my dearly-loved friends- a conviction of things which point towards salvation. 006:010 For God is not unjust so that He is unmindful of your labour and of the love which you have manifested towards Himself in having rendered services to His people and in still rendering them. 006:011 But we long for each of you to continue to manifest the same earnestness, with a view to your enjoying fulness of hope to the very End; 006:012 so that you may not become half-hearted, but be imitators of those who through faith and patient endurance are now heirs to the promises. 006:013 For when God gave the promise to Abraham, since He had no one greater to swear by, He swore by Himself, 006:014 saying, "Assuredly I will bless you and bless you, I will increase you and increase you." 006:015 And so, as the result of patient waiting, our forefather obtained what God had promised. 006:016 For men swear by what is greater than themselves; and with them an oath in confirmation of a statement always puts an end to a dispute. 006:017 In the same way, since it was God's desire to display more convincingly to the heirs of the promise how unchangeable His purpose was, 006:018 He added an oath, in order that, through two unchangeable things, in which it is impossible for Him to prove false, we may possess mighty encouragement-we who, for safety, have hastened to lay hold of the hope set before us. 006:019 That hope we have as an anchor of the soul-an anchor that can neither break nor drag. It passes in behind the veil, 006:020 where Jesus has entered as a forerunner on our behalf, having become, like Melchizedek, a High Priest for ever. 007:001 For this man, Melchizedek, King of Salem and priest of the Most High God-he who when Abraham was returning after defeating the kings met him and pronounced a blessing on him- 007:002 to whom also Abraham presented a tenth part of all- being first, as his name signifies, King of righteousness, and secondly King of Salem, that is, King of peace: 007:003 with no father or mother, and no record of ancestry: having neither beginning of days nor end of life, but made a type of the Son of God-this man Melchizedek remains a priest for ever. 007:004 Now think how great this priest-king must have been to whom Abraham the patriarch gave a tenth part of the best of the spoil. 007:005 And those of the descendants of Levi who receive the priesthood are authorized by the Law to take tithes from the people, that is, from their brethren, though these have sprung from Abraham. 007:006 But, in this instance, one who does not trace his origin from them takes tithes from Abraham, and pronounces a blessing on him to whom the promises belong. 007:007 And beyond all dispute it is always the inferior who is blessed by the superior. 007:008 Moreover here frail mortal men receive tithes: there one receives them about whom there is evidence that he is alive. 007:009 And Levi too-if I may so speak-pays tithes through Abraham: 007:010 for Levi was yet in the loins of his forefather when Melchizedek met Abraham. 007:011 Now if the crowning blessing was attainable by means of the Levitical priesthood-for as resting on this foundation the people received the Law, to which they are still subject- what further need was there for a Priest of a different kind to be raised up belonging to the order of Melchizedek instead of being said to belong to the order of Aaron? 007:012 For when the priesthood changes, a change of Law also of necessity takes place. 007:013 He, however, to whom that prophecy refers is associated with a different tribe, not one member of which has anything to do with the altar. 007:014 For it is undeniable that our Lord sprang from Judah, a tribe of which Moses said nothing in connection with priests. 007:015 And this is still more abundantly clear when we read that it is as belonging to the order of Melchizedek that a priest of a different kind is to arise, 007:016 and hold His office not in obedience to any temporary Law, but by virtue of an indestructible Life. 007:017 For the words are in evidence, "Thou art a priest for ever, belonging to the order of Melchizedek." 007:018 On the one hand we have here the abrogation of an earlier code because it was weak and ineffective- 007:019 for the Law brought no perfect blessing-but on the other hand we have the bringing in of a new and better hope by means of which we draw near to God. 007:020 And since it was not without an oath being taken- 007:021 for these men hold office without any oath having been taken, but He holds it attested by an oath from Him who said to Him, "The Lord has sworn and will not recall His words, Thou art a Priest for ever"- 007:022 so much the more also is the Covenant of which Jesus has become the guarantor, a better covenant. 007:023 And they have been appointed priests many in number, because death prevents their continuance in office: 007:024 but He, because He continues for ever, has a priesthood which does not pass to any successor. 007:025 Hence too He is able to save to the uttermost those who come to God through Him, seeing that He ever lives to plead for them. 007:026 Moreover we needed just such a High Priest as this- holy, guileless, undefiled, far removed from sinful men and exalted above the heavens; 007:027 who, unlike other High Priests, is not under the necessity of offering up sacrifices day after day, first for His own sins, and afterwards for those of the people; for this latter thing He did once for all when He offered up Himself. 007:028 For the Law constitutes men High Priests-men with all their infirmity-but the utterance of the oath, which came later than the Law, constitutes High Priest a Son who has been made for ever perfect. 008:001 Now in connexion with what we have been saying the chief point is that we have a High Priest who has taken His seat at the right hand of the throne of God's Majesty in the heavens, 008:002 and ministers in the Holy place and in the true tabernacle which not man, but the Lord pitched. 008:003 Every High Priest, however, is appointed to offer both bloodless gifts and sacrifices. Therefore this High Priest also must have some offering to present. 008:004 If then He were still on earth, He would not be a priest at all, since here there are already those who present the offerings in obedience to the Law, 008:005 and serve a copy and type of the heavenly things, just as Moses was divinely instructed when about to build the tabernacle. For God said, "See that you make everything in imitation of the pattern shown you on the mountain." 008:006 But, as a matter of fact, the ministry which Christ has obtained is all the nobler a ministry, in that He is at the same time the negotiator of a sublimer covenant, based upon sublimer promises. 008:007 For if that first Covenant had been free from imperfection, there would have been no attempt to introduce another. 008:008 For, being dissatisfied with His people, God says, "`There are days coming,' says the Lord, `When I will establish with the house of Israel and with the house of Judah a new Covenant- 008:009 a Covenant unlike the one which I made with their forefathers on the day when I took them by the hand to lead them out from the land of Egypt; for they would not remain faithful to that.' `So I turned from them,' says the Lord. 008:010 `But this is the Covenant that I will covenant with the house of Israel after those days,' says the Lord: I will put My laws into their minds and will write them upon their hearts. And I will indeed be their God and they shall be My People. 008:011 And there shall be no need for them to teach each one his fellow citizen and each one his brother, saying, Know the Lord. For all will know Me from the least of them to the greatest; 008:012 Because I will be merciful to their wrongdoings, and their sins I will remember no longer.'" 008:013 By using the words, "a new Covenant," He has made the first one obsolete; but whatever is decaying and showing signs of old age is not far from disappearing altogether. 009:001 Now even the first Covenant had regulations for divine worship, and had also its sanctuary-a sanctuary belonging to this world. 009:002 For a sacred tent was constructed-the outer one, in which were the lamp and the table and the presented loaves; and this is called the Holy place. 009:003 And behind the second veil was a sacred tent called the Holy of holies. 009:004 This had a censer of gold, and the ark of the Covenant lined with gold and completely covered with gold, and in it were a gold vase which held the manna, and Aaron's rod which budded and the tables of the Covenant. 009:005 And above the ark were the Cherubim denoting God's glorious presence and overshadowing the Mercy-seat. But I cannot now speak about all these in detail. 009:006 These arrangements having long been completed, the priests, when conducting the divine services, continually enter the outer tent. 009:007 But into the second, the High Priest goes only on one day of the year, and goes alone, taking with him blood, which he offers on his own behalf and on account of the sins which the people have ignorantly committed. 009:008 And the lesson which the Holy Spirit teaches is this-that the way into the true Holy place is not yet open so long as the outer tent still remains in existence. 009:009 And this is a figure-for the time now present-answering to which both gifts and sacrifices are offered, unable though they are to give complete freedom from sin to him who ministers. 009:010 For their efficacy depends only on meats and drinks and various washings, ceremonies pertaining to the body and imposed until a time of reformation. 009:011 But Christ appeared as a High Priest of the blessings that are soon to come by means of the greater and more perfect Tent of worship, a tent which has not been built with hands- that is to say does not belong to this material creation- 009:012 and once for all entered the Holy place, taking with Him not the blood of goats and calves, but His own blood, and thus procuring eternal redemption for us. 009:013 For if the blood of goats and bulls and the ashes of a heifer sprinkling those who have contracted defilement make them holy so as to bring about ceremonial purity, 009:014 how much more certainly shall the blood of Christ, who strengthened by the eternal Spirit offered Himself to God, free from blemish, purify your consciences from lifeless works for you to serve the ever-living God? 009:015 And because of this He is the negotiator of a new

Covenant, in order that, since a life has been given in atonement for the offences committed under the first Covenant, those who have been called may receive the eternal inheritance which has been promised to them. 009:016 For where there is a legal `will,' there must also be a death brought forward in evidence-the death of him who made it. 009:017 And a will is only of force in the case of a deceased person, being never of any avail so long as he who made it lives. 009:018 Accordingly we find that the first Covenant was not inaugurated without blood. 009:019 For when Moses had proclaimed to all the people every commandment contained in the Law, he took the blood of the calves and of the goats and with them water, scarlet wool and hyssop, and sprinkled both the book itself and all the people, 009:020 saying, "This is the blood which confirms the Covenant that God has made binding upon you." 009:021 And in the same way he also sprinkled blood upon the Tent of worship and upon all the vessels used in the ministry. 009:022 Indeed we may almost say that in obedience to the Law everything is sprinkled with blood, and that apart from the outpouring of blood there is no remission of sins. 009:023 It was needful therefore that the copies of the things in Heaven should be cleansed in this way, but that the heavenly things themselves should be cleansed with more costly sacrifices. 009:024 For not into a Holy place built by men's hands-a mere copy of the reality-did Christ enter, but He entered Heaven itself, now to appear in the presence of God on our behalf. 009:025 Nor did He enter for the purpose of many times offering Himself in sacrifice, just as the High Priest enters the Holy place, year after year, taking with him blood not his own. 009:026 In that case Christ would have needed to suffer many times, from the creation of the world onwards; but as a matter of fact He has appeared once for all, at the Close of the Ages, in order to do away with sin by the sacrifice of Himself. 009:027 And since it is reserved for all mankind once to die, and afterwards to be judged; 009:028 so the Christ also, having been once offered in sacrifice in order that He might bear the sins of many, will appear a second time, separated from sin, to those who are eagerly expecting Him, to make their salvation complete. 010:001 For, since the Law exhibits only an outline of the blessings to come and not a perfect representation of the things themselves, the priests can never, by repeating the same sacrifices which they continually offer year after year, give complete freedom from sin to those who draw near. 010:002 For then would not the sacrifices have ceased to be offered, because the consciences of the worshippers-who in that case would now have been cleansed once for all-would no longer be burdened with sins? 010:003 But in those sacrifices sins are recalled to memory year after year. 010:004 For it is impossible for the blood of bulls and goats to take away sins. 010:005 That is why, when He comes into the world, He says, "Sacrifice and offering Thou has not desired, but a body Thou hast prepared for Me. 010:006 In whole burnt-offerings and in sin-offerings Thou hast taken no pleasure. 010:007 Then I said, `I have come-in the roll of the book it is written concerning Me-to do Thy will, O God.'" 010:008 After saying the words I have just quoted, "Sacrifices and offerings or whole burnt-offerings and sin-offerings Thou hast not desired or taken pleasure in"-all such being offered in obedience to the Law- 010:009 He then adds, "I have come to do Thy will." He does away with the first in order to establish the second. 010:010 It is through that divine will that we have been set free from sin, through the offering of Jesus Christ as our sacrifice once for all. 010:011 And while every priest stands ministering, day after day, and constantly offering the same sacrifices-though such can never rid us of our sins- 010:012 this Priest, on the contrary, after offering for sins a single sacrifice of perpetual efficacy, took His seat at God's right hand, 010:013 waiting from that time onward until His enemies be put as a footstool under His feet. 010:014 For by a single offering He has for ever completed the blessing for those whom He is setting free from sin. 010:015 And the Holy Spirit also gives us His testimony; for when He had said, 010:016 "`This is the Covenant that I will make with them after those days,' says the Lord: `I will put My laws upon their hearts and will write them on their minds;'" 010:017 He adds, "And their sins and offences I will remember no longer." 010:018 But where these have been forgiven no further offering for sin is required. 010:019 Since then, brethren, we have free access to the Holy place through the blood of Jesus, 010:020 by the new and ever-living way which He opened up for us through the rending of the veil-that is to say, of His earthly nature- 010:021 and since we have a great Priest who has authority over the house of God, 010:022 let us draw near with sincerity and unfaltering faith, having had our hearts sprinkled, once for all, from consciences oppressed with sin, and our bodies bathed in pure water. 010:023 Let us hold firmly to an unflinching avowal of our hope, for He is faithful who gave us the promises. 010:024 And let us bestow thought on one another with a view to arousing one another to brotherly love and right conduct; 010:025 not neglecting-as some habitually do-to meet together, but encouraging one another, and doing this all the more since you can see the day of Christ approaching. 010:026 For if we wilfully persist in sin after having received the full knowledge of the truth, there no longer remains in reserve any other sacrifice for sins. 010:027 There remains nothing but a certain awful expectation of judgement, and the fury of a fire which before long will devour the enemies of the truth. 010:028 Any one who bids defiance to the Law of Moses is put to death without mercy on the testimony of two or three witnesses. 010:029 How much severer punishment, think you, will he be held to deserve who has trampled under foot the Son of God, has not regarded as holy that Covenant-blood with which he was set free from sin, and has insulted the Spirit from whom comes grace? 010:030 For we know who it is that has said, "Vengeance belongs to Me: I will pay back;" and again, "The Lord will be His people's judge." 010:031 It is an awful thing to fall into the hands of the ever-living God. 010:032 But continually recall to mind the days now past, when on being first enlightened you went through a great conflict and many sufferings. 010:033 This was partly through allowing yourselves to be made a public spectacle amid reproaches and persecutions, and partly through coming forward to share the sufferings of those who were thus treated. 010:034 For you not only showed sympathy with those who were imprisoned, but you even submitted with joy when your property was taken from you, being well aware that you have in your own selves a more valuable possession and one which will remain. 010:035 Therefore do not cast from you your confident hope, for it will receive a vast reward. 010:036 For you stand in need of patient endurance, so that, as the result of having done the will of God, you may receive the promised blessing. 010:037 For there is still but a short time and then "The coming One will come and will not delay. 010:038 But it is by faith that My righteous servant shall live; and if he shrinks back, My soul takes no pleasure in him." 010:039 But we are not people who shrink back and perish, but are among those who believe and gain possession of their souls. 011:001 Now faith is a well-grounded assurance of that for which we hope, and a conviction of the reality of things which we do not see. 011:002 For by it the saints of old won God's approval. 011:003 Through faith we understand that the worlds came into being, and still exist, at the command of God, so that what is seen does not owe its existence to that which is visible. 011:004 Through faith Abel offered to God a more acceptable sacrifice than Cain did, and through this faith he obtained testimony that he was righteous, God giving the testimony by accepting his gifts; and through it, though he is dead, he still speaks. 011:005 Through faith Enoch was taken from the earth so that he did not see death, and he could not be found, because God had taken him; for before he was taken we have evidence that he truly pleased God. 011:006 But where there is no faith it is impossible truly to please Him; for the man who draws near to God must believe that there is a God and that He proves Himself a rewarder of those who earnestly try to find Him. 011:007 Through faith Noah, being divinely taught about things as yet unseen, reverently gave heed and built an ark for the safety of his family, and by this act he condemned the world, and became an heir of the righteousness which depends on faith. 011:008 Through faith Abraham, upon being called to leave home and go into a land which he was soon to receive for an inheritance, obeyed; and he went out, not knowing where he was going to. 011:009 Through faith he came and made his home for a time in a land which had been promised to him, as if in a foreign country, living in tents together with Isaac and Jacob, sharers with him in the same promise; 011:010 for he continually looked forward to the city which has the foundations, whose architect and builder is God. 011:011 Through faith even Sarah herself received strength to become a mother-although she was past the time of life for this- because she judged Him faithful who had given the promise. 011:012 And thus there sprang from one man, and him practically dead, a nation like the stars of the sky in number, and like the sands on the sea shore which cannot be counted. 011:013 All these died in the possession of faith. They had not received the promised blessings, but had seen them from a distance and had greeted them, and had acknowledged themselves to be foreigners and strangers here on earth; 011:014 for men who acknowledge this make it manifest that they are seeking elsewhere a country of their own. 011:015 And if they had cherished the remembrance of the country they had left, they would have found an opportunity to return; 011:016 but, as it is, we see them eager for a better land, that is to say, a heavenly one. For this reason God is not ashamed to be called their God, for He has now prepared a city for them. 011:017 Through faith Abraham, as soon as God put him to the test, offered up Isaac. Yes, he who had joyfully welcomed the promises was on the point of sacrificing his only son 011:018 with regard to whom he had been told, "It is through Isaac that your posterity shall be traced." 011:019 For he reckoned that God is even able to raise a man up from among the dead, and, figuratively speaking, it was from among the dead that he received Isaac again. 011:020 Through faith Isaac blessed Jacob and Esau, even in connexion with things soon to come. 011:021 Through faith Jacob, when dying, blessed each of Joseph's sons, and, leaning on the top of his staff, worshipped God. 011:022 Through faith Joseph, when he was near his end, made mention of the departure of the descendants of Israel, and gave orders about his own body. 011:023 Through faith the child Moses was hid for three months by his parents, because they saw his rare beauty; and the king's edict had no terror for them. 011:024 Through faith Moses, when he grew to manhood, refused to be known as Pharaoh's daughter's son, 011:025 having determined to endure ill-treatment along with the people of God rather than enjoy the short-lived pleasures of sin; 011:026 because he deemed the reproaches which he might meet with in the service of the Christ to be greater riches than all the treasures of Egypt; for he fixed his gaze on the coming reward. 011:027 Through faith he left Egypt, not being frightened by the king's anger; for he held on his course as seeing the unseen One. 011:028 Through faith he instituted the Passover, and the sprinkling with blood so that the destroyer of the firstborn might not touch the Israelites. 011:029 Through faith they passed through the Red Sea as though they were passing over dry land, but the Egyptians, when they tried to do the same, were swallowed up. 011:030 Through faith the walls of Jericho fell to the ground after being surrounded for seven days. 011:031 Through faith the notorious sinner Rahab did not perish along with the disobedient, for she had welcomed the spies and had sheltered them. 011:032 And why need I say more? For time will fail me if I tell the story of Gideon, Barak, Samson, Jephthah, and of David and Samuel and the Prophets; 011:033 men who, as the result of faith, conquered whole kingdoms, brought about true justice, obtained promises from God, stopped lions' mouths, 011:034 deprived fire of its power, escaped being killed by the sword, out of weakness were made strong, became mighty in war, put to flight foreign armies. 011:035 Women received back their dear ones alive from the dead; and others were put to death with torture, refusing the deliverance offered to them-that they might secure a better resurrection. 011:036 Others again were tested by cruel mockery and by scourging; yes, and by chains and imprisonment. 011:037 They were stoned, they were sawn asunder, they were tried by temptation, they were killed with the sword. They went from place to place in sheepskins or goatskins, enduring want, oppression and cruelty. 011:038 (They were men of whom the world was not worthy.) They wandered across deserts and mountains, or hid themselves in caves and in holes in the ground. 011:039 And although by their faith all these people won God's approval, none of them received the fulfilment of His great promise; 011:040 for God had provided for them and us something better, so that apart from us they were not to attain to full blessedness. 012:001 Therefore, surrounded as we are by such a vast cloud of witnesses, let us fling aside every encumbrance and the sin that so readily entangles our feet. And let us run with patient endurance the race that lies before us, 012:002 simply fixing our gaze upon Jesus, our Prince Leader in the faith, who will also award us the prize. He, for the sake of the joy which lay before Him, patiently endured the cross, looking with contempt upon its shame, and afterwards seated Himself- where He still sits-at the right hand of the throne of God. 012:003 Therefore, if you would escape becoming weary and faint-hearted, compare your own sufferings with those of Him who endured such hostility directed against Him by sinners. 012:004 In your struggle against sin you have not yet resisted so as to endanger your lives; 012:005 and you have quite forgotten the encouraging words which are addressed to you as sons, and which say, "My son, do not think lightly of the Lord's discipline, and do not faint when He corrects you; 012:006 for those whom the Lord loves He disciplines: and He scourges every son whom He acknowledges." 012:007 The sufferings that you are enduring are for your discipline. God is dealing with you as sons; for what son is there whom his father does not discipline? 012:008 And if you are left without discipline, of which every true son has had a share, that shows that you are bastards, and not true sons. 012:009 Besides this, our earthly fathers used to discipline us and we treated them with respect, and shall we not be still more submissive to the Father of our spirits, and live? 012:010 It is true that they disciplined us for a few years according as they thought fit; but He does it for our certain good, in order that we may become sharers in His own holy character. 012:011 Now, at the time, discipline seems to be a matter not for joy, but for grief; yet it afterwards yields to those who have passed through its training a result full of peace-namely, righteousness. 012:012 Therefore strengthen the drooping hands and paralysed knees, 012:013 and make straight paths for your feet, so that what is lame may not be put entirely out of joint 012:014 but may rather be restored. Persistently strive for peace with all men, and for that growth in holiness apart from which no one will see the Lord. 012:015 Be carefully on your guard lest there be any one who falls back from the grace of God; lest any root bearing bitter fruit spring up and cause trouble among you, and through it the whole brotherhood be defiled; 012:016 lest there be a fornicator, or an ungodly person like Esau, who, in return for a single meal, parted with the birthright which belonged to him. 012:017 For you know that even afterwards, when he wished to secure the blessing, he was rejected; for he found no opportunity for undoing what he had done, though he sought the blessing earnestly with tears. 012:018 For you have not come to a material object all ablaze with fire, and to gloom and darkness and storm and trumpet-blast and the sound of words- 012:019 a sound of such a kind that those who heard it entreated that no more should be added. 012:020 For they could not endure the order which had been given, "Even a wild beast, if it touches the mountain, shall be stoned to death;" 012:021 and so terrible was the scene that Moses said, "I tremble with fear." 012:022 On the contrary you have come to Mount Zion, and to the city of the ever-living God, the heavenly Jerusalem, to countless hosts of angels, 012:023 to the great festal gathering and Church of the first-born, whose names are recorded in Heaven, and to a Judge who is God of all, and to the spirits of righteous men made perfect, 012:024 and to Jesus the negotiator of a new Covenant, and to the sprinkled blood which speaks in more gracious tones than that of Abel. 012:025 Be careful not to refuse to listen to Him who is speaking to you. For if they of old did not escape unpunished when they refused to listen to him who spoke on earth, much less shall we escape who turn a deaf ear to Him who now speaks from Heaven. 012:026 His voice then shook the earth, but now we have His promise, "Yet again I will, once for all, cause not only the earth to tremble, but Heaven also." 012:027 Here the words "Yet again, once for all" denote the removal of the things which can be shaken-created things-in order that the things which cannot be shaken may remain. 012:028 Therefore, receiving, as we now do, a kingdom which cannot be shaken, let us cherish thankfulness so that we may ever offer to God an acceptable service, with godly reverence and awe. 012:029 For our God is also a consuming fire. 013:001 Let brotherly love always continue. 013:002 Do not neglect to show kindness to strangers; for, in this way, some, without knowing it, have had angels as their guests. 013:003 Remember prisoners, as if you were in prison with them; and remember those suffering ill-treatment, for you yourselves also are still in the body. 013:004 Let marriage be held in honour among all, and let the marriage bed be unpolluted; for fornicators and adulterers God will judge. 013:005 Your lives should be untainted by love for money. Be content with what you have; for God Himself has said, "I will never, never let go your hand: I will never never forsake you." 013:006 So that we fearlessly say, "The Lord is my helper; I will not be afraid: what can man do to me?" 013:007 Remember your former leaders-it was they who brought you God's Message. Bear in mind how they ended their lives, and imitate their faith. 013:008 Jesus Christ is the same yesterday and to-day-yes, and to the ages to come. 013:009 Do not be drawn aside by all sorts of strange teaching; for it is well to have the heart made stedfast through God's grace, and not by special kinds of food, from which those who scrupulously attend to them have derived no benefit. 013:010 We Christians have an altar from which the ministers of the Jewish Tent have no right to eat. 013:011 For the bodies of those animals of which the blood is carried by the High Priest into the Holy place as an offering for sin, are burned outside the camp. 013:012 And for this reason Jesus also, in order, by His own blood, to set the people free from sin, suffered outside the gate. 013:013 Therefore let us go to Him outside the camp, sharing the insults directed against Him. 013:014 For we have no permanent city here, but we are longing for the city which is soon to be ours. 013:015 Through Him, then, let us continually lay on the altar a sacrifice of praise to God, namely, the utterance of lips that give thanks to His Name. 013:016 And do not forget to be kind and liberal; for with sacrifices of that sort God is greatly pleased. 013:017 Obey your leaders and be submissive to them. For they are keeping watch over your souls as those who will have to give account; that they may do this with joy and not with lamentation. For that would be of no advantage to you. 013:018 Keep on praying for us; for we are sure that we have clear consciences, and we desire to live nobly in every respect. 013:019 I specially urge this upon you in order that I may be the more speedily restored to you. 013:020 Now may God who gives peace, and brought Jesus, our Lord, up again from among the dead-even Him who, by virtue of the blood of the eternal Covenant, is the great Shepherd of the sheep- 013:021 fully equip you with every grace that you may need for the doing of His will, producing in us that which will truly please Him through Jesus Christ. To Him be the glory to the Ages of the Ages! Amen. 013:022 Bear with me, brethren, when I thus exhort you; for, in fact, it is but a short letter that I have written to you. 013:023 You will rejoice to hear that our brother Timothy has been set at liberty. If he comes soon, I will see you with him. 013:024 Greet all your leaders and all God's people. The brethren from Italy send you greetings. 013:025 Grace be with you all! Amen.

BOOK 59 JAMES

001:001 James, a bondservant of God and of the Lord Jesus Christ: to the twelve tribes who are scattered over the world. All good wishes. 001:002 Reckon it nothing but joy, my brethren, whenever you find yourselves hedged in by various trials. 001:003 Be assured that the testing of your faith leads to power of endurance. 001:004 Only let endurance have perfect results so that you may become perfect and complete, deficient in nothing. 001:005 And if any one of you is deficient in wisdom, let him ask God for it, who gives with open hand to all men, and without upbraiding; and it will be given him. 001:006 But let him ask in faith and have no doubts; for he who has doubts is like the surge of the sea, driven by the wind and tossed into spray. 001:007 A person of that sort must not expect to receive anything from the Lord- 001:008 such a one is a man of two minds, undecided in every step he takes. 001:009 Let a brother in humble life rejoice when raised to a higher position; 001:010 but a rich man should rejoice in being brought low, for like flowers among the herbage rich men will pass away. 001:011 The sun rises with his scorching heat and dries up the herbage, so that its flowers drop off and the beauty of its appearance perishes, and in the same way rich men with all their prosperity will fade away. 001:012 Blessed is he who patiently endures trials; for when he has stood the test, he will gain the victor's crown-even the crown of Life- which the Lord has promised to those who love Him. 001:013 Let no one say when passing through trial, "My temptation is from God;" for God is incapable of being tempted to do evil, and He Himself tempts no one. 001:014 But when a man is tempted, it is his own passions that carry him away and serve as a bait. 001:015 Then the passion conceives, and becomes the parent of sin; and sin, when fully matured, gives birth to death. 001:016 Do not be deceived, my dearly-loved brethren. 001:017 Every gift which is good, and every perfect boon, is from above, and comes down from the

Father, who is the source of all Light. In Him there is no variation nor the slightest suggestion of change. 001:018 In accordance with His will He made us His children through the Message of the truth, so that we might, in a sense, be the Firstfruits of the things which He has created. 001:019 You know this, my dearly-loved brethren. But let every one be quick to hear, slow to speak, and slow to be angry. 001:020 For a man's anger does not lead to action which God regards as righteous. 001:021 Ridding yourselves, therefore, of all that is vile and of the evil influences which prevail around you, welcome in a humble spirit the Message implanted within you, which is able to save your souls. 001:022 But prove yourselves obedient to the Message, and do not be mere hearers of it, imposing a delusion upon yourselves. 001:023 For if any one listens but does not obey, he is like a man who carefully looks at his own face in a mirror. 001:024 Although he has looked carefully at himself, he goes away, and has immediately forgotten the sort of man he is. 001:025 But he who looks closely into the perfect Law-the Law of freedom- and continues looking, he, being not a hearer who forgets, but an obedient doer, will as the result of his obedience be blessed. 001:026 If a man thinks that he is scrupulously religious, although he is not curbing his tongue but is deceiving himself, his religious service is worthless. 001:027 The religious service which is pure and stainless in the sight of our God and Father is to visit fatherless children and widowed women in their time of trouble, and to keep one's own self unspotted from the world. 002:001 My brethren, you must not make distinctions between one man and another while you are striving to maintain faith in the Lord Jesus Christ, who is our glory. 002:002 For suppose a man comes into one of your meetings wearing gold rings and fine clothes, and there also comes in a poor man wearing shabby clothes, 002:003 and you pay court to the one who wears the fine clothes, and say, "Sit here; this is a good place;" while to the poor man you say, "Stand there, or sit on the floor at my feet;" 002:004 is it not plain that in your hearts you have little faith, seeing that you have become judges full of wrong thoughts? 002:005 Listen, my dearly-loved brethren. Has not God chosen those whom the world regards as poor to be rich in faith and heirs of the Kingdom which He has promised to those that love Him? 002:006 But *you* have put dishonour upon the poor man. Yet is it not the rich who grind you down? Are not they the very people who drag you into the Law courts?- 002:007 and the very people who speak evil of the noble Name by which you are called? 002:008 If, however, you are keeping the Law as supreme, in obedience to the Commandment which says "You are to love your fellow man just as you love yourself," you are acting rightly. 002:009 But if you are making distinctions between one man and another, you are guilty of sin, and are convicted by the Law as offenders. 002:010 A man who has kept the Law as a whole, but has failed to keep some one command, has become guilty of violating all. 002:011 For He who said, "Do not commit adultery," also said, "Do not commit murder," and if you are a murderer, although not an adulterer, you have become an offender against the Law. 002:012 Speak and act as those should who are expecting to be judged by the Law of freedom. 002:013 For he who shows no mercy will have judgement given against him without mercy; but mercy triumphs over judgement. 002:014 What good is it, my brethren, if a man professes to have faith, and yet his actions do not correspond? Can such faith save him? 002:015 Suppose a Christian brother or sister is poorly clad or lacks daily food, 002:016 and one of you says to them, "I wish you well; keep yourselves warm and well fed," and yet you do not give them what they need; what is the use of that? 002:017 So also faith, if it is unaccompanied by obedience, has no life in it-so long as it stands alone. 002:018 Nay, some one will say, "You have faith, I have actions: prove to me your faith apart from corresponding actions and I will prove mine to you by my actions. 002:019 You believe that God is one, and you are quite right: evil spirits also believe this, and shudder." 002:020 But, idle boaster, are you willing to be taught how it is that faith apart from obedience is worthless? Take the case of Abraham our forefather. 002:021 Was it, or was it not, because of his actions that he was declared to be righteous as the result of his having offered up his son Isaac upon the altar? 002:022 You notice that his faith was co-operating with his actions, and that by his actions his faith was perfected; 002:023 and the Scripture was fulfilled which says, "And Abraham believed God, and his faith was placed to his credit as righteousness," and he received the name of `God's friend.' 002:024 You all see that it is because of actions that a man is pronounced righteous, and not simply because of faith. 002:025 In the same way also was not the notorious sinner Rahab declared to be righteous because of her actions when she welcomed the spies and hurriedly helped them to escape another way? 002:026 For just as a human body without a spirit is lifeless, so also faith is lifeless if it is unaccompanied by obedience. 003:001 Do not be eager, my brethren, for many among you to become teachers; for you know that we teachers shall undergo severer judgement. 003:002 For we often stumble and fall, all of us. If there is any one who never stumbles in speech, that man has reached maturity of character and is able to curb his whole nature. 003:003 Remember that we put the horses' bit into their mouths to make them obey us, and so we turn their whole bodies round. 003:004 So too with ships, great as they are, and often driven along by strong gales, yet they can be steered with a very small rudder in whichever direction the caprice of the man at the helm chooses. 003:005 In the same way the tongue is an insignificant part of the body, but it is immensely boastful. Remember how a mere spark may set a vast forest in flames. 003:006 And the tongue is a fire. That world of iniquity, the tongue, is placed within us spotting and soiling our whole nature, and setting the whole round of our lives on fire, being itself set on fire by Gehenna. 003:007 For brute nature under all its forms-beasts and birds, reptiles and fishes-can be subjected and kept in subjection by human nature. 003:008 But the tongue no man or woman is able to tame. It is an ever-busy mischief, and is full of deadly poison. 003:009 With it we bless the Lord and Father, and with it we curse men, who are made in God's likeness. 003:010 Out of the same mouth there proceed blessing and cursing. My brethren, this ought not to be. 003:011 In a fountain, are fresh water and bitter sent forth from the same opening? 003:012 Can a fig-tree, my brethren, yield olives, or a vine yield figs? No; and neither can salt water yield sweet. 003:013 Which of you is a wise and well-instructed man? Let him prove it by a right life with conduct guided by a wisely teachable spirit. 003:014 But if in your hearts you have bitter feelings of envy and rivalry, do not speak boastfully and falsely, in defiance of the truth. 003:015 That is not the wisdom which comes down from above: it belongs to earth, to the unspiritual nature, and to evil spirits. 003:016 For where envy and rivalry are, there also are unrest and every vile deed. 003:017 The wisdom from above is first of all pure, then peaceful, courteous, not self-willed, full of compassion and kind actions, free from favouritism and from all insincerity. 003:018 And peace, for those who strive for peace, is the seed of which the harvest is righteousness. 004:001 What causes wars and contentions among you? Is it not the cravings which are ever at war within you for various pleasures? 004:002 You covet things and yet cannot get them; you commit murder; you have passionate desires and yet cannot gain your end; you begin to fight and make war. You have not, because you do not pray; 004:003 or you pray and yet do not receive, because you pray wrongly, your object being to waste what you get on some pleasure or another. 004:004 You unfaithful women, do you not know that friendship with the world means enmity to God? Therefore whoever is bent on being friendly with the world makes himself an enemy to God. 004:005 Or do you suppose that it is to no purpose that the Scripture says, "The Spirit which He has caused to dwell in our hearts yearns jealously over us"? 004:006 But He gives more abundant grace, as is implied in His saying, "God sets Himself against the haughty, but to the lowly He gives grace." 004:007 Submit therefore to God: resist the Devil, and he will flee from you. 004:008 Draw near to God, and He will draw near to you. Cleanse your hands, you sinners, and make your hearts pure, you who are half-hearted towards God. 004:009 Afflict yourselves and mourn and weep aloud; let your laughter be turned into grief, and your gladness into shame. 004:010 Humble yourselves in the presence of the Lord, and He will exalt you. 004:011 Do not speak evil of one another, brethren. The man who speaks evil of a brother-man or judges his brother-man speaks evil of the Law and judges the Law. But if you judge the Law, you are no longer one who obeys the Law, but one who judges it. 004:012 The only real Lawgiver and Judge is He who is able to save or to destroy. Who are you to sit in judgement on your fellow man? 004:013 Come, you who say, "To-day or to-morrow we will go to this or that city, and spend a year there and carry on a successful business," 004:014 when, all the while, you do not even know what will happen to-morrow. For what is the nature of your life? Why, it is but a mist, which appears for a short time and then is seen no more. 004:015 Instead of that you ought to say, "If it is the Lord's will, we shall live and do this or that." 004:016 But, as the case stands, it is in mere self-confidence that you boast: all such boasting is evil. 004:017 If, however, a man knows what it is right to do and yet does not do it, he commits a sin. 005:001 Come, you rich men, weep aloud and howl for your sorrows which will soon be upon you. 005:002 Your treasures have rotted, and your piles of clothing are moth-eaten; 005:003 your gold and your silver have become covered with rust, and the rust on them will give evidence against you, and will eat your flesh like fire. You have hoarded up wealth in these last days. 005:004 I tell you that the pay of the labourers who have gathered in your crops-pay which you are keeping back-is calling out against you; and the outcries of those who have been your reapers have entered into the ears of the Lord of the armies of Heaven. 005:005 Here on earth you have lived self-indulgent and profligate lives. You have stupefied yourselves with gross feeding; but a day of slaughter has come. 005:006 You have condemned-you have murdered-the righteous man: he offers no resistance. 005:007 Be patient therefore, brethren, until the Coming of the Lord. Notice how eagerly a farmer waits for a valuable crop! He is patient over it till it has received the early and the later rain. 005:008 So you also must be patient: keeping up your courage; for the Coming of the Lord is now close at hand. 005:009 Do not cry out in condemnation of one another, brethren, lest you come under judgement. I tell you that the Judge is standing at the door. 005:010 In illustration, brethren, of persecution patiently endured take the Prophets who have spoken as messengers from the Lord. 005:011 Remember that we call those blessed who endured what they did. You have also heard of Job's patient endurance, and have seen the issue of the Lord's dealings with him- how full of tenderness and pity the Lord is. 005:012 But above all things, my brethren, do not swear, either by Heaven or by the earth, or with any other oath. Let your `yes' be simply `yes,' and your `no' be simply `no;' that you may not come under condemnation. 005:013 Is one of you suffering? Let him pray. Is any one in good spirits? Let him sing a psalm. 005:014 Is any one ill? Let him send for the Elders of the Church, and let them pray over him, after anointing him with oil in the name of the Lord. 005:015 And the prayer of faith will restore the sick man, and the Lord will raise him up to health; and if he has committed sins, they shall be forgiven. 005:016 Therefore confess your sins to one another, and pray for one another, so that you may be cured. The heartfelt supplication of a righteous man exerts a mighty influence. 005:017 Elijah was a man with a nature similar to ours, and he earnestly prayed that there might be no rain: and no rain fell on the land for three years and six months. 005:018 Again he prayed, and the sky gave rain and the land yielded its crops. 005:019 My brethren, if one of you strays from the truth and some one brings him back, 005:020 let him know that he who brings a sinner back from his evil ways will save the man's soul from death and throw a veil over a multitude of sins.

BOOK 43 JOHN

001:001 In the beginning was the Word, and the Word was with God, and the Word was God. 001:002 He was in the beginning with God. 001:003 All things came into being through Him, and apart from Him nothing that exists came into being. 001:004 In Him was Life, and that Life was the Light of men. 001:005 The Light shines in the darkness, and the darkness has not overpowered it. 001:006 There was a man sent from God, whose name was John. 001:007 He came as a witness, in order that he might give testimony concerning the Light-so that all might believe through him. 001:008 He was not the Light, but he existed that he might give testimony concerning the Light. 001:009 The true Light was that which illumines every man by its coming into the world. 001:010 He was in the world, and the world came into existence through Him, and the world did not recognize Him. 001:011 He came to the things that were His own, and His own people gave Him no welcome. 001:012 But all who have received Him, to them-that is, to those who trust in His name-He has given the privilege of becoming children of God; 001:013 who were begotten as such not by human descent, nor through an impulse of their own nature, nor through the will of a human father, but from God. 001:014 And the Word came in the flesh, and lived for a time in our midst, so that we saw His glory-the glory as of the Father's only Son, sent from His presence. He was full of grace and truth. 001:015 John gave testimony concerning Him and cried aloud, saying, "This is He of whom I said, `He who is coming after me has been put before me,' for He was before me." 001:016 For He it is from whose fulness we have all received, and grace upon grace. 001:017 For the Law was given through Moses; grace and truth came through Jesus Christ. 001:018 No human eye has ever seen God: the only Son, who is in the Father's bosom-He has made Him known. 001:019 This also is John's testimony, when the Jews sent to him a deputation of Priests and Levites from Jerusalem to ask him who he was. 001:020 He avowed-he did not conceal the truth, but avowed, "I am not the Christ." 001:021 "What then?" they inquired; "are you Elijah?" "I am not," he said. "Are you the Prophet?" "No," he answered. 001:022 So they pressed the question. "Who are you?" they said-"that we may take an answer to those who sent us. What account do you give of yourself?" 001:023 "I am the voice," he replied, "of one crying aloud, `Make straight the Lord's way in the Desert,' fulfilling the words of the Prophet Isaiah." 001:024 They were Pharisees who had been sent. 001:025 Again they questioned him. "Why then do you baptize," they said, "if you are neither the Christ nor Elijah nor the Prophet?" 001:026 "I baptize in water only," John answered, "but in your midst stands One whom you do not know- 001:027 He who is to come after me, and whose sandal-strap I am not worthy to unfasten." 001:028 This conversation took place at Bethany beyond the Jordan, where John was baptizing. 001:029 The next day John saw Jesus coming towards him and exclaimed, "Look, that is the Lamb of God who is to take away the sin of the world! 001:030 This is He about whom I said, `After me is to come One who has been put before me, because He was before me.' 001:031 I did not yet know Him; but that He may be openly shown to Israel is the reason why I have come baptizing in water." 001:032 John also gave testimony by stating: "I have seen the Spirit coming down like a dove out of Heaven; and it remained upon Him. 001:033 I did not yet know Him, but He who sent me to baptize in water said to me, "`The One on whom you see the Spirit coming down, and remaining, He it is who baptizes in the Holy Spirit.' 001:034 "This I have seen, and I have become a witness that He is the Son of God." 001:035 Again the next day John was standing with two of his disciples, 001:036 when he saw Jesus passing by, and said, "Look! that is the Lamb of God!" 001:037 The two disciples heard his exclamation, and they followed Jesus. 001:038 Then Jesus turned round, and seeing them following He asked them, "What is your wish?" "Rabbi," they replied-`Rabbi' means `Teacher'-"where are you staying?" 001:039 "Come and you shall see," He said. So they went and saw where He was staying, and they remained and spent that day with Him. It was then about ten o'clock in the morning. 001:040 Andrew, Simon Peter's brother, was one of the two who heard John's exclamation and followed Jesus. 001:041 He first found his own brother Simon, and said to him, "We have found the Messiah!"-that is to say, the Anointed One. 001:042 He brought him to Jesus. Jesus looked at him and said, "You are Simon, son of John: you shall be called Cephas"-that is to say, Peter (or `Rock'). 001:043 The next day, having decided to leave Bethany and go into Galilee, Jesus found Philip, and invited him to follow Him. 001:044 (Now Philip came from Bethsaida, the same town as Andrew and Peter.) 001:045 Then Philip found Nathanael, and said to him, "We have found him about whom Moses in the Law wrote, as well as the

Prophets-Jesus, the son of Joseph, a man of Nazareth." 001:046 "Can anything good come out of Nazareth?" replied Nathanael. "Come and see," said Philip. 001:047 Jesus saw Nathanael approaching, and said of him, "Look! here is a true Israelite, in whom there is no deceitfulness!" 001:048 "How do you know me?" Nathanael asked. "Before Philip called you," said Jesus, "when you were under the fig-tree I saw you." 001:049 "Rabbi," cried Nathanael, "you are the Son of God, you are Israel's King!" 001:050 "Because I said to you, `I saw you under the fig-tree,'" replied Jesus, "do you believe? You shall see greater things than that." 001:051 "I tell you all in most solemn truth," He added, "that you shall see Heaven opened wide, and God's angels going up, and coming down to the Son of Man." 002:001 Two days later there was a wedding at Cana in Galilee, and the mother of Jesus was there, 002:002 and Jesus also was invited and His disciples. 002:003 Now the wine ran short; whereupon the mother of Jesus said to Him, "They have no wine." 002:004 "Leave the matter in my hands," He replied; "the time for me to act has not yet come." 002:005 His mother said to the attendants, "Whatever he tells you to do, do it." 002:006 Now there were six stone jars standing there (in accordance with the Jewish regulations for purification), each large enough to hold twenty gallons or more. 002:007 Jesus said to the attendants, "Fill the jars with water." And they filled them to the brim. 002:008 Then He said, "Now, take some out, and carry it to the President of the feast." 002:009 So they carried some to him. And no sooner had the President tasted the water now turned into wine, than-not knowing where it came from, though the attendants who had drawn the water knew- he called to the bridegroom 002:010 and said to him, "It is usual to put on the good wine first, and when people have drunk freely, then that which is inferior. But you have kept the good wine till now." 002:011 This, the first of His miracles, Jesus performed at Cana in Galilee, and thus displayed His glorious power; and His disciples believed in Him. 002:012 Afterwards He went down to Capernaum-He, and His mother, and His brothers, and His disciples; and they made a short stay there. 002:013 But the Jewish Passover was approaching, and for this Jesus went up to Jerusalem. 002:014 And He found in the Temple the dealers in cattle and sheep and in pigeons, and the money-changers sitting there. 002:015 So He plaited a whip of rushes, and drove all-both sheep and bullocks-out of the Temple. The small coin of the brokers He upset on the ground and overturned their tables. 002:016 And to the pigeon-dealers He said, "Take these things away. Do not turn my Father's house into a market." 002:017 This recalled to His disciples the words of Scripture, "My zeal for Thy House will consume me." 002:018 So the Jews asked Him, "What proof of your authority do you exhibit to us, seeing that you do these things?" 002:019 "Demolish this Sanctuary," said Jesus, "and in three days I will rebuild it." 002:020 "It has taken forty-six years," replied the Jews, "to build this Sanctuary, and will you rebuild it in three days?" 002:021 But He was speaking of the Sanctuary of His body. 002:022 When however He had risen from among the dead, His disciples recollected that He had said this; and they believed the Scripture and the teaching which Jesus had given them. 002:023 Now when He was in Jerusalem, at the Festival of the Passover, many became believers in Him through watching the miracles He performed. 002:024 But for His part, Jesus did not trust Himself to them, because He knew them all, 002:025 and did not need any one's testimony concerning a man, for He of Himself knew what was in the man. 003:001 Now there was one of the Pharisees whose name was Nicodemus- a ruler among the Jews. 003:002 He came to Jesus by night and said, "Rabbi, we know that you are a teacher from God; for no one can do these miracles which you are doing, unless God is with him. 003:003 "In most solemn truth I tell you," answered Jesus, "that unless a man is born anew he cannot see the Kingdom of God." 003:004 "How is it possible," Nicodemus asked, "for a man to be born when he is old? Can he a second time enter his mother's womb and be born?" 003:005 "In most solemn truth I tell you," replied Jesus, "that unless a man is born of water and the Spirit, he cannot enter the Kingdom of God. 003:006 Whatever has been born of the flesh is flesh, and whatever has been born of the Spirit is spirit. 003:007 Do not be astonished at my telling you, `You must all be born anew.' 003:008 The wind blows where it chooses, and you hear its sound, but you do not know where it comes from or where it is going. So is it with every one who has been born of the Spirit." 003:009 "How is all this possible?" asked Nicodemus. 003:010 "Are you," replied Jesus, "`the Teacher of Israel,' and yet do you not understand these things? 003:011 In most solemn truth I tell you that we speak what we know, and give testimony of that of which we were eye-witnesses, and yet you all reject our testimony. 003:012 If I have told you earthly things and none of you believe me, how will you believe me if I tell you of things in Heaven? 003:013 There is no one who has gone up to Heaven, but there is One who has come down from Heaven, namely the Son of Man whose home is in Heaven. 003:014 And just as Moses lifted high the serpent in the Desert, so must the Son of Man be lifted up, 003:015 in order that every one who trusts in Him may have the Life of the Ages." 003:016 For so greatly did God love the world that He gave His only Son, that every one who trusts in Him may not perish but may have the Life of Ages. 003:017 For God did not send His Son into the world to judge the world, but that the world might be saved through Him. 003:018 He who trusts in Him does not come up for judgement. He who does not trust has already received sentence, because he has not his trust resting on the name of God's only Son. 003:019 And this is the test by which men are judged-the Light has come into the world, and men loved the darkness more than they loved the Light, because their deeds were wicked. 003:020

For every wrongdoer hates the light, and does not come to the light, for fear his actions should be exposed and condemned. 003:021 But he who does what is honest and right comes to the light, in order that his actions may be plainly shown to have been done in God. 003:022 After this Jesus and His disciples went into Judaea; and there He made a stay in company with them and baptized. 003:023 And John too was baptizing at Aenon, near Salim, because there were many pools of water there; and people came and received baptism. 003:024 (For John was not yet in prison.) 003:025 As the result, a discussion having arisen on the part of John's disciples with a Jew about purification, 003:026 they came to John and reported to him, "Rabbi, he who was with you on the other side of the Jordan and to whom you bore testimony is now baptizing, and great numbers of people are resorting to him." 003:027 "A man cannot obtain anything," replied John, "unless it has been granted to him from Heaven. 003:028 You yourselves can bear witness to my having said, `I am not the Christ,' but `I am His appointed forerunner.' 003:029 He who has the bride is the bridegroom; and the bridegroom's friend who stands by his side and listens to him, rejoices heartily on account of the bridegroom's happiness. Therefore this joy of mine is now complete. 003:030 He must grow greater, but I must grow less. 003:031 He who comes from above is above all. He whose origin is from the earth is not only himself from the earth, his teaching also is from the earth. He who comes from Heaven is above all. 003:032 What He has seen and heard, to that He bears witness; but His testimony no one receives. 003:033 Any man who has received His testimony has solemnly declared that God is true. 003:034 For He whom God has sent speaks God's words; for God does not give the Spirit with limitations." 003:035 The Father loves the Son and has entrusted everything to His hands. 003:036 He who believes in the Son has the Life of the Ages; he who disobeys the Son will not enter into Life, but God's anger remains upon him. 004:001 Now as soon as the Master was aware that the Pharisees had heard it said, "Jesus is gaining and baptizing more disciples than John"- 004:002 though Jesus Himself did not baptize them, but His disciples did- 004:003 He left Judaea and returned to Galilee. 004:004 His road lay through Samaria, 004:005 and so He came to Sychar, a town in Samaria near the piece of land that Jacob gave to his son Joseph. 004:006 Jacob's Well was there: and accordingly Jesus, tired out with His journey, sat down by the well to rest. It was about six o'clock in the evening. 004:007 Presently there came a woman of Samaria to draw water. Jesus asked her to give Him some water; 004:008 for His disciples were gone to the town to buy provisions. 004:009 "How is it," replied the woman, "that a Jew like you asks me, who am a woman and a Samaritan, for water?" (For Jews have no dealings with Samaritans.) 004:010 "If you had known God's free gift," replied Jesus, "and who it is that said to you, `Give me some water,' you would have asked Him, and He would have given you living water." 004:011 "Sir," she said, "you have nothing to draw with, and the well is deep; so where can you get the living water from? 004:012 Are you greater than our forefather Jacob, who gave us the well, and himself drank from it, as did also his sons and his cattle?" 004:013 "Every one," replied Jesus, "who drinks any of this water will be thirsty again; 004:014 but whoever drinks any of the water that I shall give him will never, never thirst. But the water that I shall give him will become a fountain within him of water springing up for the Life of the Ages." 004:015 "Sir," said the woman, "give me that water, that I may never be thirsty, nor continually come all the way here to draw from the well." 004:016 "Go and call your husband," said Jesus; "and come back." 004:017 "I have no husband," she replied. "You rightly say that you have no husband," said Jesus; 004:018 "for you have had five husbands, and the man you have at present is not your husband. You have spoken the truth in saying that." 004:019 "Sir," replied the woman, "I see that you are a Prophet. 004:020 Our forefathers worshipped on this mountain, but you Jews say that the place where people must worship is in Jerusalem." 004:021 "Believe me," said Jesus, "the time is coming when you will worship the Father neither on this mountain nor in Jerusalem. 004:022 You worship One of whom you know nothing. We worship One whom we know; for salvation comes from the Jews. 004:023 But a time is coming-nay, has already come-when the true worshippers will worship the Father with true spiritual worship; for indeed the Father desires such worshippers. 004:024 God is Spirit; and those who worship Him must bring Him true spiritual worship." 004:025 "I know," replied the woman, "that Messiah is coming-`the Christ,' as He is called. When He has come, He will tell us everything." 004:026 "I am He," said Jesus-"I who am now talking to you." 004:027 Just then His disciples came, and were surprised to find Him talking with a woman. Yet not one of them asked Him, "What is your wish?" or "Why are you talking with her?" 004:028 The woman however, leaving her pitcher, went away to the town, and called the people. 004:029 "Come," she said, "and see a man who has told me everything I have ever done. Can this be the Christ, do you think?" 004:030 They left the town and set out to go to Him. 004:031 Meanwhile the disciples were urging Jesus. "Rabbi," they said, "eat something." 004:032 "I have food to eat," He replied, "of which you do not know." 004:033 So the disciples began questioning one another. "Can it be," they said, "that some one has brought Him something to eat?" 004:034 "My food," said Jesus, "is to be obedient to Him who sent me, and fully to accomplish His work. 004:035 Do you not say, `It wants four months yet to the harvest'? But look round, I tell you, and observe these plains- they are already ripe for the sickle. 004:036 The reaper gets pay and gathers in a crop in preparation for the Life of the Ages, that so the sower and the reapers may rejoice together.

004:037 For it is in this that you see the real meaning of the saying, `The sower is one person, and the reaper is another.' 004:038 I sent you to reap a harvest which is not the result of your own labours. Others have laboured, and you are getting benefit from their labours." 004:039 Of the Samaritan population of that town a good many believed in Him because of the woman's statement when she declared, "He has told me all that I have ever done." 004:040 When however the Samaritans came to Him, they asked Him on all sides to stay with them; and He stayed there two days. 004:041 Then a far larger number of people believed because of His own words, 004:042 and they said to the woman, "We no longer believe in Him simply because of your statements; for we have now heard for ourselves, and we know that this man really is the Saviour of the world." 004:043 After the two days He departed, and went into Galilee; 004:044 though Jesus Himself declared that a Prophet has no honour in his own country. 004:045 When however He reached Galilee, the Galilaeans welcomed Him eagerly, having been eye-witnesses of all that He had done in Jerusalem at the Festival; for they also had been to the Festival. 004:046 So He came once more to Cana in Galilee, where He had made the water into wine. Now there was a certain officer of the King's court whose son was ill at Capernaum. 004:047 Having heard that Jesus had come from Judaea to Galilee, he came to Him and begged Him to go down and cure his son; for he was at the point of death. 004:048 "Unless you and others see miracles and marvels," said Jesus, "nothing will induce you to believe." 004:049 "Sir," pleaded the officer, "come down before my child dies." 004:050 "You may return home," replied Jesus; "your son has recovered." He believed the words of Jesus, and started back home; 004:051 and he was already on his way down when his servants met him and told him that his son was alive and well. 004:052 So he inquired of them at what hour he had shown improvement. "Yesterday, about seven o'clock," they replied, "the fever left him." 004:053 Then the father recollected that that was the time at which Jesus had said to him, "Your son has recovered," and he and his whole household became believers. 004:054 This is the second miracle that Jesus performed, after coming from Judaea into Galilee. 005:001 After this there was a Festival of the Jews, and Jesus went up to Jerusalem. 005:002 Now there is in Jerusalem near the Sheep Gate a pool, called in Hebrew `Bethesda.' It has five arcades. 005:003 In these there used to lie a great number of sick persons, and of people who were blind or lame or paralyzed. 005:004 [] 005:005 And there was one man there who had been an invalid for thirty-eight years. 005:006 Jesus saw him lying there, and knowing that he had been a long time in that condition, He asked him, "Do you wish to have health and strength?" 005:007 "Sir," replied the sufferer, "I have no one to put me into the pool when the water is moved; but while I am coming some one else steps down before me." 005:008 "Rise," said Jesus, "take up your mat and walk." 005:009 Instantly the man was restored to perfect health, and he took up his mat and began to walk. 005:010 That day was a Sabbath. So the Jews said to the man who had been cured, "It is the Sabbath: you must not carry your mat." 005:011 "He who cured me," he replied, "said to me, `Take up your mat and walk.'" 005:012 "Who is it," they asked, "that said to you, `Take up your mat and walk'?" 005:013 But the man who had been cured did not know who it was; for Jesus had passed out unnoticed, there being a crowd in the place. 005:014 Afterwards Jesus found him in the Temple and said to him, "You are now restored to health. Do not sin any more, or a worse thing may befall you." 005:015 The man went and told the Jews that it was Jesus who had restored him to health; 005:016 and on this account the Jews began to persecute Jesus- because He did these things on the Sabbath. 005:017 His reply to their accusation was, "My Father works unceasingly, and so do I." 005:018 On this account then the Jews were all the more eager to put Him to death-because He not only broke the Sabbath, but also spoke of God as being in a special sense His Father, thus putting Himself on a level with God. 005:019 "In most solemn truth I tell you," replied Jesus, "that the Son can do nothing of Himself-He can only do what He sees the Father doing; for whatever He does, that the Son does in like manner. 005:020 For the Father loves the Son and reveals to Him all that He Himself is doing. And greater deeds than these will He reveal to Him, in order that you may wonder. 005:021 For just as the Father awakens the dead and gives them life, so the Son also gives life to whom He wills. 005:022 The Father indeed does not judge any one, but He has entrusted all judgement to the Son, 005:023 that all may honour the Son even as they honour the Father. The man who withholds honour from the Son withholds honour from the Father who sent Him. 005:024 "In most solemn truth I tell you that he who listens to my teaching and believes Him who sent me, has the Life of the Ages, and does not come under judgement, but has passed over out of death into Life. 005:025 "In most solemn truth I tell you that a time is coming- nay, has already come-when the dead will hear the voice of the Son of God, and those who hear it will live. 005:026 For just as the Father has life in Himself, so He has also given to the Son to have life in Himself. 005:027 And He has conferred on Him authority to act as Judge, because He is the Son of Man. 005:028 Wonder not at this. For a time is coming when all who are in the graves will hear His voice and will come forth- 005:029 they who have done what is right to the resurrection of Life, and they whose actions have been evil to the resurrection of judgement. 005:030 "I can of my own self do nothing. As I am bidden, so I judge; and mine is a just judgement, because it is not my own will that guides me, but the will of Him who sent me. 005:031 "If I give testimony concerning myself, my testimony cannot be accepted. 005:032 There is Another who gives testimony concerning me, and I know

that the testimony is true which He offers concerning me. 005:033 "You
sent to John, and he both was and still is a witness to the truth. 005:034 But
the testimony on my behalf which I accept is not from man; though I say all
this in order that you may be saved. 005:035 He was the lamp that burned
and shone, and for a time you were willing to be gladdened by his light.
005:036 "But the testimony which I have is weightier than that of John; for
the work the Father has assigned to me for me to bring it to completion-the
very work which I am doing- affords testimony concerning me that the
Father has sent me. 005:037 And the Father who sent me, *He* has given
testimony concerning me. None of you have ever either heard His voice or
seen what He is like. 005:038 Nor have you His word dwelling within you,
for you refuse to believe Him whom *He* has sent. 005:039 "You search
the Scriptures, because you suppose that in them you will find the Life of
the Ages; and it is those Scriptures that yield testimony concerning me;
005:040 and yet you are unwilling to come to me that you may have Life.
005:041 "I do not accept glory from man, 005:042 but I know you well, and
I know that in your hearts you do not really love God. 005:043 I have come
as my Father's representative, and you do not receive me. If some one else
comes representing only himself, him you will receive. 005:044 How is it
possible for you to believe, while you receive glory from one another and
have no desire for the glory that comes from the only God? 005:045 "Do
not suppose that I will accuse you to the Father. There is one who accuses
you, namely Moses, on whom your hope rests. 005:046 For if you believe
Moses, you would believe me; for he wrote about me. 005:047 But if you
disbelieve his writings, how are you to believe my words?" 006:001 After
this Jesus went away across the Lake of Galilee (that is, the Lake of
Tiberias). 006:002 A vast multitude followed Him, because they witnessed
the miracles on the sick which He was constantly performing. 006:003 Then
Jesus went up the hill, and sat there with His disciples. 006:004 The Jewish
Festival, the Passover, was at hand. 006:005 And when He looked round
and saw an immense crowd coming towards Him, He said to Philip,
"Where shall we buy bread for all these people to eat?" 006:006 He said this
to put Philip to the test, for He Himself knew what He was going to do.
006:007 "Seven pounds' worth of bread," replied Philip, "is not enough for
them all to get even a scanty meal." 006:008 One of His disciples, Andrew,
Simon Peter's brother, said to Him, 006:009 "There is a boy here with five
barley loaves and a couple of fish: but what is that among so many?"
006:010 "Make the people sit down," said Jesus. The ground was covered
with thick grass; so they sat down, the adult men numbering about 5,000.
006:011 Then Jesus took the loaves, and after giving thanks He distributed
them to those who were resting on the ground; and also the fish in like
manner-as much as they desired. 006:012 When all were fully satisfied, He
said to His disciples, "Gather up the broken portions that remain over, so

that nothing be lost." 006:013 Accordingly they gathered them up; and with the fragments of the five barley loaves-the broken portions that remained over after they had done eating-they filled twelve baskets. 006:014 Thereupon the people, having seen the miracle He had performed, said, "This is indeed the Prophet who was to come into the world." 006:015 Perceiving, however, that they were about to come and carry Him off by force to make Him a king, Jesus withdrew again up the hill alone by Himself. 006:016 When evening came on, His disciples went down to the Lake. 006:017 There they got on board a boat, and pushed off to cross the Lake to Capernaum. By this time it had become dark, and Jesus had not yet joined them. 006:018 The Lake also was getting rough, because a strong wind was blowing. 006:019 When, however, they had rowed three or four miles, they sáw Jesus walking on the water and coming near the boat. 006:020 They were terrified; but He called to them. "It is I," He said, "do not be afraid." 006:021 Then they were willing to take Him on board; and in a moment the boat reached the shore at the point to which they were going. 006:022 Next morning the crowd who were still standing about on the other side of the Lake found that there had been but one small boat there, and they had seen that Jesus did not go on board with His disciples, but that His disciples went away without Him. 006:023 Yet a number of small boats came from Tiberias to the neighbourhood of the place where they had eaten the bread after the Lord had given thanks. 006:024 When however the crowd saw that neither Jesus nor His disciples were there, they themselves also took boats and came to Capernaum to look for Jesus. 006:025 So when they had crossed the Lake and had found Him, they asked Him, "Rabbi, when did you come here?" 006:026 "In most solemn truth I tell you," replied Jesus, "that you are searching for me not because you have seen miracles, but because you ate the loaves and had a hearty meal. 006:027 Bestow your pains not on the food which perishes, but on the food that remains unto the Life of the Ages- that food which will be the Son of Man's gift to you; for on Him the Father, God, has set His seal." 006:028 "What are we to do," they asked, "in order to carry out the things that God requires?" 006:029 "This," replied Jesus, "is above all the thing that God requires- that you should be believers in Him whom He has sent." 006:030 "What miracle then," they asked, "do you perform for us to see and become believers in you? What do you *do*? 006:031 Our forefathers ate the manna in the Desert, as it is written, `He gave them bread out of Heaven to eat'." 006:032 "In most solemn truth I tell you," replied Jesus, "that Moses did not give you the bread out of Heaven, but my Father is giving you the bread-the true bread-out of Heaven. 006:033 For God's bread is that which comes down out of Heaven and gives Life to the world." 006:034 "Sir," they said, "always give us that bread." 006:035 "I am the bread of Life," replied Jesus; "he who comes to me shall never hunger, and he who believes in me shall never, never thirst. 006:036 But it is as I have said to you: you have seen me and yet you do not believe. 006:037 Every one whom the Father gives me will come to me, and him who comes to me I will never on any account drive away. 006:038 For I have left Heaven and have come down to earth not to seek my own pleasure, but to do the will of Him who sent me. 006:039 And this is the will of Him who sent me, that of all that He has given me I should lose nothing, but should raise it to life on the last day. 006:040 For this is my Father's will, that every one who fixes his gaze on the Son of God and believes in Him should have the Life of the Ages, and I will raise him to life on the last day." 006:041 Now the Jews began to find fault about Him because of His claiming to be the bread which came down out of Heaven. 006:042 They kept asking, "Is not this man Joseph's son? Is he not Jesus, whose father and mother we know? What does he mean by now saying, `I have come down out of Heaven'?" 006:043 "Do not thus find fault among yourselves," replied Jesus; 006:044 "no one can come to me unless the Father who sent me draws him; then I will raise him to life on the last day. 006:045 It stands written in the Prophets, `And they shall all of them be taught by God'. Every one who listens to the Father and learns from Him comes to me. 006:046 No one has ever seen the Father-except Him who is from God. He has seen the Father. 006:047 "In most solemn truth I tell you that he who believes has the Life of the Ages. 006:048 I am the bread of Life. 006:049 Your forefathers ate the manna in the Desert, and they died. 006:050 Here is the bread that comes down out of Heaven that a man may eat it and not die. 006:051 I am the living bread come down out of Heaven. If a man eats this bread, he shall live for ever. Moreover the bread which I will give is my flesh given for the life of the world." 006:052 This led to an angry debate among the Jews. "How can this man," they argued, "give us his flesh to eat?" 006:053 "In most solemn truth I tell you," said Jesus, "that unless you eat the flesh of the Son of Man and drink His blood, you have no Life in you. 006:054 He who eats my flesh and drinks my blood has the Life of the Ages, and I will raise him up on the last day. 006:055 For my flesh is true food, and my blood is true drink. 006:056 He who eats my flesh and drinks my blood remains in union with me, and I remain in union with him. 006:057 As the ever-living Father has sent me, and I live because of the Father, so also he who eats me will live because of me. 006:058 This is the bread which came down out of Heaven; it is unlike that which your forefathers ate-for they ate and yet died. He who eats this bread shall live for ever." 006:059 Jesus said all this in the synagogue while teaching at Capernaum. 006:060 Many therefore of His disciples, when they heard it, said, "This is hard to accept. Who can listen to such teaching?" 006:061 But, knowing in Himself that His disciples were dissatisfied about it, Jesus asked them, 006:062 "Does this seem incredible to you? What then if you were to see the Son of Man ascending again where He was before?

006:063 It is the spirit which gives Life. The flesh confers no benefit whatever. The words I have spoken to you are spirit and are Life. 006:064 But there are some of you who do not believe." For Jesus knew from the beginning who those were that did not believe, and who it was that would betray Him. 006:065 So He added, "That is why I told you that no one can come to me unless it be granted him by the Father." 006:066 Thereupon many of His disciples left Him and went away, and no longer associated with Him. 006:067 Jesus therefore appealed to the Twelve. "Will you go also?" He asked. 006:068 "Master," replied Simon Peter, "to whom shall we go? Your teachings tell us of the Life of the Ages. 006:069 And we have come to believe and know that *you* are indeed the Holy One of God." 006:070 "Did not I choose you-the Twelve?" said Jesus, "and even of you one is a devil." 006:071 He alluded to Judas, the son of Simon the Iscariot. For he it was who, though one of the Twelve, was afterwards to betray Him. 007:001 After this Jesus moved from place to place in Galilee. He would not go about in Judaea, because the Jews were seeking an opportunity to kill Him. 007:002 But the Jewish Festival of the Tent-Pitching was approaching. 007:003 So His brothers said to Him, "Leave these parts and go into Judaea, that not only we but your disciples also may witness the miracles which you perform. 007:004 For no one acts in secret, desiring all the while to be himself known publicly. Since you are doing these things, show yourself openly to the world." 007:005 For even His brothers were not believers in Him. 007:006 "My time," replied Jesus, "has not yet come, but for you any time is suitable. 007:007 It is impossible for the world to hate you; but me it does hate, because I give testimony concerning it that its conduct is evil. 007:008 As for you, go up to the Festival. I do not now go up to this Festival, because my time is not yet fully come." 007:009 Such was His answer, and He remained in Galilee. 007:010 When however His brothers had gone up to the Festival, then He also went up, not openly, but as it were privately. 007:011 Meanwhile the Jews at the Festival were looking for Him and were inquiring, "Where is he?" 007:012 Among the mass of the people there was much muttered debate about Him. Some said, "He is a good man." Others said, "Not so: he is imposing on the people." 007:013 Yet for fear of the Jews no one spoke out boldly about Him. 007:014 But when the Festival was already half over, Jesus went up to the Temple and commenced teaching. 007:015 The Jews were astonished. "How does this man know anything of books," they said, "although he has never been at any of the schools?" 007:016 Jesus answered their question by saying, "My teaching does not belong to me, but comes from Him who sent me. 007:017 If any one is willing to do His will, he shall know about the teaching, whether it is from God or originates with me. 007:018 The man whose teaching originates with himself aims at his own glory. He who aims at the glory of Him who sent him teaches the truth, and there is no deception in him. 007:019 Did not Moses give you the Law? And yet not a man of you obeys the Law. Why do you want to kill me?" 007:020 "You are possessed by a demon," replied the crowd; "no one wants to kill you." 007:021 "One deed I have done," replied Jesus, "and you are all full of wonder. 007:022 Consider therefore. Moses gave you the rite of circumcision (not that it began with Moses, but with your earlier forefathers), and even on a Sabbath day you circumcise a child. 007:023 If a child is circumcised even on a Sabbath day, are you bitter against me because I have restored a man to perfect health on a Sabbath day? 007:024 Do not form superficial judgements, but form the judgements that are just." 007:025 Some however of the people of Jerusalem said, "Is not this the man they are wanting to kill? 007:026 But here he is, speaking openly and boldly, and they say nothing to him! Can the Rulers really have ascertained that this man is the Christ? 007:027 And yet we know this man, and we know where he is from; but as for the Christ, when He comes, no one can tell where He is from." 007:028 Jesus therefore, while teaching in the Temple, cried aloud, and said, "Yes, you know me, and you know where I am from. And yet I have not come of my own accord; but there is One who has sent me, an Authority indeed, of whom you have no knowledge. 007:029 I know Him, because I came from Him, and He sent me." 007:030 On hearing this they wanted to arrest Him; yet not a hand was laid on Him, because His time had not yet come. 007:031 But from among the crowd a large number believed in Him. "When the Christ comes," they said, "will He perform more miracles than this teacher has performed?" 007:032 The Pharisees heard the people thus expressing their various doubts about Him, and the High Priests and the Pharisees sent some officers to apprehend Him. 007:033 So Jesus said, "Still for a short time I am with you, and then I go my way to Him who sent me. 007:034 You will look for me and will not find me, and where I am you cannot come." 007:035 The Jews therefore said to one another, "Where is he about to betake himself, so that we shall not find him? Will he betake himself to the Dispersion among the Gentiles, and teach the Gentiles? 007:036 What do those words of his mean, `You will look for me, but will not find me, and where I am you cannot come'?" 007:037 On the last day of the Festival-the great day-Jesus stood up and cried aloud. "Whoever is thirsty," He said, "let him come to me and drink. 007:038 He who believes in me, from within him-as the Scripture has said-rivers of living water shall flow." 007:039 He referred to the Spirit which those who believed in Him were to receive; for the Spirit was not bestowed as yet, because Jesus had not yet been glorified. 007:040 After listening to these discourses, some of the crowd began to say, "This is beyond doubt the Prophet." 007:041 Others said, "He is the Christ." But others again, "Not so, for is the Christ to come from Galilee? 007:042 Has not the Scripture declared that the Christ is to come of the family of David and from Bethlehem, David's village?" 007:043 So there was a violent dissension among the people on His account. 007:044 Some of them wanted at once to arrest Him, but no one laid hands upon Him. 007:045 Meanwhile the officers returned to the High Priests and Pharisees, who asked them, "Why have you not brought him?" 007:046 "No mere man has ever spoken as this man speaks," said the officers. 007:047 "Are *you* deluded too?" replied the Pharisees; 007:048 "has any one of the Rulers or of the Pharisees believed in him? 007:049 But this rabble who understand nothing about the Law are accursed!" 007:050 Nicodemus interposed-he who had formerly gone to Jesus, being himself one of them. 007:051 "Does our Law," he asked, "judge a man without first hearing what he has to say and ascertaining what his conduct is?" 007:052 "Do you also come from Galilee?" they asked in reply. "Search and see for yourself that no Prophet is of Galilaean origin." 007:053 [So they went away to their several homes; 008:001 but Jesus went to the Mount of Olives. 008:002 At break of day however He returned to the Temple, and there the people came to Him in crowds. He seated Himself; 008:003 and was teaching them when the Scribes and the Pharisees brought to Him a woman who had been found committing adultery. They made her stand in the centre of the court, and they put the case to Him. 008:004 "Rabbi," they said, "this woman has been found in the very act of committing adultery. 008:005 Now, in the Law, Moses has ordered us to stone such women to death. But what do you say?" 008:006 They asked this in order to put Him to the test, so that they might have some charge to bring against Him. But Jesus leant forward and began to write with His finger on the ground. 008:007 When however they persisted with their question, He raised His head and said to them, "Let the sinless man among you be the first to throw a stone at her." 008:008 Then He leant forward again, and again began to write on the ground. 008:009 They listened to Him, and then, beginning with the eldest, took their departure, one by one, till all were gone. And Jesus was left behind alone-and the woman in the centre of the court. 008:010 Then, raising His head, Jesus said to her, "Where are they? Has no one condemned you?" 008:011 "No one, Sir," she replied. "And *I* do not condemn you either," said Jesus; "go, and from this time do not sin any more."] 008:012 Once more Jesus addressed them. "I am the Light of the world," He said; "the man who follows me shall certainly not walk in the dark, but shall have the light of Life." 008:013 "You are giving testimony about yourself," said the Pharisees; "your testimony is not true." 008:014 "Even if I am giving testimony about myself," replied Jesus, "my testimony is true; for I know where I came from and where I am going, but you know neither of these two things. 008:015 You judge according to appearances: I am judging no one. 008:016 And even if I do judge, my judgement is just; for I am not alone, but the Father who sent me is with me. 008:017 In your own Law, too, it is written that the testimony of two men is true. 008:018 I am one giving testimony about myself, and the Father who sent me gives testimony about me." 008:019 "Where is your Father?" they asked. "You know my Father as little as you know me." He replied; "if you knew me, you would know my Father also." 008:020 These sayings He uttered in the Treasury, while teaching in the Temple; yet no one arrested Him, because His time had not yet come. 008:021 Again He said to them, "I am going away. Then you will try to find me, but you will die in your sins. Where I am going, it is impossible for you to come." 008:022 The Jews began to ask one another, "Is he going to kill himself, do you think, that he says, `Where I am going, it is impossible for you to come'?" 008:023 "You," He continued, "are from below, I am from above: you are of this present world, I am not of this present world. 008:024 That is why I told you that you will die in your sins; for, unless you believe that I am He, that is what will happen." 008:025 "You-who are you?" they asked. "How is it that I am speaking to you at all?" replied Jesus. 008:026 "Many things I have to speak and to judge concerning you. But He who sent me is true, and the things which I have heard from Him are those which I have come into the world to speak." 008:027 They did not perceive that He was speaking to them of the Father. 008:028 So Jesus added, "When you have lifted up the Son of Man, then you will know that I am He. Of myself I do nothing; but as the Father has taught me, so I speak. 008:029 And He who sent me is with me. He has not left me alone: for I do always what is pleasing to Him." 008:030 As He thus spoke, many became believers in Him. 008:031 Jesus therefore said to those of the Jews who had now believed in Him, "As for you, if you hold fast to my teaching, then you are truly my disciples; 008:032 and you shall know the Truth, and the Truth will make you free." 008:033 "We are descendants of Abraham," they answered, "and have never at any time been in slavery to any one. What do those words of yours mean, `You shall become free'?" 008:034 "In most solemn truth I tell you," replied Jesus, "that every one who commits sin is the slave of sin. 008:035 Now a slave does not remain permanently in his master's house, but a son does. 008:036 If then the Son shall make you free, you will be free indeed. 008:037 You are descendants of Abraham, I know; but you want to kill me, because my teaching gains no ground within you. 008:038 The words I speak are those I have learnt in the presence of the Father. Therefore you also should do what you have heard from your father." 008:039 "Our father is Abraham," they said. "If you were Abraham's children," replied Jesus, "it is Abraham's deeds that you would be doing. 008:040 But, in fact, you are longing to kill me, a man who has spoken to you the truth which I have heard from God. Abraham did not do that. 008:041 You are doing the deeds of your father." "We," they replied, "are not illegitimate children. We have one Father, namely God." 008:042 "If God were your Father," said Jesus, "you would love me; for it is from

God that I came and I am now here. I have not come of myself, but *He* sent me. 008:043 How is it you do not understand me when I speak? It is because you cannot bear to listen to my words. 008:044 The father whose sons you are is the Devil; and you desire to do what gives him pleasure. *He* was a murderer from the beginning, and does not stand firm in the truth-for there is no truth in him. Whenever he utters his lie, he utters it out of his own store; for he is a liar, and the father of lies. 008:045 But because I speak the truth, you do not believe me. 008:046 Which of *you* convicts me of sin? If I speak the truth, why do you not believe me? 008:047 He who is a child of God listens to God's words. You do not listen to them: and why? It is because you are not God's children." 008:048 "Are we not right," answered the Jews, "in saying that you are a Samaritan and are possessed by a demon?" 008:049 "I am not possessed by a demon," replied Jesus. "On the contrary I honour my Father, and you dishonour me. 008:050 I, however, am not aiming at glory for myself: there is One who aims at glory for me-and who judges. 008:051 In most solemn truth I tell you that if any one shall have obeyed my teaching he shall in no case ever see death." 008:052 "Now," exclaimed the Jews, "we know that you are possessed by a demon. Abraham died, and so did the Prophets, and yet *you* say, `If any one shall have obeyed my teaching, he shall in no case ever taste death.' 008:053 Are you really greater than our forefather Abraham? For he died. And the prophets died. Who do you make yourself out to be?" 008:054 "Were I to glorify myself," answered Jesus, "I should have no real glory. There is One who glorifies me-namely my Father, who you say is your God. 008:055 You do not know Him, but I know Him perfectly; and were I to deny my knowledge of Him, I should resemble you, and be a liar. On the contrary I do know Him, and I obey His commands. 008:056 Abraham your forefather exulted in the hope of seeing my day: and he saw it, and was glad." 008:057 "You are not yet fifty years old," cried the Jews, "and have you seen Abraham?" 008:058 "In most solemn truth," answered Jesus, "I tell you that before Abraham came into existence, I am." 008:059 Thereupon they took up stones with which to stone Him, but He hid Himself and went away out of the Temple. 009:001 As He passed by, He saw a man who had been blind from his birth. 009:002 So His disciples asked Him, "Rabbi, who sinned-this man or his parents-that he was born blind?" 009:003 "Neither he nor his parents sinned," answered Jesus, "but he was born blind in order that God's mercy might be openly shown in him. 009:004 We must do the works of Him who sent me while there is daylight. Night is coming on, when no one can work. 009:005 When I am in the world, I am the Light of the world." 009:006 After thus speaking, He spat on the ground, and then, kneading the dust and spittle into clay, He smeared the clay over the man's eyes and said to him, 009:007 "Go and wash in the pool of Siloam"-the name means `Sent.' So he went and washed his eyes, and returned able to see. 009:008 His neighbours, therefore, and the other people to whom he had been a familiar object because he was a beggar, began asking, "Is not this the man who used to sit and beg?" 009:009 "Yes it is," replied some of them. "No it is not," said others, "but he is like him." His own statement was, "I am the man." 009:010 "How then were your eyes opened?" they asked. 009:011 "He whose name is Jesus," he answered, "made clay and smeared my eyes with it, and then told me to go to Siloam and wash. So I went and washed and obtained sight." 009:012 "Where is he?" they inquired, but the man did not know. 009:013 They brought him to the Pharisees-the man who had been blind. 009:014 Now the day on which Jesus made the clay and opened the man's eyes was the Sabbath. 009:015 So the Pharisees renewed their questioning as to how he had obtained his sight. "He put clay on my eyes," he replied, "and I washed, and now I can see." 009:016 This led some of the Pharisees to say, "That man has not come from God, for he does not keep the Sabbath." "How is it possible for a bad man to do such miracles?" argued others. 009:017 And there was a division among them. So again they asked the once blind man, "What is your account of him?-for he opened your eyes." "He is a Prophet," he replied. 009:018 The Jews, however, did not believe the statement concerning him- that he had been blind and had obtained his sight-until they called his parents and asked them, 009:019 "Is this your son, who you say was born blind? How is it then that he can now see?" 009:020 "We know," replied the parents, "that this is our son and that he was born blind; 009:021 but how it is that he can now see or who has opened his eyes we do not know. Ask him himself; he is of full age; he himself will give his own account of it." 009:022 Such was their answer, because they were afraid of the Jews; for the Jews had already settled among themselves that if any one should acknowledge Jesus as the Christ, he should be excluded from the synagogue. 009:023 That was why his parents said, "He is of full age: ask him himself." 009:024 A second time therefore they called the man who had been blind, and said, "Give God the praise: we know that that man is a sinner." 009:025 "Whether he is a sinner or not, I do not know," he replied; "one thing I know-that I was once blind and that now I can see." 009:026 "What did he do to you?" they asked; "how did he open your eyes?" 009:027 "I have told you already," he replied, "and you did not listen to me. Why do you want to hear it again? Do you also mean to be disciples of his?" 009:028 Then they railed at him, and said, "You are that man's disciple, but we are disciples of Moses. 009:029 We know that God spoke to Moses; but as for this fellow we do not know where he comes from." 009:030 "Why, this is marvellous!" the man replied; "you do not know where he comes from, and yet he has opened my eyes! 009:031 We know that God does not listen to bad people, but that if any one is a God-fearing man and obeys Him, to him He listens. 009:032 From the beginning of the world such a thing was never heard of as that any one should open the eyes of a man blind from his birth. 009:033 Had that man not come from God, he could have done nothing." 009:034 "You," they replied, "were wholly begotten and born in sin, and do *you* teach *us*?" And they put him out of the synagogue. 009:035 Jesus heard that they had done this. So having found him, He asked him, "Do you believe in the Son of God?" 009:036 "Who is He, Sir?" replied the man. "Tell me, so that I may believe in Him." 009:037 "You have seen Him," said Jesus; "and not only so: He is now speaking to you." 009:038 "I believe, Sir," he said. And he threw himself at His feet. 009:039 "I came into this world," said Jesus, "to judge men, that those who do not see may see, and that those who do see may become blind." 009:040 These words were heard by those of the Pharisees who were present, and they asked Him, "Are *we* also blind?" 009:041 "If you were blind," answered Jesus, "you would have no sin; but as a matter of fact you boast that you see. So your sin remains!" 010:001 "In most solemn truth I tell you that the man who does not enter the sheepfold by the door, but climbs over some other way, is a thief and a robber. 010:002 But he who enters by the door is the shepherd of the sheep. 010:003 To him the porter opens the door, and the sheep hear his voice; and he calls his own sheep by their names and leads them out. 010:004 When he has brought out his own sheep-all of them- he walks at the head of them; and the sheep follow him, because they know his voice. 010:005 But a stranger they will by no means follow, but will run away from him, because they do not know the voice of strangers." 010:006 Jesus spoke to them in this figurative language, but they did not understand what He meant. 010:007 Again therefore Jesus said to them, "In most solemn truth I tell you that I am the Door of the sheep. 010:008 All who have come before me are thieves and robbers; but the sheep would not listen to them. 010:009 I am the Door. If any one enters by me, he will find safety, and will go in and out and find pasture. 010:010 The thief comes only to steal and kill and destroy: I have come that they may have Life, and may have it in abundance. 010:011 "I am the Good Shepherd. A good shepherd lays down his very life for the sheep. 010:012 The hired servant-one who is not a shepherd and does not own the sheep-no sooner sees the wolf coming than he leaves the sheep and runs away; and the wolf worries and scatters them. 010:013 For he is only a hired servant and cares nothing for the sheep. 010:014 "I am the Good Shepherd. And I know my sheep and my sheep know me, 010:015 just as the Father knows me and I know the Father; and I am laying down my life for the sheep. 010:016 I have also other sheep-which do not belong to this fold. Those also I must bring, and they will listen to my voice; and they shall become one flock under one Shepherd. 010:017 For this reason my Father loves me, because I am laying down my life in order to receive it back again. 010:018 No one is taking it away from me, but I myself am laying it down. I am authorized to lay it down, and I am authorized to receive it back again. This is the command I received from my Father." 010:019 Again there arose a division among the Jews because of these words. 010:020 Many of them said, "He is possessed by a demon and is mad. Why do you listen to him?" 010:021 Others argued, "That is not the language of a demoniac: and can a demon open blind men's eyes?" 010:022 The Dedication Festival came on in Jerusalem. It was winter, 010:023 and Jesus was walking in the Temple in Solomon's Portico, 010:024 when the Jews gathered round Him and kept asking Him, "How long do you mean to keep us in suspense? If you are the Christ, tell us so plainly." 010:025 "I have told you," answered Jesus, "and you do not believe. The deeds that I do in my Father's name-they give testimony about me. 010:026 But you do not believe, because you are not my sheep. 010:027 My sheep listen to my voice, and I know them, and they follow me. 010:028 I give them the Life of the Ages, and they shall never, never perish, nor shall any one wrest them from my hand. 010:029 What my Father has given me is more precious than all besides; and no one is able to wrest anything from my Father's hand. 010:030 I and the Father are one." 010:031 Again the Jews brought stones with which to stone Him. 010:032 Jesus remonstrated with them. "Many good deeds," He said, "have I shown you as coming from the Father; for which of them are you going to stone me?" 010:033 "For no good deed," the Jews replied, "are we going to stone you, but for blasphemy, and because you, who are only a man, are making yourself out to be God." 010:034 "Does it not stand written in your Law," replied Jesus, "`I said, you are gods'? 010:035 If those to whom God's word was addressed are called gods (and the Scripture cannot be annulled), 010:036 how is it that you say to one whom the Father consecrated and sent into the world, `You are blaspheming,' because I said, `I am God's Son'? 010:037 If the deeds I do are not my Father's deeds, do not believe me. 010:038 But if they are, then even if you do not believe me, at least believe the deeds, that you may know and see clearly that the Father is in me, and that I am in the Father." 010:039 This made them once more try to arrest Him, but He withdrew out of their power. 010:040 Then He went away again to the other side of the Jordan, to the place where John had been baptizing at first; and there He stayed. 010:041 Large numbers of people also came to Him. Their report was, "John did not work any miracle, but all that John said about this Teacher was true." 010:042 And many became believers in Him there. 011:001 Now a certain man, named Lazarus, of Bethany, was lying ill- Bethany being the village of Mary and her sister Martha. 011:002 (It was the Mary who poured the perfume over the Lord and wiped His feet with her hair, whose brother Lazarus was ill.) 011:003 So the sisters sent to Him to say, "Master, he whom you hold dear is ill." 011:004 Jesus received the message and said, "This illness is not to end in death, but is to promote the glory of God, in order that the Son of

God may be glorified by it." 011:005 Now Jesus loved Martha, and her sister, and Lazarus. 011:006 When, however, He heard that Lazarus was ill, He still remained two days in that same place. 011:007 Then, after that, He said to the disciples, "Let us return to Judaea." 011:008 "Rabbi," exclaimed the disciples, "the Jews have just been trying to stone you, and do you think of going back there again?" 011:009 "Are there not twelve hours in the day?" replied Jesus. "If any one walks in the daytime, he does not stumble-because he sees the light of this world. 011:010 But if a man walks by night, he does stumble, because the light is not in him." 011:011 He said this, and afterwards He added, "Our friend Lazarus is sleeping, but I will go and wake him." 011:012 "Master," said the disciples, "if he is asleep he will recover." 011:013 Now Jesus had spoken of his death, but they thought He referred to the rest taken in ordinary sleep. 011:014 So then He told them plainly, 011:015 "Lazarus is dead; and for your sakes I am glad I was not there, in order that you may believe. But let us go to him." 011:016 "Let us go also," Thomas, the Twin, said to his fellow disciples, "that we may die with him." 011:017 On His arrival Jesus found that Lazarus had already been three days in the tomb. 011:018 Bethany was near Jerusalem, the distance being a little less than two miles; 011:019 and a considerable number of the Jews were with Martha and Mary, having come to express sympathy with them on the death of their brother. 011:020 Martha, however, as soon as she heard the tidings, "Jesus is coming," went to meet Him; but Mary remained sitting in the house. 011:021 So Martha came and spoke to Jesus. "Master, if you had been here," she said, "my brother would not have died. 011:022 And even now I know that whatever you ask God for, God will give you." 011:023 "Your brother shall rise again," replied Jesus. 011:024 "I know," said Martha, "that he will rise again at the resurrection, on the last day." 011:025 "I am the Resurrection and the Life," said Jesus; "he who believes in me, even if he has died, he shall live; 011:026 and every one who is living and is a believer in me shall never, never die. Do you believe this?" 011:027 "Yes, Master," she replied; "I thoroughly believe that you are the Christ, the Son of God, who was to come into the world." 011:028 After saying this, she went and called her sister Mary privately, telling her, "The Rabbi is here and is asking for you." 011:029 So she, on hearing that, rose up quickly to go to Him. 011:030 Now Jesus was not yet come into the village, but was still at the place where Martha had met Him. 011:031 So the Jews who were with Mary in the house sympathizing with her, when they saw that she had risen hastily and had gone out, followed her, supposing that she was going to the tomb to weep aloud there. 011:032 Mary then, when she came to Jesus and saw Him, fell at His feet and exclaimed, "Master, if you had been here, my brother would not have died." 011:033 Seeing her weeping aloud, and the Jews in like manner weeping who had come with her, Jesus, curbing the strong emotion of His spirit, 011:034 though deeply troubled, asked them, "Where have you laid him?" "Master, come and see," was their reply. 011:035 Jesus wept. 011:036 "See how dear he held him," said the Jews. 011:037 But others of them asked, "Was this man who opened the blind man's eyes unable to prevent this man from dying?" 011:038 Jesus, however, again restraining His strong feeling, came to the tomb. It was a cave, and a stone had been laid against the mouth of it. 011:039 "Take away the stone," said Jesus. Martha, the sister of the dead man, exclaimed, "Master, by this time there is a foul smell; for it is three days since he died." 011:040 "Did I not promise you," replied Jesus, "that if you believe, you shall see the glory of God?" 011:041 So they removed the stone. Then Jesus lifted up His eyes and said, "Father, I thank Thee that Thou hast heard me. 011:042 I know that Thou always hearest me; but for the sake of the crowd standing round I have said this-that they may believe that Thou didst send me." 011:043 After speaking thus, He called out in a loud voice, "Lazarus, come out." 011:044 The dead man came out, his hands and feet wrapped in cloths, and his face wrapped round with a towel. "Untie him," said Jesus, "and let him go free." 011:045 Thereupon a considerable number of the Jews-namely those who had come to Mary and had witnessed His deeds- became believers in Him; 011:046 though some of them went off to the Pharisees and told them what He had done. 011:047 Therefore the High Priests and the Pharisees held a meeting of the Sanhedrin. "What steps are we taking?" they asked one another; "for this man is performing a great number of miracles. 011:048 If we leave him alone in this way, everybody will believe in him, and the Romans will come and blot out both our city and our nation." 011:049 But one of them, named Caiaphas, being High Priest that year, said, "You know nothing about it. 011:050 You do not reflect that it is to your interest that one man should die for the people rather than the whole nation perish." 011:051 It was not as a mere man that he thus spoke. But being High Priest that year he was inspired to declare that Jesus was to die for the nation, 011:052 and not for the nation only, but in order to unite into one body all the far-scattered children of God. 011:053 So from that day forward they planned and schemed in order to put Him to death. 011:054 Therefore Jesus no longer went about openly among the Jews, but He left that neighbourhood and went into the district near the Desert, to a town called Ephraim, and remained there with the disciples. 011:055 The Jewish Passover was coming near, and many from that district went up to Jerusalem before the Passover, to purify themselves. 011:056 They therefore looked out for Jesus, and asked one another as they stood in the Temple, "What do you think?-will he come to the Festival at all?" 011:057 Now the High Priests and the Pharisees had issued orders that if any one knew where He was, he should give information, so that they might arrest Him. 012:001 Jesus, however, six days before the Passover, came to Bethany, where Lazarus was whom He had raised from the dead. 012:002 So they gave a dinner there in honour of Jesus, at which Martha waited at table, but Lazarus was one of the guests who were with Him. 012:003 Availing herself of the opportunity, Mary took a pound weight of pure spikenard, very costly, and poured it over His feet, and wiped His feet with her hair, so that the house was filled with the fragrance of the perfume. 012:004 Then said Judas (the Iscariot, one of the Twelve-the one who afterwards betrayed Jesus), 012:005 "Why was not that perfume sold for 300 shillings and the money given to the poor?" 012:006 The reason he said this was not that he cared for the poor, but that he was a thief, and that being in charge of the money-box, he used to steal what was put into it. 012:007 But Jesus interposed. "Do not blame her," He said, "allow her to have kept it for the time of my preparation for burial. 012:008 For the poor you always have with you, but you have not me always." 012:009 Now it became widely known among the Jews that Jesus was there; but they came not only on His account, but also in order to see Lazarus whom He had brought back to life. 012:010 The High Priests, however, consulted together to put Lazarus also to death, 012:011 for because of him many of the Jews left them and became believers in Jesus. 012:012 The next day a great crowd of those who had come to the Festival, hearing that Jesus was coming to Jerusalem, 012:013 took branches of the palm trees and went out to meet Him, shouting as they went, "God save him! Blessings on him who comes in the name of the Lord-even on the King of Israel!" 012:014 And Jesus, having procured a young ass, sat upon it, just as the Scripture says, 012:015 "Fear not, Daughter of Zion! See, thy King is coming riding on an ass's colt." 012:016 The meaning of this His disciples did not understand at the time; but after Jesus was glorified they recollected that this was written about Him, and that they had done this to Him. 012:017 The large number of people, however, who had been present when He called Lazarus out of the tomb and brought him back to life, related what they had witnessed. 012:018 This was also why the crowd came to meet Him, because they had heard of His having performed that miracle. 012:019 The result was that the Pharisees said among themselves, "Observe how idle all your efforts are! The world is gone after him!" 012:020 Now some of those who used to come up to worship at the Festival were Greeks. 012:021 They came to Philip, of Bethsaida in Galilee, with the request, "Sir, we wish to see Jesus." 012:022 Philip came and told Andrew: Andrew and Philip told Jesus. 012:023 His answer was, "The time has come for the Son of Man to be glorified. 012:024 In most solemn truth I tell you that unless the grain of wheat falls into the ground and dies, it remains what it was- a single grain; but that if it dies, it yields a rich harvest. 012:025 He who holds his life dear, is destroying it; and he who makes his life of no account in this world shall keep it to the Life of the Ages. 012:026 If a man wishes to be my servant, let him follow me; and where I am, there too shall my servant be. If a man wishes to be my servant, the Father will honour him. 012:027 Now is my soul full of trouble; and what shall I say? Father, save me from this hour. But for this purpose I have come to this hour. 012:028 Father, glorify Thy name." Thereupon there came a voice from the sky, "I have glorified it and will also glorify it again." 012:029 The crowd that stood by and heard it, said that there had been thunder. Others said, "An angel spoke to him." 012:030 "It is not for my sake," said Jesus, "that that voice came, but for your sakes. 012:031 Now is a judgement of this world: now will the Prince of this world be driven out. 012:032 And I-if I am lifted up from the earth-will draw all men to me." 012:033 He said this to indicate the kind of death He would die. 012:034 The crowd answered Him, "We have heard out of the Law that the Christ remains for ever. In what sense do you say that the Son of Man must be lifted up? Who is that Son of Man?" 012:035 "Yet a little while," He replied, "the light is among you. Be faithful to the light that you have, for fear darkness should overtake you; for a man who walks in the dark does not know where he is going. 012:036 In the degree that you have light, believe in the Light, so that you may become sons of Light." Jesus said this, and went away and hid Himself from them. 012:037 But though He had performed such great miracles in their presence, they did not believe in Him- 012:038 in order that the words of Isaiah the Prophet might be fulfilled, "Lord, who has believed our preaching? And the arm of the Lord-to whom has it been unveiled?" 012:039 For this reason they were unable to believe-because Isaiah said again, 012:040 "He has blinded their eyes and made their minds callous, lest they should see with their eyes and perceive with their minds, and should turn, and I should heal them." 012:041 Isaiah uttered these words because he saw His glory; and he spoke of Him. 012:042 Nevertheless even from among the Rulers many believed in Him. But because of the Pharisees they did not avow their belief, for fear they should be shut out from the synagogue. 012:043 For they loved the glory that comes from men rather than the glory that comes from God. 012:044 But Jesus cried aloud, "He who believes in me, believes not so much in me, as in Him who sent me; 012:045 and he who sees me sees Him who sent me. 012:046 I have come like light into the world, in order that no one who believes in me may remain in the dark. 012:047 And if any one hears my teachings and regards them not, I do not judge him; for I did not come to judge the world, but to save the world. 012:048 He who sets me at naught and does not receive my teachings is not left without a judge: the Message which I have spoken will judge him on the last day. 012:049 Because I have not spoken on my own authority; but the Father who sent me, Himself gave me a command what to say and in what words to speak. 012:050 And I know that His command is the Life of the Ages. What therefore I speak, I speak just as the Father has bidden me." 013:001 Now just before the Feast of the Passover this incident took place. Jesus knew that the time had come for Him to leave this world and go to the Father; and having loved His own who were in the world, He loved them to the end. 013:002 While supper was proceeding, the Devil having by this time suggested to Judas Iscariot, the son of Simon, the thought of betraying Him, Jesus, 013:003 although He knew that the Father had put everything into His hands, and that He had come forth from God and was now going to God, 013:004 rose from the table, threw off His upper garments, and took a towel and tied it round Him. 013:005 Then He poured water into a basin, and proceeded to wash the feet of the disciples and to wipe them with the towel which He had put round Him. 013:006 When He came to Simon Peter, Peter objected. "Master," he said, "are *you* going to wash my feet?" 013:007 "What I am doing," answered Jesus, "for the present you do not know, but afterwards you shall know." 013:008 "Never, while the world lasts," said Peter, "shall you wash my feet." "If I do not wash you," replied Jesus, "you have no share with me." 013:009 "Master," said Peter, "wash not only my feet, but also my hands and my head." 013:010 "Any one who has lately bathed," said Jesus, "does not need to wash more than his feet, but is clean all over. And you my disciples are clean, and yet this is not true of all of you." 013:011 For He knew who was betraying Him, and that was why He said, "You are not all of you clean." 013:012 So after He had washed their feet, put on His garments again, and returned to the table, He said to them, "Do you understand what I have done to you? 013:013 You call me `The Rabbi' and `The Master,' and rightly so, for such I am. 013:014 If I then, your Master and Rabbi, have washed your feet, it is also your duty to wash one another's feet. 013:015 For I have set you an example in order that you may do what I have done to you. 013:016 In most solemn truth I tell you that a servant is not superior to his master, nor is a messenger superior to him who sent him. 013:017 If you know all this, blessed are you if you act accordingly. 013:018 I am not speaking of all of you. I know whom I have chosen, but things are as they are in order that the Scripture may be fulfilled, which says, `He who eats my bread has lifted up his heel against me.' 013:019 From this time forward I tell you things before they happen, in order that when they do happen you may believe that I am He. 013:020 In most solemn truth I tell you that he who receives whoever I send receives me, and that he who receives me receives Him who sent me." 013:021 After speaking thus Jesus was troubled in spirit and said with deep earnestness, "In most solemn truth I tell you that one of you will betray me." 013:022 The disciples began looking at one another, at a loss to know to which of them He was referring. 013:023 There was at table one of His disciples-the one Jesus loved- reclining with his head on Jesus's bosom. 013:024 Making a sign therefore to him, Simon Peter said, "Tell us to whom he is referring." 013:025 So he, having his head on Jesus's bosom, leaned back and asked,

"Master, who is it?" 013:026 "It is the one," answered Jesus, "for whom I shall dip this piece of bread and to whom I shall give it." Accordingly He dipped the piece of bread, and took it and gave it to Judas, the son of the Iscariot Simon. 013:027 Then, after Judas had received the piece of bread, Satan entered into him. "Lose no time about it," said Jesus to him. 013:028 But why He said this no one else at the table understood. 013:029 Some, however, supposed that because Judas had the money-box Jesus meant, "Buy what we require for the Festival," or that he should give something to the poor. 013:030 So Judas took the piece of bread and immediately went out. And it was night. 013:031 So when he was gone out, Jesus said, "Now is the Son of Man glorified, and God is glorified in Him. 013:032 Moreover God will glorify Him in Himself, and will glorify Him without delay. 013:033 Dear children, I am still with you a little longer. You will seek me, but, as I said to the Jews, `Where I am going you cannot come,' so for the present I say to you. 013:034 A new commandment I give you, to love one another; that as I have loved you, you also may love one another. 013:035 It is by this that every one will know that you are my disciples- if you love one another." 013:036 "Master," inquired Simon Peter, "where are you going?" "Where I am going," replied Jesus, "you cannot be my follower now, but you shall be later." 013:037 "Master," asked Peter again, "why cannot I follow you now? I will lay down my life on your behalf. 013:038 "You say you will lay down your life on my behalf!" said Jesus; "in most solemn truth I tell you that the cock will not crow before you have three times disowned me." 014:001 "Let not your hearts be troubled. Trust in God: trust in me also. 014:002 In my Father's house there are many resting-places. Were it otherwise, I would have told you; for I am going to make ready a place for you. 014:003 And if I go and make ready a place for you, I will return and take you to be with me, that where I am you also may be. 014:004 And where I am going, you all know the way." 014:005 "Master," said Thomas, "we do not know where you are going. In what sense do we know the way?" 014:006 "I am the Way," replied Jesus, "and the Truth and the Life. No one comes to the Father except through me. 014:007 If you-all of you-knew me, you would fully know my Father also. From this time forward you know Him and have seen Him." 014:008 "Master," said Philip, "cause us to see the Father: that is all we need." 014:009 "Have I been so long among you," Jesus answered, "and yet you, Philip, do not know me? He who has seen me has seen the Father. How can *you* ask me, `Cause us to see the Father'? 014:010 Do you not believe that I am in the Father and that the Father is in me? The things that I tell you all I do not speak on my own authority: but the Father dwelling within me carries on His own work. 014:011 Believe me, all of you, that I am in the Father and that the Father is in me; or at any rate, believe me because of what I do. 014:012 In most solemn truth I tell you that he who trusts in me- the things which I do he shall do also; and greater things than these he shall do, because I am going to the Father. 014:013 And whatever any of you ask in my name, I will do, in order that the Father may be glorified in the Son. 014:014 If you make any request of me in my name, I will do it. 014:015 "If you love me, you will obey my commandments. 014:016 And I will ask the Father, and He will give you another Advocate to be for ever with you-the Spirit of truth. 014:017 That Spirit the world cannot receive, because it does not see Him or know Him. You know Him, because He remains by your side and is in you. 014:018 I will not leave you bereaved: I am coming to you. 014:019 Yet a little while and the world will see me no more, but you will see me: because I live, you also shall live. 014:020 At that time you will know that I am in my Father, and that you are in me, and that I am in you. 014:021 He who has my commandments and obeys them-he it is who loves me. And he who loves me will be loved by my Father, and I will love him and will clearly reveal myself to him." 014:022 Judas (not the Iscariot) asked, "Master, how is it that you will reveal yourself clearly to us and not to the world?" 014:023 "If any one loves me," replied Jesus, "he will obey my teaching; and my Father will love him, and we will come to him and make our home with him. 014:024 He who has no love for me does not obey my teaching; and yet the teaching to which you are listening is not mine, but is the teaching of the Father who sent me. 014:025 "All this I have spoken to you while still with you. 014:026 But the Advocate, the Holy Spirit whom the Father will send at my request, will teach you everything, and will bring to your memories all that I have said to you. 014:027 Peace I leave with you: my own peace I give to you. It is not as the world gives its greetings that I give you peace. Let not your hearts be troubled or dismayed. 014:028 "You heard me say to you, `I am going away, and yet I am coming to you.' If you loved me, you would have rejoiced because I am going to the Father; for the Father is greater than I am. 014:029 I have now told you before it comes to pass, that when it has come to pass you may believe. 014:030 In future I shall not talk much with you, for the Prince of this world is coming. And yet in me he has nothing; 014:031 but it is in order that the world may know that I love the Father, and that it is in obedience to the command which the Father gave me that I thus act. Rise, let us be going." 015:001 "I am the Vine-the True Vine, and my Father is the vine-dresser. 015:002 Every branch in me-if it bears no fruit, He takes away; and every branch that bears fruit He prunes, that it may bear more fruit. 015:003 Already you are cleansed-through the teaching which I have given you. 015:004 Continue in me, and let me continue in you. Just as the branch cannot bear fruit of itself-that is, if it does not continue in the vine-so neither can you if you do not continue in me. 015:005 I am the Vine, you are the branches. He who continues in me and in whom I continue bears abundant fruit, for apart from me you can do nothing. 015:006 If any one does not continue in me, he is like the unfruitful branch which is at once thrown away and then withers up. Such branches they gather up and throw into the fire and they are burned. 015:007 "If you continue in me and my sayings continue in you, ask what you will and it shall be done for you. 015:008 By this is God glorified-by your bearing abundant fruit and thus being true disciples of mine. 015:009 As the Father has loved me, I have also loved you: continue in my love. 015:010 If you obey my commands, you will continue in my love, as I have obeyed my Father's commands and continue in His love. 015:011 "These things I have spoken to you in order that I may have joy in you, and that your joy may become perfect. 015:012 This is my commandment to you, to love one another as I have loved you. 015:013 No one has greater love than this-a man laying down his life for his friends. 015:014 You are my friends, if you do what I command you. 015:015 No longer do I call you servants, because a servant does not know what his master is doing; but I have called you friends, because all that I have heard from the Father I have made known to you. 015:016 It is not you who chose me, but it is I who chose you and appointed you that you might go and be fruitful and that your fruit might remain; so that whatever petition you present to the Father in my name He may give you. 015:017 "Thus I command you to love one another. 015:018 If the world hates you, remember that it has first had me as the fixed object of its hatred. 015:019 If you belonged to the world, the world would love its own property. But because you do not belong to the world, and I have chosen you out of the world-for that reason the world hates you. 015:020 Bear in mind what I said to you, `A servant is not superior to his master.' If they have persecuted me, they will also persecute you: if they have obeyed my teaching, they will obey yours also. 015:021 But they will inflict all this suffering upon you on account of your bearing my name-because they do not know Him who sent me. 015:022 "If I had not come and spoken to them, they would have had no sin; but as the case stands they are without excuse for their sin. 015:023 He who hates me hates my Father also. 015:024 If I had not done among them, as I have, such miracles as no one else ever did, they would have had no sin; but they have in fact seen and also hated both me and my Father. 015:025 But this has been so, in order that the saying may be fulfilled which stands written in their Law, `They have hated me without any reason.' 015:026 "When the Advocate is come whom I will send to you from the Father's presence-the Spirit of Truth who comes forth from the Father's presence-He will be a witness concerning me. 015:027 And you also are witnesses, because you have been with me from the first. 016:001 "These things I have spoken to you in order to clear stumbling-blocks out of your path. 016:002 You will be excluded from the synagogues; nay more, the time is coming when any one who has murdered one of you will suppose he is offering service to God. 016:003 And they will do these things because they have failed to recognize the Father and to discover who I am. 016:004 But I have spoken these things to you in order that when the time for their accomplishment comes you may remember them, and may recollect that I told you. I did not, however, tell you all this at first, because I was still with you. 016:005 But now I an returning to Him who sent me; and not one of you asks me where I am going. 016:006 But grief has filled your hearts because I have said all this to you. 016:007 "Yet it is the truth that I am telling you-it is to your advantage that I go away. For unless I go away, the Advocate will not come to you; but if I go, I will send Him to you. 016:008 And He, when He comes, will convict the world in respect of sin, of righteousness, and of judgement;- 016:009 of sin, because they do not believe in me; 016:010 of righteousness, because I am going to the Father, and you will no longer see me; 016:011 of judgement, because the Prince of this world is under sentence. 016:012 "I have much more to say to you, but you are unable at present to bear the burden of it. 016:013 But when He has come-the Spirit of Truth-He will guide you into all the truth. For He will not speak as Himself originating what He says, but all that He hears He will speak, and He will make known the future to you. 016:014 He will glorify me, because He will take of what is mine and will make it known to you. 016:015 Everything that the Father has is mine; that is why I said that the Spirit of Truth takes of what is mine and will make it known to you. 016:016 "A little while and you see me no more, and again a little while and you shall see me." 016:017 Some of His disciples therefore said to one another, "What does this mean which He is telling us, `A little while and you do not see me, and again a little while and you shall see me,' and `Because I am going to the Father'?" 016:018 So they asked one another repeatedly, "What can that `little while' mean which He speaks of? We do not understand His words." 016:019 Jesus perceived that they wanted to ask Him, and He said, "Is this what you are questioning one another about- my saying, `A little while and you do not see me, and again a little while and you shall see me'? 016:020 In most solemn truth I tell you that you will weep aloud and lament, but the world will be glad. You will mourn, but your grief will be turned into gladness. 016:021 A woman, when she is in labour, has sorrow, because her time has come. But when she has given birth to the babe, she no longer remembers the pain, because of her joy at a child being born into the world. 016:022 So you also now have sorrow; but I shall see you again, and your hearts will be glad, and your gladness no one will take away from you. 016:023 You will put no questions to me then. "In most solemn truth I tell you that whatever you ask the Father for in my name He will give you. 016:024 As yet you have not asked for anything in my name: ask, and you shall receive, that your hearts may be filled with gladness. 016:025 "All this I have spoken to you in veiled language. The time is coming when I shall no longer speak to you in veiled language, but will tell you about the Father in plain words. 016:026 At that time you will make your requests in my name; and I do not promise to ask the Father on your behalf, 016:027 for the Father Himself holds you dear, because you have held me dear and have believed that I came from the Father's presence. 016:028 I came from the Father and have come into the world. Again I am leaving the world and am going to the Father." 016:029 "Ah, now you are using plain language," said His disciples, "and are uttering no figure of speech! 016:030 Now we know that you have all knowledge, and do not need to be pressed with questions. Through this we believe that you came from God." 016:031 "Do you at last believe?" replied Jesus. 016:032 "Remember that the time is coming, nay, has already come, for you all to be dispersed each to his own home and to leave me alone. And yet I am not alone, for the Father is with me. 016:033 "I have spoken all this to you in order that in me you may have peace. In the world you have affliction. But keep up your courage: *I* have won the victory over the world." 017:001 When Jesus had thus spoken, He raised his eyes towards Heaven and said, "Father, the hour has come. Glorify Thy Son that the Son may glorify Thee; 017:002 even as Thou hast given Him authority over all mankind, so that on all whom Thou hast given Him He may bestow the Life of the Ages. 017:003 And in this consists the Life of the Ages-in knowing Thee the only true God and Jesus Christ whom Thou hast sent. 017:004 I have glorified Thee on earth, having done perfectly the work which by Thine appointment has been mine to do. 017:005 And now, Father, do Thou glorify me in Thine own presence, with the glory that I had in Thy presence before the world existed. 017:006 "I have revealed Thy perfections to the men whom Thou gavest me out of the world. Thine they were, and Thou gavest them to me, and they have obeyed Thy message. 017:007 Now they know that whatever Thou hast given me is from Thee. 017:008 For the truths which Thou didst teach me I have taught them. And they have received them, and have known for certain that I came out from Thy presence, and have believed that Thou didst send me. 017:009 "I am making request for them: for the world I do not make any request, but for those whom Thou hast given me. Because they are Thine, 017:010 and everything that is mine is Thine, and everything that is Thine is mine; and I am crowned with glory in them. 017:011 I am now no longer in the world, but they are in the world and I am coming to Thee. "Holy Father, keep them true to Thy name- the name which Thou hast given me to bear-that they may be one, even as we are. 017:012 While I was with them, I kept them true to Thy name-the name Thou hast given me to bear-and I kept watch over them, and not one of them is lost but only he who is doomed to destruction- that the Scripture may be fulfilled. 017:013 "But now I am coming to Thee, and I speak these words while I am in the world, in order that they may have my gladness within them filling their hearts. 017:014 I have given them Thy Message, and the world has hated them, because they do not belong to the world, just as I do not belong to the world. 017:015 I do not ask that Thou wilt remove them out of the world, but that Thou wilt protect them from the Evil one. 017:016 They do not belong to the world, just as I do not belong to the world. 017:017 Make them holy in the truth: Thy Message is truth. 017:018 Just as Thou didst send me into the world, I also have sent them; 017:019 and on their behalf I consecrate myself, in order that they may become perfectly consecrated in truth. 017:020 "Nor is it for them alone that I make request. It is also for those who trust in me through their teaching; 017:021 that they may all be one, even as Thou art in me, O Father, and I am in Thee; that they also may be in us; that the world may believe that Thou didst send me. 017:022 And the glory which Thou hast given me I have given them, that they may be one, just as we are one: 017:023 I in them and Thou in me; that they may stand perfected in one; that the world may come to understand that Thou didst send me and hast loved them with the same love as that with which Thou hast loved me. 017:024 "Father, those whom Thou hast given me-I desire that where I am they also may be with me, that they may see the glory- my glory-my gift from Thee, which Thou hast given me because Thou didst love me before the creation of the world. 017:025 And, righteous Father, though the world has failed to recognize Thee, I have known Thee, and these have perceived that Thou didst send me. 017:026 And I have made known Thy name to them and will make it known, that the love with which Thou hast loved me may be in them, and that I may be in them." 018:001 After offering this prayer Jesus went out with His disciples to a place on the further side of the Ravine of the Cedars, where there was a garden which He entered- Himself and His disciples. 018:002 Now Judas also, who at that very time was betraying Him, knew the place, for Jesus had often resorted there with His disciples. 018:003 So Judas, followed by the battalion and by a detachment of the Temple police sent by the High Priests and Pharisees, came there with torches and lamps and weapons. 018:004 Jesus therefore, knowing all that was about to befall Him, went out to meet them. "Who are you looking for?" He asked them. 018:005 "For Jesus the Nazarene," was the answer. "I am he," He replied. (Now Judas who was betraying Him was also standing with them.) 018:006 As soon then as He said to them, "I am he," they went backwards and fell to the ground. 018:007 Again therefore He asked them, "Who are you looking for?" "For Jesus the Nazarene," they said. 018:008 "I have told you," replied Jesus, "that I am he. If therefore you are looking for me, let these my disciples go their way." 018:009 He made this request in order that the words He had spoken might be fulfilled, "As for those whom Thou hast given me, I have not lost one." 018:010 Simon Peter, however, having a sword, drew it, and, aiming at the High Priest's servant, cut off his right ear. The servant's name was Malchus. 018:011 Jesus therefore said to

Peter, "Put back your sword. Shall I refuse to drink the cup of sorrow which the Father has given me to drink?" 018:012 So the battalion and their tribune and the Jewish police closed in, and took Jesus and bound Him. 018:013 They then brought Him to Annas first; for Annas was the father-in-law of Caiaphas who was High Priest that year. 018:014 (It was this Caiaphas who had advised the Jews, saying, "It is to your interest that one man should die for the People.") 018:015 Meanwhile Simon Peter was following Jesus, and so also was another disciple. The latter was known to the High Priest, and went in with Jesus into the court of the High Priest's palace. 018:016 But Peter remained standing outside the door, till the disciple who was acquainted with the High Priest came out and induced the portress to let Peter in. 018:017 This led the girl, the portress, to ask Peter, "Are you also one of this man's disciples?" "No, I am not," he replied. 018:018 Now because it was cold the servants and the police had lighted a charcoal fire, and were standing and warming themselves; and Peter too remained with them, standing and warming himself. 018:019 So the High Priest questioned Jesus about His disciples and His teaching. 018:020 "As for me," replied Jesus, "I have spoken openly to the world. I have continually taught in some synagogue or in the Temple where all the Jews are wont to assemble, and I have said nothing in secret. 018:021 Why do you question me? Question those who heard what it was I said to them: these witnesses here know what I said." 018:022 Upon His saying this, one of the officers standing by struck Him with his open hand, asking Him as he did so, "Is that the way you answer the High Priest?" 018:023 "If I have spoken wrongly," replied Jesus, "bear witness to it as wrong; but if rightly, why that blow?" 018:024 So Annas sent Him bound to Caiaphas the High Priest. 018:025 But Simon Peter remained standing and warming himself, and this led to their asking him, "Are you also one of his disciples?" He denied it, and said, "No, I am not." 018:026 One of the High Priest's servants, a relative of the man whose ear Peter had cut off, said, "Did I not see you in the garden with him?" 018:027 Once more Peter denied it, and immediately a cock crowed. 018:028 So they brought Jesus from Caiaphas's house to the Praetorium. It was the early morning, and they would not enter the Praetorium themselves for fear of defilement, and in order that they might be able to eat the Passover. 018:029 Accordingly Pilate came out to them and inquired, "What accusation have you to bring against this man?" 018:030 "If the man were not a criminal," they replied, "we would not have handed him over to you." 018:031 "Take him yourselves," said Pilate, "and judge him by your Law." "We have no power," replied the Jews, "to put any man to death." 018:032 They said this that the words might be fulfilled in which Jesus predicted the kind of death He was to die. 018:033 Re-entering the Praetorium, therefore, Pilate called Jesus and asked Him, "Are *you* the King of the Jews?" 018:034 "Do you say this of yourself, or have others told it you about me?" replied Jesus. 018:035 "Am I a Jew?" exclaimed Pilate; "it is your own nation and the High Priests who have handed you over to me. What have you done?" 018:036 "My kingdom," replied Jesus, "does not belong to this world. If my kingdom did belong to this world, my subjects would have resolutely fought to save me from being delivered up to the Jews. But, as a matter of fact, my kingdom has not this origin." 018:037 "So then *you* are a king!" rejoined Pilate. "Yes," said Jesus, "you say truly that I am a king. For this purpose I was born, and for this purpose I have come into the world- to give testimony for the truth. Every one who is a friend of the truth listens to my voice." 018:038 "What is truth?" said Pilate. But no sooner had he spoken the words than he went out again to the Jews and told them, "I find no crime in him. 018:039 But you have a custom that I should release one prisoner to you at the Passover. So shall I release to you the King of the Jews?" 018:040 With a roar of voices they again cried out, saying, "Not this man, but Barabbas!" Now Barabbas was a robber. 019:001 Then Pilate took Jesus and scourged Him. 019:002 And the soldiers, twisting twigs of thorn into a wreath, put it on His head, and threw round Him a crimson cloak. 019:003 Then they began to march up to Him, saying in a mocking voice, "Hail King of the Jews!" And they struck Him with the palms of their hands. 019:004 Once more Pilate came out and said to the Jews, "See, I am bringing him out to you to let you clearly understand that I find no crime in him." 019:005 So Jesus came out, wearing the wreath of thorns and the crimson cloak. And Pilate said to them, "See, there is the man." 019:006 As soon then as the High Priests and the officers saw Him, they shouted "To the cross! To the cross!" "Take him yourselves and crucify him," said Pilate; "for I, at any rate, find no crime in him." 019:007 "We," replied the Jews, "have a Law, and in accordance with that Law he ought to die, for having claimed to be the Son of God." 019:008 More alarmed than ever, Pilate no sooner heard these words than he re-entered the Praetorium and began to question Jesus. 019:009 "What is your origin?" he asked. But Jesus gave him no answer. 019:010 "Do you refuse to speak even to me?" asked Pilate; "do you not know that I have it in my power either to release you or to crucify you?" 019:011 "You would have had no power whatever over me," replied Jesus, "had it not been granted you from above. On that account he who has delivered me up to you is more guilty than you are." 019:012 Upon receiving this answer, Pilate was for releasing Him. But the Jews kept shouting, "If you release this man, you are no friend of Caesar's. Every one who sets himself up as king declares himself a rebel against Caesar." 019:013 On hearing this, Pilate brought Jesus out, and sat down on the judge's seat in a place called the Pavement- or in Hebrew, Gabbatha. 019:014 It was the day of Preparation for the Passover, about six o'clock in the morning. Then he said to the Jews, "There is your king!" 019:015 This caused a storm of outcries, "Away with him! Away with him! Crucify him!" "Am I to crucify your king?" Pilate asked. "We have no king, except Caesar," answered the High Priests. 019:016 Then Pilate gave Him up to them to be crucified. Accordingly they took Jesus; 019:017 and He went out carrying His own cross, to the place called Skull-place-or, in Hebrew, Golgotha- 019:018 where they nailed Him to a cross, and two others at the same time, one on each side and Jesus in the middle. 019:019 And Pilate wrote a notice and had it fastened to the top of the cross. It ran thus: JESUS THE NAZARENE, THE KING OF THE JEWS. 019:020 Many of the Jews read this notice, for the place where Jesus was crucified was near the city, and the notice was in three languages-Hebrew, Latin, and Greek. 019:021 This led the Jewish High Priests to remonstrate with Pilate. "You should not write `The King of the Jews,'" they said, "but that he claimed to be King of the Jews." 019:022 "What I have written I have written," was Pilate's answer. 019:023 So the soldiers, as soon as they had crucified Jesus, took His garments, including His tunic, and divided them into four parts- one part for each soldier. The tunic was without seam, woven from the top in one piece. 019:024 So they said to one another, "Do not let us tear it. Let us draw lots for it." This happened that the Scripture might be fulfilled which says, "They shared my garments among them, and drew lots for my clothing." That was just what the soldiers did. 019:025 Now standing close to the cross of Jesus were His mother and His mother's sister, Mary the wife of Clopas, and Mary of Magdala. 019:026 So Jesus, seeing His mother, and seeing the disciple whom He loved standing near, said to His mother, "Behold, your son!" 019:027 Then He said to the disciple, "Behold, your mother!" And from that time the disciple received her into his own home. 019:028 After this, Jesus, knowing that everything was now brought to an end, said-that the Scripture might be fulfilled, "I am thirsty." 019:029 There was a jar of wine standing there. With this wine they filled a sponge, put it on the end of a stalk of hyssop, and lifted it to His mouth. 019:030 As soon as Jesus had taken the wine, He said, "It is finished." And then, bowing His head, He yielded up His spirit. 019:031 Meanwhile the Jews, because it was the day of Preparation for the Passover, and in order that the bodies might not remain on the crosses during the Sabbath (for that Sabbath was one of special solemnity), requested Pilate to have the legs of the dying men broken, and the bodies removed. 019:032 Accordingly the soldiers came and broke the legs of the first man and also of the other who had been crucified with Jesus. 019:033 Then they came to Jesus Himself: but when they saw that He was already dead, they refrained from breaking His legs. 019:034 One of the soldiers, however, made a thrust at His side with a lance, and immediately blood and water flowed out. 019:035 This statement is the testimony of an eye-witness, and it is true. He knows that he is telling the truth-in order that you also may believe. 019:036

For all this took place that the Scripture might be fulfilled which declares, "Not one of His bones shall be broken." 019:037 And again another Scripture says, "They shall look on Him whom they have pierced." 019:038 After this, Joseph of Arimathaea, who was a disciple of Jesus, but for fear of the Jews a secret disciple, asked Pilate's permission to carry away the body of Jesus; and Pilate gave him leave. So he came and removed the body. 019:039 Nicodemus too-he who at first had visited Jesus by night-came bringing a mixture of myrrh and aloes, in weight about seventy or eighty pounds. 019:040 Taking down the body they wrapped it in linen cloths along with the spices, in accordance with the Jewish mode of preparing for burial. 019:041 There was a garden at the place where Jesus had been crucified, and in the garden a new tomb, in which no one had yet been buried. 019:042 Therefore, because it was the day of Preparation for the Jewish Passover, and the tomb was close at hand, they put Jesus there. 020:001 On the first day of the week, very early, while it was still dark, Mary of Magdala came to the tomb and saw that the stone had been removed from it. 020:002 So she ran, as fast as she could, to find Simon Peter and the other disciple-the one who was dear to Jesus- and to tell them, "They have taken the Master out of the tomb, and we do not know where they have put Him." 020:003 Peter and the other disciple started at once to go to the tomb, both of them running, 020:004 but the other disciple ran faster than Peter and reached it before he did. 020:005 Stooping and looking in, he saw the linen cloths lying there on the ground, but he did not go in. 020:006 Simon Peter, however, also came, following him, and entered the tomb. There on the ground he saw the cloths; 020:007 and the towel, which had been placed over the face of Jesus, not lying with the cloths, but folded up and put by itself. 020:008 Then the other disciple, who had been the first to come to the tomb, also went in and saw and was convinced. 020:009 For until now they had not understood the inspired teaching, that He must rise again from among the dead. 020:010 Then they went away and returned home. 020:011 Meanwhile Mary remained standing near the tomb, weeping aloud. She did not enter the tomb, but as she wept she stooped and looked in, 020:012 and saw two angels clothed in white raiment, sitting one at the head and one at the feet where the body of Jesus had been. 020:013 They spoke to her. "Why are you weeping?" they asked. "Because," she replied, "they have taken away my Lord, and I do not know where they have put him." 020:014 While she was speaking, she turned round and saw Jesus standing there, but did not recognize Him. 020:015 "Why are you weeping?" He asked; "who are you looking for?" She, supposing that He was the gardener, replied, "Sir, if you have carried him away, tell me where you have put him and I will remove him." 020:016 "Mary!" said Jesus. She turned to Him. "Rabboni!" she cried in Hebrew: the word means `Teacher!' 020:017 "Do not cling to me," said Jesus, "for I have not yet ascended to

the Father. But take this message to my brethren: `I am ascending to my
Father and your Father, to my God and your God.'" 020:018 Mary of
Magdala came and brought word to the disciples. "I have seen the Master,"
she said. And she told them that He had said these things to her. 020:019
On that same first day of the week, when it was evening and, for fear of the
Jews, the doors of the house where the disciples were, were locked, Jesus
came and stood in their midst, and said to them, "Peace be to you!" 020:020
Having said this He showed them His hands and also His side; and the
disciples were filled with joy at seeing the Master. 020:021 A second time,
therefore, He said to them, "Peace be to you! As the Father sent me, I also
now send you." 020:022 Having said this He breathed upon them and said,
"Receive the Holy Spirit. 020:023 If you remit the sins of any persons, they
remain remitted to them. If you bind fast the sins of any, they remain
bound." 020:024 Thomas, one of the twelve-surnamed `the Twin'-was not
among them when Jesus came. 020:025 So the rest of the disciples told him,
"We have seen the Master!" His reply was, "Unless I see in his hands the
wound made by the nails and put my finger into the wound, and put my
hand into his side, I will never believe it." 020:026 A week later the disciples
were again in the house, and Thomas was with them, when Jesus came-
though the doors were locked- and stood in their midst, and said, "Peace be
to you." 020:027 Then He said to Thomas, "Bring your finger here and feel
my hands; bring you hand and put it into my side; and do not be ready to
disbelieve but to believe." 020:028 "My Lord and my God!" replied
Thomas. 020:029 "Because you have seen me," replied Jesus, "you have
believed. Blessed are those who have not seen and yet have believed."
020:030 There were also a great number of other signs which Jesus
performed in the presence of the disciples, which are not recorded in this
book. 020:031 But these have been recorded in order that you may believe
that He is the Christ, the Son of God, and that, through believing, you may
have Life through His name. 021:001 After this, Jesus again showed
Himself to the disciples. It was at the Lake of Tiberias. The circumstances
were as follows. 021:002 Simon Peter was with Thomas, called the Twin,
Nathanael of Cana in Galilee, the sons of Zabdi, and two others of the
Master's disciples. 021:003 Simon Peter said to them, "I am going fishing."
"We will go too," said they. So they set out and went on board their boat;
but they caught nothing that night. 021:004 When, however, day was now
dawning, Jesus stood on the beach, though the disciples did not know that
it was Jesus. 021:005 He called to them. "Children," He said, "have you any
food there?" "No," they answered. 021:006 "Throw the net in on the right
hand side," He said, "and you will find fish." So they threw the net in, and
now they could scarcely drag it along for the quantity of fish. 021:007 This
made the disciple whom Jesus loved say to Peter, "It is the Master." Simon
Peter therefore, when he heard the words, "It is the Master," drew on his

fisherman's shirt- for he had not been wearing it-put on his girdle, and sprang into the water. 021:008 But the rest of the disciples came in the small boat (for they were not far from land-only about a hundred yards off), dragging the net full of fish. 021:009 As soon as they landed, they saw a charcoal fire burning there, with fish broiling on it, and bread close by. 021:010 Jesus told them to fetch some of the fish which they had just caught. 021:011 So Simon Peter went on board the boat and drew the net ashore full of large fish, 153 in number; and yet, although there were so many, the net had not broken. 021:012 "Come this way and have breakfast," said Jesus. But not one of the disciples ventured to question Him as to who He was, for they felt sure that it was the Master. 021:013 Then Jesus came and took the bread and gave them some, and the fish in the same way. 021:014 This was now the third occasion on which Jesus showed Himself to the disciples after He had risen from among the dead. 021:015 When they had finished breakfast, Jesus asked Simon Peter, "Simon, son of John, do you love me more than these others do?" "Yes, Master," was his answer; "you know that you are dear to me." "Then feed my lambs," replied Jesus. 021:016 Again a second time He asked him, "Simon, son of John, do you love me?" "Yes, Master," he said, "you know that you are dear to me." "Then be a shepherd to my sheep," He said. 021:017 A third time Jesus put the question: "Simon, son of John, am I dear to you?" It grieved Peter that Jesus asked him the third time, "Am I dear to you?" "Master," he replied, "you know everything, you can see that you are dear to me." "Then feed my much-loved sheep," said Jesus. 021:018 "In most solemn truth I tell you that whereas, when you were young, you used to put on your girdle and walk whichever way you chose, when you have grown old you will stretch out your arms and some one else will put a girdle round you and carry you where you have no wish to go." 021:019 This He said to indicate the kind of death by which that disciple would bring glory to God; and after speaking thus He said to him, "Follow me." 021:020 Peter turned round and noticed the disciple whom Jesus loved following-the one who at the supper had leaned back on His breast and had asked, "Master, who is it that is betraying you?" 021:021 On seeing him, Peter asked Jesus, "And, Master, what about him?" 021:022 "If I desire him to remain till I come," replied Jesus, "what concern is that of yours? You, yourself, must follow me." 021:023 Hence the report spread among the brethren that that disciple would never die. Yet Jesus did not say, "He is not to die," but, "If I desire him to remain till I come, what concern is that of yours?" 021:024 That is the disciple who gives his testimony as to these matters, and has written this history; and we know that his testimony is true. 021:025 But there are also many other things which Jesus did-so vast a number indeed that if they were all described in detail, I suppose that the world itself could not contain the books that would have to be written.

BOOK 65 JUDE

001:001 Jude, a bondservant of Jesus Christ and a brother of James: To those who are in God the Father, enfolded in His love, and kept for Jesus Christ, and called. 001:002 May mercy, peace and love be abundantly granted to you. 001:003 Dear friends, since I am eager to begin a letter to you on the subject of our common salvation, I find myself constrained to write and cheer you on to the vigorous defense of the faith delivered once for all to God's people. 001:004 For certain persons have crept in unnoticed-men spoken of in ancient writings as pre-destined to this condemnation-ungodly men, who pervert the grace of our God into an excuse for immorality, and disown Jesus Christ, our only Sovereign and Lord. 001:005 I desire to remind you-although the whole matter is already familiar to you-that the Lord saved a people out of the land of Egypt, but afterwards destroyed those who had no faith. 001:006 And angels-those who did not keep the position originally assigned to them, but deserted their own proper abode- He reserves in everlasting bonds, in darkness, in preparation for the judgement of the great day. 001:007 So also Sodom and Gomorrah-and the neighboring towns in the same manner-having been guilty of gross fornication and having gone astray in pursuit of unnatural vice, are now before us as a specimen of the fire of the Ages in the punishment which they are undergoing. 001:008 Yet in just the same way these dreamers also pollute the body, while they set authority at naught and speak evil of dignities. 001:009 But Michael the Archangel, when contending with the Devil and arguing with him about the body of Moses, did not dare to pronounce judgement on him in abusive terms, but simply said, "The Lord rebuke you." 001:010 Yet these men are abusive in matters of which they know nothing, and in things which, like the brutes, they understand instinctively- in all these they corrupt themselves. 001:011 Alas for them; for they have followed in the steps of Cain; for the sake of gain they have rushed on headlong in the evil ways of Balaam; and have perished in rebellion like that of Korah! 001:012 These men-sunken rocks!-are those who share the pleasure of your love-feasts, unrestrained by fear while caring only for themselves; clouds without water, driven away by the winds; trees that cast their fruit, barren, doubly dead, uprooted; 001:013 wild waves of the sea, foaming out their own shame; wandering stars, for whom is reserved dense darkness of age-long duration. 001:014 It was also about these that Enoch, who belonged to the seventh generation from Adam, prophesied, saying, "The Lord has come, attended by myriads of His people, to execute judgement upon all, 001:015 and to convict all the ungodly of all the ungodly deeds which in their ungodliness they have committed, and of all the hard words which they, ungodly sinners as they are, have spoken against Him." 001:016 These men are murmurers, ever bemoaning their lot. Their lives are guided by their evil passions, and their mouths are full of big, boastful words, while they treat individual men with admiring reverence for the sake of the advantage they can gain. 001:017 But as for you, my dearly-loved friends, remember the words that before now were spoken by the Apostles of our Lord Jesus Christ- 001:018 how they declared to you, "In the last times there shall be scoffers, obeying only their own ungodly passions." 001:019 These are those who cause divisions. They are men of the world, wholly unspiritual. 001:020 But you, my dearly-loved friends, building yourselves up on the basis of your most holy faith and praying in the Holy Spirit, 001:021 must keep yourselves safe in the love of God, waiting for the mercy of our Lord Jesus Christ which will result in the Life of the Ages. 001:022 Some, when they argue with you, you must endeavor to convince; 001:023 others you must try to save, as brands plucked from the flames; and on others look with pity mingled with fear, while you hate every trace of their sin. 001:024 But to Him who is able to keep you safe from stumbling, and cause you to stand in the presence of His glory free from blemish and full of exultant joy- 001:025 to the only God our Saviour-through Jesus Christ our Lord, be ascribed glory, majesty, might, and authority, as it was before all time, is now, and shall be to all the Ages! Amen.

BOOK 42 LUKE

001:001 Seeing that many have attempted to draw up a narrative of the facts which are received with full assurance among us 001:002 on the authority of those who were from the beginning eye-witnesses and were devoted to the service of the divine Message, 001:003 it has seemed right to me also, after careful investigation of the facts from their commencement, to write for you, most noble Theophilus, a connected account, 001:004 that you may fully know the truth of the things which you have been taught by word of mouth. 001:005 There was in the time of Herod, the king of Judaea, a priest of the name of Zechariah, belonging to the class of Abijah. He had a wife who was a descendant of Aaron, and her name was Elizabeth. 001:006 They were both of them upright before God, blamelessly obeying all the Lord's precepts and ordinances. 001:007 But they had no child, because Elizabeth was barren; and both of them were far advanced in life. 001:008 Now while he was doing priestly duty before God in the prescribed course of his class, 001:009 it fell to his lot-according to the custom of the priesthood- to go into the Sanctuary of the Lord and burn the incense; 001:010 and the whole multitude of the people were outside praying, at the hour of incense. 001:011 Then there appeared to him an angel of the Lord standing on the right side of the altar of incense; 001:012 and Zechariah on seeing him was agitated and terrified. 001:013 But the angel said to him, "Do not be afraid, Zechariah, for your petition has been heard: and your wife Elizabeth will bear you a son, and you are to call his name John. 001:014 Gladness and exultant joy shall be yours, and many will rejoice over his birth. 001:015 For he will be great in the sight of the Lord; no wine or fermented drink shall he ever drink; but he will be filled with the Holy Spirit from the very hour of his birth. 001:016 Many of the descendants of Israel will he turn to the Lord their God; 001:017 and he will be His forerunner in the spirit and power of Elijah, to turn fathers' hearts to the children, and cause the rebellious to walk in the wisdom of the upright, to make a people perfectly ready for the lord." 001:018 "By what proof," asked Zechariah, "shall I know this? For I am an old man, and my wife is far advanced in years." 001:019 "I am Gabriel, who stand in the presence of God," answered the angel, "and I have been sent to talk with you and tell you this good news. 001:020 And now you will be dumb and unable to speak until the day when this has taken place; because you did not believe my words- words which will be fulfilled at their appointed time." 001:021 Meanwhile the people were waiting for Zechariah, and were surprised that he stayed so long in the Sanctuary. 001:022 When, however, he came out, he was unable to speak to them; and they knew that he must have seen a vision in the Sanctuary; but he kept making signs to them and continued dumb. 001:023 When his days of service were at an end, he went to his home; 001:024 and in course of time his wife Elizabeth conceived, and kept herself secluded five months. 001:025 "Thus has the Lord dealt with me," she said, "now that He has graciously taken away my reproach among men." 001:026 Now in the sixth month the angel Gabriel was sent from God to a town in Galilee called Nazareth, 001:027 to a maiden betrothed to a man of the name of Joseph, a descendant of David. The maiden's name was Mary. 001:028 So Gabriel went into the house and said to her, "Joy be to you, favoured one! the Lord is with you." 001:029 She was greatly agitated at his words, and wondered what such a greeting meant. 001:030 But the angel said, "Do not be frightened, Mary, for you have found favour with God. 001:031 You will conceive in your womb and bear a son; and you are to call His name JESUS. 001:032 He will be great and He will be called `Son of the Most High.' And the Lord God will give Him the throne of His forefather David; 001:033 and He will be King over the House of Jacob for the Ages, and of His Kingdom there will be no end." 001:034 "How can this be," Mary replied, "seeing that I have no husband?" 001:035 The angel answered, "The Holy Spirit will come upon you, and the power of the Most High will overshadow you; and for this reason your holy offspring will be called `the Son of God.' 001:036 And see, your relative Elizabeth-she also has conceived a son in her old age; and this is the sixth month with her who was called barren. 001:037 For no promise from God will be impossible of fulfilment." 001:038 "I am the Lord's maidservant," Mary replied; "may it be with me in accordance with your words!" And then the angel left her. 001:039 Not long after this, Mary rose up and went in haste into the hill country to a town in Judah. 001:040 Here she came to the house of Zechariah and greeted Elizabeth; 001:041 and as soon as Elizabeth heard Mary's greeting, the babe leapt within her. And Elizabeth was filled with the Holy Spirit, 001:042 and uttered a loud cry of joy. "Blest among women are you," she said, "and the offspring of your body is blest! 001:043 But why is this honour done me, that the mother of my Lord should come to me? 001:044 For, the moment your greeting reached my ears, the babe within me leapt for joy. 001:045 And blessed is she who has believed, for the word spoken to her from the Lord shall be fulfilled." 001:046 Then Mary said: "My soul extols the Lord, 001:047 And my spirit triumphs in God my Saviour; 001:048 Because He has not turned from His maidservant in her lowly position; For from this time forward all generations will account me happy, 001:049 Because the mighty One has done great things for me- Holy is His name!- 001:050 And His compassion is, generation after generation, Upon those who fear Him. 001:051 He has manifested His supreme strength. He has scattered those who were haughty in the thoughts of their hearts. 001:052 He has cast monarchs down from their thrones, And exalted men of low estate. 001:053 The hungry He has satisfied with choice gifts, But the rich He has sent empty-handed away. 001:054 His servant Israel He has helped, Remembering His compassion- 001:055 In fulfillment of His promises to our forefathers-For Abraham and his posterity for ever." 001:056 So Mary stayed with Elizabeth about three months, and then returned home. 001:057 Now when Elizabeth's full time was come, she gave birth to a son; 001:058 and her neighbours and relatives heard how the Lord had had great compassion on her; and they rejoiced with her. 001:059 And on the eighth day they came to circumcise the child, and were going to call him Zechariah, after his father. 001:060 His mother, however, said, "No, he is to be called John." 001:061 "There is not one of your family," they said, "who has that name." 001:062 They asked his father by signs what he wished him to be called. 001:063 So he asked for a writing-tablet, and wrote, "His name is John." And they all wondered. 001:064 Instantly his mouth and his tongue were set free, and he began to speak and bless God. 001:065 And all who lived round about them were filled with awe, and throughout the hill country of Judaea reports of all these things were spread abroad. 001:066 All who heard the story treasured it in their memories. "What then will this child be?" they said. For the lord's hand was indeed with him. 001:067 And Zechariah his father was filled with the Holy Spirit, and spoke in a rapture of praise. 001:068 "Blessed be the Lord, the God of Israel," he said, "Because He has not forgotten His people but has effected redemption for them, 001:069 And has raised up a mighty Deliverer for us In the house of David His servant- 001:070 As He has spoken from all time by the lips of His holy Prophets- 001:071 To deliver us from our foes and from the power of all who hate us. 001:072 He dealt pitifully with our forefathers, And remembered His holy covenant, 001:073 The oath which He swore to Abraham our forefather, 001:074 To grant us to be rescued from the power of our foes And so render worship to Him free from fear, 001:075 In piety and uprightness before Him all our days. 001:076 And you moreover, O child, shall be called Prophet of the Most High; For you shall go on in front before the Lord to prepare the way for

Him, 001:077 To give to His People a knowledge of salvation In the forgiveness of their sins, 001:078 Through the tender compassion of our God, Through which the daybreak from on high will come to us, 001:079 Dawning on those who now dwell in the darkness and shadow of death- To direct our feet into the path of peace." 001:080 And the child grew and became strong in character, and lived in the Desert till the time came for him to appear publicly to Israel. 002:001 Just at this time an edict was issued by Caesar Augustus for the registration of the whole Empire. 002:002 It was the first registration made during the governorship of Quirinius in Syria; 002:003 and all went to be registered-every one to the town to which he belonged. 002:004 So Joseph went up from Galilee, from the town of Nazareth, to Judaea, to David's town of Bethlehem, because he was of the house and lineage of David, 002:005 to have himself registered together with Mary, who was betrothed to him and was with child. 002:006 But while they were there, her full time came, 002:007 and she gave birth to her first-born son, and wrapped Him round, and laid Him in a manger, because there was no room for them in the inn. 002:008 Now there were shepherds in the same part of the country, keeping watch over their sheep by night in the open fields, 002:009 when suddenly an angel of the Lord stood by them, and the glory of the Lord shone round them; and they were filled with terror. 002:010 But the angel said to them, "Put away all fear; for I am bringing you good news of great joy-joy for all the People. 002:011 For a Saviour who is the Anointed Lord is born to you to-day, in the town of David. 002:012 And this is the token for you: you will find a babe wrapped in swaddling clothes and lying in a manger." 002:013 And immediately there was with the angel a multitude of the army of Heaven praising God and saying, 002:014 "Glory be to God in the highest Heavens, And on earth peace among men who please Him!" 002:015 Then, as soon as the angels had left them and returned to Heaven, the shepherds said to one another, "Let us now go over as far as Bethlehem and see this that has happened, which the Lord has made known to us." 002:016 So they made haste and came and found Mary and Joseph, with the babe lying in the manger. 002:017 And when they saw the child, they told what had been said to them about Him; 002:018 and all who listened were astonished at what the shepherds told them. 002:019 But Mary treasured up all these things, often dwelling on them in her mind. 002:020 And the shepherds returned, glorifying and praising God for all that they had heard and seen in accordance with the announcement made to them. 002:021 When eight days had passed and the time for circumcising Him had come, He was called JESUS, the name given Him by the angel before His conception in the womb. 002:022 And when the days for their purification appointed by the Law of Moses had passed, they took Him up to Jerusalem to present Him to the Lord- 002:023 as it is written in the Law of the Lord: "Every first-born male shall be called holy to the Lord." 002:024 And they also offered a sacrifice as commanded in the Law of the Lord, "a pair of turtle doves or two young pigeons." 002:025 Now there was a man in Jerusalem of the name of Symeon, an upright and God-fearing man, who was waiting for the consolation of Israel, and the Holy Spirit was upon him. 002:026 To him it had been revealed by the Holy Spirit that he should not see death until he had seen the Lord's Anointed One. 002:027 Led by the Spirit he came to the Temple; and when the parents brought in the child Jesus to do with regard to Him according to the custom of the Law, 002:028 he took Him up in his arms and blessed God and said, 002:029 "Now, O Sovereign Lord, Thou dost send Thy servant away in peace, in fulfilment of Thy word, 002:030 Because mine eyes have seen Thy salvation, 002:031 Which Thou hast made ready in the sight of all nations- 002:032 A light to shine upon the Gentiles, And the glory of Thy people Israel." 002:033 And while the child's father and mother were wondering at the words of Symeon concerning Him, 002:034 Symeon blessed them and said to Mary the mother, "This child is appointed for the falling and the uprising of many in Israel and for a token to be spoken against; 002:035 and a sword will pierce through your own soul also; that the reasonings in many hearts may be revealed." 002:036 There was also Anna, a prophetess, the daughter of Phanuel, belonging to the tribe of Asher. She was of a very great age, having had after her maidenhood seven years of married life, 002:037 and then being a widow of eighty-four years. She was never absent from the Temple, but worshipped, by day and by night, with fasting and prayer. 002:038 And coming up just at that moment, she gave thanks to God, and spoke about the child to all who were expecting the deliverance of Jerusalem. 002:039 Then, as soon as they had accomplished all that the Law required, they returned to Galilee to their own town of Nazareth. 002:040 And the child grew and became strong and full of wisdom, and the favour of God rested upon Him. 002:041 Now His parents used to go up year by year to Jerusalem at the Feast of the Passover. 002:042 And when He was twelve years old they went up as was customary at the time of the Feast, and, 002:043 after staying the full number of days, when they started back home the boy Jesus remained behind in Jerusalem. His parents did not discover this, 002:044 but supposing Him to be in the travelling company, they proceeded a day's journey. Then they searched up and down for Him among their relatives and acquaintances; 002:045 but being unable to find Him they returned to Jerusalem, making anxious inquiry for Him. 002:046 On the third day they found Him in the Temple sitting among the Rabbis, both listening to them and asking them questions, 002:047 while all who heard Him were astonished at His intelligence and at the answers He gave. 002:048 When they saw Him, they were smitten with amazement, and His mother said to Him, "My child, why have you behaved thus to us? Your father and I have been searching for you in anguish." 002:049 "Why is it that you have been searching for me?" He replied; "did you not know that it is my duty to be engaged upon my Father's business?" 002:050 But they did not understand the significance of these words. 002:051 Then He went down with them and came to Nazareth, and was always obedient to them; but His mother carefully treasured up all these incidents in her memory. 002:052 And as Jesus grew older He gained in both wisdom and stature, and in favour with God and man. 003:001 Now in the fifteenth year of the reign of Tiberius Caesar, Pontius Pilate being Governor of Judaea, Herod Tetrarch of Galilee, his brother Philip Tetrarch of Ituraea and Trachonitis, and Lysanias Tetrarch of Abilene, 003:002 during the High-priesthood of Annas and Caiaphas, a message from God came to John, the son of Zechariah, in the Desert. 003:003 John went into all the district about the Jordan proclaiming a baptism of the penitent for the forgiveness of sins; 003:004 as it is written in the book of the prophet Isaiah, "The voice of one crying aloud! `In the Desert prepare ye a road for the Lord: make His highway straight. 003:005 Every ravine shall be filled up, and every mountain and hill levelled down, the crooked places shall be turned into straight roads, and the rugged ways into smooth; 003:006 and then shall all mankind see God's salvation.'" 003:007 Accordingly John used to say to the crowds who came out to be baptized by him, "O vipers' brood, who has warned you to flee from the coming wrath? 003:008 Live lives which shall prove your change of heart; and do not begin to say to yourselves, `We have Abraham as our forefather,' for I tell you that God can raise up descendants for Abraham from these stones. 003:009 And even now the axe is lying at the root of the trees, so that every tree which fails to yield good fruit will quickly be hewn down and thrown into the fire." 003:010 The crowds repeatedly asked him, "What then are we to do?" 003:011 "Let the man who has two coats," he answered, "give one to the man who has none; and let the man who has food share it with others." 003:012 There came also a party of tax-gatherers to be baptized, and they asked him, "Rabbi, what are we to do?" 003:013 "Do not exact more than the legal amount," he replied. 003:014 The soldiers also once and again inquired of him, "And we, what are we to do?" His answer was, "Neither intimidate any one nor lay false charges; and be content with your pay." 003:015 And while the people were in suspense and all were debating in their minds whether John might possibly be the Anointed One, 003:016 he answered the question by saying to them all, "As for me, I am baptizing you with water, but One mightier than I is coming, whose very sandal-strap I am not worthy to unfasten: He will baptize you in the Holy Spirit and with fire. 003:017 His winnowing-shovel is in His hand to clear out His threshing-floor, and to gather the wheat into His storehouse; but the chaff He will burn up in fire unquenchable." 003:018 With many exhortations besides these he declared the Good News to the people. 003:019 But Herod the Tetrarch, being repeatedly rebuked by him about Herodias his brother's wife, and about all the wicked deeds that he had done, 003:020 now added this to crown all the rest, that he threw John into prison. 003:021 Now when all the people had been baptized, and Jesus also had been baptized and was praying, the sky opened, 003:022 and the Holy Spirit came down in bodily shape, like a dove, upon Him, and a voice came from Heaven, which said, "Thou art My Son, dearly loved: in Thee is My delight." 003:023 And He-Jesus-when He began His ministry, was about thirty years old. He was the son (it was supposed) of Joseph, son of Heli, 003:024 son of Matthat, son of Levi, son of Melchi, son of Jannai, son of Joseph, 003:025 son of Mattathias, son of Amos, son of Nahum, son of Esli, son of Naggai, 003:026 son of Mahath, son of Mattathias, son of Semein, son of Josech, son of Joda, 003:027 son of Johanan, son of Resa, son of Zerubbabel, son of Shealtiel, son of Neri, 003:028 son of Melchi, son of Addi, son of Cosam, son of Elmadam, son of Er, 003:029 son of Joshua, son of Eliezar, son of Jorim, son of Maththat, son of Levi, 003:030 son of Symeon, son of Judah, son of Joseph, son of Jonam, son of Eliakim, son of 003:031 Melea, son of Menna, son of Mattatha, son of Nathan, son of David, 003:032 son of Jesse, son of Obed, son of Boaz, son of Salmon, son of Nahshon, 003:033 son of Amminadab, son of Admin, son of Arni, son of Hezron, son of Perez, son of Judah, 003:034 son of Jacob, son of Isaac, son of Abraham, son of Terah, son of Nahor, 003:035 son of Serug, son of Reu, son of Peleg, son of Eber, son of Shelah, 003:036 son of Cainan, son of Arpachshad, son of Shem, son of Noah, son of Lamech, 003:037 son of Methuselah, son of Enoch, son of Jared, son of Mahalalel, son of Kenan, 003:038 son of Enosh, son of Seth, son of Adam, son of God. 004:001 Then Jesus, full of the Holy Spirit, returned from the Jordan, and was led about by the Spirit in the Desert for forty days, 004:002 tempted all the while by the Devil. During those days He ate nothing, and at the close of them He suffered from hunger. 004:003 Then the Devil said to Him, "If you are God's Son, tell this stone to become bread." 004:004 "It is written," replied Jesus, "`It is not on bread alone that a man shall live.'" 004:005 The Devil next led Him up and caused Him to see at a glance all the kingdoms of the world. 004:006 And the Devil said to Him, "To you will I give all this authority and this splendour; for it has been handed over to me, and on whomsoever I will I bestow it. 004:007 If therefore you do homage to me, it shall all be yours.' 004:008 Jesus answered him, "It is written, `To the Lord thy God thou shalt do homage, and to Him alone shalt thou render worship.'" 004:009 Then he brought Him to Jerusalem and caused Him to stand on the roof of the Temple, and said to Him, "If you are God's Son, throw yourself down from here; for it is written, 004:010 `He will give orders to His angels concerning thee, to guard thee safely;' 004:011 and `On their hands they shall bear thee up, Lest at any moment thou shouldst strike thy foot against a stone.'" 004:012 The reply of Jesus was, "It is said, `Thou shalt not put the Lord they God to the proof.'" 004:013 So the Devil, having fully tried every kind of temptation on Him, left Him for a time. 004:014 Then Jesus returned in the Spirit's power to Galilee; and His fame spread through all the adjacent districts. 004:015 And He proceeded to teach in their synagogues, winning praise from all. 004:016 He came to Nazareth also, where He had been brought up; and, as was His custom, He went to the synagogue on the Sabbath, and stood up to read. 004:017 And there was handed to Him the book of the Prophet Isaiah, and, opening the book, He found the place where it was written, 004:018 "The Spirit of the Lord is upon me, because He has anointed me to proclaim Good News to the poor; He has sent me to announce release to the prisoners of war and recovery of sight to the blind: to send away free those whom tyranny has crushed, 004:019 to proclaim the year of acceptance with the Lord." 004:020 And rolling up the book, He returned it to the attendant, and sat down-to speak. And the eyes of all in the synagogue were fixed on Him. 004:021 Then He proceeded to say to them, "To-day is this Scripture fulfilled in your hearing." 004:022 And they all spoke well of Him, wondering at the sweet words of kindness which fell from His lips, while they asked one another, "Is not this Joseph's son?" 004:023 "Doubtless," said He, "you will quote to me the proverb, `Physician, cure yourself: all that we hear that you have done at Capernaum, do here also in your native place.'" 004:024 "I tell you in solemn truth," He added, "that no Prophet is welcomed among his own people. 004:025 But I tell you in truth that there was many a widow in Israel in the time of Elijah, when there was no rain for three years and six months and there came a severe famine over all the land; 004:026 and yet to not one of them was Elijah sent: he was only sent to a widow at Zarephath in the Sidonian country. 004:027 And there was also many a leper in Israel in the time of the Prophet Elisha, and yet not one of them was cleansed, but Naaman the Syrian was." 004:028 Then all in the synagogue, while listening to these words, were filled with fury. 004:029 They rose, hurried Him outside the town, and brought Him to the brow of the hill on which their town was built, to throw Him down the cliff; 004:030 but He passed through the midst of them and went His way. 004:031 So He came down to Capernaum, a town in Galilee, where He frequently taught the people on the Sabbath days. 004:032 And they were greatly impressed by His teaching, because He spoke with the language of authority. 004:033 But in the synagogue there was a man possessed by the spirit of a foul demon. In a loud voice he cried out, 004:034 "Ha! Jesus the Nazarene, what have you to do with us? I know who you are-God's Holy One!" 004:035 But Jesus rebuked the demon. "Silence!" He exclaimed; "come out of him." Upon this, the demon hurled the man into the midst of them, and came out of him without doing him any harm. 004:036 All were astonished and awe-struck; and they asked one another, "What sort of language is this? For with authority and real power He gives orders to the foul spirits and they come out." 004:037 And the talk about Him spread into every part of the neighbouring country. 004:038 Now when He rose and left the synagogue He went to Simon's house. Simon's mother-in-law was suffering from an acute attack of fever; and they consulted Him about her. 004:039 Then standing over her He rebuked the fever, and it left her; and she at once rose and waited on them. 004:040 At sunset all who had friends suffering from any illness brought them to Him, and He laid His hands on them all, one by one, and cured them. 004:041 Demons also came out of many, loudly calling out, "You are the Son of God." But He rebuked them and forbad them to speak, because they knew Him to be the Christ. 004:042 Next morning, at daybreak, He left the town and went away to a solitary place; but the people flocked out to find Him, and, coming to the place where He was, they endeavoured to detain Him that He might not leave them. 004:043 But He said to them, "I have to tell the Good News of the Kingdom of God to the other towns also, because for this purpose I was sent." 004:044 And for some time He preached in the synagogues in Galilee. 005:001 On one occasion the crowd was pressing on Him and listening to God's Message, while He was standing by the Lake of Gennesaret. 005:002 He, however, saw two fishing-boats drawn up on the beach (for the men had gone away from them and were washing the nets), 005:003 and going on board one of them, which was Simon's He asked him to push out a little from land. Then He sat down and taught the crowd of people from the boat. 005:004 When He had finished speaking, He said to Simon, "Push out into deep water, and let down your nets for a haul." 005:005 "Rabbi," replied Peter, "all night long we have worked hard and caught nothing; but at your command I will let down the nets." 005:006 This they did, and enclosed a vast number of fish; and their nets began to break. 005:007 So they signalled to their partners in the other boat to come and help them; they came, and they filled both the boats so that they almost sank. 005:008 When Simon Peter saw this, he fell down at the knees of Jesus, and exclaimed, "Master, leave my boat, for I am a sinful man." 005:009 (For he was astonished and terrified-he and all his companions- at the haul of fish which they had taken; 005:010 and so were Simon's partners James and John, the sons of Zabdi.) But Jesus replied to Simon, "Fear not: from this time you shall be a catcher of men." 005:011 Then, after bringing their boats to land, they left everything and followed Him. 005:012 On another occasion, when He was in one of the towns, there was a man there covered with leprosy, who, seeing Jesus, threw himself at His feet and implored Him, saying, "Sir, if only you are willing, you are able to make me clean." 005:013 Reaching out His hand and touching him, Jesus said, "I am willing; be cleansed!" And instantly the leprosy left him. 005:014 He ordered him to tell no one. "But go," He said, "show yourself to the Priest, and make the offering for your purification which Moses appointed, as evidence for them." 005:015 But all the more the report about Him spread abroad, and great multitudes crowded to hear Him and to be cured of their diseases; 005:016 but Jesus Himself constantly withdrew into the Desert and there prayed. 005:017 One day He was teaching, and there were Pharisees and teachers of the Law sitting there who had come from every village in Galilee and Judaea and from Jerusalem. And the power of the Lord was present for Him to cure people. 005:018 And a party of men came carrying a palsied man on a bed, and they endeavoured to bring him in and lay him before Jesus. 005:019 But when they could find no way of doing so because of the crowd, they went up on the roof and let him down through the tiling- bed and all-into the midst, in front of Jesus. 005:020 He saw their faith and said to him, "Friend, your sins are forgiven." 005:021 Then the Scribes and Pharisees began to cavil, asking, "Who is this, uttering blasphemies? Who but God alone can forgive sins?" 005:022 Well aware of their reasonings, Jesus answered their questions by asking in turn, "What is this that you are debating in your hearts? 005:023 Which is easier?-to say, `Your sins are forgiven,' or to say, `Rise and walk'? 005:024 But to prove to you that the Son of Man has authority on earth to forgive sins"-Turning to the paralytic He said, "I bid you, Rise, take up your bed, and go home." 005:025 Instantly he stood up in their presence, took up the mattress on which he had been lying, and went away to his home, giving glory to God. 005:026 Amazement seized them all. "Glory to God!" was the abiding feeling. Yet fear flashed through their minds and they said, "We have seen strange things to-day." 005:027 After this He went out and noticed a tax-gatherer, Levi by name, sitting at the Toll office; and He said to him, "Follow me." 005:028 He rose, left everything, and followed Him. 005:029 Levi also gave a great entertainment at his house in honour of Jesus, and there was a large party of tax-gatherers and others at table with them. 005:030 This led the Pharisees and Scribes of their party to expostulate with His disciples and ask, "Why are you eating and drinking with these tax-gatherers and notorious sinners?" 005:031 But Jesus replied to them, "It is not men in good health who require a physician, but the sick. 005:032 I have not come to call the righteous to repentance, but sinners." 005:033 Again they said to Him, "John's disciples fast often and pray, as do also those of the pharisees; but yours eat and drink." 005:034 "Can you compel the bridal party to fast," replied Jesus, "so long as they have the bridegroom among them? 005:035 But a time for this will come, when the Bridegroom has been taken away from them: then, at that time, they will fast." 005:036 He also spoke in figurative language to them. "No one," He said, "tears a piece from a new garment to mend an old one. Otherwise he would not only spoil the new, but the patch from the new would not match the old. 005:037 Nor does any one pour new wine into old wine-skins. Otherwise the new wine would burst the skins, the wine itself would be spilt, and the skins be destroyed. 005:038 But new wine must be put into fresh wineskins. 005:039 Nor does any one after drinking old wine wish for new; for he says, `The old is better.'" 006:001 Now on the second-first Sabbath while He was passing through the wheatfields, His disciples were plucking the ears and rubbing them with their hands to eat the grain. 006:002 And some of the Pharisees asked, "Why are you doing what the Law forbids on the Sabbath?" 006:003 "Have you never read so much as this," answered Jesus- "what David did when he and his followers were hungry; 006:004 how he entered the house of God and took and ate the Presented Loaves and gave some to his followers-loaves which none but the Priests are allowed to eat?" 006:005 "The Son of Man," He added, "is Lord of the Sabbath also." 006:006 On another Sabbath He had gone to the synagogue and was teaching there; and in the congregation was a man whose right arm was withered. 006:007 The Scribes and the Pharisees were on the watch to see whether He would cure him on the Sabbath that they might be able to bring an accusation against Him. 006:008 He knew their thoughts, and said to the man with the withered arm, "Rise, and stand there in the middle." And he rose and stood there. 006:009 Then Jesus said to them, "I put it to you all whether we are allowed to do good on the Sabbath, or to do evil; to save a life, or to destroy it." 006:010 And looking round upon them all He said to the man, "Stretch out your arm." He did so, and the arm was restored. 006:011 But they were filled with madness, and began to discuss with one another what they should do to Jesus. 006:012 About that time He went out on one occasion into the hill country to pray; and He remained all night in prayer to God. 006:013 When it was day, He called His disciples; and He selected from among them twelve, whom He also named Apostles. 006:014 These were Simon, to whom also He had given the name of Peter, and Andrew his brother; James and John; Philip and Bartholomew; 006:015 Matthew and Thomas; James the son of Alphaeus and Simon called the Zealot; 006:016 James's relative Judas, and Judas Iscariot who proved to be a traitor. 006:017 With these He came down till He reached a level place, where there was a great crowd of His disciples, and a multitude of people from every part of Judaea, from Jerusalem, and from the sea-side district of Tyre and Sidon, who came to hear Him and to be cured of their diseases; 006:018 and those who were tormented by foul spirits were cured. 006:019 The whole crowd were eager to touch Him, because power went forth from him and cured every one. 006:020 Then fixing His eyes upon His disciples, Jesus said to them, "Blessed are you poor, because the Kingdom of God is yours. 006:021 "Blessed are you who hunger now, because your hunger shall be satisfied. "Blessed are you who now weep aloud, because you shall laugh. 006:022 "Blessed are you when men shall hate you and exclude you from their society and insult you, and spurn your very names as evil things, for the Son of Man's sake. 006:023 "Be glad at such a time, and dance for joy; for your reward is great in Heaven; for that is just the way their forefathers behaved to the Prophets! 006:024 "But alas for you rich men, because you already have your consolation! 006:025 "Alas for you who now have plenty to eat, because you will be hungry! "Alas for you who laugh now, because you will mourn and weep aloud! 006:026 "Alas for you when men shall all have spoken well of you; for that is just the way their forefathers behaved to the false Prophets! 006:027 "But to you who are listening to me I say, Love your enemies; seek the welfare of those who hate you; 006:028 bless those who curse you; pray for those who revile you. 006:029 To him who gives you a blow on one side of the face offer the other side also; and to him who is robbing you of your outer garment refuse not the under one also. 006:030 To every one who asks, give; and from him who takes away your property, do not demand it back. 006:031 And behave to your fellow men just as you would have them behave to you. 006:032 "If you love those who love you, what credit is it to you? Why, even bad men love those who love them. 006:033 And if you are kind to those who are kind to you, what credit is it to you? Even bad men act thus. 006:034 And if you lend to those from whom you hope to receive, what credit is it to you? Even bad men lend to their fellows so as to receive back an equal amount. 006:035 Nevertheless love your enemies, be beneficent; and lend without hoping for any repayment. Then your recompense shall be great, and you will be sons of the Most High; for He is kind to the ungrateful and wicked. 006:036 Be compassionate just as your Father is compassionate. 006:037 "Judge not, and you shall not be judged; condemn not, and you shall not be condemned; pardon, and you shall be pardoned; 006:038 give, and gifts shall be bestowed on you. Full measure, pressed, shaken down, and running over, shall they pour into your laps; for with the same measure that you use they shall measure to you in return." 006:039 He also spoke to them in figurative language. "Can a blind man lead a blind man?" He asked; "would not both fall into the ditch? 006:040 There is no disciple who is superior to his teacher; but every one whose instruction is complete will be like his teacher. 006:041 "And why look at the splinter in your brother's eye instead of giving careful attention to the beam in your own? 006:042 How can you say to your brother, `Brother, let me take that splinter out of your eye,' when all the while you yourself do not see the beam in your own eye? Vain pretender! take the beam out of your own eye first, and then you will see clearly to take the splinter out of your brother's eye. 006:043 "There is no good tree that yields unsound fruit, nor again any unsound tree that yields good fruit. 006:044 Every tree is known by its own fruit. It is not from thorns that men gather figs, nor from the bramble that they can get a bunch of grapes. 006:045 A good man from the good stored up in his heart brings out what is good; and an evil man from the evil stored up brings out what is evil; for from the overflow of his heart his mouth speaks. 006:046 "And why do you all call me `Master, Master' and yet not do what I tell you? 006:047 Every one who comes to me and listens to my words and puts them in practice, I will show you whom he is like. 006:048 He is like a man building a house, who digs and goes deep, and lays the foundation on the rock; and when a flood comes, the torrent bursts upon that house, but is unable to shake it, because it is securely built. 006:049 But he who has heard and not practised is like a man who has built a house upon the soft soil without a foundation, against which the torrent bursts, and immediately it collapses, and terrible is the wreck and ruin of that house." 007:001 After He had finished teaching all these things in the hearing of the people, He went into Capernaum. 007:002 Here the servant of a certain Captain, a man dear to his master, was ill and at the point of death; 007:003 and the Captain, hearing about Jesus, sent to Him some of the Jewish Elders, begging Him to come and restore his servant to health. 007:004 And they, when they came to Jesus, earnestly entreated Him, pleading, "He deserves to have this favour granted him, 007:005 for he loves our nation, and at his own expense he built our synagogue for us." 007:006 Then Jesus went with them. But when He was not far from the house, the Captain sent friends to Him with the message: "Sir, do not trouble to come. I am not worthy of having you come under my roof; 007:007 and therefore I did not deem myself worthy to come to you. Only speak the word, and let my young man be cured. 007:008 For I too am a man obedient to authority, and have soldiers under me; and I say to one, `Go,' and he goes; to another, `Come,' and he comes; and to my slave, `Do this or that,' and he does it." 007:009 Jesus listened to the Captain's message and was astonished at him, and He turned and said to the crowd that followed Him, "I tell you that not even in Israel have I found faith like that." 007:010 And the friends who had been sent, on returning to the house, found the servant in perfect health. 007:011 Shortly afterwards He went to a town called Nain, attended by His disciples and a great crowd of people. 007:012 And just as He reached the gate of the town, they happened to be bringing out for burial a dead man who was his mother's only son; and she was a widow; and a great number of the townspeople were with her. 007:013 The Lord saw her, was moved with pity for her, and said to her, "Do not weep." 007:014 Then He went close and touched the bier, and the bearers halted. "Young man," He said, "I command you, wake!" 007:015 The dead man sat up and began to speak; and He restored him to his mother. 007:016 All were awe-struck, and they gave glory to God-some saying, "A Prophet, a great Prophet, has risen up among us." Others said, "God has not forgotten His People." 007:017 And the report of what Jesus had done spread through the whole of Judaea and in all the surrounding districts. 007:018 John's disciples brought him an account of all these things; 007:019 so John called two of his disciples and sent them to the Lord. "Are you the Coming One?" he asked, "or is there another that we are to expect?" 007:020 The men came to Jesus and said, "John the Baptist has sent us to you with this question: `Are you the Coming One, or is there another that we are to expect?'" 007:021 He immediately cured many of diseases, severe pain, and evil spirits, and to many who were blind He gave the gift of sight. 007:022 Then He answered the messengers, "Go and report to John what you have seen and heard. Blind men receive sight, the lame walk, lepers are purified, deaf persons hear, the dead are raised to life, the poor have the Good News proclaimed to them. 007:023 And blessed is every one who does not stumble and fall because of my claims." 007:024 When John's messengers were gone, He proceeded to say to the multitude concerning John, "What did you go out into the Desert to gaze at? A reed waving in the wind? 007:025 But what did you go out to see? A man wearing luxurious clothes? People who are gorgeously dressed and live in luxury are found in palaces. 007:026 But what did you go out to see? A Prophet? Aye, I tell you, and far more than a Prophet. 007:027 John is the man about whom it is written, `See, I am sending My messenger before thy face, and he shall make ready thy way before thee.' 007:028 "I tell you that among all of women born there is not one greater than John. Yet one who is of lower rank in the Kingdom of God is greater than he. 007:029 And all the people, including the tax-gatherers, when they listened to him upheld the righteousness of God, by being baptized with John's baptism. 007:030 But the Pharisees and expounders of the Law have frustrated God's purpose as to their own lives, by refusing to be baptized. 007:031 "To what then shall I compare the men of the present generation, and what do they resemble? 007:032 They are like children sitting in the public square and calling out to one another, `We have played the flute to you, and you have not danced: we have sung dirges, and you have not shown sorrow.' 007:033 For John the Baptist has come eating no bread and drinking no wine, and you say, `He has a demon!' 007:034 The Son of Man has come eating and drinking, and you say, `Look, there is a man who is overfond of eating and drinking- he is a friend of tax-gatherers and notorious sinners!' 007:035 But wisdom is justified by all who are truly wise." 007:036 Now one of the Pharisees repeatedly invited Him to a meal at his house; so He entered the house and reclined at the table. 007:037 And there was a woman in the town who was a notorious sinner. Having learnt that Jesus was at table in the Pharisee's house she brought a flask of perfume, 007:038 and, standing behind close to His feet, weeping, began to wet His feet with her tears; and with her hair she wiped the tears away again, while she lovingly kissed His feet and poured the perfume over them. 007:039 Noticing this, the Pharisee, His host, said to himself, "This man, if he were really a Prophet, would know who and what sort of person this woman is who is touching him- and would know that she is an immoral woman." 007:040 In answer to his thoughts Jesus said to him, "Simon, I have a word to say to you." "Rabbi, say on," he replied. 007:041 "There were once two men in debt to one money-lender," said Jesus; "one owed him five hundred shillings and the other fifty. 007:042 But neither of them could pay anything; so he freely forgave them both. Tell me, then, which of them will love him most?" 007:043 "I suppose," replied Simon, "the one to whom he forgave most." "You have judged rightly," Jesus rejoined. 007:044 Then turning towards the woman He said to Simon, "Do you see this woman? I came into your house: you gave me no water for my feet; but she has made my feet wet with her tears, and then wiped the tears away with her hair. 007:045 No kiss did you give me; but she from the moment I came in has not left off tenderly kissing my feet. 007:046 No oil did you pour even on my head; but she has poured perfume upon my feet. 007:047 This is the reason why I tell you that her sins, her many sins, are forgiven- because she has loved much; but he who is forgiven little, loves little." 007:048 And He said to her, "Your sins are forgiven." 007:049 Then the other guests began to say to themselves, "Who can this man be who even forgives sins?" 007:050 But He said to the woman, "Your faith has cured you: go, and be at peace." 008:001 Shortly after this He visited town after town, and village after village, proclaiming His Message and telling the Good News of the Kingdom of God. The Twelve were with Him, 008:002 and certain women whom He had delivered from evil spirits and various diseases-Mary of Magdala, out of whom seven demons had come, 008:003 and Joanna the wife of Chuza, Herod's steward, and Susanna, and many other women, all of whom contributed to the support of Jesus and His Apostles. 008:004 And when a great crowd was assembling, and was receiving additions from one town after another, He spoke a parable to them. 008:005 "The sower," He said, "goes out to sow his seed; and as he sows, some of the seed falls by the way-side, and is trodden upon, or the birds of the air come and peck it up. 008:006 Another part drops upon the rock, and after growing up it withers away for want of moisture. 008:007 Another part falls among the thorns, and the thorns grow up with it and stifle it. 008:008 But some of the seed falls into good ground, and grows up and yields a return of a hundred for one." While thus speaking, He cried aloud and said, "Listen, every one who has ears to listen with!" 008:009 The disciples proceeded to ask Him what this parable meant. 008:010 "To you," He replied, "it is granted to know the secrets of the Kingdom of God; but all others are taught by parables, in order that they may see and yet not see, and may hear and yet not understand. 008:011 The meaning of the parable is as follows. The seed is God's Message. 008:012 Those by the way-side are those who have heard, and then the Devil comes and carries away the

Message from their hearts, lest they should believe and be saved. 008:013 Those on the rock are the people who on hearing the Message receive it joyfully; but they have no root: for a time they believe, but when trial comes they fall away. 008:014 That which fell among the thorns means those who have heard, but as they go on their way, the Message is stifled by the anxieties, wealth and gaieties of time, and they yield nothing in perfection. 008:015 But as for that in the good ground, it means those who, having listened to the Message with open minds and in a right spirit, hold it fast, and patiently yield a return. 008:016 "When any one lights a lamp, he does not cover it with a vessel or hide it under a couch; he puts it on a lampstand, that people who enter the room may see the light. 008:017 There is nothing hidden, which shall not be openly seen; nor anything secret, which shall not be known and come into the light of day. 008:018 Be careful, therefore, how you hear; for whoever has anything, to him more shall be given, and whoever has nothing, even that which he thinks he has shall be taken away from him." 008:019 Then came to Him His mother and His brothers, but could not get near Him for the crowd. 008:020 But He was told, "Your mother and brothers are standing on the edge of the crowd, and want to see you." 008:021 "My mother and my brothers," He replied, "are these who hear God's Message and obey it." 008:022 One day He went on board a boat-both He and his disciples; and He said to them, "Let us cross over to the other side of the Lake." So they set sail. 002:023 During the passage He fell asleep, and there came down a squall of wind on the Lake, so that the boat began to fill and they were in deadly peril. 008:024 So they came and woke Him, crying, "Rabbi, Rabbi, we are drowning." Then He roused Himself and rebuked the wind and the surging of the water, and they ceased and there was a calm. 008:025 "Where is your faith?" He asked them. But they were filled with terror and amazement, and said to one another, "Who then is this? for He gives orders both to wind and waves, and they obey Him." 008:026 Then they put in to shore in the country of the Gerasenes, which lies opposite to Galilee. 008:027 Here, on landing, He was met by one of the townsmen who was possessed by demons-for a long time he had not put on any garment, nor did he live in a house, but in the tombs. 008:028 When he saw Jesus, he cried out and fell down before Him, and said in a loud voice, "What have you to do with me, Jesus, Son of God Most High? Do not torture me, I beseech you." 008:029 For already He had been commanding the foul spirit to come out of the man. For many a time it had seized and held him, and they had repeatedly put him in chains and fetters and kept guard over him, but he used to break the chains to pieces, and, impelled by the demon, to escape into the Desert. 008:030 "What is your name?" Jesus asked him. "Legion," he replied-because a great number of demons had entered into him; 008:031 and they besought Him not to command them to be gone into the Bottomless Pit.

008:032 Now there was a great herd of swine there feeding on the hill-side; and the demons begged Him to give them leave to go into them, and He gave them leave. 008:033 The demons came out of the man and left him, and entered into the swine; and the herd rushed violently over the cliff into the Lake and were drowned. 008:034 The swineherds, seeing what had happened, fled and reported it both in town and country; 008:035 whereupon the people came out to see what had happened. They came to Jesus, and they found the man from whom the demons had gone out sitting at the feet of Jesus, clothed and in his right mind; and they were terrified. 008:036 And those who had seen it told them how the demoniac was cured. 008:037 Then the whole population of the Gerasenes and of the adjacent districts begged Him to depart from them; for their terror was great. So He went on board and returned. 008:038 But the man from whom the demons had gone out earnestly asked permission to go with Him; but He sent him away. 008:039 "Return home," He said, "and tell there all that God has done for you." So he went and published through the whole town all that Jesus had done for him. 008:040 Now when Jesus was returning, the people gave Him a warm welcome; for they had all been looking out for Him. 008:041 Just then there came a man named Jair, a Warden of the Synagogue, who threw himself at the feet of Jesus, and entreated Him to come to his house; 008:042 for he had an only daughter, about twelve years old, and she was dying. And as He went, the dense throng crowded on Him. 008:043 And a woman who for twelve years had been afflicted with haemorrhage- and had spent on doctors all she had, but none of them had been able to cure her- 008:044 came close behind Him and touched the tassel of His robe; and instantly her flow of blood stopped. 008:045 "Who is it touched me?" Jesus asked. And when all denied having done so, Peter and the rest said, "Rabbi, the crowds are hemming you in and pressing on you." 008:046 "Some one has touched me," Jesus replied, "for I feel that power has gone out from me." 008:047 Then the woman, perceiving that she had not escaped notice, came trembling, and throwing herself down at His feet she stated before all the people the reason why she had touched Him and how she was instantly cured. 008:048 "Daughter," said He, "your faith has cured you; go, and be at peace." 008:049 While He was still speaking, some one came to the Warden of the Synagogue from his house and said, "Your daughter is dead; trouble the Rabbi no further." 008:050 Jesus heard the words and said to him, "Have no fear. Only believe, and she shall be restored to life." 008:051 So He came to the house, but allowed no one to go in with Him but Peter and John and James and the girl's father and mother. 008:052 The people were all weeping aloud and beating their breasts for her; but He said, "Leave off wailing; for she is not dead, but asleep." 008:053 And they jeered at Him, knowing that she was dead. 008:054 He, however, took her by the hand and called aloud, "Child, awake!" 008:055 And her spirit returned, and instantly she stood up; and He directed them to give her some food. 008:056 Her parents were astounded; but He forbad them to mention the matter to any one. 009:001 Then calling the Twelve together He conferred on them power and authority over all the demons and to cure diseases; 009:002 and sent them out to proclaim the Kingdom of God and to cure the sick. 009:003 And He commanded them, "Take nothing for your journey; neither stick nor bag nor bread nor money; and do not have an extra under garment. 009:004 Whatever house you enter, make that your home, and from it start afresh. 009:005 Wherever they refuse to receive you, as you leave that town shake off the very dust from your feet as a protest against them." 009:006 So they departed and visited village after village, spreading the Good News and performing cures everywhere. 009:007 Now Herod the Tetrarch heard of all that was going on; and he was bewildered because of its being said by some that John had come back to life, 009:008 by others that Elijah had appeared, and by others that some one of the ancient Prophets had come back to life. 009:009 And Herod said, "John I have beheaded; but who is this, of whom I hear such reports?" And he sought for an opportunity of seeing Jesus. 009:010 The Apostles, on their return, related to Jesus all they had done. Then He took them and withdrew to a quiet retreat, to a town called Bethsaida. 009:011 But the immense crowd, aware of this, followed Him; and receiving them kindly He proceeded to speak to them of the Kingdom of God, and those who needed to be restored to health, He cured. 009:012 Now when the day began to decline, the Twelve came to Him and said, "Send the people away, that they may go to the villages and farms round about and find lodging and a supply of food; because here we are in an uninhabited district." 009:013 "You yourselves," He said, "must give them food." "We have nothing," they replied, "but five loaves and a couple of fish, unless indeed we were to go and buy provisions for all this host of people." 009:014 (For there were about 5,000 adult men.) But He said to His disciples, "Make them sit down in parties of about fifty each." 009:015 They did so, making them all, without exception, sit down. 009:016 Then He took the five loaves and the two fish, and looking up to Heaven He blessed them and broke them into portions which He gave to the disciples to distribute to the people. 009:017 So they ate and were fully satisfied, all of them; and what they had remaining over was gathered up, twelve baskets of fragments. 009:018 One day when He was praying by Himself the disciples were present; and He asked them, "Who do the people say that I am?" 009:019 "John the Baptist," they replied; "but others say Elijah; and others that some one of the ancient Prophets has come back to life." 009:020 "But you," He asked, "who do you say that I am?" "God's Anointed One," replied Peter. 009:021 And Jesus strictly forbad them to tell this to any one; 009:022 and He said, "The Son of Man must suffer much cruelty, be rejected by the Elders and

High Priests and Scribes, and be put to death, and on the third day be raised to life again." 009:023 And He said to all, "If any one is desirous of following me, let him ignore self and take up his cross day by day, and so be my follower. 009:024 For whoever desires to save his life shall lose it, and whoever loses his life for my sake shall save it. 009:025 Why, what benefit is it to a man to have gained the whole world, but to have lost or forfeited his own self. 009:026 For whoever shall have been ashamed of me and my teachings, of him the Son of Man will be ashamed when He comes in His own and the Father's glory and in that of the holy angels. 009:027 I tell you truly that there are some of those who stand here who will certainly not taste death till they have seen the Kingdom of God." 009:028 It was about eight days after this that Jesus, taking with Him Peter, John, and James, went up the mountain to pray. 009:029 And while He was praying the appearance of His face underwent a change, and His clothing became white and radiant. 009:030 And suddenly there were two men conversing with Him, who were Moses and Elijah. 009:031 They came in glory, and kept speaking about His death, which He was so soon to undergo in Jerusalem. 009:032 Now Peter and the others were weighed down with sleep; but, keeping themselves awake all through, they saw His glory, and the two men standing with Him. 009:033 And when they were preparing to depart from Him, Peter said to Jesus, "Rabbi, we are thankful to you that we are here. Let us put up three tents-one for you, one for Moses, and one for Elijah." He did not know what he was saying. 009:034 But while he was thus speaking, there came a cloud which spread over them; and they were awe-struck when they had entered into the cloud. 009:035 Then there came a voice from within the cloud: "This is My Son, My Chosen One: listen to Him." 009:036 After this voice had spoken, Jesus was found alone. They kept it to themselves, and said not a word to any one at that time about what they had seen. 009:037 On the following day, when they were come down from the mountain, a great crowd came to meet Him; 009:038 and a man from the crowd called out, "Rabbi, I beg you to pity my son, for he is my only child. 009:039 At times a spirit seizes him and he suddenly cries out. It convulses him, and makes him foam at the mouth, and does not leave him till it has well-nigh covered him with bruises. 009:040 I entreated your disciples to expel the spirit, but they could not." 009:041 "O unbelieving and perverse generation!" replied Jesus; "how long shall I be with you and bear with you? Bring your son here to me." 009:042 Now while the youth was coming, the spirit dashed him to the ground and cruelly convulsed him. But Jesus rebuked the foul spirit, and cured the youth and gave him back to his father. 009:043 And all were awe-struck at the mighty power of God. And while every one was expressing wonder at all that He was doing, He said to his disciples, 009:044 "As for you, store these my sayings in your memory; for, before long, the Son of Man will be betrayed into the hands of men." 009:045 But they did not understand His meaning: it was veiled from them that they might not perceive it, and they were afraid to ask Him about it. 009:046 Now there arose a dispute among them, which of them was to be the greatest. 009:047 And Jesus, knowing the reasoning that was in their hearts, took a young child and made him stand by His side 009:048 and said to them, "Whoever for my sake receives this little child, receives me; and whoever receives me, receives Him who sent me. For the lowliest among you all-he is the greatest." 009:049 "Rabbi," replied John, "we have seen a man making use of your name to expel demons; and we forbad him, because he does not come with us." 009:050 "Do not forbid him," said Jesus, "for he who is not against you is on your side." 009:051 Now when the time drew near for Him to be received up again into Heaven, He proceeded with fixed purpose towards Jerusalem, and sent messengers before Him. 009:052 They went and entered a village of the Samaritans to make ready for Him. 009:053 But the people there would not receive Him, because He was evidently going to Jerusalem. 009:054 When the disciples James and John saw this, they said, "Master, do you wish us to order fire to come down from Heaven and consume them?" 009:055 But He turned and rebuked them. 009:056 And they went to another village. 009:057 And, as they proceeded on their way, a man came to Him and said, "I will follow you wherever you go." 009:058 "The foxes have holes," said Jesus, "and the birds of the air have nests; but the Son of Man has nowhere to lay His head." 009:059 "Follow me," He said to another. "Master," the man replied, "allow me first to go and bury my father." 009:060 "Leave the dead," Jesus rejoined, "to bury their own dead; but you must go and announce far and wide the coming of the Kingdom of God." 009:061 "Master," said yet another, "I will follow you; but allow me first to go and say good-bye to my friends at home." 009:062 Jesus answered him, "No one who has put his hand to the plough, and then looks behind him, is fit for the Kingdom of God. 010:001 After this the Lord appointed seventy others, and sent them before Him, by twos, to go to every town or place which He Himself intended to visit. 010:002 And He addressed them thus: "The harvest is abundant, but the reapers are few: therefore entreat the Owner of the harvest to send out more reapers into His fields. And now go. 010:003 Remember that I am sending you out as lambs into the midst of wolves. 010:004 Carry no purse, bag, nor change of shoes; and salute no one on your way." 010:005 "Whatever house you enter, first say, `Peace be to this house!' 010:006 And if there is a lover of peace there, your peace shall rest upon it; otherwise come back upon you. 010:007 And in that same house stay, eating and drinking at their table; for the labourer deserves his wages. Do not move from one house to another. 010:008 "And whatever town you come to and they receive you, eat what they put before you. 010:009 Cure the sick in that town, and tell them, "`The Kingdom of God is now at your door.' 010:010 "But whatever town you come to and they will not receive you, go out into the broader streets and say, 010:011 "`The very dust of your town that hangs about us we wipe off as a protest. Only be sure of this, that the Kingdom of God is close at hand.' 010:012 "I tell you that it will be more endurable for Sodom on the great day than for that town. 010:013 "Alas for thee, Chorazin! Alas for thee, Bethsaida! For had the miracles been performed in Tyre and Sidon which have been performed in you, long ere now they would have repented, sitting in sackcloth and ashes. 010:014 However, for Tyre and Sidon it will be more endurable at the Judgement than for you. 010:015 And thou, Capernaum, shalt thou be lifted high as Heaven? Thou shalt be driven down as low as Hades. 010:016 "He who listens to you listens to me; and he who disregards you disregards me, and he who disregards me disregards Him who sent me." 010:017 When the Seventy returned, they exclaimed joyfully, "Master, even the demons submit to us when we utter your name." 010:018 "I saw Satan fall like a lightning-flash out of Heaven," He replied. 010:019 "I have given you power to tread serpents and scorpions underfoot, and to trample on all the power of the Enemy; and in no case shall anything do you harm. 010:020 Nevertheless rejoice not at this, that the spirits submit to you; but rejoice that your names are registered in Heaven." 010:021 On that same occasion Jesus was filled by the Holy Spirit with rapturous joy. "I give Thee fervent thanks," He exclaimed, "O Father, Lord of Heaven and earth, that Thou hast hidden these things from sages and men of understanding, and hast revealed them to babes. Yes, Father, for such has been Thy gracious will. 010:022 All things are delivered to me by my Father; and no one knows who the Son is but the Father, nor who the Father is but the Son, and he to whom the Son may choose to reveal Him." 010:023 And He turned towards His disciples and said to them apart, "Blessed are the eyes which see what you see! 010:024 For I tell you that many Prophets and kings have desired to see the things you see, and have not seen them, and to hear the things you hear, and have not heard them." 010:025 Then an expounder of the Law stood up to test Him with a question. "Rabbi," he asked, "what shall I do to inherit the Life of the Ages?" 010:026 "Go to the Law," said Jesus; "what is written there? how does it read?" 010:027 "`Thou shalt love the Lord thy God,'" he replied, "`with thy whole heart, thy whole soul, thy whole strength, and thy whole mind; and thy fellow man as much as thyself.'" 010:028 "A right answer," said Jesus; "do that, and you shall live." 010:029 But he, desiring to justify himself, said, "But what is meant by my `fellow man'?" 010:030 Jesus replied, "A man was once on his way down from Jerusalem to Jericho when he fell among robbers, who after both stripping and beating him went away, leaving him half dead. 010:031 Now a priest happened to be going down that way, and on seeing him passed by on the other side. 010:032 In like manner a Levite also came to the place, and seeing him passed by on the other side. 010:033 But a certain Samaritan, being on a journey, came where he lay, and seeing him was moved with pity. 010:034 He went to him, and dressed his wounds with oil and wine and bound them up. Then placing him on his own mule he brought him to an inn, where he bestowed every care on him. 010:035 The next day he took out two shillings and gave them to the innkeeper. "`Take care of him,' he said, `and whatever further expense you are put to, I will repay it you at my next visit.' 010:036 "Which of those three seems to you to have acted like a fellow man to him who fell among the robbers?" 010:037 "The one who showed him pity," he replied. "Go," said Jesus, "and act in the same way." 010:038 As they pursued their journey He came to a certain village, where a woman named Martha welcomed Him to her house. 010:039 She had a sister called Mary, who seated herself at the Lord's feet and listened to His teaching. 010:040 Martha meanwhile was busy and distracted in waiting at table, and she came and said, "Master, do you not care that my sister is leaving me to do all the waiting? Tell her to assist me." 010:041 "Martha, Martha," replied Jesus, "you are anxious and worried about a multitude of things; 010:042 and yet only one thing is really necessary. Mary has chosen the good portion and she shall not be deprived of it." 011:001 At one place where He was praying, when He rose from His knees one of His disciples said to Him, "Master, teach us to pray, just as John taught his disciples." 011:002 So He said to them, "When you pray, say, `Father may Thy name be kept holy; let Thy Kingdom come; 011:003 give us day after day our bread for the day; 011:004 and forgive us our sins, for we ourselves also forgive every one who fails in his duty to us; and bring us not into temptation.'" 011:005 And He said to them, "Which of you shall have a friend and shall go to him in the middle of the night and say, "`Friend, lend me three loaves of bread; 011:006 for a friend of mine has just come to my house from a distance, and I have nothing for him to eat'? 011:007 "And he from indoors shall answer, "`Do not pester me. The door is now barred, and I am here in bed with my children. I cannot get up and give you bread.' 011:008 "I tell you that even if he will not rise and give him the loaves because he is his friend, at any rate because of his persistency he will rouse himself and give him as many as he requires. 011:009 "So I say to you, `Ask, and what you ask for shall be given to you; seek, and you shall find; knock, and the door shall be opened to you.' 011:010 For every one who asks, receives; and he who seeks, finds; and to him who knocks, the door shall be opened. 011:011 And what father is there among you, who, if his son asks for a slice of bread, will offer him a stone? or if he asks for a fish, will instead of a fish offer him a snake? 011:012 or if he asks for an egg, will offer him a scorpion? 011:013 If you then, with all your human frailty, know how to give your children gifts that are good for them, how much more certainly will your Father who is in Heaven give the Holy Spirit

to those who ask Him!" 011:014 On once occasion He was expelling a
dumb demon; and when the demon was gone out the dumb man could
speak, and the people were astonished. 011:015 But some among them said,
"It is by the power of Baal-zebul, the Prince of the demons, that he expels
the demons." 011:016 Others, to put Him to the test, asked Him for a sign
in the sky. 011:017 And, knowing their thoughts, He said to them, "Every
kingdom in which civil war rages goes to ruin: family attacks family and is
overthrown. 011:018 And if Satan really has engaged in fierce conflict with
himself, how shall his kingdom stand?-because you say that I expel demons
by the power of Baal-zebul. 011:019 And if it is by the power of Baal-zebul
that I expel the demons, by whom do your disciples expel them? They
therefore shall be your judges. 011:020 But if it is by the power of God that
I drive out the demons, it is evident that the Kingdom of God has come
upon you. 011:021 "Whenever a strong man, fully armed and equipped, is
guarding his own castle, he enjoys peaceful possession of his property;
011:022 but as soon as another stronger than he attacks him and overcomes
him, he takes away that complete armour of his in which he trusted, and
distributes the plunder he has collected. 011:023 Whoever is not with me is
against me, and whoever is not gathering with me is scattering abroad.
011:024 "When a foul spirit has left a man, it roams about in the Desert,
seeking a resting-place; but, unable to find any, it says, `I will return to the
house I have left;" 011:025 and when it comes, it finds the house swept
clean and in good order. 011:026 Then it goes and brings with it seven
other spirits more malignant than itself, and they enter and dwell there; and
in the end that man's condition becomes worse than it was at first. 011:027
As He thus spoke a woman in the crowd called out in a loud voice,
"Blessed is the mother who carried you, and the breasts that you have
sucked." 011:028 "Nay rather," He replied, "they are blessed who hear
God's Message and carefully keep it." 011:029 Now when the crowds came
thronging upon Him, He proceeded to say, "The present generation is a
wicked generation: it requires some sign, but no sign shall be given to it
except that of Jonah. 011:030 For just as Jonah became a sign to the men of
Nineveh, so the Son of Man will be a token to the present generation.
011:031 The Queen of the South will awake at the Judgement together with
the men of the present generation, and will condemn them; because she
came from the extremity of the earth to hear the wisdom of Solomon; but
mark! One greater than Solomon is here. 011:032 There will stand up men
of Nineveh at the Judgement together with the present generation, and will
condemn it; because they repented at the preaching of Jonah; and mark!
One greater than Jonah is here. 011:033 "When any one lights a lamp, he
never puts it in the cellar or under the bushel, but on the lampstand, that
people who come in may see the light. 011:034 The lamp of the body is the
eye. When your eyesight is good, your whole body also is lighted up; but

when it is defective, your body is darkened. 011:035 Consider therefore whether the light that is in you is anything but mere darkness. 011:036 If, however, your whole body is penetrated with light, and has no part dark, it will be so lighted, all of it, as when the lamp with its bright shining gives you light." 011:037 When He had thus spoken, a Pharisee invited Him to breakfast at his house; so He entered and took His place at table. 011:038 Now the Pharisee saw to his surprise that He did not wash His hands before breakfasting. 011:039 The Master however said to him, "Here we see how you Pharisees clean the outside of the cup or plate, while your secret hearts are full of greed and selfishness. 011:040 Foolish men! Did not He who made the outside make the inside also? 011:041 But as to what is within, give alms, and instantly all is clean in you. 011:042 "But alas for you Pharisees! for you pay tithes on your mint and rue and every kind of garden vegetable, and are indifferent to justice and the love of God. These are the things you ought to have attended to, while not neglecting the others. 011:043 Alas for you Pharisees! for you love the best seats in the synagogues, and you like to be bowed to in places of public resort. 011:044 Alas for you! for you are like the tombs which lie hidden, and the people who walk over them are not aware of their existence." 011:045 Hereupon one of the expounders of the Law exclaimed, "Rabbi, in saying such things you reproach us also." 011:046 "Alas too for you expounders of the Law!" replied Jesus, "for you load men with cumbrous burdens which you yourselves will not touch with one of your fingers. 011:047 Alas for you! for you repair the tombs of the Prophets, whom your forefathers killed. 011:048 It follows that you bear testimony to the actions of your forefathers and that you fully approve thereof. They slew, you build. 011:049 "For this reason also the Wisdom of God has said, `I will send Prophets and Apostles to them, of whom they will kill some and persecute others,' 011:050 so that the blood of all the Prophets, that is being shed from the creation of the world onwards, may be required from the present generation. 011:051 Yes, I tell you that, from the blood of Abel down to the blood of Zechariah who perished between the altar and the House, it shall all be required from the present generation. 011:052 "Alas for you expounders of the Law! for you have taken away the key of knowledge: you yourselves have not entered, and those who wanted to enter you have hindered." 011:053 After He had left the house, the Scribes and Pharisees commenced a vehement attempt to entangle Him and make Him give off-hand answers on numerous points, 011:054 lying in wait to catch some unguarded expression from His lips. 012:001 Meanwhile the people had come streaming towards Him by tens of thousands, so that they were trampling one another under foot. And now He proceeded to say to His disciples first, "Beware of the yeast of the Pharisees, that is to say, beware of hypocrisy. 012:002 There is nothing that is covered up which will not be uncovered, nor hidden which will not become known. 012:003 Whatever therefore you have said in the dark, will be heard in the light; and what you have whispered within closed doors will be proclaimed from the house-tops. 012:004 "But to you who are my friends I say, "`Be not afraid of those who kill the body and after that can do nothing further. 012:005 I will warn you whom to fear: fear him who after killing has power to throw into Gehenna: yes, I say to you, fear him. 012:006 Are not five sparrows sold for a penny? and yet not one of them is a thing forgotten in God's sight. 012:007 But the very hairs on your heads are all counted. Away with fear: you are more precious than a multitude of sparrows.' 012:008 "And I tell you that every man who shall have acknowledged me before men, the Son of Man will also acknowledge before the angels of God. 012:009 But he who disowns me before men will be disowned before the angels of God. 012:010 "Moreover every one who shall speak against the Son of Man, may obtain forgiveness; but he who blasphemes the Holy Spirit will never obtain forgiveness. 012:011 And when they are bringing you before synagogues and magistrates and governors, do not anxiously ponder the manner or matter of your defence, nor what you are to say; 012:012 for the Holy Spirit shall teach you at that very moment what you must say." 012:013 Just then a man in the crowd appealed to Him. "Rabbi," he said, "tell my brother to give me a share of the inheritance." 012:014 "Man," He replied, "who has constituted me a judge or arbitrator over you?" 012:015 And to the people He said, "Take care, be on your guard against all covetousness, for no one's life consists in the superabundance of his possessions." 012:016 And He spoke a parable to them. "A certain rich man's lands," He said, "yielded abundant crops, 012:017 and he debated within himself, saying, "`What am I to do? for I have no place in which to store my crops.' 012:018 "And he said to himself, "`This is what I will do: I will pull down my barns and build larger ones, and in them I will store up all my harvest and my wealth; 012:019 and I will say to my life, "`Life, you have ample possessions laid up for many years to come: take your ease, eat, drink, enjoy yourself.' 012:020 "But God said to him, "`Foolish man, this night your life is demanded from you; and these preparations-for whom shall they be?' 012:021 "So is it with him who amasses treasure for himself, but has no riches in God." 012:022 Then turning to His disciples He said, "For this reason I say to you, `Dismiss all anxious care for your lives, inquiring what you are to eat, and for your bodies, what you are to put on.' 012:023 For life is a greater gift than food, and the body is a greater gift than clothing. 012:024 Observe the ravens. They neither sow nor reap, and have neither store-chamber nor barn. And yet God feeds them. How far more precious are you than the birds! 012:025 And which of you is able by anxious thought to add a moment to his life? 012:026 If then you are unable to do even a very little thing, why be over-anxious about other matters? 012:027 Observe the lilies, how they grow. They neither labour nor spin. And yet I tell you that not even Solomon in all his splendour was as beautifully dressed as one of these. 012:028 But if God so clothes the vegetation in the fields, that blooms to-day and to-morrow will be thrown into the oven, how much more certainly will He clothe you, you men of feeble faith! 012:029 "Therefore, do not be asking what you are to eat nor what you are to drink; and do not waver between hope and fear. 012:030 For though the nations of the world pursue these things, as for you, your Father knows that you need them. 012:031 But make His Kingdom the object of your pursuit, and these things shall be given you in addition. 012:032 "Dismiss your fears, little flock: your Father finds a pleasure in giving you the Kingdom. 012:033 Sell your possessions and give alms. Provide yourselves with purses that will never wear out, a treasure inexhaustible in Heaven, where no thief can come nor moth consume. 012:034 For where your wealth is stored, there also will your heart be. 012:035 "Have your girdles on, and let your lamps be alight; 012:036 and be yourselves like men waiting for their master- on the look-out till he shall return from the wedding feast- that, when he comes and knocks, they may open the door instantly. 012:037 Blessed are those servants, whom their Master when He comes shall find on the watch. I tell you in solemn truth, that He will tie an apron round Him, and will bid them recline at table while He comes and waits on them. 012:038 And whether it be in the second watch or in the third that He comes and finds them so, blessed are they. 012:039 Of this be sure, that if the master of the house had known what time the robber was coming, he would have kept awake and not have allowed his house to be broken into. 012:040 Be you also ready, for at an hour when you are not expecting Him the Son of Man will come." 012:041 "Master," said Peter, "are you addressing this parable to us, or to all alike?" 012:042 "Who, then," replied the Lord, "is the faithful and intelligent steward whom his Master will put in charge of His household to serve out their rations at the proper times? 012:043 Blessed is that servant whom his Master when He comes shall find so doing. 012:044 I tell you truly that He will put him in authority over all His possessions. 012:045 But if that servant should say in his heart, `My Master is a long time in coming,' and should begin to beat the menservants and the maids, and to eat and drink, drinking even to excess; 012:046 that servant's Master will come on a day when he is not expecting Him and at an hour that he knows not of, and will punish him severely, and make him share the lot of the unfaithful. 012:047 And that servant who has been told his Master's will and yet made no preparation and did not obey His will, will receive many lashes. 012:048 But he who had not been told it and yet did what deserved the scourge, will receive but few lashes. To whomsoever much has been given, from him much will be required; and to whom much has been entrusted, of him a larger amount will be demanded. 012:049 "I came to throw fire upon the earth, and what is my desire? Oh that it were even now kindled! 012:050 But I have a baptism to undergo; and how am I pent up till it is accomplished! 012:051 Do you suppose that I came to give peace on earth? No, I tell you that I came to bring dissension. 012:052 For from this time there will be in one house five persons split into parties. Three will form a party against two and two will form a party against three; 012:053 father against son and son against father; mother attacking daughter and daughter her mother, mother-in-law her daughter-in-law, and daughter-in-law her mother-in-law." 012:054 Then He said to the people also, "When you see a cloud rising in the west, you immediately say, `There is to be a shower;' and it comes to pass. 012:055 And when you see a south wind blowing, you say, `It will be burning hot;' and it comes to pass. 012:056 Vain pretenders! You know how to read the aspect of earth and sky. How is it you cannot read this present time? 012:057 "Why, too, do you not of yourselves arrive at just conclusions? 012:058 For when, with your opponent, you are going before the magistrate, on the way take pains to get out of his power; for fear that, if he should drag you before the judge, the judge may hand you over to the officer of the court, and the officer lodge you in prison. 012:059 Never, I tell you, will you get free till you have paid the last farthing." 013:001 Just at that time people came to tell Him about the Galilaeans whose blood Pilate had mingled with their sacrifices. 013:002 "Do you suppose," He asked in reply, "that those Galilaeans were worse sinners than the mass of the Galilaeans, because this happened to them? 013:003 I tell you, certainly not. On the contrary, if you are not penitent you will all perish as they did. 013:004 Or those eighteen on whom the tower at Siloam fell, do you suppose they had failed in their duty more than all the rest of the people who live in Jerusalem? 013:005 I tell you, certainly not. On the contrary, if you do not repent you will all perish just as they did." 013:006 And He gave them the following parable. "A man," He said, "who had a fig-tree growing in his garden came to look for fruit on it and could find none. 013:007 So he said to the gardener, "`See, this is the third year I have come to look for fruit on this fig-tree and cannot find any. Cut it down. Why should so much ground be actually wasted?' 013:008 "But the gardener pleaded, "`Leave it, Sir, this year also, till I have dug round it and manured it. 013:009 If after that it bears fruit, well and good; if it does not, then you shall cut it down.'" 013:010 Once He was teaching on the Sabbath in one of the synagogues 013:011 where a woman was present who for eighteen years had been a confirmed invalid: she was bent double, and was unable to lift herself to her full height. 013:012 But Jesus saw her, and calling to her, He said to her, "Woman, you are free from your weakness." 013:013 And He put His hands on her, and she immediately stood upright and began to give glory to God. 013:014 Then the Warden of the Synagogue, indignant that Jesus had cured her on a Sabbath, said to the crowd, "There are six days in the week on which people ought to work. On those days therefore come and get yourselves cured, and not on the Sabbath day." 013:015 But the Lord's reply to him was, "Hypocrites, does not each of you on the Sabbath untie his bullock or his ass from the stall and lead him to water? 013:016 And this woman, daughter of Abraham as she is, whom Satan had bound for no less than eighteen years, was she not to be loosed from this chain because it is the Sabbath day?" 013:017 When He had said this, all His opponents were ashamed, while the whole multitude was delighted at the many glorious things continually done by Him. 013:018 This prompted Him to say, "What is the Kingdom of God like? and to what shall I compare it? 013:019 It is like a mustard seed which a man drops into the soil in his garden, and it grows and becomes a tree in whose branches the birds roost." 013:020 And again He said, "To what shall I compare the Kingdom of God? 013:021 It is like yeast which a woman takes and buries in a bushel of flour, to work there till the whole is leavened." 013:022 He was passing through town after town and village after village, steadily proceeding towards Jerusalem, 013:023 when some one asked Him, "Sir, are there but few who are to be saved?" 013:024 "Strain every nerve to force your way in through the narrow gate," He answered; "for multitudes, I tell you, will endeavour to find a way in and will not succeed. 013:025 As soon as the Master of the house shall have risen and shut the door, and you have begun to stand outside and knock at the door and say, "`Sir, open the door for us'-"`I do not know you,' He answers; `you are no friends of mine.' 013:026 "Then you will plead, "`We have eaten and drunk in your company and you have taught in our streets.' 013:027 "But He will reply, "`I tell you that you are no friends of mine. Begone from me, all of you, wrongdoers that you are.' 013:028 "There will be the weeping and gnashing of teeth, when you see Abraham and Isaac and Jacob and all the Prophets in the Kingdom of God, and yourselves being driven far away. 013:029 They will come from east and west, from north and south, and will sit down at the banquet in the Kingdom of God. 013:030 And I tell you that some now last will then be first, and some now first will then be last." 013:031 Just at that time there came some Pharisees who warned Him, saying, "Leave this place and continue your journey; Herod means to kill you." 013:032 "Go," He replied, "and take this message to that fox: "`See, to-day and to-morrow I am driving out demons and effecting cures, and on the third day I finish my course.' 013:033 "Yet I must continue my journey to-day and to-morrow and the day following; for it is not conceivable that a Prophet should perish outside of Jerusalem. 013:034 O Jerusalem, Jerusalem, thou who murderest the Prophets and stonest those who have been sent to thee, how often have I desired to gather thy children just as a hen gathers her brood under her wings, and you would not come! 013:035 See, your house is left to you. But I tell you that you will never see me again until you say, `Blessed is He who comes in the name of the Lord!'" 014:001 One day-it was a Sabbath-He was taking a meal at the house of one of the Rulers of the Pharisee party, while they were closely watching Him. 014:002 In front of Him was a man suffering from dropsy. 014:003 This led Jesus to ask the lawyers and Pharisees, "Is it allowable to cure people on the Sabbath?" 014:004 They gave Him no answer; so He took hold of the man, cured him, and sent him away. 014:005 Then He turned to them and said, "Which of you shall have a child or an ox fall into a well on the Sabbath day, and will not immediately lift him out?" 014:006 To this they could make no reply. 014:007 Then, when He noticed that the invited guests chose the best seats, He used this as an illustration and said to them, 014:008 "When any one invites you to a wedding banquet, do not take the best seat, lest perhaps some more honoured guest than you may have been asked, 014:009 and the man who invited you both will come and will say to you, `Make room for this guest,' and then you, ashamed, will move to the lowest place. 014:010 On the contrary, when you are invited go and take the lowest place, that when your host comes round he may say to you, `My friend, come up higher.' This will be doing you honour in the presence of all the other guests. 014:011 For whoever uplifts himself will be humbled, and he who humbles himself will be uplifted. 014:012 Also to His host, who had invited Him, He said, "When you give a breakfast or a dinner, do not invite your friends or brothers or relatives or rich neighbours, lest perhaps they should invite you in return and a requital be made you. 014:013 But when you entertain, invite the poor, the crippled, the lame, and the blind; 014:014 and you will be blessed, because they have no means of requiting you, but there will be requital for you at the Resurrection of the righteous." 014:015 After listening to this teaching, one of His fellow guests said to Him, "Blessed is he who shall feast in God's Kingdom." 014:016 "A man once gave a great dinner," replied Jesus, "to which he invited a large number of guests. 014:017 At dinner-time he sent his servant to announce to those who had been invited, "`Come, for things are now ready.' 014:018 "But they all without exception began to excuse themselves. The first told him, "`I have purchased a piece of land, and must of necessity go and look at it. Pray hold me excused.' 014:019 "A second pleaded, "`I have bought five yoke of oxen, and am on my way to try them. Pray hold me excused.' 014:020 "Another said, "`I am just married. It is impossible for me to come.' 014:021 "So the servant came and brought these answers to his master, and they stirred his anger. "`Go out quickly,' he said, `into the streets of the city-the wide ones and the narrow. You will see poor men, and crippled, blind, lame: fetch them all in here.' 014:022 "Soon the servant reported the result, saying, "`Sir, what you ordered is done, and there is room still.' 014:023 "`Go out,' replied the master, `to the high roads and hedge-rows, and compel the people to come in, so that my house may be filled. 014:024 For I tell you that not one of those who were invited shall taste my dinner.'" 014:025 On His journey vast crowds attended Him, towards whom He turned and said, 014:026 "If any one is coming to me who does not hate his father and mother, wife and children, brothers and sisters, yes and his own life also, he cannot be a disciple of mine. 014:027 No one who does not carry his own cross and come after me can be a disciple of mine. 014:028 "Which of you, desiring to build a tower, does not sit down first and calculate the cost, asking if he has the means to finish it?- 014:029 lest perhaps, when he has laid the foundation and is unable to finish, all who see it shall begin to jeer at him, 014:030 saying, `This man began to build, but could not finish.' 014:031 Or what king, marching to encounter another king in war, does not first sit down and deliberate whether he is able with ten thousand men to meet the one who is advancing against him with twenty thousand? 014:032 If not, while the other is still a long way off, he sends messengers and sues for peace. 014:033 Just as no one of you who does not detach himself from all that belongs to him can be a disciple of mine. 014:034 "Salt is good: but if even the salt has become tasteless, what will you use to season it? 014:035 Neither for land nor dunghill is it of any use; they throw it away. Listen, every one who has ears to listen with!" 015:001 Now the tax-gatherers and the notorious sinners were everywhere in the habit of coming close to Him to listen to Him; 015:002 and this led the Pharisees and the Scribes indignantly to complain, saying, "He gives a welcome to notorious sinners, and joins them at their meals!" 015:003 So in figurative language He asked them, 015:004 "Which of you men, if he has a hundred sheep and has lost one of them, does not leave the ninety-nine in their pasture and go in search of the lost one till he finds it? 015:005 And when he has found it, he lifts it on his shoulder, glad at heart. 015:006 Then coming home he calls his friends and neighbours together, and says, `Congratulate me, for I have found my sheep- the one I had lost.' 015:007 I tell you that in the same way there will be rejoicing in Heaven over one repentant sinner-more rejoicing than over ninety-nine blameless persons who have no need of repentance. 015:008 "Or what woman who has ten silver coins, if she loses one of them, does not light a lamp and sweep the house and search carefully till she finds it? 015:009 And when she has found it, she calls together her friends and neighbours, and says, "`Congratulate me, for I have found the coin which I had lost.' 015:010 "I tell you that in the same way there is rejoicing in the presence of the angels of God over one repentant sinner." 015:011 He went on to say, "There was a man who had two sons. 015:012 The younger of them said to his father, "`Father, give me the share of the property that comes to me.' "So he divided his wealth between them. 015:013 No long time afterwards the younger son got all together and travelled to a distant country, where he wasted his money in debauchery and excess. 015:014 At last, when he had spent everything, there came a terrible famine throughout that country, and he began to feel the pinch of want. 015:015 So he went and hired himself to one of the inhabitants of that country, who sent him on to his farm to tend swine; 015:016 and he longed to make a hearty meal of the pods the swine were eating, but no one gave him any. 015:017 "But on coming to himself he said, "`How many of my father's hired men have more bread than they want, while I here am dying of hunger! 015:018 I will rise and go to my father, and will say to him, Father, I have sinned against Heaven and before you: 015:019 I no longer deserve to be called a son of yours: treat me as one of your hired men.' 015:020 "So he rose and came to his father. But while he was still a long way off, his father saw him and pitied him, and ran and threw his arms round his neck and kissed him tenderly. 015:021 "`Father,' cried the son, `I have sinned against Heaven and before you: no longer do I deserve to be called a son of yours.' 015:022 "But the father said to his servants, "`Fetch a good coat quickly- the best one-and put it on him; and bring a ring for his finger and shoes for his feet. 015:023 Fetch the fat calf and kill it, and let us feast and enjoy ourselves; 015:024 for my son here was dead and has come to life again: he was lost and has been found.' "And they began to be merry. 015:025 "Now his elder son was out on the farm; and when he returned and came near home, he heard music and dancing. 015:026 Then he called one of the lads to him and asked what all this meant. 015:027 "`Your brother has come,' he replied; `and your father has had the fat calf killed, because he has got him home safe and sound.' 015:028 "Then he was angry and would not go in. But his father came out and entreated him. 015:029 "`All these years,' replied the son, `I have been slaving for you, and I have never at any time disobeyed any of your orders, and yet you have never given me so much as a kid, for me to enjoy myself with my friends; 015:030 but now that this son of yours is come who has eaten up your property among his bad women, you have killed the fat calf for him.' 015:031 "`You my dear son,' said the father, `are always with me, and all that is mine is also yours. 015:032 We are bound to make merry and rejoice, for this brother of yours was dead and has come back to life, he was lost and has been found.'" 016:001 He said also to His disciples: "There was a rich man who had a steward, about whom a report was brought to him, that he was wasting his property. 016:002 He called him and said, "`What is this I hear about you? Render an account of your stewardship, for I cannot let you hold it any longer.' 016:003 "Then the steward said within himself, "`What am I to do? For my master is taking away the stewardship from me. I am not strong enough for field labour: to beg, I should be ashamed. 016:004 I see what to do, in order that when I am discharged from the stewardship they may give me a home in their own houses.' 016:005 "So he called all his master's debtors, one by one, and asked the first, `How much are you in debt to my master?' 016:006 "`A hundred firkins of oil,' he replied. "`Here is your account,' said the steward: `sit down quickly and change it into fifty firkins.' 016:007 "To a second he said, "`And how much do you owe?' "`A hundred quarters of wheat,' was the answer. "`Here is your account,' said he: `change it into eighty quarters.' 016:008 "And the master praised the dishonest steward for his shrewdness; for, in relation to their own contemporaries, the men of this age are shrewder than the sons of Light. 016:009 "But I charge you, so to use the wealth which is ever tempting to dishonesty as to win friends who, when it fails, shall welcome you to the tents that never perish. 016:010 The man who is honest in a very small matter is honest in a great one also; and he who is dishonest in a very small matter is dishonest in a great one also. 016:011 If therefore you have not proved yourselves faithful in dealing with the wealth that is tainted with fraud, who will entrust to you the true good? 016:012 And if you have not been faithful in dealing with that which is not your own, who will give you that which is your own? 016:013 "No servant can be in bondage to two masters. For either he will hate one and love the other, or else he will cling fast to one and scorn the other. You cannot be bondservants both of God and of gold." 016:014 To all this the Pharisees listened, bitterly jeering at Him; for they were lovers of money. 016:015 "You are they," He said to them, "who boast of their own goodness before men, but God sees your hearts; for that which holds a proud position among men is detestable in God's sight. 016:016 The Law and the Prophets continued until John came: from that time the Good News of the Kingdom of God has been spreading, and all classes have been forcing their way into it. 016:017 But it is easier for earth and sky to pass away than for one smallest detail of the Law to fall to the ground. 016:018 Every man who divorces his wife and marries another commits adultery; and he who marries her when so divorced from her husband commits adultery. 016:019 "There was once a rich man who habitually arrayed himself in purple and fine linen, and enjoyed a splendid banquet every day, 016:020 while at his outer door there lay a beggar, Lazarus by name, 016:021 covered with sores and longing to make a full meal off the scraps flung on the floor from the rich man's table. Nay, the dogs, too, used to come and lick his sores. 016:022 "But in course of time the beggar died; and he was carried by the angels into Abraham's bosom. The rich man also died, and had a funeral. 016:023 And in Hades, being in torment, he looked and saw Abraham in the far distance, and Lazarus resting in his arms. 016:024 So he cried aloud, and said, "`Father Abraham, take pity on me and send Lazarus to dip the tip of his finger in water and cool my tongue, for I am in agony in this flame.' 016:025 "`Remember, my child,' said Abraham, `that you had all your good things during your lifetime, and that Lazarus in like manner had his bad things. But, now and here, he is receiving consolation and you are in agony.

016:026 And, besides all this, a vast chasm is immovably fixed between us and you, put there in order that those who desire to cross from this side to you may not be able, nor any be able to cross over from your side to us.' 016:027 "`I entreat you then, father,' said he, `to send him to my father's house. 016:028 For I have five brothers. Let him earnestly warn them, lest they also come to this place of torment.' 016:029 "`They have Moses and the Prophets,' replied Abraham; `let them hear them.' 016:030 "`No, father Abraham,' he pleaded; `but if some one goes to them from the dead, they will repent.' 016:031 "`If they are deaf to Moses and the Prophets,' replied Abraham, `they would not be led to believe even if some one should rise from the dead.'" 017:001 Jesus said to His disciples, "It is inevitable that causes of stumbling should come; but alas for him through whom they come! 017:002 It would be well for him if, with a millstone round his neck, he were lying at the bottom of the sea, rather than that he should cause even one of these little ones to fall. 017:003 Be on your guard. "If your brother acts wrongly, reprove him; and if he is sorry, forgive him; 017:004 and if seven times in a day he acts wrongly towards you, and seven times turns again to you and says, `I am sorry,' you must forgive him." 017:005 And the Apostles said to the Lord, "Give us faith." 017:006 "If your faith," replied the Lord, "is like a mustard seed, you might command this black-mulberry-tree, `Tear up your roots and plant yourself in the sea,' and instantly it would obey you. 017:007 But which of you who has a servant ploughing, or tending sheep, will say to him when he comes in from the farm, `Come at once and take your place at table,' 017:008 and will not rather say to him, `Get my dinner ready, make yourself tidy, and wait upon me till I have finished my dinner, and then you shall have yours'? 017:009 Does he thank the servant for obeying his orders? 017:010 So you also, when you have obeyed all the orders given you, must say, "`There is no merit in our service: what we have done is only what we were in duty bound to do.'" 017:011 As they pursued their journey to Jerusalem, He passed through Samaria and Galilee. 017:012 And as He entered a certain village, ten men met Him who were lepers and stood at a distance. 017:013 In loud voices they cried out, "Jesus, Rabbi, take pity on us." 017:014 Perceiving this, He said to them, "Go and show yourselves to the Priests." And while on their way to do this they were made clean. 017:015 One of them, seeing that he was cured, came back, adoring and praising God in a loud voice, 017:016 and he threw himself at the feet of Jesus, thanking Him. He was a Samaritan. 017:017 "Were not all ten made clean?" Jesus asked; "but where are the nine? 017:018 Have none been found to come back and give glory to God except this foreigner?" 017:019 And He said to him, "Rise and go: your faith has cured you." 017:020 Being asked by the Pharisees when the Kingdom of God was coming, He answered, "The Kingdom of God does not so come that you can stealthily watch for it. 017:021 Nor will they say,

`See here!' or `See there!'-for the Kingdom of God is within you." 017:022
Then, turning to His disciples, He said, "There will come a time when you
will wish you could see a single one of the days of the Son of Man, but will
not see one. 017:023 And they will say to you, `See there!' `See here!' Do
not start off and go in pursuit. 017:024 For just as the lightning, when it
flashes, shines from one part of the horizon to the opposite part, so will the
Son of Man be on His day. 017:025 But first He must endure much
suffering, and be rejected by the present generation. 017:026 "And as it was
in the time of Noah, so will it also be in the time of the Son of Man.
017:027 Men were eating and drinking, taking wives and giving wives, up to
the very day on which Noah entered the Ark, and the Deluge came and
destroyed them all. 017:028 The same was true in the time of Lot: they were
eating and drinking, buying and selling, planting and building; 017:029 but
on the day that Lot left Sodom, God rained fire and brimstone from the sky
and destroyed them all. 017:030 Exactly so will it be on the day that the veil
is lifted from the Son of Man. 017:031 "On that day, if a man is on the roof
and his property indoors, let him not go down to fetch it; and, in the same
way, he who is in the field, let him not turn back. 017:032 Remember Lot's
wife. 017:033 Any man who makes it his object to keep his own life safe,
will lose it; but whoever loses his life will preserve it. 017:034 On that night,
I tell you, there will be two men in one bed: one will be taken away and the
other left behind. 017:035 There will be two women turning the mill
together: one will be taken away and the other left behind." 017:036 []
017:037 "Where, Master?" they inquired. "Where the dead body is," He
replied, "there also will the vultures flock together." 018:001 He also taught
them by a parable that they must always pray and never lose heart. 018:002
"In a certain town," He said, "there was a judge who had no fear of God
and no respect for man. 018:003 And in the same town was a widow who
repeatedly came and entreated him, saying, "`Give me justice and stop my
oppressor.' 018:004 "For a time he would not, but afterwards he said to
himself, "`Though I have neither reverence for God nor respect for man,
018:005 yet because she annoys me I will give her justice, to prevent her
from constantly coming to pester me.'" 018:006 And the Lord said, "Hear
those words of the unjust judge. 018:007 And will not God avenge the
wrongs of His own People who cry aloud to Him day and night, although
He seems slow in taking action on their behalf? 018:008 Yes, He will soon
avenge their wrongs. Yet, when the Son of Man comes, will He find faith
on earth?" 018:009 And to some who relied on themselves as being
righteous men, and looked down upon all others, He addressed this parable.
018:010 "Two men went up to the Temple to pray," He said; "one being a
Pharisee and the other a tax-gatherer. 018:011 The Pharisee, standing erect,
prayed as follows by himself: "`O God, I thank Thee that I am not like
other people- I am not a thief nor a cheat nor an adulterer, nor do I even

resemble this tax-gatherer. 018:012 I fast twice a week. I pay the tithe on all my gains.' 018:013 "But the tax-gatherer, standing far back, would not so much as lift his eyes to Heaven, but kept beating his breast and saying, "`O God, be reconciled to me, sinner that I am.' 018:014 "I tell you that this man went home more thoroughly absolved from guilt than the other; for every one who uplifts himself will be humbled, but he who humbles himself will be uplifted." 018:015 On one occasion people also brought with them their infants, for Him to touch them; but the disciples, noticing this, proceeded to find fault with them. 018:016 Jesus however called the infants to Him. "Let the little children come to me," He said; "do not hinder them; for it is to those who are childlike that the Kingdom of God belongs. 018:017 I tell you in solemn truth that, whoever does not receive the Kingdom of God like a little child will certainly not enter it." 018:018 The question was put to Him by a Ruler: "Good Rabbi, what shall I do to inherit the Life of the Ages?" 018:019 "Why do you call me good?" replied Jesus; "there is no one good but One, namely God. 018:020 You know the Commandments: `Do not commit adultery;' `Do not murder;' `Do not steal;' `Do not lie in giving evidence;' `Honour thy father and thy mother.'" 018:021 "All of those," he replied, "I have kept from my youth." 018:022 On receiving this answer Jesus said to him, "There is still one thing wanting in you. Sell everything you possess and give the money to the poor, and you shall have wealth in Heaven; and then come, follow me." 018:023 But on hearing these words he was deeply sorrowful, for he was exceedingly rich. 018:024 Jesus saw his sorrow, and said, "With how hard a struggle do the possessors of riches ever enter the Kingdom of God! 018:025 Why, it is easier for a camel to go through a needle's eye than for a rich man to enter the Kingdom of God." 018:026 "Who then can be saved?" exclaimed the hearers. 018:027 "Things impossible with man," He replied, "are possible with God." 018:028 Then Peter said, "See, we have given up our homes and have followed you." 018:029 "I solemnly tell you," replied Jesus, "that there is no one who has left house or wife, or brothers or parents or children, for the sake of God's Kingdom, 018:030 who shall not certainly receive many times as much in this life, and in the age that is coming the Life of the Ages." 018:031 Then He drew the Twelve to Him and said, "See, we are going up to Jerusalem, and everything written in the Prophets which refers to the Son of Man will be fulfilled. 018:032 For He will be given up to the Gentiles, and be mocked, outraged and spit upon. 018:033 They will scourge Him and put Him to death, and on the third day He will rise to life again." 018:034 Nothing of this did they understand. The words were a mystery to them, nor could they see what He meant. 018:035 As Jesus came near to Jericho, there was a blind man sitting by the way-side begging. 018:036 He heard a crowd of people going past, and inquired what it all meant. 018:037 "Jesus the Nazarene is passing by," they told him. 018:038

Then, at the top of his voice, he cried out, "Jesus, son of David, take pity on me." 018:039 Those in front reproved him and tried to silence him; but he continued shouting, louder than ever, "Son of David, take pity on me." 018:040 At length Jesus stopped and desired them to bring the man to Him; and when he had come close to Him He asked him, 018:041 "What shall I do for you?" "Sir," he replied, "let me recover my sight." 018:042 "Recover your sight," said Jesus: "your faith has cured you." 018:043 No sooner were the words spoken than the man regained his sight and followed Jesus, giving glory to God; and all the people, seeing it, gave praise to God. 019:001 So He entered Jericho and was passing through the town. 019:002 There was a man there called Zacchaeus, who was the local surveyor of taxes, and was wealthy. 019:003 He was anxious to see what sort of man Jesus was; but he could not because of the crowd, for he was short in stature. 019:004 So he ran on in front and climbed up a mulberry tree to see Him; for He was about to pass that way. 019:005 As soon as Jesus came to the place, He looked up and said to him, "Zacchaeus, come down quickly, for I must stay at your house to-day." 019:006 So he came down in haste, and welcomed Him joyfully. 019:007 When they all saw this, they began to complain with indignation. "He has gone in to be the guest of a notorious sinner!" they said. 019:008 Zacchaeus however stood up, and addressing the Lord said, "Here and now, Master, I give half my property to the poor, and if I have unjustly exacted money from any man, I pledge myself to repay to him four times the amount." 019:009 Turning towards him, Jesus replied, "To-day salvation has come to this house, seeing that he too is a son of Abraham. 019:010 For the Son of Man has come to seek and to save that which was lost." 019:011 As they were listening to His words, He went on to teach them by a parable, because He was near to Jerusalem and they supposed that the Kingdom of God was going to appear immediately. 019:012 So He said to them, "A man of noble family travelled to a distant country to obtain the rank of king, and to return. 019:013 And he called ten of his servants and gave each of them a pound, instructing them to trade with the money during his absence. 019:014 "Now his countrymen hated him, and sent a deputation after him to say, `We are not willing that he should become our king.' 019:015 And upon his return, after he had obtained the sovereignty, he ordered those servants to whom he had given the money to be summoned before him, that he might learn their success in trading. 019:016 "So the first came and said, "`Sir, your pound has produced ten pounds more.' 019:017 "`Well done, good servant,' he replied; `because you have been faithful in a very small matter, be in authority over ten towns.' 019:018 "The second came, and said, "`Your pound, Sir, has produced five pounds.' 019:019 "So he said to this one also, "`And you, be the governor of five towns.' 019:020 "The next came. "`Sir,' he said, `here is your pound, which I have kept wrapt up in a cloth. 019:021 For I was afraid of you, because you are a severe man: you take up what you did not lay down, and you reap what you did not sow.' 019:022 "`By your own words,' he replied, `I will judge you, you bad servant. You knew me to be a severe man, taking up what I did not lay down, and reaping what I did not sow: 019:023 why then did you not put my money into a bank, that when I came I might have received it back with interest? 019:024 "And he said to those who stood by, "`Take the pound from him and give it to him who has the ten pounds.' 019:025 ("They said to him, "`Sir, he already has ten pounds.') 019:026 "`I tell you that to every one who has anything, more shall be given; and from him who has not anything, even what he has shall be taken away. 019:027 But as for those enemies of mine who were unwilling that I should become their king, bring them here, and cut them to pieces in my presence.'" 019:028 After thus speaking, He journeyed onward, proceeding up to Jerusalem. 019:029 And when he was come near Bethphage and Bethany, at the Mount called the Oliveyard, He sent two of the disciples on in front, 019:030 saying to them, "Go into the village facing you. On entering it you will find an ass's foal tied up which no one has ever yet ridden: untie it, and bring it here. 019:031 And if any one asks you, `Why are you untying the colt?' simply say, `The Master needs it.'" 019:032 So those who were sent went and found things as He had told them. 019:033 And while they were untying the colt the owners called out, "Why are you untying the colt?" 019:034 and they replied, "The Master needs it." 019:035 Then they brought it to Jesus, and after throwing their outer garments on the colt they placed Jesus on it. 019:036 So He rode on, while they carpeted the road with their garments. 019:037 And when He was now getting near Jerusalem, and descending the Mount of Olives, the whole multitude of the disciples began in their joy to praise God in loud voices for all the mighty deeds they had witnessed. 019:038 "Blessed is the King," they cried, "who comes in the name of the Lord: in Heaven peace, and glory in the highest realms." 019:039 Thereupon some of the Pharisees in the crowd appealed to Him, saying, "Rabbi, reprove your disciples." 019:040 "I tell you," He replied, "that if *they* became silent, the very stones would cry out." 019:041 When He came into full view of the city, He wept aloud over it, and exclaimed, 019:042 "O that at this time thou hadst known-yes even thou- what makes peace possible! But now it is hid from thine eyes. 019:043 For the time is coming upon thee when thy foes will throw up around thee earthworks and a wall, investing thee and hemming thee in on every side. 019:044 And they will dash thee to the ground and thy children within thee, and will not leave one stone upon another within thee; because thou hast not recognized the time of thy visitation." 019:045 Then Jesus entered the Temple and proceeded to drive out the dealers. 019:046 "It is written," He said, "`And My house shall be the House of Prayer,' but you have made it a robbers' cave." 019:047 And day after day He taught in the Temple, while the High Priests and the Scribes were devising some means of destroying Him, as were also the leading men of the people. 019:048 But they could not find any way of doing it, for the people all hung upon His lips. 020:001 On one of those days while He was teaching the people in the Temple and proclaiming the Good News, the High Priests came upon Him, and the Scribes, 020:002 together with the Elders, and they asked Him, "Tell us, By what authority are you doing these things? And who is it that gave you this authority?" 020:003 "I also will put a question to you, "He said; 020:004 "was John's baptism of Heavenly or of human origin?" 020:005 So they debated the matter with one another. "If we say `Heavenly,'" they argued, "he will say, `Why did you not believe him?' 020:006 And if we say, `human,' the people will all stone us; for they are thoroughly convinced that John was a Prophet." 020:007 And they answered that they did not know the origin of it. 020:008 "Nor will I tell you," said Jesus, "by what authority I do these things." 020:009 Then He proceeded to speak a parable to the people. "There was a man," He said, "who planted a vineyard, let it out to vine-dressers, and went abroad for a considerable time. 020:010 At vintage-time he sent a servant to the vine-dressers, for them to give him a share of the crop; but the vine-dressers beat him cruelly and sent him away empty-handed. 020:011 Then he sent a second servant; and him too they beat and ill treated and sent away empty-handed. 020:012 Then again he sent a third; and this one also they wounded and drove away. 020:013 Then the owner of the vineyard said, "`What am I to do? I will send my son-my dearly-loved son: they will probably respect him.' 020:014 "But when the vine-dressers saw him, they discussed the matter with one another, and said, "`This is the heir: let us kill him, that the inheritance may be ours.' 020:015 "So they turned him out of the vineyard and murdered him. What then will the owner of the vineyard do to them? 020:016 He will come and put these vine-dressers to death, and give the vineyard to others." "God forbid!" exclaimed the hearers. 020:017 He looked at them and said, "What then does that mean which is written, "`The Stone which the builders rejected has been made the cornerstone'? 020:018 Every one who falls on that stone will be severely hurt, but on whomsoever it falls, he will be utterly crushed." 020:019 At this the Scribes and the High Priests wanted to lay hands on Him, then and there; only they were afraid of the people. For they saw that in this parable He had referred to them. 020:020 So, after impatiently watching their opportunity, they sent spies who were to act the part of good and honest men, that they might fasten on some expression of His, so as to hand Him over to the ruling power and the Governor's authority. 020:021 So they put a question to Him. "Rabbi," they said, "we know that you say and teach what is right and that you make no distinctions between one man and another, but teach God's way truly. 020:022 Is it allowable to pay a tax to Caesar, or not?" 020:023 But He saw through their knavery and replied,

020:024 "Show me a shilling; whose likeness and inscription does it bear?" "Caesar's," they said. 020:025 "Pay therefore," He replied, "what is Caesar's to Caesar- and what is God's to God." 020:026 There was nothing here that they could lay hold of before the people, and marvelling at His answer they said no more. 020:027 Next some of the Sadducees came forward (who deny that there is a Resurrection), and they asked Him, 020:028 "Rabbi, Moses made it a law for us that if a man's brother should die, leaving a wife but no children, the man shall marry the widow and raise up a family for his brother. 020:029 Now there were seven brothers. The first of them took a wife and died childless. 020:030 The second and the third also took her; 020:031 and all seven, having done the same, left no children when they died. 020:032 Finally the woman also died. 020:033 The woman, then-at the Resurrection-whose wife shall she be? for they all seven married her." 020:034 "The men of this age," replied Jesus, "marry, and the women are given in marriage. 020:035 But as for those who shall have been deemed worthy to find a place in that other age and in the Resurrection from among the dead, the men do not marry and the women are not given in marriage. 020:036 For indeed they cannot die again; they are like angels, and are sons of God through being sons of the Resurrection. 020:037 But that the dead rise to life even Moses clearly implies in the passage about the Bush, where he calls the Lord `The God of Abraham, the God of Isaac, and the God of Jacob.' 020:038 He is not a God of dead, but of living men, for to Him are all living." 020:039 Then some of the Scribes replied, "Rabbi, you have spoken well." 020:040 From that time, however, no one ventured to challenge Him with a single question. 020:041 But He asked them, "How is it they say that the Christ is a son of David? 020:042 Why, David himself says in the Book of Psalms, "`The Lord said to my Lord, Sit at My right hand 020:043 Until I have made thy foes a footstool under they feet.' 020:044 "David himself therefore calls Him Lord, and how can He be his son?" 020:045 Then, in the hearing of all the people, He said to the disciples, 020:046 "Beware of the Scribes, who like to walk about in long robes, and love to be bowed to in places of public resort and to occupy the best seats in the synagogues or at a dinner party; 020:047 who swallow up the property of widows and mask their wickedness by making long prayers. They will be punished far more severely than others." 021:001 Looking up He saw the people throwing their gifts into the Treasury- the rich people. 021:002 He also saw a poor widow dropping in two farthings, 021:003 and He said, "In truth I tell you that this widow, so poor, has thrown in more than any of them. 021:004 For from what they could well spare they have all of them contributed to the offerings, but she in her need has thrown in all she had to live on." 021:005 When some were remarking about the Temple, how it was embellished with beautiful stones and dedicated gifts, He said, 021:006 "As to these things which you now admire, the time is coming when there will not be one stone left here upon another which will not be pulled down." 021:007 "Rabbi, when will this be?" they asked Him, "and what will be the token given when these things are about to take place?" 021:008 "See to it," He replied, "that you are not misled; for many will come assuming my name and professing, `I am He,' or saying, `The time is close at hand.' Do not go and follow them. 021:009 But when you hear of wars and turmoils, be not afraid; for these things must happen first, but the end does not come immediately." 021:010 Then He said to them, "Nation will rise in arms against nation, and kingdom against kingdom. 021:011 And there will be great earthquakes, and in places famines and pestilence; and there will be terrible sights and wonderful tokens from Heaven. 021:012 "But before all these things happen they will lay hands on you and persecute you. They will deliver you up to synagogues and to prison, and you will be brought before kings and governors for my sake. 021:013 In the end all this will be evidence of your fidelity. 021:014 "Make up your minds, however, not to prepare a defence beforehand, 021:015 for I will give you utterance and wisdom which none of your opponents will be able to withstand or reply to. 021:016 You will be betrayed even by parents, brothers, relatives, friends; and some of you they will put to death. 021:017 You will be the objects of universal hatred because you are called by my name; 021:018 and yet not a hair of your heads shall perish. 021:019 By your patient endurance you will purchase your lives. 021:020 "But when you see Jerusalem with armies encamping round her on every side, then be certain that her overthrow is close at hand. 021:021 Then let those who shall be in Judaea escape to the hills; let those who are in the city leave it, and those who are in the country not enter in. 021:022 For those are the days of vengeance and of fulfilling all that is written. 021:023 "Alas for the women who at that time are with child or who have infants; for there will be great distress in the land, and anger towards this People. 021:024 They will fall by the sword, or be carried off into slavery among all the Gentiles. And Jerusalem will be trampled under foot by the Gentiles, till the appointed times of the Gentiles have expired. 021:025 "There will be signs in sun, moon, and stars; and on earth anguish among the nations in their bewilderment at the roaring of the sea and its billows; 021:026 while men's hearts are fainting for fear, and for anxious expectation of what is coming on the world. For the forces which control the heavens will be disordered and disturbed. 021:027 And then will they see the Son of Man coming in a cloud with great power and glory. 021:028 But when all this is beginning to take place, grieve no longer. Lift up your heads, because your deliverance is drawing near." 021:029 And He spoke a parable to them. "See," He said, "the fig-tree and all the trees. 021:030 As soon as they have shot out their leaves, you know at a glance that summer is now near. 021:031 So also, when you see these things happening, you may be sure that the Kingdom of

God is near. 021:032 I tell you in solemn truth that the present generation will certainly not pass away without all these things having first taken place. 021:033 Earth and sky will pass away, but it is certain that my words will not pass away. 021:034 "But take heed to yourselves, lest your souls be weighed down with self-indulgence and drunkenness or the anxieties of this life, and that day come upon you, suddenly, like a falling trap; 021:035 for it will come on all dwellers on the face of the whole earth. 021:036 But beware of slumbering; and every moment pray that you may be fully strengthened to escape from all these coming evils, and to take your stand in the presence of the Son of Man." 021:037 His habit at this time was to teach in the Temple by day, but to go out and spend the night on the Mount called the Oliveyard. 021:038 And all the people came to Him in the Temple, early in the morning, to listen to Him. 022:001 Meanwhile the Festival of the Unleavened Bread, called the Passover, was approaching, 022:002 and the High Priests and the Scribes were contriving how to destroy Him. But they feared the people. 022:003 Satan, however, entered into Judas (the man called Iscariot) who was one of the Twelve. 022:004 He went and conferred with the High Priests and Commanders as to how he should deliver Him up to them. 022:005 This gave them great pleasure, and they agreed to pay him. 022:006 He accepted their offer, and then looked out for an opportunity to betray Him when the people were not there. 022:007 When the day of the Unleavened Bread came-the day for the Passover lamb to be sacrificed- 022:008 Jesus sent Peter and John with instructions. "Go," He said, "and prepare the Passover for us, that we may eat it." 022:009 "Where shall we prepare it?" they asked. 022:010 "You will no sooner have entered the city," He replied, "than you will meet a man carrying a pitcher of water. Follow him into the house to which he goes, 022:011 and say to the master of the house, "`The Rabbi asks you, Where is the room where I can eat the Passover with my disciples?' 022:012 "And he will show you a large furnished room upstairs. There make your preparations." 022:013 So they went and found all as He had told them; and they got the Passover ready. 022:014 When the time was come, and He had taken His place at table, and the Apostles with Him, 022:015 He said to them, "Earnestly have I longed to eat this Passover with you before I suffer; 022:016 for I tell you that I certainly shall not eat one again till its full meaning has been brought out in the Kingdom of God." 022:017 Then, having received the cup and given thanks, He said, "Take this and share it among yourselves; 022:018 for I tell you that from this time I will never drink the produce of the vine till the Kingdom of God has come." 022:019 Then, taking a Passover biscuit, He gave thanks and broke it, and gave it to them, saying, "This is my body which is being given on your behalf: this do in remembrance of me." 022:020 He gave them the cup in like manner, when the meal was over. "This cup," He said, "is the new Covenant ratified by my blood which is to be poured out on your behalf. 022:021 Yet the hand of him who is betraying me is at the table with me. 022:022 For indeed the Son of Man goes on His way-His pre-destined way; yet alas for that man who is betraying Him!" 022:023 Thereupon they began to discuss with one another which of them it could possibly be who was about to do this. 022:024 There arose also a dispute among them which of them should be regarded as greatest. 022:025 But He said to them, "The kings of the Gentiles are their masters, and those who exercise authority over them are called Benefactors. 022:026 With you it is not so; but let the greatest among you be as the younger, and the leader be like him who serves. 022:027 For which is the greater-he who sits at table, or he who waits on him? Is it not he who sits at table? But my position among you is that of one who waits on others. 022:028 You however have remained with me amid my trials; 022:029 and I covenant to give you, as my Father has covenanted to give me, a Kingdom- 022:030 so that you shall eat and drink at my table in my Kingdom, and sit on thrones as judges over the twelve tribes of Israel. 022:031 "Simon, Simon, I tell you that Satan has obtained permission to have all of you to sift as wheat is sifted. 022:032 But *I* have prayed for *you* that your faith may not fail, and you, when at last you have come back to your true self, must strengthen your brethren." 022:033 "Master," replied Peter, "with you I am ready to go both to prison and to death." 022:034 "I tell you, Peter," said Jesus, "that the cock will not crow to-day till you have three times denied that you know me." 022:035 Then He asked them, "When I sent you out without purse or bag or shoes, was there anything you needed?" "No, nothing," they replied. 022:036 "But now," said He, "let the one who has a purse take it, and he who has a bag must do the same. And let him who has no sword sell his outer garment and buy one. 022:037 For I tell you that those words of Scripture must yet find their fulfilment in me: `And He was reckoned among the lawless'; for indeed that saying about me has its accomplishment." 022:038 "Master, here are two swords," they exclaimed. "That is enough," He replied. 022:039 On going out, He proceeded as usual to the Mount of Olives, and His disciples followed Him. 022:040 But when He arrived at the place, He said to them, "Pray that you may not come into temptation." 022:041 But He Himself withdrew from them about a stone's throw, and knelt down and prayed repeatedly, saying, 022:042 "Father, if it be Thy will, take this cup away from me; yet not my will but Thine be done!" 022:043 And there appeared to Him an angel from Heaven, strengthening Him; 022:044 while He-an agony of distress having come upon Him- prayed all the more with intense earnestness, and His sweat became like clots of blood dropping on the ground. 022:045 When He rose from his prayer and came to His disciples, He found them sleeping for sorrow. 022:046 "Why are you sleeping?" He said; "stand up; and pray that you may not come into temptation." 022:047

While He was still speaking there came a crowd with Judas, already mentioned as one of the Twelve, at their head. He went up to Jesus to kiss Him. 022:048 "Judas," said Jesus, "are you betraying the Son of Man with a kiss?" 022:049 Those who were about Him, seeing what was likely to happen, asked Him, "Master, shall we strike with the sword?" 022:050 And one of them struck a blow at the High Priest's servant and cut off his right ear. 022:051 "Permit me thus far," said Jesus. And He touched the ear and healed it. 022:052 Then Jesus said to the High Priests and Commanders of the Temple and Elders, who had come to arrest Him, "Have you come out as if to fight with a robber, with swords and cudgels? 022:053 While day after day I was with you in the Temple, you did not lay hands upon me; but to you belongs this hour- and the power of darkness." 022:054 And they arrested Him and led Him away, and brought Him to the High Priest's house, while Peter followed a good way behind. 022:055 And when they had lighted a fire in the middle of the court and had seated themselves in a group round it, Peter was sitting among them, 022:056 when a maidservant saw him sitting by the fire, and, looking fixedly at him, she said, "This man also was with him." 022:057 But he denied it, and declared, "Woman, I do not know him." 022:058 Shortly afterwards a man saw him and said, "You, too, are one of them." "No, man, I am not," said Peter. 022:059 After an interval of about an hour some one else stoutly maintained: "Certainly this fellow also was with him, for in fact he is a Galilaean." 022:060 "Man, I don't know what you mean," replied Peter. No sooner had he spoken than a cock crowed. 022:061 The Master turned and looked on Peter; and Peter recollected the Master's words, how He had said to him, "This very day, before the cock crows, you will disown me three times." 022:062 And he went out and wept aloud bitterly. 022:063 Meanwhile the men who held Jesus in custody repeatedly beat Him in cruel sport, 022:064 or blindfolded Him, and then challenged Him. "Prove to us," they said, "that you are a prophet, by telling us who it was that struck you." 022:065 And they said many other insulting things to Him. 022:066 As soon as it was day, the whole body of the Elders, both High Priests and Scribes, assembled. Then He was brought into their Sanhedrin, and they asked Him, 022:067 "Are you the Christ? Tell us." "If I tell you," He replied, "you will certainly not believe; 022:068 and if I ask you questions, you will certainly not answer. 022:069 But from this time forward the Son of Man will be seated at the right hand of God's omnipotence." 022:070 Thereupon they cried out with one voice, "You, then, are the Son of God?" "It is as you say," He answered; "I am He." 022:071 "What need have we of further evidence?" they said; "for we ourselves have heard it from his own lips." 023:001 Then the whole assembly rose and brought Him to Pilate, and began to accuse Him. 023:002 "We have found this man," they said, "an agitator among our nation, forbidding the payment of tribute to Caesar, and claiming to be himself an anointed king." 023:003 Then Pilate asked Him, "You, then, are the King of the Jews?" "It is as you say," He replied. 023:004 Pilate said to the High Priests and to the crowd, "I can find no crime in this man." 023:005 But they violently insisted. "He stirs up the people," they said, "throughout all Judaea with His teaching-even from Galilee (where He first started) to this city." 023:006 On hearing this, Pilate inquired, "Is this man a Galilaean?" 023:007 And learning that He belonged to Herod's jurisdiction he sent Him to Herod, for he too was in Jerusalem at that time. 023:008 To Herod the sight of Jesus was a great gratification, for, for a long time, he had been wanting to see Him, because he had heard so much about Him. He hoped also to see some miracle performed by Him. 023:009 So he put a number of questions to Him, but Jesus gave him no reply. 023:010 Meanwhile the High Priests and the Scribes were standing there and vehemently accusing Him. 023:011 Then, laughing to scorn the claims of Jesus, Herod (and his soldiers with him) made sport of Him, dressed Him in a gorgeous costume, and sent Him back to Pilate. 023:012 And on that very day Herod and Pilate became friends again, for they had been for some time at enmity. 023:013 Then calling together the High Priests and the Rulers and the people, Pilate said, 023:014 "You have brought this man to me on a charge of corrupting the loyalty of the people. But, you see, I have examined him in your presence and have discovered in the man no ground for the accusations which you bring against him. 023:015 No, nor does Herod; for he has sent him back to us; and, you see, there is nothing he has done that deserves death. 023:016 I will therefore give him a light punishment and release him." 023:017 [] 023:018 Then the whole multitude burst out into a shout. "Away with this man," they said, "and release Barabbas to us" 023:019 -Barabbas! who had been lodged in jail for some time in connexion with a riot which had occurred in the city, and for murder. 023:020 But Pilate once more addressed them, wishing to set Jesus free. 023:021 They, however, persistently shouted, "Crucify, crucify him!" 023:022 A third time he appealed to them: "Why, what crime has the man committed? I have discovered in him nothing that deserves death. I will therefore give him a light punishment and release him." 023:023 But they urgently insisted, demanding with frantic outcries that He should be crucified; and their clamour prevailed. 023:024 So Pilate gave judgement, yielding to their demand. 023:025 The man who was lying in prison charged with riot and murder and for whom they clamoured he set free, but Jesus he gave up to be dealt with as they desired. 023:026 As soon as they led Him away, they laid hold on one Simon, a Cyrenaean, who was coming in from the country, and on his shoulders they put the cross, for him to carry it behind Jesus. 023:027 A vast crowd of the people also followed Him, and of women who were beating their breasts and wailing for Him. 023:028 But Jesus turned towards them and said, "Daughters of Jerusalem, weep not for me, but weep for yourselves and for your children. 023:029 For a time is coming when they will say, `Blessed are the women who never bore children, and the breasts which have never given nourishment.' 023:030 Then will they begin to say to the mountains, `Fall on us;' and to the hills, `Cover us.' 023:031 For if they are doing these things in the case of the green tree, what will be done in that of the dry?" 023:032 They brought also two others, criminals, to put them to death with Him. 023:033 When they reached the place called `The Skull,' there they nailed Him to the cross, and the criminals also, one at His right hand and one at His left. 023:034 Jesus prayed, "Father, forgive them, for they know not what they are doing." And they divided His garments among them, drawing lots for them; 023:035 and the people stood looking on. The Rulers, too, repeatedly uttered their bitter taunts. "This fellow," they said, "saved others: let him save himself, if he is God's Anointed, the Chosen One." 023:036 And the soldiers also made sport of Him, coming and offering Him sour wine and saying, 023:037 "Are *you* the King of the Jews? Save yourself, then!" 023:038 There was moreover a writing over His head: THIS IS THE KING OF THE JEWS. 023:039 Now one of the criminals who had been crucified insulted Him, saying, "Are not you the Christ? Save yourself and us." 023:040 But the other, answering, reproved him. "Do you also not fear God," he said, "when you are actually suffering the same punishment? 023:041 And we indeed are suffering justly, for we are receiving due requital for what we have done. But He has done nothing amiss." 023:042 And he said, "Jesus, remember me when you come in your Kingdom." 023:043 "I tell you in solemn truth," replied Jesus, "that this very day you shall be with me in Paradise." 023:044 It was now about noon, and a darkness came over the whole country till three o'clock in the afternoon. 023:045 The sun was darkened, and the curtain of the Sanctuary was torn down the middle, 023:046 and Jesus cried out in a loud voice, and said, "Father, to Thy hands I entrust my spirit." And after uttering these words He yielded up His spirit. 023:047 The Captain, seeing what had happened, gave glory to God, saying, "Beyond question this man was innocent." 023:048 And all the crowds that had come together to this sight, after seeing all that had occurred, returned to the city beating their breasts. 023:049 But all His acquaintances, and the women who had been His followers after leaving Galilee, continued standing at a distance and looking on. 023:050 There was a member of the Council of the name of Joseph, a kind-hearted and upright man, 023:051 who came from the Jewish town of Arimathaea and was awaiting the coming of the Kingdom of God. He had not concurred in the design or action of the Council, 023:052 and now he went to Pilate and asked for the body of Jesus. 023:053 Then, taking it down, he wrapped it in a linen sheet and laid it in a tomb in the rock, where no one else had yet been put. 023:054 It was the Preparation Day, and the Sabbath was near at hand.

023:055 The women-those who had come with Jesus from Galilee-followed close behind, and saw the tomb and how His body was placed. 023:056 Then they returned, and prepared spices and perfumes. On the Sabbath they rested in obedience to the Commandment. 024:001 And, on the first day of the week, at early dawn, they came to the tomb bringing the spices they had prepared. 024:002 But they found the stone rolled back from the tomb, 024:003 and on entering they found that the body of the Lord Jesus was not there. 024:004 At this they were in great perplexity, when suddenly there stood by them two men whose raiment flashed like lightning. 024:005 The women were terrified; but, as they stood with their faces bowed to the ground, the men said to them, "Why do you search among the dead for Him who is living? 024:006 He is not here. He has come back to life. Remember how He spoke to you while He was still in Galilee, 024:007 when He told you that the Son of Man must be betrayed into the hands of sinful men, and be crucified, and on the third day rise again." 024:008 Then they remembered His words, 024:009 and returning from the tomb they reported all this to the Eleven and to all the rest. 024:010 The women were Mary of Magdala, Joanna, and Mary the mother of James; and they and the rest of the women related all this to the Apostles. 024:011 But the whole story seemed to them an idle tale; they could not believe the women. 024:012 Peter, however, rose and ran to the tomb. Stooping and looking in, he saw nothing but the linen cloths: so he went away to his own home, wondering at what had happened. 024:013 On that same day two of the disciples were walking to Emmaus, a village seven or eight miles from Jerusalem, 024:014 and were conversing about all these recent events; 024:015 and, in the midst of their conversation and discussion, Jesus Himself came and joined them, 024:016 though they were prevented from recognizing Him. 024:017 "What is the subject," He asked them, "on which you are talking so earnestly, as you walk?" And they stood still, looking full of sorrow. 024:018 Then one of them, named Cleopas, answered, "Are you a stranger lodging alone in Jerusalem, that you have known nothing of the things that have lately happened in the city?" 024:019 "What things?" He asked. "The things about Jesus the Nazarene," they said, "who was a Prophet powerful in work and word before God and all the people; 024:020 and how our High Priests and Rulers delivered Him up to be sentenced to death, and crucified Him. 024:021 But we were hoping that it was He who was about to ransom Israel. Yes, and moreover it was the day before yesterday that these things happened. 024:022 And, besides, some of the women of our company have amazed us. They went to the tomb at daybreak, 024:023 and, finding that His body was not there, they came and declared to us that they had also seen a vision of angels who said that He was alive. 024:024 Thereupon some of our party went to the tomb and found things just as the women had said; but Jesus Himself they did not see." 024:025 "O dull-witted men," He replied, "with minds so slow to believe all that the Prophets have spoken! 024:026 Was there not a necessity for the Christ thus to suffer, and then enter into His glory?" 024:027 And, beginning with Moses and all the Prophets, He explained to them the passages in Scripture which refer to Himself. 024:028 When they had come near the village to which they were going, He appeared to be going further. 024:029 But they pressed Him to remain with them. "Because," said they, "it is getting towards evening, and the day is nearly over." So He went in to stay with them. 024:030 But as soon as He had sat down with them, and had taken the bread and had blessed and broken it, and was handing it to them, 024:031 their eyes were opened and they recognized Him. But He vanished from them. 024:032 "Were not our hearts," they said to one another, "burning within us while He talked to us on the way and explained the Scriptures to us?" 024:033 So they rose and without an hour's delay returned to Jerusalem, and found the Eleven and the rest met together, who said to them, 024:034 "Yes, it is true: the Master has come back to life. He has been seen by Simon." 024:035 Then they related what had happened on the way, and how He had been recognized by them in the breaking of the bread. 024:036 While they were thus talking, He Himself stood in their midst and said, "Peace be to you!" 024:037 Startled, and in the utmost alarm, they thought they were looking at a spirit; 024:038 but He said to them, "Why such alarm? And why are there such questionings in your minds? 024:039 See my hands and my feet-it is my very self. Feel me and see, for a spirit has not flesh and bones as you see I have." 024:040 And then He showed them His hands and His feet. 024:041 But, while they still could not believe it for joy and were full of astonishment, He asked them, "Have you any food here?" 024:042 And they gave Him a piece of roasted fish, 024:043 and He took it and ate it in their presence. 024:044 And He said to them, "This is what I told you while I was still with you-that everything must be fulfilled that is written in the Law of Moses and in the Prophets and the Psalms concerning me." 024:045 Then He opened their minds to understand the Scriptures, 024:046 and He said, "Thus it is written that the Christ would suffer and on the third day rise again from among the dead; 024:047 and that proclamation would be made, in His name, of repentance and forgiveness of sins to all the nations, beginning in Jerusalem. 024:048 You are witnesses as to these things. 024:049 And remember that I am about to send out my Father's promised gift to rest upon you. But, as for you, wait patiently in the city until you are clothed with power from on high." 024:050 And He brought them out to within view of Bethany, and then lifted up His hands and blessed them. 024:051 And while He was blessing them, He parted from them and was carried up into Heaven. 024:052 They worshipped Him, and returned to Jerusalem with great joy. 024:053 Afterwards they were continually in attendance at the Temple, blessing God.

BOOK 41 MARK

001:001 The beginning of the Good News of Jesus Christ the Son of God. 001:002 As it is written in Isaiah the Prophet, "See, I am sending My messenger before Thee, Who will prepare Thy way"; 001:003 "The voice of one crying aloud: `In the Desert prepare a road for the Lord: Make His highways straight.'" 001:004 So John the Baptizer came, and was in the Desert proclaiming a baptism of the penitent for forgiveness of sins. 001:005 There went out to him people of all classes from Judaea, and the inhabitants of Jerusalem of all ranks, and were baptized by him in the river Jordan, making open confession of their sins. 001:006 As for John, his garment was of camel's hair, and he wore a loincloth of leather; and his food was locusts and wild honey. 001:007 His announcement was, "There is One coming after me mightier than I-One whose sandal-strap I am unworthy to stoop down and unfasten. 001:008 I have baptized you with water, but He will baptize you with the Holy Spirit." 001:009 At that time Jesus came from Nazareth in Galilee and was baptized by John in the Jordan; 001:010 and immediately on His coming up out of the water He saw an opening in the sky, and the Spirit like a dove coming down to Him; 001:011 and a voice came from the sky, saying, "Thou art My Son dearly loved: in Thee is My delight." 001:012 At once the Spirit impelled Him to go out into the Desert, 001:013 where He remained for forty days, tempted by Satan; and He was among the wild beasts, but the angels waited upon Him. 001:014 Then, after John had been thrown into prison, Jesus came into Galilee proclaiming God's Good News. 001:015 "The time has fully come," He said, "and the Kingdom of God is close at hand: repent, and believe this Good News. 001:016 One day, passing along the shore of the Lake of Galilee, He saw Simon and Andrew, Simon's brother, throwing their nets in the Lake; for they were fisherman. 001:017 "Come and follow me," said Jesus, "and I will make you fishers for men." 001:018 At once they left their nets and followed Him. 001:019 Going on a little further He saw James the son of Zabdi and his brother John: they also were in the boat mending the nets, and He immediately called them. 001:020 They therefore left their father Zabdi in the boat with the hired men, and went and followed Him. 001:021 So they came to Capernaum, and on the next Sabbath He went to the synagogue and began to teach. 001:022 The people listened with amazement to His teaching- for there was authority about it: it was very different from that of the Scribes- 001:023 when all at once, there in their synagogue, a man under the power of a foul spirit screamed out: 001:024 "What have you to do with us, Jesus the Nazarene? Have you come to destroy us? I know who you are-God's Holy One." 001:025 But Jesus reprimanded him, saying, "Silence! come out of him." 001:026 So the foul spirit, after throwing the man into convulsions, came out of him with a loud cry. 001:027 And all were amazed and awe-struck, so they began to ask one another, "What does this mean? Here is a new sort of teaching- and a tone of authority! And even to foul spirits he issues orders and they obey him!" 001:028 And His fame spread at once everywhere in all that part of Galilee. 001:029 Then on leaving the synagogue they came at once, with James and John, to the house of Simon and Andrew. 001:030 Now Simon's mother-in-law was ill in bed with a fever, and without delay they informed Him about her. 001:031 So He went to her, and taking her hand He raised her to her feet: the fever left her, and she began to wait upon them. 001:032 When it was evening, after sunset people came bringing Him all who were sick and the demoniacs; 001:033 and the whole town was assembled at the door. 001:034 Then He cured numbers of people who were ill with various diseases, and He drove out many demons; not allowing the demons to speak, because they knew who He was. 001:035 In the morning He rose early, while it was still quite dark, and leaving the house He went away to a solitary place and there prayed. 001:036 And Simon and the others searched everywhere for Him. 001:037 When they found Him they said, "Every one is looking for you." 001:038 "Let us go elsewhere, to the neighbouring country towns," He replied, "that I may proclaim my Message there also; because for that purpose I came from God." 001:039 And He went through all Galilee, preaching in the synagogues and expelling the demons. 001:040 One day there came a leper to Jesus entreating Him, and pleading on his knees. "If you are willing," he said, "you are able to cleanse me." 001:041 Moved with pity Jesus reached out His hand and touched him. "I am willing," He said; "be cleansed." 001:042 The leprosy at once left him, and he was cleansed. 001:043 Jesus at once sent him away, strictly charging him, 001:044 and saying, "Be careful not to tell any one, but go and show yourself to the Priest, and for your purification present the offerings that Moses appointed as evidence for them." 001:045 But the man, when he went out, began to tell every one and to publish the matter abroad, so that it was no longer possible for Jesus to go openly into any town; but He had to remain outside in unfrequented places, where people came to Him from all parts. 002:001 After some days He entered Capernaum again, and it soon became known that He was at home; 002:002 and such numbers of people came together that there was no longer room for them even round the door. He was speaking His Message to them, 002:003 when there came a party of people bringing a paralytic- four men carrying him. 002:004 Finding themselves unable, however, to bring him to Jesus because of the crowd, they untiled the roof just over His head, and after clearing an opening they lowered the mat on which the paralytic was lying. 002:005 Seeing their faith, Jesus said to the paralytic, "My son, your sins are pardoned." 002:006 Now there were some of the Scribes sitting there, and reasoning in their hearts. 002:007 "Why does this man use such words?" they said; "he is blaspheming. Who can pardon sins but One-that is, God?" 002:008 At once perceiving by His spirit that they were reasoning within themselves, Jesus asked them, "Why do you thus argue in your minds? 002:009 Which is easier?-to say to this paralytic, `Your sins are pardoned,' or to say, `Rise, take up your mat, and walk?' 002:010 But that you may know that the Son of Man has authority on earth to pardon sins"-He turned to the paralytic, and said, 002:011 "To you I say, `Rise, take up your mat and go home.'" 002:012 The man rose, and immediately under the eyes of all took up his mat and went out, so that they were all filled with astonishment, gave the glory to God, and said, "We never saw anything like this." 002:013 Again He went out to the shore of the Lake, and the whole multitude kept coming to Him, and He taught them. 002:014 And as He passed by, He saw Levi the son of Alphaeus sitting at the Toll Office, and said to him, "Follow me." So he rose and followed Him. 002:015 When He was sitting at table in Levi's house, a large number of tax-gatherers and notorious sinners were at table with Jesus and His disciples; for there were many such who habitually followed Him. 002:016 But when the Scribes of the Pharisee sect saw Him eating with the sinners and the tax-gatherers, they said to His disciples, "He is eating and drinking with the tax-gatherers and sinners!" 002:017 Jesus heard the words, and He said, "It is not the healthy who require a doctor, but the sick: I did not come to appeal to the righteous, but to sinners." 002:018 (Now John's disciples and those of the Pharisees were keeping a fast.) And they came and asked Him, "How is it that John's disciples and those of the Pharisees are fasting, and yours are not?" 002:019 "Can a wedding party fast while the bridegroom is among them?" replied Jesus. "So long as they have the bridegroom with them, fasting is impossible. 002:020 But a time will come when the Bridegroom will be taken away from them; then they will fast. 002:021 No one mends an old garment with a piece of unshrunk cloth. Otherwise, the patch put on would tear away from it- the new from the old-and a worse hole would be made. 002:022 And no one pours new wine into old wineskins. Otherwise the wine would burst the skins, and both wine and skins would be lost. New wine needs fresh skins!" 002:023 One Sabbath He was walking through the wheatfields when His disciples began to pluck the ears of wheat as they went. 002:024 So the Pharisees said to Him, "Look! why are they doing what on the Sabbath is unlawful?" 002:025 "Have you never read," Jesus replied, "what David did when the necessity arose and he and his men were hungry: 002:026 how he entered the house of God in the High-priesthood of Abiathar, and ate the Presented Loaves-which none but the priests are allowed to eat-and gave some to his men also?" 002:027 And Jesus said to them: "The Sabbath was made for man, not man for the Sabbath; 002:028 so that the Son of Man is Lord even of the Sabbath." 003:001 At another time, when He went to the synagogue, there was a man there with one arm shrivelled up. 003:002 They closely watched Him to see whether He would cure him on the Sabbath-so as to have a charge to bring against Him. 003:003 "Come forward," said He to the man with the shrivelled arm. 003:004 Then He asked them, "Are we allowed to do good on the Sabbath, or to do evil? to save a life, or to destroy one?" They remained silent. 003:005 Grieved and indignant at the hardening of their hearts, He looked round on them with anger, and said to the man, "Stretch out your arm." He stretched it out, and the arm was completely restored. 003:006 But no sooner had the Pharisees left the synagogue than they held a consultation with the Herodians against Jesus, to devise some means of destroying Him. 003:007 Accordingly Jesus withdrew with His disciples to the Lake, and a vast crowd of people from Galilee followed Him; 003:008 and from Judaea and Jerusalem and Idumaea and from beyond the Jordan and from the district of Tyre and Sidon there came to Him a vast crowd, hearing of all that He was doing. 003:009 So He gave directions to His disciples to keep a small boat in constant attendance on Him because of the throng- to prevent their crushing Him. 003:010 For He had cured many of the people, so that all who had any ailments pressed upon Him, to touch Him. 003:011 And the foul spirits, whenever they saw Him, threw themselves down at His feet, screaming out: "You are the Son of God." 003:012 But He many a time checked them, forbidding them to say who He was. 003:013 Then He went up the hill; and those whom He Himself chose He called, and they came to Him. 003:014 He appointed twelve of them, that they might be with Him, and that He might also send them to proclaim His Message, 003:015 with authority to expel the demons. 003:016 These twelve were Simon (to whom He gave the surname of Peter), 003:017 James the son of Zabdi and John the brother of James (these two He surnamed Boanerges, that is `Sons of Thunder'), 003:018 Andrew, Philip, Bartholomew, Matthew, Thomas, James the son of Alphaeus, Thaddaeus, Simon the Cananaean, 003:019 and Judas Iscariot, the man who also betrayed Him. 003:020 And He went into a house. But again the crowd assembled, so that there was no opportunity for them even to snatch a meal. 003:021 Hearing of this, His relatives came to seize Him by force, for they said, "He is out of his mind." 003:022 The Scribes, too, who had come down from Jerusalem said, "He has Baal-zebul in him; and it is by the power of the Prince of the demons that he expels the demons." 003:023 So He called them to Him, and using figurative language He appealed to them, saying, "How is it possible for Satan to expel Satan? 003:024 For if civil war breaks out in a kingdom, nothing can make that kingdom last; 003:025 and if a family splits into parties, that family cannot continue. 003:026 So if Satan has risen in arms and has made war upon himself, stand he cannot, but meets his end. 003:027 Nay, no one can go into a strong man's house and carry off his property, unless he first binds the strong man, and then he will plunder his house. 003:028 In solemn truth I tell you that all their sins may be pardoned to the sons of men, and all their blasphemies, however they may have blasphemed; 003:029 but whoever blasphemes against the Holy Spirit, he remains for ever unabsolved: he is guilty of a sin of the Ages." 003:030 This was because they said, "He is possessed by a foul spirit." 003:031 By this time His mother and His brothers arrive, and standing outside they send a message to Him to call Him. 003:032 Now a crowd was sitting round Him; so they tell Him, "Your mother and your brothers and sisters are outside, inquiring for you." 003:033 "Who are my mother and my brothers?" He replied. 003:034 And, fixing His eyes on the people who were sitting round Him in a circle, He said, 003:035 "Here are my mother and my brothers. For wherever there is one who has been obedient to God, there is my brother- my sister-and my mother." 004:001 Once more He began to teach by the side of the Lake, and a vast multitude of people came together to listen to Him. He therefore went on board the boat and sat there, a little way from the land; and all the people were on the shore close to the water. 004:002 Then He proceeded to teach them many lessons in figurative language; and in His teaching He said, 004:003 "Listen: the sower goes out to sow. 004:004 As he sows, some of the seed falls by the way-side, and the birds come and peck it up. 004:005 Some falls on the rocky ground where it finds but little earth, and it shoots up quickly because it has no depth of soil; 004:006 but when the sun is risen, it is scorched, and through having no root it withers away. 004:007 Some, again, falls among the thorns; and the thorns spring up and stifle it, so that it yields no crop. 004:008 But some of the seed falls into good ground, and gives a return: it comes up and increases, and yields thirty, sixty, or a hundred-fold." 004:009 "Listen," He added, "every one who has ears to listen with!" 004:010 When He was alone, the Twelve and the others who were about Him requested Him to explain His figurative language. 004:011 "To you," He replied, "has been entrusted the secret truth concerning the Kingdom of God; but to those others outside your number all this is spoken in figurative language; 004:012 that "'They may look and look but not see, and listen and listen but not understand, lest perchance they should return and be pardoned.'" 004:013 "Do you all miss the meaning of this parable?" He added; "how then will you understand the rest of my parables?" 004:014 "What the sower sows is the Message. 004:015 Those who receive the seed by the way-side are those in whom the Message is sown, but, when they have heard it, Satan comes at once and carries away the Message sown in them. 004:016 In the same way those who receive the seed on the rocky places are those who, when they have heard the Message, at once accept it joyfully, 004:017 but they have no root within them. They last for a time; then, when suffering or persecution comes because of the Message, they are immediately overthrown. 004:018 Others there are who receive the seed among the thorns: these are they who have heard the Message, 004:019 but worldly cares and the deceitfulness of wealth and the excessive pursuit of other objects come in and stifle the Message, and it becomes unfruitful. 004:020 Those, on the other hand, who have received the seed on the good ground, are all who hear the Message and welcome it, and yield a return of thirty, sixty, or a hundred fold." 004:021 He went on to say, "Is the lamp brought in in order to be put under the bushel or under the bed? Is it not rather in order that it may be placed on the lampstand? 004:022 Why, there is nothing hidden except with a view to its being ultimately disclosed, nor has anything been made a secret but that it may at last come to light. 004:023 Listen, every one who has ears to listen with!" 004:024 He also said to them, "Take care what you hear. With what measure you measure, it will be measured to you, and that with interest. 004:025 For those who have will have more given them; and from those who have not, even what they have will be taken away." 004:026 Another saying of His was this: "The Kingdom of God is as if a man scattered seed over the ground: 004:027 he spends days and nights, now awake, now asleep, while the seed sprouts and grows tall, he knows not how. 004:028 Of itself the land produces the crop-first the blade, then the ear; afterwards the perfect grain is seen in the ear. 004:029 But no sooner is the crop ripe, than he sends the reapers, because the time of harvest has come." 004:030 Another saying of His was this: "How are we to picture the Kingdom of God? or by what figure of speech shall we represent it? 004:031 It is like a mustard-seed, which, when sown in the earth, is the smallest of all the seeds in the world; 004:032 yet when sown it springs up and becomes larger than all the herbs, and throws out great branches, so that the birds build under its shadow." 004:033 With many such parables He used to speak the Message to them according to their capacity for receiving it. 004:034 But except in figurative language He spoke nothing to them; while to His own disciples He expounded everything, in private. 004:035 The same day, in the evening, He said to them, "Let us cross to the other side." 004:036 So they got away from the crowd, and took Him-as He was- in the boat; and other boats accompanied Him. 004:037 But a heavy squall came on, and the waves were now dashing into the boat, so that it was fast filling. 004:038 But He Himself was in the stern asleep, with His head on the cushion: so they woke Him. "Rabbi," they cried, "is it nothing to you that we are drowning?" 004:039 So He roused Himself and rebuked the wind, and said to the waves, "Silence! Be still!" The wind sank, and a perfect calm set in. 004:040 "Why are you so timid?" He asked; "have you still no faith?" 004:041 Then they were filled with terror, and began to say to one another, "Who is this, then? For even wind and sea obey Him." 005:001 So they arrived at the opposite shore of the Lake, in the country of the Gerasenes. 005:002 At once, on His landing, there came from the tombs to meet Him a man possessed by a foul spirit. 005:003 This man lived among the tombs, nor could any one now secure him even with a chain; 005:004 for many a time he had been left securely bound in fetters and chains, but afterwards the chains lay torn link from link, and the fetters in fragments, and there was no one strong enough to master him. 005:005 And constantly, day and night, he remained among the tombs or on the hills, shrieking, and mangling himself with sharp stones. 005:006 And when he saw Jesus in the distance, he ran and threw himself at His feet, 005:007 crying out in a loud voice, "What hast Thou to do with me, Jesus, Son of God Most High? In God's name I implore Thee not to torment me." 005:008 For He had said to him, "Foul spirit, come out of the man." 005:009 Jesus also questioned him. "What is your name?" He said. "Legion," he replied, "for there are a host of us." 005:010 And he earnestly entreated Him not to send them away out of the country. 005:011 Feeding there, on the mountain slope, was a great herd of swine. 005:012 So they besought Jesus. "Send us to the swine," they said, "so that we may enter into them." 005:013 He gave them leave; and the foul spirits came out and entered into the swine, and the herd-about 2,000 in number- rushed headlong down the cliff into the Lake and were drowned in the Lake. 005:014 The swineherds fled, and spread the news in town and country. So the people came to see what it was that had happened; 005:015 and when they came to Jesus, they beheld the demoniac quietly seated, clothed and of sane mind-the man who had had the legion; and they were awe-stricken. 005:016 And those who had seen it told them the particulars of what had happened to the demoniac, and all about the swine. 005:017 Then they began entreating Him to depart from their district. 005:018 As He was embarking, the man who had been possessed asked permission to accompany Him. 005:019 But He would not allow it. "Go home to your family," He said, "and report to them all that the Lord has done for you, and the mercy He has shown you." 005:020 So the man departed, and related publicly everywhere in the Ten Towns all that Jesus had done for him; and all were astonished. 005:021 When Jesus had re-crossed in the boat to the other side, a vast multitude came crowding to Him; and He was on the shore of the Lake, 005:022 when there came one of the Wardens of the Synagogue- he was called Jair-who, on beholding Him, threw himself at His feet, 005:023 and besought Him with many entreaties. "My little daughter," he said, "is at the point of death: I pray you come and lay your hands upon her, that she may recover and live." 005:024 And Jesus went with him. And a dense crowd followed Him, and thronged Him on all sides. 005:025 Now a woman who for twelve years had suffered from haemorrhage, 005:026 and had undergone many different treatments under a number of doctors and had spent all she had without receiving benefit but on the contrary growing worse, 005:027 heard of Jesus. And she came in the crowd behind Him and touched His cloak; 005:028 for she said, "If I but touch His clothes, I shall be cured." 005:029 In a moment the flow of her blood ceased, and she felt in herself that her complaint was cured. 005:030 Immediately Jesus, well knowing that healing power had gone from within Him, turned round in the crowd and asked, "Who touched my clothes?" 005:031 "You see the multitude pressing you on all sides," His disciples exclaimed, "and yet you ask, `Who touched me?'" 005:032 But He continued looking about to see the person who had done this, 005:033 until the woman, frightened and trembling, knowing what had happened to her, came and threw herself at His feet, and told Him all the truth. 005:034 "Daughter," He said, "your faith has cured you: go in peace, and be free from your complaint." 005:035 While He is yet speaking, men come from the house to the Warden, and say, "Your daughter is dead: why trouble the Rabbi further?" 005:036 But Jesus, overhearing the words, said to the Warden, "Do not be afraid; only have faith." 005:037 And He allowed no one to accompany Him except Peter and the brothers James and John. 005:038 So they come to the Warden's house. Here He gazes on a scene of uproar, with people weeping aloud and wailing. 005:039 He goes in. "Why all this outcry and loud weeping?" He asks; "the child is asleep, not dead." 005:040 To this their reply is a scornful laugh. He, however, puts them all out, takes the child's father and mother and those He has brought with Him, and enters the room where the child lies. 005:041 Then, taking her by the hand, He says to her, "Talitha, koum;" that is to say, "Little girl, I command you to wake!" 005:042 Instantly the little girl rises to her feet and begins to walk (for she was twelve years old). They were at once beside themselves with utter astonishment; 005:043 but He gave strict injunctions that the matter should not be made known, and directed them to give her something to eat. 006:001 Leaving that place He came into His own country, accompanied by His disciples. 006:002 On the Sabbath He proceeded to teach in the synagogue; and many, as they heard Him, were astonished. "Where did he acquire all this?" they asked. "What is this wisdom that has been given to him? And what are these marvellous miracles which his hands perform? 006:003 Is not this the carpenter, Mary's son, the brother of James and Joses, Jude and Simon? And do not his sisters live here among us?" So they turned angrily away. 006:004 But Jesus said to them, "There is no Prophet without honour except in his own country, and among his own relatives, and in his own home." 006:005 And He could not do any miracle there, except that He laid His hands on a few who were out of health and cured them; and 006:006 He wondered at their unbelief. So He went round the adjacent villages, teaching. 006:007 Then summoning the Twelve to Him, He proceeded to send them out by twos, and gave them authority over the foul spirits. 006:008 He charged them to take nothing for the journey except a stick; no bread, no bag, and not a penny in their pockets, 006:009 but to go wearing sandals. "And do not," He said, "put on an extra under garment. 006:010 Wherever you enter a house, make it your home till you leave that place. 006:011 But wherever they will not receive you or listen to you, when you leave shake off the very dust from under your feet to bear witness concerning them." 006:012 So they set out, and preached in order that men might repent. 006:013 Many demons they expelled, and many invalids they anointed with oil and cured. 006:014 King Herod heard of all this (for the name of Jesus had become widely known), and he kept saying, "John the Baptizer has come back to life, and that is why these miraculous Powers are working in him." 006:015 Others asserted that He was Elijah. Others again said, "He is a Prophet, like one of the great Prophets." 006:016 But when Herod heard of Him, he said, "The John, whom I beheaded, has come back to life." 006:017 For Herod himself had sent and had had John arrested and had kept him in prison in chains, for the sake of Herodias, his brother Philip's wife; because he had married her. 006:018 For John had repeatedly told Herod, "You have no right to be living with your brother's wife." 006:019 Therefore Herodias hated him and wished to take his life, but could not; 006:020 for Herod stood in awe of John, knowing him to be an upright and holy man, and he protected him. After listening to him he was in great perplexity, and yet he found a pleasure in listening. 006:021 At length Herodias found her opportunity. Herod on his birthday gave a banquet to the nobles of his court and to the tribunes and the principal people in Galilee, 006:022 at which Herodias's own daughter came in and danced, and so charmed Herod and his guests that he said to her, "Ask me for anything you please, and I will give it to you." 006:023 He even swore to her, "Whatever you ask me for I will give you, up to half my kingdom." 006:024 She at once went out and said to her mother: "What shall I ask for?" "The head of John the Baptizer," she replied. 006:025 The girl immediately came in, in haste, to the King and made her request. "My desire is," she said, "that you will give me, here and now, on a dish, the head of John the Baptist." 006:026 Then the

King, though intensely sorry, yet for the sake of his oaths, and of his guests, would not break faith with her. 006:027 He at once sent a soldier of his guard with orders to bring John's head. So he went and beheaded him in the prison, 006:028 and brought his head on a dish and gave it to the young girl, who gave it to her mother. 006:029 When John's disciples heard of it, they came and took away his body and laid it in a tomb. 006:030 When the Apostles had re-assembled round Jesus, they reported to Him all they had done and all they had taught. 006:031 Then He said to them, "Come away, all of you, to a quiet place, and rest awhile." For there were many coming and going, so that they had no time even for meals. 006:032 Accordingly they sailed away in the boat to a solitary place apart. 006:033 But the people saw them going, and many knew them; and coming by land they ran together there from all the neighbouring towns, and arrived before them. 006:034 So when Jesus landed, He saw a vast multitude; and His heart was moved with pity for them, because they were like sheep which have no shepherd, and He proceeded to teach them many things. 006:035 By this time it was late; so His disciples came to Him, and said, "This is a lonely place, and the hour is now late: 006:036 send them away that they may go to the farms and villages near here and buy themselves something to eat." 006:037 "Give them food yourselves," He replied. "Are we," they asked, "to go and buy two hundred shillings' worth of bread and give them food?" 006:038 "How many loaves have you?" He inquired; "go and see." So they found out, and said, "Five; and a couple of fish." 006:039 So He directed them to make all sit down in companies on the green grass. 006:040 And they sat down in rows of hundreds and of fifties. 006:041 Then He took the five loaves and the two fish, and lifting His eyes to Heaven He blessed the food. Then He broke the loaves into portions which He went on handing to the disciples to distribute; giving pieces also of the two fish to them all. 006:042 All ate and were fully satisfied. 006:043 And they carried away broken portions enough to fill twelve baskets, besides pieces of the fish. 006:044 Those who ate the bread were 5,000 adult men. 006:045 Immediately afterwards He made His disciples go on board the boat and cross over to Bethsaida, leaving Him behind to dismiss the crowd. 006:046 He then bade the people farewell, and went away up the hill to pray. 006:047 When evening was come, the boat was half way across the Lake, while he Himself was on shore alone. 006:048 But when He saw them distressed with rowing (for the wind was against them), towards morning He came towards them walking on the Lake, as if intending to pass them. 006:049 They saw Him walking on the water, and thinking that it was a spirit they cried out; 006:050 for they all saw Him and were terrified. He, however, immediately spoke to them. "There is no danger," He said; "it is I; be not alarmed." 006:051 Then He went up to them on board the boat, and the wind lulled; and they were beside themselves with silent amazement.

006:052 For they had not learned the lesson taught by the loaves, but their minds were dull. 006:053 Having crossed over they drew to land in Gennesaret and came to anchor. 006:054 But no sooner had they gone ashore than the people immediately recognized Him. 006:055 Then they scoured the whole district, and began to bring Him the sick on their mats wherever they heard He was. 006:056 And enter wherever He might-village or town or hamlet- they laid their sick in the open places, and entreated Him to let them touch were it but the tassel of His robe; and all, whoever touched Him, were restored to health. 007:001 Then the Pharisees, with certain Scribes who had come from Jerusalem, came to Him in a body. 007:002 They had noticed that some of His disciples were eating their food with `unclean' (that is to say, unwashed) hands. 007:003 (For the Pharisees and all the Jews-being, as they are, zealous for the traditions of the Elders-never eat without first carefully washing their hands, 007:004 and when they come from market they will not eat without bathing first; and they have a good many other customs which they have received traditionally and cling to, such as the rinsing of cups and pots and of bronze utensils, and the washing of beds.) 007:005 So the Pharisees and Scribes put the question to Him: "Why do your disciples transgress the traditions of the Elders, and eat their food with unclean hands?" 007:006 "Rightly did Isaiah prophesy of you hypocrites," He replied; "as it is written, "`This People honour Me with their lips, while their hearts are far away from Me: 007:007 But idle is their devotion while they lay down precepts which are mere human rules.' 007:008 "You neglect God's Commandment: you hold fast to men's traditions." 007:009 "Praiseworthy indeed!" He added, "to set at nought God's Commandment in order to observe your own traditions! 007:010 For Moses said, `Honour thy father and thy mother' and again, `He who curses father or mother, let him die the death.' 007:011 But *you* say, `If a man says to his father or mother, It is a Korban (that is, a thing devoted to God), whatever it is, which otherwise you would have received from me-' 007:012 And so you no longer allow him to do anything for his father or mother, 007:013 thus nullifying God's precept by your tradition which you have handed down. And many things of that kind you do." 007:014 Then Jesus called the people to Him again. "Listen to me, all of you," He said, "and understand. 007:015 There is nothing outside a man which entering him can make him unclean; but it is the things which come out of a man that make him unclean." 007:016 [] 007:017 After He had left the crowd and gone indoors, His disciples began to ask Him about this figure of speech. 007:018 "Have *you* also so little understanding?" He replied; "do you not understand that anything whatever that enters a man from outside cannot make him unclean, 007:019 because it does not go into his heart, but into his stomach, and passes away ejected from him?" By these words Jesus pronounced all kinds of food clean. 007:020 "What comes out of a man,"

He added, "that it is which makes him unclean. 007:021 For from within, out of men's hearts, their evil purposes proceed- fornication, theft, murder, adultery, 007:022 covetousness, wickedness, deceit, licentiousness, envy, reviling, pride, reckless folly: 007:023 all these wicked things come out from within and make a man unclean." 007:024 Then He rose and left that place and went into the neighbourhood of Tyre and Sidon. Here He entered a house and wished no one to know it, but He could not escape observation. 007:025 Forthwith a woman whose little daughter was possessed by a foul spirit heard of Him, and came and flung herself at His feet. 007:026 She was a Gentile woman, a Syro-phoenician by nation: and again and again she begged Him to expel the demon from her daughter. 007:027 "Let the children first eat all they want," He said; "it is not right to take the children's bread and throw it to the dogs." 007:028 "True, Sir," she replied, "and yet the dogs under the table eat the children's scraps." 007:029 "For those words of yours, go home," He replied; "the demon has gone out of your daughter." 007:030 So she went home, and found the child lying on the bed, and the demon gone. 007:031 Returning from the neighbourhood of Tyre, He came by way of Sidon to the Lake of Galilee, passing through the district of the Ten Towns. 007:032 Here they brought to Him a deaf man that stammered, on whom they begged Him to lay His hands. 007:033 So Jesus taking him aside, apart from the crowd, put His fingers into his ears, and spat, and moistened his tongue; 007:034 and looking up to Heaven He sighed, and said to him, "Ephphatha!" (that is, "Open!") 007:035 And the man's ears were opened, and his tongue became untied, and he began to speak perfectly. 007:036 Then Jesus charged them to tell no one; but the more He charged them, all the more did they spread the news far and wide. 007:037 The amazement was extreme. "He succeeds in everything he attempts," they exclaimed; "he even makes deaf men hear and dumb men speak!" 008:001 About that time there was again an immense crowd, and they found themselves with nothing to eat. So He called His disciples to Him. 008:002 "My heart yearns over the people," He said; "for this is now the third day they have remained with me, and they have nothing to eat. 008:003 If I were to send them home hungry, they would faint on the way, some of them having come a great distance." 008:004 "Where can we possibly get bread here in this remote place to satisfy such a crowd?" answered His disciples. 008:005 "How many loaves have you?" He asked. "Seven," they said. 008:006 So He passed the word to the people to sit down on the ground. Then taking the seven loaves He blessed them, and broke them into portions and proceeded to give them to His disciples for them to distribute, and they distributed them to the people. 008:007 They had also a few small fish. He blessed them, and He told His disciples to distribute these also. 008:008 So the people ate an abundant meal; and what remained over they picked up and carried away-seven hampers of broken pieces. 008:009 The number fed were about 4,000. Then He sent them away, 008:010 and at once going on board with His disciples He came into the district of Dalmanutha. 008:011 The Pharisees followed Him and began to dispute with Him, asking Him for a sign in the sky, to make trial of Him. 008:012 Heaving a deep and troubled sigh, He said, "Why do the men of to-day ask for a sign? In solemn truth I tell you that no sign will be given to the men of to-day." 008:013 So He left them, went on board again, and came away to the other side. 008:014 Now they had forgotten to take bread, nor had they more than a single loaf with them in the boat; 008:015 and when He admonished them, "See to it, be on your guard against the yeast of the Pharisees and the yeast of Herod," 008:016 they explained His words to one another by saying, "We have no bread!" 008:017 He perceived what they were saying, and He said to them, "What is this discussion of yours about having no bread? Do you not yet see and understand? Are your minds so dull of comprehension? 008:018 You have eyes! can you not see? You have ears! can you not hear? and have you no memory? 008:019 When I broke up the five loaves for the 5,000 men, how many baskets did you carry away full of broken portions?" "Twelve," they said. 008:020 "And when the seven for the 4,000, how many hampers full of portions did you take away?" "Seven," they answered. 008:021 "Do you not yet understand?" He said. 008:022 And they came to Bethsaida. And a blind man was brought to Jesus and they entreated Him to touch him. 008:023 So He took the blind man by the arm and brought him out of the village, and spitting into his eyes He put His hands on him and asked him, "Can you see anything?" 008:024 He looked up and said, "I can see the people: I see them like trees-only walking." 008:025 Then for the second time He put His hands on the man's eyes, and the man, looking steadily, recovered his sight and saw everything distinctly. 008:026 So He sent him home, and added, "Do not even go into the village." 008:027 From that place Jesus and His disciples went to the villages belonging to Caesarea Philippi. On the way He began to ask His disciples, "Who do people say that I am?" 008:028 "John the Baptist," they replied, "but others say Elijah, and others, that it is one of the Prophets." 008:029 Then He asked them pointedly, "But you yourselves, who do you say that I am?" "You are the Christ," answered Peter. 008:030 And He strictly forbad them to tell this about Him to any one. 008:031 And now for the first time He told them, "The Son of Man must endure much suffering, and be rejected by the Elders and the High Priests and the Scribes, and be put to death, and after two days rise to life." 008:032 This He told them plainly; whereupon Peter took Him and began to remonstrate with Him. 008:033 But turning round and seeing His disciples, He rebuked Peter. "Get behind me, Adversary," He said, "for your thoughts are not God's thoughts, but men's." 008:034 Then calling to Him the crowd and also His disciples, He said to them, "If any one is desirous of following me, let him ignore self and take up his cross, and so be my follower. 008:035 For whoever is bent on securing his life will lose it, but he who loses his life for my sake, and for the sake of the Good News, will secure it. 008:036 Why, what does it benefit a man to gain the whole world and forfeit his life? 008:037 For what could a man give to buy back his life? 008:038 Every one, however, who has been ashamed of me and of my teachings in this faithless and sinful age, of him the Son of Man also will be ashamed when He comes in His Father's glory with the holy angels." 009:001 He went on to say, "In solemn truth I tell you that some of those who are standing here will certainly not taste death till they have seen the Kingdom of God already come in power." 009:002 Six days later, Jesus took with Him Peter, James, and John, and brought them alone, apart from the rest, up a high mountain; and in their presence His appearance underwent a change. 009:003 His garments also became dazzling with brilliant whiteness- such whiteness as no bleaching on earth could give. 009:004 Moreover there appeared to them Elijah accompanied by Moses; and the two were conversing with Jesus, 009:005 when Peter said to Jesus, "Rabbi, we are thankful to you that we are here. Let us put up three tents- one for you, one for Moses, and one for Elijah." 009:006 For he knew not what to say: they were filled with such awe. 009:007 Then there came a cloud spreading over them, and a voice issued from the cloud, "This is my Son, dearly loved: listen to Him." 009:008 Instantly they looked round, and now they could no longer see any one, but themselves and Jesus. 009:009 As they were coming down from the mountain, He very strictly forbad them to tell any one what they had seen "until after the Son of Man has risen from among the dead." 009:010 So they kept the matter to themselves, although frequently asking one another what was meant by the rising from the dead. 009:011 They also asked Him, "How is it that the Scribes say that Elijah must first come?" 009:012 "Elijah," He replied, "does indeed come first and reforms everything; but how is it that it is written of the Son of Man that He will endure much suffering and be held in contempt? 009:013 Yet I tell you that not only has Elijah come, but they have also done to him whatever they chose, as the Scriptures say about him." 009:014 As they came to rejoin the disciples, they saw an immense crowd surrounding them and a party of Scribes disputing with them. 009:015 Immediately the whole multitude on beholding Him were astonished and awe-struck, and yet they ran forward and greeted Him. 009:016 "What is the subject you are discussing?" He asked them. 009:017 "Rabbi," answered one of the crowd, "I have brought you my son. He has a dumb spirit in him; 009:018 and wherever it comes upon him, it dashes him to the ground, and he foams at the mouth and grinds his teeth, and he is pining away. I begged your disciples to expel it, but they had not the power." 009:019 "O unbelieving generation!" replied Jesus; "how long must I be with you? how long must I have patience with you? Bring the boy to me." 009:020 So they brought him to Jesus. And the spirit, when he saw Jesus, immediately threw the youth into convulsions, so that he fell on the ground and rolled about, foaming at the mouth. 009:021 Then Jesus asked the father, "How long has he been like this?" "From early childhood," he said; 009:022 "and often it has thrown him into the fire or into pools of water to destroy him. But, if you possibly can, have pity on us and help us." 009:023 "`If I possibly can!'" replied Jesus; "why, everything is possible to him who believes." 009:024 Immediately the father cried out, "I do believe: strengthen my weak faith." 009:025 Then Jesus, seeing that an increasing crowd was running towards Him, rebuked the foul spirit, and said to it, "Dumb and deaf spirit, *I* command you, come out of him and never enter into him again." 009:026 So with a loud cry he threw the boy into fit after fit, and came out. The boy looked as if he were dead, so that most of them said he was dead; 009:027 but Jesus took his hand and raised him up, and he stood on his feet. 009:028 After the return of Jesus to the house His disciples asked Him privately, "How is it that we could not expel the spirit?" 009:029 "An evil spirit of this kind," He answered, "can only be driven out by prayer." 009:030 Departing thence they passed through Galilee, and He was unwilling that any one should know it; 009:031 for He was teaching His disciples, and telling them, "The Son of Man is to be betrayed into the hands of men, and they will put Him to death; and after being put to death, in three days He will rise to life again." 009:032 They, however, did not understand what He meant, and were afraid to question Him. 009:033 So they came to Capernaum; and when in the house He asked them, "What were you arguing about on the way?" 009:034 But they remained silent; for on the way they had debated with one another who was the chief of them. 009:035 Then sitting down He called the Twelve, and said to them, "If any one wishes to be first, he must be last of all and servant of all." 009:036 And taking a young child He made him stand in their midst, then threw His arms round him and said, 009:037 "Whoever for my sake receives one such young child as this, receives me; and whoever receives me, receives not so much me as Him who sent me." 009:038 "Rabbi," said John to Him, "we saw a man making use of your name to expel demons, and we tried to hinder him, on the ground that he did not follow us." 009:039 "You should not have tried to hinder him," replied Jesus, "for there is no one who will use my name to perform a miracle and be able the next minute to speak evil of me. 009:040 He who is not against us is for us; 009:041 and whoever gives you a cup of water to drink because you belong to Christ, I solemnly tell you that he will certainly not lose his reward. 009:042 "And whoever shall occasion the fall of one of these little ones who believe, he would be better off if, with a millstone round his neck, he were lying at the bottom of the sea. 009:043 If your hand should cause you to sin, cut it off: it would be better for you to enter into Life maimed, than remain in possession of both your hands and go away into Gehenna, into the fire which cannot be put out. 009:044 [] 009:045 Or if your foot should cause you to sin, cut it off: it would be better for you to enter into Life crippled, than remain in possession of both your feet and be thrown into Gehenna. 009:046 [] 009:047 Or if your eye should cause you to sin, tear it out. It would be better for you to enter into the Kingdom of God half-blind than remain in possession of two eyes and be thrown into Gehenna, 009:048 where their worm does not die and the fire does not go out. 009:049 Every one, however, will be salted with fire. 009:050 Salt is a good thing, but if the salt should become tasteless, what will you use to give it saltness? Have salt within you and live at peace with one another." 010:001 Soon on His feet once more, He enters the district of Judaea and crosses the Jordan: again the people flock to Him, and ere long, as was usual with Him, He was teaching them once more. 010:002 Presently a party of Pharisees come to Him with the question- seeking to entrap Him, "May a man divorce his wife?" 010:003 "What rule did Moses lay down for you?" He answered. 010:004 "Moses," they said, "permitted a man to draw up a written notice of divorce, and to send his wife away." 010:005 "It was in consideration of your stubborn hearts," said Jesus, "that Moses enacted this law for you; 010:006 but from the beginning of the creation the rule was, `Male and female did God make them. 010:007 For this reason a man shall leave his father and his mother, and shall cling to his wife, 010:008 and the two shall be one'; so that they are two no longer, but `one.' 010:009 What, therefore, God has joined together let not man separate." 010:010 Indoors the disciples began questioning Jesus again on the same subject. 010:011 He replied, "Whoever divorces his wife and marries another woman, commits adultery against the first wife; 010:012 and if a woman puts away her husband and marries another man, she commits adultery." 010:013 One day people were bringing young children to Jesus for Him to touch them, but the disciples interfered. 010:014 Jesus, however, on seeing this, was moved to indignation, and said to them, "Let the little children come to me: do not hinder them; for to those who are childlike the Kingdom of God belongs. 010:015 In solemn truth I tell you that no one who does not receive the Kingdom of God like a little child will by any possibility enter it." 010:016 Then He took them in His arms and blessed them lovingly, one by one, laying His hands upon them. 010:017 As He went out to resume His journey, there came a man running up to Him, who knelt at His feet and asked, "Good Rabbi, what am I to do in order to inherit the Life of the Ages?" 010:018 "Why do you call me good?" asked Jesus in reply; "there is no one truly good except One-that is, God. 010:019 You know the Commandments-`Do not murder;' `Do not commit adultery;' `Do not steal;' `Do not lie in giving evidence;' `Do not defraud;' `Honour thy father and thy mother.'" 010:020 "Rabbi," he replied, "all these Commandments I have carefully obeyed from my youth." 010:021 Then Jesus looked at him and loved him, and said, "One thing is lacking in you: go, sell all you possess and give the proceeds to the poor, and you shall have riches in Heaven; and come and be a follower of mine." 010:022 At these words his brow darkened, and he went away sad; for he was possessed of great wealth. 010:023 Then looking round on His disciples Jesus said, "With how hard a struggle will the possessors of riches enter the Kingdom of God!" 010:024 The disciples were amazed at His words. Jesus, however, said again, "Children, how hard a struggle is it for those who trust in riches to enter the Kingdom of God! 010:025 It is easier for a camel to go through the eye of a needle than for a rich man to enter the Kingdom of God." 010:026 They were astonished beyond measure, and said to one another, "Who then *can* be saved?" 010:027 Jesus looking on them said, "With men it is impossible, but not with God; for everything is possible with God." 010:028 "Remember," said Peter to Him, "that we forsook everything and have become your followers." 010:029 "In solemn truth I tell you," replied Jesus, "that there is no one who has forsaken house or brothers or sisters, or mother or father, or children or lands, for my sake and for the sake of the Good News, 010:030 but will receive a hundred times as much now in this present life- houses, brothers, sisters, mothers, children, lands- and persecution with them-and in the coming age the Life of the Ages. 010:031 But many who are now first will be last, and the last, first." 010:032 They were still on the road going up to Jerusalem, and Jesus was walking ahead of them; they were full of wonder, and some, though they followed, did so with fear. Then, once more calling to Him the Twelve, He began to tell them what was about to happen to Him. 010:033 "See," He said, "we are going up to Jerusalem, where the Son of Man will be betrayed to the High Priests and the Scribes. They will condemn Him to death, and will hand Him over to the Gentiles; 010:034 they will insult Him in cruel sport, spit on Him, scourge Him, and put Him to death; but on the third day He will rise to life again." 010:035 Then James and John, the sons of Zabdi, came up to Him and said, "Rabbi, we wish you would grant us whatever request we make of you." 010:036 "What would you have me do for you?" He asked. 010:037 "Allow us," they replied, "to sit one at your right hand and the other at your left hand, in your glory." 010:038 "You know not," said He, "what you are asking. Are you able to drink out of the cup from which I am to drink, or to be baptized with the baptism with which I am to be baptized?" 010:039 "We are able," they replied. "Out of the cup," said Jesus, "from which I am to drink you shall drink, and with the baptism with which I am to be baptized you shall be baptized; 010:040 but as to sitting at my right hand or at my left, that is not mine to give: it will be for those for whom it is reserved." 010:041 The other ten, hearing of it, were at first highly indignant with James and John. 010:042 Jesus, however, called them to Him and said to them, "You are aware how those who are deemed rulers among the Gentiles lord it over them, and their great men make them feel their authority; 010:043 but it is not to be so among you. No, whoever desires to be great among you must be your servant; 010:044 and whoever desires to be first among you must be the bondservant of all. 010:045 For the Son of Man also did not come to be waited upon, but to wait on others, and to give His life as the redemption-price for a multitude of people." 010:046 They came to Jericho; and as He was leaving that town- Himself and His disciples and a great crowd-Bartimaeus (the son of Timaeus), a blind beggar, was sitting by the way-side. 010:047 Hearing that it was Jesus the Nazarene, he began to cry out, "Son of David, Jesus, have pity on me." 010:048 Many angrily told him to leave off shouting; but he only cried out all the louder, "Son of David, have pity on me." 010:049 Then Jesus stood still. "Call him," He said. So they called the blind man. "Cheer up," they said; "rise, he is calling you." 010:050 The man flung away his outer garment, sprang to his feet, and came to Jesus. 010:051 "What shall I do for you?" said Jesus. "Rabboni," replied the blind man, "let me recover my sight." 010:052 "Go," said Jesus, "your faith has cured you." Instantly he regained his sight, and followed Him along the road. 011:001 When they were getting near Jerusalem and had arrived at Bethphage and Bethany, on the Mount of Olives, Jesus sent two of his disciples on in front, with these instructions. 011:002 "Go," He said, "to the village facing you, and immediately on entering it you will find an ass's foal tied up which no one has ever yet ridden: untie him and bring him here. 011:003 And if any one asks you, `Why are you doing that?' say, `The Master needs it, and will send it back here without delay.'" 011:004 So they went and found a young ass tied up at the front door of a house. They were untying it, 011:005 when some of the bystanders called out, "What are you doing, untying the foal?" 011:006 But on their giving the answer that Jesus had bidden them give, they let them take it. 011:007 So they brought the foal to Jesus, and threw their outer garments over him; and Jesus mounted. 011:008 Then many spread their outer garments to carpet the road, and others leafy branches which they had cut down in the fields; 011:009 while those who led the way and those who followed kept shouting "God save Him!" Blessed be He who comes in the Lord's name. 011:010 Blessings on the coming Kingdom of our forefather David! God in the highest Heavens save Him!" 011:011 So He came into Jerusalem and into the Temple; and after looking round upon everything there, the hour being now late He went out to Bethany with the Twelve. 011:012 The next day, after they had left Bethany, He was hungry. 011:013 But in the distance He saw a fig-tree in full leaf, and went to see whether perhaps He could find some figs on it. When however He came to it, He found nothing but leaves (for it was not fig time); 011:014

and He said to the tree, "Let no one ever again eat fruit from thee!" And His disciples heard this. 011:015 They reached Jerusalem, and entering the Temple He began to drive out the buyers and sellers, and upset the money-changers' tables and the stools of the pigeon-dealers, 011:016 and would not allow any one to carry anything through the Temple. 011:017 And He remonstrated with them. "Is it not written," He said, "`My House shall be called The House of Prayer for all the nations?' But you have made it what it now is-a robbers' cave." 011:018 This the High Priests and Scribes heard, and they began to devise means to destroy Him. For they were afraid of Him, because of the deep impression produced on all the people by His teaching. 011:019 When evening came on, Jesus and His disciples used to leave the city. 011:020 In the early morning, as they passed by, they saw the fig-tree withered to the roots; 011:021 and Peter, recollecting, said to Him, "Look, Rabbi, the fig-tree which you cursed is withered up." 011:022 Jesus said to them, "Have faith in God. 011:023 In solemn truth I tell you that if any one shall say to this mountain, `Remove, and hurl thyself into the sea,' and has no doubt about it in his heart, but stedfastly believes that what he says will happen, it shall be granted him. 011:024 That is why I tell you, as to whatever you pray and make request for, if you believe that you have received it it shall be yours. 011:025 But whenever you stand praying, if you have a grievance against any one, forgive it, so that your Father in Heaven may also forgive you your offences." 011:026 [] 011:027 They came again to Jerusalem; and as He was walking in the Temple, the High Priests, Scribes and Elders came to Him 011:028 and asked, "By what authority are you doing these things? and who gave you authority to do them?" 011:029 "And I will put a question to you," replied Jesus; "answer me, and then I will tell you by what authority I do these things. 011:030 John's Baptism-was it of Heavenly or of human origin? Answer me." 011:031 So they debated the matter with one another. "Suppose we say, `Heavenly,'" they argued, "he will ask, `Why then did you not believe him?' 011:032 Or should we say, `human?'" They were afraid of the people; for all agreed in holding John to have been really a Prophet. 011:033 So they answered Jesus, "We do not know." "Nor do I tell you," said Jesus, "by what authority I do these things." 012:001 Then He began to speak to them in figurative language. "There was once a man," He said, "who planted a vineyard, fenced it round, dug a pit for the wine-tank, and built a strong lodge. Then he let the place to vine-dressers and went abroad. 012:002 At vintage-time he sent one of his servants to receive from the vine-dressers a share of the grapes. 012:003 But they seized him, beat him cruelly and sent him away empty-handed. 012:004 Again he sent to them another servant: and as for him, they wounded him in the head and treated him shamefully. 012:005 Yet a third he sent, and him they killed. And he sent many besides, and them also they ill-treated, beating some and killing others. 012:006 He had still one left whom he could send, a dearly-loved son: him last of all he sent, saying, "`They will treat my son with respect.' 012:007 "But those men-the vine-dressers-said to one another, "`Here is the heir: come, let us kill him, and then the property will one day be ours.' 012:008 "So they took him and killed him, and flung his body outside the vineyard. 012:009 What, therefore, will the owner of the vineyard do?" "He will come and put the vine-dressers to death," they said; "and will give the vineyard to others." 012:010 "Have you not read even this passage," He added, "`The stone which the builders rejected has become the Cornerstone: 012:011 this Cornerstone came from the Lord, and is wonderful in our esteem?'" 012:012 And they kept looking out for an opportunity to seize Him, but were afraid of the people; for they saw that in this parable He had referred to *them*. So they left Him and went away. 012:013 Their next step was to send to Him some of the Pharisees and of Herod's partisans to entrap Him in conversation. 012:014 So they came to Him. "Rabbi," they said, "we know that you are a truthful man and you do not fear any one; for you do not recognize human distinctions, but teach God's way truly. Is it allowable to pay poll-tax to Caesar, or not? 012:015 Shall we pay, or shall we refuse to pay?" But He, knowing their hypocrisy, replied, "Why try to ensnare me? Bring me a shilling for me to look at." 012:016 They brought one; and He asked them, "Whose is this likeness and this inscription?" "Caesar's," they replied. 012:017 "What is Caesar's," replied Jesus, "pay to Caesar-and what is God's, pay to God." And they wondered exceedingly at Him. 012:018 Then came to Him a party of Sadducees, a sect which denies that there is any Resurrection; and they proceeded to question Him. 012:019 "Rabbi," they said, "Moses made it a law for us: `If a man's brother should die and leave a wife, but no child, the man shall marry the widow and raise up a family for his brother.' 012:020 There were once seven brothers, the eldest of whom married a wife, but at his death left no family. 012:021 The second married her, and died, leaving no family; and the third did the same. 012:022 And so did the rest of the seven, all dying childless. Finally the woman also died. 012:023 At the Resurrection whose wife will she be? For they all seven married her." 012:024 "Is not this the cause of your error," replied Jesus-"your ignorance alike of the Scriptures and of the power of God? 012:025 For when they have risen from among the dead, men do not marry and women are not given in marriage, but they are as angels are in Heaven. 012:026 But as to the dead, that they rise to life, have you never read in the Book of Moses, in the passage about the Bush, how God said to him, `I am the God of Abraham, the God of Isaac, and the God of Jacob?' 012:027 He is not the God of dead, but of living men. You are in grave error." 012:028 Then one of the Scribes, who had heard them disputing and well knew that Jesus had given them an answer to the point, and a forcible one, came forward and asked Him, "Which is the chief of all the

Commandments?" 012:029 "The chief Commandment," replied Jesus, "is this: `Hear, O Israel! The Lord our God is one Lord; 012:030 and thou shalt love the Lord thy God with thy whole heart, thy whole soul, thy whole mind, and thy whole strength.' 012:031 "The second is this: `Thou shalt love thy fellow man as thou lovest thyself.' "Other Commandment greater than these there is none." 012:032 So the Scribe said to Him, "Rightly, in very truth, Rabbi, have you said that He stands alone, and there is none but He; 012:033 and To love Him with all one's heart, with all one's understanding, and with all one's strength, and to love one's fellow man no less than oneself, is far better than all our whole burnt-offerings and sacrifices." 012:034 Perceiving that the Scribe had answered wisely Jesus said to him, "You are not far from the Kingdom of God." No one from that time forward ventured to put any question to Him. 012:035 But, while teaching in the Temple, Jesus asked, "How is it the Scribes say that the Christ is a son of David? 012:036 David himself said, taught by the Holy Spirit, "`The Lord said to my Lord, Sit at My right hand, until I have made thy foes a footstool under thy feet.' 012:037 "David himself calls Him `Lord:' how then can He be his son?" And the mass of people found pleasure in listening to Jesus. 012:038 Moreover in the course of His teaching He said, "Be on your guard against the Scribes who like to walk about in long robes and to be bowed to in places of public resort, 012:039 and to occupy the best seats in the synagogues and at dinner parties, 012:040 and who swallow up the property of widows and then mask their wickedness by making long prayers: these men will receive far heavier punishment." 012:041 Having taken a seat opposite the Treasury, He observed how the people were dropping money into the Treasury, and that many of the wealthy threw in large sums. 012:042 But there came one poor widow and dropped in two farthings, equal in value to a halfpenny. 012:043 So He called His disciples to Him and said, "In solemn truth I tell you that this widow, poor as she is, has thrown in more than all the other contributors to the Treasury; 012:044 for they have all contributed out of what they could well spare, but she out of her need has thrown in all she possessed- all she had to live on." 013:001 As He was leaving the Temple, one of His disciples exclaimed, "Look, Rabbi, what wonderful stones! what wonderful buildings!" 013:002 "You see all these great buildings?" Jesus replied; "not one stone will be left here upon another-not thrown down." 013:003 He was sitting on the Mount of Olives opposite to the Temple, when Peter, James, John, and Andrew, apart from the others asked Him, 013:004 "Tell us, When will these things be? and what will be the sign when all these predictions are on the point of being fulfilled?" 013:005 So Jesus began to say to them: "Take care that no one misleads you. 013:006 Many will come assuming my name and saying, `I am He;' and they will mislead many. 013:007 But when you hear of wars and rumours of wars, do not be alarmed: come they must, but the End is not yet. 013:008 For nation will rise in arms against nation, and kingdom against kingdom. There will be earthquakes in various places; there will be famines. These miseries are but like the early pains of childbirth. 013:009 "You yourselves must be on your guard. They will deliver you up to Sanhedrins; you will be brought into synagogues and cruelly beaten; and you will stand before governors and kings for my sake, to be witnesses to them for me. 013:010 But the proclamation of the Good News must be carried to all the Gentiles before the End comes. 013:011 When however they are marching you along under arrest, do not be anxious beforehand about what you are to say, but speak what is given you when the time comes; for it will not be you who speak, but the Holy Spirit. 013:012 "Brother will betray brother to be killed, and fathers will betray children; and children will rise against their parents and have them put to death. 013:013 You will be objects of universal hatred because you are called by my name, but those who stand firm to the End will be saved. 013:014 "As soon, however, as you see the Abomination of Desolation standing where he ought not"-let the reader observe these words-"then let those in Judaea escape to the hills; 013:015 let him who is on the roof not come down and enter the house to fetch anything out of it; 013:016 and let not him who is in the field turn back to pick up his outer garment. 013:017 And alas for the women who at that time are with child or have infants! 013:018 "But pray that it may not come in the winter. 013:019 For those will be times of suffering the like of which has never been from the first creation of God's world until now, and assuredly never will be again; 013:020 and but for the fact that the Lord has cut short those days, no one would escape; but for the sake of His own People whom He has chosen for Himself He has cut short the days. 013:021 "At that time if any one says to you, `See, here is the Christ!' or `See, He is there!' do not believe it. 013:022 For there will rise up false Christs and false prophets, displaying signs and prodigies with a view to lead astray- if indeed that were possible- even God's own People. 013:023 But as for yourselves, be on your guard: I have forewarned you of everything. 013:024 "At that time, however, after that distress, the sun will be darkened and the moon will not shed her light; 013:025 the stars will be seen falling from the firmament, and the forces which are in the heavens will be disordered and disturbed. 013:026 And then will they see the Son of Man coming in clouds with great power and glory. 013:027 Then He will send forth the angels and gather together His chosen People from north, south, east and west, from the remotest parts of the earth and the sky. 013:028 "Learn from the fig-tree the lesson it teaches. As soon as its branch has become soft and it is bursting into leaf, you know that summer is near. 013:029 So also do you, when you see these things happening, be sure that He is near, at your very door. 013:030 I tell you in solemn truth that the present generation will certainly not pass away without all these things having first taken place. 013:031 Earth and sky will pass away, but it is certain that my words will not pass away. 013:032 "But as to that day or the exact time no one knows-not even the angels in Heaven, nor the Son, but the Father alone. 013:033 Take care, be on the alert, and pray; for you do not know when it will happen. 013:034 It is like a man living abroad who has left his house, and given the management to his servants-to each one his special duty- and has ordered the porter to keep awake. 013:035 Be wakeful therefore, for you know not when the master of the house is coming-in the evening, at midnight, at cock-crow, or at dawn. 013:036 Beware lest He should arrive unexpectedly and find you asleep. 013:037 Moreover, what I say to you I say to all-Be wakeful!" 014:001 It was now two days before the Passover and the feast of Unleavened Bread, and the High Priests and Scribes were bent on finding how to seize Him by stratagem and put Him to death. 014:002 But they said, "Not on the Festival-day, for fear there should be a riot among the people." 014:003 Now when He was at Bethany, in the house of Simon the Leper, while He was at table, there came a woman with a jar of pure, sweet-scented ointment very costly: she broke the jar and poured the ointment over His head. 014:004 But there were some who said indignantly among themselves, "Why has the ointment been thus wasted? 014:005 For that ointment might have been sold for fifteen pounds or more, and the money have been given to the poor." And they were exceedingly angry with her. 014:006 But Jesus said, "Leave her alone: why are you troubling her? She has done a most gracious act towards me. 014:007 For you always have the poor among you, and whenever you choose you can do acts of kindness to them; but me you have not always. 014:008 What she could she did: she has perfumed my body in preparation for my burial. 014:009 And I solemnly tell you that wherever in the whole world the Good News shall be proclaimed, this which she has done shall also be told in remembrance of her." 014:010 But Judas Iscariot, already mentioned as one of the Twelve, went to the High Priests to betray Jesus to them. 014:011 They gladly listened to his proposal, and promised to give him a sum of money. So he looked out for an opportunity to betray Him. 014:012 On the first day of the feast of Unleavened Bread-the day for killing the Passover lamb-His disciples asked Him, "Where shall we go and prepare for you to eat the Passover?" 014:013 So He sent two of His disciples with instructions, saying, "Go into the city, and you will meet a man carrying a pitcher of water: follow him, 014:014 and whatever house he enters, tell the master of the house, `The Rabbi asks, Where is my room where I can eat the Passover with my disciples?' 014:015 Then he will himself show you a large room upstairs, ready furnished: there make preparation for us." 014:016 So the disciples went out and came to the city, and found everything just as He had told them; and they got the Passover ready. 014:017 When it was evening, He came with the Twelve.

014:018 And while they were at table Jesus said, "I solemnly tell you that one of you will betray me-one who is eating with me." 014:019 They were filled with sorrow, and began asking Him, one by one, "Not I, is it?" 014:020 "It is one of the Twelve," He replied; "he who is dipping his fingers in the dish with me. 014:021 For the Son of Man is going His way as it is written about Him; but alas for the man by whom the Son of Man is betrayed! It had been a happy thing for that man, had he never been born." 014:022 Also during the meal He took a Passover biscuit, blessed it, and broke it. He then gave it to them, saying, "Take this, it is my body." 014:023 Then He took the cup, gave thanks, and handed it to them, and they all of them drank from it. 014:024 "This is my blood," He said, "which is to be poured out on behalf of many-the blood which makes the Covenant sure. 014:025 I solemnly tell you that never again will I taste the produce of the vine till I shall drink the new wine in the Kingdom of God." 014:026 After singing a hymn, they went out to the Mount of Olives. 014:027 Then said Jesus to them, "All of you are about to stumble and fall, for it is written, `I will strike down the Shepherd, and the sheep will be scattered in all directions.' 014:028 But after I have risen to life again I will go before you into Galilee." 014:029 "All may stumble and fall," said Peter, "yet I never will." 014:030 "I solemnly tell you," replied Jesus, "that to-day-this night-before the cock crows twice, you yourself will three times disown me." 014:031 "Even if I must die with you," declared Peter again and again, "I will never disown you." In like manner protested also all the disciples. 014:032 So they came to a place called Gethsemane. There He said to His disciples, "Sit down here till I have prayed." 014:033 Then He took with Him Peter and James and John, and began to be full of terror and distress, 014:034 and He said to them, "My heart is oppressed with anguish to the very point of death: wait here and keep awake." 014:035 Going forward a short distance He threw Himself upon His face and prayed repeatedly that, if it was possible, He might be spared that time of agony; 014:036 and He said, "Abba! my Father! all things are possible for Thee: take this cup of suffering away from me: and yet not what I desire, but what Thou desirest." 014:037 Then He came and found them asleep, and He said to Peter, "Simon, are you asleep? Had you not strength to keep awake a single hour? 014:038 Be wakeful, all of you, and keep on praying, that you may not come into temptation: the spirit is right willing, but the body is frail." 014:039 He again went away and prayed, using the very same words. 014:040 When He returned He again found them asleep, for they were very tired; and they knew not how to answer Him. 014:041 A third time He came, and then He said, "Sleep on and rest. Enough! the hour has come. Even now they are betraying the Son of Man into the hands of sinful men. 014:042 Rouse yourselves, let us be going: my betrayer is close at hand." 014:043 Immediately, while He was still speaking, Judas, one of the Twelve, came and with him a crowd of men armed with swords and cudgels, sent by the High Priests and Scribes and Elders. 014:044 Now the betrayer had arranged a signal with them. "The one I kiss," he said, "is the man: lay hold of him, and take him safely away." 014:045 So he came, and going straight to Jesus he said, "Rabbi!" and kissed Him with seeming affection; 014:046 whereupon they laid hands on Him and held Him firmly. 014:047 But one of those who stood by drew his sword and struck a blow at the High Priest's servant, cutting off his ear. 014:048 "Have you come out," said Jesus, "with swords and cudgels to arrest me, as if you had to fight with a robber? 014:049 Day after day I used to be among you in the Temple teaching, and you never seized me. But this is happening in order that the Scriptures may be fulfilled.' 014:050 Then His friends all forsook Him and fled. 014:051 One youth indeed did follow Him, wearing only a linen cloth round his bare body. Of him they laid hold, 014:052 but he left the linen cloth in their hands and fled without it. 014:053 So they led Jesus away to the High Priest, and with him there assembled all the High Priests, Elders, and Scribes. 014:054 Peter followed Jesus at a distance, as far as the outer court of the High Priest's palace. But there he remained sitting among the officers, and warming himself by the fire. 014:055 Meanwhile the High Priests and the entire Sanhedrin were endeavouring to get evidence against Jesus in order to put Him to death, but could find none; 014:056 for though many gave false testimony against Him, their statements did not tally. 014:057 Then some came forward as witnesses and falsely declared, 014:058 "We have heard him say, `I will pull down this Sanctuary built by human hands, and three days afterwards I will erect another built without hands.'" 014:059 But not even in this shape was their testimony consistent. 014:060 At last the High Priest stood up, and advancing into the midst of them all, asked Jesus, "Have you no answer to make? What is the meaning of all this that these witnesses allege against you?" 014:061 But He remained silent, and gave no reply. A second time the High Priest questioned Him. "Are you the Christ, the Son of the Blessed One?" he said. 014:062 "I am," replied Jesus, "and you and others will see the Son of Man sitting at the right hand of the divine Power, and coming amid the clouds of the sky." 014:063 Rending his garments the High Priest exclaimed, "What need have we of witnesses after that? 014:064 You all heard his impious words. What is your judgement?" Then with one voice they condemned Him as deserving of death. 014:065 Thereupon some began to spit on Him, and to blindfold Him, while striking Him with their fists and crying, "Prove that you are a prophet." The officers too struck Him with open hands as they took Him in charge. 014:066 Now while Peter was below in the quadrangle, one of the High Priest's maidservants came, 014:067 and seeing Peter warming himself she looked at him and said, "You also were with Jesus, the Nazarene." 014:068 But he denied it, and said, "I don't know-I don't understand- What do you mean?" And then he went out into the outer court. Just then a cock crowed. 014:069 Again the maidservant saw him, and again began to say to the people standing by, "He is one of them." 014:070 A second time he repeatedly denied it. Soon afterwards the bystanders again accused Peter, saying, "You are surely one of them, for you too are a Galilaean." 014:071 But he broke out into curses and oaths, declaring, "I know nothing of the man you are talking about." 014:072 No sooner had he spoken than a cock crowed for the second time, and Peter recollected the words of Jesus, "Before the cock crows twice, you will three times disown me." And as he thought of it, he wept aloud. 015:001 At earliest dawn, after the High Priests had held a consultation with the Elders and Scribes, they and the entire Sanhedrin bound Jesus and took Him away and handed Him over to Pilate. 015:002 So Pilate questioned Him. "Are *you* the King of the Jews?" he asked. "I am," replied Jesus. 015:003 Then, as the High Priests went on heaping accusations on Him, 015:004 Pilate again and again asked Him, "Do you make no reply? Listen to the many charges they are bringing against you." 015:005 But Jesus made no further answer: so that Pilate wondered. 015:006 Now at the Festival it was customary for Pilate to release to the Jews any one prisoner whom they might beg off from punishment; 015:007 and at this time a man named Barabbas was in prison among the insurgents-persons who in the insurrection had committed murder. 015:008 So the people came crowding up, asking Pilate to grant them the usual favour. 015:009 "Shall I release for you the King of the Jews?" answered Pilate. 015:010 For he could see that it was out of sheer spite that the High Priests had handed Him over. 015:011 But the High Priests urged on the crowd to obtain Barabbas's release in preference; 015:012 and when Pilate again asked them, "What then shall I do to the man you call King of the Jews?" 015:013 they once more shouted out, "Crucify Him!" 015:014 "Why, what crime has he committed?" asked Pilate. But they vehemently shouted, "Crucify Him!" 015:015 So Pilate, wishing to satisfy the mob, released Barabbas for them, and after scourging Jesus handed Him over for crucifixion. 015:016 Then the soldiers led Him away into the court of the Palace (the Praetorium), and calling together the whole battalion 015:017 they arrayed Him in crimson, placed on His head a wreath of thorny twigs which they had twisted, 015:018 and went on to salute Him with shouts of "Long live the King of the Jews." 015:019 Then they began to beat Him on the head with a cane, to spit on Him, and to do Him homage on bended knees. 015:020 At last, having finished their sport, they took the robe off Him, put His own clothes on Him, and led Him out to crucify Him. 015:021 One Simon, a Cyrenaean, the father of Alexander and Rufus, was passing along, coming from the country: him they compelled to carry His cross. 015:022 So they brought Him to the place called Golgotha, which, being translated, means `Skull-ground.' 015:023

Here they offered Him wine mixed with myrrh; but He refused it. 015:024 Then they crucified Him. This done, they divided His garments among them, drawing lots to decide what each should take. 015:025 It was nine o'clock in the morning when they crucified Him. 015:026 Over His head was the notice in writing of the charge against Him: THE KING OF THE JEWS. 015:027 And together with Jesus they crucified two robbers, one at His right hand and one at His left. 015:028 [] 015:029 And all the passers-by reviled Him. They shook their heads at Him and said, "Ah! you who were for destroying the Sanctuary and building a new one in three days, 015:030 come down from the cross and save yourself." 015:031 In the same way the High Priests also, as well as the Scribes, kept on scoffing at Him, saying to one another, "He has saved others: himself he cannot save! 015:032 This Christ, the King of Israel, let him come down now from the cross, that we may see and believe." Even the men who were being crucified with Him heaped insults on Him. 015:033 At noon there came a darkness over the whole land, lasting till three o'clock in the afternoon. 015:034 But at three o'clock Jesus cried out with a loud voice, "Elohi, Elohi, lama sabachthani?" which means, "My God, My God, why hast Thou forsaken me?" 015:035 Some of the bystanders, hearing Him, said, "Listen, he is calling for Elijah!" 015:036 Then a man ran to fill a sponge with sour wine, and he put it on the end of a cane and placed it to His lips, saying at the same time, "Wait! let us see whether Elijah will come and take him down." 015:037 But Jesus uttered a loud cry and yielded up His spirit. 015:038 And the curtain in the Sanctuary was torn in two, from top to bottom. 015:039 And when the Centurion who stood in front of the cross saw that He was dead, he exclaimed, "This man was indeed God's Son." 015:040 There were also a party of women looking on from a distance; among them being both Mary of Magdala and Mary the mother of James the Little and of Joses, and Salome- 015:041 all of whom in the Galilaean days had habitually been with Him and cared for Him, as well as many other women who had come up to Jerusalem with Him. 015:042 Towards sunset, as it was the Preparation-that is, the day preceding the Sabbath- 015:043 Joseph of Arimathaea came, a highly respected member of the Council, who himself also was living in expectation of the Kingdom of God. He summoned up courage to go in to see Pilate and beg for the body of Jesus. 015:044 But Pilate could hardly believe that He was already dead. He called, however, for the Centurion and inquired whether He had been long dead; 015:045 and having ascertained the fact he granted the body to Joseph. 015:046 He, having bought a sheet of linen, took Him down, wrapped Him in the sheet and laid Him in a tomb hewn in the rock; after which he rolled a stone against the entrance to the tomb. 015:047 Mary of Magdala and Mary the mother of Joses were looking on to see where He was put. 016:001 When the Sabbath was over, Mary of Magdala, Mary the mother of James, and Salome, bought spices, in order to come and anoint His body. 016:002 So, very soon after sunrise on the first day of the week, they came to the tomb; 016:003 and they were saying to one another, `Who will roll away the stone for us from the entrance to the tomb?" 016:004 But then, looking up, they saw that the stone was already rolled back: for it was of immense size. 016:005 Upon entering the tomb, they saw a young man sitting at their right hand, clothed in a long white robe. They were astonished and terrified. 016:006 But he said to them, "Do not be terrified. It is Jesus you are looking for-the Nazarene who has been crucified. He has come back to life: He is not here: this is the place where they laid Him. 016:007 But go and tell His disciples and Peter that He is going before you into Galilee: and that there you will see Him, as He told you." 016:008 So they came out, and fled from the tomb, for they were greatly agitated and surprised; and they said not a word to any one, for they were afraid. 016:009 [But He rose to life early on the first day of the week, and appeared first to Mary of Magdala from whom He had expelled seven demons. 016:010 She went and brought the tidings to those who had been with Him, as they were mourning and weeping. 016:011 But they, when they were told that He was alive and that she had seen Him, could not believe it. 016:012 Afterwards He showed Himself in another form to two of them as they were walking, on their way into the country. 016:013 These, again, went and told the news to the rest; but not even them did they believe. 016:014 Later still He showed Himself to the Eleven themselves whilst they were at table, and He upbraided them with their unbelief and obstinacy in not having believed those who had seen Him alive. 016:015 Then He said to them, "Go the whole world over, and proclaim the Good News to all mankind. 016:016 He who believes and is baptized shall be saved, but he who disbelieves will be condemned. 016:017 And signs shall attend those who believe, even such as these. By making use of my name they shall expel demons. They shall speak new languages. 016:018 They shall take up venomous snakes, and if they drink any deadly poison it shall do them no harm whatever. They shall lay their hands on the sick, and the sick shall recover." 016:019 So the Lord Jesus after having thus spoken to them was taken up into Heaven, and sat down at the right hand of God. 016:020 But they went out and made proclamation everywhere, the Lord working with them and confirming their Message by the signs which accompanied it.]

BOOK 40 MATTHEW

001:001 The Genealogy of Jesus Christ, the son of David, the son of Abraham. 001:002 Abraham was the father of Isaac; Isaac of Jacob; Jacob of Judah and his brothers. 001:003 Judah was the father (by Tamar) of Perez and Zerah; Perez of Hezron; Hezron of Ram; 001:004 Ram of Amminadab; Amminadab of Nahshon; Nahshon of Salmon; 001:005 Salmon (by Rahab) of Boaz; Boaz (by Ruth) of Obed; Obed of Jesse; 001:006 Jesse of David-the King. David (by Uriah's widow) was the father of Solomon; 001:007 Solomon of Rehoboam; Rehoboam of Abijah; Abijah of Asa; 001:008 Asa of Jehoshaphat; Jehoshaphat of Jehoram; Jehoram of Uzziah; 001:009 Uzziah of Jotham; Jotham of Ahaz; Ahaz of Hezekiah; 001:010 Hezekiah of Manasseh; Manasseh of Amon; Amon of Josiah; 001:011 Josiah of Jeconiah and his brothers at the period of the Removal to Babylon. 001:012 After the Removal to Babylon Jeconiah had a son Shealtiel; Shealtiel was the father of Zerubbabel; 001:013 Zerubbabel of Abiud; Abiud of Eliakim; Eliakim of Azor; 001:014 Azor of Zadok; Zadok of Achim; Achim of Eliud; 001:015 Eliud of Eleazar; Eleazar of Matthan; Matthan of Jacob; 001:016 and Jacob of Joseph the husband of Mary, who was the mother of JESUS who is called CHRIST. 001:017 There are therefore, in all, fourteen generations from Abraham to David; fourteen from David to the Removal to Babylon; and fourteen from the Removal to Babylon to the Christ. 001:018 The circumstances of the birth of Jesus Christ were these. After his mother Mary was betrothed to Joseph, before they were united in marriage, she was found to be with child through the Holy Spirit. 001:019 But Joseph her husband, being a kind-hearted man and unwilling publicly to disgrace her, had determined to release her privately from the betrothal. 001:020 But while he was contemplating this step, an angel of the Lord appeared to him in a dream and said, "Joseph, son of David, do not be afraid to bring home your wife Mary, for she is with child through the Holy Spirit. 001:021 She will give birth to a Son, and you are to call His name JESUS for He it is who will save His People from their sins." 001:022 All this took place in fulfilment of what the Lord had spoken through the Prophet, 001:023 "Mark! The maiden will be with child and will give birth to a son, and they will call His name Immanuel"-a word which signifies `God with us'. 001:024 When Joseph awoke, he did as the angel of the Lord had commanded, and brought home his wife, 001:025 but did not live with her until she had given birth to a son. The child's name he called JESUS. 002:001 Now after the birth of Jesus, which took place at Bethlehem in Judaea in the reign of King Herod, excitement was produced in Jerusalem by the arrival of certain Magi from the east, 002:002 inquiring, "Where is the newly born king of the Jews? For we have seen his Star in the east, and have come here to do him homage." 002:003 Reports of this soon reached the king, and greatly agitated not only him but all the people of Jerusalem. 002:004 So he assembled all the High Priests and Scribes of the people, and anxiously asked them where the Christ was to be born. 002:005 "At Bethlehem in Judaea," they replied; "for so it stands written in the words of the Prophet, 002:006 "`And thou, Bethlehem in the land of Judah, by no means the least honorable art thou among princely places in Judah! For from thee shall come a prince-one who shall be the Shepherd of My People Israel.'" 002:007 Thereupon Herod sent privately for the Magi and ascertained from them the exact time of the star's appearing. 002:008 He then directed them to go to Bethlehem, adding, "Go and make careful inquiry about the child, and when you have found him, bring me word, that I too may come and do him homage." 002:009 After hearing what the king said, they went to Bethlehem, while, strange to say, the star they had seen in the east led them on until it came and stood over the place where the babe was. 002:010 When they saw the star, the sight filled them with intense joy. 002:011 So they entered the house; and when they saw the babe with His mother Mary, they prostrated themselves and did Him homage, and opening their treasure-chests offered gifts to Him- gold, frankincense, and myrrh. 002:012 But being forbidden by God in a dream to return to Herod, they went back to their own country by a different route. 002:013 When they were gone, and angel of the Lord appeared to Joseph in a dream and said, "Rise: take the babe and His mother and escape to Egypt, and remain there till I bring you word. For Herod is about to make search for the child in order to destroy Him." 002:014 So Joseph roused himself and took the babe and His mother by night and departed into Egypt. 002:015 There he remained till Herod's death, that what the Lord had said through the Prophet might be fulfilled, "Out of Egypt I called My Son." 002:016 Then Herod, finding that the Magi had trifled with him, was furious, and sent and massacred all the boys under two years of age, in Bethlehem and all its neighbourhood, according to the date he had so carefully ascertained from the Magi. 002:017 Then were these words, spoken by the Prophet Jeremiah, fulfilled, 002:018 "A voice was heard in Ramah, wailing and bitter lamentation: It was Rachel bewailing her children, and she refused to be comforted because there were no more." 002:019 But after Herod's death an angel of the Lord appeared in a dream to Joseph in Egypt, and said to him, 002:020 "Rise from sleep, and take the child and His mother, and go into the land of Israel, for those who were seeking the child's life are dead." 002:021 So he roused himself and took the child and His mother and came into the land of Israel. 002:022 But hearing that Archelaus had succeeded his father Herod on the throne of Judaea, he was afraid to go there; and being instructed by God in a dream he withdrew into Galilee, 002:023 and went and settled in a town called Nazareth, in order that these words spoken through the Prophets might be fulfilled, "He shall be called a Nazarene." 003:001 About this time John the Baptist made his appearance, preaching in the Desert of Judaea. 003:002 "Repent," he said, "for the Kingdom of the Heavens is now close at hand." 003:003 He it is who was spoken of through the Prophet Isaiah when he said, "The voice of one crying aloud, `In the desert prepare ye a road for the Lord: make His highway straight.'" 003:004 This man John wore a garment of camel's hair, and a loincloth of leather; and he lived upon locusts and wild honey. 003:005 Then large numbers of people went out to him-people from Jerusalem and from all Judaea, and from the whole of the Jordan valley- 003:006 and were baptized by him in the Jordan, making full confession of their sins. 003:007 But when he saw many of the Pharisees and Sadducees coming for baptism, he exclaimed, "O vipers' brood, who has warned you to flee from the coming wrath? 003:008 Therefore let your lives prove your change of heart; 003:009 and do not imagine that you can say to yourselves,

`We have Abraham as our forefather,' for I tell you that God can raise up descendants for Abraham from these stones. 003:010 And already the axe is lying at the root of the trees, so that every tree which does not produce good fruit will quickly be hewn down and thrown into the fire. 003:011 I indeed am baptizing you in water on a profession of repentance; but He who is coming after me is mightier than I: His sandals I am not worthy to carry for a moment; He will baptize you in the Holy Spirit and in fire. 003:012 His winnowing-shovel is in His hand, and He will make a thorough clearance of His threshing-floor, gathering His wheat into the storehouse, but burning up the chaff in unquenchable fire." 003:013 Just at that time Jesus, coming from Galilee to the Jordan, presents Himself to John to be baptized by him. 003:014 John protested. "It is I," he said, "who have need to be baptized by you, and do you come to me?" 003:015 "Let it be so on this occasion," Jesus replied; "for so we ought to fulfil every religious duty." Then he consented; 003:016 and Jesus was baptized, and immediately went up from the water. At that moment the heavens opened, and he saw the Spirit of God descending like a dove and alighting upon Him, 003:017 while a voice came from Heaven, saying, "This is My Son, the dearly loved, in whom is My delight." 004:001 At that time Jesus was led up by the Spirit into the Desert in order to be tempted by the Devil. 004:002 There He fasted for forty days and nights; and after that He suffered from hunger. 004:003 So the Tempter came and said, "If you are the Son of God, command these stones to turn into loaves." 004:004 "It is written," replied Jesus, "`It is not on bread alone that a man shall live, but on whatsoever God shall appoint.'" 004:005 Then the Devil took Him to the Holy City and caused Him to stand on the roof of the Temple, 004:006 and said, "If you are God's Son, throw yourself down; for it is written, "`To His angels He will give orders concerning thee, and on their hands they shall bear thee up, lest at any moment thou shouldst strike thy foot against a stone.'" 004:007 "Again it is written," replied Jesus, "`Thou shalt not put the Lord thy God to the proof.'" 004:008 Then the Devil took Him to the top of an exceedingly lofty mountain, from which he caused Him to see all the Kingdoms of the world and their splendour, 004:009 and said to Him, "All this I will give you, if you will kneel down and do me homage." 004:010 "Begone, Satan!" Jesus replied; "for it is written, `To the Lord thy God thou shalt do homage, and to Him alone shalt thou render worship.'" 004:011 Thereupon the Devil left Him, and angels at once came and ministered to

Him. 004:012 Now when Jesus heard that John was thrown into prison, He withdrew into Galilee, 004:013 and leaving Nazareth He went and settled at Capernaum, a town by the Lake on the frontiers of Zebulun and Naphtali, 004:014 in order that these words, spoken through the Prophet Isaiah, might be fulfilled, 004:015 "Zebulun's land and Naphtali's land; the road by the Lake; the country beyond the Jordan; Galilee of the Nations! 004:016 The people who were dwelling in darkness have seen a brilliant light; and on those who were dwelling in the region of the shadow of death, on them light has dawned." 004:017 From that time Jesus began to preach. "Repent," He said, "for the Kingdom of the Heavens is now close at hand." 004:018 And walking along the shore of the Lake of Galilee He saw two brothers-Simon called Peter and his brother Andrew- throwing a drag-net into the Lake; for they were fishers. 004:019 And He said to them, "Come and follow me, and I will make you fishers of men." 004:020 So they immediately left their nets and followed Him. As He went further on, 004:021 He saw two other brothers, James the son of Zabdi and his brother John, in the boat with their father Zabdi mending their nets; and He called them. 004:022 And they at once left the boat and their father, and followed Him. 004:023 Then Jesus travelled through all Galilee, teaching in their synagogues and proclaiming the Good News of the Kingdom, and curing every kind of disease and infirmity among the people. 004:024 Thus His fame spread through all Syria; and they brought all the sick to Him, the people who were suffering from various diseases and pains-demoniacs, epileptics, paralytics; and He cured them. 004:025 And great crowds followed Him, coming from Galilee, from the Ten Towns, from Jerusalem, and from beyond the district on the other side of the Jordan. 005:001 Seeing the multitude of people, Jesus went up the Hill. There He seated Himself, and when His disciples came to Him, 005:002 He proceeded to teach them, and said: 005:003 "Blessed are the poor in spirit, for to them belongs the Kingdom of the Heavens. 005:004 "Blessed are the mourners, for they shall be comforted. 005:005 "Blessed are the meek, for they as heirs shall obtain possession of the earth. 005:006 "Blessed are those who hunger and thirst for righteousness, for they shall be completely satisfied. 005:007 "Blessed are the compassionate, for they shall receive compassion. 005:008 "Blessed are the pure in heart, for they shall see God. 005:009 "Blessed are the peacemakers, for it is they who will be recognized as sons of God. 005:010 "Blessed are those who have borne persecution in the cause of

Righteousness, for to them belongs the Kingdom of the Heavens. 005:011 "Blessed are you when they have insulted and persecuted you, and have said every cruel thing about you falsely for my sake. 005:012 Be joyful and triumphant, because your reward is great in the Heavens; for so were the Prophets before you persecuted. 005:013 "*You* are the salt of the earth; but if salt has become tasteless, in what way can it regain its saltness? It is no longer good for anything but to be thrown away and trodden on by the passers by. 005:014 *You* are the light of the world; a town cannot be hid if built on a hill-top. 005:015 Nor is a lamp lighted to be put under a bushel, but on the lampstand; and then it gives light to all in the house. 005:016 Just so let your light shine before all men, in order that they may see your holy lives and may give glory to your Father who is in Heaven. 005:017 "Do not for a moment suppose that I have come to abrogate the Law or the Prophets: I have not come to abrogate them but to give them their completion. 005:018 Solemnly I tell you that until Heaven and earth pass away, not one iota or smallest detail will pass away from the Law until all has taken place. 005:019 Whoever therefore breaks one of these least commandments and teaches others to break them, will be called the least in the Kingdom of the Heavens; but whoever practises them and teaches them, he will be acknowledged as great in the Kingdom of the Heavens. 005:020 For I assure you that unless your righteousness greatly surpasses that of the Scribes and the Pharisees, you will certainly not find entrance into the Kingdom of the Heavens. 005:021 "You have heard that it was said to the ancients, `Thou shalt not commit murder', and whoever commits murder will be answerable to the magistrate. 005:022 But I say to you that every one who becomes angry with his brother shall be answerable to the magistrate; that whoever says to his brother `Raca,' shall be answerable to the Sanhedrin; and that whoever says, `You fool!' shall be liable to the Gehenna of Fire. 005:023 If therefore when you are offering your gift upon the altar, you remember that your brother has a grievance against you, 005:024 leave your gift there before the altar, and go and make friends with your brother first, and then return and proceed to offer your gift. 005:025 Come to terms without delay with your opponent while you are yet with him on the way to the court; for fear he should obtain judgement from the magistrate against you, and the magistrate should give you in custody to the officer and you be thrown into prison. 005:026 I solemnly tell you that you will certainly not be released till you have paid the very last farthing.

005:027 "You have heard that it was said, `Thou shalt not commit adultery.'
005:028 But I tell you that whoever looks at a woman and cherishes lustful
thoughts has already in his heart become guilty with regard to her. 005:029
If therefore your eye, even the right eye, is a snare to you, tear it out and
away with it; it is better for you that one member should be destroyed
rather than that your whole body should be thrown into Gehenna. 005:030
And if your right hand is a snare to you, cut it off and away with it; it is
better for you that one member should be destroyed rather than that your
whole body should go into Gehenna. 005:031 "It was also said, `If any man
puts away his wife, let him give her a written notice of divorce.' 005:032 But
I tell you that every man who puts away his wife except on the ground of
unfaithfulness causes her to commit adultery, and whoever marries her
when so divorced commits adultery. 005:033 "Again, you have heard that it
was said to the ancients, `Thou shalt not swear falsely, but shalt perform thy
vows to the Lord.' 005:034 But I tell you not to swear at all; neither by
Heaven, for it is God's throne; 005:035 nor by the earth, for it is the
footstool under His feet; nor by Jerusalem, for it is the City of the Great
King. 005:036 And do not swear by your head, for you cannot make one
hair white or black. 005:037 But let your language be, `Yes, yes,' or `No,
no.' Anything in excess of this comes from the Evil one. 005:038 "You have
heard that it was said, `Eye for eye, tooth for tooth.' 005:039 But I tell you
not to resist a wicked man, but if any one strikes you on the right cheek,
turn the other to him as well. 005:040 If any one wishes to go to law with
you and to deprive you of your under garment, let him take your outer one
also. 005:041 And whoever shall compel you to convey his goods one mile,
go with him two. 005:042 To him who asks, give: from him who would
borrow, turn not away. 005:043 "You have heard that it was said, `Thou
shalt love thy neighbour and hate thine enemy.' 005:044 But I command
you all, love your enemies, and pray for your persecutors; 005:045 that so
you may become true sons of your Father in Heaven; for He causes His sun
to rise on the wicked as well as the good, and sends rain upon those who do
right and those who do wrong. 005:046 For if you love only those who love
you, what reward have you earned? Do not even the tax-gatherers do that?
005:047 And if you salute only your near relatives, what praise is due to
you? Do not even the Gentiles do the same? 005:048 You however are to
be complete in goodness, as your Heavenly Father is complete. 006:001
"But beware of doing your good actions in the sight of men, in order to

attract their gaze; if you do, there is no reward for you with your Father who is in Heaven. 006:002 `When you give in charity, never blow a trumpet before you as the hypocrites do in the synagogues and streets in order that their praises may be sung by men. I solemnly tell you that they already have their reward. 006:003 But when you are giving in charity, let not your left hand perceive what your right hand is doing, 006:004 that your charities may be in secret; and then your Father-He who sees in secret-will recompense you. 006:005 "And when praying, you must not be like the hypocrites. They are fond of standing and praying in the synagogues or at the corners of the wider streets, in order that men may see them. I solemnly tell you that they already have their reward. 006:006 But you, whenever you pray, go into your own room and shut the door: then pray to your Father who is in secret, and your Father-He who sees in secret-will recompense you. 006:007 "And when praying, do not use needless repetitions as the Gentiles do, for they expect to be listened to because of their multitude of words. 006:008 Do not, however, imitate them; for your Father knows what things you need before ever you ask Him. 006:009 "In this manner therefore pray: `Our Father who art in Heaven, may Thy name be kept holy; 006:010 let Thy kingdom come; let Thy will be done, as in Heaven so on earth; 006:011 give us to-day our bread for the day; 006:012 and forgive us our shortcomings, as we also have forgiven those who have failed in their duty towards us; 006:013 and bring us not into temptation, but rescue us from the Evil one.' 006:014 "For if you forgive others their offences, your Heavenly Father will forgive you also; 006:015 but if you do not forgive others their offences, neither will your Father forgive yours. 006:016 "When any of you fast, never assume gloomy looks as the hypocrites do; for they disfigure their faces in order that it may be evident to men that they are fasting. I solemnly tell you that they already have their reward. 006:017 But, whenever you fast, pour perfume on your hair and wash your face, 006:018 that it may not be apparent to men that you are fasting, but to your Father who is in secret; and your Father-He who sees in secret-will recompense you. 006:019 "Do not lay up stores of wealth for yourselves on earth, where the moth and wear-and-tear destroy, and where thieves break in and steal. 006:020 But amass wealth for yourselves in Heaven, where neither the moth nor wear-and-tear destroys, and where thieves do not break in and steal. 006:021 For where your wealth is, there also will your heart be. 006:022 "The eye is the lamp of the body. If then your eyesight is good, your whole body will be well lighted; 006:023 but if your eyesight is bad, your whole body will be dark. If however the very light within you is darkness, how dense must the darkness be! 006:024 "No man can be the bondservant of two masters; for either he will dislike one and like the other, or he will attach himself to one and think slightingly of the other. You cannot be the bondservants both of God and of gold. 006:025 For this reason I charge you not to be over-anxious about your lives, inquiring what you are to eat or what you are to drink, nor yet about your bodies, inquiring what clothes you are to put on. Is not the life more precious than its food, and the body than its clothing? 006:026 Look at the birds which fly in the air: they do not sow or reap or store up in barns, but your Heavenly Father feeds them: are not you of much greater value than they? 006:027 Which of you by being over-anxious can add a single foot to his height? 006:028 And why be anxious about clothing? Learn a lesson from the wild lilies. Watch their growth. They neither toil nor spin, 006:029 and yet I tell you that not even Solomon in all his magnificence could array himself like one of these. 006:030 And if God so clothes the wild herbage which to-day flourishes and to-morrow is thrown into the oven, is it not much more certain that He will clothe you, you men of little faith? 006:031 Do not be over-anxious, therefore, asking `What shall we eat?' or `What shall we drink?' or `What shall we wear?' 006:032 For all these are questions that Gentiles are always asking; but your Heavenly Father knows that you need these things- all of them. 006:033 But make His Kingdom and righteousness your chief aim, and then these things shall all be given you in addition. 006:034 Do not be over-anxious, therefore, about to-morrow, for to-morrow will bring its own cares. Enough for each day are its own troubles. 007:001 "Judge not, that you may not be judged; 007:002 for your own judgement will be dealt-and your own measure meted-to yourselves. 007:003 And why do you look at the splinter in your brother's eye, and not notice the beam which is in your own eye? 007:004 Or how say to your brother, `Allow me to take the splinter out of your eye,' while the beam is in your own eye? 007:005 Hypocrite, first take the beam out of your own eye, and then you will see clearly how to remove the splinter from your brother's eye. 007:006 "Give not that which is holy to the dogs, nor throw your pearls to the swine; otherwise they will trample them under their feet and then turn and attack you. 007:007 "Ask, and it will be given to you; seek, and you will find; knock, and the door will be opened to you. 007:008 For it is always he who asks that receives, he who seeks that finds, and he who knocks that has the door opened to him. 007:009 What man is there among you, who if his son shall ask him for bread will offer him a stone? 007:010 Or if the son shall ask him for a fish will offer him a snake? 007:011 If you then, imperfect as you are, know how to give good gifts to your children, how much more will your Father in Heaven give good things to those who ask Him! 007:012 Everything, therefore, be it what it may, that you would have men do to you, do you also the same to them; for in this the Law and the Prophets are summed up. 007:013 "Enter by the narrow gate; for wide is the gate and broad the road which leads to ruin, and many there are who enter by it; 007:014 because narrow is the gate and contracted the road which leads to Life, and few are those who find it. 007:015 "Beware of the false teachers-men who come to you in sheep's fleeces, but beneath that disguise they are ravenous wolves. 007:016 By their fruits you will easily recognize them. Are grapes gathered from thorns or figs from brambles? 007:017 Just so every good tree produces good fruit, but a poisonous tree produces bad fruit. 007:018 A good tree cannot bear bad fruit, nor a poisonous tree good fruit. 007:019 Every tree which does not yield good fruit is cut down and thrown aside for burning. 007:020 So by their fruits at any rate, you will easily recognize them. 007:021 "Not every one who says to me, `Master, Master,' will enter the Kingdom of the Heavens, but only those who are obedient to my Father who is in Heaven. 007:022 Many will say to me on that day, "`Master, Master, have we not prophesied in Thy name, and in Thy name expelled demons, and in Thy name performed many mighty works?' 007:023 "And then I will tell them plainly, "`I never knew you: begone from me, you doers of wickedness.' 007:024 "Every one who hears these my teachings and acts upon them will be found to resemble a wise man who builds his house upon rock; 007:025 and the heavy rain falls, the swollen torrents come, and the winds blow and beat against the house; yet it does not fall, for its foundation is on rock. 007:026 And every one who hears these my teachings and does not act upon them will be found to resemble a fool who builds his house upon sand. 007:027 The heavy rain descends, the swollen torrents come, and the winds blow and burst upon the house, and it falls; and disastrous is the fall." 007:028 When Jesus had concluded this discourse, the crowds were filled with amazement at His teaching, 007:029 for He had been teaching them as one who had authority, and not as their Scribes taught. 008:001 Upon descending from the hill country He was followed by immense crowds. 008:002 And a leper came to Him, and throwing himself at His feet, said, "Sir, if only you are willing you are able to cleanse me." 008:003 So Jesus put out His hand and touched him, and said, "I am willing: be cleansed." Instantly he was cleansed from his leprosy; 008:004 and Jesus said to him, "Be careful to tell no one, but go and show yourself to the priest, and offer the gift which Moses appointed as evidence for them." 008:005 After His entry into Capernaum a Captain came to Him, and entreated Him. 008:006 "Sir," he said, "my servant at home is lying ill with paralysis, and is suffering great pain." 008:007 "I will come and cure him," said Jesus. 008:008 "Sir," replied the Captain, "I am not a fit person to receive you under my roof: merely say the word, and my servant will be cured. 008:009 For I myself am also under authority, and have soldiers under me. To one I say `Go,' and he goes, to another `Come,' and he comes, and to my slave `Do this or that,' and he does it." 008:010 Jesus listened to this reply, and was astonished, and said to the people following Him, "I solemnly tell you that in no Israelite have I found faith as great as this. 008:011 And I tell you that many will come from the east and from the west and will recline at table with Abraham, Isaac and Jacob in the Kingdom of the Heavens, 008:012 while the natural heirs of the Kingdom will be driven out into the darkness outside: there will be the weeping aloud and the gnashing of teeth." 008:013 And Jesus said to the Captain, "Go, and just as you have believed, so be it for you." And the servant recovered precisely at that time. 008:014 After this Jesus went to the house of Peter, whose mother-in-law he found ill in bed with fever. 008:015 He touched her hand and the fever left her: and then she rose and waited upon Him. 008:016 In the evening many demoniacs were brought to Him, and with a word He expelled the demons; and He cured all the sick, 008:017 in order that this prediction of the Prophet Isaiah might be fulfilled, "He took on Him our weaknesses, and bore the burden of our diseases." 008:018 Seeing great crowds about Him Jesus had given directions to cross to the other side of the Lake, 008:019 when a Scribe came and said to Him, "Teacher, I will follow you wherever you go." 008:020 "Foxes have holes," replied Jesus, "and birds have nests; but the Son of Man has nowhere to lay His head." 008:021 Another of the disciples said to Him, "Sir, allow me first to go and bury my father." 008:022 "Follow me," said Jesus, "and leave the dead to bury their own dead." 008:023 Then He went on board a fishing-boat, and His disciples followed Him. 008:024 But suddenly there arose a great storm on the Lake, so that the waves threatened to engulf the boat; but He was asleep. 008:025 So they came and woke Him, crying, "Master, save us, we are drowning!" 008:026 "Why are you so easily frightened," He replied, "you men of little faith?" Then He rose and reproved the winds and the waves, and there was a perfect calm; 008:027 and the men, filled with amazement, exclaimed, "What kind of man is this? for the very winds and waves obey him!" 008:028 On His arrival at the other side, in the country of the Gadarenes, there met Him two men possessed by demons, coming from among the tombs: they were so dangerously fierce that no one was able to pass that way. 008:029 They cried aloud, "What hast Thou to do with us, Thou Son of God? Hast Thou come here to torment us before the time?" 008:030 Now at some distance from them a vast herd of swine were feeding. 008:031 So the demons entreated Him. "If Thou drivest us out," they said, "send us into the herd of swine." 008:032 "Go," He replied. Then they came out from the men and went into the swine, whereupon the entire herd instantly rushed down the cliff into the Lake and perished in the water. 008:033 The swineherds fled, and went and told the whole story in the town, including what had happened to the demoniacs. 008:034 So at once the whole population came out to meet Jesus; and when they saw Him, they besought Him to leave their country. 009:001 Accordingly He went on board, and crossing over came to His own town. 009:002 Here they brought to Him a paralytic lying on a bed. Seeing their faith Jesus said to the paralytic, "Take courage, my child; your sins are pardoned." 009:003 "Such language is impious," said some of the Scribes among themselves. 009:004 Knowing their thoughts Jesus said, "Why are you cherishing evil thoughts in your hearts? 009:005 Why, which is easier?-to say, `Your sins are pardoned,' or to say `Rise up and walk'? 009:006 But, to prove to you that the Son of Man has authority on earth to pardon sins"-He then says to the paralytic, "Rise, and take up your bed and go home." 009:007 And he got up, and went off home. 009:008 And the crowds were awe-struck when they saw it, and ascribed the glory to God who had entrusted such power to a man. 009:009 Passing on thence Jesus saw a man called Matthew sitting at the Toll Office, and said to him, "Follow me." And he arose, and followed Him. 009:010 And while He was reclining at table, a large number of tax-gathers and notorious sinners were of the party with Jesus and His disciples. 009:011 The Pharisees noticed this, and they inquired of His disciples, "Why does your Teacher eat with the tax-gatherers and notorious sinners?"

009:012 He heard the question and replied, "It is not men in good health who require a doctor, but the sick. 009:013 But go and learn what this means, `It is mercy that I desire, not sacrifice'; for I did not come to appeal to the righteous, but to sinners." 009:014 At that time John's disciples came and asked Jesus, "Why do we and the Pharisees fast, but your disciples do not?" 009:015 "Can the bridegroom's party mourn," He replied, "as long as the bridegroom is with them? But other days will come (when the Bridegroom has been taken from them) and then they will fast. 009:016 No one ever mends an old cloak with a patch of newly woven cloth. Otherwise, the patch put on would tear away some of the old, and a worse hole would be made. 009:017 Nor do people pour new wine into old wineskins. Otherwise, the skins would split, the wine would escape, and the skins be destroyed. But they put new wine into fresh skins, and both are saved." 009:018 While He was thus speaking, a Ruler came up and profoundly bowing said, "My daughter is just dead; but come and put your hand upon her and she will return to life." 009:019 And Jesus rose and followed him, as did also His disciples. 009:020 But a woman who for twelve years had been afflicted with haemorrhage came behind Him and touched the tassel of His cloak; 009:021 for she said to herself, "If I but touch His cloak, I shall be cured." 009:022 And Jesus turned and saw her, and said, "Take courage, daughter; your faith has cured you." And the woman was restored to health from that moment. 009:023 Entering the Ruler's house, Jesus saw the flute-players and the crowd loudly wailing, 009:024 and He said, "Go out of the room; the little girl is not dead, but asleep." And they laughed at Him. 009:025 When however the place was cleared of the crowd, Jesus went in, and on His taking the little girl by the hand, she rose up. 009:026 And the report of this spread throughout all that district. 009:027 As Jesus passed on, two blind men followed Him, shouting and saying, "Pity us, Son of David." 009:028 And when He had gone indoors, they came to Him. "Do you believe that I can do this?" He asked them. "Yes, Sir," they replied. 009:029 So He touched their eyes and said, "According to your faith let it be to you." 009:030 Then their eyes were opened. And assuming a stern tone Jesus said to them, "Be careful to let no one know." 009:031 But they went out and published His fame in all that district. 009:032 And as they were leaving His presence a dumb demoniac was brought to Him. 009:033 When the demon was expelled, the dumb man could speak. And the crowds exclaimed in astonishment, "Never was such a thing seen in Israel."

009:034 But the Pharisees maintained, "It is by the power of the Prince of the demons that he drives out the demons." 009:035 And Jesus continued His circuits through all the towns and the villages, teaching in their synagogues and proclaiming the Good News of the Kingdom, and curing every kind of disease and infirmity. 009:036 And when He saw the crowds He was touched with pity for them, because they were distressed and were fainting on the ground like sheep which have no shepherd. 009:037 Then He said to His disciples, "The harvest is abundant, but the reapers are few; 009:038 therefore entreat the Owner of the Harvest to send out reapers into His fields." 010:001 Then He called to Him His twelve disciples and gave them authority over foul spirits, to drive them out; and to cure every kind of disease and infirmity. 010:002 Now the names of the twelve Apostles were these: first, Simon called Peter, and his brother Andrew; James the son of Zabdi, and his brother John; 010:003 Philip and Bartholomew, Thomas and Matthew the tax-gatherer, James the son of Alphaeus, and Thaddaeus; 010:004 Simon the Cananaean, and Judas the Iscariot, who also betrayed Him. 010:005 These twelve Jesus sent on a mission, after giving them their instructions: "Go not," He said, "among the Gentiles, and enter no Samaritan town; 010:006 but, instead of that, go to the lost sheep of Israel's race. 010:007 And as you go, preach and say, `The Kingdom of the Heavens is close at hand.' 010:008 Cure the sick, raise the dead to life, cleanse lepers, drive out demons: you have received without payment, give without payment. 010:009 "Provide no gold, nor even silver nor copper to carry in your pockets; 010:010 no bag for your journey, nor change of linen, nor shoes, nor stick; for the labourer deserves his food. 010:011 "Whatever town or village you enter, inquire for some good man; and make his house your home till you leave the place. 010:012 When you enter the house, salute it; 010:013 and if the house deserves it, the peace you invoke shall come upon it. If not, your peace shall return to you. 010:014 And whoever refuses to receive you or even to listen to your Message, as you leave that house or town, shake off the very dust from your feet. 010:015 I solemnly tell you that it will be more endurable for the land of Sodom and Gomorrah on the day of Judgement than for that town. 010:016 "Remember it is I who am sending you out, as sheep into the midst of wolves; prove yourselves as sagacious as serpents, and as innocent as doves. 010:017 But beware of men; for they will deliver you up to appear before Sanhedrins, and will flog you in their synagogues; 010:018 and you will even be put on trial before governors and kings for my sake, to bear witness to them and to the Gentiles. 010:019 But when they have delivered you up, have no anxiety as to how you shall speak or what you shall say; for at that very time it shall be given you what to say; 010:020 for it is not you who will speak: it will be the Spirit of your Father speaking through you. 010:021 Brother will betray brother to death, and father, child; and children will rise against their own parents and will put them to death. 010:022 And you will be objects of universal hatred because you are called by my name; but he who holds out to the End- he will be saved. 010:023 Whenever they persecute you in one town, escape to the next; for I solemnly tell you that you will not have gone the round of all the towns of Israel before the Son of Man comes. 010:024 "The learner is never superior to his teacher, and the servant is never superior to his master. 010:025 Enough for the learner to be on a level with his teacher, and for the servant to be on a level with his master. If they have called the master of the house Baal-zebul, how much more will they slander his servants? 010:026 Fear them not, however; there is nothing veiled which will not be uncovered, nor secret which will not become known. 010:027 What I tell you in the dark, speak in the light; and what is whispered into your ear, proclaim upon the roofs of the houses. 010:028 "And do not fear those who kill the body, but cannot kill the soul; but rather fear him who is able to destroy both soul and body in Gehenna. 010:029 Do not two sparrows sell for a halfpenny? Yet not one of them will fall to the ground without your Father's leave. 010:030 But as for you, the very hairs on your heads are all numbered. 010:031 Away then with fear; you are more precious than a multitude of sparrows. 010:032 "Every man who acknowledges me before men I also will acknowledge before my Father who is in Heaven. 010:033 But whoever disowns me before men I also will disown before my Father who is in Heaven. 010:034 "Do not suppose that I came to bring peace to the earth: I did not come to bring peace but a sword. 010:035 For I came to set a man against his father, a daughter against her mother, and a daughter-in-law against her mother-in-law; 010:036 and a man's own family will be his foes. 010:037 Any one who loves father or mother more than me is not worthy of me, and any one who loves son or daughter more than me is not worthy of me; 010:038 and any one who does not take up his cross and follow where I lead is not worthy of me. 010:039 To save your life is to lose it, and to lose your life for my sake is to save it. 010:040 "Whoever receives you receives me, and whoever receives me receives Him who sent me. 010:041 Every one who receives a prophet, because he is a prophet, will receive a prophet's reward, and every one who receives a righteous man, because he is a righteous man, will receive a righteous man's reward. 010:042 And whoever gives one of these little ones even a cup of cold water to drink because he is a disciple, I solemnly tell you that he will not lose his reward." 011:001 When Jesus had concluded His instructions to His twelve disciples, He left in order to teach and to proclaim His Message in the neighbouring towns. 011:002 Now John had heard in prison about the Christ's doings, and he sent some of his disciples to inquire: 011:003 "Are you the Coming One, or is it a different person that we are to expect?" 011:004 "Go and report to John what you see and hear," replied Jesus; 011:005 "blind eyes receive sight, and cripples walk; lepers are cleansed, and deaf ears hear; the dead are raised to life, and the poor have the Good News proclaimed to them; 011:006 and blessed is every one who does not stumble and fall because of my claims." 011:007 When the messengers had taken their leave, Jesus proceeded to say to the multitude concerning John, "What did you go out into the Desert to gaze at? A reed waving in the wind? 011:008 But what did you go out to see? A man luxuriously dressed? Those who wear luxurious clothes are to be found in kings' palaces. 011:009 But why did you go out? To see a prophet? Yes, I tell you, and far more than a prophet. 011:010 This is he of whom it is written, "`See I am sending My messenger before Thy face, and he will make Thy road ready before Thee.' 011:011 "I solemnly tell you that among all of woman born no greater has ever been raised up than John the Baptist; yet one who is of lower rank in the Kingdom of the Heavens is greater than he. 011:012 But from the time of John the Baptist till now, the Kingdom of the Heavens has been suffering violent assault, and the violent have been seizing it by force. 011:013 For all the Prophets and the Law taught until John. 011:014 And (if you are willing to receive it) he is the Elijah who was to come. 011:015 Listen, every one who has ears! 011:016 "But to what shall I compare the present generation? It is like children sitting in the open places, who call to their playmates. 011:017 "`We have played the flute to you,' they say, `and you have not danced: we have sung dirges, and you have not beaten your breasts.' 011:018 "For John came neither eating nor drinking, and they say, `He has a demon.' 011:019 The Son of Man came eating and drinking, and they exclaim, `See this man!-given to gluttony and tippling, and a friend of tax-gatherers and notorious sinners!' And yet

Wisdom is vindicated by her actions." 011:020 Then began He to upbraid the towns where most of His mighty works had been done-because they had not repented. 011:021 "Alas for thee, Chorazin!" He cried. "Alas for thee, Bethsaida! For had the mighty works been done in Tyre and Sidon which have been done in both of you, they would long ere now have repented, covered with sackcloth and ashes. 011:022 Only I tell you that it will be more endurable for Tyre and Sidon on the day of Judgement than for you. 011:023 And thou, Capernaum, shalt thou be exalted even to Heaven? Even to Hades shalt thou descend. For had the mighty works been done in Sodom which have been done in thee, it would have remained until now. 011:024 Only I tell you all, that it will be more endurable for the land of Sodom on the day of Judgement than for thee." 011:025 About that time Jesus exclaimed, "I heartily praise Thee, Father, Lord of Heaven and of earth, that Thou hast hidden these things from sages and men of discernment, and hast unveiled them to babes. 011:026 Yes, Father, for such has been Thy gracious will. 011:027 "All things have been handed over to me by my Father, and no one fully knows the Son except the Father, nor does any one fully know the Father except the Son and all to whom the Son chooses to reveal Him. 011:028 "Come to me, all you toiling and burdened ones, and *I* will give you rest. 011:029 Take my yoke upon you and learn from me; for I am gentle and lowly in heart, and you will find rest for your souls. 011:030 For it is good to bear my yoke, and my burden is light." 012:001 About that time Jesus passed on the Sabbath through the wheatfields; and His disciples became hungry, and began to gather ears of wheat and eat them. 012:002 But the Pharisees saw it and said to Him, "Look! your disciples are doing what the Law forbids them to do on the Sabbath." 012:003 "Have you never read," He replied, "what David did when he and his men were hungry? 012:004 how he entered the House of God and ate the Presented Loaves, which it was not lawful for him or his men to eat, nor for any except the priests? 012:005 And have you not read in the Law how on the Sabbath the priests in the Temple break the Sabbath without incurring guilt? 012:006 But I tell you that there is here that which is greater than the Temple. 012:007 And if you knew what this means, `It is mercy I desire, not sacrifice', you would not have condemned those who are without guilt. 012:008 For the Son of Man is the Lord of the Sabbath." 012:009 Departing thence He went to their synagogue, 012:010 where there was a man with a shrivelled arm. And they questioned Him, "Is it right to cure people on the Sabbath?" Their intention was to bring a charge against Him. 012:011 "Which of you is there," He replied, "who, if he has but a single sheep and it falls into a hole on the Sabbath, will not lay hold of it and lift it out? 012:012 Is not a man, however, far superior to a sheep? Therefore it is right to do good on the Sabbath." 012:013 Then He said to the man, "Stretch out your arm." And he stretched it out, and it was restored quite sound like the other. 012:014 But the Pharisees after leaving the synagogue consulted together against Him, how they might destroy Him. 012:015 Aware of this, Jesus departed elsewhere; and a great number of people followed Him, all of whom He cured. 012:016 But He gave them strict injunctions not to blaze abroad His doings, 012:017 that those words of the Prophet Isaiah might be fulfilled, 012:018 "This is My servant whom I have chosen, My dearly loved One in whom My soul takes pleasure. I will put My spirit upon Him, and He will announce justice to the nations. 012:019 He will not wrangle or raise His voice, nor will His voice be heard in the broadways. 012:020 A crushed reed He will not utterly break, nor will He quench the still smouldering wick, until He has led on Justice to victory. 012:021 And on His name shall the nations rest their hopes." 012:022 At that time a demoniac was brought to Him, blind and dumb; and He cured him, so that the dumb man could speak and see. 012:023 And the crowds of people were all filled with amazement and said, "Can this be the Son of David?" 012:024 The Pharisees heard it and said, "This man only expels demons by the power of Baal-zebul, the Prince of demons." 012:025 Knowing their thoughts He said to them, "Every kingdom in which civil war has raged suffers desolation; and every city or house in which there is internal strife will be brought low. 012:026 And if Satan is expelling Satan, he has begun to make war on himself: how therefore shall his kingdom last? 012:027 And if it is by Baal-zebul's power that I expel the demons, by whose power do your disciples expel them? They therefore shall be your judges. 012:028 But if it is by the power of the Spirit of God that I expel the demons, it is evident that the Kingdom of God has come upon you. 012:029 Again, how can any one enter the house of a strong man and carry off his goods, unless first of all he masters and secures the strong man: then he will ransack his house. 012:030 "The man who is not with me is against me, and he who is not gathering with me is scattering abroad. 012:031 This is why I tell you that men may find forgiveness for every other sin and impious word, but that for impious speaking against the Holy Spirit they shall find no forgiveness. 012:032 And whoever shall speak against the Son of Man may obtain forgiveness; but whoever speaks against the Holy Spirit, neither in this nor in the coming age shall he obtain forgiveness." 012:033 "Either grant the tree to be wholesome and its fruit wholesome, or the tree poisonous and its fruit poisonous; for the tree is known by its fruit. 012:034 O vipers' brood, how can you speak what is good when you are evil? For it is from the overflow of the heart that the mouth speaks. 012:035 A good man from his good store produces good things, and a bad man from his bad store produces bad things. 012:036 But I tell you that for every careless word that men shall speak they will be held accountable on the day of Judgement. 012:037 For each of you by his words shall be justified, or by his words shall be condemned." 012:038 Then He was accosted by some of the Scribes and of the Pharisees who said, "Teacher, we wish to see a sign given by you." 012:039 "Wicked and faithless generation!" He replied, "they clamour for a sign, but none shall be given to them except the sign of the Prophet Jonah. 012:040 For just as Jonah was three days in the sea-monster's belly, so will the Son of Man be three days in the heart of the earth. 012:041 There will stand up men of Nineveh at the Judgement together with the present generation, and will condemn it; because they repented at the preaching of Jonah, and mark! there is One greater than Jonah here. 012:042 The Queen of the south will awake at the Judgement together with the present generation, and will condemn it; because she came from the ends of the earth to hear the wisdom of Solomon, and mark! there is One greater than Solomon here. 012:043 "No sooner however has the foul spirit gone out of the man, then he roams about in places where there is no water, seeking rest but finding none. 012:044 Then he says, `I will return to my house that I left;' and he comes and finds it unoccupied, swept clean, and in good order. 012:045 Then he goes and brings back with him seven other spirits more wicked than himself, and they come in and dwell there; and in the end that man's condition becomes worse than it was at first. So will it be also with the present wicked generation." 012:046 While He was still addressing the people His mother and His brothers were standing on the edge of the crowd desiring to speak to Him. 012:047 So some one told Him, "Your mother and your brothers are standing outside, and desire to speak to you." 012:048 "Who is my mother?" He said to the man; "and who are my brothers?" 012:049 And pointing to His disciples He added, "See here are my mother and my brothers. 012:050 To obey my

Father who is in Heaven-that is to be my brother and my sister and my mother." 013:001 That same day Jesus had left the house and was sitting on the shore of the Lake, 013:002 when a vast multitude of people crowded round Him. He therefore went on board a boat and sat there, while all the people stood on the shore. 013:003 He then spoke many things to them in figurative language. "The sower goes out," He said, "to sow. 013:004 As he sows, some of the seed falls by the way-side, and the birds come and peck it up. 013:005 Some falls on rocky ground, where it has but scanty soil. It quickly shows itself above ground, because it has no depth of earth; 013:006 but when the sun is risen, it is scorched by the heat, and through having no root it withers up. 013:007 Some falls among the thorns; but the thorns spring up and stifle it. 013:008 But a portion falls upon good ground, and gives a return, some a hundred for one, some sixty, some thirty. 013:009 Listen, every one who has ears!" 013:010 (And His disciples came and asked Him, "Why do you speak to them in figurative language?" 013:011 "Because," He replied, "while to you it is granted to know the secrets of the Kingdom of the Heavens, to them it is not. 013:012 For whoever has, to him more shall be given, and he shall have abundance; but whoever has not, from him even what he has shall be taken away. 013:013 I speak to them in figurative language for this reason, that while looking they do not see, and while hearing they neither hear nor understand. 013:014 And in regard to them the prophecy of Isaiah is receiving signal fulfilment: "`You will hear and hear and by no means understand, and you will look and look and by no means see. 013:015 For this people's mind is stupefied, their hearing has become dull, and their eyes they have closed; to prevent their ever seeing with their eyes, or hearing with their ears, or understanding with their minds, and turning back, so that I might heal them.' 013:016 "But as for you, blessed are your eyes, for they see, and your ears, for they hear. 013:017 For I solemnly tell you that many Prophets and holy men have longed to see the sights you see, and have not seen them, and to hear the words you hear, and have not heard them. 013:018 "To you then I will explain the parable of the Sower. 013:019 When a man hears the Message concerning the Kingdom and does not understand it, the Evil one comes and catches away what has been sown in his heart. This is he who has received the seed by the road-side. 013:020 He who has received the seed on the rocky ground is the man who hears the Message and immediately receives it with joy. 013:021 It has struck no root, however, within him. He

continues for a time, but when suffering comes, or persecution, because of
the Message, he at once stumbles and falls. 013:022 He who has received
the seed among the thorns is the man who hears the Message, but the cares
of the present age and the delusions of riches quite stifle the Message, and it
becomes unfruitful. 013:023 But he who has received the seed on good
ground is he who hears and understands. Such hearers give a return, and
yield one a hundred for one, another sixty, another thirty.") 013:024
Another parable He put before them. "The Kingdom of the Heavens," He
said, "may be compared to a man who has sown good seed in his field,
013:025 but during the night his enemy comes, and over the first seed he
sows darnel among the wheat, and goes away. 013:026 But when the blade
shoots up and the grain is formed, then appears the darnel also. 013:027
"So the farmer's men come and ask him, "`Sir, was it not good seed that
you sowed on your land? Where then does the darnel come from?' 013:028
"`Some enemy has done this,' he said. "`Shall we go, and collect it?' the men
inquire. 013:029 "`No,' he replied, `for fear that while collecting the darnel
you should at the same time root up the wheat with it. 013:030 Leave both
to grow together until the harvest, and at harvest-time I will direct the
reapers, Collect the darnel first, and make it up into bundles to burn it, but
bring all the wheat into my barn.'" 013:031 Another parable He put before
them. "The Kingdom of the Heavens," He said, "is like a mustard-seed,
which a man takes and sows in his ground. 013:032 It is the smallest of all
seeds, and yet when full-grown it is larger than any herb and forms a tree,
so that the birds come and build in its branches." 013:033 Another parable
He spoke to them. "The Kingdom of the Heavens," He said, "is like yeast
which a woman takes and buries in a bushel of flour, for it to work there till
the whole mass has risen." 013:034 All this Jesus spoke to the people in
figurative language, and except in figurative language He spoke nothing to
them, 013:035 in fulfilment of the saying of the Prophet, "I will open my
mouth in figurative language, I will utter things kept hidden since the
creation of all things." 013:036 When He had dismissed the people and had
returned to the house, His disciples came to Him with the request, "Explain
to us the parable of the darnel sown in the field." 013:037 "The sower of
the good seed," He replied, "is the Son of Man; 013:038 the field is the
world; the good seed-these are the sons of the Kingdom; the darnel, the
sons of the Evil one. 013:039 The enemy who sows the darnel is *the
Devil*; the harvest is the Close of the Age; the reapers are the angels.

013:040 As then the darnel is collected together and burnt up with fire, so will it be at the Close of the Age. 013:041 The Son of Man will commission His angels, and they will gather out of His Kingdom all causes of sin and all who violate His laws; 013:042 and these they will throw into the fiery furnace. There will be the weeping aloud and the gnashing of teeth. 013:043 Then will the righteous shine out like the sun in their Father's Kingdom. Listen, every one who has ears! 013:044 "The Kingdom of the Heavens is like treasure buried in the open country, which a man finds, but buries again, and, in his joy about it, goes and sells all he has and buys that piece of ground. 013:045 "Again the Kingdom of the Heavens is like a jewel merchant who is in quest of choice pearls. 013:046 He finds one most costly pearl; he goes away; and though it costs all he has, he buys it. 013:047 "Again the Kingdom of the Heavens is like a draw-net let down into the sea, which encloses fish of all sorts. 013:048 When full, they haul it up on the beach, and sit down and collect the good fish in baskets, while the worthless they throw away. 013:049 So will it be at the Close of the Age. The angels will go forth and separate the wicked from among the righteous, 013:050 and will throw them into the fiery furnace. There will be the weeping aloud and the gnashing of teeth." 013:051 "Have you understood all this?" He asked. "Yes," they said. 013:052 "Therefore," He said, "remember that every Scribe well trained for the Kingdom of the Heavens is like a householder who brings out of his storehouse new things and old." 013:053 Jesus concluded this series of parables and then departed. 013:054 And He came into His own country and proceeded to teach in their synagogue, so that they were filled with astonishment and exclaimed, "Where did he obtain such wisdom, and these wondrous powers? 013:055 Is not this the carpenter's son? Is not his mother called Mary? And are not his brothers, James, Joseph, Simon and Judah? 013:056 And his sisters-are they not all living here among us? Where then did he get all this?" 013:057 So they turned angrily away from Him. But Jesus said to them, "There is no prophet left without honour except in his own country and among his own family." 013:058 And He performed but few mighty deeds there because of their want of faith. 014:001 About that time Herod the Tetrarch heard of the fame of Jesus, 014:002 and he said to his courtiers, "This is John the Baptist: he has come back to life-and that is why these miraculous Powers are working in him." 014:003 For Herod had arrested John, and had put him in chains, and imprisoned him, for the sake of Herodias his brother

Philip's wife, 014:004 because John had persistently said to him, "It is not lawful for you to have her." 014:005 And he would have liked to put him to death, but was afraid of the people, because they regarded John as a Prophet. 014:006 But when Herod's birthday came, the daughter of Herodias danced before all the company, and so pleased Herod 014:007 that with an oath he promised to give her whatever she asked. 014:008 So she, instigated by her mother, said, "Give me here on a dish the head of John the Baptist." 014:009 The king was deeply vexed, yet because of his repeated oath and of the guests at his table he ordered it to be given her, 014:010 and he sent and beheaded John in the prison. 014:011 The head was brought on a dish and given to the young girl, and she took it to her mother. 014:012 Then John's disciples went and removed the body and buried it, and came and informed Jesus. 014:013 Upon receiving these tidings, Jesus went away by boat to an uninhabited and secluded district; but the people heard of it and followed Him in crowds from the towns by land. 014:014 So Jesus went out and saw an immense multitude, and felt compassion for them, and cured those of them who were out of health. 014:015 But when evening was come, the disciples came to Him and said, "This is an uninhabited place, and the best of the day is now gone; send the people away to go into the villages and buy something to eat." 014:016 "They need not go away," replied Jesus; "you yourselves must give them something to eat." 014:017 "We have nothing here," they said, "but five loaves and a couple of fish." 014:018 "Bring them here to me," He said, 014:019 and He told all the people to sit down on the grass. Then He took the five loaves and the two fish, and after looking up to heaven and blessing them, He broke up the loaves and gave them to the disciples, and the disciples distributed them to the people. 014:020 So all ate, and were fully satisfied. The broken portions that remained over they gathered up, filling twelve baskets. 014:021 Those who had eaten were about 5,000 adult men, without reckoning women and children. 014:022 Immediately afterwards He made the disciples go on board the boat and cross to the opposite shore, leaving Him to dismiss the people. 014:023 When He had done this, He climbed the hill to pray in solitude. Night came on, and he was there alone. 014:024 Meanwhile the boat was far out on the Lake, buffeted and tossed by the waves, the wind being adverse. 014:025 But towards daybreak He went to them, walking over the waves. 014:026 When the disciples saw Him walking on the waves, they were greatly alarmed. "It is a spirit," they exclaimed, and they cried out with terror. 014:027 But instantly Jesus spoke to them, and said, "There is no danger; it is I; do not be afraid." 014:028 "Master," answered Peter, "if it is you, bid me come to you upon the water." 014:029 "Come," said Jesus. Then Peter climbed down from the boat and walked upon the water to go to Him. 014:030 But when he felt the wind he grew frightened, and beginning to sink he cried out, "Master, save me." 014:031 Instantly Jesus stretched out His hand and caught hold of him, saying to him, "O little faith, why did you doubt?" 014:032 So they climbed into the boat, and the wind lulled; 014:033 and the men on board fell down before him and said, "You are indeed God's Son." 014:034 When they had quite crossed over, they put ashore at Gennesaret; 014:035 and the men of the place, recognizing Him, sent word into all the country round. So they brought all the sick to Him, 014:036 and they entreated Him that they might but touch the tassel of His outer garment; and all who did so were restored to perfect health. 015:001 Then there came to Jesus a party of Pharisees and Scribes from Jerusalem, who inquired, 015:002 "Why do your disciples transgress the tradition of the Elders by not washing their hands before meals?" 015:003 "Why do you, too," He retorted, "transgress God's commands for the sake of your tradition? 015:004 For God said, `Honour thy father and thy mother'; and `Let him who reviles father or mother be certainly put to death'; 015:005 but you-this is what you say: `If a man says to his father or mother, That is consecrated, whatever it is, which otherwise you should have received from me- 015:006 he shall be absolved from honouring his father'; and so you have abrogated God's Word for the sake of your tradition. 015:007 Hypocrites! well did Isaiah prophesy of you, 015:008 "`This is a People who honour Me with their lips, while their heart is far away from Me; 015:009 but it is in vain they worship Me, while they lay down precepts which are mere human rules.'" 015:010 Then, when He had called the people to Him, Jesus said, "Hear and understand. 015:011 It is not what goes into a man's mouth that defiles him; but it is what comes out of his mouth-that* defiles a man." 015:012 Then His disciples came and said to Him, "Do you know that the Pharisees were greatly shocked when they heard those words?" 015:013 "Every plant," He replied, "which my Heavenly Father has not planted will be rooted up. 015:014 Leave them alone. They are blind guides of the blind; and if a blind man leads a blind man, both will fall into some pit." 015:015 "Explain to us this figurative language," said Peter. 015:016 "Are even you," He answered, "still without intellingence? 015:017 Do you not understand that whatever enters the mouth passes into the stomach and is afterwards ejected from the body? 015:018 But the things that come out of the mouth proceed from the heart, and it is these that defile the man. 015:019 For out of the heart proceed wicked thoughts, murder, adultery, fornication, theft, perjury, impiety of speech. 015:020 These are the things which defile the man; but eating with unwashed hands does not defile." 015:021 Leaving that place, Jesus withdrew into the vicinity of Tyre and Sidon. 015:022 Here a Canaanitish woman of the district came out and persistently cried out, "Sir, Son of David, pity me; my daughter is cruelly harassed by a demon." 015:023 But He answered her not a word. Then the disciples interposed, and begged Him, saying, "Send her away because she keeps crying behind us." 015:024 "I have only been sent to the lost sheep of the house of Israel," He replied. 015:025 Then she came and threw herself at His feet and entreated Him. "O Sir, help me," she said. 015:026 "It is not right," He said, "to take the children's bread and throw it to the dogs." 015:027 "Be it so, Sir," she said, "for even the dogs eat the scraps which fall from their masters' tables." 015:028 "O woman," replied Jesus, "great is your faith: be it done to you as you desire." And from that moment her daughter was restored to health. 015:029 Again, moving thence, Jesus went along by the Lake of Galilee; and ascending the hill, He sat down there. 015:030 Soon great crowds came to Him, bringing with them those who were crippled in feet or hands, blind or dumb, and many besides, and they hastened to lay them at His feet. And He cured them, 015:031 so that the people were amazed to see the dumb speaking, the maimed with their hands perfect, the lame walking, and the blind seeing; and they gave the glory to the God of Israel. 015:032 But Jesus called His disciples to Him and said, "My heart yearns over this mass of people, for it is now the third day that they have been with me and they have nothing to eat. I am unwilling to send them away hungry, lest they should faint on the road." 015:033 "Where can we," asked the disciples, "get bread enough in this remote place to satisfy so vast a multitude?" 015:034 "How many loaves have you?" Jesus asked. "Seven," they said, "and a few small fish." 015:035 So He bade all the people sit down on the ground, 015:036 and He took the seven loaves and the fish, and after giving thanks He broke them up and then distributed them to the disciples, and they to the people. 015:037 And they all ate and were satisfied. The broken portions that remained over they took up-seven full hampers. 015:038

Those who ate were 4,000 adult men, without reckoning women and children. 015:039 He then dismissed the people, went on board the boat, and came into the district of Magadan. 016:001 Here the Pharisees and Sadducees came to Him; and, to make trial of Him, they asked Him to show them a sign in the sky. 016:002 He replied, "In the evening you say, `It will be fine weather, for the sky is red;' 016:003 and in the morning, `It will be rough weather to-day, for the sky is red and murky.' You learn how to distinguish the aspect of the heavens, but the signs of the times you cannot. 016:004 A wicked and faithless generation are eager for a sign; but none shall be given to them except the sign of Jonah." and He left them and went away. 016:005 When the disciples arrived at the other side of the Lake, they found that they had forgotten to bring any bread; 016:006 and when Jesus said to them, "See to it: beware of the yeast of the Pharisees and Sadducees," 016:007 they reasoned among themselves, saying, "It is because we have not brought any bread." 016:008 Jesus perceived this and said, "Why are you reasoning among yourselves, you men of little faith, because you have no bread? 016:009 Do you not yet understand? nor even remember the 5,000 and the five loaves, and how many basketfuls you carried away, 016:010 nor the 4,000 and the seven loaves, and how many hampers you carried away? 016:011 How is it you do not understand that it was not about bread that I spoke to you? But beware of the yeast of the Pharisees and Sadducees." 016:012 Then they perceived that He had not warned them against bread-yeast, but against the teaching of the Pharisees and Sadducees. 016:013 When He arrived in the neighbourhood of Caesarea Philippi, Jesus questioned His disciples. "Who do people say that the Son of Man is?" He asked. 016:014 "Some say John the Baptist," they replied; "others Elijah; others Jeremiah or one of the Prophets." 016:015 "But you, who do you say that I am?" He asked again. 016:016 "You," replied Simon Peter, "are the Christ, the Son of the ever-living God." 016:017 "Blessed are you, Simon Bar-jonah," said Jesus; "for mere human nature has not revealed this to you, but my Father in Heaven. 016:018 And I declare to you that you are Peter, and that upon this Rock I will build my Church, and the might of Hades shall not triumph over it. 016:019 I will give you the keys of the Kingdom of the Heavens; and whatever you bind on earth shall remain bound in Heaven, and whatever you loose on earth shall remain loosed in Heaven." 016:020 Then He urged His disciples to tell no one that He was the Christ. 016:021 From this time Jesus began to explain to His disciples that He must go to Jerusalem, and suffer much cruelty from the Elders and the High Priests and the Scribes, and be put to death, and on the third day be raised to life again. 016:022 Then Peter took Him aside and began taking Him to task. "Master," he said, "God forbid; this will not be your lot." 016:023 But He turned and said to Peter, "Get behind me, Adversary; you are a hindrance to me, because your thoughts are not God's thoughts, but men's." 016:024 Then Jesus said to His disciples, "If any one desires to follow me, let him renounce self and take up his cross, and so be my follower. 016:025 For whoever desires to save his life shall lose it, and whoever loses his life for my sake shall find it. 016:026 Why, what benefit will it be to a man if he gains the whole world but forfeits his life? Or what shall a man give to buy back his life? 016:027 For the Son of Man is soon to come in the glory of the Father with His angels, and then will He requite every man according to his actions. 016:028 I solemnly tell you that some of those who are standing here will certainly not taste death till they have seen the Son of Man coming in His Kingdom." 017:001 Six day later, Jesus took with Him Peter and the brothers James and John, and brought them up a high mountain to a solitary place. 017:002 There in their presence His form underwent a change; His face shone like the sun, and His raiment became as white as the light. 017:003 And suddenly Moses and Elijah appeared to them conversing with Him. 017:004 Then Peter said to Jesus, "Master, we are thankful to you that we are here. If you approve, I will put up three tents here, one for you, one for Moses, and one for Elijah." 017:005 He was still speaking when a luminous cloud spread over them; and a voice was heard from within the cloud, which said, "This is My Son dearly beloved, in whom is My delight. Listen to Him." 017:006 On hearing this voice, the disciples fell on their faces and were filled with terror. 017:007 But Jesus came and touched them, and said, "Rouse yourselves and have no fear." 017:008 So they looked up, and saw no one but Jesus. 017:009 As they were descending the mountain, Jesus laid a command upon them. "Tell no one," He said, "of the sight you have seen till the Son of Man has risen from among the dead." 017:010 "Why then," asked the disciples, "do the Scribes say that Elijah must first come?" 017:011 "Elijah was indeed to come," He replied, "and would reform everything. 017:012 But I tell you that he has already come, and they did not recognize him, but dealt with him as they chose. And before long the Son of Man will be treated by them in a similar way." 017:013 Then it

dawned upon the disciples that it was John the Baptist about whom He had
spoken to them. 017:014 When they had returned to the people, there came
to Him a man who fell on his knees before Him and besought Him.
017:015 "Sir," he said, "have pity on my son, for he is an epileptic and is
very ill. Often he falls into the fire and often into the water. 017:016 I have
brought him to your disciples, and they have not been able to cure him."
017:017 "O unbelieving and perverse generation!" replied Jesus; "how long
shall I be with you? how long shall I endure you? Bring him to me."
017:018 Then Jesus reprimanded the demon, and it came out and left him;
and the boy was cured from that moment. 017:019 Then the disciples came
to Jesus privately and asked Him, "Why could not we expel the demon?"
017:020 "Because your faith is so small," He replied; "for I solemnly declare
to you that if you have faith like a mustard-seed, you shall say to this
mountain, `Remove from this place to that,' and it will remove; and nothing
shall be impossible to you. 017:021 But an evil spirit of this kind is only
driven out by prayer and fasting." 017:022 As they were travelling about in
Galilee, Jesus said to them, "The Son of Man is about to be betrayed into
the hands of men; 017:023 they will put Him to death, but on the third day
He will be raised to life again." And they were exceedingly distressed.
017:024 After their arrival at Capernaum the collectors of the half-shekel
came and asked Peter, "Does not your Teacher pay the half-shekel?"
017:025 "Yes," he replied, and then went into the house. But before he
spoke a word Jesus said, "What think you, Simon? From whom do this
world's kings receive customs or capitation tax? from their own children, or
from others?" 017:026 "From others," he replied. "Then the children go
free," said Jesus. 017:027 "However, lest we cause them to sin, go and
throw a hook into the Lake, and take the first fish that comes up. When you
open its mouth, you will find a shekel in it: bring that coin and give it to
them for yourself and me." 018:001 Just then the disciples came to Jesus
and asked, "Who ranks higher than others in the Kingdom of the
Heavens?" 018:002 So He called a young child to Him, and, bidding him
stand in the midst of them, 018:003 said, "In solemn truth I tell you that
unless you turn and become like little children, you will in no case be
admitted into the Kingdom of the Heavens. 018:004 Whoever therefore
shall humble himself as this young child, he it is who is superior to others in
the Kingdom of the Heavens. 018:005 And whoever for my sake receives
one young child such as this, receives me. 018:006 But whoever shall

occasion the fall of one of these little ones who believe in me, it would be better for him to have a millstone hung round his neck and to be drowned in the depths of the sea. 018:007 "Alas for the world because of causes of falling! They cannot but come, but alas for each man through whom they come! 018:008 If your hand or your foot is causing you to fall into sin, cut it off and away with it. It is better for you to enter into Life crippled in hand or foot than to remain in possession of two sound hands or feet but be thrown into the fire of the Ages. 018:009 And if your eye is causing you to fall into sin, tear it out and away with it; it is better for you to enter into Life with only one eye, than to remain in possession of two eyes but be thrown into the Gehenna of fire. 018:010 "Beware of ever despising one of these little ones, for I tell you that in Heaven their angels have continual access to my Father who is in Heaven. 018:011 [] 018:012 What do you yourselves think? Suppose a man gets a hundred sheep and one of them strays away, will he not leave the ninety-nine on the hills and go and look for the one that is straying? 018:013 And if he succeeds in finding it, in solemn truth I tell you that he rejoices over it more than he does over the ninety-nine that have not gone astray. 018:014 Just so it is not the will of your Father in Heaven that one of these little ones should be lost. 018:015 "If your brother acts wrongly towards you, go and point out his fault to him when only you and he are there. If he listens to you, you have gained your brother. 018:016 But if he will not listen to you, go again, and ask one or two to go with you, that every word spoken may be attested by two or three witnesses. 018:017 If he refuses to hear them, appeal to the Church; and if he refuses to hear even the Church, regard him just as you regard a Gentile or a tax-gatherer. 018:018 I solemnly tell you that whatever you as a Church bind on earth will in Heaven be held as bound, and whatever you loose on earth will in Heaven be held to be loosed. 018:019 I also solemnly tell you that if two of you here on earth agree together concerning anything whatever that they shall ask, the boon will come to them from my Father who is in Heaven. 018:020 For where there are two or three assembled in my name, there am I in the midst of them." 018:021 At this point Peter came to Him with the question, "Master, how often shall my brother act wrongly towards me and I forgive him? seven times?" 018:022 "I do not say seven times," answered Jesus, "but seventy times seven times. 018:023 "For this reason the Kingdom of the Heavens may be compared to a king who determined to have a settlement of accounts with his servants. 018:024 But as soon as he began the settlement, one was brought before him who owed 10,000 talents, 018:025 and was unable to pay. So his master ordered that he and his wife and children and everything that he had should be sold, and payment be made. 018:026 The servant therefore falling down, prostrated himself at his feet and entreated him. "`Only give me time,' he said, `and I will pay you the whole.' 018:027 "Whereupon his master, touched with compassion, set him free and forgave him the debt. 018:028 But no sooner had that servant gone out, than he met with one of his fellow servants who owed him 100 shillings; and seizing him by the throat and nearly strangling him he exclaimed, "`Pay me all you owe.' 018:029 "His fellow servant therefore fell at his feet and entreated him, "`Only give me time,' he said, `and I will pay you.' 018:030 "He would not, however, but went and threw him into prison until he should pay what was due. 018:031 His fellow servants, therefore, seeing what had happened, were exceedingly angry; and they came and told their master without reserve all that had happened. 018:032 At once his master called him and said, "`Wicked servant, I forgave you all that debt, because you entreated me: 018:033 ought not you also to have had pity on your fellow servant, just as I had pity on you?' 018:034 "So his master, greatly incensed, handed him over to the jailers until he should pay all he owed him. 018:035 "In the same way my Heavenly Father will deal with you, if you do not all of you forgive one another from your hearts." 019:001 When Jesus had finished these discourses, He removed from Galilee and came into that part of Judaea which lay beyond the Jordan. 019:002 And a vast multitude followed him, and He cured them there. 019:003 Then came some of the Pharisees to Him to put Him to the proof by the question, "Has a man a right to divorce his wife whenever he chooses?" 019:004 "Have you not read," He replied, "that He who made them `made them' from the beginning `male and female, 019:005 and said, For this reason a man shall leave his father and mother and be united to his wife, and the two shall be one'? 019:006 Thus they are no longer two, but `one'! What therefore God has joined together, let not man separate." 019:007 "Why then," said they, "did Moses command the husband to give her `a written notice of divorce,' and so put her away?" 019:008 "Moses," He replied, "in consideration of the hardness of your nature permitted you to put away your wives, but it has not been so from the beginning. 019:009 And I tell you that whoever divorces his wife for any reason except her unfaithfulness, and marries another woman, commits adultery." 019:010 "If

this is the case with a man in relation to his wife," said the disciples to Him,
"it is better not to marry." 019:011 "It is not every man," He replied, "who
can receive this teaching, but only those on whom the grace has been
bestowed. 019:012 There are men who from their birth have been disabled
from marriage, others who have been so disabled by men, and others who
have disabled themselves for the sake of the Kingdom of the Heavens. He
who is able to receive this, let him receive it." 019:013 Then young children
were brought to Him for Him to put His hands on them and pray; but the
disciples interfered. 019:014 Jesus however said, "Let the little children
come to me, and do not hinder them; for it is to those who are childlike
that the Kingdom of the Heavens belongs." 019:015 So He laid His hands
upon them and went away. 019:016 "Teacher," said one man, coming up to
Him, "what that is good shall I do in order to win the Life of the Ages?"
019:017 "Why do you ask me," He replied, "about what is good? There is
only One who is truly good. But if you desire to enter into Life, keep the
Commandments." 019:018 "Which Commandments?" he asked. Jesus
answered, "`Thou shalt not kill;' `Thou shalt not commit adultery;' `Thou
shalt not steal;' `Thou shalt not lie in giving evidence;' 019:019 `Honour thy
father and thy mother'; and `Thou shalt love thy fellow man as much as
thyself.'" 019:020 "All of these," said the young man, "I have carefully kept.
What do I still lack?" 019:021 "If you desire to be perfect," replied Jesus,
"go and sell all that you have, and give to the poor, and you shall have
wealth in Heaven; and come, follow me." 019:022 On hearing those words
the young man went away much cast down; for he had much property.
019:023 So Jesus said to His disciples, "I solemnly tell you that it is with
difficulty that a rich man will enter the Kingdom of the Heavens. 019:024
Yes, I tell you, it is easier for a camel to go through the eye of a needle than
for a rich man to enter the Kingdom of God." 019:025 These words utterly
amazed the disciples, and they asked, "Who then can be saved?" 019:026
Jesus looked at them and said, "With men this is impossible, but with God
everything is possible." 019:027 Then Peter said to Jesus, "See, *we* have
forsaken everything and followed you; what then will be *our* reward?"
019:028 "I solemnly tell you," replied Jesus, "that in the New Creation,
when the Son of Man has taken His seat on His glorious throne, all of you
who have followed me shall also sit on twelve thrones and judge the twelve
tribes of Israel. 019:029 And whoever has forsaken houses, or brothers or
sisters, or father or mother, or children or lands, for my sake, shall receive

many times as much and shall have as his inheritance the Life of the Ages. 019:030 "But many who are now first will be last, and many who are now last will be first. 020:001 "For the Kingdom of the Heavens is like an employer who went out early in the morning to hire men to work in his vineyard, 020:002 and having made an agreement with them for a shilling a day, sent them into his vineyard. 020:003 About nine o'clock he went out and saw others loitering in the market-place. 020:004 To these also he said, "`You also, go into the vineyard, and whatever is right I will give you.' 020:005 "So they went. Again about twelve, and about three o'clock, he went out and did the same. 020:006 And going out about five o'clock he found others loitering, and he asked them, "`Why have you been standing here all day long, doing nothing?' 020:007 "`Because no one has hired us,' they replied. "`You also, go into the vineyard,' he said. 020:008 "When evening came, the master said to his steward, "`Call the men and pay them their wages. Begin with the last set and finish with the first.' 020:009 "When those came who had begun at five o'clock, they received a shilling apiece; 020:010 and when the first came, they expected to get more, but they also each got the shilling. 020:011 So when they had received it, they grumbled against the employer, saying, 020:012 "`These who came last have done only one hour's work, and you have put them on a level with us who have worked the whole day and have borne the scorching heat.' 020:013 "`My friend,' he answered to one of them, `I am doing you no injustice. Did you not agree with me for a shilling? 020:014 Take your money and go. I choose to give this last comer just as much as I give you. 020:015 Have I not a right to do what I choose with my own property? Or are you envious because I am generous?' 020:016 "So the last shall be first, and the first last." 020:017 Jesus was now going up to Jerusalem, and He took the twelve disciples aside by themselves, and on the way He said to them, 020:018 "We are going up to Jerusalem, and there the Son of Man will be betrayed to the High Priests and Scribes. They will condemn Him to death, 020:019 and hand Him over to the Gentiles to be made sport of and scourged and crucified; and on the third day He will be raised to life." 020:020 Then the mother of the sons of Zabdi came to Him with her sons, and knelt before Him to make a request of Him. 020:021 "What is it you desire?" He asked. "Command," she replied, "that these my two sons may sit one at your right hand and one at your left in your Kingdom." 020:022 "None of you know what you are asking for," said Jesus; "can you drink out of the cup from which I am about to drink?" "We can," they replied. 020:023 "You shall drink out of my cup," He said, "but a seat at my right hand or at my left it is not for me to allot, but it belongs to those for whom it has been prepared by my Father." 020:024 The other ten heard of this, and their indignation was aroused against the two brothers. 020:025 But Jesus called them to Him, and said, "You know that the rulers of the Gentiles lord it over them, and their great men exercise authority over them. 020:026 Not so shall it be among you; but whoever desires to be great among you shall be your servant, 020:027 and whoever desires to be first among you shall be your bondservant; 020:028 just as the Son of Man came not to be served but to serve, and to give His life as the redemption-price for many." 020:029 As they were leaving Jericho, an immense crowd following Him, 020:030 two blind men sitting by the roadside heard that it was Jesus who was passing by, and cried aloud, "Sir, Son of David, pity us." 020:031 The people angrily tried to silence them, but they cried all the louder. "O Sir, Son of David, pity us," they said. 020:032 So Jesus stood still and called to them. "What shall I do for you?" He asked. 020:033 "Sir, let our eyes be opened," they replied. 020:034 Moved with compassion, Jesus touched their eyes, and immediately they regained their sight and followed Him. 021:001 When they were come near Jerusalem and had arrived at Bethphage and the Mount of Olives, Jesus sent two of the disciples on in front, 021:002 saying to them, "Go to the village you see facing you, and as you enter it you will find a she-ass tied up and a foal with her. Untie her and bring them to me. 021:003 And if any one says anything to you, say, `The Master needs them,' and he will at once send them." 021:004 This took place in order that the Prophet's prediction might be fulfilled: 021:005 "Tell the Daughter of Zion, `See, thy King is coming to thee, gentle, and yet mounted on an ass, even on a colt the foal of a beast of burden.'" 021:006 So the disciples went and did as Jesus had instructed them: 021:007 they brought the she-ass and the foal, and threw their outer garments on them. So He sat on them; 021:008 and most of the crowd kept spreading their garments along the road, while others cut branches from the trees and carpeted the road with them, 021:009 and the multitudes-some of the people preceding Him and some following-sang aloud, "God save the Son of David! Blessings on Him who comes in the Lord's name! God in the highest Heavens save Him!" 021:010 When He thus entered Jerusalem, the whole city was thrown into commotion, every one inquiring, "Who is this?" 021:011 "This is Jesus, the

Prophet, from Nazareth in Galilee," replied the crowds. 021:012 Entering the Temple, Jesus drove out all who were buying and selling there, and overturned the money-changers' tables and the seats of the pigeon-dealers. 021:013 "It is written," He said, "`My House shall be called the House of Prayer', but you are making it a robbers' cave." 021:014 And the blind and the lame came to Him in the Temple, and He cured them. 021:015 But when the High Priests and the Scribes saw the wonderful things that He had done and the children who were crying aloud in the Temple, "God save the Son of David," they were filled with indignation. 021:016 "Do you hear," they asked Him, "what these children are saying?" "Yes," He replied; "have you never read, `Out of the mouths of infants and of babes at the breast Thou hast brought forth the praise which is due'?" 021:017 So He left them and went out of the city to Bethany and passed the night there. 021:018 Early in the morning as He was on His way to return to the city He was hungry, 021:019 and seeing a fig-tree on the road-side He went up to it, but found nothing on it but leaves. "On you," He said, "no fruit shall ever again grow." And immediately the fig-tree withered away. 021:020 When the disciples saw it they exclaimed in astonishment, "How instantaneously the fig-tree has withered away!" 021:021 "I solemnly tell you," said Jesus, "that if you have an unwavering faith, you shall not only perform such a miracle as this of the fig-tree, but that even if you say to this mountain, `Be thou lifted up and hurled into the sea,' it shall be done; 021:022 and everything, whatever it be, that you ask for in your prayers, if you have faith, you shall obtain." 021:023 He entered the Temple; and while He was teaching, the High Priests and the Elders of the people came to Him and asked Him, "By what authority are you doing these things? and who gave you this authority?" 021:024 "And I also have a question to ask *you*," replied Jesus, "and if you answer me, I in turn will tell you by what authority I do these things. 021:025 John's Baptism, whence was it?-had it a heavenly or a human origin?" So they debated the matter among themselves. "If we say `a heavenly origin,'" they argued, "he will say, `Why then did you not believe him?' 021:026 and if we say `a human origin' we have the people to fear, for they all hold John to have been a Prophet." 021:027 So they answered Jesus, "We do not know." "Nor do I tell you," He replied, "by what authority I do these things." 021:028 "But give me your judgement. There was a man who had two sons. He came to the elder of them, and said, "`My son, go and work in the vineyard to-day.' 021:029 "`I will not,' he replied. "But afterwards he was sorry, and went. 021:030 He came to the second and spoke in the same manner. His answer was, "`I will go, Sir.' "But he did not go. 021:031 Which of the two did as his father desired?" "The first," they said. "I solemnly tell you,' replied Jesus, "that the tax-gatherers and the notorious sinners are entering the Kingdom of God in front of you. 021:032 For John came to you observing all sorts of ritual, and you put no faith in him: the tax-gatherers and the notorious sinners did put faith in him, and you, though you saw this example set you, were not even afterwards sorry so as to believe him. 021:033 "Listen to another parable. There was a householder who planted a vineyard, made a fence round it, dug a wine-tank in it, and built a strong lodge; then let the place to vine-dressers, and went abroad. 021:034 When vintage-time approached, he sent his servants to the vine-dressers to receive his share of the grapes; 021:035 but the vine-dressers seized the servants, and one they cruelly beat, one they killed, one they pelted with stones. 021:036 Again he sent another party of servants more numerous than the first; and these they treated in the same manner. 021:037 Later still he sent to them his son, saying, "`They will respect my son.' 021:038 "But the vine-dressers, when they saw the son, said to one another, "`Here is the heir: come, let us kill him and get his inheritance.' 021:039 "So they seized him, dragged him out of the vineyard, and killed him. 021:040 When then the owner of the vineyard comes, what will he do to those vine-dressers?" 021:041 "He will put the wretches to a wretched death," was the reply, "and will entrust the vineyard to other vine-dressers who will render the produce to him at the vintage season." 021:042 "Have you never read in the Scriptures," said Jesus, "`The Stone which the builders rejected has been made the Cornerstone: this Cornerstone came from the Lord, and is wonderful in our eyes'? 021:043 "That, I tell you, is the reason why the Kingdom of God will be taken away from you, and given to a nation that will exhibit the power of it. 021:044 He who falls on this stone will be severely hurt; but he on whom it falls will be utterly crushed." 021:045 After listening to His parables the High Priests and the Pharisees perceived that He was speaking about them; 021:046 but though they were eager to lay hands upon Him, they were afraid of the people, for by them He was regarded as a Prophet. 022:001 Again Jesus spoke to them in figurative language. 022:002 "The Kingdom of the Heavens," He said, "may be compared to a king who celebrated the marriage of his son, 022:003 and sent his servants to call the invited guests to the wedding, but they were unwilling to come. 022:004 "Again he sent other servants with a message to those who were invited. "`My breakfast is now ready," he said, `my bullocks and fat cattle are killed, and every preparation is made: come to the wedding.' 022:005 "They however gave no heed, but went, one to his home in the country, another to his business; 022:006 and the rest seized the king's servants, maltreated them, and murdered them. 022:007 So the king's anger was stirred, and he sent his troops and destroyed those murderers and burnt their city. 022:008 Then he said to his servants, "`The wedding banquet is ready, but those who were invited were unworthy of it. 022:009 Go out therefore to the crossroads, and everybody you meet invite to the wedding.' 022:010 "So they went out into the roads and gathered together all they could find, both bad and good, and the banqueting hall was filled with guests. 022:011 "Now the king came in to see the guests; and among them he discovered one who was not wearing a wedding-robe. 022:012 "`My friend,' he said, `how is it that you came in here without a wedding robe?' 022:013 "The man stood speechless. Then the king said to the servants, "`Bind him hand and foot and fling him into the darkness outside: there will be the weeping aloud and the gnashing of teeth.' 022:014 "For there are many called, but few chosen." 022:015 Then the Pharisees went and consulted together how they might entrap Him in His conversation. 022:016 So they sent to Him their disciples together with the Herodians; who said, "Teacher, we know that you are truthful and that you faithfully teach God's truth; and that no fear of man misleads you, for you are not biased by men's wealth or rank. 022:017 Give us your judgement therefore: is it allowable for us to pay a poll-tax to Caesar, or not?" 022:018 Perceiving their wickedness, Jesus replied, "Why are you hypocrites trying to ensnare me? 022:019 Show me the tribute coin." And they brought Him a shilling. 022:020 "Whose likeness and inscription," He asked, "is this?" 022:021 "Caesar's," they replied. "Pay therefore," He rejoined, "what is Caesar's to Caesar; and what is God's to God." 022:022 They heard this, and were astonished; then left Him, and went their way. 022:023 On the same day a party of Sadducees came to Him, contending that there is no resurrection. And they put this case to Him. 022:024 "Teacher," they said, "Moses enjoined, `If a man die childless, his brother shall marry his widow, and raise up a family for him.' 022:025 Now we had among us seven brothers. The eldest of them married, but died childless, leaving his wife to his brother. 022:026 So also did the second and the third, down to the seventh, 022:027 till the woman also died, after surviving them all. 022:028 At the Resurrection, therefore, whose wife of the seven will she be? for they all married her." 022:029 The reply of Jesus was, "You are in error, through ignorance of the Scriptures and of the power of God. 022:030 For in the Resurrection, men neither marry nor are women given in marriage, but they are like angels in Heaven. 022:031 But as to the Resurrection of the dead, have you never read what God says to you, 022:032 `I am the God of Abraham, the God of Isaac, and the God of Jacob'? He is not the God of dead, but of living men." 022:033 All the crowd heard this, and were filled with amazement at His teaching. 022:034 Now the Pharisees came up when they heard that He had silenced the Sadducees, 022:035 and one of them, an expounder of the Law, asked Him as a test question, 022:036 "Teacher, which is the greatest Commandment in the Law?" 022:037 "`Thou shalt love the Lord thy God,'" He answered, "`with thy whole heart, thy whole soul, thy whole mind.' 022:038 This is the greatest and foremost Commandment. 022:039 And the second is similar to it: `Thou shalt love thy fellow man as much as thyself.' 022:040 The whole of the Law and the Prophets is summed up in these two Commandments." 022:041 While the Pharisees were still assembled there, Jesus put a question to them. 022:042 "What think you about the Christ," He said, "whose son is He?" "David's," they replied. 022:043 "How then," He asked, "does David, taught by the Spirit, call Him Lord, when he says, 022:044 "`The Lord said to my Lord, sit at My right hand until I have put thy foes beneath thy feet'? 022:045 "If therefore David calls Him Lord, how can He be his son?" 022:046 No one could say a word in reply, nor from that day did any one venture again to put a question to Him. 023:001 Then Jesus addressed the crowds and His disciples. 023:002 "The Scribes," He said, "and the Pharisees sit in the chair of Moses. 023:003 Therefore do and observe everything that they command you; but do not imitate their lives, for though they tell others what to do, they do not do it themselves. 023:004 Heavy and cumbrous burdens they bind together and load men's shoulders with them, while as for themselves, not with one finger do they choose to lift them. 023:005 And everything they do they do with a view to being observed by men; for they widen their phylacteries and make the tassels large, 023:006 and love the best seats at a dinner party or in the synagogues, 023:007 and like to be bowed to in places of public resort, and to be addressed by men as `Rabbi.' 023:008 "As for you, do not accept the title of `Rabbi,' for one alone is your

Teacher, and you are all brothers. 023:009 And call no one on earth your Father, for One alone is your Father- the Heavenly Father. 023:010 And do not accept the name of `leader,' for your Leader is one alone-the Christ. 023:011 He who is the greatest among you shall be your servant; 023:012 and one who exalts himself shall be abased, while one who abases himself shall be exalted. 023:013 "But alas for you, Scribes and Pharisees, hypocrites, for you lock the door of the Kingdom of the Heavens against men; you yourselves do not enter, nor do you allow those to enter who are seeking to do so. 023:014 [] 023:015 "Alas for you, Scribes and Pharisees, hypocrites, for you scour sea and land in order to win one convert-and when he is gained, you make him twice as much a son of Gehenna as yourselves. 023:016 "Alas for you, you blind guides, who say, "`Whoever swears by the Sanctuary it is nothing; but whoever swears by the gold of the Sanctuary, is bound by the oath.' 023:017 "Blind fools! Why, which is greater?-the gold, or the Sanctuary which has made the gold holy? 023:018 And you say, "`Whoever swears by the altar, it is nothing; but whoever swears by the offering lying on it is bound by the oath.' 023:019 "You are blind! Why, which is greater?-the offering, or the altar which makes the offering holy? 023:020 He who swears by the altar swears both by it and by everything on it; 023:021 he who swears by the Sanctuary swears both by it and by Him who dwells in it; 023:022 and he who swears by Heaven swears both by the throne of God and by Him who sits upon it. 023:023 "Alas for you, Scribes and Pharisees, hypocrites, for you pay the tithe on mint, dill, and cumin, while you have neglected the weightier requirements of the Law-just judgement, mercy, and faithful dealing. These things you ought to have done, and yet you ought not to have left the others undone. 023:024 You blind guides, straining out the gnat while you gulp down the camel! 023:025 "Alas for you, Scribes and Pharisees, hypocrites, for you wash clean the outside of the cup or dish, while within they are full of greed and self-indulgence. 023:026 Blind Pharisee, first wash clean the inside of the cup or dish, and then the outside will be clean also. 023:027 "Alas for you, Scribes and Pharisees, hypocrites, for you are just like whitewashed sepulchres, the outside of which pleases the eye, though inside they are full of dead men's bones and of all that is unclean. 023:028 The same is true of you: outwardly you seem to the human eye to be good and honest men, but, within, you are full of insincerity and disregard of God's Law. 023:029 "Alas for you, Scribes and Pharisees, hypocrites, for you repair the sepulchres of the

Prophets and keep in order the tombs of the righteous, 023:030 and your boast is, "`If we had lived in the time of our forefathers, we should not have been implicated with them in the murder of the Prophets.' 023:031 "So that you bear witness against yourselves that you are descendants of those who murdered the Prophets. 023:032 Fill up the measure of your forefathers' guilt. 023:033 O serpents, O vipers' brood, how are you to escape condemnation to Gehenna? 023:034 "For this reason I am sending to you Prophets and wise men and Scribes. Some of them you will put to death-nay, crucify; some of them you will flog in your synagogues and chase from town to town; 023:035 that all the innocent blood shed upon earth may come on you, from the blood of righteous Abel to the blood of Zechariah the son of Berechiah whom you murdered between the Sanctuary and the altar. 023:036 I tell you in solemn truth that all these things will come upon the present generation. 023:037 "O Jerusalem, Jerusalem! thou who murderest the Prophets and stonest those who have been sent to thee! how often have I desired to gather thy children to me, just as a hen gathers her chickens under her wings, and you would not come! 023:038 See, your house will now be left to you desolate! 023:039 For I tell you that you will never see me again until you say, `Blessed be He who comes in the name of the Lord.'" 024:001 Jesus had left the Temple and was going on His way, when His disciples came and called His attention to the Temple buildings. 024:002 "You see all these?" He replied; "in solemn truth I tell you that there will not be left here one stone upon another that will not be pulled down." 024:003 Afterwards He was on the Mount of Olives and was seated there when the disciples came to Him, apart from the others, and said, "Tell us when this will be; and what will be the sign of your Coming and of the Close of the Age?" 024:004 "Take care that no one misleads you," answered Jesus; 024:005 "for many will come assuming my name and saying `I am the Christ;' and they will mislead many. 024:006 And before long you will hear of wars and rumours of wars. Do not be alarmed, for such things must be; but the End is not yet. 024:007 For nation will rise in arms against nation, kingdom against kingdom, and there will be famines and earthquakes in various places; 024:008 but all these miseries are but like the early pains of childbirth. 024:009 "At that time they will deliver you up to punishment and will put you to death; and you will be objects of hatred to all the nations because you are called by my name. 024:010 Then will many stumble and fall, and they will betray one another and hate one another. 024:011 Many false prophets will rise up and lead multitudes astray; 024:012 and because of the prevalent disregard of God's law the love of the great majority will grow cold; 024:013 but those who stand firm to the End shall be saved. 024:014 And this Good News of the Kingdom shall be proclaimed throughout the whole world to set the evidence before all the Gentiles; and then the End will come. 024:015 "When you have seen (to use the language of the Prophet Daniel) the `Abomination of Desolation', standing in the Holy Place"- let the reader observe those words- 024:016 "then let those who are in Judaea escape to the hills; 024:017 let him who is on the roof not go down to fetch what is in his house; 024:018 nor let him who is outside the city stay to pick up his outer garment. 024:019 And alas for the women who at that time are with child or have infants! 024:020 "But pray that your flight may not be in winter, nor on the Sabbath; 024:021 for it will be a time of great suffering, such as never has been from the beginning of the world till now, and assuredly never will be again. 024:022 And if those days had not been cut short, no one would escape; but for the sake of God's own People those days will be cut short. 024:023 "If at that time any one should say to you, `See, here is the Christ!' or `Here!' give no credence to it. 024:024 For there will rise up false Christs and false prophets, displaying wonderful signs and prodigies, so as to deceive, were it possible, even God's own People. 024:025 Remember, I have forewarned you. 024:026 If therefore they should say to you, `See, He is in the Desert!' do not go out there: or `See, He is indoors in the room!' do not believe it. 024:027 For just as the lightning flashes in the east and is seen to the very west, so will be the Coming of the Son of Man. 024:028 Wherever the dead body is, there will the vultures flock together. 024:029 "But immediately after those times of distress the sun will be darkened, the moon will not shed her light, the stars will fall from the firmament, and the forces which control the heavens will be disordered and disturbed. 024:030 Then will appear the Sign of the Son of Man in the sky; and then will all the nations of the earth lament, when they see the Son of Man coming on the clouds of the sky with great power and glory. 024:031 And He will send out His angels with a loud trumpet-blast, and they will bring together His own People to Him from north, south, east and west-from one extremity of the world to the other. 024:032 "Now learn from the fig-tree the lesson it teaches. As soon as its branches have now become soft and it is bursting into leaf, you all know that summer is near. 024:033 So you also, when you

see all these signs, may be sure that He is near-at your very door. 024:034 I
tell you in solemn truth that the present generation will certainly not pass
away without all these things having first taken place. 024:035 Earth and sky
will pass away, but it is certain that my words will not pass away. 024:036
"But as to that day and the exact time no one knows-not even the angels of
heaven, nor the Son, but the Father alone. 024:037 `For as it was in the
time of Noah, so it will be at the Coming of the Son of Man. 024:038 At
that time, before the Deluge, men were busy eating and drinking, taking
wives or giving them, up to the very day when Noah entered the Ark,
024:039 nor did they realise any danger till the Deluge came and swept
them all away; so will it be at the Coming of the Son of Man. 024:040 Then
will two men be in the open country: one will be taken away, and one left
behind. 024:041 Two women will be grinding at the mill: one will be taken
away, and one left behind. 024:042 Be on the alert therefore, for you do not
know the day on which your Lord is coming. 024:043 But of this be
assured, that if the master of the house had known the hour at which the
robber was coming, he would have kept awake, and not have allowed his
house to be broken into. 024:044 Therefore you also must be ready; for it is
at a time when you do not expect Him that the Son of Man will come.
024:045 "Who therefore is the loyal and intelligent servant to whom his
master has entrusted the control of his household to give them their rations
at the appointed time? 024:046 Blessed is that servant whom his master
when he comes shall find so doing! 024:047 In solemn truth I tell you that
he will give him the management of all his wealth. 024:048 But if the man,
being a bad servant, should say in his heart, `My master is a long time in
coming,' 024:049 and should begin to beat his fellow servants, while he eats
and drinks with drunkards; 024:050 the master of that servant will arrive on
a day when he is not expecting him and at an hour of which he has not
been informed; 024:051 he will treat him with the utmost severity and
assign him a place among the hypocrites: there will be the weeping and the
gnashing of teeth. 025:001 "Then will the Kingdom of the Heavens be
found to be like ten bridesmaids who took their torches and went out to
meet the bridegroom. 025:002 Five of them were foolish and five were
wise. 025:003 For the foolish, when they took their torches, did not provide
themselves with oil; 025:004 but the wise, besides their torches, took oil in
their flasks. 025:005 The bridegroom was a long time in coming, so that
meanwhile they all became drowsy and fell asleep. 025:006 But at midnight

there is a loud cry, "`The bridegroom! Go out and meet him!' 025:007 "Then all those bridesmaids roused themselves and trimmed their torches. 025:008 "`Give us some of your oil,' said the foolish ones to the wise, `for our torches are going out.' 025:009 "`But perhaps,' replied the wise, `there will not be enough for all of us. Go to the shops rather, and buy some for yourselves.' 025:010 "So they went to buy. But meanwhile the bridegroom came; those bridesmaids who were ready went in with him to the wedding banquet; and the door was shut. 025:011 "Afterwards the other bridesmaids came and cried, "`Sir, Sir, open the door to us.' 025:012 "`In solemn truth I tell you,' he replied, `I do not know you.' 025:013 "Keep awake therefore; for you know neither the day nor the hour. 025:014 "Why, it is like a man who, when going on his travels, called his bondservants and entrusted his property to their care. 025:015 To one he gave five talents, to another two, to another one- to each according to his individual capacity; and then started from home. 025:016 Without delay the one who had received the five talents went and employed them in business, and gained five more. 025:017 In the same way he who had the two gained two more. 025:018 But the man who had received the one went and dug a hole and buried his master's money. 025:019 "After a long lapse of time the master of those servants returned, and had a reckoning with them. 025:020 The one who had received the five talents came and brought five more, and said, "`Sir, it was five talents that you entrusted to me: see, I have gained five more.' 025:021 "`You have done well, good and trustworthy servant,' replied his master; `you have been trustworthy in the management of a little, I will put you in charge of much: share your master's joy.' 025:022 "The second, who had received the two talents, came and said, "`Sir, it was two talents you entrusted to me: see, I have gained two more.' 025:023 "`Good and trustworthy servant, you have done well,' his master replied; `you have been trustworthy in the management of a little, I will put you in charge of much: share your master's joy.' 025:024 "But, next, the man who had the one talent in his keeping came and said, "`Sir, I knew you to be a severe man, reaping where you had not sown and garnering what you had not winnowed. 025:025 So being afraid I went and buried your talent in the ground: there you have what belongs to you.' 025:026 "`You wicked and slothful servant,' replied his master, `did you know that I reap where I have not sown, and garner what I have not winnowed? 025:027 Your duty then was to deposit my money in some bank, and so when I came I should have got back my property with interest. 025:028 So take away the talent from him, and give it to the man who has the ten.' 025:029 (For to every one who has, more shall be given, and he shall have abundance; but from him who has nothing, even what he has shall be taken away.) 025:030 `But as for this worthless servant, put him out into the darkness outside: *there* will be the weeping and the gnashing of teeth.' 025:031 "When the Son of Man comes in His glory, and all the angels with Him, then will He sit upon His glorious throne, 025:032 and all the nations will be gathered into His presence. And He will separate them from one another, just as a shepherd separates the sheep from the goats; 025:033 and will make the sheep stand at His right hand, and the goats at His left. 025:034 "Then the King will say to those at His right, "`Come, my Father's blessed ones, receive your inheritance of the Kingdom which has been divinely intended for you ever since the creation of the world. 025:035 For when I was hungry, you gave me food; when I was thirsty, you gave me drink; when I was homeless, you gave me a welcome; 025:036 when I was ill-clad, you clothed me; when I was sick, you visited me; when I was in prison, you came to see me.' 025:037 "`When, Lord,' the righteous will reply, `did we see Thee hungry, and feed Thee; or thirsty, and give Thee drink? 025:038 When did we see Thee homeless, and give Thee a welcome? or ill-clad, and clothe Thee? 025:039 When did we see Thee sick or in prison, and come to see Thee?' 025:040 "But the King will answer them, "`In solemn truth I tell you that in so far as you rendered such services to one of the humblest of these my brethren, you rendered them to myself.' 025:041 "Then will He say to those at His left, "`Begone from me, with the curse resting upon you, into the Fire of the Ages, which has been prepared for the Devil and his angels. 025:042 For when I was hungry, you gave me nothing to eat; when thirsty, you gave me nothing to drink; 025:043 when homeless, you gave me no welcome; ill-clad, you clothed me not; sick or in prison, you visited me not.' 025:044 "Then will they also answer, "`Lord, when did we see Thee hungry or thirsty or homeless or ill-clad or sick or in prison, and not come to serve Thee?' 025:045 "But he will reply, "`In solemn truth I tell you that in so far as you withheld such services from one of the humblest of these, you withheld them from me.' 025:046 "And these shall go away into the Punishment of the Ages, but the righteous into the Life of the Ages." 026:001 When Jesus had ended all these discourses, He said to His disciples, 026:002 "You know that in two days' time the Passover comes. And the Son of Man will be delivered up to be crucified." 026:003 Then the High Priests and Elders of the People assembled in the court of the palace of the High Priest Caiaphas, 026:004 and consulted how to get Jesus into their power by stratagem and put Him to death. 026:005 But they said, "Not during the Festival, lest there be a riot among the people." 026:006 Now when Jesus was come to Bethany and was at the house of Simon the Leper, 026:007 a woman came to Him with a jar of very costly, sweet-scented ointment, which she poured over His head as He reclined at table. 026:008 "Why such waste?" indignantly exclaimed the disciples; 026:009 "for this might have been sold for a considerable sum, and the money given to the poor." 026:010 But Jesus heard it, and said to them, "Why are you vexing her? For she has done a most gracious act towards me. 026:011 The poor you always have with you, but me you have not always. 026:012 In pouring this ointment over me, her object was to prepare me for burial. 026:013 In solemn truth I tell you that wherever in the whole world this Good News shall be proclaimed, this deed of hers shall be spoken of in memory of her." 026:014 At that time one of the Twelve, the one called Judas Iscariot, went to the High Priests 026:015 and said, "What are you willing to give me if I betray him to you?" So they weighed out to him thirty shekels, 026:016 and from that moment he was on the look out for an opportunity to betray Him. 026:017 On the first day of the Unleavened Bread the disciples came to Jesus with the question, "Where shall we make preparations for you to eat the Passover?" 026:018 "Go into the city," He replied, "to a certain man, and tell him, `The Teacher says, My time is close at hand. It is at your house that I shall keep the Passover with my disciples.'" 026:019 The disciples did as Jesus directed them, and got the Passover ready. 026:020 When evening came, He was at table with the twelve disciples, 026:021 and the meal was proceeding, when Jesus said, "In solemn truth I tell you that one of you will betray me." 026:022 Intensely grieved they began one after another to ask Him, "Can it be I, Master?" 026:023 "The one who has dipped his fingers in the bowl with me," He answered, "is the man who will betray me. 026:024 The Son of Man is indeed going as is written concerning Him; but alas for that man by whom the Son of Man is betrayed! It had been a happy thing for that man if he had never been born." 026:025 Then Judas, the disciple who was betraying Him, asked, "Can it be I, Rabbi?" "It is you," He replied. 026:026 During the meal Jesus took a Passover biscuit, blessed it and broke it. He then gave it to the disciples, saying, "Take this and eat it: it is my

body." 026:027 And He took the cup and gave thanks, and gave it to them
saying, "Drink from it, all of you; 026:028 for this is my blood which is to
be poured out for many for the remission of sins-the blood which ratifies
the Covenant. 026:029 I tell you that I will never again take the produce of
the vine till that day when I shall drink the new wine with you in my
Father's Kingdom." 026:030 So they sang the hymn and went out to the
Mount of Olives. 026:031 Then said Jesus, "This night all of you will
stumble and fail in your fidelity to me; for it is written, `I will strike the
Shepherd, and the sheep of the flock will be scattered in all directions.'
026:032 But after I have risen to life again I will go before you into Galilee."
026:033 "All may stumble and fail," said Peter, "but I never will." 026:034
"In solemn truth I tell you," replied Jesus, "that this very night, before the
cock crows, you will three times disown me." 026:035 "Even if I must die
with you," declared Peter, "I will never disown you." In like manner
protested all the disciples. 026:036 Then Jesus came with them to a place
called Gethsemane. And He said to the disciples, "Sit down here, whilst I
go yonder and there pray." 026:037 And He took with Him Peter and the
two sons of Zabdi. Then He began to be full of anguish and distress,
026:038 and He said to them, "My soul is crushed with anguish to the very
point of death; wait here, and keep awake with me." 026:039 Going forward
a short distance He fell on His face and prayed. "My Father," He said, "if it
is possible, let this cup pass away from me; nevertheless, not as I will, but as
Thou willest." 026:040 Then He came to the disciples and found them
asleep, and He said to Peter, "Alas, none of you could keep awake with me
for even a single hour! 026:041 Keep awake, and pray that you may not
enter into temptation: the spirit is right willing, but the body is frail."
026:042 Again a second time He went away and prayed, saying, "My Father,
if it is impossible for this cup to pass without my drinking it, Thy will be
done." 026:043 He came and again found them asleep, for they were very
tired. 026:044 So He left them, and went away once more and prayed a
third time, again using the same words. 026:045 Then He came to the
disciples and said, "Sleep on and rest. See, the moment is close at hand
when the Son of Man is to be betrayed into the hands of sinful men.
026:046 Rouse yourselves. Let us be going. My betrayer is close at hand."
026:047 He had scarcely finished speaking when Judas came- one of the
Twelve-accompanied by a great crowd of men armed with swords and
bludgeons, sent by the High Priests and Elders of the People. 026:048 Now

the betrayer had agreed upon a sign with them, to direct them. He had said, "The one whom I kiss is the man: lay hold of him." 026:049 So he went straight to Jesus and said, "Peace to you, Rabbi!" And he kissed Him eagerly. 026:050 "Friend," said Jesus, "carry out your intention." Then they came and laid their hands on Jesus and seized Him firmly. 026:051 But one of those with Jesus drew his sword and struck the High Priest's servant, cutting off his ear. 026:052 "Put back your sword again," said Jesus, "for all who draw the sword shall perish by the sword. 026:053 Or do you suppose I cannot entreat my Father and He would instantly send to my help more than twelve legions of angels? 026:054 In that case how are the Scriptures to be fulfilled which declare that thus it must be?" 026:055 Then said Jesus to the crowds, "Have you come out as if to fight with a robber, with swords and bludgeons to apprehend me? Day after day I have been sitting teaching in the Temple, and you did not arrest me. 026:056 But all this has taken place in order that the writings of the Prophets may be fulfilled." At this point the disciples all left Him and fled. 026:057 But the officers who had laid hold of Jesus led Him away to Caiaphas the High Priest, at whose house the Scribes and the Elders had assembled. 026:058 And Peter kept following Him at a distance, till he came even to the court of the High Priest's palace, where he entered and sat down among the officers to see the issue. 026:059 Meanwhile the High Priests and the whole Sanhedrin were seeking false testimony against Jesus in order to put Him to death; 026:060 but they could find none, although many false witnesses came forward. At length there came two 026:061 who testified, "This man said, `I am able to pull down the Sanctuary of God and three days afterwards to build a new one.'" 026:062 Then the High Priest stood up and asked Him, "Have you no answer to make? What is it these men are saying in evidence against you?" 026:063 Jesus however remained silent. Again the High Priest addressed Him. "In the name of the ever-living God," he said, "I now put you on your oath. Tell us whether you are the Christ, the Son of God." 026:064 "I am He," replied Jesus. "But I tell you that, later on, you will see the Son of Man sitting at the right hand of Omnipotence, and coming on the clouds of the sky." 026:065 Then the High Priest tore his robes and exclaimed, "Impious language! What further need have we of witnesses! See, you have now heard the impiety. 026:066 What is your verdict?" "He deserves to die," they replied. 026:067 Then they spat in His face, and struck Him-some with the fist, some with the open hand- 026:068 while they taunted Him, saying, "Christ, prove yourself a Prophet by telling us who it was that struck you." 026:069 Peter meanwhile was sitting outside in the court of the palace, when one of the maidservants came over to him and said, "You too were with Jesus the Galilaean." 026:070 He denied it before them all, saying, "I do not know what you mean." 026:071 Soon afterwards he went out and stood in the gateway, when another girl saw him, and said, addressing the people there, "This man was with Jesus the Nazarene." 026:072 Again he denied it with an oath. "I do not know the man," he said. 026:073 A short time afterwards the people standing there came and said to Peter, "Certainly you too are one of them, for your brogue shows it." 026:074 Then with curses and oaths he declared, "I do not know the man." Immediately a cock crowed, 026:075 and Peter recollected the words of Jesus, how He had said, "Before the cock crows you will three times disown me." And he went out and wept aloud, bitterly. 027:001 When morning came all the High Priests and the Elders of the people consulted together against Jesus to put Him to death; 027:002 and binding Him they led Him away and handed Him over to Pilate the Governor. 027:003 Then when Judas, who had betrayed Him, saw that He was condemned, smitten with remorse he brought back the thirty shekels to the High Priests and Elders 027:004 and said, "I have sinned, in betraying to death one who is innocent." "What does that matter to us?" they replied; it is your business." 027:005 Flinging the shekels into the Sanctuary he left the place, and went and hanged himself. 027:006 When the High Priests had gathered up the money they said, "It is illegal to put it into the Treasury, because it is the price of blood." 027:007 So after consulting together they spent the money in the purchase of the Potter's Field as a burial place for people not belonging to the city; 027:008 for which reason that piece of ground received the name, which it still bears, of `the Field of Blood.' 027:009 Then were fulfilled the words spoken by the Prophet Jeremiah, "And I took the thirty shekels, the price of the prized one on whom Israelites had set a price, 027:010 and gave them for the potter's field, as the Lord directed me." 027:011 Meanwhile Jesus was brought before the Governor, and the latter put the question, "Are you the King of the Jews?" "I am their King," He answered. 027:012 When however the High Priests and the Elders kept bringing their charges against Him, He said not a word in reply. 027:013 "Do you not hear," asked Pilate, "what a mass of evidence they are bringing against you?" 027:014 But He made no reply to a single accusation, so that the Governor was greatly astonished. 027:015 "Now it was the Governor's custom at the Festival to release some one prisoner, whomsoever the populace desired; 027:016 and at this time they had a notorious prisoner called Barabbas. 027:017 So when they were now assembled Pilate appealed to them. "Whom shall I release to you," he said, "Barabbas, or Jesus the so-called Christ?" 027:018 For he knew that it was from envious hatred that Jesus had been brought before him. 027:019 While he was sitting on the tribunal a message came to him from his wife. "Have nothing to do with that innocent man," she said, "for during the night I have suffered terribly in a dream through him." 027:020 The High Priests, however, and the Elders urged the crowd to ask for Barabbas and to demand the death of Jesus. 027:021 So when the Governor a second time asked them, "Which of the two shall I release to you?"-they cried, "Barabbas!" 027:022 "What then," said Pilate, "shall I do with Jesus, the so-called Christ?" With one voice they shouted, "Let him be crucified!" 027:023 "Why, what crime has he committed?" asked Pilate. But they kept on furiously shouting, "Let him be crucified!" 027:024 So when he saw that he could gain nothing, but that on the contrary there was a riot threatening, he called for water and washed his hands in sight of them all, saying, "I am not responsible for this murder: you must answer for it." 027:025 "His blood," replied all the people, "be on us and on our children!" 027:026 Then he released Barabbas to them, but Jesus he ordered to be scourged, and gave Him up to be crucified. 027:027 Then the Governor's soldiers took Jesus into the Praetorium, and called together the whole battalion to make sport of Him. 027:028 Stripping off His garments, they put on Him a general's short crimson cloak. 027:029 They twisted a wreath of thorny twigs and put it on His head, and they put a sceptre of cane in His right hand, and kneeling to Him they shouted in mockery, "Long live the King of the Jews!" 027:030 Then they spat upon Him, and taking the cane they repeatedly struck Him on the head with it. 027:031 At last, having finished their sport, they took off the cloak, clothed Him again in His own garments, and led Him away for crucifixion. 027:032 Going out they met a Cyrenaean named Simon; whom they compelled to carry His cross, 027:033 and so they came to a place called Golgotha, which means `Skull-ground.' 027:034 Here they gave Him a mixture of wine and gall to drink, but having tasted it He refused to drink it. 027:035 After crucifying Him, they divided His garments among them by lot, 027:036 and sat down there on guard. 027:037 Over His head they placed a written statement of the charge against Him: THIS IS JESUS THE KING OF THE JEWS. 027:038 At the same time two robbers were crucified with Him, one at His right hand and the other at His left. 027:039 And the passers-by reviled Him. They shook their heads at Him 027:040 and said, "You who would pull down the Sanctuary and build a new one within three days, save yourself. If you are God's Son, come down from the cross." 027:041 In like manner the High Priests also, together with the Scribes and the Elders, taunted Him. 027:042 "He saved others," they said, "himself he cannot save! He is the King of Israel! Let him now come down from the cross, and we will believe in him. 027:043 His trust is in God: let God deliver him now, if He will have him; for he said, `I am God's Son.'" 027:044 Insults of the same kind were heaped on Him even by the robbers who were being crucified with Him. 027:045 Now from noon until three o'clock in the afternoon there was darkness over the whole land; 027:046 but about three o'clock Jesus cried out in a loud voice, "Eli, Eli, lama sabachthani?" that is to say, "My God, My God, why hast Thou forsaken me?" 027:047 "The man is calling for Elijah," said some of the bystanders. 027:048 One of them ran forthwith, and filling a sponge with sour wine put it on the end of a cane and offered it Him to drink; 027:049 while the rest said, "Let us see whether Elijah is coming to deliver him." 027:050 But Jesus uttered another loud cry and then yielded up His spirit. 027:051 Immediately the curtain of the Sanctuary was torn in two from top to bottom: the earth quaked; the rocks split; 027:052 the tombs opened; and many of God's people who were asleep in death awoke. 027:053 And coming out of their tombs after Christ's resurrection they entered the holy city and showed themselves to many. 027:054 As for the Captain and the soldiers who were with Him keeping guard over Jesus, when they witnessed the earthquake and the other occurrences they were filled with terror, and exclaimed, "Assuredly he was God's Son." 027:055 And there were a number of women there looking on from a distance, who had followed Jesus from Galilee ministering to His necessities; 027:056 among them being Mary of Magdala, Mary the mother of James and Joses, and the mother of the sons of Zabdi. 027:057 Towards sunset there came a wealthy inhabitant of Arimathaea, named Joseph, who himself also had become a disciple of Jesus. 027:058 He went to Pilate and begged to have the body of Jesus, and Pilate ordered it to be given to him. 027:059 So Joseph took the body and wrapped it in a clean sheet of fine linen. 027:060 He then laid it in his own new tomb which he had hewn in the solid rock, and after rolling a great stone against the door of the tomb he went home. 027:061 Mary of Magdala and the other Mary were both present there, sitting opposite to the sepulchre. 027:062 On the next day, the day after the Preparation, the High Priests and the Pharisees came in a body to Pilate. 027:063 "Sir," they said, "we recollect that during his lifetime that impostor pretended that after two days he was to rise to life again. 027:064 So give orders for the sepulchre to be securely guarded till the third day, for fear his disciples should come by night and steal the body, and then tell the people that he has come back to life; and so the last imposture will be more serious than the first." 027:065 "You can have a guard," said Pilate: "go and make all safe, as best you can." 027:066 So they went and made the sepulchre secure, sealing the stone besides setting the guard. 028:001 After the Sabbath, in the early dawn of the first day of the week, Mary of Magdala and the other Mary came to see the sepulchre. 028:002 But to their amazement there had been a great earthquake; for an angel of the Lord had descended from Heaven, and had come and rolled back the stone, and was sitting upon it. 028:003 His appearance was like lightning, and his raiment white as snow. 028:004 For fear of him the guards trembled violently, and became like dead men. 028:005 But the angel said to the women, "As for you, dismiss your fears. I know that it is Jesus that you are looking for- the crucified One. 028:006 He is not here: He has come back to life, as He foretold. Come and see the place where He lay. 028:007 And go quickly and tell His disciples that He has risen from the dead and is going before you into Galilee: there you shall see Him. Remember, I have told you." 028:008 They quickly left the tomb and ran, still terrified but full of unspeakable joy, to carry the news to His disciples. 028:009 And then suddenly they saw Jesus coming to meet them. "Peace be to you," He said. And they came and clasped His feet, bowing to the ground before Him. 028:010 Then He said, "Dismiss all fear! Go and take word to my brethren to go into Galilee, and there they shall see me." 028:011 While they went on this errand, some of the guards came into the city and reported to the High Priests every detail of what had happened. 028:012 So the latter held a conference with the Elders, and after consultation with them they heavily bribed the soldiers, 028:013 telling them to say, "His disciples came during the night and stole his body while we were asleep." 028:014 "And if this," they added, "is reported to the Governor, we will satisfy him and screen you from punishment." 028:015

So they took the money and did as they were instructed; and this story was
noised about among the Jews, and is current to this day. 028:016 As for the
eleven disciples, they proceeded into Galilee, to the hill where Jesus had
arranged to meet them. 028:017 There they saw Him and prostrated
themselves before Him. Yet some doubted. 028:018 Jesus however came
near and said to them, "All power in Heaven and over the earth has been
given to me. 028:019 Go therefore and make disciples of all the nations;
baptize them into the name of the Father, and of the Son, and of the Holy
Spirit; 028:020 and teach them to obey every command which I have given
you. And remember, I am with you always, day by day, until the Close of
the Age."

BOOK 57 PHILEMON

001:001 Paul, a prisoner for Christ Jesus, and Timothy our brother: To Philemon our dearly-loved fellow labourer- 001:002 and to our sister Apphia and our comrade Archippus- as well as to the Church in your house. 001:003 May grace be granted to you all, and peace, from God our Father and the Lord Jesus Christ. 001:004 I give continual thanks to my God while making mention of you, my brother, in my prayers, 001:005 because I hear of your love and of the faith which you have towards the Lord Jesus and which you manifest towards all God's people; 001:006 praying as I do, that their participation in your faith may result in others fully recognizing all the right affection that is in us toward Christ. 001:007 For I have found great joy and comfort in your love, because the hearts of God's people have been, and are, refreshed through you, my brother. 001:008 Therefore, though I might with Christ's authority speak very freely and order you to do what is fitting, 001:009 it is for love's sake that-instead of that-although I am none other than Paul the aged, and am now also a prisoner for Christ Jesus, 001:010 I entreat you on behalf of my own child whose father I have become while in my chains-I mean Onesimus. 001:011 Formerly he was useless to you, but now-true to his name- he is of great use to you and to me. 001:012 I am sending him back to you, though in so doing I send part of myself. 001:013 It was my wish to keep him at my side for him to attend to my wants, as your representative, during my imprisonment for the Good News. 001:014 Only I wished to do nothing without your consent, so that his kind action of yours might not be done under pressure, but might be a voluntary one. 001:015 For perhaps it was for this reason he was parted from you for a time, that you might receive him back wholly and for ever yours; 001:016 no longer as a slave, but as something better than a slave- a brother peculiarly dear to me, and even dearer to you, both as a servant and as a fellow Christian. 001:017 If

therefore you regard me as a comrade, receive him as if he were I myself.
001:018 And if he was ever dishonest or is in your debt, debit me with the
amount. 001:019 I Paul write this with my own hand-I will pay you in full.
(I say nothing of the fact that you owe me even your own self.) 001:020
Yes, brother, do me this favour for the Lord's sake. Refresh my heart in
Christ. 001:021 I write to you in the full confidence that you will meet my
wishes, for I know you will do even more than I say. 001:022 And at the
same time provide accommodation for me; for I hope that through your
prayers I shall be permitted to come to you. 001:023 Greetings to you, my
brother, from Epaphras my fellow prisoner for the sake of Christ Jesus;
001:024 and from Mark, Aristarchus, Demas, and Luke, my fellow workers.
001:025 May the grace of our Lord Jesus Christ be with the spirit of every
one of you.

BOOK 50 PHILIPPIANS

001:001 Paul and Timothy, bondservants of Christ Jesus: To all God's people in Christ Jesus who are at Philippi, with the ministers of the Church and their assistants. 001:002 May grace and peace be granted to you from God our Father and the Lord Jesus Christ. 001:003 I thank my God at my every remembrance of you- 001:004 always when offering any prayer on behalf of you all, finding a joy in offering it. 001:005 I thank my God, I say, for your cooperation in spreading the Good News, from the time it first came to you even until now. 001:006 For of this I am confident, that He who has begun a good work within you will go on to perfect it in preparation for the day of Jesus Christ. 001:007 And I am justified in having this confidence about you all, because, both during my imprisonment and when I stand up in defence of the Good News or to confirm its truth, I have you in my heart, sharers as you all are in the same grace as myself. 001:008 For God is my witness how I yearn over all of you with tender Christian affection. 001:009 And it is my prayer that your love may be more and more accompanied by clear knowledge and keen perception, for testing things that differ, 001:010 so that you may be men of transparent character, and may be blameless, in preparation for the day of Christ, 001:011 being filled with these fruits of righteousness which come through Jesus Christ-to the glory and praise of God. 001:012 Now I would have you know, brethren, that what I have gone through has turned out to the furtherance of the Good News rather than otherwise. 001:013 And thus it has become notorious among all the Imperial Guards, and everywhere, that it is for the sake of Christ that I am a prisoner; 001:014 and the greater part of the brethren, made confident in the Lord through my imprisonment, now speak of God's Message without fear, more boldly than ever. 001:015 Some indeed actually preach Christ out of envy and contentiousness but there are also others who do it from good will. 001:016 These latter preach Him from love to me, knowing that I am here for the defence of the Good News; 001:017 while the others proclaim Him from motives of rivalry, and insincerely, supposing that by this they are embittering my imprisonment. 001:018 What does it matter, however? In any case Christ is preached-either perversely or in honest truth; and in that I rejoice, yes, and will rejoice. 001:019 For I know that it will result in my salvation through your prayers and a bountiful supply of the Spirit of Jesus Christ, 001:020 in fulfilment of my eager expectation and hope that I shall never have reason to feel ashamed, but that by my perfect freedom of speech Christ will be glorified in me, now as always, either by my life or by my death. 001:021 For, with me, to live is Christ and to die is gain. 001:022 But since to live means a longer stay on earth, that implies more labour for me-and not unsuccessful labour; and which I am to choose I cannot tell. 001:023 I am in a dilemma, my earnest desire being to depart and be with Christ, for that is far, far better. 001:024 But for your sakes it is more important that I should still remain in the body. 001:025 I am convinced of this, and I know that I shall remain, and shall go on working side by side with you all, to promote your progress and joy in the faith; 001:026 so that, as Christians, you may have additional reason for glorying about me as the result of my being with you again. 001:027 Only let the lives you live be worthy of the Good News of the Christ, in order that, whether I come and see you or, being absent, only hear of you, I may know that you are standing fast in one spirit and with one mind, fighting shoulder to shoulder for the faith of the Good News. 001:028 Never for a moment quail before your antagonists. Your fearlessness will be to them a sure token of impending destruction, but to you it will be a sure token of your salvation- a token coming from God. 001:029 For you have had the privilege granted you on behalf of Christ- not only to believe in Him, but also to suffer on His behalf; 001:030 maintaining, as you do, the same kind of conflict that you once saw in me and which you still hear that I am engaged in. 002:001 If then I can appeal to you as the followers of Christ, if there is any persuasive power in love and any common sharing of the Spirit, or if you have any tender-heartedness and compassion, make my joy complete by being of one mind, 002:002 united by mutual love, with harmony of feeling giving your minds to one and the same object. 002:003 Do nothing in a spirit of factiousness or of vainglory, but, with true humility, let every one regard the rest as being of more account than himself; 002:004 each fixing his attention, not simply on his own interests, but on those of others also. 002:005 Let the same disposition be in you which was in Christ Jesus. 002:006 Although from the beginning He had the nature of God He did not reckon His equality with God a treasure to be tightly grasped. 002:007 Nay, He stripped Himself of His glory, and took on Him the nature of a bondservant by becoming a man like other men. 002:008 And being recognized as truly human, He humbled Himself and even stooped to die; yes, to die on a cross. 002:009 It is in consequence of this that God has also so highly exalted Him, and has conferred on Him the Name which is supreme above every other, 002:010 in order that in the Name of JESUS every knee should bow, of beings in Heaven, of those on the earth, and of those in the underworld, 002:011 and that every tongue should confess that JESUS CHRIST is LORD, to the glory of God the Father. 002:012 Therefore, my dearly-loved friends, as I have always found you obedient, labour earnestly with fear and trembling-not merely as though I were present with you, but much more now since I am absent from you-labour earnestly, I say, to make sure of your own salvation. 002:013 For it is God Himself whose power creates within you the desire to do His gracious will and also brings about the accomplishment of the desire. 002:014 Be ever on your guard against a grudging and contentious spirit, 002:015 so that you may always prove yourselves to be blameless and spotless- irreproachable children of God in the midst of a crooked and perverse generation, among whom you are seen as heavenly lights in the world, 002:016 holding out to them a Message of Life. It will then be my glory on the day of Christ that I did not run my race in vain nor toil in vain. 002:017 Nay, even if my life is to be poured as a libation upon the sacrificial offering of your faith, I rejoice, and I congratulate you all. 002:018 And I bid you also share my gladness, and congratulate me. 002:019 But, if the Lord permits it, I hope before long to send Timothy to you, that I, in turn, may be cheered by getting news of you. 002:020 For I have no one likeminded with him, who will cherish a genuine care for you. 002:021 Everybody concerns himself about his own interests, not about those of Jesus Christ. 002:022 But you know Timothy's approved worth-how, like a child working with his father, he has served with me in furtherance of the Good News. 002:023 So it is he that I hope to send as soon as ever I see how things go with me; 002:024 but trusting, as I do, in the Lord, I believe that I shall myself also come to you before long. 002:025 Yet I deem it important to send Epaphroditus to you now- he is my brother and comrade both in labour and in arms, and is your messenger who has ministered to my needs. 002:026 I send him because he is longing to see you all and is distressed at your having heard of his illness. 002:027 For it is true that he has been ill, and was apparently at the point of death; but God had pity on him, and not only on him, but also on me, to save me from having sorrow upon sorrow. 002:028 I am therefore all the more eager to send him, in the hope that when you see him again you may be glad and I may have the less sorrow. 002:029 Receive him therefore with heartfelt Christian joy, and hold in honour men like him; 002:030 because it was for the sake of Christ's work that he came so near death, hazarding, as he did, his very life in endeavouring to make good any deficiency that there might be in your gifts to me. 003:001 In conclusion, my brethren, be joyful in the

Lord. For me to give you the same warnings as before is not irksome to me, while so far as you are concerned it is a safe precaution. 003:002 Beware of `the dogs,' the bad workmen, the self-mutilators. 003:003 For we are the true circumcision-we who render to God a spiritual worship and make our boast in Christ Jesus and have no confidence in outward ceremonies: 003:004 although I myself might have some excuse for confidence in outward ceremonies. If any one else claims a right to trust in them, far more may I: 003:005 circumcised, as I was, on the eighth day, a member of the race of Israel and of the tribe of Benjamin, a Hebrew sprung from Hebrews; as to the Law a Pharisee; 003:006 as to zeal, a persecutor of the Church; as to the righteousness which comes through Law, blameless. 003:007 Yet all that was gain to me-for Christ's sake I have reckoned it loss. 003:008 Nay, I even reckon all things as pure loss because of the priceless privilege of knowing Christ Jesus my Lord. And for His sake I have suffered the loss of everything, and reckon it all as mere refuse, in order that I may win Christ and be found in union with Him, 003:009 not having a righteousness of my own, derived from the Law, but that which arises from faith in Christ-the righteousness which comes from God through faith. 003:010 I long to know Christ and the power which is in His resurrection, and to share in His sufferings and die even as He died; 003:011 in the hope that I may attain to the resurrection from among the dead. 003:012 I do not say that I have already won the race or have already reached perfection. But I am pressing on, striving to lay hold of the prize for which also Christ has laid hold of me. 003:013 Brethren, I do not imagine that I have yet laid hold of it. But this one thing I do-forgetting everything which is past and stretching forward to what lies in front of me, 003:014 with my eyes fixed on the goal I push on to secure the prize of God's heavenward call in Christ Jesus. 003:015 Therefore let all of us who are mature believers cherish these thoughts; and if in any respect you think differently, that also God will make clear to you. 003:016 But whatever be the point that we have already reached, let us persevere in the same course. 003:017 Brethren, vie with one another in imitating me, and carefully observe those who follow the example which we have set you. 003:018 For there are many whom I have often described to you, and I now even with tears describe them, as being enemies to the Cross of Christ. 003:019 Their end is destruction, their bellies are their God, their glory is in their shame, and their minds are devoted to earthly things. 003:020 We, however, are free citizens of Heaven, and we are waiting with longing expectation for the coming from Heaven of a Saviour, the Lord Jesus Christ, 003:021 who, in the exercise of the power which He has even to subject all things to Himself, will transform this body of our humiliation until it resembles His own glorious body. 004:001 Therefore, my brethren, dearly loved and longed for, my joy and crown, so stand firm in the Lord, my dearly-loved ones. 004:002 I entreat Euodia, and I entreat Syntyche, to be of one mind, as sisters in Christ. 004:003 Yes, and I beg you also, my faithful yoke-fellow, to help these women who have shared my toil in connection with the Good News, together with Clement and the rest of my fellow labourers, whose names are recorded in the Book of Life. 004:004 Always be glad in the Lord: I will repeat it, be glad. 004:005 Let your forbearing spirit be known to every one- the Lord is near. 004:006 Do not be over-anxious about anything, but by prayer and earnest pleading, together with thanksgiving, let your request be unreservedly made known in the presence of God. 004:007 And then the peace of God, which transcends all our powers of thought, will be a garrison to guard your hearts and minds in union with Christ Jesus. 004:008 Finally, brethren, whatever is true, whatever wins respect, whatever is just, whatever is pure, whatever is lovable, whatever is of good repute-if there is any virtue or anything deemed worthy of praise-cherish the thought of these things. 004:009 The doctrines and the line of conduct which I taught you- both what you heard and what you saw in me-hold fast to them; and God who gives peace will be with you. 004:010 But I rejoice with a deep and holy joy that now at length you have revived your thoughtfulness for my welfare. Indeed you have always been thoughtful for me, although opportunity failed you. 004:011 I do not refer to this through fear of privation, for (for my part) I have learned, whatever be my outward experiences, to be content. 004:012 I know both how to live in humble circumstances and how to live amid abundance. I am fully initiated into all the mysteries both of fulness and of hunger, of abundance and of want. 004:013 I have strength for anything through Him who gives me power. 004:014 Yet I thank you for taking your share in my troubles. 004:015 And you men and women of Philippi also know that at the first preaching of the Good News, when I had left Macedonia, no other Church except yourselves held communication with me about giving and receiving; 004:016 because even in Thessalonica you sent several times to minister to my needs. 004:017 Not that I crave for gifts from you, but I do want to see abundant fruit bring you honour. 004:018 I have enough of everything-and more than enough. My wants are fully satisfied now that I have received from the hands of Epaphroditus the generous gifts which you sent me-they are a fragrant odor, an acceptable sacrifice, truly pleasing to God. 004:019 But my God-so great is His wealth of glory in Christ Jesus- will fully supply every need of yours. 004:020 And to our God and Father be the glory throughout the Ages of the Ages! Amen. 004:021 My Christian greetings to every one of God's people. The brethren who are with me send their greetings. 004:022 All God's people here greet you-especially the members of Caesar's household. 004:023 May the grace of our Lord Jesus Christ be with your spirits.

Preface to the First Edition

The Translation of the New Testament here offered to English-speaking Christians is a bona fide translation made directly from the Greek, and is in no sense a revision. The plan adopted has been the following.

1. An earnest endeavour has been made (based upon more than sixty years' study of both the Greek and English languages, besides much further familiarity gained by continual teaching) to ascertain the exact meaning of every passage not only by the light that Classical Greek throws on the langruage used, but also by that which the Septuagint and the Hebrew Scriptures afford; aid being sought too from Versions and Commentators ancient and modern, and from the ample et cetera of apparatus grammaticus and theological and Classical reviews and magazines-or rather, by means of occasional excursions into this vast prairie.

2. The sense thus seeming to have been ascertained, the next step has been to consider how it could be most accurately and naturally exhibited in the English of the present day; in other words, how we can with some approach to probability suppose that the inspired writer himself would have expressed his thoughts, had he been writing in our age and country. /1

3. Lastly it has been evidently desirable to compare the results thus attained with the renderings of other scholars, especially of course witll the Authorized and Revised Versions. But alas, the great majority of even "new translations," so called, are, in reality, only Tyndale's immortal work a little-often very litLle-modernized!

4. But in the endeavour to find in Twentieth Century English a precise equivalent for a Greek word, phrase, or sentence there are two dangers to be guarded against. There are a Scylla and a Charybdis. On the one hand there is the English of Society, on the other hand that of the utterly uneducated, each of these patois having also its own special, though expressive, borderland which we name 'slang.' But all these salient angles (as a professor of fortification might say) of our language are forbidden ground to the reverent translator of Holy Scripture.

5. But again, a modern translation-does this imply that no words or phrases in any degree antiquated are to be admitted? Not so, for great numbers of such words and phrases are still in constant use. To be antiquated is not the same thing as to be obsolete or even obsolescent, and without at least a tinge of antiquity it is scarcely possible that there should be that dignity of style that befits the sacred themes with which the Evangelists and Apostles deal.

6. It is plain that this attempt to bring out the sense of the Sacred Writings naturally as well as accurately in present-day English does not permit, except to a limited extent, the method of literal rendering-the verbo

verbum reddere at which Horace shrugs his shoulders. Dr. Welldon, recently Bishop of Calcutta, in the Preface (p. vii) to his masterly translation of the Nicomachean Ethics of Aristotle, writes, "I have deliberately rejected the principle of trying to translate the same Greek word by the same word in English, and where circumstances seemed to call for it I have sometimes used two English words to represent one word of the Greek;"-and he is perfectly right. With a slavish literality delicate shades of meaning cannot be reproduced, nor allowance be made for the influence of interwoven thought, or of the writer's ever shifting-not to say changing-point of view. An utterly ignorant or utterly lazy man, if possessed of a little ingenuity, can with the help of a dictionary and grammar give a word-for-word rendering, whether intelligible or not, and print 'Translation' on his title-page. On the other hand it is a melancholy spectacle to see men of high ability and undoubted scholarship toil and struggle at translation under a needless restriction to literality, as in intellectual handcuffs and fetters, when they might with advantage snap the bonds and fling them away, as Dr. Welldon has done: more melancholy still, if they are at the same time racking their brains to exhibit the result of their laboursa splendid but idle philological tour de force -in what was English nearly 300 years before.

7. Obviously any literal translation cannot but carry idioms of the earlier language into the later, where they will very probably not be understood; /2 and more serious still is the evil when, as in the Jewish Greek of the N T, the earlier language of the two is itself composite and abounds in forms of speech that belong to one earlier still. For the N.T. Greek, even in the writings of Luke, contains a large number of Hebrew idioms; and a literal rendering into English cannot but partially veil, and in some degree distort, the true sense, even if it does not totally obscure it (and that too where perfect clearness should be attained, if possible), by this admixture of Hebrew as well as Greek forms of expression.

8. It follows that the reader who is bent upon getting a literal rendering, such as he can commonly find in the R.V. or (often a better one) in Darby's New Testament, should always be on his guard against its strong tendency to mislead.

9. One point however can hardly be too emphatically stated. It is not the present Translator's ambition to supplant the Versions already in general use, to which their intrinsic merit or long familiarity or both have caused all Christian minds so lovingly to cling. His desire has rather been to furnish a succinct and compressed running commentary (not doctrinal) to be used sidc by side with its elder compeers. And yet there has been something of a remoter hope. It can scarcely be doubted that some day the attempt will be renewed to produce a satisfactory English Bible-one in some respects perhaps (but assuredly with great and important deviations) on the lines of the Revision of 1881, or even altogether to supersede both the A.V. and the

R.V.; and it may be that the Translation here offered will contribute some materials that may be built into that far grander edifice.

10. THE GREEK TEXT here followed is that given in the Translator's Resultant Greek Testament.

11. Of the VARIOUS READINGS only those are here given which seem the most important, and which affect the rendering into English. They are in the footnotes, with V.L. (varia lectio) prefixed. As to the chief modern critical editions full details will be found in the Resultant Greek Testament, while for the original authorities-MSS., Versions, Patristic quotations-the reader must of necessity consult the great works of Lachmann, Tregelles, Tischendorf, and others, or the numerous monographs on separate Books. /3 In the margin of the R.V. a distinction is made between readings supported by "a few ancient authorities," "some ancient authorities," "many ancient authorities," and so on. Such valuation is not attempted in this work.

12. Considerable pains have been bestowed on the exact rendering of the tenses of the Greek verb; for by inexactness in this detail the true sense cannot but be missed. That the Greek tenses do not coincide, and cannot be expected to coincide with those of the English verb; that-except in narrative-the aorist as a rule is more exactly represented in English by our perfect with "have" than by our simple past tense; and that in this particular the A.V. is in scores of instances more correct than the R.V.; the present Translator has contended (with arguments which some of the best scholars in Britain and in America hold to be "unanswerable" and "indisputable") in a pamphlet On the Rendering into English of the Greek Aorist and Perfect. Even an outline of the argument cannot be given in a Preface such as this.

13. But he who would make a truly English translation of a foreign book must not only select the right nouns, adjectives, and verbs, insert the suitable prepositions and auxiliaries, and triumph (if he can) over the seductions and blandishments of idioms with which he has been familiar from his infancy, but which, though forcible or beautiful with other surroundings, are for all that part and parcel of that other language rather than of English: he has also to beware of connecting his sentences in an un-English fashion.

Now a careful examination of a number of authors (including Scottish, Irish, and American) yields some interesting results. Taking at haphazard a passage from each of fifty-six authors, and counting on after some full stop till fifty finite verbs-i. e. verbs in the indicative, imperative, or subjunctive mood-have been reached (each finite verb, as every schoolboy knows, being the nucleus of one sentence or clause), it has been found that the connecting links of the fifty-six times fifty sentences are about one-third conjunctions, about one-third adverbs or relative and interrogative pronouns, while in the case of the remaining third there is what the grammarians call an asyndeton-no formal grammatical connexion at all. But in the writers of the N.T. nearly two-thirds of the connecting links are conjunctions. It follows that in order to make the style of a translation true idiomatic English many of these conjunctions must be omitted, and for others adverbs, &c., must be substituted.

The two conjunctions for and therefore are discussed at some length in two Appendices to the above-mentioned pamphlet on the Aorist, to which the reader is referred.

14. The NOTES, with but few exceptions, are not of the nature of a general commentary. Some, as already intimated, refer to the readings here followed, but the great majority are in vindication or explanation of the renderings given. Since the completion of this new version nearly two years ago, ill-health has incapacitated the Translator from undertaking even the lightest work. He has therefore been obliged to entrust to other hands the labour of critically examining and revising the manuscript and of seeing it through the press. This arduous task has been undertaken by Rev. Ernest Hampden-Cook, M.A., St. John's College, Cambridge, of Sandhach, Cheshire, with some co-operation from one of the Translator's sons; and the Translator is under deep obligations to these two gentlemen for their kindness in the matter. He has also most cordially to thank Mr. Hampden-Cook for making the existence of the work known to various members of the OLD MILLHILIANS' CLUB and other former pupils of the Translator, who in a truly substantial manner have manifested a generous determination to enable the volume to see the light. Very grateful does the Translator feel to them for this signal mark of their friendship.

Mr. Hampden-Cook is responsible for the headings of the paragraphs, and at my express desire has inserted some additional notes.

I have further to express my gratitude to Rev. Frank Baliard, M.A., B.Sc., Lond., at present of Sharrow, Sheffield, for some very valuable assistance which he has most kindly given in connexion with the Introductions to the several books.

I have also the pleasure of acknowledging the numerous valuable and suggestive criticisms with which I have been favoured on some parts of the work, by an old friend, Rev. Sydney Thelwall, B.A., of Leamington, a clergyman of the Church of England, whom I have known for many years as a painstaking and accurate scholar, a well-read theologian. and a thoughtful and devout student of Scripture.

I am very thankful to Mr. H. L. Gethin. Mr. S. Hales, Mr. J. A. Latham, and Rev. T. A. Seed, for the care with which they have read the proof sheets.

And now this Translation is humbly and prayerfully commended to God's gracious blessing.

R.F.W.

/1. I am aware of what Proffessor Blackie has written on this subject (Aeschylus, Pref. p. viii) but the problem endeavoured to be solved in this Translation is as above stated.

/2. A flagrant instance is the "having in a readiness" of 2 Cor. 10.6, A.V. althoglgh in Tyndale we find "and are redy to take vengeaunce," and even Wiclif writes "and we han redi to venge."

/3 Such as McClellan's Four Gospels; Westcott on John's Gospel, John's Epistles, and Hebrews; Hackett on Acts, Lightfoot, and also Ellicott, on various Epistles: Mayor on James; Edwards on I Corinthians and Hebrews; Sanday and Headlam on Romans. Add to these Scrivener's very valuable Introduction to the Criticism of the N.T.

Preface to the Third Edition

For the purposes of this edition the whole volume has been re-set in new type, and, in the hope of increasing the interest and attractiveness of the Translation, all conversations have been spaced out in accordance with modern custom. A freer use than before has been made of capital letters, and by means of small, raised figures, prefixed to words in the text, an indication has been griven whenever there is a footnote. "Capernaum" and "Philadelphia" have been substituted for the less familiar but more literal "Capharnahum" and "Philadelpheia." Many errata have been corrected, and a very considerable number of what seemed to be infelicities or slight inaccuracies in the English have been removed. A few additional footnotes have been inserted, and, for the most part, those for which the Editor is responsible have now the letters ED. added to them.

Sincere thanks are tendered to the many kind friends who have expressed their appreciation of this Translation, or have helped to make it better known, and to the many correspondents who have sent criticisms of the previous editions, and made useful suggestions for the improvement of the volume.

E.H.C.

Abbreviations Used in the Notes

Aorist. Dr. Weymouth's Pamphlet on the Rendering of the Greek Aorist and Perfect Tenses into English.
A.V. Authorised English Version, 1611.
Cp. Compare.

ED. Notes for which the Editor is responsible, wholly or in part.
I.E. That is.
Lit. Literally.
LXX. The Septuagint (Greek) Version of the Old Testament.
n. Note.
nn. Notes.
N.T. New Testament.
O.T. Old Testament.
R.V. Revised English Version, 1881-85.
S.H. Sanday and Headlam's Commentary on 'Romans.'
V.L. Varia Lectio. An alternative reading found in some
Manuscripts of the New Testament.
V.V. Verses.

In accordance with modern English custom, ITALICS are used to indicate emphasis.

Old Testament quotations are printed in small capitals.

During Christ's earthly ministry even His disciples did not always recognize His super-human nature and dignity. Accordingly, in the Gospels of this Translation, it is only when the Evangelists themselves use of Him the words "He," "Him," "His," that these are spelt with capital initial letters.

The spelling of "me" and "my" with small initial letters, when used by Christ Himself in the Gospels, is explained by the fact that, before His Resurrection, He did not always emphasize His own super-human nature and dignity.

The Good News as Recorded by Matthew

There are ample reasons for accepting the uniform tradition which from earliest times has ascribed this Gospel to Levi the son of Alphaeus, who seems to have changed his name to 'Matthew' on becoming a disciple of Jesus. Our information as to his subsequent life is very scanty. After the feast which he made for his old friends (Lu 5:29) his name only appears in the New Testament in the list of the twelve Apostles. Early Christian writers add little to our knowledge of him, but his life seems to have been quiet and somewhat ascetic. He is also generally represented as having died a natural death. Where his Gospel was written, or where he himself laboured, we cannot say.

Not a little controversy has arisen as to the form in which this Gospel first appeared, that is, as to whether we have in the Greek MSS. an original document or a translation from an earlier Aramaic writing. Modern scholarship inclines to the view that the book is not a translation, but was probably written in Greek by Matthew himself, upon the basis of a previously issued collection of "Logia" or discourses, to the existence of which Papias, Irenaeus, Pantaenus, Origen, Eusebius and Jerome all testify.

The date of the Gospel, as we know it, is somewhat uncertain, but the best critical estimates are included between 70 and 90, A.D. Perhaps, with Harnack, we may adopt 75, A.D.

The book was evidently intended for Jewish converts, and exhibits Jesus as the God-appointed Messiah and King, the fulfiller of the Law and of the highest expectations of the Jewish nation. This speciality of aim rather enhances than diminishes its general value. Renan found reason for pronouncing it "the most important book of Christendom- the most important book which has ever been written." Its aim is manifestly didactic rather than chronological.

The Good News as Recorded by Mark

This Gospel is at once the briefest and earliest of the four. Modern research confirms the ancient tradition that the author was Barnabas's cousin, "John, whose other name was Mark," who during Paul's first missionary tour "departed from them" at Pamphylia, "and returned to Jerusalem" (see Ac 12:12,25; 15:37,39; Co 4:1O; 2Ti 4:11; Phm 1:24; 1Pe 5:13). His defection appeared to Paul sufficiently serious to warrant an emphatic refusal to take him with him on a second tour, but in after years the breach was healed and we find Mark with Paul again when he writes to Colossae, and he is also mentioned approvingly in the second Letter to Timothy.

Scholars are now almost unanimous in fixing the date of this Gospel between 63 and 70, A. D. There is no valid reason for questioning the usual view that it was written in Rome. Clement, Eusebius, Jerome and Epiphanius, all assert that this was so. That the book was mainly intended for Gentiles, and especially Romans, seems probable from internal evidence. Latin forms not occurring in other Gospels, together with explanations of Jewish terms and customs, and the omission of all reference to the Jewish Law, point in this direction. Its vividness of narration and pictorial minuteness of observation bespeak the testimony of an eye-witness, and the assertion of Papias, quoted by Eusebius, that Mark was "the interpreter of Peter" is borne out by the Gospel itself no less than by what we otherwise know of Mark and Peter.

In a real though not mechanical sense, this is "the Gospel of Peter," and its admitted priority to the Gospels of Matthew and Luke affords substantial reason for the assumption that it is to some extent the source whence they derive their narratives, although Papias distinctly affirms that Mark made no attempt at giving a carefully arranged history such as that at which Luke confessedly aimed.

In spite of the witness of most uncial MSS. and the valiant pleading of Dean Burgon and others, modern scholars are well nigh unanimous in asserting that the last twelve verses of this Gospel are an appendix. Yet less cannot honestly be said than that they "must have been of very early date," and that they embody "a true apostolic tradition which may have been written by some companion or successor of the original author." In one Armenian MS. they are attributed to Aristion.

The Good News as Recorded by Luke

Modern research has abundantly confirmed the ancient tradition that the anonymous author of the third Gospel is none other than "Luke the beloved physician" and the narrator of the "Acts of the Apostles" (see. Col 4:14; 2Ti 4:11; Phm 1:24). Even Renan acknowledges this, and the objections of a few extremists appear to have been sufficiently answered.

The date is not easy to settle. The main problem is whether the book was written before or after the destruction of Jerusalem in 70, A.D. Not a few scholars whose views merit great respect still think that it preceded that event, but the majority of critics believe otherwise. Three principal dates have been suggested, 63, A.D., 80, A.D., 100, A.D. If we accept 80, A. D., we shall be in substantial accord with Harnack, McGiffert, and Plummer, who fairly represent the best consensus of scholarly opinion.

There is no evidence as to where this Gospel was composed, although its general style suggests the influence of some Hellenic centre. Its special characteristics are plain. It is written in purer Greek than the other Gospels, and is manifestly the most historic and artistic. It has also the widest outlook, having obviously been compiled for Gentiles, and, especially, for Greeks. The Author was evidently an educated man and probably a physician, and was also a close observer.

Eighteen of the parables and six of the miracles found here are not recorded elsewhere. Those "portions of the Gospel narrative which Luke alone has preserved for us, are among the most beautiful treasures which we possess, and we owe them in a great measure to his desire to make his collection as full as possible." Luke's object was rather to write history than construct an "apology" and for this reason his order is generally chronological.

This Gospel is often termed, and not without reason, "the Gospel of Paul." Luke's close association with the great Apostle-an association to which the record in the Acts and also the Pauline Letters bear testimony-at once warrants and explains the ancient assumption that we have here a writing as truly coloured by the influence of Paul as that of Mark was by Peter. This is especially the Gospel of gratuitous and universal salvation. Its integrity has recently been placed beyond dispute. Marcion's edition of it in 140, A.D., was a mutilation of the original!

The Good News as Recorded by John

In spite of its rejection by Marcion and the Alogi, the fourth Gospel was accepted by most Christians at the end of the second century as having been written by the Apostle John. In the present day the preponderating tendency among scholars favours the traditional authorship. On the other hand the most recent scrutiny asserts: "Although many critics see no adequate reason for accepting the tradition which assigns the book to the Apostle John, and there are several cogent reasons to the contrary, they would hardly deny that nevertheless the volume is Johannine-in the sense that any historical element throughout its pages may be traced back directly or indirectly to that Apostle and his school."

As regards the date, no more definite period can be indicated than that suggested by Harnack-between 80, A.D., and 110, A.D. But that it was written in Ephesus is practically certain, and there is evidence that it was composed at the request of Elders and believers belonging to the Churches of Roman Asia.

The special characteristics which render the book unique in literature are unmistakable, but scarcely admit of brief expression. It is manifestly supplementary to the other Gospels and assumes that they are known and are true. The differences between the fourth Gospel and the other three may be easily exaggerated, but it must be acknowledged that they exist. They relate, (1) to the ministry of Christ, and (2) to His person. As to the former it is impossible to correlate all the references to distinct events, for whilst the Synoptics appear to contemplate little more than the life and work of a single year, from John's standpoint there can scarcely have been less than three years concerned. As to the person of Christ, it must be owned that although the fourth Gospel makes no assertion which contradicts the character of Teacher and Reformer attributed to Him by the Synoptics, it presents to us a personage so enwrapped in mystery and dignity as altogether to transcend ordinary human nature. This transcendent Personality is indeed the avowed centre of the whole record, and His portrayal is its avowed purpose. Yet whilst the writer never clearly reveals to us who he himself is, it is equally manifest that his own convictions constitute the matrix in which the discourses and events are imbedded, and that there is nothing in this matrix to render that which it contains unreal or untrustworthy.

The Acts of the Apostles

The authorship of this book has been much discussed, but it may now be affirmed with certainty that the writer of our third Gospel is also the author of "the Acts," and that he speaks from the standpoint of an eye-witness in the four we sections (16:10-17; 20:5-15; 21:1-18; 27:1-28:16), and is known in Paul's Letters as "Luke the beloved physician" (Col 4:14; 2Ti 4:11; Phm 1:24). The date necessarily depends upon that of the third Gospel. If the latter was written before the destruction of Jerusalem, then Luke's second work may well have been issued between 66 and 70, A.D. But the tendency, in the present day, is to date the Gospel somewhere between 75 and 85, A.D., after the destruction of the city. In that case "the Acts" may be assigned to any period between 80 and 90, A.D. The latter conclusion, though by no means certain, is perhaps the more probable.

The familiar title of the book is somewhat unfortunate, for it is manifestly not the intention of the writer to describe the doings of the Apostles generally, but rather just so much of the labours of Peter and Paul-and especially the latter-as will serve to illustrate the growth of the early Church, and at the same time exhibit the emancipation of Christianity from its primitive Judaic origin and environment.

It is plain that the writer was contemporary with the events he describes, and although his perfect ingenuousness ceaselessly connects his narrative with history, in no case has he been proved to be in error. The intricacy of the connexions between this record and the Pauline Letters will be best estimated from a study of Paley's Horae Paulinae. We know nothing definite as to the place where the Acts was written, nor the sources whence the information for the earlier portion of the narrative was obtained. But it may be truthfully affirmed that from the modern critical ordeal the work emerges as a definite whole, and rather confirmed than weakened in regard to its general authenticity.

Paul's Letter to the Romans

The four books of the New Testament known as the Letters to the Romans, Corinthians, and Galatians, are allowed by practically all critics, including some of the most "destructive," to be genuine productions of the Apostle Paul. Opinions vary as to the order of their composition. The latest research tends to put 'Galatians' first, and 'Romans' last, in the period between 53 and 58 A. D. The date generally assigned to the Roman Letter is 58 A.D., but recently Harnack, McGiffert, Clemen and others have shown cause for putting it some four years earlier. The chronology of the period is necessarily very complicated. It must suffice, therefore, to regard this Letter as having been written, at either of these dates, from Corinth, where Paul was staying in the course of his third missionary tour. He was hoping to go to Rome, by way of Jerusalem, and then proceed to Spain (15:24; Ac 24:21).

The object of this Letter was to prepare the Christians in Rome for his visit, and make a clear statement of the new doctrines which he taught. It is probable that the crisis in Galatia, to which the Letter sent thither bears witness, had driven the Apostle's thoughts in the direction of the subject of Justification, and he was apparently much troubled by the persistence of Jewish unbelief. Hence the present Letter has been well termed "the Gospel according to Paul."

We know really nothing about the Christians then in Rome beyond what we find here. It is, however, fairly certain that reports concerning the Saviour would be taken to that city by proselytes, both before and after the events described in Acts 2, and we know that there was a large Jewish population there amongst whom the seed would be sown. Some critics have thought "that a note addressed to Ephesus lies embedded in the 16th chapter," because, they say, it is "inconceivable that Paul could have intimately known so many individuals in a Church like that in Rome to which he was personally a stranger." But this is by no means demonstrated, nor is there evidence that the Church there was founded by any other Apostle.

Paul's First Letter to the Corinthians

The genuineness of the two Letters to the Corinthians has never been seriously disputed. The first was written by the Apostle Paul, probably in the early spring of 56 A.D., just before he left Ephesus for Troas in the course of his third missionary tour (Ac 19). The Church in Corinth had been founded by him during his previous tour (Ac 18). After some hesitation he had been induced to preach in Corinth, and in spite of the opposition of the Jews such great success attended his efforts that he remained there for more than eighteen months. The furious attack upon him which was frustrated by Gallio gave impetus to the new cause, so that when the Apostle left, there was a comparatively strong Church there, consisting mostly of Greeks, but including not a few Jews also. The dangers, however, arising out of the temperament and circumstances of the Corinthians soon manifested themselves. The city was the capital of Roman Greece, a wealthy commercial centre, and the home of a restless, superficial intellectualism. Exuberant verbosity, selfish display, excesses at the Lord's table, unseemly behaviour of women at meetings for worship, and also abuse of spiritual gifts, were complicated by heathen influences and the corrupting customs of idolatry. Hence the Apostle's pleas, rebukes, and exhortations. Most noteworthy of all is his forceful treatment of the subject of the Resurrection of Christ; and this only a quarter of a century after the event. Of the Letter mentioned in 5:9 we know nothing.

Paul's Second Letter to the Corinthians

The second Letter to the Corinthians was probably written in the autumn of 56 A.D., the first Letter to them having been sent in the spring of that year. But there are other letters of which we have no clear account. One, lost to us, evidently preceded the first Letter (1Co 5:9). In our "second" Letter we find mention (2:2,4) of a severe communication which could not but give pain. Can this have been our "first" to the Corinthians? Some think not, in which case there must have been an "intermediate" letter. This some students find in 2Co 10 1-8:1O. If so, there must have been four letters. Some have thought that in 2Co 6:14-7:1, and 8, 9, yet another is embedded, making possibly five in all. The reader must form his own conclusions, inasmuch as the evidence is almost entirely internal. On the whole it would seem that our first Letter, conveyed by Titus, had produced a good effect in the Corinthian Church, but that this wore off, and that Titus returned to the Apostle in Ephesus with such disquieting news that a visit of Paul just then to Corinth would have been very embarrassing, alike for the Church and the Apostle. Hence, instead of going, he writes a "painful" letter and sends it by the same messenger, proceeding himself to Troas and thence to Macedonia, where, in great tension of spirit, he awaits the return of Titus. At last there comes a reassuring account, the relief derived from which is so great that our second Letter is written, with the double purpose of comforting those who had been so sharply rebuked and of preventing the recurrence of the evils which had called forth the remonstrance. In this way both the tenderness and the severity of the present Letter may be explained.

Paul's Letter to the Galatians

There is no question as to the genuineness of this Pauline Letter, but unlike most other writings of the Apostle it was addressed to "Churches" rather than to a single community.

Formerly it was not easy to decide the precise meaning of the term "Galatia." Opinions differed on the subject. The "North Galatian theory," contended for by some German scholars, maintained that the Letter was addressed to the Churches of Ancyra, Tavium, Pessinus and possibly to those in other cities. The "South Galatian theory," which now holds the field in English-speaking countries, is to the effect that the congregations intended were those of Pisidian Antioch, Iconium, Derbe and Lystra; and this is strongly supported by the unique resemblance between this Letter and Paul's sermon in Pisidian Antioch (Ac 13:14-41). In any case the population was very mixed, consisting of Phrygians, Greeks, Romans, Gauls and Jews.

The date of the Letter cannot be exactly fixed. The periods assigned by recent scholarship vary from 46 A.D. to 58 A.D., but the medium estimate of 53 A.D., adopted by Harnack and

Ramsay, satisfies all the requirements of the case.

The Apostle certainly visited Galatia during his second missionary tour, perhaps about 51 A. D., and, although suffering from illness, was received with enthusiasm. After a short stay he departed cherishing a joyful confidence as to his converts there. But when, less than three years afterwards, he came again, he found that the leaven of Judaism had produced a definite apostasy, insomuch that both the freedom of individual believers and his own Apostolic authority were in danger.

Even his personal presence (Ac 18:23) did not end the difficulty. Hence, possibly during his journey between Macedonia and Achaia, he sent this Letter. Its rugged and incoherent style shows that it was dictated under great stress of feeling, and the doctrine of justification by faith is stated more emphatically than in any other of his writings. But his earnest insistence upon the "fruit borne by the Spirit" proves that his ideal of practical holiness was rather strengthened than impaired by his plea for Faith as the mainspring of Christian life.

Paul's Letter to the Ephesians

This appears to have been a kind of circular Letter to the Churches in Roman Asia, and was not addressed exclusively to the Church in Ephesus.

Ephesus was a well-known seaport and the principal city in Roman Asia. It was famous alike for its wonderful temple, containing the shrine of Artemis, and for its vast theatre, which was capable of accommodating 50,000 persons.

Paul was forbidden at first to preach in Roman Asia (Ac 16:6), but he afterwards visited Ephesus in company with Priscilla and Aquila (Ac 18:19). About three years later (Ac 19:1) he came again and remained for some time-probably from 54 to 57 A. D.-preaching and arguing in the school of Tyrannus, until driven away through the tumult raised by Demetrius. He then went to Jerusalem, by way of Miletus, but was arrested in the uproar created by the Jews and was taken first to Caesarea (Ac 23:23), and thence to Rome (Ac 28:16). This was probably in the spring of 61 A.D.

Late in 62 or early in 63 A.D., this Letter was written, together with the companion Letters to the Colossians and Philemon.

Paul's Letter to the Philippians

This Letter was written shortly before that to the Ephesians, probably late in 61 or early in 62 A.D. Epaphroditus had been sent to Rome to assure the Apostle, in his imprisonment, of the tender and practical sympathy of the Philippian disciples (Php 2:25; 4:15,16). The messenger, however, fell ill upon his arrival, and only on his recovery could Paul, as in this Letter, express his appreciation of the thoughtful love of the Philippians.

The Apostle appears to have visited the city three times. In 52 A.D. it was the place of his first preaching in Europe (Ac 16:12); but he came again in 57 and in 58 A.D. (Ac 20:2,6), on the last occasion spending the Passover season there.

Two special traits in the Macedonian character are recognized by the Apostle in this Letter; the position and influence of women, and the financial liberality of the Philippians. It is remarkable that a Church displaying such characteristics, and existing in a Roman "colonia," should have lived, as this one did, "without a history, and have perished without a memorial."

Paul's Letter to the Colossians

This Letter belongs to the same group as those to the Ephesians and Philemon, and was probably written from Rome about 63 A. D. Colossae was a town in Phrygia (Roman Asia), on the river Lycus, and was destroyed by an earthquake in the seventh year of Nero's reign. The Church there was not founded by Paul himself (Col 2:1), but by Epaphras (Col 1:7; 4:12), and this Letter arose out of a visit which Epaphras paid to the Apostle, for the purpose of discussing with him the development, at Colossae, of certain strange doctrines which may possibly have been a kind of early Gnosticism. Paul here writes to support the authority and confirm the teaching of Epaphras.

Paul's First Letter to the Thessalonians

During his second missionary tour (Ac 17), Paul came to Thessalonica and preached the Good News there with no little success. The city-which had had its name given it by Cassander, after his wife, the sister of Alexander the Great-was the most populous in Macedonia, besides being a "free city" and the seat of the Roman pro-consular administration. Its modern name is Saloniki.

Very soon the unbelieving Jews stirred up the mob against Paul and Silas, and dragged Jason before the magistrates. Hence the brethren sent the missionaries away by night to Beroea, being alarmed for their safety. As the Apostle was naturally anxious about the persecuted flock which he had been obliged to leave behind, he made two attempts to return to them, but these being frustrated (1Th 2:18), he then sent Timothy, from Athens, to inquire after their welfare and encourage them.

The report brought back was on the whole satisfactory, but left occasion for the self-defence, the warnings and the exhortations of this Letter, which was then sent from Corinth, probably in 53 A.D.

Paul's Second Letter to the Thessalonians

This Letter was written from Corinth not long after the preceding one, and probably in the year 54 A.D. Its occasion was the reception of tidings from Thessalonica which showed that there had been a measure of misapprehension of the Apostle's teaching in regard to the Return of the Lord Jesus, and also that there was a definitely disorderly section in the Church there, capable of doing great harm.

Hence Paul writes to correct the error into which his converts had fallen, and at the same time he uses strong language as to the treatment to be dealt out to those members of the Church who were given to idleness and insubordination.

Paul's First Letter to Timothy

There has never been any real doubt among Christian people as to the authorship of the three "pastoral" Letters. But definite objections to their genuineness have been made in recent times upon the ground of such internal evidence as their style, the indications they present of advanced organization, their historic standpoint and their references to developed heresy.

Says one scholar, "While there is probably nothing in them to which the Apostle would have objected, they must be regarded on account of their style as the product of one who had been taught by Paul and now desired to convey certain teachings under cover of his name. The date need not be later than 80 A.D."

Yet a thorough examination of the matter does not support such objections. It is certain that the three Letters stand or fall together, and there is no sufficient reason for dismissing the ancient conclusion that they are all the genuine work of Paul, and belong to the last years of his life, 66-67 A.D.

This first Letter was probably written from Macedonia.

Paul's Second Letter to Timothy

The marks of genuineness in this Letter are very pronounced. For instance, the thanksgiving, the long list of proper names-twenty-three in number-the personal details and the manifest tone of sincerity and earnestness. Hence it is accepted as Paul's even by some who reject the former Letter and that addressed to Titus. But it is inseparable from the others, and was probably written from Rome during the Apostle's second imprisonment. It is his last Letter known to us, and its apparent date is 67 A.D.

Paul's Letter to Titus

This Letter was probably written from Ephesus in 67 A.D. Titus, who was a Greek by birth, is mentioned in eleven other places in the Pauline Letters and always with marked approval (2Co 2:13; 7:6,13,14; 8:6,16,23; 12:18; Ga 2:1,3; 2Ti 4:10). He was often a trusted messenger to the Churches, his last errand being to Dalmatia. Tradition confirms the inference commonly drawn from this Letter that he was long the Bishop of the Church in Crete, and regards Candia as having been his birthplace.

Paul's Letter to Philemon

This Letter (63 A.D.) was written as the result of Paul's deep interest in Onesimus, a slave who had fled from Colossae to Rome to get free from Philemon his master (Col 4:9).

"A Phrygian slave was one of the lowest known types to be found in the Roman world, displaying all the worst features of character which the servile condition developed. Onesimus had proved no exception. He ran away from his master, and, as Paul thought probable (verses 18,19), not without helping himself to a share of his master's possessions. By the help of what he had stolen, and by the cleverness which afterwards made him so helpful to Paul, he made his way to Rome, naturally drawn to the great centre, and prompted both by a desire to hide himself and by a youthful yearning to see the utmost the world could show of glory and of vice.

"But whether feeling his loneliness, or wearied with a life of vice, or impoverished and reduced to want, or seized with a fear of detection, he made his way to Paul, or unbosomed himself to some Asiatic he saw on the street. And as he stepped out of the coarse debauchery and profanity of the crowded resorts of the metropolis into the room hallowed by the presence of Paul, he saw the foulness of the one life and the beauty of the other, and was persuaded to accept the gospel he had so often heard in his master's house.

"How long he remained with Paul does not appear, but it was long enough to impress on the Apostle's mind that this slave was no common man. Paul had devoted and active friends by him, but this slave, trained to watch his master's wants and to execute promptly all that was entrusted to him, became almost indispensable to the Apostle. But to retain him, he feels, would be to steal him, or at any rate to deprive Philemon of the pleasure of voluntarily sending him to minister to him (verse 14). He therefore sends him back with this Letter, so exquisitely worded that it cannot but have secured the forgiveness and cordial reception of Onesimus" (Marcus Dods, D.D., New Testament Introduction).

The Letter to the Hebrews

As regards the date of this Letter, the only sure conclusion appears to be that it was before 70 A.D. The book itself claims to have been written at the end of the Jewish Age (1:2; 9:26), whilst the earthly temple was still in existence (9:8), and it is inconceivable that such an overwhelming comment upon the writer's whole position as that afforded by the destruction of Jerusalem would have been overlooked, had it been available. Hence 67-68 A.D. may with probability be alleged as the time of composition. The only fact clear as to the author is that he was not the Apostle Paul. The early Fathers did not attribute the book to Paul, nor was it until the seventh century that the tendency to do this, derived from Jerome, swelled into an ecclesiastical practice. From the book itself we see that the author must have been a Jew and a Hellenist, familiar with Philo as well as with the Old Testament, a friend of Timothy and well-known to many of those whom he addressed, and not an Apostle but decidedly acquainted with Apostolic thoughts; and that he not only wrote before the destruction of Jerusalem but apparently himself was never in Palestine. The name of Barnabas, and also that of Priscilla, has been suggested, but in reality all these distinctive marks appear to be found only in Apollos. So that with Luther, and not a few modern scholars, we must either attribute it to him or give up the quest.

There has never been any question as to the canonicity of this Letter, nor can there be any doubt as to its perennial value to the Church of Christ. Where it was written cannot be decided. "The brethren from Italy" (13:24) proves nothing. Nor is it possible to decide to whom it was sent. "The Hebrews," to whom it was addressed, may have been resident in Jerusalem, Alexandria, Ephesus, or Rome. The most remarkable feature of the Letter is manifestly its references to the old Covenant. Here there is a mingling of reverence and iconoclasm. The unquestionably divine origin of the Jewish dispensation is made use of for laying emphasis upon the infinitely superior glory of the Christian order. Thus an a fortiori argument pervades the whole -if the shadow was divine, how much more must the substance be! "The language of the Epistle, both in vocabulary and style, is purer and more vigorous than that of any other book of the New Testament" (Westcott).

James's Letter

Four persons bearing the name of 'James' are mentioned in the New Testament.

(1) The Apostle, the son of Zabdi. (2) The Apostle, the son of Alphaeus. (3) The son of Mary the wife of Clopas. (4) The Lord's brother, mentioned as such along with Joses, Simon and Judah, and prominent in the Acts (12:17; 15:13; 21:18).

The last-named was also known as 'James the Just' and is represented by tradition as having led an ascetic life, which ended in martyrdom. He was undoubtedly Bishop, or President, of the Church in Jerusalem and in all probability this Letter was written by him from that city.

There has been some difference of opinion as to the date of the book. The majority of scholars insist that both the internal and external evidence point to its having been written between 44 and 50 A. D., before the earliest of Paul's Letters. But, on the other hand, the solemn emphasis which the author lays upon the immediateness of the Lord's Return (5:7,8,9) may be regarded as a moral proof of a date very much nearer the winding up of the Mosaic dispensation in 70 A. D.

The Letter may have been a Jewish one, addressed to the Christian converts from Judaism who were scattered abroad, within or beyond the limits of the Roman Empire. Luther deemed it "an Epistle of straw," by reason of its insistence upon the vital importance of 'works.' But its practical ideal assumes the same basis of Christian faith as is found in the Letters of Paul. The opening references to severe trial seem to show that the persecution begun by Herod Agrippa had already been repeated elsewhere. If the later date of the book be admitted, the persecution must then, of course, have been that under Nero.

Peter's First Letter

The state of things described in this Letter answers to what we find in the first Letter to Timothy, and points to the same period. The "fiery trial" referred to is probably the persecution which, begun by Nero, in 64 A.D., in order to divert attention from himself, was continued throughout the Roman Empire.

The Letter seems to be primarily addressed to those who regarded Peter as the Apostle to the Jews, although it is manifest that he did not think of these alone. The fact that it is "full of Pauline thought and Pauline language," is accounted for by the well-grounded supposition that Peter arrived in Rome shortly before Paul was released. So that this Letter, probably written about 65-66 A.D., was definitely intended to set before the Churches of Roman Asia "the inspiring vision of the two Apostles working and planning together in the capital."

This would be at once the clearest lesson the Churches could have concerning their unity, and a great encouragement to those then undergoing tribulation and persecution on behalf of Christ.

Peter's Second Letter

It is impossible to speak with any certainty as to either the date or the authorship of this Letter. From the beginning there have been doubts as to its genuineness and canonicity, and these are represented to-day in the differing judgements of critics equally able and sincere.

It has, however, unquestionably had a place in the canon of the New Testament since the Council of Laodicea in 372 A.D., and there is certainly no such decisive evidence against it as to warrant our omitting it from the New Testament.

It would appear that the writer, whoever he was, had seen the Letter from Jude, and bore it in mind in this his plea for such character and conduct on the part of believers as were worthy of their faith and would prepare them for the Coming of the Lord. The whole Letter constitutes an earnest appeal for practical holiness.

John's First Letter

That this Letter was the actual work of the Apostle John, the son of Zabdi, has been abundantly testified from the very earliest times.

Some modern critics have doubted it, on the ground of internal evidence. But a calm survey of the whole case does not bear out their objections. Dr. Salmon well says that no explanation of the origin of the Epistle fits the facts so well as the one which has always prevailed. It seems to have been addressed to the Church at large, with perhaps special reference to the Churches in Roman Asia.

The connexion between this Letter and the fourth Gospel is "intimate and organic. The Gospel is objective and the Epistle subjective. The Gospel suggests principles of conduct which the Epistle lays down explicitly. The

Epistle implies facts which the Gospel states as historically true."

This Letter appears to have been written from Ephesus, and critics have usually assigned 95 A. D., or some other year equally late in the Apostolic age, as the probable date of its composition. On the other hand the internal evidence points to a date immediately preceding the destruction of Jerusalem in 70 A.D. See 2:8 (last clause); 2:18; 4:3; and note the expectation of a speedy Coming of Christ (2:28; 3:2)-an expectation which seems almost to have ceased in the early Church after that date.

John's Second Letter

Although we are unable to fix the exact date of this Letter or the place at which it was written, there is sufficient evidence, both external and internal, to warrant our acceptance of it as a genuine work of the Apostle John.

Some have thought that the "lady" addressed stands for an unknown Church, but upon careful consideration it appears more reasonable and natural to regard the Letter as having been a private one. It is impossible to discover the name of the individual to whom it was sent, but both this and the following Letter may be taken as "precious specimens of the private correspondence of the beloved Apostle."

John's Third Letter

There can be no doubt that this Letter was addressed to an individual person. We cannot affix to it a definite date, or place, but the most natural supposition-which there is nothing to contradict-is that it came from the Apostle in Ephesus, about the same time as the preceding Letter.

The special mention of Diotrephes and his behaviour points indeed to a somewhat advanced development in the Church to which Galus belonged, but such characters are all too possible at any juncture to afford in this instance any guarantee of a later date.

In this, as in the preceding Letters, the writer's great concern is that transcendental truth should be embodied in practical holiness.

Jude's Letter

Of the time and place of the composition of this Letter we know nothing beyond what may be inferred from its contents. These seem to show that it was written in Palestine, and the absence of any reference to so striking an event as the destruction of Jerusalem points to a date earlier than 70 A. D.

It has, however, been thought that such a rebuke of error and licentiousness as that which this Letter contains can only apply to the forms of Gnosticism known to have existed in the first quarter of the second century. But there is no reason to doubt that the author was the man he asserts he was, the brother of James, the head of the Church in Jerusalem. He was, therefore, not an Apostle but one of the Lord's brothers.

The abiding value of the Letter consists in its severe condemnation of merely professional Christianity, and its remarkably beautiful doxology.

The Revelation of John

The Apocalypse was written either in 67, or in 96, A.D. An oft-quoted statement of Irenaeus that it, or its author- there is no word inserted to indicate which of the two he meant-"was seen" about the end of the reign of Domitian, is regarded by many as a conclusive proof of the later date. On the other hand, the "internal evidence"-the evidence, that is, furnished by the contents of the book itself-appears to point even more unmistakably to the earlier date. E.g-., in 11:1,2,8, the Holy City and the earthly Temple are spoken of as being still in existence, and as about to be trodden under foot by the Gentiles.

The language of the book has also a bearing upon the problem of its date. Although other explanations have been suggested, the many Hebrew idioms that it contains as compared with the much purer Greek of the fourth Gospel- which was probably by the same author-seem to indicate that it was written long before that Gospel, at a time when the Apostle had as yet only an imperfect acquaintance with the Greek language.

Dr. Stuart Russell, in his work The Parousia, has contended for the belief that the fall of Jerusalem and Judaism in 70 A.D. marked a stupendous epoch in the unseen world, a personal-although unrecorded-return of the Saviour to the earth then taking place (cp. Ac 7:55; 9:7; 1Co 9:1), accompanied by a spiritual judgement of bygone generations, a resurrection from Hades to Heaven of the faithful of past ages, and an ingathering of saints then on earth into the Father's House of many mansions (Mt 24:31; Joh 14:3; 1Th 4:17; 2Th 2:1).

If this belief ever obtains general acceptance the earlier date of the Apocalypse will also be regarded as fully established. For it will then be seen that the book describes beforehand events which took place in 70 A.D. and the years immediately preceding, partly on earth and partly in the spiritual world, and is mainly concerned with the downfall of the earthly Jerusalem and the setting up of Christ's heavenly Kingdom-the new Jerusalem. And its many mysterious symbols will be seen to have been a cipher of which the first Christians held the key, but which hid its meaning from their enemies.

Many scholars, however, regard the book as a document of Nero's time carefully incorporated in one written about 90 A.D.: "a Jewish Apocalypse in a Christian framework;" both perhaps being by the same author.-EDITOR.

BOOK 66 REVELATION

001:001 The revelation given by Jesus Christ, which God granted Him, that He might make known to His servants certain events which must shortly come to pass: and He sent His angel and communicated it to His servant John. 001:002 This is the John who taught the truth concerning the Word of God and the truth told us by Jesus Christ-a faithful account of what he had seen. 001:003 Blessed is he who reads and blessed are those who listen to the words of this prophecy and lay to heart what is written in it; for the time for its fulfillment is now close at hand. 001:004 John sends greetings to the seven Churches in the province of Asia. May grace be granted to you, and peace, from Him who is and was and evermore will be; and from the seven Spirits which are before His throne; 001:005 and from Jesus Christ, the truthful witness, the first of the dead to be born to Life, and the Ruler of the kings of the earth. To Him who loves us and has freed us from our sins with His own blood, 001:006 and has formed us into a Kingdom, to be priests to God, His Father- to Him be ascribed the glory and the power until the Ages of the Ages. Amen. 001:007 He is coming in the clouds, and every eye will see Him, and so will those who pierced Him; and all the nations of the earth will gaze on Him and mourn. Even so. Amen. 001:008 "I am the Alpha and the Omega," says the Lord God, "He who is and was and evermore will be-the Ruler of all." 001:009 I John, your brother, and a sharer with you in the sorrows and Kingship and patient endurance of Jesus, found myself in the island of Patmos, on account of the Word of God and the truth told us by Jesus. 001:010 In the Spirit I found myself present on the day of the Lord, and I heard behind me a loud voice which resembled the blast of a trumpet. 001:011 It said, "Write forthwith in a roll an account of what you see, and send it to the seven Churches-to Ephesus, Smyrna, Pergamum, Thyateira, Sardis, Philadelphia and Laodicea." 001:012 I turned to see who it was that was speaking to me; and then I saw seven golden lampstands, 001:013 and in the center of the lampstands some One resembling the Son of Man, clothed in a robe which reached to His feet, and with a girdle of gold across His breast. 001:014 His head and His hair were white, like white wool-as white as snow; and His eyes resembled a flame of fire. 001:015 His feet were like silver-bronze, when it is white-hot in a furnace; and His voice resembled the sound of many waters. 001:016 In His right hand He held seven stars, and a sharp, two-edged sword was seen coming from His mouth; and His glance resembled the sun when it is shining with its full strength. 001:017 When I saw Him, I fell at His feet as if I were dead. But He laid His right hand upon me and said, "Do not be afraid: I am the First and the Last, and the ever-living One. 001:018 I died; but I am now alive until the Ages of the Ages, and I have the keys of the gates of Death and of Hades! 001:019 Write down therefore the things you have just seen, and those which are now taking place, and those which are soon to follow: 001:020 the secret meaning of the seven stars which you have seen in My right hand, and of the seven lampstands of gold. The seven stars are the ministers of the seven Churches, and the seven lampstands are the seven Churches. 002:001 "To the minister of the Church in Ephesus write as follows: "`This is what He who holds the seven stars in the grasp of His right hand says-He who walks to and fro among the seven lampstands of gold. 002:002 I know your doings and your toil and patient suffering. And I know that you cannot tolerate wicked men, but have put to the test those who say that they themselves are Apostles but are not, and you have found them to be liars. 002:003 And you endure patiently and have borne burdens for My sake and have never grown weary. 002:004 Yet I have this against you-that you no longer love Me as you did at first. 002:005 Be mindful, therefore, of the height from which you have fallen. Repent at once, and act as you did at first, or else I will surely come and remove your lampstand out of its place- unless you repent. 002:006 Yet this you have in your favor: you hate the doings of the Nicolaitans, which I also hate. 002:007 "`Let all who have ears give heed to what the Spirit is saying to the Churches. To him who overcomes I will give the privilege of eating the fruit of the Tree of Life, which is in the Paradise of God.' 002:008 "To the minister of the Church at Smyrna write as follows: "`This is what the First and the Last says-He who died and has returned to life. 002:009 Your sufferings I know, and your poverty-but you are rich- and the evil name given you by those who say that they themselves are Jews, and are not, but are Satan's synagogue. 002:010 Dismiss your fears concerning all that you are about to suffer. I tell you that the Devil is about to throw some of you into prison that you may be put to the test, and for ten days you will have to endure persecution. Be faithful to the End, even if you have to die, and then I will give you the victor's Wreath of Life. 002:011 "`Let all who have ears give heed to what the Spirit is saying to the Churches. He who overcomes shall be in no way hurt by the Second Death.' 002:012 "To the minister of the Church at Pergamum write as follows: "`This is what He who has the sharp, two-edged sword says. I know where you dwell. 002:013 Satan's throne is there; and yet you are true to Me, and did not deny your faith in Me, even in the days of Antipas My witness and faithful friend, who was put to death among you, in the place where Satan dwells. 002:014 Yet I have a few things against you, because you have with you some that cling to the teaching of Balaam, who taught Balak to put a stumbling-block in the way of the descendants of Israel- to eat what had been sacrificed to idols, and commit fornication. 002:015 So even you have some that cling in the same way to the teaching of the Nicolaitans. 002:016 Repent, at once; or else I will come to you quickly, and will make war upon them with the sword which is in My mouth. 002:017 "`Let all who have ears give heed to what the Spirit is saying to the Churches. He who overcomes-to him I will give some of the hidden Manna, and a white stone; and-written upon the stone and known only to him who receives it-a new name.' 002:018 "To the minister of the Church at Thyateira write as follows: "`This is what the Son of God says-He who has eyes like a flame of fire, and feet resembling silver-bronze. 002:019 I know your doings, your love, your faith, your service, and your patient endurance; and that of late you have toiled harder than you did at first. 002:020 Yet I have this against you, that you tolerate the woman Jezebel, who calls herself a prophetess and by her teaching leads astray My servants, so that they commit fornication and eat what has been sacrificed to idols. 002:021 I have given her time to repent, but she is determined not to repent of her fornication. 002:022 I tell you that I am about to cast her upon a bed of sickness, and I will severely afflict those who commit adultery with her, unless they repent of conduct such as hers. 002:023 Her children too shall surely die; and all the Churches shall come to know that I am He who searches into men's inmost thoughts; and to each of you I will give a requital which shall be in accordance with what your conduct has been. 002:024 But to you, the rest of you in Thyateira, all who do not hold this teaching and are not the people who have learnt the "deep things," as they call them (the deep things of Satan!)- to you I say that I lay no other burden on you. 002:025 Only that which you already possess, cling to until I come. 002:026 "`And to him who overcomes and obeys My commands to the very end, I will give authority over the nations of the earth. 002:027 And he shall be their shepherd, ruling them with a rod of iron, just as earthenware jars are broken to pieces; and his power over them shall be like that which I Myself have received from My Father; 002:028 and I will give him the Morning Star. 002:029 Let all who have ears give heed to what the Spirit is saying to the Churches.' 003:001 "To the minister of the Church at Sardis write as follows: "`This is what He who has the seven Spirits of God and the seven stars says. I know your doings-you are supposed to be alive, but in reality you are dead. 003:002 Rouse yourself and keep awake, and strengthen those things which remain but have well-nigh perished; for I have found no doings of yours free from imperfection in the sight of My God. 003:003 Be mindful, therefore, of the lessons you have received and heard. Continually lay them to heart, and repent. If, however, you fail to rouse yourself and keep awake, I shall come upon you suddenly like a thief, and you will certainly not know the hour at which I shall come to judge you. 003:004 Yet you have in Sardis a few who have not soiled their garments; and they shall walk with Me in white; for they are worthy. 003:005 "`In this way he who overcomes shall be clothed in white garments; and I will certainly not blot out his name from the Book of Life, but will acknowledge him in the presence of My Father and His angels. 003:006 Let all who have ears give heed to what the Spirit is saying to the Churches.' 003:007 "To the minister of the Church at Philadelphia write as follows: "`This is what the holy One and the true says-He who has the key of David-He who opens and no one shall shut, and shuts and no one shall open. 003:008 I know your doings. I have put an opened door in front of you, which no one can shut; because you have but a little power, and yet you have guarded My word and have not disowned Me. 003:009 I will cause some belonging to Satan's synagogue who say that they themselves are Jews, and are not, but are liars- I will make them come and fall at your feet and know for certain that I have loved you. 003:010 Because in spite of suffering you have guarded My word, I in turn will guard you from that hour of trial which is soon coming upon the whole world, to put to the test the inhabitants of the earth. 003:011 I am coming quickly: cling to that which you already possess, so that your wreath of victory be not taken away from you. 003:012 "`He who overcomes-I will make him a pillar in the sanctuary of My God, and he shall never go out from it again. And I will write on him the name of My God, and the name of the city of My God, the new Jerusalem, which is to come down out of Heaven from My God, and My own new name. 003:013 Let all who have ears give heed to what the Spirit is saying to the Churches.' 003:014 "And to the minister of the Church at Laodicea write as follows: "`This is what the Amen says-the true and faithful witness, the Beginning and Lord of God's Creation. 003:015 I know your doings-you are neither cold nor hot; I would that you were cold or hot! 003:016 Accordingly, because you are lukewarm and neither hot nor cold, before long I will vomit you out of My mouth. 003:017 You say, I am rich, and have wealth stored up, and I stand in need of nothing; and you do not know that if there is a wretched creature it is *you*-pitiable, poor, blind, naked. 003:018 Therefore I counsel you to buy of Me gold refined in the fire that you may become rich, and white robes to put on, so as to hide your shameful nakedness, and eye-salve to anoint your eyes with, so that you may be able to see. 003:019 All whom I hold dear, I reprove and chastise;

therefore be in earnest and repent. 003:020 I am now standing at the door and am knocking. If any one listens to My voice and opens the door, I will go in to be with him and will feast with him, and he shall feast with Me. 003:021 "`To him who overcomes I will give the privilege of sitting down with Me on My throne, as I also have overcome and have sat down with My Father on His throne. 003:022 Let all who have ears give heed to what the Spirit is saying to the Churches.'" 004:001 After all this I looked and saw a door in Heaven standing open, and the voice that I had previously heard, which resembled the blast of a trumpet, again spoke to me and said, "Come up here, and I will show you things which are to happen in the future." 004:002 Immediately I found myself in the Spirit, and saw a throne in Heaven, and some One sitting on the throne. 004:003 The appearance of Him who sat there was like jasper or sard; and encircling the throne was a rainbow, in appearance like an emerald. 004:004 Surrounding the throne there were also twenty-four other thrones, on which sat twenty-four Elders clothed in white robes, with victors' wreaths of gold upon their heads. 004:005 Out from the throne there came flashes of lightning, and voices, and peals of thunder, while in front of the throne seven blazing lamps were burning, which are the seven Spirits of God. 004:006 And in front of the throne there seemed to be a sea of glass, resembling crystal. And midway between the throne and the Elders, and surrounding the throne, were four living creatures, full of eyes in front and behind. 004:007 The first living creature resembled a lion, the second an ox, the third had a face like that of a man, and the fourth resembled an eagle flying. 004:008 And each of the four living creatures had six wings, and in every direction, and within, are full of eyes; and day after day, and night after night, they never cease saying, "Holy, holy, holy, Lord God, the Ruler of all, who wast and art and evermore shalt be." 004:009 And whenever the living creatures give glory and honor and thanks to Him who is seated on the throne, and lives until the Ages of the Ages, 004:010 the twenty-four Elders fall down before Him who sits on the throne and worship Him who lives until the Ages of the Ages, and they cast their wreaths down in front of the throne, 004:011 saying, "It is fitting, O our Lord and God, That we should ascribe unto Thee the glory and the honor and the power; For Thou didst create all things, And because it was Thy will they came into existence, and were created." 005:001 And I saw lying in the right hand of Him who sat on the throne a book written on both sides and closely sealed with seven seals. 005:002 And I saw a mighty angel who was exclaiming in a loud voice, "Who is worthy to open the book and break its seals?" 005:003 But no one in Heaven, or on earth, or under the earth, was able to open the book or look into it. 005:004 And while I was weeping bitterly, because no one was found worthy to open the book or look into it, 005:005 one of the Elders said to me, "Do not weep. The Lion which belongs to the tribe of Judah, the Root of David, has triumphed, and will open the book and break its seven seals." 005:006 Then, midway between the throne and the four living creatures, I saw a Lamb standing among the Elders. He looked as if He had been offered in sacrifice, and He had seven horns and seven eyes. The last-named are the seven Spirits of God, and have been sent far and wide into all the earth. 005:007 So He comes, and now He has taken the book out of the right hand of Him who is seated on the throne. 005:008 And when He had taken the book, the four living creatures and the twenty-four Elders fell down before the Lamb, having each of them a harp and bringing golden bowls full of incense, which represent the prayers of God's people. 005:009 And now they sing a new song. "It is fitting," they say, "that Thou shouldst be the One to take the book And break its seals; Because Thou hast been offered in sacrifice, And hast purchased for God with Thine own blood Some out of every tribe and language and people and nation, 005:010 And hast formed them into a Kingdom to be priests to our God, And they reign over the earth." 005:011 And I looked, and heard what seemed to be the voices of countless angels on every side of the throne, and of the living creatures and the Elders. Their number was myriads of myriads and thousands of thousands, 005:012 and in loud voices they were singing, "It is fitting that the Lamb which has been offered in sacrifice should receive all power and riches and wisdom and might and honor and glory and blessing." 005:013 And as for every created thing in Heaven and on earth and under the earth and on the sea, and everything that was in any of these, I heard them say, "To Him who is seated on the throne, And to the Lamb, Be ascribed all blessing and honor And glory and might, Until the Ages of the Ages!" 005:014 Then the four living creatures said "Amen," and the Elders fell down and worshipped. 006:001 And when the Lamb broke one of the seven seals I saw it, and I heard one of the four living creatures say, as if in a voice of thunder, "Come." 006:002 And I looked and a white horse appeared, and its rider carried a bow; and a victor's wreath was given to him; and he went out conquering and in order to conquer. 006:003 And when the Lamb broke the second seal, I heard the second living creature say, "Come." 006:004 And another horse came out-a fiery-red one; and power was given to its rider to take peace from the earth, and to cause men to kill one another; and a great sword was given to him. 006:005 When the Lamb broke the third seal, I heard the third living creature say, "Come." I looked, and a black horse appeared, its rider carrying a balance in his hand. 006:006 And I heard what seemed to be a voice speaking in the midst of the four living creatures, and saying, "A quart of wheat for a shilling, and three quarts of barley for a shilling; but do not injure either the oil or the wine." 006:007 When the Lamb broke the fourth seal I heard the voice of the fourth living creature say, "Come." 006:008 I looked and a pale-colored horse appeared. Its rider's name was Death, and Hades came close behind

him; and authority was given to them over the fourth part of the earth, to
kill with the sword or with famine or pestilence or by means of the wild
beasts of the earth. 006:009 When the Lamb broke the fifth seal, I saw at
the foot of the altar the souls of those whose lives had been sacrificed
because of the word of God and of the testimony which they had given.
006:010 And now in loud voices they cried out, saying, "How long, O
Sovereign Lord, the holy One and the true, dost Thou delay judgment and
the taking of vengeance upon the inhabitants of the earth for our blood?"
006:011 And there was given to each of them a long white robe, and they
were bidden to wait patiently for a short time longer, until the full number
of their fellow bondservants should also complete-namely of their brethren
who were soon to be killed just as they had been. 006:012 When the Lamb
broke the sixth seal I looked, and there was a great earthquake, and the sun
became as dark as sackcloth, and the whole disc of the moon became like
blood. 006:013 The stars in the sky also fell to the earth, as when a fig-tree,
upon being shaken by a gale of wind, casts its unripe figs to the ground.
006:014 The sky too passed away, as if a scroll were being rolled up, and
every mountain and island was removed from its place. 006:015 The kings
of the earth and the great men, the military chiefs, the wealthy and the
powerful-all, whether slaves or free men- hid themselves in the caves and in
the rocks of the mountains, 006:016 while they called to the mountains and
the rocks, saying, "Fall on us and hide us from the presence of Him who
sits on the throne and from the anger of the Lamb; 006:017 for the day of
His anger-that great day-has come, and who is able to stand?" 007:001 After
this I saw four angels standing at the four corners of the earth, and holding
back the four winds of the earth so that no wind should blow over the earth
or the sea or upon any tree. 007:002 And I saw another angel coming from
the east and carrying a seal belonging to the ever-living God. He called in a
loud voice to the four angels whose work it was to injure the earth and the
sea. 007:003 "Injure neither land nor sea nor trees," he said, "until we have
sealed the bondservants of our God upon their foreheads." 007:004 When
the sealing was finished, I heard how many were sealed out of the tribes of
the descendants of Israel. They were 144,000. 007:005 Of the tribe of
Judah, 12,000 were sealed; Of the tribe of Reuben, 12,000; Of the tribe of
Gad, 12,000; 007:006 Of the tribe of Asher, 12,000; Of the tribe of
Naphtali, 12,000; Of the tribe of Manasseh, 12,000; 007:007 Of the tribe of
Symeon, 12,000; Of the tribe of Levi, 12,000; Of the tribe of Issachar,
12,000; 007:008 Of the tribe of Zebulun, 12,000; Of the tribe of Joseph,
12,000; Of the tribe of Benjamin, 12,000. 007:009 After this I looked, and a
vast host appeared which it was impossible for anyone to count, gathered
out of every nation and from all tribes and peoples and languages, standing
before the throne and before the Lamb, clothed in long white robes, and
carrying palm-branches in their hands. 007:010 In loud voices they were

exclaiming, "It is to our God who is seated on the throne, and to the Lamb, that we owe our salvation!" 007:011 All the angels were standing in a circle round the throne and round the Elders and the four living creatures, and they fell on their faces in front of the throne and worshipped God. 007:012 "Even so!" they cried: "The blessing and the glory and the wisdom and the thanks and the honor and the power and the might are to be ascribed to our God, until the Ages of the Ages! Even so!" 007:013 Then, addressing me, one of the Elders said, "Who are these people clothed in the long white robes? And where have they come from?" 007:014 "My lord, you know," I replied. "They are those," he said, "who have just passed through the great distress, and have washed their robes and made them white in the blood of the Lamb. 007:015 For this reason they stand before the very throne of God, and render Him service, day after day and night after night, in His sanctuary, and He who is sitting upon the throne will shelter them in His tent. 007:016 They will never again be hungry or thirsty, and never again will the sun or any scorching heat trouble them. 007:017 For the Lamb who is in front of the throne will be their Shepherd, and will guide them to watersprings of Life, and God will wipe every tear from their eyes." 008:001 When the Lamb broke the seventh seal, there was silence in Heaven for about half an hour. 008:002 Then I saw the seven angels who are in the presence of God, and seven trumpets were given to them. 008:003 And another angel came and stood close to the altar, carrying a censer of gold; and abundance of incense was given to him that he might place it with the prayers of all God's people upon the golden altar which was in front of the throne. 008:004 And the smoke of the incense rose into the presence of God from the angel's hand, and mingled with the prayers of His people. 008:005 So the angel took the censer and filled it with fire from the altar and flung it to the earth; and there followed peals of thunder, and voices, and flashes of lightning, and an earthquake. 008:006 Then the seven angels who had the seven trumpets made preparations for blowing them. 008:007 The first blew his trumpet; and there came hail and fire, mixed with blood, falling upon the earth; and a third part of the earth was burnt up, and a third part of the trees and all the green grass. 008:008 The second angel blew his trumpet; and what seemed to be a great mountain, all ablaze with fire, was hurled into the sea; and a third part of the sea was turned into blood. 008:009 And a third part of the creatures that were in the sea-those that had life-died; and a third part of the ships were destroyed. 008:010 The third angel blew his trumpet; and there fell from Heaven a great star, which was on fire like a torch. It fell upon a third part of the rivers and upon the springs of water. 008:011 The name of the star is `Wormwood;' and a third part of the waters were turned into wormwood, and vast numbers of the people died from drinking the water, because it had become bitter. 008:012 Then the fourth angel blew his trumpet; and a curse fell upon a third part of the sun, a third part of the moon, and a third part of the stars, so that a third part of them were darkened and for a third of the day, and also of the night, there was no light. 008:013 Then I looked, and I heard a solitary eagle crying in a loud voice, as it flew across the sky, "Alas, alas, alas, for the inhabitants of the earth, because of the significance of the remaining trumpets which the three angels are about to blow!" 009:001 The fifth angel blew his trumpet; and I saw a Star which had fallen from Heaven to the earth; and to him was given the key of the depths of the bottomless pit, 009:002 and he opened the depths of the bottomless pit. And smoke came up out of the pit resembling the smoke of a vast furnace, so that the sun was darkened, and the air also, by reason of the smoke of the pit. 009:003 And from the midst of the smoke there came locusts on to the earth, and power was given to them resembling the power which earthly scorpions possess. 009:004 And they were forbidden to injure the herbage of the earth, or any green thing, or any tree. They were only to injure human beings- those who have not the seal of God on their foreheads. 009:005 Their mission was not to kill, but to cause awful agony for five months; and this agony was like that which a scorpion inflicts when it stings a man. 009:006 And at that time people will seek death, but will by no possibility find it, and will long to die, but death evades them. 009:007 The appearance of the locusts was like that of horses equipped for war. On their heads they had wreaths which looked like gold. 009:008 Their faces seemed human and they had hair like women's hair, but their teeth resembled those of lions. 009:009 They had breast-plates which seemed to be made of steel; and the noise caused by their wings was like that of a vast number of horses and chariots hurrying into battle. 009:010 They had tails like those of scorpions, and also stings; and in their tails lay their power of injuring mankind for five months. 009:011 The locusts had a king over them-the angel of the bottomless pit, whose name in Hebrew is `Abaddon,' while in the Greek he is called `Apollyon.' 009:012 The first woe is past; two other woes have still to come. 009:013 The sixth angel blew his trumpet; and I heard a single voice speaking from among the horns of the golden incense altar which is in the presence of God. 009:014 It said to the sixth angel-the angel who had the trumpet, "Set at liberty the four angels who are prisoners near the great river Euphrates." 009:015 And the four angels who had been kept in readiness for that hour, day, month, and year, were set at liberty, so that they might kill a third part of mankind. 009:016 The number of the cavalry was two hundred millions; I heard their number. 009:017 And this was the appearance of the horses which I saw in my vision- and of their riders. The body-armour of the riders was red, blue and yellow; and the horses' heads were shaped like the heads of lions, while from their mouths there came fire and smoke and sulphur. 009:018 By these three plagues a third part of mankind were destroyed- by the fire and the smoke, and by the sulphur which came from their mouths. 009:019 For the power of the horses is in their mouths and in their tails; their tails being like serpents, and having heads, and it is with them that they inflict injury. 009:020 But the rest of mankind who were not killed by these plagues, did not even then repent and leave the things they had made, so as to cease worshipping the demons, and the idols of gold and silver, bronze, stone, and wood, which can neither see nor hear, nor move. 009:021 Nor did they repent of their murders, their practice of magic, their fornication, or their thefts. 010:001 Then I saw another strong angel coming down from Heaven. He was robed in a cloud, and over his head was the rainbow. His face was like the sun, and his feet resembled pillars of fire. 010:002 In his hand he held a small scroll unrolled; and, planting his right foot on the sea and his left foot on the land, 010:003 he cried out in a loud voice which resembled the roar of a lion. And when he had cried out, each of the seven peals of thunder uttered its own message. 010:004 And when the seven peals of thunder had spoken, I was about to write down what they had said; but I heard a voice from Heaven which told me to keep secret all that the seven peals of thunder had said, and not write it down. 010:005 Then the angel that I saw standing on the sea and on the land, lifted his right hand toward Heaven. 010:006 And in the name of Him who lives until the Ages of the Ages, the Creator of Heaven and all that is in it, of the earth and all that is in it, and of the sea and all that is in it, he solemnly declared, 010:007 "There shall be no further delay; but in the days when the seventh angel blows his trumpet-when he begins to do so- then the secret purposes of God are realized, in accordance with the good news which He gave to His servants the Prophets." 010:008 Then the voice which I had heard speaking from Heaven once more addressed me. It said, "Go and take the little book which lies open in the hand of the angel who is standing on the sea and on the land." 010:009 So I went to the angel and asked him to give me the little book. "Take it," he said, "and eat the whole of it. You will find it bitter when you have eaten it, although in your mouth it will taste as sweet as honey." 010:010 So I took the roll out of the angel's hand and ate the whole of it; and in my mouth it was as sweet as honey, but when I had eaten it I found it very bitter. 010:011 And a voice said to me, "You must prophesy yet further concerning peoples, nations, languages, and many kings." 011:001 Then a reed was given me to serve as a measuring rod; and a voice said, "Rise, and measure God's sanctuary- and the altar-and count the worshipers who are in it. 011:002 But as for the court which is outside the sanctuary, pass it over. Do not measure it; for it has been given to the Gentiles, and for forty-two months they will trample the holy city under foot. 011:003 And I will authorize My two witnesses to prophesy for 1,260 days, clothed in sackcloth. 011:004 "These witnesses are the two olive-trees, and they are the two lamps which stand in the presence of the Lord of the earth. 011:005

And if any one seeks to injure them-fire comes from their mouths and devours their enemies; and if any one seeks to injure them, he will in this way certainly be killed. 011:006 They have power given to them to seal up the sky, so that no rain may fall so long as they continue to prophesy; and power over the waters to turn them into blood, and to smite the earth with various plagues whenever they choose to do so. 011:007 "And when they have fully delivered their testimony, the Wild Beast which is to rise out of the bottomless pit will make war upon them and overcome them and kill them. 011:008 And their dead bodies are to lie in the broad street of the great city which spiritually is designated `Sodom' and `Egypt,' where indeed their Lord was crucified. 011:009 And men belonging to all peoples, tribes, languages and nations gaze at their dead bodies for three days and a half, but they refuse to let them be laid in a tomb. 011:010 The inhabitants of the earth rejoice over them and are glad and will send gifts to one another; for these two Prophets had greatly troubled the inhabitants of the earth." 011:011 But at the end of the three days and a half the breath of life from God entered into them, and they rose to their feet; and all who saw them were terrified. 011:012 Then they heard a loud voice calling to them out of Heaven, and bidding them come up; and they went up to Heaven in the cloud, and their enemies saw them go. 011:013 And just as that time there was a great earthquake, and a tenth part of the city was overthrown. 7,000 people were killed in the earthquake, and the rest were terrified and gave glory to the God of Heaven. 011:014 The second Woe is past; the third Woe will soon be here. 011:015 The seventh angel blew his trumpet; and there followed loud voices in Heaven which said, "The sovereignty of the world now belongs to our Lord and His Christ; and He will be King until the Ages of the Ages." 011:016 Then the twenty-four Elders, who sit on thrones in the presence of God, fell on their faces and worshipped God, 011:017 saying, "We give thee thanks, O Lord God, the Ruler of all, Who art and wast, because Thou hast exerted Thy power, Thy great power, and hast become King. 011:018 The nations grew angry, and Thine anger has come, and the time for the dead to be judged, and the time for Thee to give their reward to Thy servants the Prophets and to Thy people, and to those who fear Thee, the small and the great, and to destroy those who destroy the earth." 011:019 Then the doors of God's sanctuary in Heaven were opened, and the Ark, in which His Covenant was, was seen in His sanctuary; and there came flashes of lightning, and voices, and peals of thunder, and an earthquake, and heavy hail. 012:001 And a great marvel was seen in Heaven-a woman who was robed with the sun and had the moon under her feet, and had also a wreath of stars round her head, was with child, 012:002 and she was crying out in the pains and agony of childbirth. 012:003 And another marvel was seen in Heaven-a great fiery-red Dragon, with seven heads and ten horns; and on his heads were seven kingly crowns. 012:004 His tail was drawing after it a third part of the stars of Heaven, and it dashed them to the ground. And in front of the woman who was about to become a mother, the Dragon was standing in order to devour the child as soon as it was born. 012:005 She gave birth to a son-a male child, destined before long to rule all nations with an iron scepter. But her child was caught up to God and His throne, 012:006 and the woman fled into the Desert, there to be cared for, for 1,260 days, in a place which God had prepared for her. 012:007 And war broke out in Heaven, Michael and his angels engaging in battle with the Dragon. 012:008 The Dragon fought and so did his angels; but they were defeated, and there was no longer any room found for them in Heaven. 012:009 The great Dragon, the ancient serpent, he who is called `the Devil' and `the Adversary' and leads the whole earth astray, was hurled down: he was hurled down to the earth, and his angels were hurled down with him. 012:010 Then I heard a loud voice speaking in Heaven. It said, "The salvation and the power and the Kingdom of our God have now come, and the sovereignty of His Christ; for the accuser of our brethren has been hurled down-he who, day after day and night after night, was wont to accuse them in the presence of God. 012:011 But they have gained the victory over him because of the blood of the Lamb and of the testimony which they have borne, and because they held their lives cheap and did not shrink even from death. 012:012 For this reason be glad, O Heaven, and you who live in Heaven! Alas for the earth and the sea! For the Devil has come down to you; full of fierce anger, because he knows that his appointed time is short." 012:013 And when the Dragon saw that he was hurled down to the earth, he went in pursuit of the woman who had given birth to the male child. 012:014 Then, the two wings of a great eagle were given to the woman to enable her to fly away into the Desert to the place assigned her, there to be cared for, for a period of time, two periods of time, and half a period of time, beyond the reach of the serpent. 012:015 And the serpent poured water from his mouth-a very river it seemed- after the woman, in the hope that she would be carried away by its flood. 012:016 But the earth came to the woman's help: it opened its mouth and drank up the river which the Dragon had poured from his mouth. 012:017 This made the Dragon furiously angry with the woman, and he went elsewhere to make war upon her other children-those who keep God's commandments and hold fast to the testimony of Jesus. 013:001 And he took up a position upon the sands of the sea-shore. Then I saw a Wild Beast coming up out of the sea, and he had ten horns and seven heads. On his horns were ten kingly crowns, and inscribed on his heads were names full of blasphemy. 013:002 The Wild Beast which I saw resembled a leopard, and had feet like the feet of a bear, and his mouth was like the mouth of a lion; and it was to the Dragon that he owed his power and his throne and his wide dominion. 013:003 I saw that one of his heads seemed to have been mortally wounded; but his mortal wound was healed, and the whole world was amazed and followed him. 013:004 And they offered worship to the Dragon, because it was to him that the Wild Beast owed his dominion; and they also offered worship to the Wild Beast, and said, "Who is there like him? And who is able to engage in battle with him?" 013:005 And there was given him a mouth full of boastful and blasphemous words; and liberty of action was granted him for forty-two months. 013:006 And he opened his mouth to utter blasphemies against God, to speak evil of His name and of His dwelling-place- that is to say, of those who dwell in Heaven. 013:007 And permission was given him to make war upon God's people and conquer them; and power was given him over every tribe, people, language and nation. 013:008 And all the inhabitants of the earth will be found to be worshipping him: every one whose name is not recorded in the Book of Life-the Book of the Lamb who has been offered in sacrifice ever since the creation of the world. 013:009 Let all who have ears give heed. 013:010 If any one is eager to lead others into captivity, he must himself go into captivity. If any one is bent on killing with the sword, he must himself be killed by the sword. Here is an opportunity for endurance, and for the exercise of faith, on the part of God's people. 013:011 Then I saw another Wild Beast, coming up out of the earth. He had two horns like those of a lamb, but he spoke like a dragon. 013:012 And the authority of the first Wild Beast-the whole of that authority-he exercises in his presence, and he causes the earth and its inhabitants to worship the first Wild Beast, whose mortal wound had been healed. 013:013 He also works great miracles, so as even to make fire come down from Heaven to earth in the presence of human beings. 013:014 And his power of leading astray the inhabitants of the earth is due to the marvels which he has been permitted to work in the presence of the Wild Beast. And he told the inhabitants of the earth to erect a statue to the Wild Beast who had received the sword-stroke and yet had recovered. 013:015 And power was granted him to give breath to the statue of the Wild Beast, so that the statue of the Wild Beast could even speak and cause all who refuse to worship it to be put to death. 013:016 And he causes all, small and great, rich and poor, free men and slaves, to have stamped upon them a mark on their right hands or on their foreheads, 013:017 in order that no one should be allowed to buy or sell unless he had the mark-either the name of the Wild Beast or the number which his name represents. 013:018 Here is scope for ingenuity. Let people of shrewd intelligence calculate the number of the Wild Beast; for it indicates a certain man, and his number is 666. 014:001 Then I looked, and I saw the Lamb standing upon Mount Zion, and with Him 144,000 people, having His name and His Father's name written on their foreheads. 014:002 And I heard music from Heaven which resembled the sound of many waters and the roar of loud thunder; and the music which I heard was like that of harpists playing upon their harps. 014:003 And they were singing what seemed to be a new song, in front of the throne and in the presence of the four living creatures and the Elders; and no one was able to learn that song except the 144,000 people who had been redeemed out of the world. 014:004 These are those who had not defiled themselves with women: they are as pure as virgins. They follow the Lamb wherever He goes. They have been redeemed from among men, as firstfruits to God and to the Lamb. 014:005 And no lie has ever been found upon their lips: they are faultless. 014:006 And I saw another angel flying across the sky, carrying the Good News of the Ages to tell to every nation, tribe, language and people, among those who live on the earth. 014:007 He said in a loud voice, "Fear God and give Him glory, because the time of His judgment has come; and worship Him who made sky and earth, the sea and the water-springs." 014:008 And another, a second angel, followed, exclaiming, "Great Babylon has fallen, has fallen-she who made all the nations drink the wine of the anger provoked by her fornication." 014:009 And another, a third angel, followed them, exclaiming in a loud voice, "If any one worships the Wild Beast and his statue, and receives a mark on his forehead or on his hand, 014:010 he shall drink the wine of God's anger which stands ready, undiluted, in the cup of His fury, and he shall be tormented with fire and sulphur in the presence of the holy angels and of the Lamb. 014:011 And the smoke of their torment goes up until the Ages of the Ages; and the worshipers of the Wild Beast and his statue have no rest day or night, nor has any one who receives the mark of his name. 014:012 Here is an opportunity for endurance on the part of God's people, who carefully keep His commandments and the faith of Jesus!" 014:013 And I heard a voice speaking from Heaven. It said, "Write as follows: "`Blessed are the dead who die in the Lord from this time onward. Yes, says the Spirit, let them rest from their sorrowful labours; for what they have done goes with them.'" 014:014 Then I looked, and a white cloud appeared, and sitting on the cloud was some One resembling the Son of Man, having a wreath of gold upon His head and in His hand a sharp sickle. 014:015 And another, an angel, came out of the sanctuary, calling in a loud voice to Him who sat on the cloud, and saying, "Use your sickle and reap the harvest, for the hour for reaping it has come: the harvest of the earth is over-ripe." 014:016 Then He who sat on the cloud flung His sickle on the earth, and the earth had its harvest reaped. 014:017 And another angel came out from the sanctuary in Heaven, and he too carried a sharp sickle. 014:018 And another angel came out from the altar-he who had power over fire-and he spoke in a loud voice to him who had the sharp sickle, saying, "Use your sharp sickle, and gather the bunches from the vine of the earth, for its grapes are now quite ripe." 014:019 And the angel flung his sickle down to the earth, and reaped the vine of the earth and threw the grapes into the great winepress of God's anger. 014:020 And the winepress was trodden outside the city, and out of it came blood reaching the horses' bridles for a distance of 200 miles. 015:001 Then I saw another marvel in Heaven, great and wonderful- there were seven angels bringing seven plagues. These are the last plagues, because in them God's anger has found full expression. 015:002 And I saw what seemed to be a sea of glass mingled with fire, and those who had gained the victory over the Wild Beast and over his statue and the number of his name, standing by the sea of glass and having harps which belonged to God. 015:003 And they were singing the song of Moses, God's servant, and the song of the Lamb. Their words were, "Great and wonderful are Thy works, O Lord God, the Ruler of all. Righteous and true are Thy ways, O King of the nations. 015:004 Who shall not be afraid, O Lord, and glorify Thy name? For Thou alone art holy. All nations shall come and shall worship Thee, because the righteousness of all that Thou hast done has been made manifest." 015:005 After this, when the doors of the sanctuary of the tent of witness in Heaven were opened, I looked; 015:006 and there came out of the sanctuary the seven angels who were bringing the seven plagues. The angels were clad in pure, bright linen, and had girdles of gold across their breasts. 015:007 And one of the four living creatures gave the seven angels seven bowls of gold, full of the anger of God who lives until the Ages of the Ages. 015:008 And the sanctuary was filled with smoke from the glory of God and from His power; and no one could enter the sanctuary till the seven plagues brought by the seven angels were at an end. 016:001 Then I heard a loud voice from the sanctuary say to the seven angels, "Go and pour on to the earth the seven bowls of the anger of God." 016:002 So the first angel went away and poured his bowl on to the earth; and it brought a bad and painful sore upon the men who had on them the mark of the Wild Beast and worshipped his statue. 016:003 The second angel poured his bowl into the sea, and it became blood, like a dead man's blood, and every living creature in the sea died. 016:004 The third angel poured his bowl into the rivers and springs of water, and they became blood. 016:005 And I heard the angel of the waters say, "Righteous art Thou, who art and wast, the holy One, because Thou hast thus taken vengeance. 016:006 For they poured out the blood of Thy people and of the Prophets, and in return Thou hast given them blood to drink. And this they deserved." 016:007 And I heard a voice from the altar say, "Even so, O Lord God, the Ruler of all, true and righteous are Thy judgments." 016:008 Then the fourth angel poured his bowl on to the sun, and power was given to it to scorch men with fire. 016:009 And the men were severely burned; and yet they spoke evil of God who had power over the plagues, and they did not repent so as to give Him glory. 016:010 The fifth angel poured his bowl on to the throne of the Wild Beast; and his kingdom became darkened. People gnawed their tongues because of the pain, 016:011 and they spoke evil of the God in Heaven because of their pains and their sores, and did not repent of their misconduct. 016:012 The sixth angel poured his bowl into that great river, the Euphrates; and its stream was dried up in order to clear the way for the kings who are to come from the east. 016:013 Then I saw three foul spirits, resembling frogs, issue from the mouth of the Dragon, from the mouth of the Wild Beast, and from the mouth of the false Prophet. 016:014 For they are the spirits of demons working marvels- spirits that go out to control the kings of the whole earth, to assemble them for the battle which is to take place on the great day of God, the Ruler of all. 016:015 ("I am coming like a thief. Blessed is the man who keeps awake and guards his raiment for fear he walk about ill-clad, and his uncomeliness become manifest.") 016:016 And assemble them they did at the place called in Hebrew `Har-Magedon.' 016:017 Then the seventh angel poured his bowl into the air; and a loud voice came out of the sanctuary from the throne, saying, "Everything is now ready." 016:018 Flashes of lightning followed, and voices, and peals of thunder, and an earthquake more dreadful than there had ever been since there was a man upon the earth-so terrible was it, and so great! 016:019 The great city was split into three parts; the cities of the nations fell; and great Babylon came into remembrance before God, for Him to make her drink from the wine-cup of His fierce anger. 016:020 Every island fled away, and there was not a mountain anywhere to be seen. 016:021 And heavy hail, that seemed to be a talent in weight, fell from the sky upon the people; and they spoke evil of God on account of the plague of the hail-because the plague of it was exceedingly severe. 017:001 Then one of the seven angels who were carrying the seven bowls came and spoke to me. "Come with me," he said, "and I will show you the doom of the great Harlot who sits upon many waters. 017:002 The kings of the earth have committed fornication with her, and the inhabitants of the earth have been made drunk with the wine of her fornication." 017:003 So he carried me away in the Spirit into a desert, and there I saw a woman sitting on a scarlet-colored Wild Beast which was covered with names of blasphemy and had seven heads and ten horns. 017:004 The woman was clothed in purple and scarlet, and was brilliantly attired with gold and jewels and pearls. She held in her hand a cup of gold, full of abominations, and she gave filthy indications of her fornication. 017:005 And on her forehead was a name written: "I am a symbol of great Babylon, the mother of the harlots and of the abominations of the earth." 017:006 And I saw the woman drinking herself drunk with the blood of the saints, and with the blood of the witnesses of Jesus. And when I saw her I was filled with utter astonishment. 017:007 Then the angel said to me, "Why are you so astonished? I will explain to you the secret meaning of the woman and of the seven-headed, ten-horned Wild Beast which carries her. 017:008 "The Wild Beast which you have seen was, and is not, and yet is destined to re-ascend, before long, out of the bottomless pit and go his way into perdition. And the inhabitants of the earth will be filled with amazement- all whose names are not in the Book of Life, having been recorded there ever since the creation of the world- when they see the Wild Beast: because he was, and is not, and yet is to come. 017:009 Here is scope for the exercise of a mind that has wisdom! The seven heads are the seven hills on which the woman sits. 017:010 And they are seven kings: five of them have fallen, and the one is still reigning. The seventh has not yet come, but when he comes he must continue for a short time. 017:011 And the Wild Beast which once existed but does not now exist- he is an eighth king and yet is one of the seven and he goes his way into perdition. 017:012 "And the ten horns which you have seen are ten kings who have not yet come to the throne, but for a single hour they are to receive authority as kings along with the Wild Beast. 017:013 They have one common policy, and they are to give their power and authority to the Wild Beast. 017:014 They will make war upon the Lamb, and the Lamb will triumph over them; for He is Lord of lords and King of kings. And those who accompany Him- called, as they are, and chosen, and faithful-shall share in the victory." 017:015 He also said to me, "The waters which you have seen, on which the Harlot sits, are peoples and multitudes, nations and languages. 017:016 And the ten horns that you have seen-and the Wild Beast- these will hate the Harlot, and they will cause her to be laid waste and will strip her bare. They will eat her flesh, and burn her up with fire. 017:017 For God has put it into their hearts to carry out His purpose, and to carry out a common purpose and to give their kingdom to the Wild Beast until God's words have come to pass. 017:018 And the woman whom you have seen is the great city which has kingly power over the kings of the earth." 018:001 After these things I saw another angel coming down from Heaven, armed with great power. The earth shone with his splendor, 018:002 and with a mighty voice he cried out, saying, "Great Babylon has fallen, has fallen, and has become a home for demons and a stronghold for every kind of foul spirit and for every kind of foul and hateful bird. 018:003 For all the nations have drunk the wine of the anger provoked by her fornication, and the kings of the earth have committed fornication with her, and the merchants of the earth have grown rich through her excessive luxury." 018:004 Then I heard another voice from Heaven, which said, "Come out of her, My people, that you may not become partakers in her sins, nor receive a share of her plagues. 018:005 For her sins are piled up to the sky, and God has called to mind her unrighteous deeds. 018:006 Give back to her as she has given; repay her in accordance with her doings, twice as much; in the bowl that she has mixed, mix twice as much for her. 018:007 She has freely glorified herself and revelled in luxury; equally freely administer torment to her, and woe. For in her heart she boasts, saying, `I sit enthroned as Queen: no widow am I: I shall never know sorrow.' 018:008 "For this reason calamities shall come thick upon her on a single day- death and sorrow and famine- and she shall be burned to the ground. For strong is the Lord God who has judged her. 018:009 The kings of the earth who have committed fornication with her, and have revelled in luxury, shall weep aloud and lament over her when they see the smoke of her burning, 018:010 while they stand afar off because of their terror at her heavy punishment, and say, `Alas, alas, thou great city, O Babylon, the mighty city! For in one short hour thy doom has come!' 018:011 And the merchants of the earth weep aloud and lament over her, because now there is no sale for their cargoes- 018:012 cargoes of gold and silver, of jewels and pearls, of fine linen, purple and silk, and of scarlet stuff; all kinds of rare woods, and all kinds of goods in ivory and in very costly wood, in bronze, steel and marble. 018:013 Also cinnamon and amomum; odors to burn as incense or for perfume; frankincense, wine, oil; fine flour, wheat, cattle and sheep; horses and carriages and slaves; and the lives of men. 018:014 The dainties that thy soul longed for are gone from thee, and all thine elegance and splendor have perished, and never again shall they be found. 018:015 Those who traded in these things, who grew wealthy through her, will stand afar off, struck with terror at her punishment, 018:016 weeping aloud and sorrowing, and saying, `Alas, alas, for this great city, which was brilliantly arrayed in fine linen, and purple and scarlet stuff, and beautified with gold, jewels and pearls; 018:017 because in one short hour all this great wealth has been laid waste!' And every shipmaster and every passenger by sea and the crews and all who ply their trade on the sea, 018:018 stood afar off, and cried aloud when they saw the smoke of her burning. And they said, `What city is like this great city?' 018:019 And they threw dust upon their heads, and cried out, weeping aloud and sorrowing. `Alas, alas,' they said, `for this great city, in which, through her vast wealth, the owners of all the ships on the sea have grown rich; because in one short hour she has been laid waste!' 018:020 Rejoice over her, O Heaven, and you saints and Apostles and Prophets; for God has taken vengeance upon her because of you." 018:021 Then a single angel of great strength took a stone which resembled a huge millstone, and hurled it into the sea, saying, "So shall Babylon, that great city, be violently hurled down and never again be found. 018:022 No harp or song, no flute or trumpet, shall ever again be heard in thee; no craftsman of any kind shall ever again be found in thee; nor shall the grinding of the mill ever again be heard in thee. 018:023 Never again shall the light of a lamp shine in thee, and never again shall the voice of a bridegroom or of a bride be heard in thee. For thy merchants were the great men of the earth, and with the magic which thou didst practise all nations were led astray. 018:024 And in her was found the blood of Prophets and of God's people and of all who had been put to death on the earth." 019:001 After this I seemed to hear the

far-echoing voices of a great multitude in Heaven, who said, "Hallelujah!
The salvation and the glory and the power belong to our God. 019:002
True and just are His judgments, because He has judged the great Harlot
who was corrupting the whole earth with her fornication, and He has taken
vengeance for the blood of His bondservants which her hands have shed."
019:003 And a second time they said, "Hallelujah! For her smoke ascends
until the Ages of the Ages." 019:004 And the twenty-four Elders and the
four living creatures fell down and worshipped God who sits upon the
throne. "Even so," they said; "Hallelujah!" 019:005 And from the throne
there came a voice which said, "Praise our God, all you His bondservants-
you who fear Him, both the small and the great." 019:006 And I seemed to
hear the voices of a great multitude and the sound of many waters and of
loud peals of thunder, which said, "Hallelujah! Because the Lord our God,
the Ruler of all, has become King. 019:007 Let us rejoice and triumph and
give Him the glory; for the time for the marriage of the Lamb has come,
and His Bride has made herself ready." 019:008 And she was permitted to
array herself in fine linen, shining and spotless; the fine linen being the
righteous actions of God's people. 019:009 And he said to me, "Write as
follows: `Blessed are those who receive an invitation to the Marriage Supper
of the Lamb.'" And he added, still addressing me, "These are truly the
words of God." 019:010 Then I fell at his feet to worship him. But he
exclaimed, "Oh, do not do that. I am a fellow bondservant of yours and a
fellow bondservant of your brethren who have borne testimony to Jesus.
Worship God." Testimony to Jesus is the spirit which underlies Prophecy.
019:011 Then I saw a door open in Heaven, and a white horse appeared. Its
rider was named "Faithful and True"-being One who in righteousness acts
as Judge, and makes war. 019:012 His eyes were like a flame of fire, and on
His head were many kingly crowns; and He has a name written upon Him
which no one but He Himself knows. 019:013 The outer garment in which
He is clad has been dipped in blood and His name is THE WORD OF
GOD. 019:014 The armies in Heaven followed Him-mounted on white
horses and clothed in fine linen, white and spotless. 019:015 From His
mouth there comes a sharp sword with which He will smite the nations;
and He will Himself be their Shepherd, ruling them with a scepter of iron;
and it is His work to tread the winepress of the fierce anger of God, the
Ruler of all. 019:016 And on His outer garment and on His thigh He has a
name written, KING OF KINGS AND LORD OF LORDS. 019:017 And
I saw a single angel standing in the full light of the sun, who cried in a loud
voice to all the birds that flew across the sky, "Come and be present at
God's great supper, 019:018 that you may feast on the flesh of kings and
the flesh of generals and the flesh of mighty men, on the flesh of horses
and their riders, and on the flesh of all mankind, whether they are free men
or slaves, great men or small." 019:019 And I saw the Wild Beast, and the

kings of the earth, and their armies, all assembled to make war, once for all, against the Rider upon the horse and against His army. And the Wild Beast was captured, and with him the false Prophet 019:020 who had done the miracles in his presence with which he had led astray those who had received the mark of the Wild Beast, and those who worshipped his statue. Both of them were thrown alive into the Lake of fire that was all ablaze with sulphur. 019:021 But the rest were killed with the sword that came from the mouth of the Rider on the horse. And the birds all fed ravenously upon their flesh. 020:001 Then I saw an angel coming down from Heaven, having the key of the bottomless pit, and upon his arm he carried a great chain. 020:002 He laid hold of the Dragon-the ancient serpent-who is the Devil and the Adversary, and bound him for a thousand years, and hurled him into the bottomless pit. 020:003 He closed the entrance and put a seal upon him in order that he might be unable to lead the nations astray any more until the thousand years were at an end. Afterwards he is to be set at liberty for a short time. 020:004 And I saw thrones, and some who were seated on them, to whom judgment was entrusted. And I saw the souls of those who had been beheaded on account of the testimony that they had borne to Jesus and on account of God's Message, and also the souls of those who had not worshipped the Wild Beast or his statue, nor received his mark on their foreheads or on their hands; and they came to Life and were kings with Christ for a thousand years. 020:005 No one else who was dead rose to Life until the thousand years were at an end. This is the First Resurrection. 020:006 Blessed and holy are those who share in the First Resurrection. The Second Death has no power over them, but they shall be priests to God and to Christ, and shall be kings with Christ for the thousand years. 020:007 But when the thousand years are at an end, the Adversary will be released from his imprisonment, 020:008 and will go out to lead astray the nations in all the four corners of the earth, Gog and Magog, and assemble them for war, and they are like the sands on the seashore in number. 020:009 And they went up over the whole breadth of the earth and surrounded the encampment of God's people and the beloved city. But fire came down from Heaven and consumed them; 020:010 and the Devil, who had been leading them astray, was thrown into the Lake of fire and sulphur where the Wild Beast and the false Prophet were, and day and night they will suffer torture until the Ages of the Ages. 020:011 Then I saw a great white throne and One who was seated on it, from whose presence earth and sky fled away, and no place was found for them. 020:012 And I saw the dead, the great and the small, standing in front of the throne. And books were opened; and so was another book-namely, the Book of Life; and the dead were judged by the things recorded in the books in accordance with what their conduct had been. 020:013 Then the sea yielded up the dead who were in it, Death and Hades yielded up the dead who were in them, and each man was judged in accordance with what his conduct had been. 020:014 Then Death and Hades were thrown into the Lake of fire; this is the Second Death-the Lake of fire. 020:015 And if any one's name was not found recorded in the Book of Life he was thrown into the Lake of fire. 021:001 And I saw a new Heaven and a new earth; for the first Heaven and the first earth were gone, and the sea no longer exists. 021:002 And I saw the holy city, the new Jerusalem, coming down out of Heaven from God and made ready like a bride attired to meet her husband. 021:003 And I heard a loud voice, which came from the throne, say, "God's dwelling place is among men and He will dwell among them and they shall be His peoples. Yes, God Himself will be among them. 021:004 He will wipe every tear from their eyes. Death shall be no more; nor sorrow, nor wail of woe, nor pain; for the first things have passed away." 021:005 Then He who was seated on the throne said, "I am re-creating all things." And He added, "Write down these words, for they are trustworthy and true." 021:006 He also said, "They have now been fulfilled. I am the Alpha and the Omega, the Beginning and the End. To those who are thirsty I will give the privilege of drinking from the well of the Water of Life without payment. 021:007 All this shall be the heritage of him who overcomes, and I will be his God and he shall be one of My sons. 021:008 But as for cowards and the unfaithful, and the polluted, and murderers, fornicators, and those who practise magic or worship idols, and all liars-the portion allotted to them shall be in the Lake which burns with fire and sulphur. This is the Second Death." 021:009 Then there came one of the seven angels who were carrying the seven bowls full of the seven last plagues. "Come with me," he said, "and I will show you the Bride, the Lamb's wife." 021:010 So in the Spirit he carried me to the top of a vast, lofty mountain, and showed me the holy city, Jerusalem, coming down out of Heaven from God, 021:011 and bringing with it the glory of God. It shone with a radiance like that of a very precious stone-such as a jasper, bright and transparent. 021:012 It has a wall, massive and high, with twelve large gates, and in charge of the gates were twelve angels. And overhead, above the gates, names were inscribed which are those of the twelve tribes of the descendants of Israel. 021:013 There were three gates on the east, three on the north, three on the south, and three on the west. 021:014 The wall of the city had twelve foundation stones, and engraved upon them were twelve names-the names of the twelve Apostles of the Lamb. 021:015 Now he who was speaking to me had a measuring-rod of gold, with which to measure the city and its gates and its wall. 021:016 The plan of the city is a square, the length being the same as the breadth; and he measured the city furlong by furlong, with his measuring rod-it is twelve hundred miles long, and the length and the breadth and the height of it are equal. 021:017 And he measured the wall of it-a wall of a hundred and forty-four cubits, according to human measure, which was also that of the angel. 021:018 The solid fabric of the wall was jasper; and the city itself was made of gold, resembling transparent glass. 021:019 As for the foundation-stones of the city wall, which were beautified with various kinds of precious stones, the first was jasper, the second sapphire, the third chalcedony, the fourth emerald, the fifth sardonyx, the sixth sardius, 021:020 the seventh chrysolite, the eighth beryl, the ninth topaz, the tenth chrysoprase, the eleventh jacinth, the twelfth amethyst. 021:021 And the twelve gates were twelve pearls; each of them consisting of a single pearl. And the main street of the city was made of pure gold, resembling transparent glass. 021:022 I saw no sanctuary in the city, for the Lord God, the Ruler of all, is its Sanctuary, and so is the Lamb. 021:023 Nor has the city any need of the sun or of the moon, to give it light; for the glory of God has shone upon it and its lamp is the Lamb. 021:024 The nations will live their lives by its light; and the kings of the earth are to bring their glory into it. 021:025 And in the daytime (for there will be no night there) the gates will never be closed; 021:026 and the glory and honor of the nations shall be brought into it. 021:027 And no unclean thing shall ever enter it, nor any one who is guilty of base conduct or tells lies, but only they whose names stand recorded in the Lamb's Book of Life. 022:001 Then he showed me the river of the Water of Life, bright as crystal, issuing from the throne of God and of the Lamb. 022:002 On either side of the river, midway between it and the main street of the city, was the Tree of Life. It produced twelve kinds of fruit, yielding a fresh crop month by month, and the leaves of the tree served as medicine for the nations. 022:003 "In future there will be no curse," he said, "but the throne of God and of the Lamb will be in that city. And His servants will render Him holy service and will see His face, 022:004 and His name will be on their foreheads. 022:005 And there will be no night there; and they have no need of lamplight or sunlight, for the Lord God will shine upon them, and they will be kings until the Ages of the Ages." 022:006 And he said to me, "These words are trustworthy and true; and the Lord, the God of the spirits of the Prophets, sent His angel to make known to His servants the things which must soon happen. 022:007 `I am coming quickly.' Blessed is he who is mindful of the predictions contained in this book." 022:008 I John heard and saw these things; and when I had heard and seen them, I fell at the feet of the angel who was showing me them- to worship him. 022:009 But he said to me, "Oh, do not do that. I am a fellow bondservant of yours, and a fellow bondservant of your brethren the Prophets and of those who are mindful of the teachings of this book. Worship God." 022:010 "Make no secret," he added, "of the meaning of the predictions contained in this book; for the time for their fulfillment is now close at hand. 022:011 Let the dishonest man act dishonestly still; let the filthy make himself filthy still; let the righteous practise righteousness still; and let the holy be made holy still." 022:012 "I am coming quickly; and My reward is with Me, that I may requite every man in accordance with what his conduct has been. 022:013 I am the Alpha and the Omega, the First and the Last, the Beginning and the End. 022:014 Blessed are those who wash their robes clean, that they may have a right to the Tree of Life, and may go through the gates into the city. 022:015 The unclean are shut out, and so are all who practise magic, all fornicators, all murderers, and those who worship idols, and every one who loves falsehood and tells lies. 022:016 "I Jesus have sent My angel for him solemnly to declare these things to you among the Churches. I am the Root and the offspring of David, the bright Morning Star. 022:017 The Spirit and the Bride say, `Come;' and whoever hears, let him say, `Come;' and let those who are thirsty come. Whoever will, let him take the Water of Life, without payment. 022:018 "I solemnly declare to every one who hears the words of the prophecy contained in this book, that if any one adds to those words, God will add to him the plagues spoken of in this book; 022:019 and that if any one takes away from the words of the book of this prophecy, God will take from him his share in the Tree of Life and in the holy city-the things described in this book. 022:020 "He who solemnly declares all this says, "`Yes, I am coming quickly.'" Amen. Come, Lord Jesus. 022:021 The grace of the Lord Jesus be with God's people.

BOOK 45 ROMANS

001:001 Paul, a bondservant of Jesus Christ, called to be an Apostle, set apart to proclaim God's Good News, 001:002 which God had already promised through His Prophets in Holy Writ, concerning His Son, 001:003 who, as regards His human descent, belonged to the posterity of David, 001:004 but as regards the holiness of His Spirit was decisively proved by His Resurrection to be the Son of God-I mean concerning Jesus Christ our Lord, 001:005 through whom we have received grace and Apostleship in His service in order to win men to obedience to the faith, among all Gentile peoples, 001:006 among whom you also, called, as you have been, to belong to Jesus Christ, are numbered: 001:007 To all God's loved ones who are in Rome, called to be saints. May grace and peace be granted to you from God our Father and the Lord Jesus Christ. 001:008 First of all, I thank my God through Jesus Christ for what He has done for all of you; for the report of your faith is spreading through the whole world. 001:009 I call God to witness-to whom I render priestly and spiritual service by telling the Good News about His Son-how unceasingly I make mention of you in His presence, 001:010 always in my prayers entreating that now, at length, if such be His will, the way may by some means be made clear for me to come to you. 001:011 For I am longing to see you, in order to convey to you some spiritual help, so that you may be strengthened; 001:012 in other words that while I am among you we may be mutually encouraged by one another's faith, yours and mine. 001:013 And I desire you to know, brethren, that I have many a time intended to come to you-though until now I have been disappointed- in order that among you also I might gather some fruit from my labours, as I have already done among the rest of the Gentile nations. 001:014 I am already under obligations alike to Greek-speaking races and to others, to cultured and to uncultured people: 001:015 so that for my part I am willing and eager to proclaim the Good News to you also who are in Rome. 001:016 For I am not ashamed of the Good News. It is God's power which is at work for the salvation of every one who believes- the Jew first, and then the Gentile. 001:017 For in the Good News a righteousness which comes from God is being revealed, depending on faith and tending to produce faith; as the Scripture has it, "The righteous man shall live by faith." 001:018 For God's anger is being revealed from Heaven against all impiety and against the iniquity of men who through iniquity suppress the truth. God is angry: 001:019 because what may be known about Him is plain to their inmost consciousness; for He Himself has made it plain to them. 001:020 For, from the very creation of the world, His invisible perfections- namely His eternal power and divine nature-have been rendered intelligible and clearly visible by His works, so that these men are without excuse. 001:021 For when they had come to know God, they did not give Him glory as God nor render Him thanks, but they became absorbed in useless discussions, and their senseless minds were darkened. 001:022 While boasting of their wisdom they became utter fools, 001:023 and, instead of worshipping the imperishable God, they worshipped images resembling perishable man or resembling birds or beasts or reptiles. 001:024 For this reason, in accordance with their own depraved cravings, God gave them up to uncleanness, allowing them to dishonour their bodies among themselves with impurity. 001:025 For they had bartered the reality of God for what is unreal, and had offered divine honours and religious service to created things, rather than to the Creator- He who is for ever blessed. Amen. 001:026 This then is the reason why God gave them up to vile passions. For not only did the women among them exchange the natural use of their bodies for one which is contrary to nature, but the men also, 001:027 in just the same way-neglecting that for which nature intends women- burned with passion towards one another, men practising shameful vice with men, and receiving in their own selves the reward which necessarily followed their misconduct. 001:028 And just as they had refused to continue to have a full knowledge of God, so it was to utterly worthless minds that God gave them up, for them to do things which should not be done. 001:029 Their hearts overflowed with all sorts of dishonesty, mischief, greed, malice. They were full of envy and murder, and were quarrelsome, crafty, and spiteful. 001:030 They were secret backbiters, open slanderers; hateful to God, insolent, haughty, boastful; inventors of new forms of sin, disobedient to parents, destitute of common sense, 001:031 faithless to their promises, without natural affection, without human pity. 001:032 In short, though knowing full well the sentence which God pronounces against actions such as theirs, as things which deserve death, they not only practise them, but even encourage and applaud others who do them. 002:001 You are therefore without excuse, O man, whoever you are who sit in judgement upon others. For when you pass judgement on your fellow man, you condemn yourself; for you who sit in judgement upon others are guilty of the same misdeeds; 002:002 and we know that God's judgement against those who commit such sins is in accordance with the truth. 002:003 And you who pronounce judgement upon those who do such things although your own conduct is the same as theirs- do you imagine that you yourself will escape unpunished when God judges? 002:004 Or is it that you think slightingly of His infinite goodness, forbearance and patience, unaware that the goodness of God is gently drawing you to repentance? 002:005 The fact is that in the stubbornness of your impenitent heart you are treasuring up against yourself anger on the day of Anger-the day when the righteousness of God's judgements will stand revealed. 002:006 To each man He will make an award corresponding to his actions; 002:007 to those on the one hand who, by lives of persistent right-doing, are striving for glory, honour and immortality, the Life of the Ages; 002:008 while on the other hand upon the self-willed who disobey the truth and obey unrighteousness will fall anger and fury, affliction and awful distress, 002:009 coming upon the soul of every man and woman who deliberately does wrong-upon the Jew first, and then upon the Gentile; 002:010 whereas glory, honour and peace will be given to every one who does what is good and right-to the Jew first and then to the Gentile. 002:011 For God pays no attention to this world's distinctions. 002:012 For all who have sinned apart from the Law will also perish apart from the Law, and all who have sinned whilst living under the Law, will be judged by the Law. 002:013 It is not those that merely hear the Law read who are righteous in the sight of God, but it is those that obey the Law who will be pronounced righteous. 002:014 For when Gentiles who have no Law obey by natural instinct the commands of the Law, they, without having a Law, are a Law to themselves; 002:015 since they exhibit proof that a knowledge of the conduct which the Law requires is engraven on their hearts, while their consciences also bear witness to the Law, and their thoughts, as if in mutual discussion, accuse them or perhaps maintain their innocence- 002:016 on the day when God will judge the secrets of men's lives by Jesus Christ, as declared in the Good News as I have taught it. 002:017 And since you claim the name of Jew, and find rest and satisfaction in the Law, and make your boast in God, 002:018 and know the supreme will, and can test things that differ- being a man who receives instruction from the Law- 002:019 and have persuaded yourself that, as for you, you are a guide to the blind, a light to those who are in darkness, 002:020 a schoolmaster for the dull and ignorant, a teacher of the young, because in the Law you possess an outline of real knowledge and an outline of the truth: 002:021 you then who teach your fellow man, do you refuse to teach yourself? You who cry out against stealing, are you yourself a thief? 002:022 You who forbid adultery, do you commit adultery? You who loathe idols, do you plunder their temples? 002:023 You who make your boast in the Law, do you offend against its commands and so dishonour God? 002:024 For the name of God is blasphemed among the Gentile nations because of you, as Holy Writ declares. 002:025 Circumcision does indeed profit, if you obey the Law; but if you are a Law-breaker, the fact that you have been circumcised counts for nothing. 002:026 In the same way if an uncircumcised man pays attention to the just requirements of the Law, shall not his lack of circumcision be overlooked, and, 002:027 although he is a Gentile by birth, if he scrupulously obeys the Law, shall he not sit in judgement upon you who, possessing, as you do, a written Law and circumcision, are yet a Law-breaker? 002:028 For the true Jew is not the man who is simply a Jew outwardly, and true circumcision is not that which is outward and bodily. 002:029 But the true Jew is one inwardly, and true circumcision is heart-circumcision-not literal, but spiritual; and such people receive praise not from men, but from God. 003:001 What special privilege, then, has a Jew? Or what benefit is to be derived from circumcision? 003:002 The privilege is great from every point of view. First of all, because the Jews were entrusted with God's truth. 003:003 For what if some Jews have proved unfaithful? Shall their faithlessness render God's faithfulness worthless? 003:004 No, indeed; let us hold God to be true, though every man should prove to be false. As it stands written, "That Thou mayest be shown to be just in the sentence Thou pronouncest, and gain Thy cause when Thou contendest." 003:005 But if our unrighteousness sets God's righteousness in a clearer light, what shall we say? (Is God unrighteous- I speak in our everyday language-when He inflicts punishment? 003:006 No indeed; for in that case how shall He judge all mankind?) 003:007 If, for instance, a falsehood of mine has made God's truthfulness more conspicuous, redounding to His glory, why am I judged all the same as a sinner? 003:008 And why should we not say-for so they wickedly misrepresent us, and so some charge us with arguing-"Let us do evil that good may come"? The condemnation of those who would so argue is just. 003:009 What then? Are we Jews more highly estimated than they? Not in the least; for we have already charged all Jews and Gentiles alike with being in thraldom to sin. 003:010 Thus it stands written, "There is not one righteous man. 003:011 There is not one who is really wise, nor one who is a diligent seeker after God. 003:012 All have turned aside from the right path; they have every one of them become corrupt. There is no one who does what is right-no, not so much as one." 003:013 "Their throats resemble an opened grave; with their tongues they have been talking deceitfully." "The venom of vipers lies hidden behind their lips." 003:014 "Their mouths are full of cursing and bitterness." 003:015 "Their feet move swiftly to shed blood. 003:016 Ruin and misery mark their path; 003:017 and the way to peace they have not known." 003:018 "There is no fear of God before their eyes."

003:019 But it cannot be denied that all that the Law says is addressed to those who are living under the Law, in order that every mouth may be stopped, and that the whole world may await sentence from God. 003:020 For on the ground of obedience to Law no man living will be declared righteous before Him. Law simply brings a sure knowledge of sin. 003:021 But now a righteousness coming from God has been brought to light apart from any Law, both Law and Prophets bearing witness to it- 003:022 a righteousness coming from God, which depends on faith in Jesus Christ and extends to all who believe. No distinction is made; 003:023 for all alike have sinned, and all consciously come short of the glory of God, 003:024 gaining acquittal from guilt by His free unpurchased grace through the deliverance which is found in Christ Jesus. 003:025 He it is whom God put forward as a Mercy-seat, rendered efficacious through faith in His blood, in order to demonstrate His righteousness-because of the passing over, in God's forbearance, of the sins previously committed- 003:026 with a view to demonstrating, at the present time, His righteousness, that He may be shown to be righteous Himself, and the giver of righteousness to those who believe in Jesus. 003:027 Where then is there room for your boasting? It is for ever shut out. On what principle? On the ground of merit? No, but on the ground of faith. 003:028 For we maintain that it is as the result of faith that a man is held to be righteous, apart from actions done in obedience to Law. 003:029 Is God simply the God of the Jews, and not of the Gentiles also? He is certainly the God of the Gentiles also, 003:030 unless you can deny that it is one and the same God who will pronounce the circumcised to be acquitted on the ground of faith, and the uncircumcised to be acquitted through the same faith. 003:031 Do we then by means of this faith abolish the Law? No, indeed; we give the Law a firmer footing. 004:001 What then shall we say that Abraham, our earthly forefather, has gained? 004:002 For if he was held to be righteous on the ground of his actions, he has something to boast of; but not in the presence of God. 004:003 For what says the Scripture? "And Abraham believed God, and this was placed to his credit as righteousness." 004:004 But in the case of a man who works, pay is not reckoned a favour but a debt; 004:005 whereas in the case of a man who pleads no actions of his own, but simply believes in Him who declares the ungodly free from guilt, his faith is placed to his credit as righteousness. 004:006 In this way David also tells of the blessedness of the man to whose credit God places righteousness, apart from his actions. 004:007 "Blessed," he says, "are those whose iniquities have been forgiven, and whose sins have been covered over. 004:008 Blessed is the man of whose sin the Lord will not take account." 004:009 This declaration of blessedness, then, does it come simply to the circumcised, or to the uncircumcised as well? For Abraham's faith-so we affirm-was placed to his credit as righteousness. 004:010 What then were the circumstances under which this took place? Was it after he had been circumcised, or before? 004:011 Before, not after. And he received circumcision as a sign, a mark attesting the reality of the faith-righteousness which was his while still uncircumcised, that he might be the forefather of all those who believe even though they are uncircumcised- in order that this righteousness might be placed to their credit; 004:012 and the forefather of the circumcised, namely of those who not merely are circumcised, but also walk in the steps of the faith which our forefather Abraham had while he was as yet uncircumcised. 004:013 Again, the promise that he should inherit the world did not come to Abraham or his posterity conditioned by Law, but by faith-righteousness. 004:014 For if it is the righteous through Law who are heirs, then faith is useless and the promise counts for nothing. 004:015 For the Law inflicts punishment; but where no Law exists, there can be no violation of Law. 004:016 All depends on faith, and for this reason-that acceptance with God might be an act of pure grace, 004:017 so that the promise should be made sure to all Abraham's true descendants; not merely to those who are righteous through the Law, but to those who are righteous through a faith like that of Abraham. Thus in the sight of God in whom he believed, who gives life to the dead and makes reference to things that do not exist, as though they did, Abraham is the forefather of all of us. As it is written, "I have appointed you to be the forefather of many nations." 004:018 Under utterly hopeless circumstances he hopefully believed, so that he might become the forefather of many nations, in agreement with the words "Equally numerous shall your posterity be." 004:019 And, without growing weak in faith, he could contemplate his own vital powers which had now decayed-for he was nearly 100 years old-and Sarah's barrenness. 004:020 Nor did he in unbelief stagger at God's promise, but became mighty in faith, giving glory to God, 004:021 and being absolutely certain that whatever promise He is bound by He is able also to make good. 004:022 For this reason also his faith was placed to his credit as righteousness. 004:023 Nor was the fact of its being placed to his credit put on record for his sake only; 004:024 it was for our sakes too. Faith, before long, will be placed to the credit of us also who are believers in Him who raised Jesus, our Lord, from the dead, 004:025 who was surrendered to death because of the offences we had committed, and was raised to life because of the acquittal secured for us. 005:001 Standing then acquitted as the result of faith, let us enjoy peace with God through our Lord Jesus Christ, 005:002 through whom also, as the result of faith, we have obtained an introduction into that state of favour with God in which we stand, and we exult in hope of some day sharing in God's glory. 005:003 And not only so: we also exult in our sufferings, knowing as we do, that suffering produces fortitude; 005:004 fortitude, ripeness of character; and ripeness of character, hope; 005:005 and that this hope never disappoints, because God's love for us floods our hearts through the Holy Spirit who has been given to us. 005:006 For already, while we were still helpless, Christ at the right moment died for the ungodly. 005:007 Why, it is scarcely conceivable that any one would die for a simply just man, although for a good and lovable man perhaps some one, here and there, will have the courage even to lay down his life. 005:008 But God gives proof of His love to us in Christ's dying for us while we were still sinners. 005:009 If therefore we have now been pronounced free from guilt through His blood, much more shall we be delivered from God's anger through Him. 005:010 For if while we were hostile to God we were reconciled to Him through the death of His Son, it is still more certain that now that we are reconciled, we shall obtain salvation through Christ's life. 005:011 And not only so, but we also exult in God through our Lord Jesus Christ, through whom we have now obtained that reconciliation. 005:012 What follows? This comparison. Through one man sin entered into the world, and through sin death, and so death passed to all mankind in turn, in that all sinned. 005:013 For prior to the Law sin was already in the world; only it is not entered in the account against us when no Law exists. 005:014 Yet Death reigned as king from Adam to Moses even over those who had not sinned, as Adam did, against Law. And in Adam we have a type of Him whose coming was still future. 005:015 But God's free gift immeasurably outweighs the transgression. For if through the transgression of the one individual the mass of mankind have died, infinitely greater is the generosity with which God's grace, and the gift given in His grace which found expression in the one man Jesus Christ, have been bestowed on the mass of mankind. 005:016 And it is not with the gift as it was with the results of one individual's sin; for the judgement which one individual provoked resulted in condemnation, whereas the free gift after a multitude of transgressions results in acquittal. 005:017 For if, through the transgression of the one individual, Death made use of the one individual to seize the sovereignty, all the more shall those who receive God's overflowing grace and gift of righteousness reign as kings in Life through the one individual, Jesus Christ. 005:018 It follows then that just as the result of a single transgression is a condemnation which extends to the whole race, so also the result of a single decree of righteousness is a life-giving acquittal which extends to the whole race. 005:019 For as through the disobedience of the one individual the mass of mankind were constituted sinners, so also through the obedience of the One the mass of mankind will be constituted righteous. 005:020 Now Law was brought in later on, so that transgression might increase. But where sin increased, grace has overflowed; 005:021 in order that as sin has exercised kingly sway in inflicting death, so grace, too, may exercise kingly sway in bestowing a righteousness which results in the Life of the Ages through Jesus Christ our Lord. 006:001 To what conclusion, then, shall we come? Are we to persist in sinning in order that the grace extended to us may be the greater? 006:002 No, indeed; how shall we who have died to sin, live in it any longer? 006:003 And do you not know that all of us who have been baptized into Christ Jesus were baptized into His death? 006:004 Well, then, we by our baptism were buried with Him in death, in order that, just as Christ was raised from among the dead by the Father's glorious power, we also should live an entirely new life. 006:005 For since we have become one with Him by sharing in His death, we shall also be one with Him by sharing in His resurrection. 006:006 This we know-that our old self was nailed to the cross with Him, in order that our sinful nature might be deprived of its power, so that we should no longer be the slaves of sin; 006:007 for he who has paid the penalty of death stands absolved from his sin. 006:008 But, seeing that we have died with Christ, we believe that we shall also live with Him; 006:009 because we know that Christ, having come back to life, is no longer liable to die. 006:010 Death has no longer any power over Him. For by the death which He died He became, once for all, dead in relation to sin; but by the life which He now lives He is alive in relation to God. 006:011 In the same way you also must regard yourselves as dead in relation to sin, but as alive in relation to God, because you are in Christ Jesus. 006:012 Let not Sin therefore reign as king in your mortal bodies, causing you to be in subjection to their cravings; 006:013 and no longer lend your faculties as unrighteous weapons for Sin to use. On the contrary surrender your very selves to God as living men who have risen from the dead, and surrender your several faculties to God, to be used as weapons to maintain the right. 006:014 For Sin shall not be lord over you, since you are subjects not of Law, but of grace. 006:015 Are we therefore to sin because we are no longer under the authority of Law, but under grace? No, indeed! 006:016 Do you not know that if you surrender yourselves as bondservants to obey any one, you become the bondservants of him whom you obey, whether the bondservants of Sin (with death as the result) or of Duty (resulting in righteousness)? 006:017 But thanks be to God that though you were once in thraldom to Sin, you have now yielded a hearty obedience to that system of truth in which you have been instructed. 006:018 You were set free from the tyranny of Sin, and became the bondservants of Righteousness- 006:019 your human infirmity leads me to employ these familiar figures- and just as you once surrendered your faculties into bondage to Impurity and ever-increasing disregard of Law, so you must now surrender them into bondage to Righteousness ever advancing towards perfect holiness. 006:020 For when you were the bondservants of sin, you were under no sort of subjection to Righteousness. 006:021 At that time, then, what benefit did you get from conduct which you now regard with shame? Why, such things finally result in death. 006:022 But now that you have been set free from the tyranny of Sin, and have become the bondservants of God, you have your reward in being made holy, and you have the Life of the Ages as the final result. 006:023 For the wages paid by Sin are death; but God's free gift is the Life of the Ages bestowed upon us in Christ Jesus our Lord. 007:001 Brethren, do you not know-for I am writing to people acquainted with the Law-that it is during our lifetime that we are subject to the Law? 007:002 A wife, for instance, whose husband is living is bound to him by the Law; but if her husband dies the law that bound her to him has now no hold over her. 007:003 This accounts for the fact that if during her husband's life she lives with another man, she will be stigmatized as an adulteress; but that if her husband is dead she is no longer under the old prohibition, and even though she marries again, she is not an adulteress. 007:004 So, my brethren, to you also the Law died through the incarnation of Christ, that you might be wedded to Another, namely to Him who rose from the dead in order that we might yield fruit to God. 007:005 For whilst we were under the thraldom of our earthly natures, sinful passions-made sinful by the Law-were always being aroused to action in our bodily faculties that they might yield fruit to death. 007:006 But seeing that we have died to that which once held us in bondage, the Law has now no hold over us, so that we render a service which, instead of being old and formal, is new and spiritual. 007:007 What follows? Is the Law itself a sinful thing? No, indeed; on the contrary, unless I had been taught by the Law, I should have known nothing of sin as sin. For instance, I should not have known what covetousness is, if the Law had not repeatedly said, "Thou shalt not covet." 007:008 Sin took advantage of this, and by means of the Commandment stirred up within me every kind of coveting; for apart from Law sin would be dead. 007:009 Once, apart from Law, I was alive, but when the Commandment came, sin sprang into life, and I died; 007:010 and, as it turned out, the very Commandment which was to bring me life, brought me death. 007:011 For sin seized the advantage, and by means of the Commandment it completely deceived me, and also put me to death. 007:012 So that the Law itself is holy, and the Commandment is holy, just and good. 007:013 Did then a thing which is good become death to me? No, indeed, but sin did; so that through its bringing about death by means of what was good, it might be seen in its true light as sin, in order that by means of the Commandment the unspeakable sinfulness of sin might be plainly shown. 007:014 For we know that the Law is a spiritual thing; but I am unspiritual- the slave, bought and sold, of sin. 007:015 For what I do, I do not recognize as my own action. What I desire to do is not what I do, but what I am averse to is what I do. 007:016 But if I do that which I do not desire to do, I admit the excellence of the Law, 007:017 and now it is no longer I that do these things, but the sin which has its home within me does them. 007:018 For I know that in me, that is, in my lower self, nothing good has its home; for while the will to do right is present with me, the power to carry it out is not. 007:019 For what I do is not the good thing that I desire to do; but the evil thing that I desire not to do, is what I constantly do. 007:020 But if I do that which I desire not to do, it can no longer be said that it is I who do it, but the sin which has its home within me does it. 007:021 I find therefore the law of my nature to be that when I desire to do what is right, evil is lying in ambush for me. 007:022 For in my inmost self all my sympathy is with the Law of God; 007:023 but I discover within me a different Law at war with the Law of my understanding, and leading me captive to the Law which is everywhere at work in my body-the Law of sin. 007:024 (Unhappy man that I am! who will rescue me from this death-burdened body? 007:025 Thanks be to God through Jesus Christ our Lord!) To sum up then, with my understanding, I-my true self-am in servitude to the Law of God, but with my lower nature I am in servitude to the Law of sin. 008:001 There is therefore now no condemnation to those who are in Christ Jesus; 008:002 for the Spirit's Law-telling of Life in Christ Jesus- has set me free from the Law that deals only with sin and death. 008:003 For what was impossible to the Law-powerless as it was because it acted through frail humanity-God effected. Sending His own Son in a body like that of sinful human nature and as a sacrifice for sin, He pronounced sentence upon sin in human nature; 008:004 in order that in our case the requirements of the Law might be fully met. For our lives are regulated not by our earthly, but by our spiritual natures. 008:005 For if men are controlled by their earthly natures, they give their minds to earthly things. If they are controlled by their spiritual natures, they give their minds to spiritual things. 008:006 Because for the mind to be given up to earthly things means death; but for it to be given up to spiritual things means Life and peace. 008:007 Abandonment to earthly things is a state of enmity to God. Such a mind does not submit to God's Law, and indeed cannot do so. 008:008 And those whose hearts are absorbed in earthly things cannot please God. 008:009 You, however, are not devoted to earthly, but to spiritual things, if the Spirit of God is really dwelling in you; whereas if any man has not the Spirit of Christ, such a one does not belong to Him. 008:010 But if Christ is in you, though your body must die because of sin, yet your spirit has Life because of righteousness. 008:011 And if the Spirit of Him who raised up Jesus from the dead is dwelling in you, He who raised up Christ from the dead will give Life also to your mortal bodies because of His Spirit who dwells in you. 008:012 Therefore, brethren, it is not to our lower natures that we are under obligation that we should live by their rule. 008:013 For if you so live, death is near; but if, through being under the sway of the spirit, you are putting your old bodily habits to death, you will live. 008:014 For those who are led by God's Spirit are, all of them, God's sons. 008:015 You have not for the second time acquired the consciousness of being-a consciousness which fills you with terror. But you have acquired a deep inward conviction of having been adopted as sons-a conviction which prompts us to cry aloud, "Abba! our Father!" 008:016 The Spirit Himself bears witness, along with our own spirits, to the fact that we are children of God; 008:017 and if children, then heirs too-heirs of God and co-heirs with Christ; if indeed we are sharers in Christ's sufferings, in order that we may also be sharers in His glory. 008:018 Why, what we now suffer I count as nothing in comparison with the glory which is soon to be manifested in us. 008:019 For all creation, gazing eagerly as if with outstretched neck, is waiting and longing to see the manifestation of the sons of God. 008:020 For the Creation fell into subjection to failure and unreality (not of its own choice, but by the will of Him who so subjected it). 008:021 Yet there was always the hope that at last the Creation itself would also be set free from the thraldom of decay so as to enjoy the liberty that will attend the glory of the children of God. 008:022 For we know that the whole of Creation is groaning together in the pains of childbirth until this hour. 008:023 And more than that, we ourselves, though we possess the Spirit as a foretaste and pledge of the glorious future, yet we ourselves inwardly sigh, as we wait and long for open recognition as sons through the deliverance of our bodies. 008:024 It is *in hope* that we have been saved. But an object of hope is such no longer when it is present to view; for when a man has a thing before his eyes, how can he be said to hope for it? 008:025 But if we hope for something which we do not see, then we eagerly and patiently wait for it. 008:026 In the same way the Spirit also helps us in our weakness; for we do not know what prayers to offer nor in what way to offer them. But the Spirit Himself pleads for us in yearnings that can find no words, 008:027 and the Searcher of hearts knows what the Spirit's meaning is, because His intercessions for God's people are in harmony with God's will. 008:028 Now we know that for those who love God all things are working together for good-for those, I mean, whom with deliberate purpose He has called. 008:029 For those whom He has known beforehand He has also pre-destined to bear the likeness of His Son, that He might be the Eldest in a vast family of brothers; 008:030 and those whom He has pre-destined He also has called; and those whom He has called He has also declared free from guilt; and those whom He has declared free from guilt He has also crowned with glory. 008:031 What then shall we say to this? If God is on our side, who is there to appear against us? 008:032 He who did not withhold even His own Son, but gave Him up for all of us, will He not also with Him freely give us all things? 008:033 Who shall impeach those whom God has chosen? God declares them free from guilt. 008:034 Who is there to condemn them? Christ Jesus died, or rather has risen to life again. He is also at the right hand of God, and is interceding for us. 008:035 Who shall separate us from Christ's love? Shall affliction or distress, persecution or hunger, nakedness or danger or the sword? 008:036 As it stands written in the Scripture, "For Thy sake they are, all day long, trying to kill us. We have been looked upon as sheep destined for slaughter." 008:037 Yet amid all these things we are more than conquerors through Him who has loved us. 008:038 For I am convinced that neither death nor life, neither the lower ranks of evil angels nor the higher, neither things present nor things future, nor the forces of nature, 008:039 nor height nor depth, nor any other created thing, will be able to separate us from the love of God which rests upon us in Christ Jesus our Lord. 009:001 I am telling you the truth as a Christian man-it is no falsehood, for my conscience enlightened, as it is, by the Holy Spirit adds its testimony to mine- 009:002 when I declare that I have deep grief and unceasing anguish of heart. 009:003 For I could pray to be accursed from Christ on behalf of my brethren, my human kinsfolk-for such the Israelites are. 009:004 To them belongs recognition as God's sons, and they have His glorious Presence and the Covenants, and the giving of the Law, and the Temple service, and the ancient Promises. 009:005 To them the Patriarchs belong, and from them in respect of His human lineage came the Christ, who is exalted above all, God blessed throughout the Ages. Amen. 009:006 Not however that God's word has failed; for all who have sprung from Israel do not count as Israel, 009:007 nor because they are Abraham's true children. But the promise was "Through Isaac shall your posterity be reckoned." 009:008 In other words, it is not the children by natural descent who count as God's children, but the children made such by the promise are regarded as Abraham's posterity. 009:009 For the words are the language of promise and run thus, "About this time next year I will come, and Sarah shall have a son." 009:010 Nor is that all: later on there was Rebecca too. She was soon to bear two children to her husband, our forefather Isaac- 009:011 and even then, though they were not then born and had not done anything either good or evil, yet in order that God's electing purpose might not be frustrated, based, as it was, not on their actions but on the will of Him who called them, she was told, 009:012 "The elder of them will be bondservant to the younger." 009:013 This agrees with the other Scripture which says, "Jacob I have loved, but Esau I have hated." 009:014 What then are we to infer? That there is injustice in God? 009:015 No, indeed; the solution is found in His words to Moses, "Wherever I show mercy it shall be nothing but mercy, and wherever I show compassion it shall be simply compassion." 009:016 And from this we learn that everything is dependent not on man's will or endeavour, but upon God who has mercy. For the Scripture said to Pharaoh, 009:017 "It is for this very purpose that I have lifted you so high- that I may make manifest in you My power, and that My name may be proclaimed far and wide in all the earth." 009:018 This is a proof that wherever He chooses He shows mercy, and wherever he chooses He hardens the heart. 009:019 "Why then does God still find fault?" you will ask; "for who is resisting His will?" 009:020

Nay, but who are you, a mere man, that you should cavil against GOD? Shall the thing moulded say to him who moulded it, "Why have you made me thus?" 009:021 Or has not the potter rightful power over the clay to make out of the same lump one vessel for more honourable and another for less honourable uses? 009:022 And what if God, while choosing to make manifest the terrors of His anger and to show what is possible with Him, has yet borne with long-forbearing patience with the subjects of His anger who stand ready for destruction, 009:023 in order to make known His infinite goodness towards the subjects of His mercy whom He has prepared beforehand for glory, 009:024 even towards us whom He has called not only from among the Jews but also from among the Gentiles? 009:025 So also in Hosea He says, "I will call that nation My People which was not My People, and I will call her beloved who was not beloved. 009:026 And in the place where it was said to them, `No people of Mine are you,' there shall they be called sons of the everliving God." 009:027 And Isaiah cries aloud concerning Israel, "Though the number of the sons of Israel be like the sands of the sea, only a remnant of them shall be saved; 009:028 for the Lord will hold a reckoning upon the earth, making it efficacious and brief." 009:029 Even as Isaiah says in an earlier place, "Were it not that the Lord, the God of Hosts, had left us some few descendants, we should have become like Sodom, and have come to resemble Gomorrah." 009:030 To what conclusion does this bring us? Why, that the Gentiles, who were not in pursuit of righteousness, have overtaken it- a righteousness, however, which arises from faith; 009:031 while the descendants of Israel, who were in pursuit of a Law that could give righteousness, have not arrived at one. 009:032 And why? Because they were pursuing a righteousness which should arise not from faith, but from what they regarded as merit. They stuck their foot against the stone which lay in their way; 009:033 in agreement with the statement of Scripture, "See, I am placing on Mount Zion a stone for people to stumble at, and a rock for them to trip over, and yet he whose faith rests upon it shall never have reason to feel ashamed." 010:001 Brethren, the longing of my heart, and my prayer to God, on behalf of my countrymen is for their salvation. 010:002 For I bear witness that they possess an enthusiasm for God, but it is an unenlightened enthusiasm. 010:003 Ignorant of the righteousness which God provides and building their hopes upon a righteousness of their own, they have refused submission to God's righteousness. 010:004 For as a means of righteousness Christ is the termination of Law to every believer. 010:005 Moses says that he whose actions conform to the righteousness required by the Law shall live by that righteousness. 010:006 But the righteousness which is based on faith speaks in a different tone. "Say not in your heart," it declares, "`Who shall ascend to Heaven?'"-that is, to bring Christ down; 010:007 "nor `Who shall go down into the abyss?'"-that is, to bring Christ up again from the grave. 010:008 But what does it say? "The Message is close to you, in your mouth and in your heart;" that is, the Message which we are publishing about the faith- 010:009 that if with your mouth you confess Jesus as Lord and in your heart believe that God brought Him back to life, you shall be saved. 010:010 For with the heart men believe and obtain righteousness, and with the mouth they make confession and obtain salvation. 010:011 The Scripture says, "No one who believes in Him shall have reason to feel ashamed." 010:012 Jew and Gentile are on precisely the same footing; for the same Lord is Lord over all, and is infinitely kind to all who call upon Him for deliverance. 010:013 For "every one, without exception, who calls on the name of the Lord shall be saved." 010:014 But how are they to call on One in whom they have not believed? And how are they to believe in One whose voice they have never heard? And how are they to hear without a preacher? 010:015 And how are men to preach unless they have been sent to do so? As it is written, "How beautiful are the feet of those who bring glad tidings of good!" 010:016 But, some will say, they have not all hearkened to the Good News. No, for Isaiah asks, "Lord, who has believed the Message they have heard from us?" 010:017 And this proves that faith comes from a Message heard, and that the Message comes through its having been spoken by Christ. 010:018 But, I ask, have they not heard? Yes, indeed: "To the whole world the preachers' voices have sounded forth, and their words to the remotest parts of the earth." 010:019 But again, did Israel fail to understand? Listen to Moses first. He says, "I will fire you with jealousy against a nation which is no nation, and with fury against a nation devoid of understanding." 010:020 And Isaiah, with strange boldness, exclaims, "I have been found by those who were not looking for Me, I have revealed Myself to those who were not inquiring of Me." 010:021 While as to Israel he says, "All day long I have stretched out My arms to a self-willed and fault-finding people." 011:001 I ask then, Has God cast off His People? No, indeed. Why, I myself am an Israelite, of the posterity of Abraham and of the tribe of Benjamin. 011:002 God has not cast off His People whom He knew beforehand. Or are you ignorant of what Scripture says in speaking of Elijah- how he pleaded with God against Israel, saying, 011:003 "Lord, they have put Thy Prophets to death, and have overthrown Thy altars; and, now that I alone remain, they are thirsting for my blood"? 011:004 But what did God say to him in reply? "I have reserved for Myself 7,000 men who have never bent the knee to Baal." 011:005 In the same way also at the present time there has come to be a remnant whom God in His grace has selected. 011:006 But if it is in His grace that He has selected them, then His choice is no longer determined by human actions. Otherwise grace would be grace no longer. 011:007 How then does the matter stand? It stands thus. That which Israel are in earnest pursuit of, they have not obtained; but God's chosen servants have obtained it, and the rest have become hardened. 011:008 And so Scripture says, "God has given them a spirit of drowsiness- eyes to see nothing with and ears to hear nothing with- even until now." 011:009 And David says, "Let their very food become a snare and a trap to them, a stumbling-block and a retribution. 011:010 Let darkness come over their eyes that they may be unable to see, and make Thou their backs continually to stoop." 011:011 I ask, however, "Have they stumbled so as to be finally ruined?" No, indeed; but by their lapse salvation has come to the Gentiles in order to arouse the jealousy of the descendants of Israel; 011:012 and if their lapse is the enriching of the world, and their overthrow the enriching of the Gentiles, will not still greater good follow their restoration? 011:013 But to you Gentiles I say that, since I am an Apostle specially sent to the Gentiles, I take pride in my ministry, 011:014 trying whether I can succeed in rousing my own countrymen to jealousy and thus save some of them. 011:015 For if their having been cast aside has carried with it the reconciliation of the world, what will their being accepted again be but Life out of death? 011:016 Now if the firstfruits of the dough are holy, so also is the whole mass; and if the root of a tree is holy, so also are the branches. 011:017 And if some of the branches have been pruned away, and you, although you were but a wild olive, have been grafted in among them and have become a sharer with others in the rich sap of the root of the olive tree, 011:018 beware of glorying over the natural branches. Or if you are so glorying, do not forget that it is not you who uphold the root: the root upholds you. 011:019 "Branches have been lopped off," you will say, "for the sake of my being grafted in." 011:020 This is true; yet it was their unbelief that cut them off, and you only stand through your faith. 011:021 Do not be puffed up with pride. Tremble rather-for if God did not spare the natural branches, neither will He spare you. 011:022 Notice therefore God's kindness and God's severity. On those who have fallen His severity has descended, but upon you His kindness has come, provided that you do not cease to respond to that kindness. Otherwise you will be cut off also. 011:023 Moreover, if they turn from their unbelief, they too will be grafted in. For God is powerful enough to graft them in again; 011:024 and if you were cut from that which by nature is a wild olive and contrary to nature were grafted into the good olive tree, how much more certainly will these natural branches be grafted on their own olive tree? 011:025 For there is a truth, brethren, not revealed hitherto, of which I do not wish to leave you in ignorance, for fear you should attribute superior wisdom to yourselves-the truth, I mean, that partial blindness has fallen upon Israel until the great mass of the Gentiles have come in; 011:026 and so all Israel will be saved. As is declared in Scripture, "From Mount Zion a Deliverer will come: He will remove all ungodliness from Jacob; 011:027 and this shall be My Covenant with them; when I have taken away their sins." 011:028 In relation to the Good News, the Jews are God's enemies for your sakes; but in relation to God's choice they are dearly loved for the sake of their forefathers. 011:029 For God does not repent of His free gifts nor of His call; 011:030 but just as you were formerly disobedient to Him, but now have received mercy at a time when they are disobedient, 011:031 so now they also have been disobedient at a time when you are receiving mercy; so that to them too there may now be mercy. 011:032 For God has locked up all in the prison of unbelief, that upon all alike He may have mercy. 011:033 Oh, how inexhaustible are God's resources and God's wisdom and God's knowledge! How impossible it is to search into His decrees or trace His footsteps! 011:034 "Who has ever known the mind of the Lord, or shared His counsels?" 011:035 "Who has first given God anything, so as to receive payment in return?" 011:036 For the universe owes its origin to Him, was created by Him, and has its aim and purpose in Him. To Him be the glory throughout the Ages! Amen. 012:001 I plead with you therefore, brethren, by the compassionsof God, to present all your faculties to Him as a living and holy sacrifice acceptable to Him. This with you will be an act of reasonable worship. 012:002 And do not follow the customs of the present age, but be transformed by the entire renewal of your minds, so that you may learn by experience what God's will is- that will which is good and beautiful and perfect. 012:003 For through the authority graciously given to me I warn every individual among you not to value himself unduly, but to cultivate sobriety of judgement in accordance with the amount of faith which God has allotted to each one. 012:004 For just as there are in the one human body many parts, and these parts have not all the same function; 012:005 so collectively we form one body in Christ, while individually we are linked to one another as its members. 012:006 But since we have special gifts which differ in accordance with the diversified work graciously entrusted to us, if it is prophecy, let the prophet speak in exact proportion to his faith; 012:007 if it is the gift of administration, let the administrator exercise a sound judgement in his duties. 012:008 The teacher must do the same in his teaching; and he who exhorts others, in his exhortation. He who gives should be liberal; he who is in authority should be energetic and alert; and he who succours the afflicted should do it cheerfully. 012:009 Let your love be perfectly sincere. Regard with horror what is evil; cling to what is right. 012:010 As for brotherly love, be affectionate to one another; in matters of worldly honour, yield to one another. 012:011 Do not be indolent when zeal is required. Be thoroughly warm-hearted, the Lord's own servants, 012:012 full of joyful hope, patient under persecution, earnest and persistent in prayer. 012:013 Relieve the necessities of God's people; always practise hospitality. 012:014 Invoke blessings on your persecutors-blessings, not curses. 012:015 Rejoice with those who rejoice; weep with those who weep. 012:016 Have full sympathy with one another. Do not give your mind to high things, but let humble ways content you. Do not be wise in your own conceits. 012:017 Pay back to no man evil for evil. Take thought for what is right and seemly in every one's esteem. 012:018 If you can, so far as it depends on you, live at peace with all the world. 012:019 Do not be revengeful, my dear friends, but give way before anger; for it is written, "`Revenge belongs to Me: I will pay back,' says the Lord." 012:020 On the contrary, therefore, if your enemy is hungry, give him food; if he is thirsty, quench his thirst. For by doing this you will be heaping burning coals upon his head. 012:021 Do not be overcome by evil, but overcome the evil with goodness. 013:001 Let every individual be obedient to those who rule over him; for no one is a ruler except by God's permission, and our present rulers have had their rank and power assigned to them by Him. 013:002 Therefore the man who rebels against his ruler is resisting God's will; and those who thus resist will bring punishment upon themselves. 013:003 For judges and magistrates are to be feared not by right-doers but by wrong-doers. You desire-do you not?-to have no reason to fear your ruler. Well, do the thing that is right, and then he will commend you. 013:004 For he is God's servant for your benefit. But if you do what is wrong, be afraid. He does not wear the sword to no purpose: he is God's servant-an administrator to inflict punishment upon evil-doers. 013:005 We must obey therefore, not only in order to escape punishment, but also for conscience' sake. 013:006 Why, this is really the reason you pay taxes; for tax-gatherers are ministers of God, devoting their energies to this very work. 013:007 Pay promptly to all men what is due to them: taxes to those to whom taxes are due, toll to those to whom toll is due, respect to those to whom respect is due, honour to those to whom honour is due. 013:008 Owe nothing to any one except mutual love; for he who loves his fellow man has satisfied the demands of Law. 013:009 For the precepts, "Thou shalt not commit adultery," "Thou shalt do no murder," "Thou shalt not steal," "Thou shalt not covet," and all other precepts, are summed up in this one command, "Thou shalt love thy fellow man as much as thou lovest thyself." 013:010 Love avoids doing any wrong to one's fellow man, and is therefore complete obedience to Law. 013:011 Carry out these injunctions because you know the critical period at which we are living, and that it is now high time, to rouse yourselves from sleep; for salvation is now nearer to us than when we first became believers. 013:012 The night is far advanced, and day is about to dawn. We must therefore lay aside the deeds of darkness, and clothe ourselves with the armour of Light. 013:013 Living as we do in broad daylight, let us conduct ourselves becomingly, not indulging in revelry and drunkenness, nor in lust and debauchery, nor in quarrelling and jealousy. 013:014 On the contrary, clothe yourselves with the Lord Jesus Christ, and make no provision for gratifying your earthly cravings. 014:001 I now pass to another subject. Receive as a friend a man whose faith is weak, but not for the purpose of deciding mere matters of opinion. 014:002 One man's faith allows him to eat anything, while a man of weaker faith eats nothing but vegetables. 014:003 Let not him who eats certain food look down upon him who abstains from it, nor him who abstains from it find fault with him who eats it; for God has received both of them. 014:004 Who are you that you should find fault with the servant of another? Whether he stands or falls is a matter which concerns his own master. But stand he will; for the Master can give him power to stand. 014:005 One man esteems one day more highly than another; another esteems all days alike. Let every one be thoroughly convinced in his own mind. 014:006 He who regards the day as sacred, so regards it for the Master's sake; and he who eats certain food eats it for the Master's sake, for he gives thanks to God; and he who refrains from eating it refrains for the Master's sake, and he also gives thanks to God. 014:007 For not one of us lives to himself, and not one dies to himself. 014:008 If we live, we live to the Lord: if we die, we die to the Lord. So whether we live or die, we belong to the Lord. 014:009 For this was the purpose of Christ's dying and coming to life- namely that He might be Lord both of the dead and the living. 014:010 But you, why do you find fault with your brother? Or you, why do you look down upon your brother? We shall all stand before God to be judged; 014:011 for it is written, "`As I live,' says the Lord, `to Me every knee shall bow, and every tongue shall make confession to God.'" 014:012 So we see that every one of us will give account of himself to God. 014:013 Therefore let us no longer judge one another; but, instead of that, you should come to this judgement-that we must not put a stumbling-block in our brother's path, nor anything to trip him up. 014:014 As one who lives in union with the Lord Jesus, I know and am certain that in its own nature no food is `impure'; but if people regard any food as impure, to them it is. 014:015 If your brother is pained by the food you are eating, your conduct is no longer controlled by love. Take care lest, by the food you eat, you lead to ruin a man for whom Christ died. 014:016 Therefore do not let the boon which is yours in common be exposed to reproach. 014:017 For the Kingdom of God does not consist of eating and drinking, but of right conduct, peace and joy, through the Holy Spirit; 014:018 and whoever in this way devotedly serves Christ, God takes pleasure in him, and men highly commend him. 014:019 Therefore let us aim at whatever makes for peace and mutual upbuilding of character. 014:020 Do not for food's sake be throwing down God's work. All food is pure; but a man is in the wrong if his food is a snare to others. 014:021 The right course is to forego eating meat or drinking wine or doing anything that tends to your brother's fall. 014:022 As for you and your faith, keep your faith to yourself in the presence of God. The man is to be congratulated who does not pronounce judgement on himself in what his actions sanction. 014:023 But he who has misgivings and yet eats meat is condemned already, because his conduct is not based on faith; for all conduct not based on faith is sinful. 015:001 As for us who are strong, our duty is to bear with the weaknesses of those who are not strong, and not seek our own pleasure. 015:002 Let each of us endeavour to please his fellow Christian, aiming at a blessing calculated to build him up. 015:003 For even the Christ did not seek His own pleasure. His principle was, "The reproaches which they addressed to Thee have fallen on me." 015:004 For all that was written of old has been written for our instruction, so that we may always have hope through the power of endurance and the encouragement which the Scriptures afford. 015:005 And may God, the giver of power of endurance and of that encouragement, grant you to be in full sympathy with one another in accordance with the example of Christ Jesus, 015:006 so that with oneness both of heart and voice you may glorify the God and Father of our Lord Jesus Christ. 015:007 Habitually therefore give one another a friendly reception, just as Christ also has received you, and thus promote the glory of God. 015:008 My meaning is that Christ has become a servant to the people of Israel in vindication of God's truthfulness-in showing how sure are the promises made to our forefathers- 015:009 and that the Gentiles also have glorified God in acknowledgment of His mercy. So it is written, "For this reason I will praise Thee among the Gentiles, and sing psalms in honour of Thy name." 015:010 And again the Psalmist says, "Be glad, ye Gentiles, in company with His People." 015:011 And again, "Praise the Lord, all ye Gentiles, and let all the people extol Him." 015:012 And again Isaiah says, "There shall be the Root of Jesse and One who rises up to rule the Gentiles. On Him shall the Gentiles build their hopes." 015:013 May God, the giver of hope, fill you with continual joy and peace because you trust in Him-so that you may have abundant hope through the power of the Holy Spirit. 015:014 But as to you, brethren, I am convinced-yes, I Paul am convinced-that, even apart from my teaching, you are already full of goodness of heart, and enriched with complete Christian knowledge, and are also competent to instruct one another. 015:015 But I write to you the more boldly-partly as reminding you of what you already know-because of the authority graciously entrusted to me by God, 015:016 that I should be a minister of Christ Jesus among the Gentiles, doing priestly duties in connexion with God's Good News so that the sacrifice-namely the Gentiles-may be acceptable to Him, being (as it is) an offering which the Holy Spirit has made holy. 015:017 I can therefore glory in Christ Jesus concerning the work for God in which I am engaged. 015:018 For I will not presume to mention any of the results that Christ has brought about by other agency than mine in securing the obedience of the Gentiles by word or deed, 015:019 with power manifested in signs and marvels, and through the power of the Holy Spirit. But-to speak simply of my own labours-beginning in Jerusalem and the outlying districts, I have proclaimed without reserve, even as far as Illyricum, the Good News of the Christ; 015:020 making it my ambition, however, not to tell the Good News where Christ's name was already known, for fear I should be building on another man's foundation. 015:021 But, as Scripture says, "Those shall see, to whom no report about Him has hitherto come, and those who until now have not heard shall understand." 015:022 And it is really this which has again and again prevented my coming to you. 015:023 But now, as there is no more unoccupied ground in this part of the world, and I have for years past been eager to pay you a visit, 015:024 I hope, as soon as ever I extend my travels into Spain, to see you on my way and be helped forward by you on my journey, when I have first enjoyed being with you for a time. 015:025 But at present I am going to Jerusalem to serve God's people, 015:026 for Macedonia and Greece have kindly contributed a certain sum in relief of the poor among God's people, in Jerusalem. 015:027 Yes, they have kindly done this, and, in fact, it was a debt they owed them. For seeing that the Gentiles have been admitted in to partnership with the Jews in their spiritual blessings, they in turn are under an obligation to render sacred service to the Jews in temporal things. 015:028 So after discharging this duty, and making sure that these kind gifts reach those for whom they are intended, I shall start for Spain, passing through Rome on my way there; 015:029 and I know that when I come to you it will be with a vast amount of blessing from Christ. 015:030 But I entreat you, brethren, in the name of our Lord Jesus Christ and by the love which His Spirit inspires, to help me by wrestling in prayer to God on my behalf, 015:031 asking that I may escape unhurt from those in Judaea who are disobedient, and that the service which I am going to Jerusalem to render may be well received by the Church there, 015:032 in order that if God be willing I may come to you with a glad heart, and may enjoy a time of rest with you. 015:033 May God, who gives peace be with you all! Amen. 016:001 Herewith I introduce our sister Phoebe to you, who is a servant of the Church at Cenchreae, 016:002 that you may receive her as a fellow Christian in a manner worthy of God's people, and may assist her in any matter in which she may need help. For she has indeed been a kind friend to many, including myself. 016:003 Greetings to Prisca and Aquila my fellow labourers in the work of Christ Jesus- 016:004 friends who have endangered their own lives for mine. I am grateful to them, and not I alone, but all the Gentile Churches also. 016:005 Greetings, too, to the Church that meets at their house. Greetings to my dear Epaenetus, who was the earliest convert to Christ in the province of Asia; 016:006 to Mary who has laboured strenuously among you; 016:007 and to Andronicus and Junia, my countrymen, who once shared my imprisonment. They are of note among the Apostles, and are Christians of longer standing than myself. 016:008 Greetings to Ampliatus, dear to me in the Lord; 016:009 to Urban, our fellow labourer in Christ, and to my dear Stachys. 016:010 Greetings to Apella, that veteran believer; and to the members of the household of Aristobulus. 016:011 Greetings to my countryman, Herodion; and to the believing members of the household of Narcissus. 016:012 Greetings to those Christian workers, Tryphaena and Tryphosa; also to dear Persis, who has laboured strenuously in the Lord's work. 016:013 Greetings to Rufus, who is one of the Lord's chosen people; and to his mother, who has also been a mother to me. 016:014 Greetings to Asyncritus, Phlegon, Hermes, Patrobas, Hermas, and to the brethren associated with them; 016:015 to Philologus and Julia, Nereus and his sister and Olympas, and to all God's people associated with them. 016:016 Salute one another with a holy kiss. All the Churches of Christ send greetings to you. 016:017 But I beseech you, brethren, to keep a watch on those who are causing the divisions among you, and are leading others into sin, in defiance of the instruction which you have received; and habitually to shun them. 016:018 For men of that stamp are not bondservants of Christ our Lord, but are slaves to their own appetites; and by their plausible words and their flattery they utterly deceive the minds of the simple. 016:019 Your fidelity to the truth is everywhere known. I rejoice over you, therefore, but I wish you to be wise as to what is good, and simple-minded as to what is evil. 016:020 And before long, God the giver of peace will crush Satan under your feet. The grace of our Lord Jesus Christ be with you! 016:021 Timothy, my fellow worker, sends you greetings, and so do my countrymen Lucius, Jason and Sosipater. 016:022 I, Tertius, who write this letter, send you Christian greetings. 016:023 Gaius, my host, who is also the host of the whole Church, greets you. So do Erastus, the treasurer of the city, and Quartus our brother. 016:024 [] 016:025 To Him who has it in His power to make you strong, as declared in the Good News which I am spreading, and the proclamation concerning Jesus Christ, in harmony with the unveiling of the Truth which in the periods of past Ages remained unuttered, 016:026 but has now been brought fully to light, and by the command of the God of the Ages has been made known by the writings of the Prophets among all the Gentiles to win them to obedience to the faith- 016:027 to God, the only wise, through Jesus Christ, even to Him be the glory through all the Ages! Amen.

BOOK 56 TITUS

001:001 Paul, a bondservant of God and an Apostle of Jesus Christ for building up the faith of God's own people and spreading a full knowledge of the truths of religion, 001:002 in hope of the Life of the Ages which God, who is never false to His word, promised before the commencement of the Ages. 001:003 And at the appointed time He clearly made known His Message in the preaching with which I was entrusted by the command of God our Saviour: 001:004 To Titus my own true child in our common faith. May grace and peace be granted to you from God the Father and Christ Jesus our Saviour. 001:005 I have left you behind in Crete in order that you may set right the things which still require attention, and appoint Elders in every town, as I directed you to do; 001:006 wherever there is a man of blameless life, true to his one wife, having children who are themselves believers and are free from every reproach of profligacy or of stubborn self-will. 001:007 For, as God's steward, a minister must be of blameless life, not over-fond of having his own way, not a man of a passionate temper nor a hard drinker, not given to blows nor greedy of gain, 001:008 but hospitable to strangers, a lover of goodness, sober-minded, upright, saintly, self-controlled; 001:009 holding fast to the faithful Message which he has received, so that he may be well qualified both to encourage others with sound teaching and to reply successfully to opponents. 001:010 For there are many that spurn authority-idle, talkative and deceitful persons, who, for the most part, are adherents of the Circumcision. 001:011 You must stop the mouths of such men, for they overthrow the faith of whole families, teaching what they ought not, just for the sake of making money. 001:012 One of their own number-a Prophet who is a countryman of theirs- has said, "Cretans are always liars, dangerous animals, idle gluttons." 001:013 This testimony is true. Therefore sternly denounce them, that they may be robust in their faith, 001:014 and not give attention to Jewish legends and the maxims of men who turn their backs on the truth. 001:015 To the pure everything is pure; but to the polluted and unbelieving nothing is pure, but on the contrary their very minds and consciences are polluted. 001:016 They profess to know God; but in their actions they disown Him, and are detestable and disobedient men, and for any good work are utterly useless. 002:001 But as for you, you must speak in a manner that befits wholesome teaching. 002:002 Exhort aged men to be temperate, grave, sober-minded, robust in their faith, their love and their patience. 002:003 In the same way exhort aged women to let their conduct be such as becomes consecrated persons. They must not be slanderers nor enslaved to wine-drinking. They must be teachers of what is right. 002:004 They should school the young women to be affectionate to their husbands and to their children, to be sober-minded, pure in their lives, 002:005 industrious in their homes, kind, submissive to their husbands, so that the Christian teaching may not be exposed to reproach. 002:006 In the same way exhort the younger men to be discreet, 002:007 and above all make your own life a pattern of right conduct, having in your teaching no taint of insincerity, but a serious tone, 002:008 and healthy language which no one can censure, so that our opponents may feel ashamed at having nothing evil to say against us. 002:009 Exhort slaves to be always obedient to their owners, and to give them satisfaction in everything, not contradicting and not pilfering, 002:010 but manifesting perfect fidelity and kind feeling, in order to bring honour to the teaching of our Saviour, God, in all things. 002:011 For the grace of God has displayed itself with healing power to all mankind, 002:012 training us to renounce ungodliness and all the pleasures of this world, and to live sober, upright, and pious lives at the present time, 002:013 in expectation of the fulfilment of our blessed hope- the Appearing in glory of our great God and Saviour Jesus Christ; 002:014 who gave Himself for us to purchase our freedom from all iniquity, and purify for Himself a people who should be specially His own, zealous for doing good works. 002:015 Thus speak, exhort, reprove, with all impressiveness. Let no one make light of your authority. 003:001 Remind people that they must submit to the rulers who are in authority over them; that they must obey the magistrates, be prepared for every right action, 003:002 not speak evil of any one, nor be contentious, but yield unselfishly to others and constantly manifest a forgiving spirit towards all men. 003:003 For there was a time when we also were deficient in understanding, obstinate, deluded, the slaves of various cravings and pleasures, spending our lives in malice and envy, hateful ourselves and hating one another. 003:004 But when the goodness of God our Saviour, and His love to man, dawned upon us, not in consequence of things which we, 003:005 as righteous men, had done, but as the result of His own mercy He saved us by means of the bath of regeneration and the renewal of our natures by the Holy Spirit, 003:006

which He poured out on us richly through Jesus Christ our Saviour; 003:007 in order that having been declared righteous through His grace we might become heirs to the Life of the Ages in fulfilment of our hopes. 003:008 This is a faithful saying, and on these various points I would have you insist strenuously, in order that those who have their faith fixed on God may be careful to set an example of good actions. For these are not only good in themselves, but are also useful to mankind. 003:009 But hold yourself aloof from foolish controversies and pedigrees and discussions and wrangling about the Law, for they are useless and vain. 003:010 After a first and second admonition, have nothing further to do with any one who will not be taught; 003:011 for, as you know, a man of that description has turned aside from the right path and is a sinner self-condemned. 003:012 After I have sent Artemas or Tychicus to you, lose no time in joining me at Nicopolis; for I have decided to pass the winter there. 003:013 Help Zenas the lawyer forward on his journey with special care, and Apollos, so that they may have all they require. 003:014 And let our people too learn to set a good example in following honest occupations for the supply of their necessities, so that they may not live useless lives. 003:015 Every one here sends you greeting. Greet the believers who hold us dear. May grace be with you all.